The Beautiful Music All Around Us

STEPHEN WADE

The Beautiful Music

All Around Us

Field Recordings and the American Experience

University of Illinois Press

Urbana, Chicago, and Springfield

Library of Congress Cataloging-in-Publication Data
Wade, Stephen.
The beautiful music all around us: field recordings
and the American experience / Stephen Wade.
p.   cm. — (Music in American life)
Includes bibliographical references and index.
ISBN 978-0-252-03688-0 (cloth)
1. Folk music—United States—History and criticism.
2. Field recordings—United States—History.
3. Archive of Folk Culture (U.S.)
I. Title.
ML3550.W34   2012
781.62'13—dc23   2011044092

For Michaelle

Contents

I don't think I had gone much past second grade when I first saw Casey Jones, the Chicken Man. This tall, kindly-eyed, toothless figure with a weathered button accordion stood at the center of a crowd that gathered on the corner of Diversey and Clark, a dense Chicago intersection near my elementary school. The commotion that surrounded him stemmed less from his music making than from the large white chicken nestled on his hat. According to a hand-lettered sign that Casey wore, he had "trained 218 chickens in Chicago." Apparently he named each one of them Mae West.

"No dime, no show," he kept repeating. Once he collected a proper amount of coinage, he removed the chicken from her perch. Then Mae began her part of the performance. She walked a tightrope, danced and bowed, drank something he gave her from a flask, and began hobbling with a drunkard's gait. "Okay Baby," said Casey, "shake that thing. Do the shimmy-she-wabble now. Do the boogie-woogie Baby."[1] In later years, along with his sign, a harmonica, a rag doll, and a bell, Casey hung a toy telephone around his neck. He'd "call" his chicken, who answered by pecking on the receiver. To repay her replies, Casey slipped the bird a few grains of corn.

One heckler chided the performer on his appearance, mocking how Casey's bunions protruded from his ragged shoes. Casey paused for a moment, then

FIGURE 1.
Casey Jones, with
Mae West, Chicago, 1973. Photo
by Ted Gray. Used
by permission.

replied, "I always say there is more room out than in."[2] His critic vanquished, Casey began the trucking dance, wagging his finger in the air and singing the huckle-buck. As he moved, he referred to his whitened hair. "I may be ninety, but folks can natcherly see that I'm not an old man. Old man sho' can't dance like this. Only one thing wrong with me. I gets tired. Sometime, that's all."[3]

Born Anderson Punch in Marshall, Texas, in 1870, Casey Jones got his moniker from the folksong he often played. He reached Chicago in 1914, where he spent nearly sixty years roaming the city's streets with his music and his succession of chickens—all of whom, he insisted, died of natural causes. Over the decades he appeared throughout the city and became a local hero, the subject of folktales, paintings, newspaper clips, and even a posthumous play.[4] When he passed away in 1974 at age 104—indigent and without family survivors—he made the front page of the *Chicago Defender*: "Street comedian, Casey Jones, dies."[5] A funeral home run by a Chicago alderman arranged a single evening's visitation before Casey's burial. The unending stream of visitors, however, soon caused a change of plans. His service took place instead at the city's Third Baptist Church, allowing many more to pay their respects to the beloved performer. "Casey," someone once told me, "was street-joy."[6]

The image of Casey Jones—"dressed like a junk man, think in terms of a scarecrow"—never seems to fade.[7] He signaled in my childhood the presence of American folklore and folklife. With his chickens called Mae West, his ceaseless stream of colloquial speech, and his squeezebox melodies of an earlier day, he indelibly demonstrated that reservoirs of culture thrive not only in institutionally sanctioned preserves such as museums and concert halls, but also in the streets and marketplaces. Casey Jones—part hustler, part Pied Piper, ever the wise fool, and not one bit crazy—could transform a sidewalk into a theatrical milieu. Despite the rush hour buses lumbering past, the prodding of policemen, and the tumult of pedestrians, Casey kept his bearings. A trouper's creed anchored him through all these currents as he reminded his listeners "I'm a showman."[8] Casey personified what folklorist Benjamin Botkin called "'living lore' . . . responsive to the mood of the moment, though it had behind it the accumulated mother wit and wisdom of generations."[9]

Botkin wrote those words to describe an endeavor he directed in the late 1930s for the Federal Writers' Project. Conceiving of folklore in ongoing rather than antiquarian terms, he launched several Living Lore units, including one in Chicago, to document current folk expression and vernacular creativity.[10] Cabbies, carnival high divers, garment workers, and tunnel diggers, among others, appear in this encyclopedic collecting effort. Botkin had in mind a specific person, too, one he found touchingly emblematic of living lore's realities: a fish peddler, who, pushing his cart down the canyons of New York's skyscrapers and tenements created interest by making up rhymes and setting them to tunes appropriate to the ethnicity of whichever enclave he entered. In November 1939 Clyde "Kingfish" Smith of East One Hundredth Street chanted catchphrases such as "I got shad, ain't you glad."[11] Up in Harlem he set this street cry and others like it to numbers such as "Jumpin' Jive," while in Jewish neighborhoods his calls gave way to lyrics wrapped in "Bei Mir Bist Du Schön." Wherever he went—switching to Spanish when he reached that community—he made up new combinations, seizing on the latest hits and familiar tunes to carry his message. He found this strategy good for business: "A lot of people wait for my individual cry."[12] The main thing required is "You gotta be in the mood. You got to put yourself in it."[13] For Clyde "Kingfish" Smith, the most ordinary transaction imaginable had become a pretext to fill the streets with sung poetry.

Kingfish and Casey shaped their performances in ways they knew their audiences would recognize. Mississippi blues greats Muddy Waters and Howlin' Wolf achieved similar rapport when they performed in Chicago's neighborhood bars. Both of these bandleaders, like Casey, arrived during the Great Migration. The amplified blues they made resonated with a new but still homegrown sound familiar to their fellow urban émigrés. In the mid-1960s, as a fledgling, preteen electric guitarist too young to enter the taverns where Muddy and Wolf appeared, I sometimes stood outside during matinees and listened to them by the front window. If I got lucky, the bouncer swung the front door open, allowing fresh air to thin the reek of Blatz beer and the fog of Salem cigarettes, and permitted me to peer inside. More than once I saw

Muddy Waters perform "Hoochie Coochie Man." In this career-defining hit, Muddy chanted his lines in a propulsive call-and-response with his band. He summoned conjure-man charms, the powers of the seventh son, and the workings of High John the Conqueror.[14] While I had little or no knowledge of these references, or their worldly implications, I saw their power, watching how audiences accepted this imagery as their own. They embraced the messages of his song and the nuances of his singing with an understanding born of shared experience.

On a lower frequency, the childhood adventures my friends and I pursued back then had parallels to that merging of life and art so evident when Muddy and his compatriots performed. For a quarter we could take the El downtown and ride it like a roller coaster. We'd lean with it as it whooshed and rolled into the damp warm corridors and we jumped between its cars when it swooped back above ground into the searing light of day, screeching perilously around the famous curves of the Loop. Once downtown, we'd climb to the top of skyscrapers by taking batteries of elevators, running up fire stairs, and edging past hissing, snapping electrical equipment. At last we'd find our way onto the building's roof. The wind from the lake bit like a bad dog, and sometimes the empty scaffolds of the window washers banged with a frightening clatter against the girders. Following the lead of my best friend, Freddy, I'd crawl out behind him to the cornice coping and look down at the sidewalks and people below. On the plain of Lake Michigan, we boys found mountains, manmade to be sure. We lived in an environment we didn't create and certainly didn't control, but we found our greatest pleasures when we somehow infused aspects of our personalities into the city's impersonal habitat. We had scaled these office buildings and transformed them into our personal observation posts. Giddily we came back to earth, fleeing the janitors and security guards who had gotten word of our trespassing. Then we reveled in our narrow escapes.

Unexpectedly, those scenes all came to mind when, as a teenager, I began listening to folk music albums published by the Library of Congress. These records, with their bureaucrat-gray jackets and decidedly noncommercial titles like *Songs and Ballads of American History and of the Assassination of Presidents,* seemed imbued with the high purpose and solemnity proper to an undertaking of the federal government. Outwardly, this series called "Folk Music of the United States" surveyed examples of our national artistic patrimony, while inherently these performances shared with field recordings everywhere an underlying theme: the location of art in human experience.

They made audible the essential fusion that Ben Botkin defined in his Living Lore project, "relating of the foreground, lore, to its background in life."[15] Sometimes on the Library's records kitchen clocks tick, trucks drive by, and roosters crow. Children laugh, and occasionally a performer or his neighbor interrupts a song to talk. This palpability struck me, and a stream of associated memories pooled around these recordings: how Casey Jones enlivened a street corner; how my friends and I rode the El like an amusement park ride; how Muddy Waters's listeners reacted so knowingly to his songs.

My banjo teacher, Fleming Brown, who suggested I listen to these recordings, set their vivid qualities in a pedagogical frame. The performers' locales, he explained, marked a vital aspect of their music. Not hearing it "in its natural environment," he added dryly, amounted to the difference between seeing a polar bear in Antarctica and one confined to the Brookfield Zoo.[16] Years earlier these same records prompted him to seek out traditional musicians, an experience he termed "a privilege." He recalled his honeymoon, driving with his bride nonstop from Chicago to western North Carolina, where they called on Bascom Lamar Lunsford, who had made a vast number of recordings for the Library's Folk Archive (originally the Archive of American Folk Song, now the Archive of Folk Culture). Later, Fleming hosted Frank Proffitt, the source of "Tom Dooley," in his home, and in October 1963 undertook a monumental set of recordings with Hobart Smith, who along with his sister Texas Gladden had appeared on the first of these Library of Congress albums. Now Fleming directed me to do the same, to "find the people who know how to play this music."[17] I began to contact traditional singers and instrumentalists at their homes, hoping to better absorb how this music should be played, set against the backdrop of their lives.

What those musicians so unstintingly offered this stranger comes back to Casey Jones. On the streets of Chicago, social histories clung to his merriment. Born early in the Jim Crow era, Casey reckoned with accumulated legacies of minstrelsy and caricature. For some his chickens called up images of raided coops and stolen food. Members of his community understandably cringed when he disarmed courtroom judges with self-deprecating humor and antics rooted in that past. Repeatedly arrested for obstructing traffic, Casey eluded the powerful and entrenched by playing to their expectations. To the extent these behaviors kept him out of jail and let him back on the street to pursue his livelihood, his resilience and rascality exceeded the confinement of those stereotypes. For Casey, nicknamed after one folksong, embodied the words of another, the spiritual that tells of "making a way out of

FIGURE 2.
Fleming Brown at
home in Chicago,
December 1981.
Photo by
Stephen Wade.

no way." This lyric, born in slavery, speaks to solutions found in the barest of circumstances. As someone literally exposed to the elements, carrying a live creature on his head, and subject to the pressures of his times from car horns to cops, he made a way out of no way. At the same time, he showed generations of bystanders that art is wherever you find it.

The singers and players who fill this book likewise made their ways out of no way. They, too, bring together lore and life, drawing from mother wit and the mood of the moment to create in their corners of America their own varieties of street-joy. My path to them began with seeing their names set in white type, spinning on the navy blue labels of some hard-to-find phonograph records. Joyously enough, this journey started years before with a man called Casey Jones and 218 trained chickens he named Mae West.

Acknowledgments

A simple thank-you cannot begin to express my gratitude to the performers presented in this book, their families, friends, and fellow musicians. They have brought rich delight into my life, and my respect for them is boundless. Their names appear in the unnumbered notes immediately preceding each chapter's endnotes. Even if family members did not know these Library of Congress recordings existed, they readily shared their kin's past, fully aware that the hard stories they told as well as the warm memories would make their way here. They wanted their parents, grandparents, and siblings remembered with a fullness of who they were, what they faced, and what they achieved. With rare exceptions, the photographs that came from them to illustrate this book, like these stories, have not previously appeared in print. I'm touched that they were so willing to share them.

One of the joys of folk music research is the chance to get to know so many wonderful people from so many walks of life. I have extended thanks to those who have helped with particular pieces in the paragraphs that precede the numbered notes. Still more names appear within those notes themselves. My deepest gratitude for wider help and support goes to friends and colleagues Norm Cohen, John Cowley, Archie Green, Ed Kahn, and Dick Spottswood. I also want to call attention to the music studies written by Edward Ives and

Bruce Jackson. They have set models of inquiry combined with grace of expression and moral integrity that extend the paths broken by such great predecessors as Phillips Barry, Samuel Bayard, Henry Belden, Benjamin A. Botkin, and Mary Wheeler.

Many institutions and their staffs have continually given of themselves throughout this research. Foremost among them is the Archive of Folk Culture at the American Folklife Center, Library of Congress. Past staffers include Jim Hardin, Joe Hickerson, Alan Jabbour, and Gerry Parsons. In more recent years their capacious spirit continues with reference librarian Ann Hoog and her colleagues, and Matthew Barton, who has since become curator of recorded sound at the Library of Congress. Craig D'Ooge, public affairs officer at the Library when *A Treasury of Library of Congress Field Recordings* appeared, made a special effort to reach out to the people and communities represented. Others include John Wheat of the Barker Texas History Center, Austin, Texas; Suzanne Flandreau of the Center for Black Music Research, Chicago, Illinois; Missy Craig of the Carnegie Public Library, Clarksdale, Mississippi; Barbara Landis of the Cumberland County Historical Society and Hamilton Library, Carlisle, Pennsylvania; Kathy Bailey of the Evans Memorial Library, Aberdeen, Mississippi; Beth Howse of Fisk University, Special Collections, Nashville, Tennessee; Bev Rodgerson, Charles Wright, and Michael Zeliff of the University of Maryland and its libraries, College Park, Maryland; Vonnie Shelton of the McCracken County Public Library, Paducah, Kentucky; Anne L. Webster of the Mississippi Department of Archives and History, Jackson, Mississippi; John Loy, Matthew Turi, and Steve Weiss of the Southern Folklife Collection at the Wilson Library, University of North Carolina, Chapel Hill, North Carolina; Sheila Limerick of the University of West Alabama; and Stephen Green of the Western Folklife Center, Elko, Nevada.

Among those ever available and always helpful were Anna Lomax Wood of the Alan Lomax Archive; Annie Johnston and Chris Strachwitz of Arhoolie Records; Mike Monseur of Bias Studios; Ron Middlebrook of Centerstream Publishing; Tom Cole of National Public Radio; Bill Nowlin of Rounder Records; Mary Monseur and Ronnie Simpkins of Smithsonian Folkways; Margie Towery of Towery Indexing Service; Joe and Teresa Leffson of Train Printing; Todd Stewart and Bridget Warren of Vertigo Books; and Elmer Addison, Pam Daniels, Linda Parker, and Laura Woodland of our local post office who heard about this project day in and day out. Doug Hood, technician extraordinaire, made all the photographic restorations.

ACKNOWLEDGMENTS

Others whose friendship and guidance has been personally sustaining include Tim Brooks, Ellsworth Brown, Clarke Buehling, Joe Bussard, Jason and Romina Byrd, Jonathan and Judith Churchill, Michael and Phyllis Courlander, Leonard Cozad, Jr., Mike Craver, Peter Danner, Mattie Jean Willingham Dodge, Steven Dodge, Dena Epstein, Barbara Evans, Michael Ferguson, Abbott Ferriss, Alma Garcia, Ervin Gladden, Chris Griffin, Owen Heiberg, Wayne Henderson, Dwight Holmes, Jordan Kaye, Ed Komara, James Leva, Kip Lornell, David Massey, Leon McCulloh, Zan McLeod, Michael Melford, J. David Miller, Larry Mintz, Roger Misiewicz, Jean Murphy, Fred Ordower, Tom Rankin, Leonard Rapport, Blair and Kathryn Reedy, John Renbourn, Neil Rosenberg, Liberty Rucker, Bob Sayers, LaMar Schlabach, Sandra Shifrin, Chris Smith, Marion Stocking, MaryE Yeomans, and Doug Wixson.

Great thanks to the remarkable University of Illinois Press: Director Willis Regier for his unwavering support, the Press's many wonderful staffers, and especially editor Laurie Matheson, who steered this effort to completion with thoughtfulness and grace. Scholars Bob Cantwell and Norm Cohen served as the manuscript's readers. Their counsel enormously improved this work. Copyeditor Deborah Oliver tirelessly took it the last long mile. Thanks beyond words are offered Judy McCulloh for her insights and encouragement over all these years. Finally, love and gratitude to my wife, Michaelle LaFond Wade, who has given so much to see this through and to whom this book is dedicated.

Introduction

IN MAY 1941, NEAR THE END OF FISK UNIVERSITY'S SEVENTY-fifth anniversary festivities, music professor John W. Work III hosted an afternoon concert in the school chapel. The program included a banjoist he first saw busking on Nashville streets, a gospel quartet he heard about from his barber, and Fisk's minister, who doubled as an old-time storyteller specializing in slave-era tales. Work delighted in knowing these artists who lived so close by, and throughout his introductory remarks he saluted their talents, prized their discovery, and valued their repertories. They attested, he said, to the unique folklore riches that Nashville offered its citizenry. At the same time, he acknowledged that these performers had creative counterparts elsewhere, that the cultural forms they represented thrived "in every corner of American life."[1]

Work stressed that earlier pastoral and isolate conditions did not adequately characterize folklore of the present day. Over the preceding fifty years, rapid movement, mass communications, monetary reward, and public literacy had permeated the countryside as it had the cities. He viewed folklore, a concept that unites specific communities with wisdom and knowledge rooted in the past, not as something inherently remote, but as something intrinsically local. The artists on the Fisk stage proved that no matter how recently their

songs originated or how identifiable their composers, folk patterns and processes extended into modern times and cosmopolitan settings. Accordingly, to this audience made up of members of the Fisk community, Work mused "if a title for this program were necessary it would be—'The Beautiful Music All Around You.'"[2] In addressing his listeners as "you," he included all of us.

Among those making a beautiful music all around us, we should count the performers who animate the chapters that follow. These twelve musicians, singers, and groups recorded between 1934 and 1942—seven black and five white—provide a baker's dozen of folksongs and traditional tunes. Apart from their surpassing artistic gifts, these individuals illuminate an America rich with local creativity. They resided in such places as Salyersville, Kentucky; Byhalia, Mississippi; and Salem, Virginia. Like the players at the Fisk concert, they confined their music making largely to their own communities. Sometimes they sang on playgrounds, sometimes while chopping cotton, and sometimes from behind bars.

At the time of these recordings, Virginia ballad singer Texas Gladden had a house full of youngsters and found music a way of calming her brood. Both the Shipp sisters and Ora Dell Graham attended school in Mississippi, where they shared their danceable game songs with their classmates and friends. Blindness afflicted two members of the Nashville Washboard Band, while the rest of the group worked day labor. Jess Morris, a classically trained violinist and former cowboy living in Dalhart, Texas, played at ranch dances throughout the Panhandle. Contest-winning fiddler Luther Strong followed a string of building jobs in Kentucky and factory work in Ohio. Singers Kelly Pace and Charlie Butler performed whatever tasks the state authorities of Arkansas and Mississippi compelled them to, tasks that included policing convicts like themselves. Kentuckian Bill Stepp worked as a logger in his younger days, but now focused his energies fiddling for neighborhood hoedowns. Banjoist Pete Steele, who began as a coal miner, had become a carpenter in a southern Ohio paper plant. Contralto-voiced Vera Hall, who sang in her church, found employment as an Alabama housemaid, and second-tenor quartet singer Bozie Sturdivant held down a job as a yard boy in Clarksdale, Mississippi, among other domestic chores. The life experiences of these performers also included prostitution, armed robbery, attempted murder, alcoholism, domestic violence, and death by partying.

Both happenstance and purposeful design surrounded the recordings they made. Two days before Pete Steele recorded "Coal Creek March," he had played at a nearby folk festival, creating a strong enough impression that collector Alan Lomax called on him at home. Jess Morris was remaking "Goodbye, Old Paint" for a second time with John A. Lomax, whom he had known for years. Vera Hall had sung for Lomax previously, too. Texas Gladden made some discs earlier for the Virginia Folklore Society, though this marked her first attempt with "One Morning in May." For the remaining singers and players, these encounters marked their inaugural and in most cases only recordings.

Occasionally they had forewarning, even if their song choices, sometimes prompted by the collectors, didn't emerge until the sessions. The Nashville Washboard Band knew to come to John Work's house on the appointed day. Christine and Katherine Shipp likewise heard from their mother to get ready. A well-placed townsperson who earlier had recommended the Shipp family singers for recording—the sisters, two of their brothers, and their mother—got word when the WPA sound truck would pass through Byhalia. The rest answered their doors to strangers they didn't expect, or else found themselves confronted by the recordists at places where they routinely spent time. News about them got to the collectors in various ways: through neighbors, local folksong aficionados, and members of the upper crust open to traditional music and interested in heritage; sheriffs, jailers, wardens, sergeants, and prisoners; schoolteachers and principals; church deacons and quartet singing coaches; and fellow musicians. All played roles in calling attention to these talents who lived among them.

The recordists, working on behalf of the Library of Congress and allied cultural agencies, used disc-cutting machines as their primary documentation tool. These phonographic devices, whose early models weighed 315 pounds when outfitted with their microphones, playback heads, and amplifiers, literally engraved aluminum or acetate surfaces as the musicians performed.[3] Family members present at these sessions unfailingly recall the spiraling coils of acetate falling away from the lathe during the recording process.

Recordings often took place in performers' homes or front yards, but others were made in public facilities such as churches, social clubs, and hotel rooms. Collectors also carried extra lead-acid batteries, weighing seventy-five pounds each, and a converter to operate the disc machine when they ventured beyond the commercial power grid. Sounds from these environments seeped into the microphones and onto the discs: children laugh in their school's auditorium, a door closes as a fiddler begins his tune, a congregation thumps a quiet cadence on a church-house floor, a prisoner urges his fellow inmate to sing with all his might. For performers and witnesses alike, this art could not be set aside from life.

Or kept from the nation. Beginning in February 1943, these performances began appearing on compilations assembled by the Archive of American Folk Song at the Library of Congress (henceforth Folk Archive).[4] "The Library," read the original press release, "has prepared seven albums containing 119 titles selected as being the best and most representative of the approximately 30,000 recorded songs in the Archive and are now ready for distribution."[5] Eight of the thirteen selections featured in these pages appeared on that first set of releases, leaving the rest, with one exception, soon to follow. Eventually the Library included all of them in Folk Music of the United States, a series that totaled seventy-one recordings in LP format. From that sampling, narrowed to pieces made only on disc-cutting recorders, I chose thirty for a 1997 compact disc called *A Treasury of Library of Congress Field Recordings*. The choices that comprise this book and its accompanying disc come from there.

These performances make good candidates for the Folk Archive "hit parade." Stemming from their initial publication in the Library recording series, and in some instances from their reissue on the *Treasury*, they have played identifiable roles in the wider culture. Several became sources for well-known popular songs and orchestral works. Others have resounded in television and film scores, found new parts in dramatic works and modern ballets, and even appeared in disco tracks and commercial jingles. I settled on these pieces not so much because of their fame but because of their capacity for renewal. Given this creative vitality, small wonder that John Work III and the Library's recordists found beautiful music all around them. The twelve singers and instrumentalists caught here on a handful of Folk Archive records show us the irrepressible admixture of music in America. Their stories are metaphors for how this country has lived.

The May 1941 concert in the Fisk Memorial Chapel marks a spiritual beginning point for the explorations that follow. John Work III's affectionate words for the omnipresent artistry he so warmly welcomed reach beyond the afternoon program his school modestly labeled "Folklore in the Fisk Community."[6] He in turn credited as his mentor and champion one who had helped build that concert's philosophical infrastructure and voiced it within these walls thirteen years earlier. This person was also his next-door neighbor and friend. "My father," John Work IV told me, "loved Charles Johnson."[7]

On October 17, 1928, Charles S. Johnson gave his maiden lecture at Fisk. A few days before, Johnson (1893–1956), an admired sociologist, editor of the National Urban League's magazine *Opportunity,* and a leading figure in the Harlem Renaissance, arrived on campus to chair its revitalized department of sociology. The previous year Fisk received a five-year grant from the Rockefeller Foundation to strengthen its social sciences department. Johnson accepted an invitation from Fisk President Thomas E. Jones to head this department, with the understanding that Fisk would become a major research hub of black life and race relations.[8] Johnson's subsequent regional studies, which combined statistical surveys with first-person testimonies, became landmark works of social science, one by-product being the 1941–42 collaboration between Fisk and the Library of Congress in their joint study of black folk music in Mississippi's Coahoma County.[9] Now, at the outset of his career at Fisk, which eventually led to his becoming the school's first black president, Johnson spoke in the chapel about matters of social status.

In a society of unequal opportunity and racial dogma, Johnson pondered aloud how black youth might best surmount these challenges. Early in his remarks he directed their attention to an available resource: "We have in Negro life a virgin world of beauty which can yield rich satisfactions and command a new order of respect, and . . . the freedom which these bring is a first condition of participation in world culture."[10] He recommended the students develop both "a cult of competence" and "a cult of beauty."[11] With the former he discussed occupational strategies, development of skills, and notions of excellence. For the latter he counseled his youthful listeners to find in common experience its sustaining values. That search, he said "is the spirit of the New America."[12]

Johnson acknowledged that the spirituals and folklore of slavery days had given America some of its most stirring art. Recently that focus had widened with the emergence of the blues and creative writers going "'back to the concrete.'"[13] In literature Johnson credited Carl Sandburg and Edwin

Arlington Robinson as instigators of this movement that found "beauty in forgotten lives." To their company he added contemporary black authors such as Langston Hughes and Jean Toomer. He quoted Toomer's "Georgia Dusk," in which men sing as their workday shifts to evening pleasures, "the chorus of the cane / Is caroling a vesper to the stars."[14] That such a scene might furnish materials of art communicated that "No life . . . is without beauty, no beginning too low."[15] Similarly, in an article published a few months earlier, Johnson applauded Langston Hughes, who took for subjects "cabaret singers, porters, street walkers, elevator boys, the long range of 'hard luck' victims, Beale Street and Railroad Avenue, prayer meetings, sinners and hard working men."[16] He compared these figures to the blues, noting the broad appeal generated from its portrayal of those "who live beneath the range of polite respect."[17] Wanting the students to cherish their culture at all levels of society, Johnson brought these outcasts and commoners, field hands and cane cutters home to the Fisk audience: "I am convinced that the road to a new freedom for us lies in the discovery of the surrounding beauties of our lives."[18]

Johnson's credo came early in his career. Assigned by a charity to research some impoverished applicants for Christmas baskets, Johnson grasped that "no man can be justly judged until you have looked at the world through his eyes."[19] Calling this the core of his social philosophy, "it led to the University of Chicago where I met . . . Robert E. Park. It was he who linked this deep and moving human concern with science and human understanding, and with the great minds that have struggled with these issues—William James, John Dewey, George Santayana, Josiah Royce, all his friends." These names that begin with Park, Johnson's sociology professor whom he later hired at Fisk, helped shape American pragmatist thought that emerged from the wounds of the Civil War. Johnson identified himself with that tradition and put his faith, as had these others, in "the power of experience to provide, in its own on-going movement, the needed principles of belief and action."[20] Johnson pressed its empiricism into the methodology that marked his research: "In working with the Negro migrants then moving in millions in a current too vast for them to comprehend, this zeal was channeled to see the world through their eyes and interpret it and them. So it has been, through each successive human problem that has become a part of my experience."[21]

A like spirit of empathy and inquiry guided John Work III in his 1941 concert. Prior to that event, Work had visited with the day's musicians, learning about their artistry as they conceived it. Equipped with this knowledge, he then explored with the chapel audience habituated to the Fisk Jubilee

Singers, heedful of Western European classical aesthetics, ways to appreciate vernacular music on its own terms. He explained how each idiom had corresponding but separate approaches to tonality, decoration, rhythm, and repetition. Work contrasted the "throaty tone" used by the folk with "our opera-set standard of head tone."[22] While the former "never sang a head tone in their lives," the latter—and he included himself among them—"no matter how glorious we think the rich head tone may be, it is . . . the product of the European concert hall and opera house." He also helped his listeners open themselves to the fiddle and banjo pieces. "When listening to a folk instrumentalist," he forewarned, "do not demand or expect a sweet, luscious, vibrant tone. The performer does not play upon a Stradivarius or Guarnerius violin. . . . If he is a good performer, he offers you instead a driving rhythm and astounding melodic patterns and ornaments, most of which he inherited from the tradition and some he invented." Musical values likewise served social practice. Work contrasted the hypnotic power of a repeated figure in a gospel song that in the classics would register as monotonous. He told of a Nashville churchgoer who exhorted a vocal quartet during an especially long song. "Keep on singing, chillun," she called out. "I ain't near tired yet."[23]

Work's affectionate musicology went further than just illuminating the artists' traditions and their skills. The sight of street banjoist Ned Frazier and hoedown fiddler Frank Patterson exhausting their guitarist Ford Britton as they plowed through a set of vintage reels in the Fisk Memorial Chapel made an implicit statement about cultural inclusion.[24] By inviting them into this sanctuary, Work had extended a position taken by his father and embodied by his grandfather. Both John Work I and John Work II played crucial roles in the formation and training of the Fisk Jubilee Singers and the dissemination of their music.[25] While Work II had at times scorned black secular styles, that dismissal fit within a larger strategy. He passionately defended the spirituals, knowing that the graceful beauties of the "sorrow songs" demonstrated black humanity to a skeptical majority.[26] The international esteem accorded the Fisk spirituals confirmed their worth not just as a racial, but as an American art form.[27] In effect, he reasoned, they made a case for social enfranchisement. At the 1941 concert Work III built upon this argument for a new generation by presenting genres and practitioners that his father could not. More than simply art appreciation surrounded his whimsical introduction of Frank Patterson's fiddling: "You will not hear any vibrato in his playing," he vowed, "although you are due to vibrate."[28] That the poetic resided in the prosaic translated here into a democratic ideal.

FIGURE 4.
Three generations.
Left to right:
John Work II,
John Work I, John
Work III. Courtesy
of John Work IV.

Johnson shaped his sociological studies and Work III pursued his musicology out of a profound respect for others, in an acceptance of differences. In May 1941 this common perspective resurfaced in another endeavor about to begin. During the same week as Work's concert, the president of Fisk and the head of the school's music department met with the Library of Congress's Alan Lomax, who had come to participate in the Fisk anniversary celebrations. These discussions led to a conference that summer in Charles Johnson's office, which John Work III also attended. There they outlined the forthcoming folk music survey of Mississippi's Coahoma County. This celebrated project, foreshadowed by Charles Johnson's research in that region, as well as Work's recent proposal to document the community folklore that emerged from a calamitous April 1940 fire in Natchez, Mississippi, centered in the Fisk social sciences department.[29] Plans called for a handful of Johnson's colleagues to do most of the field work. The task of musical interpretations and transcriptions fell largely to Work III. Alan Lomax represented the Library, bringing to the endeavor its stature and recording gear, apart from his reputation as a veteran folksong collector.

In September 1941, following an initial Mississippi collecting foray that August (which included Work III as part of the Fisk team), Lomax conducted a training session at the school. He played a series of recordings for the field-workers that mirrored the variety of genres they might find on location. He also outlined the research method:

> The history of song & music in the community can be reconstructed from a thorough cross check of the accounts of persons of varying ages.
>
> American music, being largely oral, will thus have its history written in the only way possible.
>
> If you will turn to the outline on page 10 & examine the outline of the music catalogue you will notice that our classification is largely functional—that is the songs are divided up according to the way they function in community life. This classification approximates—I believe—that which is current among the people, themselves. Our job will be to note down, copy and or record the songs and music of the community against a background of real speech of the people. The validity of this approach can be illustrated by a quote from Handy's biography.[30]

Then Lomax quoted W. C. Handy's eye-opening experience with some roughshod country musicians at a soirée in Cleveland, Mississippi. Someone had asked Handy to play some "native music."[31] That idiom lay outside his sight-reading ensemble's forte, and he deferred to a threadbare trio standing around who only had "a battered guitar, a mandolin and a worn-out bass." They played a number redolent of "cane rows and levee camps" and with it tore down the house. Listeners showered their approval on these men in silver dollars. Handy saw that these unprepossessing musicians had "touched the spot" and realized, as he had not before, that this harsh-textured music reflected a deeply felt community taste. This practical and spiritual revelation moved Handy to base his future work on folk materials. Returning to his home in Clarksdale that night he wrote "a composer was born, an *American* composer."

The inspiration that Handy took from that evening, like the Fisk social sciences department's research methods, had placed faith in the folk. Kindred trends in regionalist literature, notions of pluralism articulated in the New Deal, ethnographic description dependent on native categories, recent approaches to cultural history, as well as themes developed in the Harlem Renaissance took this direction. Under the anthropological rubric of functionalism, folklorists focused on vernacular creativity from the point of view of its listeners and makers.[32] Writing to John Work III in 1935, anthropologist George Herzog applauded their mutual approach to African American music and commended Work's affinity for his subjects.[33] While Work's forays into field recording began only in 1938, his 1930 Columbia master's thesis, where he cited Charles Johnson's 1928 "Jazz Poetry and Blues," had already demonstrated his commitment to field work and his attention to living context, echoing Johnson's pragmatist approach.

In April 1938 Herzog pointed to missing areas in American folksong study: how songs function within the communities where they are sung, what they mean to the singers who perform them, and how they are understood by those who listen to them. He added that neither compiled verses nor comparative data provided enough information to understand the music's role in its local settings. Indeed, he remarked, we may wonder "just why it is that people find delight or satisfaction in singing about things so remote as castles and kings and princes, whose existence in actual life would clash with what they know and practice of democracy."[34] That curiosity led Herzog, along with his former student Herbert Halpert, followed soon by folklorist Benjamin Botkin at the Federal Writers' Project, and eventually Alan Lomax and the Fisk team, to develop questionnaires based on this linkage of the participants' lives to their lore. The Fisk/Library of Congress Coahoma culture study was still underway during the April 1942 Washington conference, "Character and State of Studies in Folklore," where Lomax contemplated future community-centered projects elsewhere in the country: "The best interpretations of folklore may be obtained in the end from the folk themselves, and holds that the objective of the folklorist is not only an historical one, but one of recording and interpreting a living human tradition."[35]

At that time the first volumes of the Library's Folk Music of the United States series that Lomax, with the help of his division chief, Harold Spivacke, had been assembling, neared completion.[36] These endeavors also consisted of folklore obtained from the folk. To be sure, the living human traditions available on those products had previously filtered through the field collectors who made on-site decisions about whom and what they would record, and then was channeled again through Lomax's and Spivacke's editorial and auditory choices that governed these collections. Yet that winnowing did not dilute the immediacy of the performances or diminish the role of the performers. For the most part they are not anonymous. The album brochures usually identify them, and often the singers and instrumentalists spoke their names after they finished their numbers, "recorded for the benefit of the Library of Congress in Washington, D.C."

The living presence of these performers did not escape Benjamin Botkin, who became head of the Folk Archive following Alan Lomax's departure in 1942. Botkin numbered among the first to comment on the initial set of releases. Soon to edit the Archive's next four albums himself, Botkin wrote: "They give us a new understanding of the diversity of American life. They bring us into direct contact with the people—workers, prison inmates, house-wives, and school children—white, Negro, and Indian—who made these records."[37] In highlighting these transmitters, he affirmed their worth. If largely unknown as creators and interpreters, they stood outside of romantic cari-cature. Botkin did not voice Popular Front ideology that defended the folk as marginalized and overlooked. Nor did he call upon the perennial notion that folklore harbors the spirit of a people, their inner essence or soul. He also kept some distance from the folk music revival, which so often saw the folk as exotic symbols of otherness, pursuing a simple life that never was. "Although in most cases it is impossible to establish the origin of a piece of folklore," he wrote nearly a quarter century later, "we want to know as much as possible about its source, history and use in relation to the past and pres-ent experience of the people who keep it alive. This information enables us to understand the function and meaning which folklore has for those who use it and so enhances its interest and significance for others."[38] The key to understanding the products of tradition, Botkin reminds us, as Johnson and Work had earlier, is to explore the roles they have played and to learn from the people whose experience this creativity reflects, whether within a com-munity or extending beyond. This approach to the American cultural mosaic, the same that had resounded in the Fisk Memorial Chapel, guides this book.

This project began on June 3, 1994, during a telephone conversation with Ger-ald E. Parsons, Jr. For twenty-one years Gerry worked as the reference librarian of the Library of Congress's Archive of Folk Culture, and he brought to this idea, as he brought to whatever he touched, a lucid, clarifying vision. We agreed in the course of that talk to gather for a new release some of the wonderful performances that had appeared on the Library's legendary albums. Less than an hour later, a record company agreed to publish this nascent collection.[39]

Only a few minutes into that discussion with Gerry, it became clear to us both which piece should open the CD and which should end it. Start-ing with fiddler Bill Stepp's rendition of "Bonaparte's Retreat," whose strains

FIGURE 5.
Belo Cozad of
Stecker, Oklahoma,
ca. 1941. Courtesy of
Leonard Cozad Sr.

have resounded throughout the nation in diverse but wholly identifiable ways, it would end with Kiowa Indian Belo Cozad playing a cedar flute he carved himself. In the summer of 1941, during a recording he made at the Riverside Indian School in Anadarko, Oklahoma, Belo told how his tune came about. Before he played it, he described an ancestor who went up on a mountain and after four days received this music as a gift. Subsequently it transferred to Belo. Recounting this saga to the ethnomusicologist recording him, he says "Keep it. Keep it as long as you live."[40] Belo is giving this stranger operating a disc machine a place in a precious musical heritage.

I thought, as did Gerry, who loved this recording, that to close the sampler with this heartwarming alternative to the Balkanization, identity politics, and fragmentation that occupied so much current thought and effort in cultural matters expressed a message as encompassing as Bill Stepp's anthemic fanfare. I also thought that to structure the CD this way recalled an aim that had propelled the Folk Music of the United States albums from the start. The Library launched the series not only to offer the American public exemplary holdings from its Folk Archive, but also as part of an intercultural exchange program with the republics of South America. Like Belo Cozad sharing his heritage with an outsider, these releases introduced disparate peoples to one another, literally crossing borders, political as well as cultural.

The series' distribution in the Southern Hemisphere traces back to a unanimous resolution for artistic exchange passed in December 1936 during the Inter-American Conference on the Maintenance of Peace held in Buenos Aires, a commitment "founded upon a growing knowledge of, and respect for, each others' views and aspirations."[41] The subsequent establishment of a State Department division on cultural relations, and several inter-American music conferences held at the Library in 1939 and 1940 involving a range of cultural experts, advanced interest in the albums' creation.[42] Support followed, and between 1942 and 1945, the series' first eleven releases derived their principal funding from a $5,000 annual Department of State grant. Beginning in spring 1942 Alan Lomax wrote to performers seeking their permission to issue selected recordings for the initial compilations: "The Archive of American Folk Song is planning to make up a group of the best, representative American Folk Songs to be distributed in Latin America."[43]

The CD that Gerry and I now discussed focused on the aesthetic component of their cross-cultural appeal. Though the Library's albums, like most documentary field recordings, surveyed or represented various anthropological, literary, or historical principles, Gerry thought that presenting certain performances purely for their artistry, "apart from what they might represent as examples of scholars' categories," provided reason enough.[44] "A tune that helped Mississippi River roustabouts 'dance' 400 pound bales of cotton up the gangway, or a ballad that eased a lonely housewife through her day of pre-electric drudgery, or the lullaby that sang her cranky child to sleep, or the spiritual that focused the devotional energies of an old-time congregation, or the fiddle tune that brought sets in order for an evening's frolic could also speak to us as art. . . . Each of these expressions are enduring testimonials to something profoundly admirable in the human spirit."[45] Gerry's eloquence never left him, although by then cancer had stricken him. He died in the summer of 1995 at age fifty-five. To the end he passionately believed in what his folklorist colleague Edward Ives had written in an article for the American Folklife Center's *Folklife Annual*: "What I am arguing for, then, is the principle of the essential equivalence of all art forms as elements in systems of expressive culture to be taken on their own terms."[46]

Certainly artistry exceptional and representative appears throughout the Folk Music of the United States series. Sometimes the players take familiar melodies and reconstitute them in wholly individualistic ways. The sinewy, liquid slides that banjoist Wade Ward employs in the opening measures of "Old Joe Clark" make him sound like no one else, his timing in those passages and his touch on the strings unmistakably bearing his musical signature. Others, like the Shipp sisters, bring unexpected atmosphere to a children's game song, quieting its playground gyrations through the stillness of their blended voices. David "Honeyboy" Edwards takes "Worried Life Blues" through a startling succession of single-string runs, bent notes, treble licks, half-chord voicings, and boogie-woogie patterns. One man with a guitar becomes an entire orchestra. Fiddler W. E. Claunch whoops over his high-voltage "Grub Springs," the open notes of his cross-tuned violin ringing in unison with his vocal hollers. His daughter, playing the guitar, keeps close accompaniment, extending that family's multigenerational predilection for music making. "Every Claunch that ever was could play," he said at the time of the recording, referring to his grandfather, father, and his four brothers, all fiddlers.[47] No wonder five months earlier a WPA worker filling out a personal history on Claunch observed, "His everything is music. He can play any instrument he ever saw & any music he hears."[48]

During that telephone conversation with Gerry, I found myself pouring out these titles and others brimming with comparable power, beginning with Jess Morris's "Goodbye, Old Paint," Ora Dell Graham's "Pullin' the Skiff," Luther Strong's "Glory in the Meetinghouse," and Vera Hall's "Another Man Done Gone." Nearly all the numbers explored in this book got named during that initial talk. The remainder of the CD's selections required my listening to the whole LP series, but that task considerably narrowed by drawing only from those made on disc-cutting machines. Their use coincided with the Library's folksong expeditions, and consequently I tried to make choices mindful of that era's collecting practices. A Pennsylvania mining ballad, a Cajun French song, and a Creek lullaby included in the final set helped illustrate the breadth of those acquisition efforts.[49]

The other element governing the *Treasury* choices involved spoken word exchanges. These comments, sometimes short interviews, provided glimpses of the performers engaged in their art and the recording sessions at their moment of creation. Editors of the original albums often left these off, probably for reasons of time. Restored here, they attested to what recordists like the Lomaxes had witnessed firsthand: "Singing in their homes, in their churches, at their dances, they leave on these records imperishable spirals of their personalities, their singing styles, and their cultural heritage."[50] Some remarks by blind Mississippi harmonica player and street musician Turner Junior Johnson convey this imperishable poignancy. Before the disc machine began turning, he told of losing his sight at age sixteen, "I suffered with a swimmin' in my head when I was coming up."[51] Though he spent over a year and a half at Nashville's Tennessee School for the Blind and learned Braille, his condition left him no other means to survive than as a mendicant musician. The next day he sang "When I Lay My Burden Down," calling it his favorite number. By then he had set its message in context: "When you leave this old mortality," he noted, "you'll see with a spiritual eye."

By mid-July 1994 I had selected thirty-nine tracks for the CD, eighty-eight minutes of sound. The Library's Recording Laboratory soon transferred the material from the original discs to digital tape. For a single disc intended to run slightly more than seventy minutes in length, the extra songs offered some alternatives in case of rights issues, which in the end never arose. The record company set up an escrow account for performers or their designees, and the project dictated a total of thirty tracks. Of the thirty-six artists I began with at that time, the Archive had valid addresses for thirteen of them, or their survivors, and little information in general about the performers.

This absence of biographical information was not all that surprising. Many folklorists of the 1930s saw the songs they collected as critical emblems of American culture. Matters of textural and melodic variation preoccupied scholarly attention, and individual performers and their creativity formed a lesser concern. Practical considerations also played a part: the technical difficulties of disc recording and the limited amount of recording time on each disc (about four minutes per side on the ten-inch blanks recorded at 78 rpm, and four-and-a-half minutes each on the twelve-inch blanks) made the song-in-itself a scarce commodity and thereby gave it special value.[52] By contrast, musicians seemed in relatively abundant supply. Consequently the artifact—the song—often took preeminence over the artist. Late in the 1930s, however, this began to change, and the biography of folk performers emerged as a new area of academic and literary concern. Certainly Alan Lomax's 1938 recordings of Jelly Roll Morton signaled a significant step in that direction. The gathering of ex-slave narratives, the idea of history told from the bottom up, and the aim enunciated at the 1939 conference of the American Historical Association toward "the study of history from the standpoint of the total culture" help frame this shift.[53]

At the outset of this project, that past seemed to return when a number of the performers' permission forms came back "undeliverable." Many of their addresses had stayed unchanged in the Archive's files during the half century since those first letters went out informing them of the albums' distribution in Latin America. Where had these singers and musicians gone? Who were they, beyond a few words possibly spoken on a smattering of discs? What were their lives? How did they learn these songs, let alone what happened with those pieces once their performances got disseminated? Even with the Archive's resources of correspondence files, subject files on the songs, and field notes on the expeditions, along with the reference tapes to draw upon, I knew from my own ventures as a musician calling on older players—a process inspired by these very recordings—that I would take that route again: to seek out this music from the perspective of the participants, their family members, neighbors, and fellow players closest to the experience. In the same way I had learned from traditional musicians in their homes, I wanted to know what lay behind these recordings, framing the songs and tunes in what Charles Seeger called their "inner technical and outer sociological tradition."[54] With these aspirations in mind, and hoping reciprocally that the musicians and their families whose knowledge I sought might receive new recognition as well as their royalty advances, I began traveling to where each of the pieces on *A Treasury of Library of Congress Field Recordings* had been recorded.

By November 1994, Alan Jabbour, director of the American Folklife Center at the Library of Congress and past head of the Archive of Folk Culture himself, observed the flurry going on with this project and suggested this effort become a book. Two years later that led me to Judy McCulloh of the University of Illinois Press and the Music in American Life series that she stewarded for thirty-five years. As we sat in the quiet of the Folk Archive's reading room and formally launched this effort, Judy, herself a veteran of folksong study, asked, "What lessons do these songs have to teach? What do they tell us about American life? How might a given performance illuminate larger circumstances?" Judy's questions made the need for stories and the search for witnesses all the more urgent. I grabbed my tape recorder, left the banjo at home, and got back out on the road.

Heaven knows I have had my share of wonderful, frustrating, frightening, and transporting moments with the songs and singers that comprised the *Treasury.* So many scenes along the way. Some of them dark: In Huntsville, Texas, I walked in an abandoned cell block that once held not only the legendary Leadbelly, but also guitarist Smith Casey, a rich-voiced, soulful Paul Robeson of a singer. Before his conviction for first-degree murder, Casey worked as a solo street musician and in a small band despite the disfigurement of a crushed nose that horribly scarred his face. Both the Library's field notes and his prison records mentioned a radio show he did during confinement. Staffers from the Texas Department of Criminal Justice now provided more information about "Thirty Minutes behind the Walls," broadcast from the Huntsville penitentiary.

They also gave me access to two more facilities, one where he resided during the time of those broadcasts, and the other during the time of his recordings. At the first, Wynne Farm, after going through the sally port, the double-gated entrance, I turned around for some reason and saw the sign above the gate that read "No hostages past this point." That meant they weren't going to open it if someone caught me from the inside. At Clemens, where Smith Casey made his recordings, I got taken along the "ad-seg" unit—administrative segregation, or solitary confinement—warned a moment before that I might get "chunked" with feces and blood. The guard wore a raincoat, and I followed behind still in shirtsleeves, moving breathlessly down that corridor close between the cells. Later I listened in amazement as one guard told the other that in case of a foreign invasion, he thought that under some general order they were supposed to kill all the inmates. But of that he wasn't really sure.

Even more haunting was the leather cap and sponge worn during electrocutions that the warden of the James River Correctional Center at State Farm, Virginia, showed me.[55] The striations on its cracked surface cried out with the pain of every person who had worn it. I also saw a face carved of soap. A convict had stuffed a life-size figure in his bed clothes, and then placed this uncannily detailed, flesh-colored relief topped with human hair on his pillow for a nighttime escape.

That afternoon we called on a ninety-two-year-old retired prison guard. He mentioned a blind banjoist he watched over in the mid-1930s. In that completely unprompted moment the warden and I knew that he recalled Jimmie Strothers, the source of "Blood-Strained Banders," a song that many of my generation first heard from the Jefferson Airplane's singing of "Good Shepherd." Later I gave their former guitarist Jorma Kaukonen a copy of *Treasury*, which contains this number. He had taught that song to his band, but had never heard it directly. He learned it from another musician who got it from a Folk Archive album. So goes the winding path of cultural transmission.

A different journey attended Judge Learned Hand. Hand sang the "Iron Merrimac" in a typical Adirondack ballad style. But he brought something beyond that tradition to the *Treasury*. The contrast of his eminence—his family background of New York lawyers, his Harvard education, his distinguished career—with the personal, hand-me-down character of folksong made a statement all its own. A couple years after the CD came out, I received from his grandson some nearly forgotten tapes, unplayed for years and kept in a closet in the family's home. On several reels made in the 1950s, along with others containing French lessons and practice recitations, Hand's daughter Mary interviews her father. At one point she asks him to name his earliest memories growing up. Suddenly Judge Hand sings the multiplication table to the tune of "Yankee Doodle."[56]

Perhaps no one more fully gathered the threads of this work than Ella Hoffpauir Boudreaux. On an overcast day in June 1934, Ella, then ten years

old, had gone outside to play with two of her older sisters. As they often did for fun, the three girls began singing together. By chance, folksong collectors John and Alan Lomax, staying nearby, drove past the Hoffpauirs' house in New Iberia, Louisiana, and heard them. Ella's mother, Cora Lee, was home when they knocked, but as she never learned English and spoke only French, the folklorists made arrangements with the family's head and main musical force, traditional Cajun ballad singer Julien Hoffpauir. "They came in and asked if we wanted to sing," Ella said.[57] With a chuckle she added, "We were never shy about singing." The house had no electricity. The Lomaxes set up their disc-cutting machine on the porch and used aluminum blanks to make the recordings. Sixty-three years later the one they gave Ella as a keepsake still shined in her memory. "I used to love that little record."

The year before the recordings took place, Julien Hoffpauir had moved his family of twelve to New Iberia from the countryside, hoping to find new opportunities for them all. He possessed an aptitude for math and a facility with lyrics and melody but could not read or write. His increasingly ill health affected his capacity to earn a living. A former Jefferson Island salt miner and small farmer, he had developed a severely ulcerated stomach, initially contracted from smoke inhalation during a house fire when Ella was still

INTRODUCTION

an infant. He had recently lost his livestock to cholera, and with no funds to replace them, circumstances now required that the whole family chip in for their welfare. "The country was rock bottom," said Ella of those Depression years.[58] "You couldn't buy a job."

The shotgun house where they lived, two rooms and a kitchen that they rented for five dollars a month, had to serve the nine family members still at home. Julien built a shed for their cow, always kept a pig, and raised a garden. Despite his infirmities, he made sure that his family never went hungry. However, that specter stayed close by. Two years later, with no money to buy clothes, Ella left school at age twelve and began full-time work, cleaning houses for seventy-five cents a week. Sometimes she joined her mother for weeklong stays out in the country cutting sugar cane and harvesting peppers. Her voice choked up when she mentioned a one-dollar dress she purchased for Cora Lee back then. Ella set aside a quarter each week to give her this gift. "We didn't have anything," she explained. "But one thing we did have was a lot of love and respect for one another. So I think that's what made us the human beings that we are today." Raised by her family to share, she recalled a neighboring family in New Iberia to whom she sometimes brought leftover food. Those children were so hungry, they didn't wait to get utensils. They just ate with their hands.

A song that Ella and her sisters learned from their father also had to do with hunger. It reaches back centuries, a mariner's ballad found in Iceland, Denmark, Norway, Great Britain, and French Canada. He called it "Six ans sur mer," and as the title indicates, it tells of a party adrift at sea for six years. Unable to find land, they depleted the provisions aboard their ship, leaving them to eat mice and rats that occupied the hold. When all food is gone, they draw straws to determine which of them will be sacrificed. Little Jean draws the fatal straw but tells his comrades to take courage. In the next verse, he sees land all around and three pigeons flying overhead. Then he spies a prince's daughters walking along the water's edge and vows that should he ever get to shore, he'll wed the most beautiful of the three.

Ella smiles at the song's happy ending, but deeper emotions cross her face when she listens to the recording. The voices of her sisters provoke tears, their music "bringing back the past."[59] Earlier, when we discussed that past, specifically her father's German lineage, yet all of them raised in the French language, which they learned before they spoke English, Ella said, "That's what America's all about. We're all immigrants, but we're born here."[60] In another conversation she repeated this same thought, then added, "I know

I'm a mixture. . . . We're all mixtures in this part of the world . . . in the whole United States. Our ancestors had to come from overseas somewhere, and mine came from Germany and France."[61] A moment later she cast this thought in moral terms. "And that's why I just couldn't understand why Hitler, how he wanted to kill these Jews so much. Why? What was the reason? . . . We're all God's children. It's just like these black people. A lot . . . just hate them. Why? There's no reason for that. I can't see it. . . . We never thought because your color has to make you a difference of your person."

Without dismissing race or ethnicity, Ella's acceptance of others fit her sense of American society and its composite mix. She spoke from a devout religious creed—herself a Eucharistic minister—communicating an ethic she learned as a youngster. She voiced a personal response to a national matter. We hear her testimony now because of some beautiful music that Ella and her sisters made so long ago.

Each of the thirteen songs and tunes in this book is both exceptional and representative. No logic insists that the remaining seventeen from the *Treasury* had to be here, even though that drove my plan originally, and those pieces have as much to tell as these do here. I'm sure, too, that the same applies to the more than eleven hundred others that appear on the earlier Library albums, the thousands more in the Folk Archive, the tens of thousands issued on commercial hillbilly, race, and ethnic music records, and untold ones never recorded. "Any good song," said folklorist Archie Green, "deserves a case study."[62]

Mentor to this book and master of the case study approach that sets its investigative model, Archie (1917–2009) spent more than sixty years studying folksong and society. Over those decades he probed how traditional music and related forms of vernacular creativity formed a counterpart to democracy. Like Charles Johnson cherishing "the surrounding beauties of our lives," or John Work III presenting "The Beautiful Music All Around You" program, Archie welcomed the effects of cultural inclusion. "To value the separate vernaculars in American life, to stress our difference and not insist on a unified culture," he asserted, offered a way to hold together a contentious society.[63] He would have applauded Ella Hoffpauir Boudreaux's analysis of the American alloy, and the tolerance she distilled from its clangorous, sometimes clashing valences. Likewise, he would have granted that if art is wherever you find it—as the field recordings of Ella and her sisters exemplify—there follows a recognition of plural experience. "Do we ask too much by calling for equity and democracy in cultural life," Archie wrote late in his life. "The peasant fiddler is as worthy as the symphony violinist; the village cobbler more precious than a pair of boots."[64]

A nonmusician but an intensely social thinker, Archie continually asked, "What is the force of ideas embodied in the music?"[65] These works constituted community statements as well as musical systems. Thus the meaning of a song to a sharecropper, he pointed out, is different than the meaning we might find in it. That earlier meaning, too, can become completely lost to us. He knew that repertory continually crosses boundaries, that music moves from one setting to another—a road grader's wheelbarrow worksong might become a railroader's lament, a mountain fiddle tune might find a place in a formal composition. Ever the functionalist, he paid close attention to currents flowing both within their original cultural settings and outward to their reception in the larger society. Watchful of these contexts, Archie stressed that "every artistic expression has an ideology underneath."[66] For this reason, each case study has much to tell us about American life, though hardly a monolithic portrait.

Archie also said "Enjoy your scholarship." He knew from his own years of work the joys, the elation, and the serendipities that come so unexpectedly with this research, along with the frustrations, false leads, lost memories and documents, and awareness that the work will always remain incomplete. He likened folksong research to casting a fishing line into a pond. While we may learn that spot well and get a good sense of its currents and bottom, more water surrounds it. Tradition extends far beyond our view, recycling itself through time and space, changing, shifting. With his analytic tools, his rod and reel, Archie taught, we cast for origin, form, function, and meaning. Always follow the evidence, he counseled, and relish the pursuit, wherever it leads.

When I think of all the miles traveled over the long course of this book's development, and the case studies that might have been, I sometimes recollect a guitar that belonged to musician E. C. Ball and a song he used to play on it. In early September 1941 Alan and Elizabeth Lomax had just come up from Mississippi, where Alan, along with John Work III, made their first collaborative recordings. Soon Alan would return to Fisk to conduct the training sessions mentioned before. Now, in fiddler Walt Henderson's home, the only house in Rugby, Virginia, that had electricity, he recorded Ball and his band: his wife

Orna, her brother Wade Reedy, and Henderson. Ball sang by himself on "Pretty Polly," an eighteenth-century English broadside ballad he learned from a 1927 record by an eastern Kentucky banjoist. From that performance Ball (1913–78) crafted a version that combined the sonorities of his guitar with the mood of the banjo, giving new life to the song's somber tale. "I always like to use my own style near as much as I can," he later said. "I always like to feel like I was different, maybe not any better, but just different from somebody else."[67]

He applied that maxim to his prized guitar, a 1949 Martin D-28. Sylvia Henderson, Walt's widow and first cousin to Orna, kept it under her bed in the same room where fifty-five years earlier Ball sang "Pretty Polly" for the Lomaxes. She remembered that clear summer night, and then warmly remarked, "Old-time music. I lived in it."[68] We took the guitar from its case. Its handcrafted mother-of-pearl position markers, wavy and indented from use, still shined along the fingerboard. Surprisingly, its customarily plain ebony bridge also glittered with decorative inlays. Using his pocketknife, Ball had shaved some slivers from Orna's engagement ring and embedded these particles into the bridge, an otherwise black wooden strip that anchored the strings. Just as he had listened to the music and found ways to make it his own, Ball had cut into this factory-built guitar and brought something entirely personal into its very body.

Like E. C. Ball, the singers and instrumentalists in this book all exerted their own creativity on inherited forms. As Gerry Parsons characterized their artistry, they "responded by amplifying tradition's gifts through the medium of their own abilities and according to their own understanding of the human condition."[69] The chapters that follow continually balance the personal with the historical, the enduring with the evolving, the individual and the social tradition, reflecting what Ben Botkin called "a compromise between folklore as a creative expression and folklore as a cultural record."[70] One other pairing runs through here: the official with the informal, for that identifies the connection between the Library of Congress and these performers.

"The country," John Dewey wrote in 1920, "is a spread of localities, while the nation is something that exists in Washington and other seats of government."[71] Dewey had observed that while hometown newspapers dutifully make use of wire services and, from time to time, write sober editorials on matters of national import, the greater interest of these papers lay in their chronicling of nearby events, such as "fires, burglaries, murders, family jars, weddings, and banquets to esteemed fellow citizens."[72] A corresponding blend characterizes the Library's Folk Music of the United States series—an endeavor emanating from Washington that defined America locally. "Take all the localities of the United States," Dewey added, "and extract their greatest common divisor, and the result is of necessity a crackling surface."[73] Through these field recordings we hear those crackling localities, places on the American map where we can find a beautiful music all around us. On a personal level, most of the singers and players here made these recordings and returned to their lives with little contact again with the Library or its records. But wherever those albums went, with their luminous examples of "best, representative American Folk Music," by then these individuals had made a difference. One by one they show us what a single person can do in a democracy.

Bill Stepp

Retreat across America

J OHN AND BECKY ARNETT OF WEST LIBERTY, KENTUCKY, MADE
their way through Orlando International Airport and boarded the mono-
rail that would ferry them to the departure lounges. Like a futuristic ride
at nearby Disney World, the train glided past postcard views of manmade
lakes and landscaped palm trees. It coasted to a stop, and a warning tone
signaled the vehicle's computer-driven arrival. They began their trek down
the long, carpeted corridor to the plane. Gate announcements, prefaced by
the bleating of an electronic whistle, barked from the public address system.
Between the clatter of messages and noises, a crescendo of forty concert violins and a xylophone streamed from the loudspeakers. For many of Orlando's
air travelers, the melody recalled a well-known television commercial in
which images of sizzling steaks and high-spirited fun flash across the screen.
Throughout the spot, this musical arrangement plays beneath the gunmetal
voice of Robert Mitchum telling a nation, "Beef. It's what's for dinner."[1] Becky
listened to a few notes, pointed to the speakers overhead, and said, "John,
can't you hear it? That's Grandpa! That's Grandpa!"[2]

In truth, Becky's grandfather, fiddler Bill Stepp, born in rural Kentucky
twenty-five years before the close of the nineteenth century, is the creative
source of an American anthem. In 1942 his rendition of the tune "Bonaparte's

Retreat" became incorporated, nearly note for note, in the score of *Rodeo,* Aaron Copland's acclaimed modern ballet.[3] Cast in a rousing orchestral setting, the piece entered the repertory of popular American concert works. By the early 1970s it appeared as "Hoedown," an FM radio hit for Emerson, Lake and Palmer, a symphonically oriented English rock band.[4] Later, it formed the soundtrack for the beef growers' commercial, and finally, in this, an example of its continuing presence in American life, it recurs in the music piped down the hallways of a modern airport. Bill Stepp's "Bonaparte's Retreat" spans our national experience.

William Hamilton Stepp (1875–1957) began life as the illegitimate child of a locally prominent father and a half-Indian mother whose principal means of support was prostitution. As a Nottaway Indian, Lucinda Stepp (1838–1909), like her mother, Rachel Memdra Miranda Sea Horse Stepp (1813–1887), occupied the lowest rungs of eastern Kentucky society. Although both women found occasional employment as domestics, and from time to time manufactured homemade lye soap, household brooms, and corn-shuck beds, they spent their lives in poverty. In the words of Lucinda's great-granddaughter, "These women would work all day for a spool of thread."[5] Not unlike today's homeless who occupy open bus shelters, from the mid-1870s until 1912 one or another of this family (including Lucinda's youngest sister, Morning Stepp) lived under a large sandstone cliff near Beattyville in Lee County, Kentucky. In that region of the state, the Kentucky, Licking, and Red Rivers have cut a number of such formations, and indigent persons up and down the rivers once occupied these rough cave dwellings. Along with moonshiners who took advantage of the concealment (and nearby running water) the caves afforded, and pirates who, in earlier years, preyed on the flatboats that plied these waters, the Stepps lived outside conventional practices and protections, their living spaces divided by scrap lumber and tree limbs.

The cliff lies near a modern ranch-style home that boasts a spacious vegetable garden and an outdoor swimming pool. From the line of trees behind the house, the ground drops away to a sharp ravine of shelf rock concealed by bushes and trees, its depths hidden by sunlight and overgrowth. One could easily plunge from this precipice into the rocks and scrub below. Only by leaning with the trail and grasping at roots scattered along the way can a venturer safely edge down the face of the incline. There, some fifty feet beneath the highway, is the cave where Bill Stepp spent the first five years of his life. It curves in a slow arc, divided into two chambers. Pieces of rock have fallen to the dry creekbed below from a stone canopy that jutted from the cliff's entrance. A natural spring still runs through its shaded interior. Soot marks from open fires have stained the rock ceiling. One can imagine a couple huddled in a dark corner of this dwelling, hidden from public detection. Here in April 1875 Bill Stepp was born, the product of a union between William Taylor Seale, scion of a judge and nephew of a local minister, and Lucinda Stepp. Bill was one of Seale's three children with Lucinda. But Seale never acknowledged these youngsters, a fact sardonically observed by one local as "too many woods colts."[6] In the year following his birth, authorities arrested Lucinda and her mother on charges of adultery, which, in the parlance of the day, was understood as prostitution. "Don't think too hard on them," said Lizzie Seale, a local centenarian who in 1986 still remembered Lucinda and her sisters. "They did what they had to do to survive."[7]

FIGURE 8. *Left to right:* Bill Stepp's mother, Lucinda Stepp, with Newton Coomer and Priscilla Stepp, Lee County, Kentucky, 1870s. Courtesy of Becky Arnett.

By the age of five, Bill Stepp had been removed from his mother's care to the nearby home of Asa Smyth. Bill became a "bound boy," in today's terminology a foster child. "It was in this home," recalls Bill Stepp's oldest granddaughter, Dorothy Allen, "that he began to play the fiddle." In 1880, sixty-year-old landowner Asa Smyth lived along the same Long Branch road as Lucinda and Rachel Stepp, his home within a half mile of the cliff. The county census of that year reports five-year-old William Stepp's presence in the family together with Smyth's two stepsons and his young wife. According to family accounts, Smyth was expected to teach the boy a trade and provide for him until the age of eighteen. Apparently a kind man, he did not isolate Bill from his mother or her people. Bill's sister, for instance, was married under Smyth's roof. Nearby, too, lived Bill's aunt Morning Stepp (1855–1933). Morning's companion, a man named William "Greasy Bill" Tincher, had been arrested in 1876 along with Rachel and Lucinda for adultery and with them saw the case dismissed two years later by the circuit court. A generation older than Bill Stepp, "Greasy Bill" played the fiddle, and it was this common-law uncle that locals cite as the young man's first musical exemplar during the time he lived at Asa Smyth's.[8]

In the mid-1890s Bill was performing at local affairs in Lee County and later Magoffin County, where he relocated. His showmanship is still remembered. Bill's nephew Clayton Congleton described one of his uncle's appearances in Beattyville. More than a hundred people—a sizable gathering for that time—traveled from throughout the region to dance to his fiddle. As Bill played from his spot on the back porch of Congletons' home, the guests "ran figures" along the wide, flat yard that lay behind the house. For some numbers he joined them himself, standing up to clog while he continued to draw his bow. On this occasion, he tied a red ribbon to his fiddle.[9]

These years of Bill's life were not easy. In addition to his work as a musician, he rafted logs. Lumber then ranked as the chief industry in Beattyville, a small town poised above the three forks of the Kentucky River. Bill transported product upriver to the sawmill in Royalton. During this period too, his first wife, Cornelia Noe (1874–1893), died in childbirth with their unborn daughter. Mother and child were buried on Asa Smyth's farm. In the wake of these losses Bill came to Magoffin County to visit Cornelia's family. Although Lee and Magoffin counties remained separated by only one county to the east, travel to Magoffin remained difficult well into the twentieth century. Before the 1930s brought paved roads, horseback or foot was the usual form of transport. He traveled by horse to Magoffin, where for the first time he encountered Cornelia's niece Hester Arnett. "I was staying over at Grandmother Noe's," Bill told Dorothy Allen. "That's how I met your grandmother."[10] They wed in 1896 and had twelve children, who, in turn, would give them sixty-three grandchildren.

"He was a shrewd old feller," said Nannie Howard, Bill Stepp's last surviving child. "And I mean, he was shifty."[11] Although Nannie spoke affectionately of her father, her choice of words seemed surprising. In calling him a shifty man she followed a long-time regional practice, revealing ambiguities of his character—fluent and resourceful, footloose and concealed. "Shifty people," Bill's grandson explained, "don't have the formal education. But, like Grandpa,

FIGURE 9.
Fiddler Bill
mounted up,
Magoffin County,
Kentucky, 1930s.
Courtesy of Elsie
Risner and
Becky Arnett.

they are smart in their own way. You can get by on a little of nothing, get by and do it well."[12]

By all accounts Bill cared little for workaday toil. He was not, in the words of another of his grandsons, "workified."[13] While the family warmly remembers this man they call Fiddler Bill, they also acknowledge his personal uprootedness. With a fiddle balanced on his saddle, and by the light of a kerosene lantern, he would leave home without notice for two or three weeks at a time. Nannie recounted an incident during her mother Hester's final illness. After dressing himself fastidiously, Bill announced he would "step out of a night."[14] Hester rose up from her sickbed and threw the contents of her bedpan on Bill's fresh suit with the words, "Now, Bill, take that to your dance." Nannie sat back in her chair and sighed, "He was a rounder." He married, I learned, seven times in his life.

Yet as he moved from Lee County to Magoffin, and finally to Hamlet, Indiana, where he finished his days, Bill took care to live in close radius of the family he and Hester had raised. None of his descendants remember him speaking of his childhood or of the domestic rupture that scarred his beginnings. Their living memories of Bill Stepp keep returning to his high style, his appealing flamboyance. His grandchildren knew him as a man who seldom worked, yet somehow kept money in his pocket. One smiled when he described this striking figure gone some forty years: "He could walk down a road and never get mud on his shoes."[15] Bill Stepp's daily attire of ironed shirts and pressed pants did not fit the mien of an outdoor laborer. "Oh, he wasn't a committed farmer," said his grandson. "He was a committed musician."

The awning that formerly sheltered the entrance to Owen Hoskins's Lakeville, Kentucky, grocery has fallen away. In the 1930s Fiddler Bill came by horseback to play here on Saturday mornings, as his neighbors traded their crops of tobacco, ginseng, and eggs. When I first visited the area in 1997, the boarded-up business with its whitewashed wood was collapsing, abandoned since the owner's death. For several years a local gospel group had parked its bus beside the building. The rusting vehicle stood unused, its once-bright robe of purple paint fading away. Next door, children's voices clattered above the sounds of a television. Otherwise, this section of road was empty, bordered only by small tobacco fields and vacant outbuildings. Past the grocery, in the distance, mist lingered above the notch of trees. Around the curve, Stinson Creek, a branch of the Licking River, ran down behind the woods. In 1937 Bill Stepp lived along this creek in a log cabin. Fiddler Bill's granddaughter, Dorothy Allen, raised in this home, remembered days like this: "People liked him, and they liked to hear him play his music. They'd come and sit on that porch, especially on a rainy day. They'd stop by and tie their horses to the paling. Grandpa would sit out on the porch. They'd come in, sit around, sometimes they'd be ten, fifteen people sitting on that porch listening to Grandpa play fiddle."[16] Listeners, Dorothy said, wanted him to make the fiddle "hiccup like a drunkard."[17] He'd pluck the strings and stagger his bow like the uncertain steps of an inebriate. There were other tunes, too—hoedowns and hymns—that met with great favor. Sometimes he'd retune his fiddle for "Bonaparte's Retreat," but as Dorothy recalled, "that one was always last." When time came for the neighbors to leave, Bill would call inside, "Hester, don't you think we better get some dinner on the table?"

A month after Hester's death at age fifty-five from a stroke, Bill Stepp recorded for the Library of Congress. One of a handful of musicians drawn from the Lakeville community, he played seventeen pieces for the disc machine operated by Alan Lomax and his wife, Elizabeth.[18] The Lomaxes were then in the final week of a Kentucky song-collecting expedition, a venture that yielded 859 recorded items, 148 of which included the fiddle. Over the course of the trip the couple recorded a dozen fiddlers, Bill Stepp being the last. Two months before, their trip had begun with another fiddler, one whom Lomax and his father, John, had come to know some years earlier.

In August 1933 John A. and Alan Lomax were nearing the end of their first Library of Congress music expedition. On their final leg north to Washington they stopped in Harlan, Kentucky, at the invitation of song collector Harvey Fuson. A native of the state, a local poet, and an amateur scholar, Fuson had compiled *Ballads of the Kentucky Highlands* two years earlier. One of his sources was James Howard, a blind musician who sang and played the fiddle. Fuson introduced the Lomaxes to Howard, who in turn became the first fiddler they ever recorded. The following year they included several of his dance tunes and one of his mining songs in their *American Ballads and Folk Songs.*[19]

Three years later, in June 1937, Fuson again contacted the Library of Congress, inviting its recording unit to his section of Kentucky. Aware that the absence of musical notation in his book had been a shortcoming, he remarked, "I realize this was a defect and felt it at the time, but had no way of getting the music."[20] During the 1920s and 1930s portable electric disc-recording equipment constituted a specialized technology, scarcely available except to scholarly institutions such as the Library or to those commercial record labels that sent out field units in search of regional performers. In exchange for these recordings, Fuson promised to contact additional singers from other parts of Leslie and Harlan counties, as well as students at the Pine Mountain Settlement School. The recordings made early in the trip represent those performers, beginning with James Howard on September 6, 1937.

In an endeavor "as chancy as the collection of folk-songs where Acts of God, bad roads and bad tempers so often intervene," Lomax recognized that despite such vicissitudes, "Most of one's encounters here in Kentucky are as pleasant as one could well imagine. Everywhere you go you are invited to spend the night and forced to eat a meal. Indeed, on account of the fact that one cannot establish any sort of impersonal relationship with these people, it is difficult to collect songs quickly."[21] After coordinating his journey with a talent show in West Liberty that featured a number of local performers, Lomax left on October 24 for nearby Salyersville.[22] The next day he began recording Bill Stepp.

None of Fiddler Bill's family recalls these sessions. Salyersville's historical society, just three miles from his home in Lakeville, has no files on the expedition. A fire consumed whatever issues of the local newspaper might have remained from the time of the trip. My conversations with the former Elizabeth Lomax and with Alan Lomax in the mid-1990s yielded no information about Bill.[23] Apart from the recordings themselves, the documentary materials that come closest to the experience reside in notes scribbled on the sleeves of the recording blanks, in Lomax's correspondence of that time, and in a summary of the Archive of American Folk Song's activities that accompanied the Library's annual report for 1937.[24] The obscurity that surrounded these recordings included his name. Maybe from a misreading of Alan Lomax's handwriting, William Hamilton Stepp became in the Library's files "W. M. Stepp," an identifier that would follow him for years. For now, other questions remained. What or who led the Lomaxes to Bill Stepp? The local talent show in West Liberty? One of the high school superintendents to whom he had written in advance of the trip? Or was theirs a chance encounter on the road?

Hopeful of finding answers, I went to Lakeville. With Becky Arnett as my guide, I sought out the oldest persons "in good mind" who could either remember Bill Stepp or describe Lakeville of that era.[25] During my 1997 trip I visited Ollie Barnett, who still lived along the same road and overlooked the same creek that he once had shared with his neighbor Bill Stepp. In 1930 Barnett turned eighteen and was finishing his first year as a teacher in Waldo, Kentucky. As a reward for his students, he invited Fiddler Bill to play for the last day of school. Barnett warmly described how his old friend arrived on horseback, bringing with him his fiddle and "a millsack full of stick candies as a treat."[26] As for Bill's rendition of "Bonaparte's Retreat": "To me, it was just a wonderful voice and wonderful sound."

On returning for the 1999 Stepp family reunion, I wondered if we couldn't try again, this time to talk with others from that period of Bill's life. Early one morning Becky started calling the oldest folks she knew in the community, setting up appointments for later that day. After playing the banjo at the reunion—where eighty-year-old Nannie Howard had been the first to jump up and start clogging—I drove with Becky and John back to Lakeville.

Late that afternoon, we stood outside the home of one of Lakeville's most senior residents. I riffled through the Library of Congress's list of Salyersville performers, and a ballad singer identified only as "R. C. Macfarlane" appeared on the disc numbered just below "Bonaparte's Retreat."[27] The sleeve note also said that he taught English at the Salyersville High School. The woman we were talking with, whose mother we were to visit that evening, replied that a Roscoe McFarland had been her English teacher and gestured to the hillside behind me. Another McFarland, perhaps his kin, lives over the rise, just a few turns away.

In the light that remained before sunset, we drove over to the McFarlands' house. As we came around the bend, a car heading toward us stopped in the one-lane dirt road. Arnold and Lydie McFarland watched quietly as Becky and I approached them, the log sheets of the recordings waving under my arm. The McFarlands remembered Becky, as she had attended Salyersville High School with their son. They spoke briefly about him, and then Lydie spoke, looking not at me but straight ahead. "No matter what," she vowed, "I'm not going to part with any of my Buell Kazee records."[28] At that moment, this reference to the legendary musician came as a total—and thoroughly welcome—surprise. Lydie was talking about Magoffin County's most famous traditional musician, the banjoist and ballad singer who between 1927 and 1929 recorded fifty-eight sides for the Brunswick recording company.

Standing on this unpaved road with green burrs stuck all down my trouser legs, and Lydie describing her wind-up gramophone and a cabinet full of original records, I realized I was talking with a couple in direct touch with the music of their community.[29]

"Are you, by chance, kin to an 'R. MacFarlane?'"

"Well," Arnold answered, "I had a brother named Roscoe."

I looked again at the notes. "Did he teach English at the Salyersville School?"

"Yes, he did."

"Was your family from Wise County, Virginia?"

"Yes, they were."

With the Library's recording log confirmed, and the weight of uncertainty lifted, the conversation turned to Roscoe McFarland (1911–1985), an educated man, who, like Buell Kazee, found pleasure in the old ballads. Arnold spoke affectionately of his quiet older brother and the songs he sometimes performed.[30]

Becky asked him, "Did you remember hearing my Grandpa Stepp?"

"When he'd draw on a bow, you couldn't just stand and listen." Arnold began to describe a schoolhouse dance on an election day. "When he started playing, people drove like a bee to honey." Arnold said he was unequaled. "Nobody held him a light in his playing."

"Have you ever heard," I asked, "of a fiddler named Clay Walters?"

"He was my uncle. He married my daddy's sister."

Here, then, were the two fiddlers the Lomaxes had recorded near Salyersville. Clay lived at Mill Branch and Bill at Stinson, some four or five miles apart. They knew each other as friends, playing partners, and neighbors.

FIGURE 10.
Mae Porter
Puckett, Bill
Stepp's guitarist,
Salyersville, Ken-
tucky, ca. 1928.
Courtesy of Peggy
Puckett Howard.

"Now, Bill Stepp hit it at a dog race. I mean he moved along. He fiddled like he meant it. Now, Uncle Clay fiddled slow, but you could tell what he was playing all right. Just had an old style of playing. Never did change from it."[31]

We began to go through the list of remaining performers. Arnold and Lydie McFarland held an entire map in their minds of these musicians, and which family members survived them. By whatever circumstances the Lomaxes came to record Bill Stepp—the contact might have stemmed from Roscoe McFarland at the high school as easily as from Clay Walters, who sang at most of Salyersville's funerals, and with whom Lomax would later correspond—it became clear that a dense network of families and friendships linked these players together. Of all the descendants I should contact, Arnold said, "When you find Peggy Howard, you'll have found a singer."

When Peggy Howard picked up the phone, I could hear music in the background. Angular mountain voices seeped through the telephone, and from time to time Peggy would have to speak up. She had just sung "Model Church" and was running through some other numbers with her sister. Every week Peggy sings in church, and at home she hosts music get-togethers. One section of her kitchen floor is bricked in just for clogging. She chuckles about these "frolics." In the 1920s Peggy's great-grandfather, banjo player Boze Hale, also hosted a weekly jam session at his house, a log cabin at Half Mountain. "Visitors would light a lantern," she said, "and play till daylight at the Boze Hale frolic."[32] Among the musicians who came to the frolic were Peggy's father and mother, who first met there.

Peggy's mother, multi-instrumentalist Mae Porter Puckett (1913–1991), began playing the guitar at the age of ten. By her teens, Mae was being taken by her grandfather to Owen Hoskins's grocery on Saturday mornings. As neighbors traded their chickens and tobacco for groceries, the sixteen-year-old learned to accompany Fiddler Bill on banjo and guitar. Several years later, Bill's daughter Opal Stepp wed Cletus Porter, Mae's first cousin. The following year, in October 1937, twenty-four-year-old Mae, now a married woman herself, joined Bill for three Library of Congress recordings. They played two fiddle tunes and then backed Mae's sister on "The Old Ship of Zion." On these fast, high-pitched tunes, she set a chordal foundation for the fiddle's lead. At these sessions, too, Mae performed one solo song while her sister, Nell Hampton, a blind ballad singer, sang fourteen more into the Library's disc-cutter. Two days earlier their father, Harvey Porter (1871–1955), recorded three songs himself. A few days later, his best friend, town barber Basil May, performed his guitar-accompanied "Lady of Carlisle." That same day Eula Cooper, the wife of a lawyer, and described on the sleeve notes as "very hi class," recorded three lyric numbers. She, too, sang with Mae from time to time.[33]

A number of the Salyersville recordings, then, can be sorted through Mae Puckett's family. If the Archive's numerical listings accurately reflect the actual sequence of recordings, Harvey Porter made the first discs in Salyersville. He, too, could have led the Lomaxes to Bill Stepp, Clay Walters, and all the rest.

Banjoist Virginia Prater, "Winnie" in the Archive's files, led music classes at the same high school where Roscoe McFarland taught, suggesting yet another linkage. Singer Branch Higgins, eighty-seven years old at the time of the recordings, was also a well-known figure in the community, his name familiar still to both Arnold McFarland and Peggy Howard. Arnold described him as "an old man with a big family," and his performance of "The Vance Song," a lament of a condemned man, impressed the Lomaxes enough to be included a few years later in their collection *Our Singing Country*. From nearby Boardtree Hollow, banjoist Walter Williams played with Bill Stepp on some of the expedition's last recordings.[34] Williams joined Fiddler Bill on "Wild Horse" and "Mud Fence" in a display of instrumental virtuosity. Williams also recorded several songs on his own and navigated these pieces with commanding speed, displaying a knowledge that spanned the length of the fingerboard. In his final report of the trip, Lomax affectionately cited Williams, "who took all day to tune his banjo, but who was well worth waiting for."[35] One way or another, through blood ties, marriage, and social contact, the Salyersville players were entwined in one another's lives.[36]

There are more connections. Seventy-eight-year-old fiddler and banjoist Richard Whitely, who played with Fiddler Bill in the 1930s and still owned one of his fiddles, mentioned that he also played with banjoist Nora Carpenter.[37]

Carpenter's name was familiar to me because Becky and her mother had spoken of her as one of Bill's closest music partners. That friendship continued well after Bill moved to northern Indiana in the early 1940s. Carpenter would bring her banjo along on her visits. In the fall of 1937 Carpenter and her husband were operating the one hotel in Salyersville. Just as she, too, could have furnished the Lomaxes with the names of the Salyersville performers, one could speculate that it was at her lodgings that Alan Lomax penned these words: "This afternoon the best fiddler I have heard in Ky. is coming to play."[38] On the day he made that assessment, Bill Stepp recorded "Bonaparte's Retreat."

Napoleon Bonaparte's career fired the imagination of nineteenth-century America, an impression expressing itself in songs, set pieces, and marches wherever local militia drilled to the fife and drum. From "Napoleon Crossing the Rhine" to "Bonaparte's Retreat from Moscow," a profusion of tunes and titles has traced the peregrinations of the French leader. No homegrown military figure, neither Washington nor Lee, Jackson nor Grant, has been commemorated so widely in American folk music. By the twentieth century his name appeared on dozens of recordings. Kay Starr's 1950 jukebox hit that swayed couples to its dreamy refrain, "And I kissed her while the fiddles played the 'Bonaparte's Retreat,'" provides but a late example of the romance attached to Napoleon.[39] Even in the era of the internet, traditional histories continue to circulate in cyberspace, commenting on Napoleon and the music he inspired.[40]

The most famous of these accounts concerns Uncle John, a fiddler at Pine Mountain, Kentucky. After running through a few tunes for an inquiring college professor, the old-timer launched into his favorite. Taken with the beguiling melody, the scholar asked the grizzled musician for its title. The mountaineer answered, "That one's called 'Napoleon Crossing the Rockies.'" Mindful of his duty to the truth, the professor diplomatically averred, "That was a lovely tune, Uncle John, and I'm terribly grateful that you played it for me, but you do know that Napoleon never actually crossed the Rockies." After a moment's reflection, the musician replied, "Well, historians differ."

In 1937 arts educator Allen Eaton included the story in his *Handicrafts of the Southern Highlands,* where it appeared in a section covering the music and instruments of the mountains.[41] There musicologist Charles Seeger spotted the tale, and he, in turn, quoted it to Alan Lomax.[42] Lomax wrote to Eaton for the text in 1939, remarking that he and his father might want to include it in "a book of folk songs and fiddle tunes," a collection that eventually became *Our Singing Country*.[43] The book's musical notation, furnished by Seeger's wife, composer Ruth Crawford Seeger, included Bill Stepp's version of "Bonaparte's Retreat." Lomax intended to preface the tune with this story, thus providing it with an anecdotal context. By using such material in *Our Singing Country,* the Lomaxes hoped to bridge disparate domains as they brought their rural field recordings to the attention of an urbane audience. The introductory stories provided an entertaining access to the unfamiliar material.

But by 1941, when *Our Singing Country* came out, Alan Lomax had selected a different quotation, one taken from Kentucky singer and labor activist Aunt Molly Jackson.[44] Aunt Molly characterized Napoleon as a liberator, a latter-day Robin Hood who would venture from his homeland in France to protect the rights of others: "If some country like Germany," she declared, "would try to take some poor little country that was defenseless and make 'em do as they wanted 'em to do—you know, work for 'em and all that—well, he'd go and he'd fight for that country, and he'd lick Germany."[45] With Nazi aggression unloosed across Europe, her view of Napoleon as a defender of freedom invoked an older radicalism: "To the Irish composers of this tune and to American frontiersmen," Lomax later added, "Bonaparte was a hero."[46]

Public fascination with Napoleon surely played a part in fusing the instrumental tune with his name. Moscow's burning by its citizenry, Bonaparte's flight in the Russian snow, the decimation of his forces, let alone his defeat at Waterloo and his banishment to St. Helena, comprised intensely dramatic stories that found a widespread audience in the English-speaking world of the nineteenth century. Other tunes, such as "The Rights of Man," "The Battle of Waterloo," "Down with the French," and "The Battle of the Nile," also commemorate in their very titles the historical events.

In addition to serving a symbolic role, tunes like "Bonaparte's Retreat" could actually be enlisted into military service. Historian Vic Gammon cites how the British army appropriated the French revolutionary song "Ça Ira" as an aural feint intended to confuse the enemy (in England, the tune became known, ironically enough, as "The Downfall of Paris").[47] Field musicians using drums, fifes, and, later, bugles, rallied troops into formations with charges, quicksteps, and retreats. Academic inquiry into the tune began in 1944 when Samuel Bayard collected "Bonaparte's Retreat" from the whistling of a western Pennsylvania workingman, F. P. Provence. Tellingly, Bayard found that this former fiddler, who was born in the 1870s, learned the tune from a Civil War fifer who "played it as a retreat in Civil War days."[48]

The evocative melody may have derived from a particular family of Bonaparte songs known as "The Island of St. Helena" or "Boney's in St. Helena."[49] With a few melodic and metrical changes, the tune suddenly becomes "Bonaparte's Retreat" as it is commonly played today. But when Samuel Bayard included in his pioneering work on American fiddle music five distinct airs associated with three different Napoleonic titles, he connected one of these "Bonaparte" pieces to an Irish pipe march called "The Eagle's Whistle." Frank Ferrel's 1991 recording of "The Eagle's Whistle" highlights the similarities between the tunes.[50] Like most renditions of "Bonaparte's Retreat," Ferrel's piece unfolds at a slow pace, suggestive of the tune's ceremonial role. In both the high and low strains, the bow draws mournfully, answered by a brief arpeggio. With an open tuning, resonant with drones and double-stops, the fiddle imitates the stately, somber plaint of regimental bagpipes. "Bonaparte's Retreat" also employs this feature, with the drone framing the tune's slow tempo. A related tune that Bayard associated with "Bonaparte's Retreat," one sometimes called "The Old Man and Old Woman Quarrelin'," similarly alternates high and low strains. Here the fiddle re-creates a husband's low-pitched growl as he confronts the treble-voiced invective of his wife. In like manner, "Bonaparte's Retreat" fuses two lines of contrasting pitch and energy that suggest armies in motion.

In the headnote just above the transcription of Bill Stepp's "Bonaparte's Retreat" in *Our Singing Country*, Alan Lomax rightly classified the tune as imitative: "The piece," he wrote, "is descriptive—marching, wind howling, etc."[51] On the recording, in a wonderful turn of speech, Stepp draws his listeners' attention to that strain in the tune richest with military connotation. As he plays the low strings of his fiddle, he says, "That's the Bony-part, that's the Bony-part." Bascom Lunsford observed this feature, too, during his 1935 Library recording when he remarked, "The 'G' string is supposed to represent the drum in the retreat." Still other players accelerated the tune to represent the combatants' flight, an effect illustrated by the 1929 recording by Crockett's Kentucky Mountaineers. In yet another performance, one commentator said of fiddler Ed Haley's version, "If two armies could come together and hear him play that tune, they'd kill themselves in piles."[52]

The tune first appeared on a recording in 1924, played by A. A. Gray. This Alabama-born fiddler played a slow, dignified solo, not unlike a concert violin piece, intended solely for listening. Other recordings followed with performances by Crockett's Kentucky Mountaineers, the Skillet Lickers, and in 1936 Arthur Smith's graceful rendition. When the Lomaxes arrived the following year in Kentucky, they also encountered "Bonaparte's Retreat" in a variety of forms. In one seven-day span, they collected the tune from George C. Nicholson, Boyd Asher, and Luther Strong.[53]

None of these players, however, performed "Bonaparte's Retreat" as elaborately as did Bill Stepp. Like them, Bill employed the customary DADD tuning, and followed the usual "leaping" structure. He played the A or high part, followed by the B or low part. Then the A part repeats at its original pitch, after which the B part transposes an octave higher, which, in effect, places it higher than the A part. In these respects, Bill's version is perfectly conventional, but he did one other thing: he transformed the tempo from a march to a hoedown—and that made all the difference. In Alan Jabbour's words, "His is not just one more version, but a singular, racing breakdown."[54] The ringing overtones of repeated drone notes, the dexterity of his phrasing, the introduction of triplets on the first beat, the long strings of notes, and graceful changes in bow direction allowed Fiddler Bill to perform the tune at square-dance velocity. "Bonaparte's Retreat" was reborn from a slow air into a dazzling example of instrumental display.

With this inspired change from a familiar time signature to a new and radically different meter, Bill Stepp incurred his neighbors' admiration and touched the memories of his family. In a few years' time, his fiddling would quietly revitalize the cultural experience of incalculably more.

FIGURE 11. William Hamilton Stepp, Salyersville, Kentucky, late 1930s. Courtesy of Becky Arnett.

In April 1942 dancer and choreographer Agnes de Mille contacted Aaron Copland about a new ballet she had just completed. As the first American invited to choreograph for the Ballet Russe de Monte Carlo, de Mille submitted a work set in the thoroughly regional locale of frontier Texas, circa 1900.

Its plot centers on a young woman smitten with a charismatic cowboy. The Cowgirl, whom de Mille played that fall for the show's New York premiere, disguises herself as a ranch hand in order to remain near the Head Wrangler. He is attracted to another, the Ranchowner's Daughter. Undeterred, the Cowgirl tries to impress him with her derring-do, ending in a botched attempt to ride a rodeo bronco. Later that evening a dance occurs, and as couples waltz around the ranch house, the Cowgirl departs in tears, still unable to draw the attentions of the Head Wrangler. A calf escapes the corral and the cowboys quit the gathering to recover the stray. After they return, a square dance strikes up and the Cowgirl reappears, wearing a skirt and with a bow tied in her hair. To the soaring folk medley that featured "Bonaparte's Retreat," the Head Wrangler forsakes the Ranchowner's Daughter, finding his match instead with this impassioned woman. They feverishly dance, the girl falls into his arms, and he kisses her. The show closes as the dancers form a grand promenade.

This synopsis overly simplifies *Rodeo*, as the ballet would soon come to be known. Its theme concerned, in de Mille's words, womankind's perpetual question of "'how to get a suitable man.'"[55] De Mille's exultant story mirrored events that had recently transpired in her own life. "For years," Copland biographer Howard Pollack writes, "she thought her features unattractive and her body ungainly . . . leaving her dowdy in her dress and prim in her relations with men."[56] But in 1941, minding Martha Graham's firm counsel, de Mille put on her best dress, got her hair done, and fixed her makeup before meeting Graham's Texas-bred concert manager, William Prude. De Mille would liken him to Gary Cooper in his charms, and in short time the couple became engaged. If, as Pollack explains, de Mille's efforts resulted in her own romantic realization, the wearing of her dress and the transforming of her appearance, like that of Cowgirl's, signified not appeasement but personal growth. In the wake of this experience, of her finding a suitable man, de Mille wrote her ballet.

Externally, *Rodeo*'s Cinderella-like tale echoes a popular family of British and American folksongs.[57] When a young man is sent to war, a woman dresses herself in man's apparel to be near her beloved. With her "keen and slender" fingers, she brooches back her hair and enlists as an orderly, a foot soldier, or a common seaman. Determined to stay by her lover's side, she is afraid neither to wield a gun nor to face cannon fire. In the end, she removes her disguise, and the two joyously find one another. Whether de Mille drew inspiration from one such song or another lies outside this study, there's no question but that she brought to this ballet a familiarity with traditional music.[58] At her April meeting with Aaron Copland, she not only handed him a version of "Old Paint" that she notated herself, but presented him with a "time plot" calibrated to the precise beat: "Hoe-Down, 4 minutes. . . . Pause and silence for about 4 counts . . . Dance begins on walk—hit a fiddle tune hard."[59] Written as much in the terminology of fiddling as that of modern dance, these instructions would spur Copland to seek out "Bonaparte's Retreat." Agnes de Mille had chosen her composer well.

Since his days as a composition student in Paris, Aaron Copland's interest in creating a body of identifiably American symphonic music freed him from following purely belletristic models. Copland became part of a circle of New York artists and writers that convened at photographer Alfred Stieglitz's Photo-Secessionist 291 Gallery. Members of 291, including Georgia O'Keeffe, Waldo Frank, Lewis Mumford, Edmund Wilson, Paul Strand, Van Wyck Brooks, and Harold Clurman, joined other modernists who tied their work to the social surround. Over the course of their meetings, speakers articulated a gathering interest in the American idiom, an interest that emerged in the following decade under the cultural aegis of the New Deal. Many of these artists found in America's "common man" (a term that Copland artfully employed in his 1943 *Fanfare for the Common Man*) a symbol of national identity. For Copland and like-minded peers quotation from American folk music accomplished in sound what Carl Sandburg achieved in *Good Morning, America*: a modern poetics stocked with what he called "the proverbs of a people."[60]

Composer Herbert Haufrecht shared Copland's interest in folk music as well as his political sympathies. The two met in the early 1930s at New York's Composers' Collective, a forum of socially conscious conservatory musicians who debated, and sometimes ventured, a repertory for American workers. Haufrecht warmly described Copland's abilities as a folk music arranger, "as if he were steeped in it."[61] "But," he continued, "we used folk material as "germinal . . . as a basis to integrate it into [our] work." For himself, that aesthetic distance forever narrowed when he began a yearlong assignment in a rural West Virginia community established by the Resettlement Administration.[62] In 1936 Charles Seeger, director of the agency's music program (also a past member of the Composers' Collective), hired him to organize a church choir, establish a music program in the surrounding schools, and play at local square dances. Over the course of living on a "one-acre corn farm" battered by continual flooding, Haufrecht received an "introduction to impoverished farmers and miners . . . [with their] shape note hymnals," "a direct experience" he never forgot.[63] This immersion set him apart, he realized, from Aaron Copland and other schooled composers exposed to the music, but not particularly to its makers.

Copland, like most at the Composers' Collective, viewed folk melodies as building blocks for sophisticated composition. "Give me a book of tunes," he said, "and I'll immediately know what tune attracts me and what one doesn't."[64] As a professional composer, he wanted "to put fresh and unconventional harmonies to well-known melodies without spoiling their naturalness; moreover, for an orchestral score, one must expand, contract, rearrange, and superimpose the bare tunes themselves, giving them something of one's own touch. That is what I tried to do."[65] He largely sifted tunes from written texts, which allowed him to better focus on their purely thematic possibilities. At the same time this method insulated him from source musicians, the textures of their playing styles, and the contexts of their music making that colleagues like Herbert Haufrecht confronted at West Virginia's Red House Farms homestead. American folk music offered Aaron Copland a treasured inheritance certainly, and a spur to his imagination, but not one that he necessarily viewed as an individually molded creative product. Yet this singular personal artistry that animates Bill Stepp's "Bonaparte's Retreat" had everything to do with how the piece came to the composer's attention.

When Copland began working on *Rodeo,* he turned to John A. and Alan Lomax's newest book for three of his principal tune selections, which included Bill Stepp's "Bonyparte."[66] He had recently worked with their materials for a 1940 radio broadcast that Alan Lomax hosted on the Columbia *School of the Air.* In a short segment intended for young listeners, Copland wrote a variation on "John Henry" complete with train whistle and anvil, and whose basic melody he gleaned from the Lomaxes' earlier *American Ballads and Folk Songs.* Before that, in 1938, commissioned to score a ballet based on the life of Billy the Kid, he drew from sheet music editions of "[Goodbye,] Old Paint," "The Old Chisholm Trail," and "Whoopee Ti Yi Yo" collected by John A. Lomax and arranged by Oscar Fox.[67] Copland's success with that ballet had, in fact, impelled Agnes de Mille to contact him now.

Our Singing Country appeared in November 1941. From the outset reviewers lauded its music transcriptions by modernist composer and musicologist Ruth Crawford Seeger (1901–1953). An acquaintance of Copland's and a former member of the Composers' Collective herself, "Crawford," as she is called in Judith Tick's biography, worked directly from Library of Congress recordings in this effort. Her instincts as a composer where "the choice of every note involves an act of will," led to a painstaking appraisal of every disc.[68]

In her extended foreword to *Our Singing Country*—which did not appear in print until sixty years after the songbook's publication—Crawford accorded folk musicians the same legitimacy as their fine-art counterparts. She described her notational task as a link between two societies, rural and urban, one preserving, the other recapturing living musical heritage. Transcription thus provided a "bridge."[69] All the while Crawford remained conscious of its limitations to adequately describe the irregularities of this music, as well as its remoteness from the usual musical practices of those whom it represented. "A great deal," she cautioned, "depends upon just how this bridge is built."

Crawford's work on *Our Singing Country* began in the summer of 1937. It lengthened into a four-year process during which she transcribed some three hundred songs. She balanced her role as the mother of three young children with her commitments as a musician, slowing down the recordings, jotting on her notepad each pass she made. On one side stood her coal-black bottles of Higgins ink and, with it, the authority of written music. On the other, her Ansley variable-speed turntable, by which she examined these performances and probed their idiosyncrasies. Her laborious process sometimes caused friction with the book's compilers. Alan Lomax's sister, fifteen-year-old Bess, shuttled innumerable messages between the Lomaxes' office at the Library of Congress and Crawford's home in suburban Maryland:

> Bess, you tell Ruth that no blues singer God ever made would sing "redder than rouge"—it's "redder than ru(by)" with a voice break in the middle—that's why she doesn't hear it right.
>
> Now, Bess, you go back and tell Alan and your father that I have listened to this song exactly 78 times all the way through, not mentioning single verses. How many times have they listened to it? Get them to figure that out.[70]

To create her transcriptions Crawford repeatedly weighed "this question of 'common possession' versus 'individual contribution,'" giving careful thought to each entry's underlying melody as it varied from verse to verse, as well as how the same piece might fluctuate from one interpreter to another.[71] In the completed book, *Our Singing Country* keyed printed texts to specific Library of Congress field recordings.[72] Headnotes for each of the 195 entries included the final tone from the recording, the Archive's number for that item, the performer, instrumentation, location, and date, followed by textual references. These elements furthered the emphasis on individual performances. As Crawford poetically said in a letter to a friend, she sought to put on paper "the breath of the singer."[73]

As a result, "no one who has studied these or similar recordings," writes Crawford in the book's music preface, "can deny that the song and its singing are indissolubly connected."[74] In her transcription of Bill Stepp's "Bonaparte's Retreat" (along with Luther Strong's "Callahan," which follows it), Crawford did not satisfy herself with a simple notation of the basic melody. Her meticulous scoring made clear the richness and subtlety of Bill's drone notes and melodic decorations. Still, she added in a footnote, "the bowing in . . . 'Bonyparte' could not be determined with sufficient accuracy to allow its notation."[75]

Aaron Copland's interest, however, lay not in duplicating the technique of the Kentucky fiddler. He dramatically restaged the tune within a philharmonic framework. As the movement begins, Copland re-creates the cacophony of instruments tuning up. Horns and strings push with seeming dissonance. Then the instruments converge, and a western theme sets off like the sauntering of a horse. A wood block punctuates the clip-clop of the passage. Bowed basses add a comic lilt as the violins and piano play in stop-time rhythms. Then "Bonaparte's Retreat" breaks in. A horn plays the drone from the tune's third high part, followed by the central strain of the melody. A xylophone's mallets beat in time with the bowing of the strings. The orchestra powers through the lower registers of the tune while a triangle rings high above. The melody repeats three times, and the horns veer off in disparate directions. The piece becomes quiet and Copland inserts the sprightly fiddle tune "McLeod's Reel," followed for a measure by a Celtic-sounding "Gilderoy." "McLeod's Reel" repeats, trailed by yet another traditional tune, "Tip Toe, Pretty Betty Martin."[76] Copland finishes the collage with a familiar hoedown turn. A snare drum rattles, then comes a pause, and the cowboy motif returns. The piece slows with brass and woodwinds, drifting into a pensive, meditative chord. "Bonaparte's Retreat" floods back, and oboes, cymbals, and horns tap out a telegrapher's tattoo. The piece ends on a showstopping cadence.

Fiddler Bill's "Bonyparte" in *Our Singing Country* "became a signature tune for an American sound," writes Judith Tick, "after Aaron Copland swallowed it whole for the 'Hoedown' movement in the ballet suite 'Rodeo' a few years later, and Agnes de Mille's dancers moved to the upbeat triplet figures and the double-stop drones so assiduously notated by Crawford."[77] Even with tympani and horns, reeds and brass, a xylophone and wood blocks, swirling in orchestral majesty, we're hearing Bill Stepp.

The day I first met Fiddler Bill's family, I inserted a cassette of his Library of Congress performance into a tape recorder. Becky Arnett, her mother, Nannie, and I sat around their kitchen table. Her mother beamed as we listened. "Now, he really loved it," Nannie affirmed.[78] "That's the reason he was so good. He loved it." Although Becky and Nannie already knew Bill's recording, this dubbing faded his fiddle solo into the symphonic version. As the pieces flowed together, Becky's face reddened. "I'm not a musician," she said, making the connection. "But I know what you mean."[79] The score that she had casually heard so many times on television incorporated her grandfather's tune with pointed accuracy, beginning with the same key. A few months later I played this tape again for dozens of family members at their annual Stepp reunion. Everyone there knew the beef growers' commercial, but none had linked it to their forebear. It took Fiddler Bill's family by surprise, and pride filled the hall.

At suppertime we stopped our conversation to watch the evening news. That day Miloš Forman's movie, *The People vs. Larry Flynt,* premiered nationwide. Becky said, "You see, we have another famous member of this family." Magoffin County native and publisher of *Hustler* magazine, Larry Flynt is one of Becky's cousins from her mother's side. When Becky took to me to Owen Hoskins's grocery in Lakeville near Fiddler Bill's home during the time of the recordings, she pointed to an ornate iron fence atop the nearest hillside. It surrounds the grave of Flynt's wife, Althea. As I looked up at the memorial I couldn't help but think of her brief life, the notoriety of the skin trade, and Flynt's seemingly theatrical anarchy, his battles over civil liberties, political and sexual hypocrisy, and the press. Even in this misty spot in Kentucky America's mass culture hovers close by, and Bill Stepp and his family are actors on that stage. It seemed fitting when his grandchildren mentioned their hope that Larry Flynt might someday underwrite a movie about the life of Fiddler Bill.

Ahead of us, hidden by mist and mountainside, lay the remnants of Bill Stepp's cabin. I thought of him riding by horseback to a dance where he would play the fiddle. His life, which began in a Kentucky cave, and the prostitution of his Indian mother speak to grim features of our national experience. But his grandchildren also remember how proudly he told a minister as they flocked into church and filled its pews one by one, "This is my family."[80]

Behind us, in the car, a recording of *Rodeo* quietly plays. "Certainly, some songs have come 'down' (and will continue to do so) from popular and fine-art idioms, and have been made 'common' through processes of oral tradition," writes Ruth Crawford Seeger.[81] "The mere fact that we have not a written record of the reverse process should not, of itself, allow us to jump to the conclusion that 'common' songs have not also found their way 'up' (and will continue to do) from folk into popular and fine-art idioms." Crawford had foreseen what came true about Bill Stepp's "Bonaparte's Retreat." Though she could not reduce his idiomatic technique to paper, she did transfer his tune, and conservatory instrumentalists steeped in their artistic byways learned his uncommon rendition of the much-played march.

Many decades have passed since Fiddler Bill seated himself before a disc-cutting machine in Salyersville. On that October afternoon in 1937, he could not have predicted, nor indeed did he ever know, where his music would lead. But whenever the beef growers' commercial airs on national television, or Emerson, Lake and Palmer's "Hoedown" reprises on the radio, whenever a dance company performs Agnes de Mille's *Rodeo* or Aaron Copland's score resounds in concert halls around the world, W. H. Stepp, a nearly anonymous Kentucky mountain fiddler, continues to play for millions.

Kelly Pace

Coworker in the Kingdom of Culture

O N OCTOBER 1, 1934, USING ARKANSAS STATE PENITENTIARY letterhead, John Lomax wrote home, "I ought to turn up something of rare interest."[1] And over the next few days he did. Despite the malfunctions of his recording apparatus and the long drives "down the worst roads in Arkansas" to get it repaired, he could report on his very next postcard, "We are headed for fine stuff at Cummins."[2] This unit of the state's penal system, some seventy miles southeast of Little Rock, operated as a farm tended by an entirely African American workforce. There, for a second time within a week, a group of convicts performed for him a regional song that eventually became part of the American musical idiom—"Rock Island Line."

At Cummins Camp One, a charismatic twenty-one-year-old convict named Robert Kelly Pace, then serving his second term in prison, led the song with a group of seven fellow inmates. Their performance involved a closely patterned call-and-response, their voices dispersed in three- and sometimes four-part harmony. Between the choruses one of them imitated a train whistle. On the brown dust jacket of the recording disc, John Lomax noted that the singers, accompanied by a guard on horseback, had just run in from working in a cotton field, eager "'to git on dat machine.'"[3] Curiously, Lomax always associated this piece with the tasks of outdoor labor. Although he had set up his disc machine in the wood yard, and recorded several songs that day to the sounds of chopping wood, "Rock Island Line" was not among them. During his next visit to Cummins in 1939 he wrote about another group of convicts: "After several experiments with shovels and picks in an effort to get the right sound effects, a group finally recorded 'Rock Island Line' in the mess hall where the machine was set up."[4] Yet on that recording, too, no sounds of tools appear, no effects audibly related to physical toil, only voices arranged in close harmony.[5] Still later, in *The Ballad Hunter,* his 1941 recorded lecture series, and in his subsequent autobiography, Lomax depicts Kelly Pace and his companions filling their sacks to the rhythm of the song, "as if they were on an express train tearing through the cotton patch on the famous Rock Island Line."[6] When Lomax recorded them singing it one last time in September 1942, "Rock Island Line" again incorporates only vocal harmonizing as before. Nothing about these performances ties it to the essentially solitary task of cotton picking. Instead, the recordings John Lomax made of "Rock Island Line" show it to be a quartet song—unaccompanied, social, church based, arranged for singing, and staged for listening.

When Kelly Pace and his companions bounded from their labors in the cotton fields to perform for the Library's recording machine, they carried with them circumstances and conditions that freighted this song from the start. "Rock Island Line" began its journey in Little Rock, Arkansas, at the repair shops of the Chicago, Rock Island and Pacific Railroad. Based on a traditional form and arising within a commercial setting, the song, like a trunk line whose branches radiate across the countryside, soon moved beyond this work site making new stops, shifting its contents, and streamlining its load. It migrated from a gospel quartet that the Arkansas prisoners performed to a rhythmic fable that Huddie Ledbetter created as he traveled with John Lomax as chauffeur, auto mechanic, and musical demonstrator. Eventually the song reached an incalculable number of players, singers, and listeners via skiffle, rock and roll, country, pop, and the folksong revival.[7] Yet for all these crossings and couplings, "Rock Island Line" hung on to its message, emblazoned in boxcar letters of a train fleeting past, to become the poetry by which a proud railroad is still remembered.

On December 3, 1929, at Little Rock's Arch Street Missionary Baptist Church, just off the main stem of the city's black shopping district, an African American vocal quartet opened the evening's program. Known as the Rock Island Colored Booster Quartet, these singers—Clarence Wilson, Jake Mason, Walter Dennis, and Phil Garrett—worked at the nearby Biddle Shops, the central freight yard, repair works, and roundhouse for the Rock Island railroad's Arkansas-Louisiana Division. At the time, thirty-eight railroads operated state-wide. In Arkansas the Rock Island itself ran 390 freight trains monthly as well as 44 passenger trains daily on seven hundred miles of track that traversed bridges, trestles, and culverts. For railroading in general, and for the Rock Island specifically, the 1920s had been prosperous. Nevertheless, the company vied for its every passenger and payload. Ceaseless efforts to attract revenue, from the Rock Island's president to the laborers who comprised the Biddle quartet, led to this meeting at the Arch Street church. The audience that evening included several of the shop's principals: Master Mechanic C. L. Sharp as well as General Foreman C. A. Welch, along with Biddle's general car foreman, assistant car foreman, and foreman of inspectors.[8] Of the nearly three thousand then employed by the Rock Island in Arkansas, some four hundred and fifty, roughly half of whom were black, worked at the Biddle Shops. Following the performance, these shop officials spoke about "the booster movement," a companywide initiative for which singer and engine wiper Clarence Wilson had written a song. Its title was "Buy Your Ticket over Rock Island Lines":

The California Limited is the best you ever rode,
We have good engines running on the road,
We have roundhouse firemen that know they're right,
We have engine wipers to keep them bright.

> Chorus
> Rock Island Line is a mighty good road,
> Passengers get on board if you want to ride,
> Ride like you're flying, be sure you buy your ticket
> Over the Rock Island Line.

We have good engineers to run these trains,
Mr. Pard Cole is one of their names,
He is never late, always on time,
Be sure you buy your ticket over the Rock Island Line.

Engineer Kugler is a good one, too.
He blows his whistle 'til it makes you blue,
He runs a freight train on passenger time,
Be sure and buy your ticket over the Rock Island Line.

We have Pullmans, chair cars and diners, too,
We have good service all the way through;
Keep good service on your mind
And buy your ticket over the Rock Island Line.

Mr. Church leaves Little Rock and Biddle Shops,
Runs into Memphis makes just two stops;
He's never late, always on time,
The engine that he runs is 849.

Mr. Sharp, our master mechanic, is a very good man; Mr. Welch is, too,
They see that all the trains go through,
They keep the Rock Island business on their minds—
Things must go right on the Rock Island Lines.[9]

Those familiar with "Rock Island Line," as this song came to be known, will find many of these lyrics novel. Most of them dropped away as the piece moved into tradition, leaving those that remained to make a new kind of sense. Still, if forgotten today, these original verses illuminate the song's development. On an immediate level, the names celebrated persons known at the Biddle Shops. Apart from the references to officials Sharp and Welch in attendance that evening at the church, its other names, too, bore local significance. Engineer Kugler, for instance, was George J. Kugler, known throughout Little Rock and beyond as the Musical Engineer.[10] Kugler had devised a removable steam whistle attachment that allowed him to control its pitch and play whole tunes on this mechanical instrument no matter what engine he was assigned. "Fritz Kreisler or Ignace Paderewski," wrote one 1925 journalist, "have nothing on Engineer George Kugler when it comes to playing to large audiences. People all over the State of Arkansas drop their work and listen when George makes a steam pipe organ out of his locomotive whistle, and proceeds to peal out familiar melodies." With his larger-than-life music making, Kugler became a magnet for a number of legends that involved train whistles. But the truth about him was already marvelous enough. When leaving Little Rock, he typically played "Goodbye My Lover Goodbye," which he dedicated to his wife, Nannie. On his return, heading back into the Biddle roundhouse, he apparently signaled her again, taking for his homecoming theme, and regardless the hour, the tune of "Polly Put the Kettle On." Kugler died in 1945 with his hand on the throttle of the Memphis–California train named in the song. The wreck, killing eight including Kugler, took place thirty-five miles from Little Rock at a crossing during a seventy-five-mile-an-hour collision with a milk truck.[11]

This turn of events underlines a spirit already present in the piece Clarence Wilson created.

"Buy Your Ticket" emerged from the Rock Island's fraternal ethos. With eight thousand miles of track built across fourteen Midwestern states and employing over 41,000 persons, the company established in 1920 a network of so-called booster clubs. While the first Rock Island Employees Club opened in 1904 at the line's Chicago headquarters to promote closer fellowship among company officials, the idea grew to include the railroad's larger workforce, from master mechanics to shop workers (as well as the establishment of Diamond Clubs, a program for employees' children). These racially segregated organizations fostered social events that expressed the company's values. For the Rock Island's black employees, such gatherings might entail a baseball game between different Rock Island shops followed by a picnic, or else nighttime meetings hosted by the local African American church, lodge hall, or restricted YMCA. White employees, working at a higher pay scale than their black counterparts, sometimes found the means to build themselves clubhouses, as well as to stage programs that included tennis tournaments, target shooting, and track and field competitions in addition to monthly dinner dances, recitals, and banquets. Whether convened indoors or out, and whatever an employee's status, the booster clubs made the point of identifying company success with job security. Circumventing the craft unions to assert the idea of the railroad as a single family, the booster clubs exhorted Rock Island employees to gather business in the interest of all concerned. Animating this initiative, company boosterism combined with "pep"—"the thing . . . that makes the engineer wave a kiss to his sweetheart as he throws open the throttle . . . [and] the mechanic and laborer fairly dance to their jobs."[12]

The Rock Island's booster movement can be surveyed in the company's monthly magazine. In January 1920, under the banner "What It Means to Be a Rock Island Man," the word "boost" appears with its rationale: "Boost the Rock Island—let the patron know we have a good thing and that we believe in it. . . . More friends mean more patrons—more patrons assures greater revenues . . . the stockholder receives larger dividends and the employee increased salary. Is there anything more reasonable, more honest or more logical than this?"[13] By spring the idea gained enough momentum to count the railroad's female workforce: "Mr. 'Rock Island Man,' which includes our women members, too, the time has arrived for each and every one of us to come to the front and boost the 'Rock Island.'"[14] In September the magazine urged personnel to "advertise the Rock Island service on every occasion that presents itself . . . Be a 'booster.'"[15] The June 1922 issue states, "The more money our company earns, the more men they can keep at work."[16] Then, in the same article and set in capital letters, "STOP WHINING—GO AFTER BUSINESS AND BOOST."

Music played a leading role in the effort, with the company providing facilities, sometimes uniforms, and, on occasion, instruments. Under the corporate banner all sorts of ensembles arose, from saxophone quartets to large-scale choruses. A December 1923 article about the Trenton, Missouri, booster club illustrates: Immediately following a performance by the railroad's shop band, a forty-two-piece marching group that featured a company painter singing "That Wonderful Mother of Mine" to a thousand assembled Rock Island workers, the yard's master mechanic explained that "securing additional business . . . would mean better working conditions and would assist our company in retaining their present forces."[17] At the Silvis shops, located near Moline, Illinois, the company sponsored a glee club, a shop workers' band, and a Mexican boys' band drawn from the recently arrived Spanish-speaking labor force. Up in Chicago, an appropriately high-toned ensemble led by a former director of music at the University of Chicago conducted the twenty-five-piece Rock Island Railway Orchestra. That ensemble, like the Silvis Glee Club, traveled throughout the route, often appearing on radio with James E. Gorman, the Rock Island president, who discoursed about the line. Regional broadcasts featured other Rock Island talents—musical saw players, old-time string bands, and solo fiddlers—playing on programs with fellow company recitalists who specialized in popular favorites and light classics. Rock Island vocal quartets, both white and black, appeared at company events across the system. One Rock Island broadcast from Hot Springs, Arkansas, in March 1927, featured "the famous Pullman Porters Quartette of Chicago," themselves on the verge of making their own commercially released recordings.[18] All in all, music, boostering, and the Rock Island Lines made a promotional fit.

The Biddle Shops Colored Quartette began in 1924 when A. J. "Smoky" McMahon, an African American railroad mechanic with a quarter-century's service at Rock Island, organized the group. The original nine singers rehearsed weekly their repertory of spirituals.[19] They performed at a variety of public gatherings as well as company events. According to the magazine's 1925 feature, their plans included McMahon's ambition to gather all the quartets in the Arkansas-Louisiana Division to perform on "Juneteenth," the black celebration of Emancipation. The same article also mentions a thirty-piece dance band that

their membership recently launched. Seven years later, a picture of the Biddle shop ran with the caption "This club is a live organization and is instrumental in bringing much business to the Rock Island."[20] The next month a follow-up item read: "The Rock Island Colored Booster Club, Biddle, entertained with a delightful program . . . these meetings are held very often, and are for the purpose of securing business for the Rock Island Lines."[21]

By then, Rock Island employees from throughout the system had composed numerous commemorative musical and literary works. Subjects ranged from rusty but beloved locomotives reduced to scrap metal and the choice of taking the bus versus the train to the exploits, nicknames, and camaraderie of railroaders past. If one poem echoed Vachel Lindsay's sonorities, set to a throbbing tattoo of "Rock Island Lines, Rock Island Lines," others recreated the tenor of Robert Service's popular verse. Most sustained a homegrown atmosphere, espousing the sentimental, the affectionate, and, in keeping with booster-club philosophy, company loyalty.[22]

In July 1926, "The Golden State," written by a company refrigerator inspector, reads like Charlie Monroe's recording some two decades later of "Bringin' In the Georgia Mail":

Can you hear the rails a thrumming,
Can you hear the whistle shrill.
Tis our 'Golden State' a coming,
Coming up the near-by hill. . . .

Sure, our 'Golden State's' a hummer,
And it is no idle boast,
That you'll always be a booster,
If you ride her to the coast.[23]

Perhaps alert to the Biddle shop's colored quartet composition that earlier appeared in these pages, in November 1931 a pensioned conductor from Arizona sent along a piece that he called "The Rock Island Line." While it shares some of the same wording with the former, his number speaks more in the language of advertising than did the quartet's appeal to workplace fraternalism:

You are sure to have a wonderful time,
If you buy your ticket on the Rock Island Line

. . .

If you are a shipper of heavy freight,
And need it at an early date,
You are sure to get it right on time,
If you route it over the Rock Island Line.[24]

That summer the magazine included with detailed musical notation "a brand new Rock Island song" composed by a Kansas branch telegrapher. It starts like a letter: "Dear Rock Island friends I wish to state, / I used your road on an urgent date, / If all the service is good like this, / To use your lines is heavenly bliss."[25]

Clarence Wilson's 1929 "Buy Your Ticket over Rock Island Lines" finds its place within this repertory. Indeed, the magazine identified what Wilson and his Biddle Shop colleagues sang at the Arch Street church as a "booster song," affirming company values with its advice to "keep good service," its reminder to "buy your ticket," and its promise that "things must go right." But apart from the Rock Island work ethic the song expressed, the commercial motives it repeats, and the local personalities it celebrates, its lyrics, especially the last verse, which names key officials present at the church that evening, reveal a wider social condition. By working in a black religious song form and singing in a black church, the singers communicated not simply as Rock Island employees, but also within the framework of their race. That consciousness shaped the song as it made its way across Arkansas. Within four years of the December 1929 meeting at Arch Street Missionary Baptist Church, "Buy Your Ticket over Rock Island Lines" had reached beyond the Rock Island railroad and its employees. Others took it up, and in so doing, reclaimed this piece by the traditions that first shaped it.

––––––––

"A queerly assorted couple sat on that front seat—a white man hunting folk songs, a Negro ex-convict yet wearing his scanty prison clothes. A unique situation and an unusual enterprise."[26] So wrote John A. Lomax about his inaugural journey with Huddie Ledbetter, who had been pardoned from Louisiana's Angola Prison six weeks earlier. Now in late September 1934, with this legendary singer and instrumentalist better known as Leadbelly behind the wheel of Lomax's Ford sedan, the two set off from Marshall, Texas, to Little Rock to call on the governor of Arkansas. Lomax wanted access to the penitentiaries of that state, where he knew the music was "yet dammed up . . . and therefore easy to get at."

Since 1907, when Lomax began his formal canvassing efforts of cowboy material, he looked for songs "made by men . . . far removed from the restraining influences of polite society."[27] This subject matter, he said, divided into seven occupations. To the categories of lumbermen, miners, sailors, soldiers, railroaders, cowboys, and Negro balladists, he added another type: "the songs of the down-and-out classes,—the outcast girl, the dope fiend, the convict, the jailbird, and the tramp." Of them all, African American convicts, he maintained, provided the most distinctive of the American folksong styles. He hoped their worksongs of everyday life, "largely passed over as too trivial for note," might become as widely recognized as the spirituals.[28] He compared the music's power to *Green Pastures,* a recent dramatic piece filled with black religious singing. "Perhaps these labor songs," he conjectured, "will some day constitute the major theme of some notable musical composition, or be wrought into a drama to move the heart of man to sympathy for our brother in black."

On September 25, 1934, Leadbelly and Lomax arrived in Little Rock, where Governor Futrell's office had prepared a letter of introduction for Lomax to present to the Arkansas superintendent of prisons in Tucker.[29] Lomax took accommodations at a tourist cabin outside Little Rock, while Leadbelly stayed in town, searching for performers in the black neighborhoods. That evening and for two days following, the duo remained in the Arkansas capital to begin their recordings and to visit with Lomax's oldest son, Johnny Lomax Jr., then in Little Rock on bank business. Johnny's nightly visits culminated in a

FIGURE 13.
The Rock Island
Line passing over
the Third Street
viaduct at North
Little Rock,
Arkansas.
From *Rock Island
Magazine*
(October 1931).

party on September 27 "with Lead Belly singing and me interpolating."[30] As Johnny and his friends huddled in a corner of the cabin, Leadbelly presented a sampling of his songs while the sixty-six-year-old folklorist provided a running commentary on the singer's art.

Two days later, after coping with the temperamental disc recorder that required more than one trip to Pine Bluff for repairs, Lomax and Leadbelly arrived at the state prison in Tucker, Arkansas.[31] For everyone involved, conditions were challenging: "It has rained all day," he wrote in a letter home. "We have our singers rounded up but they must stand outside and our recording must wait for the rain to stop."[32] These performers, none of whom were identified in Lomax's notes, made the first recording of "Rock Island Line." The men began by singing "My Lord, My Lord, My Lord" in three slow, drawn-out cadences.[33] Then they launched in:

> Chorus:
> Leader: I said the Rock Island Line
> Group: Is a mighty good road.
> Leader: I said the Rock Island Line
> Group: Is a road to ride.
> Leader: I said the Rock Island Line

Group: Is a mighty good road,
All: If you want to ride, you got to ride it like you're flyin',
Buy your ticket at the station on the Rock Island Line.

(Repeat chorus)

Leader: Jesus died to save all of my friends.
Second voice: Glory to God we gonna meet him again.

Chorus

Leader: I said we have [inaudible] men and fireman too.
Second voice: [inaudible] and brakemen too.

Chorus

Leader: Well, the train got to Memphis just on time.
Second voice: Well, it made it back to Little Rock at 8:49.

Chorus

Chorus[34]

Even with a few words indecipherable, the Tucker recording reveals how much the song's text had changed from the original presented at the Arch Street church. No longer called "Buy Your Ticket over Rock Island Lines," but simply "Rock Island Line," its center had shifted, like its title, from trade to travel. The slow-meter religious invocation immediately reframed the song. The former booster song, meant to sell tickets, now evoked a gospel train. Instead of celebrating individuals affiliated with the Biddle Shops, names essentially unknown to outsiders, it fastened onto more widely shared experiences. Technically explicit jobs, too, like "engine wiper" have fallen away, leaving just the firemen and brakemen. As the song pared down the densely written original verses, it added a new, easily repeatable couplet, beginning "Jesus died to save all of my friends." Its buoyant gospel message fit with the song's chanted chorus, here shortened, turning its focus from the purchase of seats to the train ride itself. The engine numbered 849 that Mr. Church drove in "Buy Your Ticket" has turned into "8:49," the time the train purportedly returned to Little Rock. The text at Tucker, like the other "Rock Island Line" versions John Lomax subsequently recorded, no longer mentions the railroad's long-distance California service, but addresses a more regional concern, the better-known route between Memphis and Little Rock.

The 133 miles of track that lay between the two cities marked the oldest railroad line in the state of Arkansas, chartered in 1853. With flood plains lying outside of Memphis and six river crossings to make, the original trip took thirty-two hours. Heading eastward from Little Rock, the tracks stopped at De Valls Bluff, at which point passengers embarked on a steamboat. They landed at Clarendon, where they took a stagecoach to Madison before the tracks to Memphis resumed.[35] Direct rail service between the two cities began in April 1871 when the White River bridge was completed and the pilings along the Cache River bottoms had been fixed. This through-line trip took ten hours, passing across a rural countryside of rice farms and cotton plantations. In 1902 the Rock Island Lines took over the route (whose tracks had previously belonged to the Choctaw, Oklahoma and Gulf Railroad), and by the mid-1930s made six trips daily between Memphis and Little Rock, three in each direction. Between station stops, the train ran at speeds up to fifty miles an hour, making it a three-hour trip. Every afternoon the five o'clock train from Memphis stopped at the many small towns and flag stops that lined the route, reaching Little Rock at 8:25 P.M. Its counterpart, running in the reverse direction and starting out at nine in the morning, made the same local stops, also adding a half hour to the run. By 1953, under diesel power, the trip took two hours and made speeds up to ninety miles an hour. The Memphis–Little Rock service ended in 1967, and the Rock Island Lines liquidated in 1980. When *Time* magazine wrote about the line's receivership, it began its article, "Wreck of the Rock Island," with a lyric from the song.[36]

Like the realities of the railroad, the life of the folksong in Arkansas was powered by different engines. At the time of its earliest recordings a style of close vocal harmony drove the number. Neighborhood institutions from corner barbershops to shoeshine parlors, social clubs to fraternal lodges, along with more formal church, school, and stage settings had long provided outlets for this widespread communal activity.[37] At state prisons black inmates likewise formed their own leisure-time quartets. In October 1934 Lomax and Leadbelly left Tucker for Cummins prison farm, where they first met Kelly Pace. On his recordings then, and again in 1942, Kelly showed himself to be above all a quartet singer. Kelly's family remembered his organizing singing groups at Cummins, assigning parts much as he had done during his childhood in Camden, Arkansas, at the Good Hope Baptist Church. "Kelly told me," said his cousin Otis Sams, "'There is some guys there [at Cummins] who really can sing. Sitting around, we got together. I got to singing and they got to singing, and finally we organized our club and we just went at it.'"[38] Sometimes when Kelly and his groups performed, the guards gave them a break from their work. Singing activities under Kelly's leadership also led to occasional appearances outside the prison gates, usually at churches and often on Saturday nights. Understandably, the men crowded around Lomax's microphone now to sing "Rock Island Line":

> Chorus:
> Pace: I said the Rock Island Line
> Group: Is a mighty good road.
> Pace: I said the Rock Island Line
> Group: Is the road to ride.
> Pace: I said the Rock Island Line
> Group: Is a mighty good road.
> All: If you want to ride, you got to ride it like you're flyin',
> Buy your ticket at the station on the Rock Island Line.
>
> Train whistler
>
> Pace: Well, Jesus died to save me in all of my sin.
> Group: Well a glory to God we gonna meet him again.
>
> Chorus
>
> Train whistler
>
> Pace: Well, the train left Memphis at half past nine.
> Group: Well, it made it back to Little Rock at 8:49.
>
> Chorus
>
> Train whistler
>
> Repeat first verse
>
> Chorus
>
> Train whistler.[39]

This spirited performance attests to Kelly's observation that at Cummins there were "some guys there that really can sing." The chorus of "Rock Island Line," repeated between the short couplets, became the song's central feature. With less polish but still keeping the melody intact and nearly the same text, Joe Battle led another group of convicts through the song in Lomax's 1939 recording. Kelly was out of prison at that time, and Battle's sextet sounds closer to the Tucker version of several years before. When Lomax returned to Cummins for the last time in 1942, and Kelly was again behind bars, they recorded "Rock Island Line" once more. Kelly opened it with his own railroad whistling. But this group sang the piece with less cohesion than before, leaving Kelly to carry most of it himself. No matter the variables of rehearsal and personnel, the song had sustained. Just as the details in "Buy Your Ticket" simplified as it moved further away from the Biddle Yards, an older tradition lent the song new coherence, which in turn insured its survival.

In January 1998, I visited the Reverend Ralph Dawson, a quartet singer from Denison, Texas. In the mid-1940s, Dawson formed a group with Bozie Sturdivant, the lead performer of "Ain't No Grave Can Hold My Body Down," also recorded by the Library. Since his youth, the Reverend Dawson has participated in the genre of close-harmony sacred singing. As with many other traditionally steeped performers, his job, family needs, and professional opportunities have limited his performances to his local region. But over the years he has fastidiously listened to this style on records and radio, and closely studied those quartets that passed through his community making live appearances. During our days together, and by telephone since, the Reverend Dawson and I have worked through "Ain't No Grave Can Hold My Body Down" and other gospel quartet songs. Our conversations, which always begin with music, inevitably turn meditative as Reverend Dawson explores the byways of belief.

As soon as Dawson played Kelly Pace's 1934 "Rock Island Line" on his cassette machine, he knew it, he said, "but by another name. We called it 'pulling the whistle.'"[40] The hand-cupped voice trumpet in Kelly's recording recalled an effect that he and Bozie Sturdivant sometimes used in their own quartet performances. Dawson then demonstrated how they used to introduce one of these numbers, with a "whoa, whoa, whoa-whoa"—two long blasts followed by two short toots—evoking the signal of a train coming to a crossing. "We sang a song like that, 'This Train Is Bound for Glory.' Basically the same thing." The whistle on Kelly's record reminded Dawson of the one he did with Bozie, even though it differed in melodic contour. That, in turn, led him to consider "Rock Island Line" and its origins.

"One time Sturdivant told me [before he moved to Denison] that he formed this group out of a bunch of conductors. They were meeting at a barbershop on time off from their runs. So if this was the Rock Island line they worked for, even if it was railroad sponsored or to promote the Rock Island, he was still able to promote God and His Son in the same action." He ran the tape back and listened to it again. "Sometimes you get sponsors on programs, and there might have been a connection to that railroad, but I'm looking for what its purpose is."

Dawson probed "Rock Island Line" for its splicing of religious content with corporate self-interest, a coupling that scholars elsewhere have also reported. In the early 1980s, researchers Kip Lornell in Memphis and Brenda McCallum in Birmingham separately interviewed scores of quartet singers, the oldest of whom were active in the late 1920s when "Buy Your Ticket" was first sung.[41] Lornell and McCallum listened to their sources describe the once common practice of companies sponsoring gospel jubilee quartets. Lornell's interview with former quartet singer Will Rodgers sparked his memories of a Rock Island railroad quartet that appeared in Memphis in the 1940s. Rodgers then quoted the well-known chorus: "Rock Island is a mighty good road, / If you want to ride, ride like you're flyin', / Be sure to buy your ticket on the Rock Island Line."[42] Rodgers, who watched this group perform in churches, added, "I never will forget that song. That was their theme song." His anecdote highlighted the traditional basis of the booster club quartets. Over and above any commercial role they might have played, they arose within a religious setting, a devotional activity based in the church. As another Memphis singer of that era told Kip Lornell, "The gospel quartet is all about being a Christian."[43]

In Birmingham, Brenda McCallum found kindred sensibilities. Following the Civil War in this industrial center of the New South, various steel works, coal mines, iron foundries, and railroad lines came to sponsor a number of quartets, with the first of these groups recording in 1926. Even though "local companies often appropriated indigenous musical traditions for their own purposes," she found the quartets to be "simultaneously, an extended social and familial network, a brotherhood or fraternal organization, a benevolent society and mutual aid association, and a convocation for spiritual fellowship."[44] If like-minded singers on a job site sometimes blended their voices to pass away the hours, the core of that activity lay not with the company where they met, but with deeper community-based traditions that had nurtured this music from its start. "Harmony and love amongst the group," L. T. Smoot of the Four Eagle Gospel Singers told McCallum, "that's the main object. If you get that to work, then you can hold on, with God to help."[45]

The Reverend Dawson viewed "Rock Island Line" the same way and compared it to "The Old Ship of Zion." Dawson felt that the older spiritual, set to a similarly lively pace, offers "almost the same type of emotion, in the dramatization, in the way the singers presented it. 'If you want to get with Jesus, get on board.' You're saying that 'my mother and father followed in this tradition with faith, and they were pleased.' This was a sure route."[46] The metaphor of gospel transport, one by rail and the other by sail, ran through both songs. Dawson reversed the tape back to Kelly's opening lines of "Jesus died to save me in all of my sin / Glory to God we're gonna meet him again." To whatever degree "Rock Island Line" was a unique work, it joined this wider idiom. "When you use a different word which we call a different song,"

Dawson explained, "it's for the part of getting the attention of the people you're performing to."

"So it's a personal vision of the general message of Christianity," I said.

"Exactly."

"Different approaches to the same idea?"

"That's my point, all these songs are basically on the same platform of singing. The message of God to man is always going to be the same, in a blues song or a Christian song. I'm going deep on you now." We laughed.

"'Rock Island Line,'" Ralph Dawson paused, "is a spiritual song."

He pressed the fast-forward button of the cassette player, and our conversation turned to other matters. But he had made this much clear: Beginning with its whistle that made the Reverend Dawson think of "This Train Is Bound for Glory," and later "Old Ship of Zion," he found in "Rock Island Line" a common pattern. The metaphor of a train coupled with the verses that mention Jesus identified it as part of an allegorical tradition. From the Fisk Jubilee Singers who included "The Gospel Train is Coming" in their first songbook of 1872 to the Golden Gate Jubilee Singers, who began their illustrious career with a recording of "Gospel Train" in 1937, from street-vended broadsides to mail-order records, pulpit orators to storefront evangelists, the railroad has prolifically given, as historian Lawrence Levine has observed, "a persistent image of change, transcendence, and the possibilities of beginning again."[47]

Even as "Rock Island Line" carried a secular intent, promoting a fast moving route with poetic verve, by virtue of its being a quartet song, a form instilled with spiritual precedent, gospel associations clung to it. As "Buy Your Ticket" moved beyond Arch Street, and its immediate references fell away, those drawn to the song reasserted its underlying religious traditions. Simplified to the few vigorous stanzas that Kelly Pace led on this recording, it communicated a message of salvation that Ralph Dawson recognized. Once the song ceased to be performed as a quartet number, and found expression within a different musical framework—the one that Huddie Ledbetter engineered—these gospel associations in turn dropped away.

We can imagine how "Rock Island Line" began to change in the tourist cabin John Lomax had rented near Little Rock at the outset of their collecting trip. In September 1934, as Lomax spoke against the backdrop of Leadbelly's songs, explaining them to his son and his son's friends, Leadbelly must have seen the effect this presentation had on the young audience gathered there.

While spoken interludes have long occupied a place in folksong tradition, Leadbelly employed this device to a greater extent than many of his recorded contemporaries. These spoken-word vignettes made his material all the more accessible for the audiences he faced, largely comprised of white cosmopolitans who had scant familiarity with rural Southern black music. Even in the privacy of his New York City apartment, in later years when guests came by, Leadbelly played the "Rock Island Line" complete with the verbal interludes he had created for it. He stood in his living room as if it were a concert hall, dressed in bow tie and shirt, entertaining his visitors in ways they would assuredly understand.[48] Though Leadbelly's initial exposure to the piece lay just hours away from that September night in Little Rock, he may have already plotted its future course.

Three years later, in June 1937, Leadbelly made his first recording of the song.[49] The narrative he devised for "Rock Island Line" steered it into a work-song setting. In that recording, made without accompaniment, he begins with a meticulous depiction of "cutting in Arkansas"—of men chopping wood "down the line just like coaches." He speaks with authority, informing listeners how a work gang clears a field with axes and saws. Arkansas professor and "Rock Island Line" scholar Robert Cochran speculated that Leadbelly might have remembered songs at Cummins that did involve axes and logs and spliced that activity to this number. This seems altogether plausible.[50] It is also conceivable that Leadbelly had absorbed the Lomaxes' eagerness to find worksongs in prisons. Leadbelly went on to record the song at least five more times, shaping it as a solo, eventually creating a musical drama of a percussive freight train express bound for New Orleans. It becomes a contest between an engineer and a depot agent, replete with train whistles and calls, powered by his twelve-string guitar.[51] The click-clack of verses recreated a churning railroad train hauling a cargo load of livestock and pig iron. When "Rock Island Line" eventually entered popular culture, it arrived there as a secular, rhythmic showpiece.

In 1956, "Rock Island Line" became a transatlantic hit when Scotsman Lonnie Donegan released his performance based on Leadbelly's story song. In kinescopes from that time, Donegan's ensemble of grinning, bow-tied musicians crowd the edges of the screen, showing the wiry singer as he leaps through the alphabet to the snare-drum cadence of Leadbelly's "A-B-C double X-Y-Z." By springtime, the song reached number nine in the United States while occupying the British top twenty for nearly six months. "Rock Island Line" ignited in the British Isles a homemade music style called skiffle, lodging the guitar in the hands of such players as John Lennon and Paul McCartney well before they became Beatles. Like other youthful musicians of their generation (in later years they each recorded it), they put together a skiffle band and honed their skills to this song along with studying the latest imports of Bill Haley and Elvis Presley. When Beatle George Harrison passed away in November 2001, the *Washington Post* noted that, by his own admission, what "awoke his musical passion" was Lonnie Donegan's "Rock Island Line."[52]

Paul Oliver's 1957 profile of "Rock Island Line" appeared at the height of skiffle's popularity. As a passenger returning home to London on a commuter train, Oliver looked up to see several pairs of hands drumming on the glass and wood frame that separated his compartment from the corridor. He heard sounds of muffled voices, and when the door swung open, he found a group singing "Rock Island Line." Some of the lyrics had collapsed into rhythmic syllabic markers: "And de da diddy da is a da diddy da."[53] The singers, Oliver discovered, had little or no idea of the history behind the song. Here at the dawn of rock and roll, the "rock" in the song's title found new meanings. "Some confused thinking," Oliver writes, "had resulted in the vague idea that 'Rock' referred to bending one's knees as one sang, etc. to the rolling of a train and the rhythm of the band." Oliver goes on to sketch a history of the Rock Island railroad, the Library's recording of Kelly Pace, and Leadbelly's subsequent development of the song. He concludes by describing the recent copyrighted works to stem from the commercial success of "Rock Island Line." In one, a playlet for choral group and combo set at a railway station, the finale features a character, who, after obtaining a ticket and checking his baggage, "enters to dance a routine of a traveler."[54] Oliver ruefully notes that it might be just as well if Kelly Pace and his group never learn of these routes taken by their song.

Powered by Leadbelly's jangling locomotive, "Rock Island Line" soon headed into the timbres of country, folk, and pop. From Bobby Darin to the Brothers Four, dozens of performers recorded it. At summer camps cross-legged youngsters encircled around an evening fire yipped in gleeful unison to Leadbelly's line in the song "Cats in the cupboard, but they don't see me." His succession of recordings, performances, and broadcasts established the standard form of "Rock Island Line," and in the pluralism of the marketplace gave rise to a plethora of commercial interpretations. Johnny Horton and Johnny Cash picked it up. Stan Freberg did a parody, and in 1988, Little Richard treated it to a piano rave-up on a Grammy-winning compilation dedicated to Leadbelly. More recently, musician Bethany Yarrow, daughter of Peter Yarrow of the singing group Peter, Paul and Mary, has said of the song,

"It has to do for me with the rhythmic. Today, a lot of the music, especially R & B and HipHop is all based on the rhythm, and that's what people dance to; that's what people move to."[55]

So the Leadbelly version became dominant in popular culture, save for a brief moment in the summer of 1999, when Kelly Pace and his seven fellow inmates were again heard to sing "Rock Island Line" in a mass medium. As the misty flats of coastal Georgia spread out against the horizon seen from the air, their voices accompany the closing scenes of *The General's Daughter*, a high-budget Hollywood film starring John Travolta. The film's director, Simon West, drew on three selections taken from *A Treasury of Library of Congress Field Recordings*, including this version of "Rock Island Line." West, an Englishman born well after the skiffle craze of the fifties, had heard the song before, but only in passing, from a Johnny Cash recording. Once he heard the Kelly Pace version he knew only that it was sung by Southern black prisoners. "Rock Island Line" was, he said, "a powerful song, sad to me, but also means you can move on with life."[56] Repositioned in a framework of slide guitar and drums, with their voices stacked in a digital loop, Kelly and the others sang "Glory to God we're going to meet Him again [and] again [and] again." As John Travolta and costar Madeleine Stowe drive off, their mission accomplished and sunlight breaking through the clouds, the dark film ends with a rapid succession of shots, indicating new vistas and fresh directions. Simon West closed *The General's Daughter* with "Rock Island Line," its old voices set against new instrumentation to suggest hope for the future tempered by experience.

The downpour started just as we reached the graveyard. A few decorations, mainly plastic flowers, lay tip-sided near the headstones. Beneath some bushes at the back of the cemetery stood the small granite slab. Moss spread along its side, mottling it with dark stains. I touched the marker that bore these words: "Robert Kelly Pace, January 2, 1913—June 27, 1958." Thick drops of rain stuck to my camera lens and the flash attachment switched on automatically. In the gusting wind and indigo half-light of the storm, the ground seemed to pitch. After a couple of snapshots I jumped back in the car, and we sped off into the gathering dark.

Earlier on the afternoon of the rainstorm, guided there by Robert Cochran, I had visited Otis Sams (1908–2003), Kelly's second cousin. Eighty-nine years old, Otis lived just down the road from the cemetery where Kelly Pace is buried. A few doors away stands the Good Hope A.M.E. Church, then in its 137th year. Otis and Kelly attended this church in their youth. The church owned no hymnals back then. The boys sang in the choir, where they learned the songs, Otis said, "of their foreparents."[57] Otis stretched back on his sofa and began to chuckle over those childhood days. They would hide from the scowls of the church seniors, he told us, to listen to the latest blues records or to watch the French harp players who could "play that freight train." When the youngsters worked in the cotton fields around Camden and Kelly sang, his clear voice drew the attention of those within earshot. "He was," said Otis, "really gifted to sing."

Most of all, as Otis's own voice filled with warmth, Kelly emerged as a rascally Robin Hood, stealing from the rich for the comfort of others less well off. "Kelly was a fine boy, always in mischievious himself. That's why he was in prison. Never hurt no one. Always ready to help somebody." Otis told of Kelly's absconding down Camden's alleyways with suits that had hung on a mannequin outside a local clothes store, and of offering his neighbors a brace of stolen pistols for ten dollars apiece. Kelly, he explained, would provide you with whatever you needed. Hampered with little or no money, Kelly freely admitted he did not require cash to meet his needs. But neither did he insist his companions commit larcenies themselves. "That's me," Kelly told his cousin, "that ain't none of you."

Kelly spent over half his life behind bars. According to Arkansas prison records, his first arrest for burglary occurred in 1931. Sentenced to two years imprisonment but paroled the following year, he was next arrested in Texarkana for gambling. In November 1933, he was convicted of burglary in Tucker, Arkansas, and sent to Cummins State Farm. Discharged five years later, Kelly Pace was soon again arrested, this time for grand larceny. The sentence was forty-two years. On October 18, 1955, after serving sixteen of those years, he was discharged from prison and was never again arrested. He had a fourth-grade education and described himself in prison documents as a laborer.

A number of Kelly's thirty-seven recordings that John Lomax made in 1934 and 1942 comment on imprisonment. In one of his later solo field hollers, Kelly sang of a man severed from his home: "Well, I told my mama 'fore I left the town / Don't she let nobody tear my barrelhouse down."[58] The lyric evokes the loss of domestic stability, the disintegration of one's livelihood, and the shattering of one's place within a community. In another of his solos, with sharp vocal leaps and long dwelling notes, Kelly ends with a trenchant observation, "I would come to see you, but the white folks got me barred."[59]

One spoken-word piece, titled "Guard Talking to Convict," recorded during the 1934 session, seems to touch directly on Kelly's personal experience.[60] In it, Kelly plays the part of an inmate assigned to stack wood. The "guard," played by another convict, unidentified (as was Kelly) in the recording notes, says that he would have given him leave had he known Kelly was sick. Like fast-talking characters in a radio play, they rag one another mercilessly. Kelly rebukes his taskmaster, who expects too much. The "guard" counters that "you just barrel-housing . . . jiving . . . always giving me the downside"—a shirker. Then Kelly answers, "I'm not trying to jive you. You know this, don't you. This is Kelly Pace. You realize who I is. I'm a man like you. . . . God almighty dog, man. I'm going on. I'm gonna work long as I got a day to do here, and I got six long years." Kelly speaks without apology, sounding neither depressed nor resigned, but with directness. The exchange fits with Otis's recollections of Kelly talking to his family in those years: "'Don't worry about me. Worry about yourself, I'm making it alright.'"[61]

As Otis looked back on Kelly's experiences, he mused about his own eighty-nine years of living. "I've been on the job," he said, "a good long while." For thirty of those years, he dug graves for the Good Hope Baptist Church. Visitors still stopped at his door, asking his help to find their relatives. Otis's own grandfather, a former slave born in 1824, occupies the oldest identified plot. For many, this place is a hallowed ground. "Lots of folks buried here without no tombstone, wasn't able to buy land. Others just put up an old piece of churn." This would have been the wooden handle, like a broom stick, used in an old-time butter churn. Otis knew that if not for the family's intercession, Kelly Pace's grave could have gone this way, too.

The next morning, the sky finally quieted from the pummeling of the night before, we drove across the state to visit Kelly's one surviving brother, Lawrence Pace. A pearl light framed the sea-gray horizon. Although the fall day had now turned warm, Lawrence and his wife, Ruby, kept the windows closed and the heater running. Bad health had beset him and he needed the warmth. When we came in, Lawrence smiled quietly from his leather chair, his almond-wide eyes looking at me. He steepled his fingers. "I understand you have something for me." I said I did, and set down my tape recorder, camera, and papers.

Three days earlier, *A Treasury of Library of Congress Field Recordings* had gone into national release. As Kelly's song resounded on a portable CD player, Lawrence leafed through the booklet. Once he signed the form, I could give him his check. Ruby, a retired elementary schoolteacher and a church pianist, sat on the bench behind him. She watched over the room, talking with us,

touching his shoulder, and seeing after him. Something quiet passed between the two of them, and Ruby asked if this was all right. Lawrence's illness hindered him from clasping a pen, so she leaned over the table where the agreement lay and signed his name. As she did, Lawrence touched her hand. They looked to see if I understood—from him through her to it. In that unforgettable moment two worlds met: the symbolic and the literal, the traditional and the formal, and, like "Rock Island Line" itself, the commercial and the spiritual.

Our business completed, I turned on the tape recorder.

"My brother," said Lawrence, "was a songster. He sang all sort of songs—songs of the church, of the blues, dance songs, work songs."[62] Lawrence's voice changed, gaining vigor as he recalled his younger brother Kelly. "You couldn't beat him working. He didn't wait till the dew is off. He'd say, 'I'm going to get 400 pounds of cotton.' And when you was done half-way, he done cut out and coming back." Lawrence bit off his words in rapid gusts, as if these contests of a bygone day rushed past him again. Then he paused. "Kelly, he was something else."

Lawrence listed his brother's skills: "He sung. You couldn't beat him working. He could chunk a rock like a .22. Hit a rabbit with that rock. If he throwed it, he wasn't going to miss. He going to hit you. You couldn't beat him doing nothing; he could do it."

Until his first imprisonment, Kelly lived with his parents, six brothers, and two sisters in a four-room house fifteen miles outside of Camden. Like other black families in that section, the Paces had no electricity. For light, they burned pine splinters set out on buckets, heated their home with wood, made their own butter, refrigerated with ice, and hunted the woods for possums and wild hogs. As for organized singing, on Wednesdays and Sundays the family traveled by two-mule wagon to church.[63] As one of his last jobs before imprisonment, Kelly worked on a white-owned plantation picking cotton.

"When we was coming up," Lawrence continued, "we sung together." The three oldest boys—Henry, Lawrence, and Kelly—harmonized at Good

CHAPTER 2

Hope, eventually forming their own quartet "club." "Kelly sang all the time, did solos. Did some of everything." His recordings, meanwhile playing in the background, glimpsed that breadth, ranging from field hollers to blues, worksongs to lullabies, spirituals to quartets. We stopped for a bit to listen, how during his 1942 session, in "Samson," Kelly led his group in the style of the Golden Gate Jubilee Singers.[64] At that time the Gates had recorded the number just four years earlier. Although Kelly's lyrics differ at points from theirs, his arrangement re-created the popular rendition. As its lead singer he becomes here a storyteller, expressing with pitch and rhythm "Samson's" Bible tale. He also performed a sequence of children's songs that included "Will You Marry Me, My Pretty Little Miss."[65] The number had none of the blues notes or off-beats that characterized so many of his other pieces. Instead, it sounds Anglo-American, staying with the major chords, the syllables hitting square on the beat. On the recording John Lomax's wife, Ruby, asks him where he learned it, and Kelly answers disarmingly, "When my mother was teaching me how to sing songs."

Kelly learned songs by ear, "done all that at home," Lawrence confirmed, and while he worked outside, he made up new ones. The most gregarious of the siblings, Kelly sang throughout the day. He also danced. "He'd go to socials, swinging and dancing. He could do that, man. He sure could do that," Lawrence continued. "They had a vendor thing then."

"A jukebox?" I asked.

"Yes, punch whatever you wanted to hear. Jazz stuff. He loved that stuff." At some point too, Lawrence recalled, the family acquired a graphonola, a type of phonograph.

"He went to the pen and sung his way out." Lawrence mentioned Kelly's performances at the local churches where, under guard, he and his groups sometimes performed. "But he wouldn't stay out. He told papa, if he's in the penitentiary he didn't have to buy no clothes, no nothing." Over time, Kelly worked his way up to the job of line rider, "totin' them pistols, shotgun." In the parlance of the penal system, Kelly became a trusty, meaning he carried a weapon, which he would use if a convict tried to make an escape. For this privilege, trusties were freed from chopping cotton themselves.

"So he stayed in there the biggest part of his life. He told the warden he was going home for Christmas." The Arkansas State Penitentiary offered furloughs in exchange for good conduct, and Kelly's record reflects two such reprieves. "He'd tell him, 'If you let me go, I'll come on back. If you don't, you gonna have trouble, 'cause I ain't coming back.'" Again, Lawrence paused. "That's the way he carried himself. But I had to let him go 'cause he got out of hand for me." Lawrence spoke of Kelly's larcenies: "If you wanted that car, and you put up the money, he gonna get you that car and that's it. He could get sort of mean too. If you mess with him, he'd fight. He'd get me in a whole lot of trouble . . . I couldn't do that, I couldn't go along with him."

By 1955, the year of Kelly's discharge, "he'd changed right smart." Three years later he died at a sawmill in Texas peeling logs. "Running that thing, it hung up somewhere. Kicked back and killed him." Kelly had never before held an industrial job, having spent over half his life on a prison farm. Lawrence looked away with sadness, "God had given him a gift, but the devil won."

———

Of all the songs published in the *Rock Island Magazine*, only one, written by a black American engine wiper from Little Rock that he sang in church with three of his fellow laborers, took public hold. Cast in a traditional style, written to meet a company theme but expressed in a vernacular particular to that form, it proved attractive enough that without commercial support and sustained by a wholly voluntary process, it made its way into folk tradition. Within four years of its being sung at the Arch Street Missionary Baptist Church, inmates at various units of the Arkansas penitentiary had absorbed it and made it part of their recreation. By then, the song had become tauter, reduced to essentials, its emphasis shifted back to the tradition from which it originated. Subsequently absorbed by a musician of prodigious talent who drew it through his own artistic filter, it became known to millions.

Kelly Pace served as a crucial link in that transfer, a conduit between the booster number that the Biddle Shop quartet offered and the direction that Leadbelly took. As an interpretative artist and an African American state prisoner, Kelly negotiated another midpoint as well, evident in his relationship to John A. Lomax, whom he both accommodated and at times met head-on. The last time Kelly saw the folklorist was in September 1942, when he sang numbers like "Samson" along with "Rock Island Line" for his final recording session. By his own account, when he saw Lomax unexpectedly arrive, circling the cotton turnrows where he was at work, Kelly called out, "That's my bossman."[66] In a recorded conversation that is nothing if not coaxed, Lomax has Kelly describe his initial reactions to his appearance. Kelly obliges with appropriate enthusiasm, adding that he was also glad just to get out of the heat as the two drove around. If this recording expresses one dimension of their relationship, reprising a predictable banter determined by race, era, and confinement, other recordings made that day reveal a greater complexity, and a greater richness, that the two men shared.

While discussing the song "Pick a Bale of Cotton," Lomax asks Kelly about when he might sing it. "In the cotton patch," Kelly answers, when he's out picking cotton. Lomax then asks, "Does it help you to pick it faster?"[67] Here Kelly answers both dutifully and comically: "It makes me have a spiritual life to pick cotton." Lomax laughs, and a joke lies at hand. The question gets repeated, as does the answer. "Doesn't it make your hands move faster when you sing it," Lomax asks. "Don't you keep time with your hands when you pick cotton?" Kelly replies as before, only the volume rising in his voice. "It makes me keep time with my hands picking cotton. That makes me have a spiritual life to pick faster." Clearly, Kelly plays on the expected reply, echoing his questioner's words, while at the same time parodying it with his word play. By this point, too, Lomax has reiterated an idea he used in his 1941 *Ballad Hunter* lecture and in his autobiography, associating "Rock Island Line" with cotton picking. The concept is identical, even if the realities of hands picking cotton and keeping time with the song were not.

At another point the two confer as colleagues. About to record "Samson," which involved the largest group of singers organized that day, Lomax whispers to Kelly that when he sings the lead part the others need to lower their voices. Just as quietly, Kelly assures him they will.[68] In the course of the session, they even disagree. When Kelly sings what he calls "Bad Lazarus," Lomax questions that title. "Well, some folks call him poor Lazarus," Kelly

FIGURE 15.
Kelly Pace, Arkansas, mid-1950s.
Author's collection, with thanks to Lorine Pace Strong.

replies, holding his own, "but I'd rather call him bad Lazarus."[69] A moment later, he says, "I'm gone," then starts the song, his group falling in behind. On the recording titled "Kelly Pace Speaks" still another sentiment appears.[70] At first Kelly talks as if he's addressing a radio audience about the Library of Congress recordings, "Putting them out, over the country, far and near." Soon he finishes and seems ready to hand the microphone back. Presumably, gestured to do otherwise and to fill the silence, Kelly resumes talking. "I feel mighty fine that Mr. Lomax drove down to see me, and was glad to know that he thought that much of me. Come down to see me, and talk with me. And then we'll put out some more records for him. I guess that he'll go in today, but I'll be too glad if he'll come back again sometime." Two years later, in September 1944, Lomax wrote to the superintendent of the Arkansas penitentiary asking for Kelly's records and conduct reports.[71] That letter, like this recording, signifies more than simply a subjugated informant and his powerful visitor. Lomax evidently hoped to aid in his release.

The balance of autonomy and independence that Kelly reached with John A. Lomax, like the Biddle Shop singers performing "Buy Your Ticket" to their bosses at the Arch Street church, recalls a duality that W. E. B. DuBois explored in *The Souls of Black Folk*. Writing in 1903, DuBois pondered a condition of "twoness," of being black and American. "The American Negro," he observed, is someone who "would not Africanize America, for America has too much to teach the world and Africa. He would not bleach his Negro soul in a flood of white Americanism, for he knows that Negro blood has a message for the world. He simply wishes to make it possible for a man to be both a Negro and an American, without being cursed and spit upon by his fellows, without having the doors of Opportunity closed roughly in his face. This, then, is the end of his striving: to be a coworker in the kingdom of culture."[72] DuBois's egalitarian hope for his times, in essence, tells the story of "Rock Island Line." He expresses what its formative singers both endured and achieved.

That this joyful hymn to a railroad reached from a gospel quartet to a songster's showpiece to a rhythmic workhorse known worldwide makes engine wiper Clarence Wilson, the Rock Island Colored Booster Quartet, Kelly Pace, and Leadbelly all coworkers in the kingdom of culture. Its success attests to what DuBois saw as the end product of that cultural striving he envisioned for America and beyond. What Clarence Wilson and his companions sang that December night in 1929 involved more than just a salute to their employers. They practiced an art form that literally, physically, socially, and spiritually expressed a type of human unity. Like the Juneteenth efforts led by their quartet's founder, Smoky McMahon, to bring that celebration of freedom across Arkansas to its Rock Island black booster clubs, their harmony singing in this piece expressed values that stood beyond purely company prerogatives. In moving past the Biddle yards, the deeper spirit of "Buy Your Ticket over Rock Island Lines" never went away. It only broadened.

Ora Dell Graham

A Little Black Girl from Mississippi

S ONNY MILTON FOCUSED SILENTLY ON THE ROAD AHEAD.
Nestled between us in the cab of his pickup, set in a rusted metal frame
held fast by tacks and twine, lay a picture of someone he had always
loved. Ora Dell Graham—"Honey"—had been his favorite aunt. The hand-
colored photograph, mounted on cardboard and bent from more than a half-
century of age, shows her in late adolescence, confidently looking on with a
pixie smile. In her family, she had been the voluble one, the extrovert. "She
loved to go, she always loved to go."[1] Milton spoke quietly but emphatically.
"She was what you call a night person. She loved to have a ball. She loved
to dance. She loved to sing. That was her thing, you know." The muscles in
his jaw flickered, and there was a long pause. "And that's what killed her."

"I was playing ball with my friends," he continued, "when I first got the
news." During the summer of 1952, Ora Dell Graham and three companions
headed from her home in Drew, Mississippi, for the nightspots of Clarksdale. Three miles north of town, at the foot of a narrow highway bridge, their
car smashed into a brick embankment. "They say her neck was broken. By
the time I got there, they had taken her and the other three people in the
car away." Milton and his grandmother buried Ora Dell in the town's segregated cemetery, marking the spot with a tin badge tied with wire. She was

twenty-four years old. Her grave marker has since disappeared.

Now, forty-six years later, we scoured East St. Louis, Illinois, for a high-grade photocopier able to reproduce Ora Dell's sole portrait. A few days before, Milton first learned that his aunt had made some recordings. In the fall of 1940, the year she turned twelve, Ora Dell stood before her classmates in her school auditorium. As John A. Lomax operated a disc recorder, she performed a handful of songs that she animated with dance steps, hand clapping, and vocal effects. Three of these numbers, along with the earliest published recordings of Muddy Waters, subsequently appeared on an album of African American blues and game songs issued by the Library of Congress.[2] This news came as a surprise to Milton. He listened patiently to the story, one that included a government library that until now he had never heard of. On our way to another strip mall with possibly a better duplicator than the machine we just tried, his reserve finally gave way. "Why," he asked heatedly, "would anyone care about a little black girl from Mississippi?"

The question echoed something he had said earlier. "It was rough down there," he remembered, "very rough."[3] In the early 1950s, the years of Sonny Milton's youth, custom demanded that a black man step off the sidewalk in deference to passing white pedestrians. For that reason, he explained, he didn't wear a cap. That way he never had to tip it to any whites he met on the street. "That's why I say the good Lord didn't let me be a slave. 'Cause they'd a-had to kill me. My people took some stuff that I wouldn't have been able to take." Then he mentioned August 1955. In a town thirty-five miles southeast of Drew—fifteen months after *Brown v. Board of Education*—a fourteen-year-old Chicagoan named Emmett Till had come south to visit relatives. Till allegedly whistled at a young white woman clerking in a grocery store. Three days later her husband and brother-in-law seized Till from his great-uncle's home. After beating, facially mutilating, and shooting him, they tied a ventilator fan to his neck and sank his body in the Tallahatchie River. At the trial the defense argued that the corpse, disfigured beyond the family's ability to identify it, might not have been Till. The two who committed the crime, their guilt known throughout the community, were acquitted after sixty-seven minutes of deliberation. "Emmett Till," Milton whispered. "That hurt."

No wonder he asked why anyone would care about a little black girl from Mississippi. Yet as we drove around that afternoon we somehow found an answer. In November 1940, just three weeks after Ora Dell made her recordings, Librarian of Congress Archibald MacLeish summarized the Library's acquisition policy in the "Canons of Selection," which I read aloud with Ora Dell's picture between us: "The Library of Congress should possess all books and other materials . . . which express and record the life and achievements of the people of the United States."[4] The Library's canon embraced the entire nation, welcoming not only the papers of a president but the poetry of a schoolyard child. The recordings she made gave tangible evidence of this policy of inclusion.

I handed Milton a postcard of the Library. Inside that majestic edifice crisscrossed with marble staircases and portico busts, gold-leaf inscriptions and Greco-Roman grandeur, reside millions of items, possessions that express American life—from Thomas Jefferson's books to a print of the *Wizard of Oz,* from a draft of the Emancipation Proclamation to the sheet music for "Stars and Stripes Forever." Kept among them, too, are recordings of his aunt, a little black girl from Mississippi leading a few game songs she once played with her friends. In one of these pieces, Ora Dell portrays her world turned upside down, and in another, she rejoices with her classmates over a beloved food. These songs draw from a larger creative tradition of rituals and rhymes that have sustained the disenfranchised for centuries. This resonant heritage only adds to Sonny Milton's haunting question. The pain he knew growing up in Mississippi in the time of Emmett Till made these recordings seem improbable. That some casual playtime amusements his aunt learned during childhood and performed once into a microphone had been gathered and conserved, cataloged and disseminated, surpassed all reasonable expectation. Earlier on this drive he acknowledged a grim irony—Ora Dell's death stemmed from her yearning for music and dance. That same vitality, radiating from her recordings, became her legacy for the nation.

We swung back onto the highway still hoping to make a faithful copy of Ora Dell's picture. Sonny Milton looked over. "I see what you mean," he nodded. "Now I understand."

———

Beginning in the fall of 1939 and continuing through the following spring, John A. Lomax's son Alan hosted the *American School of the Air*, a CBS radio program that featured traditional material—sometimes live singers and sometimes their recordings—paired with the radio orchestra's folksong interpretations. During these broadcasts, Lomax invited listeners to write in with suggestions. Some did, and as part of a fall 1940 folksong collecting trip for the Library of Congress, John and Ruby Lomax followed up several of the contacts generated by Alan's radio series.[5]

One of those correspondents was a singer from Oxford, Mississippi, named Irene Williams. For local women's clubs and related civic groups, Williams presented the black folk music she knew as a youngster. Though her performances teemed with Old South sentimentalism and her singing style reflected voice-culture training, she capably imitated a variety of traditional African American songs. When the Lomaxes arrived at her home in Oxford to record her, they found she had gone to her brother-in-law's plantation a hundred miles distant, in Rome, Mississippi, a small Delta town located in Sunflower County. The Lomaxes followed her there and began documenting her repertory of cow-milking ditties, hollers, spirituals, and lullabies, though her performances did not meet John Lomax's expectations. More to his liking, Williams got him in contact with several singing field hands who resided at her brother's plantation in nearby Drew. The folklorist welcomed this opportunity to gather music from some authentic African American sources.[6]

Left with a few free hours before the workers returned for the day, Lomax ventured over to the Mississippi State Penitentiary at Parchman, which adjoins Drew on its southeast perimeter. This would have been his fifth visit to the facility, but, since he lacked an introductory letter from the governor, the warden denied him admittance. The administrator evidently turned on his heel, reminding Lomax of the low esteem that the pursuit of folk music, particularly among black sources, could be accorded. While heading back to the Williams plantation, Lomax stopped at a small brick building that faced Highway 49.

The Drew Colored School had just that year added the eleventh and twelfth grades.[7] Nicknamed Little Red because of its distinctive masonry, the six-

FIGURE 17.
Drew School girls
in lunchroom,
1949. Photo by
John E. Phay.
Used by permis-
sion of Special
Collections,
University of Mis-
sissippi Libraries.

classroom facility (plus a fair-sized auditorium) bore the town's educational responsibility for local black children. A bayou submerged one end of the two-acre property, which included a small frame outbuilding that served as the school's cafeteria, and a separate house where the principal lived. The main building, completed in 1930, replaced a four-classroom frame structure that burned down in 1926. In Drew, as elsewhere in Sunflower County, most schooling for black youngsters took place in dilapidated facilities, usually one-room churches with the students not facing a chalkboard but huddled around a woodstove. A local bond issue, combined with Chicago philanthropist Julius Rosenwald's program to establish black educational facilities throughout the South, made possible the solid progress that Little Red represented.

At the time of Lomax's visit, however, state support for its segregated schools operated at the barest level. No school buses for black children ran anywhere in Sunflower County (only two such vehicles operated by that decade's end). Nor did these schools stay open nine months a year. Instead, they were organized for shorter periods around cotton-picking schedules. School censuses of children aged six to twenty-one, the designated years of the educable population, found a significant number three years older than their grade level, reflecting their role as part-time field hands attending essentially part-time schools. The frequent movement of sharecropping families from one farm to another also resulted in overcounts. Of the available figures, the steadiest show a total of 406 black students enrolled during the 1940–41 school year in the Drew district.[8] Though black children comprised over 80 percent of the county's total student population, Drew's annual per-pupil instructional expenditure provided by the state came to $6.32, a figure 91 percent lower than the amount apportioned for white students in the same district.[9] This amount, which largely represented teachers' pay, left little to nothing for improving facilities or purchasing school supplies.[10] Students at Little Red were provided few books, they had no musical instruments to play except one aged piano, and if ball players wanted a uniform, they had to sew it themselves. Any hope of buying equipment for the football team, as Sonny Milton recalled from those years, was entirely out of the question.

Yet for all the institutional neglect that pupils and educators faced at Drew Colored School, order still marked its regimen. During Ora Dell's school years, girls were required to fix paper bows or ribbons in their hair, while boys were expected to wear bow ties and knee pants. Mornings began with devotionals, and teachers developed a handbook of singing games and rounds for classroom use. When John A. Lomax made his initial visit on October 23, 1940, he met with Earlene Hughes, the teacher responsible for the school choir and glee club. Hughes offered to assemble a group of students who could perform what Lomax called "their repertoire of native songs."[11] These were the musical games and rhymes that passed informally among the children, transmitted not from handbooks or by teachers, but among themselves. By the next morning, Hughes had organized a group of nine girls and two boys.

They began with "All Hid," a musical game of hide and seek that Lomax had recorded the day before (along with "Pullin' the Skiff") from John Grant. Grant, the young son of the plantation owner Lomax was visiting and a nephew of Irene Williams, mentioned that in this song black children "make up verses in place of verses, like white people do."[12] Seven of the Drew Colored School students then took turns, each singing made-up verses to "All Hid."[13] As the disc machine turned, Lomax instructed the youngsters to repeat their stanzas, but with greater volume. By spurring them like a schoolmaster, not always gently, he did succeed in eliciting more assertive performances and a variety of texts. The children responded, with poise and self-possession.

But none sang more confidently than Ora Dell Graham. After leading "Little Girl," a vigorous call-and-response song, Ora Dell soloed on "Pullin' the Skiff." Though Lomax requested that she, too, repeat a portion of it, he found no need to ask her to speak up.

From listening to the recording, we can readily picture Ora Dell Graham— this lithe, twelve-year-old girl, her arms akimbo, vigorously drawing them to and fro, enacting the song's lyrics:

> I went downtown,
> To get my grip.
> I come back home,
> Just a-pullin' the skiff,
> Just a-pullin' the skiff.
>
> I went upstairs,
> To make my bed.
> I made a mistake,
> And I bumped my head.
> Just a-pullin' the skiff.
> Just a-pullin' the skiff.
>
> I went downstairs,
> To milk my cow.
> I made a mistake,
> And I milked that sow.
> Just a-pullin' the skiff.
> Just a-pullin' the skiff.
>
> Tomorrow, tomorrow,
> Tomorrow never come.
> Tomorrow, tomorrow,
> Tomorrow's in the barn.
> And a hun-uh, and a hun-uh,
> And a hun-uh, hun-uh, hun-uh.[14]

The exuberance of her chant, the catch in her voice, the rhythm of her phrasing, and the tapping of her foot reveal that "Pullin' the Skiff" was a dance set to verses. Emma Deal, one of Ora Dell's classmates and later a teacher at Little Red, also knew the piece. She called it "Pulling the Skip," referring to the song's basic step. She likened its hand and body gestures to "Row, Row, Row Your Boat": "Sing the song, keep in motion with it. Use both arms and legs.

Keep that motion going, pulling the right arm and right leg back; then the left. You had to keep your step and words at the same time. It's a movement, a skip."[15] More than just the rules of the game stayed with her, too. Despite a lapse of sixty years, in 2000 Deal could still describe Ora Dell's complexion and short hair. Most of all, she remembered her verve. Ora Dell was "fast-like . . . and she liked to talk a lot"—good qualities in a song leader.

Another Mississippian, Isaac Shipp of Byhalia, whose own field recordings reside at the Library, had also led the song for his playmates. "It's kind of a fast dance," Isaac recollected, "not a slow dance like a waltz."[16] His memories corresponded with accounts given by all three of the 1939 Mississippi sources for "Pullin' the Skiff." They associated the children's song with a couples dance. "To be properly played, dance music is necessary," says one of the collector's field notes.[17] The participants face each other, according to another entry, with one of the partners singing during the dance.[18] Isaac likewise associated "Skiff" with popular music and choreography, "just like the Charleston, Black Bottom, and Camel Walk."[19] In 1998 he strode across his living room with an imaginary oar, singing verses he learned more than seventy-five years before. "It was a dance at that time," he smiled. "And you'd make up something to say."

Isaac's lyrics focus on a youngster, assigned a daily chore, who confronts a balky cow. A test of manhood ensues:

Saw a cow, back your leg,
I'm gonna milk you like grandma said.
You think you're hard,
You think you're bad.
But I'm gonna milk you at last.

I'm pulling the skiff,
It's not hard.
I'm just a man,
Gonna do my part.[20]

Folk Archive performances also portray this encounter: "Saw a cow, back your leg," intones John Grant, "I'm gonna milk it / if it kill me dead."[21] On her 1939 recording, Sarah Ann Reed from Edwards, Mississippi, sings a stanza much like John Grant and Isaac Shipp's and then adds: "Saw cow saw, back your leg / I went upstairs to fry some meat / I made a mistake and I fried my feet."[22] She also draws attention to the reluctant animal, but like Ora Dell, brings humor to the scene.

Ora Dell's "mistakes"—milking a sow instead of a cow and bumping her head while making her bed—entail more than a recitation of rhymes. Both she and Sarah Ann Reed drew from a venerable body of popular and traditional nonsense. These upsets in the daily routine fit alongside such light-hearted paradoxes as Carl Sandburg's "pancakes so thin they only had one side," or the predicament that Stephen Foster captures in "Oh Susannah" with "the sun so hot I froze to death."[23] Their quandaries also join the darker riddles of such songs as the British broadside "Nottingham Fair," within which one Ozark singer proclaims, "I set myself down on a hot frozen stone / Ten thousand around me and me all alone."[24] Childlore experts Iona and Peter Opie called this form of wordplay "tangletalk."[25] Its practitioners, they found, shape these verbal puzzles deliberately. "You can say this when you are skipping if you like," offered one twelve-year-old English girl, prefacing her verse rooted in a centuries-old mummers play: "As I walked down to the wayrail station, I met a bark and it dogged at me." Likewise, when cultural historian Hal Rammel investigated "The Big Rock Candy Mountain," the perennial hobo song with its promise of kindly cops, cigarette trees, and lemonade springs, he found that tangletalk and its traditions reached back to classical literature, citing as one example a piece of Greek satiric poetry from fourth century B.C. It told how "fishes, coming to men's houses and baking themselves, would serve themselves upon the tables."[26] Ora Dell's list of chores made topsy-turvy echo with 2,500 years of comic literature.

Perhaps Ora Dell first heard "Pullin' the Skiff" while playing with her friends. "Where did you learn that," Lomax asks Ora Dell during her recording.[27] "*I didn't,*" she answers unabashedly. "I just learned it by—just go on singing it." She put the song together, she is saying, from what she knew and heard from the social life around her. In the poetic transactions of the schoolyard, children find ways to shape their inheritance of rhyme and rhythm that fit present-day circumstances. At the time of Ora Dell's recording, Irene Williams told John A. Lomax that black workers used skiffs for transportation in that part of the Mississippi low country.[28] In times of high water a person could take this shallow draft boat straight across bends in the landscape rather than rowing all the way around to the main channel. However, water that rises is also likely to fall, and the shallow, grassy slough that afforded the traveler a shortcut at one point might be discovered on the return trip to be too shallow to float. Once into such a pass there's nothing to do but to disembark and "pull" your skiff across the mud flat. With the

Delta's many wetlands and waterways, this image would have made sense to Ora Dell and her classmates. But in lugging the boat, Ora Dell represents a more general condition than just her local environment. In this comedy of errors she repudiates the drudgeries attending childhood. Ora Dell's unplanned skiff pulling marks only the first of her thwarted plans. She responds to these pressures with energetic movement. Her hands and feet ceaselessly skip and row, a counterpoint to the weary task of hauling a boat across dry land. By the game's end she drives her ironic message home.

Ora Dell concludes with a gesture made of sounds instead of words. In keeping with her upside-down lyrics, she makes the child's equivalent of "rough music"—clangorous, public displays often expressed in ritualized parades and other attention-getting disturbances that register humorous if pointed protest.[29] Ora Dell's boldly voiced grunts, both rude and exuberant, make fun of her responsibilities, parody bodily functions, and flaunt acceptable manners. The unanimous reaction of her schoolmates reveals how effectively she has touched these socially sensitive zones. Not surprisingly, the children absolutely howl when John Lomax, the very embodiment of an adult authority figure—a portly, older white man—tries to imitate these sounds himself. In an effort to capture this piece of art on a recording, he trespassed onto the precincts of childhood.

In 1997, Henrietta Taylor, an African American quilter born the same year as Ora Dell and a native of Bolivar County, Mississippi, just west of Drew, mapped out that part of the song's imaginative territory. Taylor recalled how four or five of her friends of Ora Dell's age would get together and sing: "Mama don't allow me to pull the skiff, / Papa don't allow me to try. / I gets behind the middle of the door, / And pulls it on the sly."[30]

The "middle door" led to the center of the house, where family members socialized. "It's lots of times I'm supposed to be in the kitchen washing dishes," she explained, "but I'm behind the middle, pulling the skiff." While Henrietta Taylor didn't include Ora Dell's comic reversals in her rendition, she overturns authority by proclaiming emancipation from household toil. Henrietta's real-life reluctance to do dishes in favor of dancing and playing in the kitchen found voice in the traditional lyrics she employed.

In May 1939, Eva Grace Boone of Rankin County, Mississippi, led a group of songs that included "Pullin' the Skiff." Boone's version invokes a Mother Goose–like image of a black cow pulling a skiff. It begins, like Ora Dell's, with the narrator losing her grip (a valise) but coming back "pulling a skip." The refrain follows:

Papa don't allow me, yankey.
Mama don't allow me, yankey.
Get behind the door and pull it anyhow.
You ought to be ashamed,
To ask me to pull that skiff.[31]

FIGURE 18.
Students who sang
"Pullin' the Skiff"
with songleader
Eva Grace Boone,
Brandon, Mis-
sissippi, May 25,
1939. Photo by
Abbott Ferriss.
Used by permis-
sion of Mississippi
Department of
Archives and
History.

Like Henrietta Taylor, Boone refers to something forbidden. Six days later, this allusion becomes more explicit when a group of women inmates recorded "Pullin' the Skiff" in the sewing room at the Parchman penitentiary:

I got it, I got it
It sure was good.
Too heavy, too heavy,
Too heavy on my belly.
Papa Leman, Papa Leman,
Off, off, offer me.[32]

The women then chant a stanza of rhythmic syllables, laughing. If nervous embarrassment surrounds this outburst, they laugh uproariously next, follow-ing a set of vocables much like Ora Dell's. This refrain unmistakably suggests the sounds of lovemaking. Recordist Herbert Halpert concluded that "Pullin' the Skiff," while known as a children's game, "generally . . . is considered, from the nature of the words, an adult dance."[33] No wonder the Drew students tittered in Lomax's presence. Ora Dell's sounds signified at some level a physical, bodily awareness that the older prisoners conspicuously employ.

Another group of school-age youngsters living nearby, however, did translate that adult consciousness into the song. In late July 1942 Alan Lomax reached Friars Point, Mississippi, with the Library's recording equipment. He copied down in one of his notebooks a set of words for "Pullin' the Skiff" that some unnamed children refused to record. "The little girls," he wrote, "wouldn't sing for me."[34] Instead, they gave their verses to a woman who then passed them on to Lomax:

My mama, my mama,
Didn't wear no drawers
I saw her pull them off
She washed them in alcohol
Then she hung them upside the wall
They stink like alcohol
She gave them to Santa Claus
He said, "Uh-uh—I didn't want these funky drawers."
Aunt Lucy said, "Sho is good & juicy."
Uncle Ben said, "Sho is hairy."[35]

These pungent lines register the simmering pressures of oncoming puberty. The Friars Point girls, understandably embarrassed to record this piece, had resorted to brazen, juvenile humor. Their ribald lyrics find a place alongside the other "Pullin' the Skiff" recordings. From Ora Dell's mockery of chores to John Grant and Sarah Ann Reed's struggles with an unyielding cow, to what goes on behind the middle door that Eva Grace Boone and Emma Jane Davis reprise, to the female prisoners at Parchman who drew "Skiff" in a frank direction that suited their age and sophistication—each of these performers helps make sense of their lives through the medium of this piece.[36] In such game songs, folklorist Patrick Mullen has written, children "are drawing on the past, creating in the present, and preparing themselves for future roles."[37]

During my visit with Sonny Milton, his wife Kathleen remembered "Pullin' the Skiff" from her childhood in Jackson, Mississippi. At one point, as Ora Dell's voice rang out from the tape player, she got up and cocked her arm against her hip. She began swaying as if she again stood beside her friends, all of them keeping time with the song. Watching her, I thought of Alan

Lomax's 1942 silent footage of a group of Mississippi Delta schoolgirls doing "Pullin' the Skiff." These few seconds captured the synchronized movements that Kathleen embodied here in her dining room. "Back then they all made faces as they danced," she explained. "They put their own to it. Everyone sung it in a different way and added different things to it."[38] Then Kathleen looked intently at Sonny. "And I'm just sure that was the way his aunt was." For Kathleen Milton and her playmates—for that matter Emma Deal, Isaac Shipp, Henrietta Taylor, and no doubt Ora Dell—each ran through the steps to make this song their own. "Now," Kathleen says, "They're pulling the skip, jumping rope, and dancing too."

In the years since Ora Dell first sang "Pullin' the Skiff" into the Library disc recorder, its title, chorus, and dance steps have faded from playground use. Emma Deal recalled that in the late 1930s, when she and Ora Dell first attended the Drew Colored School, they played "Pullin' the Skiff" as a dancing game. But interest in the song subsided, Deal explained, with the installation of "playground equipment, seesaws, and such. By the time they [today's school children] hit the ground, they run to them first. They don't run to the game."[39] The dance steps once associated with "Pullin' the Skiff" have given way to another kind of metrical movement: the agile demands of rope skipping.

Succeeding collections of jump-rope rhymes, absent "Skiff"'s refrain, document the predicaments that Ora Dell expressed. As early as 1945, one youngster from Greenville, North Carolina, called out as she jumped, "I went in the kitchen to bake a pie; / I made a mistake and baked a fly."[40] In that entry, she also bumped her head against her bed and mistook her cow for a sow. Other rope-jumping texts, beginning with "I went upstairs to make my bed" and leading into a variety of rhymed mistakes, have been collected in Texas, Indiana, New York, and New Zealand.[41] A 1979 Mississippi collection repeats the pattern with what its editor calls the single most popular verse children there use to accompany their jumping games: "Cinderella, dressed in yellow / Went upstairs to see her fellow / Made a mistake and kissed a snake / How many doctors will it take."[42] In Cincinnati, a 1995 newspaper article on inner-city jump-rope activity begins with the same Cinderella snake kiss.[43] Clearly, youngsters have continued to mock the incongruities around them much as Ora Dell did in 1940.

Her performance, too, has found a lasting, if quietly hidden place in contemporary popular culture. Ora Dell's "Pullin' the Skiff" (drawn from the

Treasury) served a role in the 2003 film *Cold Mountain*. "The recording of her performance," writes John Cohen, "provided the director [Anthony Minghella] of the film . . . with a clue to the character of Ruby."[44] Just as Ora Dell's spirited singing and unbowed replies to John A. Lomax may have helped actress Renée Zellweger construct her Oscar-winning performance, Ora Dell's singing also provided a backdrop in August Wilson's celebrated drama, *Joe Turner's Come and Gone*. He appropriated Ora Dell's recording (taken from the original phonograph album) for his character Zonia Loomis, a black child of Ora Dell's age.[45] During a first-act scene, Zonia plays behind the tattered boardinghouse where she and her emotionally haunted father live. Sheltered by the quiet of her activity, Zonia finds a moment of gentle respite from the anguish that surrounds her. She sings and in some productions skips rope to "Pullin' the Skiff," using Ora Dell's precise set of verses, but with a difference.

As Wilson often did with traditional lore in his plays, he adapted Ora Dell's game song to fit the work's dramatic needs.[46] A tiny example of that shaping lies in the way he handled one of Zonia's lines. He wrote her last verse as: "Tomorrow, tomorrow / Tomorrow never comes / The marrow the marrow / The marrow in the bone."[47] While Ora Dell sings "tomorrow's in the barn," he makes an association through sound, joining "tomorrow" to "marrow" to "bone" to form a new unit of sense. Naturally, different impulses guide the requirements of a play from the needs of a playground. An authority on August Wilson's work, Samuel Hay, finds "Pullin' the Skiff" in *Joe Turner* a forecast of what Zonia will face in later years. He interprets its verses as an expression of "lamented mistakes, frustrated intentions and creeping-but-never-arriving tomorrows."[48]

By contrast, a hardier strength animates Ora Dell's own performance. Admittedly, she acknowledges a long day that never seems to end. The demands that the adult world make upon her promise to start all over again come morning. They might even begin with milking the cow, for "tomorrow's in the barn." But with her coda of noisemaking—not present in *Joe Turner*—she utterly dismisses these troubles and cares. Instead of foretelling sorrow as in the play, Ora Dell in the auditorium of the Drew Colored School turns a frustrating time on its head. Her litany of deeds gone wrong harnesses the appeal of misrule, a medieval and ultimately ancient satirizing of the social order. Ora Dell achieves in "Pullin' the Skiff" that tradition's symbolic redistribution of power. In Jean Arp's artful phrase, one that Hal Rammel uses to explain misrule's upending of roles, "'the little holds the big on a leash.'"[49] She uses the timeless resources of children's play—a dance that enjoyed local popularity, a stock of comic reversals, and a vigorous show of vocal noise—to redeem the chores and trials of an ordinary day. This transformational spirit also instills another song Ora Dell knew.

For the last piece John and Ruby Lomax recorded at the Drew Colored School, Ora Dell led her classmates in "Shortenin' Bread." By then this staple of American music suited many tastes—from a Paul Robeson concert selection to an Andrews Sisters hit. Soon it would ring out in Duke Ellington's "Happy-Go-Lucky Local" as part of the train man's steam whistle medley, while in Walt Disney's 1946 animated musical *Willie the Operatic Whale,* the title character (sung by Nelson Eddy) brings its homey appeal to a literally buoyant audience of seals and seagulls. Unlike these popular renditions, Ora Dell's "Shortenin' Bread" follows a different melody and serves another purpose. In Little Red's auditorium, it becomes a surging musical game.

Ora Dell's voice, quavering yet piercing, rides above the clapping and singing of her classmates. Akin to a railroad gang hoisting ties to a track caller's chants or churchgoers echoing back the verses their minister lines out, the children answer Ora Dell with the song's title refrain. This call-and-response establishes in "Shortenin' Bread" two separate but related rhythms. Their hand clapping adds a third marker, a pulse beneath Ora Dell's bluesy singing. By varying her pitch over the course of the song, she flattens certain notes for the words and syllables italicized below to create a tonally rich performance steeped in black folksong style:

Chorus:
I *do love,*
[group responds:] Shortenin' bread.
I *do* love,
Shortenin' bread.
*Ma*ma love,
Shortenin' bread.
*Pa*pa love,
Shortenin' bread.
*Every*body love,
Shortenin' bread.

Two little babies layin' in the *bed,*
One plays *sick* an' the *other*'n play dead.
I *do love,*
Shortenin' bread.
I *do* love,
Shortenin' bread.
Ev'ry since my dog's been *dead,*
Hogs been *rootin'* my 'ta*ter* bed.

   Chorus

Old Aunt Dinah sick in the *bed,*
Sent for the doctor, doctor *said,*
"All she *need's* some *short*enin' bread."

   Chorus

Neither Ora Dell's recording nor John A. Lomax's notes include any comments on the song itself, but other schoolhouse recordings from that time show that it did not arise in isolation. Six days after leaving Drew, Lomax reached York, Alabama, where he recorded a group of children at the Mount Powell School. They called one of their numbers "Jack, Can I Ride."[50] Pitched in the same key and employing the same call-and-response pattern, it resembles Ora Dell's "Shortenin' Bread." While the title refrain obviously differs from the one heard at Drew, little else sets apart its verses from Ora Dell's.[51] From formal structure to melodic contour, lyric content to overall feel, "Jack, Can I Ride" demonstrates that a game-song tradition interwoven with "Shortenin' Bread"'s circulated among the region's schoolchildren.

Two years later, at a Clarksdale, Mississippi, school, located in neighboring Coahoma County not far from Drew, Alan Lomax also documented "Shortenin' Bread." In August 1942, singer Ruby Smith led a rendition nearly identical to Ora Dell's. Though Smith sings without the blues notes that Ora Dell uses, she keeps the telltale "I do love" call, answered by the group's "shortenin' bread" response. The piece had apparently made the schoolhouse rounds for some time. "This game," she said, "is a stealing game. Children form a ring and steal partners. I learned this game about eighteen years ago in Friars Point School, Coahoma County, Mississippi."[52] Given the similarity of the words and music, it seems possible that Ora Dell and her classmates may have followed comparable directions themselves.

The day before Ruby Smith sang the piece into the disc cutter, an eight-year-old named Bobbie Mae Brown recorded "Shortenin' Bread" at the same Clarksdale school.[53] She had learned it from her teacher, essentially absorbing the popular music hit. With her petite child's voice, she artfully delivered its five verses in all their tunefulness. A few weeks earlier, in Friars Point, Alan Lomax recorded Emma Jane Davis leading a group of school girls in "Shortenin' Bread."[54] They, too, clapped to the melody that achieved pop success, and sang, as did Bobbie Mae Brown, nearly the same verses, beginning with "mammy's little baby loves shortenin', shortenin'."

From ring game to lullaby, these musically separate approaches—Ora Dell's blues-drenched performance and the singsong air that Bobbie Mae Brown knew—reiterate what Kathleen Milton said about "Pullin' the Skiff": individual players make the number their own. Both schoolgirls, like their counterparts Ruby Smith and Emma Jane Davis, took this essentially humorous treatment of poverty and turned it to recreational needs. This interpretative freedom with the song's melody and its function extends to other Folk Archive recordings: the old-time country dance verses that Celina Lewis sang in Alabama, the talking-guitar story-song that Tom McKinney performed in Mississippi, the swooping vocal line that Henry Truvillion used in Texas, and the falsetto cries that transformed Alabama prisoner George James's verses into a wail, let alone the numerous banjo, fiddle, harmonica, and string-band versions documented on field recordings and issued on commercial country releases.[55] All these performers transmitted a deeply rooted symbol of a regional foodstuff and the people who made it.

"Shortening bread," said Helen Marie Rowe, "is not a sweet bread. It's not a dessert at all. It's just a corn bread, a real good corn bread."[56] Helen, the last surviving niece of Wash Dennis, the bass-voiced singer on the Folk Archive's 1936 recording of "Lead Me to the Rock," grew up, like her contemporary Ora Dell Graham, in a small Mississippi town.[57] As a youngster in Okolona, located in the state's agricultural prairie region, Helen lived under the same roof as her uncle Wash. Unlike him, she never sang, nor did she learn to read or write. Helen did, however, become a storehouse of spoken lore. She possessed a seemingly endless supply of what she called jokes—anecdotes and sayings that included centuries-old riddles and tales. With sixteen children of her own, Helen often put these jokes to work, a time-tested means for settling down her brood at bedtime. Helen's memories also included old-time country recipes, and she took pleasure in naming the various dishes that made up a traditional dinner: shortening bread, neck bones, ham hocks, collard greens, okra, peas, and sweet potatoes. These foods marked for her a cultural continuity that she warmly recalled. She viewed them as both part of the modern soul food cuisine and as a piece of her family's past. Not surprisingly, Helen learned how to prepare shortening bread from her grandparents who raised her, themselves the children of former slaves.

"When you get ready to make up your bread," Helen continued, "you put your grease in it." That grease, the lard drawn from a farmyard hog, gives shortening bread its name. Preparation for this stove-top, skillet-cooked dish starts with the animal's butchering. Helen's family, like so many southern rural dwellers, kept a few hogs and chickens they fed slop and scraps. These low-maintenance animals provided for their nutritional needs while not requiring pasturing or costly feed. As a youth, Helen learned how to trim a hog, making use of all its parts, from middlings to head cheese, fatback to ham. "Don't use the hard skin," she explained. "You strip your inside meat, chip it up, and you cook that in a pot." This process makes the lard, yielding also the cracklings, small bits of meat and fat that rise to the top. Often added to the bread for taste, any unused cracklings were dried out and stored in a bucket until next time. While Helen's grandparents made their syrup from sorghum and maintained a garden planted with okra, potatoes, peas, and greens, they got their self-rising cornmeal from the country store. Helen continued: "You takes your cornmeal . . . put in just a little taste of milk and one or two eggs. Stir it up as soupy as you want it." Then she put the parts together: "Pour it in your skillet over a low fire and cover it. Let it fix like a cake. Then run a knife under it." For Helen Marie Rowe, shortening bread took its place beside cush, cornpone, and tea cakes that she had known growing up—filling foods devised for meager circumstances.

This cuisine also translated into song. Since the early decades of the nineteenth century, blackface impersonators presented musical caricatures based on authentic slave diets of hominy, yellow cornmeal, dark flour, and wild game.[58] Night-hunted possums and raccoons became regular dramatic fare, as did hoecakes and their preparation. Bare feet that serve as griddles occupy early minstrelsy along with evocations of jubilant social dancing that follow savored meals of fat meat, ash cakes, and molasses.[59] An aggregate of images associated with slavery days—the Dinah character, a name often ascribed to a slave cook or wife; the visible place of hogs and hog fat in plantation cookery; the cracked heels of a shoeless people; the gyrations of tireless dancers; and the medicinal, restorative powers of food—all appear in "Shortenin' Bread."

If the song originated in minstrelsy—so far it has not surfaced in minstrel-era song books, newspaper accounts of stage shows, or vintage recordings of blackface humor—or possibly began as a newer piece indebted to that genre's conventions, "Shortenin' Bread" had taken hold informally by the time of Helen Marie Rowe and Ora Dell's youth. Helen remembered it as a song "of the old people."[60] Her grandparents and her Uncle Wash sang it around the house. But when our conversation turned to its wider popularity, she wondered if "it was Lightnin' Hopkins or John Lee Hooker who got it out." By mentioning these musicians she heard on neighborhood jukeboxes, Helen situated "Shortenin' Bread" not only as a piece of community lore, but also as a commercial product. Indeed, both processes mark the song's history.

The year 1892 emerges as the earliest fixed date for "Shortenin' Bread." Writing thirty-four years after the fact, collector Gates Thomas recalled a group of black singers in south Texas performing "Don't Love-a Nobody" during a rural dance.[61] While some verses restate the original elements—the butchered hogs, babies asleep in bed, and cracked bare feet—the song chiefly responds to this post-Emancipation era. It speaks of "salty dogs" (a slang term for a lecher that soon appeared in a number of recorded blues), it names active train routes in Texas, and with an unmistakably modern frankness, it chuckles about out-of-wedlock births and mixed-race pregnancies. Thomas identified its singers as rounders, "shiftless and shifting day laborers and small croppers who follow Lady Luck, Aphrodite, and John Barleycorn."[62] Here the itinerant rounder addresses "his favorite theme—woman and lust."[63]

That same year, North Carolina mountain banjoist Bascom Lunsford, then ten years old, encountered "Shortenin' Bread," possibly spotting its lyrics in an 1892 newspaper. Later he absorbed the piece from some neighboring fiddlers, but by then had lost the older set of words.[64] "Jumbo's sick and Sambo's dead," Lunsford sings in one verse, while his chorus completes the theatrical stereotype: "Very last word that Sambo said, / Don't my baby love short'nin', short'nin'. / Don't my baby love short'nin' bread."[65] An alternative name he gave the song, "Wild Horse," also reaches back to minstrelsy.[66] It surfaces there as a principal piece of melody in "My Old Dad," a number that appeared in an 1844 banjo songbook printed under minstrel Dan Emmett's name.[67] Poet James Whitcomb Riley responded similarly to "Short'nin' Bread." He published the song in 1900, and in November 1913 registered its first musical copyright in his own name, rendering it in full blackface dialect: "Fotch dat dough fum the kitchin-shed—/ Rake dem coals out hot an' red—/ Putt on de oven an' putt on de led,—/ Mammy's gwineter cook some short'nin' bread."[68]

The song's presence in the closing years of the nineteenth century proved influential, too, for Bibb County, Georgia, native Reese DuPree, a black recording artist and cabaret performer.[69] In 1905, when he was fourteen, he performed the piece on excursion boats while dressed as a singing chef complete with hat and apron. "He used to sing it," continued a December 1939 *Esquire* article, "at pound parties in the South . . . community affairs given by Negroes at that time where one would bring a pound of 'vittles' of anything edible, a pound of chitterlings, of pig's feet, of hog maw, barbeque, butter—anything that contributed to the feast. It was a simple little piece, but everywhere he went they wanted him to sing it."[70] In April 1927, DuPree's colleagues, Bobbie Leecan's Need-More Band, recorded his chorus and three of his twelve verses for the Victor label.[71] To a washboard's tap-dance percussion, the guitar and harmonica-led ensemble alternated raglike breaks with vigorously bowed cello and astringent mandolin. Like DuPree, these musicians, writes Paul Oliver, "worked in the hinterland between jazz, blues and vaudeville."[72] Their performance stands as the sole prewar commercially released vernacular music recording of "Shortnin' Bread" by African Americans.[73]

Victor record producer Ralph Peer, who copyrighted DuPree's composition in September, supervised the session. Previously he had worked with Leecan and his partner Robert Cooksey at the Okeh record company, where they first recorded, as did Dupree, in 1924. That same year, Peer also produced "Shortenin' Bread"'s first-ever appearance on a record. Played on solo harmonica by white Virginia millhand Henry Whitter, it appears in a dance medley between "Hop Light Ladies" and "Turkey in the Straw."[74] Peer's awareness of the song, his personal contact with the artists involved, and his interest in promoting its sales to both hillbilly and race markets indicates that before its popular music ascendancy—launched by Jacques Wolfe's string of vocal arrangements that began appearing in 1928—"Shortenin' Bread" had already found an audience.

Not surprisingly, early scholarship located the song in white and black settings with accordingly different emphases. In 1912, Eber C. Perrow, a Harvard-trained English professor who grew up in Tye Valley, Virginia, obtained "Shortened Bread" from white residents of mountainous East Tennessee.[75] He published it three years later, marking the song's first scholarly imprint. In contrast to the self-liberated revelers in Gates Thomas's piece, Perrow's nine-verse song tells a story of mishaps—narrowing choices, thwarted progress, and a failed outcome for two black children. Its opening four verses carry the song's conventional cast and characters: babies taken ill, their mammy

nearby, and the doctor recommending a shortening bread cure. It becomes apparent that the treatment did not succeed. The children, clothed in white but appearing "black as tar," now try one means or another to get to heaven. The joke extends like a tall tale, and their vehicles dwindle down to the tail of a kite. Finally, they "tried to go to heaven in a peanut shell," the song ends, "but they went to hell." Perrow notes that the piece's melody had been adapted from the pre–Civil War "Run Nigger Run," a song about foiled escape.

Still in Tennessee, but a few counties to the west, Thomas W. Talley, an African American chemistry professor at Fisk University and former member of the Fisk Jubilee Singers, included three versions of "Shortenin' Bread" in his 1922 *Negro Folk Rhymes.* These provide the earliest published texts collected from African American sources (Gates Thomas's 1892 version did not appear until 1926). Though Talley presents his several entries without musical notation, two versions dwell on the vivacity of dance.[76] The last of them, "Little Sleeping Negroes," appears in the chapter on nursery songs.[77] He identifies it as a counting rhyme, each verse adding to the one before. Just as the first enumerates one child pretending to be asleep, the second verse counts two, "a-snorin' an' a-dreamin' of a table spread." By the fourth and

FIGURE 19. Reese DuPree's copyright lead sheet for "Shortenin' Bread." Photo by Stephen Wade.

final verse, the song announces to all those still in bed, "Ded'd better hop out, if dey wants to git fed!" These youngsters, roused from dreams of abundant food, awaken to a meal. Such dreams of plenitude "inevitably proceed," said folklorist Ben Botkin, "from having too little rather than too much."[78] For Talley's sources, some of whom held slavery in living memory and others being close descendants of those who had experienced it, nourishment loomed as a real concern. In the versions he documented, the song figures as much a celebration of freedom as of sustenance, stemming from those who possessed little of either.

For succeeding scholars, conscious of both living practice and blackface convention, the song's origins remained unsettled. Robert W. Gordon called it "genuine negro" in 1923, and music historian Sigmund Spaeth thought the same, having come in contact with the piece while editing a collection of mountain songs in 1927.[79] Conversely, in his 1928 collection Newman Ivey White avers, "I suspect that the 'Shortnin' Bread' song originated with whites."[80] Soon White addressed the subject again, deeming it a modern descendant of an older blackface.[81] Later scholarly collectors, including Vance Randolph and Frank C. Brown, located it in their minstrel and black song sections, a combined category that allowed for black creation as well as white embellishment.

It also appears that efforts by one of these scholars led to its place in American popular music. Three years after Talley's book appeared, folklorist, novelist, and teacher Dorothy Scarborough published *On the Trail of Negro Folk-Songs*. In assembling this 1925 collection, she drew from her own experience as well as a large group of correspondents who submitted songs to her and her musical collaborator. To date she offered the most detailed of "Shortenin' Bread"'s scholarship.[82] She characterized it as "another favorite hushaby song, which many Negro mammies confess to knowing, and which numerous white acquaintances remember dropping off to sleep by."[83] The first of her three entries combines a number of potentially appealing and largely familiar elements: its nursery room ambience, a singing mammy, the gal in the kitchen, a stereotypical food theft, and at the end, a tightly structured humor that turns the punishment of the crime into a jailhouse reward. Scarborough acknowledged its compelling air, despite its primary role as a pacifier: "This has a lively tune which might easily have entertained an infant enough to keep him wide awake." She credited "Short'nin' Bread"'s opening stanza, chorus, and melody to Jean Feild of Richmond, Virginia, and the remaining three verses to Wirt Williams, a Mississippi professor. It begins:

Put on de skillet,
Put on de led;
Mammy's gwine to make
A li'l short'nin' bread.
Dat ain't all
Dat she's gwine to do—
She's gwine to make
A li'l coffee, too.

> Chorus:
> Mammy's li'l baby loves short'nin', short'nin',
> Mammy's li'l baby loves short'nin' bread.
> Mammy's li'l baby loves short'nin', short'nin',
> Mammy's li'l baby loves short'nin' bread.[84]

"Shortenin' Bread"'s commercial life originated from this piece. Without crediting Scarborough or her song as his source, it seems clear that Jacques Wolfe, a white theatrical composer interested in black folklife, took this version intact for his own. He kept her melody, which had no other published or recorded equivalents, as well as her verses—which came to her from two geographically removed sources—and he preserved their exact sequence. Preserving her spelling of the title, too, he made but a few surgical changes to the music.

More substantive changes occur in the text, edited by Wolfe's collaborator, Clement Wood, a novelist and anthologist also drawn to black folk materials. "Gwine" becomes "goin'," a minute shift that a new audience of northerners could surely appreciate, let alone pronounce.[85] But the crucial change lay in turning Scarborough's "three li'l niggers" into "three little darkies." A line or two later, the doctor calls them "children" instead of the usual racial epithet. This softened language made the song more acceptable to mainstream sympathies, while rendering its characters more infantile. Wolfe subsequently channeled the song into the idiom of the musical theater and popular choral works. By February 1936 he had copyrighted it in eleven more adaptations, setting it for four-part and three-part male and female voices, mixed chorus, as a slow air with orchestra, and as a "Negro dance episode."[86] His arrangement, Sigmund Spaeth noted, became "a stand-by for concert singers who want to prove that they are human after all."[87]

A nostalgic minstrelsy had permeated American popular culture when Jacques Wolfe first offered up "Short'nin' Bread." In 1928 the conventionalized roles its characters took coincided with the blackface radio humor of *Amos 'n' Andy,* also launched that year, an era, too, when a servant's livery still remained the principal costume for blacks in film.[88] The song became prominent, Spaeth wrote in 1936, during a period of "increasing interest in the authentic Negro materials of American music, as well as the undeniable popularity of highly sophisticated, modern versions of an essentially naïve and primitive type of racial expression."[89] While this ascending aesthetic hierarchy has upended laterally in more recent years, and "Mammy's little baby" revises nowadays into the less historically burdened "Mama's little baby," the song sheds but never entirely loses its racial past.

Matters of "Shortenin' Bread'"s beginnings ultimately turn to questions of its use. The song's earliest sighting finds it in South Texas in the presence of transients and sharecroppers. They reacted to the past it signified, Gates Thomas shows, by relocating it to the times of their lives. Poised in what seems an earlier musical epoch, the fragments that Thomas Talley gathered came from black sources also living in the segregation era. They redirected the song's Jim Crow condescension into an early black pride, sharing some of its language but shifting its message from what their white East Tennessee neighbors had given E. C. Perrow. Still other implications attached to the song's high culture performances by Lawrence Tibbett and Paul Robeson, just as the Andrews Sisters, Nelson Eddy, and Johnny Mercer communicated its variable meanings to their audiences. In a phonographic study of commercial music influences on early country music, scholar Norm Cohen writes, "A more fruitful conception of folk music is obtained if one casts aside the criterion of origin and concentrates on possession; it doesn't matter where a particular song or tune originated; what does matter is what has become of it."[90] Surely this notion applies to "Shortenin' Bread" as its passes from one singer to another, whatever their idiom.[91]

During the summer of 1942 some children in Coahoma County, Mississippi, recorded "Shortenin' Bread." When Emma Jane Davis and her friends sang Jacques Wolfe's arrangement, they brought it into their world. They clapped along to it like a ring game and left his harmony parts behind. Eight-year-old Bobbie Mae Brown, who also learned his tune and all his verses, called it her favorite song. But when she sang it, it sounded like Dorothy Scarborough's hushaby all over again.

That Ora Dell Graham voiced "Shortenin' Bread" in a sound of the Delta utterly unlike the popular number bears messages too. Like "Pullin' the Skiff" with its patterns set in misrule—her tangletalk and clangor that repudiates the daily round—Ora Dell's "Shortenin' Bread" also expresses a symbolic reversal, turning poverty into plenty. In keeping with the lyrics that Thomas

Talley gathered two decades earlier, or the sentiments that Helen Marie Rowe expressed about the soul food dishes that she still prepared, Ora Dell takes a plain but desired food, rooted in subsistence, and converts it into strength. As she chants "I do love" and her classmates unanimously answer back, her "Shortenin' Bread" joins larger ceremonials of the poor. These include such rituals as the eighteenth-century Pinkster parades in New York state and the nineteenth-century John Canoe festivities along coastal North Carolina. If only for a day or two, these events suspended slavery's customs and codes, freeing up food and drink to those otherwise limited or denied it. During these jubilant periods of consumption, the world turned upside down. For carnival and its American equivalents has its origin in *carne,* meat, a rarity for its impoverished revelers.[92] In the auditorium of the Drew Colored School, "Shortenin' Bread" calls out to these traditions in ways as forceful as Ora Dell herself.

When I went to Mississippi in January 1997 to research the liner notes for the *Treasury,* I carried the hope that Ora Dell Graham was still alive. State records showed no death certificate for her, and her name didn't appear in the Social Security system. Although the state's Department of Health could not retrieve her birth certificate, the Drew school rolls at the Mississippi state archives, along with those kept by the Sunflower County School Board, indicated her to be twelve in 1940.[93] She still lived in Drew two years later, when she signed a release for her recordings and collected a small payment from the Library.[94] While that exchange marked the institution's last contact with her, it still seemed possible in the late 1990s that she might be located. By then she would have been only in her late sixties.

At the recommendation of Mississippi folklorist Tom Rankin, my first stop in Drew was the Music Mart, a small storefront shop located on the main street. For thirty years its sole proprietor was Marvin Flemmons, a white native of the town with a deep affection for black music. As we spoke, Marvin stood behind an ornate, hand-cranked cash register, ringing up purchases and answering his young customers' inquiries about the latest rap and hip-hop releases that filled the store's Plexiglas-covered bins. Overhead, rainbow-striped posters of local gospel and blues performers, their names emblazoned in thick block print, lined the store, while at eye level dozens of newspaper articles about Roebuck "Pop" Staples, a Drew native and patriarch of the Staple Singers, were pasted up. With quiet pride, Marvin mentioned the nearby Dockery plantation, legendary home to the Delta's first recorded blues star, Charley Patton, and cited the Drew-based musicians that scholar David Evans documented in *Big Road Blues*.[95] Even before I played him a cassette of Ora Dell's recordings, he remembered her songs and the Library of Congress album on which they first appeared. A moment later he thought of someone who might be able to say if she were still alive, and he picked up the phone.

One contact led to another. Just down the street, at the office of an attorney with ties in the black community, I explained my purpose to the lawyer's assistant. In Drew, like other small towns, people know each other, and often with an intricate knowledge of the blood and marriage lines that bind one to another. The question that usually faces a stranger is not whether desired biographical information exists or a person can be found, but whether the newcomer can be trusted with such knowledge. After another call or two, matters were settled, and I drove to the home of Nancy Hunter.

Mrs. Hunter, a lifelong resident of this area, attended the Drew Colored School at the same time as Ora Dell. A few years older than her, Mrs. Hunter was a member of the school's first senior class, graduating in 1941. After college, Mrs. Hunter returned there to assume a teaching position, staying for nineteen years. Moreover, Mrs. Hunter was related to Ora Dell through marriage. Her sister-in-law's aunt was Ora Dell's grandmother.

At first Mrs. Hunter seemed baffled by the idea of Ora Dell as a singer. She knew an Ora Dell Graham all right, but that Ora Dell would not have been part of any "glee club," she said.[96] Not one to be confined to the proprieties of a choir (which the Drew Colored School's glee club soon became), Ora Dell was, in her words, "a creature of the streets." As we listened to the recordings, the question of her identity and her music making soon resolved. These were "playground songs," Mrs. Hunter pointed out, products of the streets themselves. The singing provoked more memories, and Mrs. Hunter's voice tightened when she described Ora Dell's home by the tracks. Ora Dell, her mother, Sonny Milton, Ora Dell's two sisters, and her brother all lived in a three-room rented house located in the Hyde quarters, a small, segregated neighborhood on the former site of J. T. Hyde's sawmill operations near the train depot. Their house stood six blocks from Little Red. It had, Mrs. Hunter recalled, "little order and great poverty." As for Ora Dell herself, "She wasn't a fearful kind of person. She went when she got ready. Not afraid of people by no means." I asked Mrs. Hunter if she knew what happened to Ora Dell.

"Ora Dell did not live to be twenty-one," Mrs. Hunter said. While trying to rob a man who had just cashed a pension check at a store in Drew, she was shot with her own pistol. "It was that, or else she was killed in a car wreck out on 49 Highway." But of the two, she was certain it was the first. Later I reported Ora Dell's attempted robbery and death in the *Treasury*'s notes. It made sense with so much else that Mrs. Hunter shared.

"We made it," she continued, "but don't ask me how." Like Ora Dell's mother, Mrs. Hunter's also took in the laundry of white families for income. With a hot bucket of water, lye soap, and a scrub board, a day's work yielded the payment of a few dimes. Their own home lacked amenities, and she described how water, stored in a barrel and hauled on a wagon, was poured into wash pots for bathing. Like so many black residents in this part of Mississippi, Mrs. Hunter's life was marked by agriculture labor. "We would start chopping cotton the first Monday after the second Sunday in May," she recounted. "And the second week in September we'd start harvesting." Mrs. Hunter's family eventually moved into town, where her father became a barber. Our conversation turned to her experiences at the Drew Colored School.

"I taught many a hungry child, with nothing [in their stomachs] but syrup and bread, or no breakfast at all." With no books provided them, teachers like herself conducted their often combined classes from the blackboard. Frequently, older students helped out the younger ones. "On rainy days, blacks would attend, but when it was dry, they was in the fields." This, she explained, is why it took so many years for the school to develop its first senior class.

Throughout our visit, Mrs. Hunter sat with her terrier poodle in her lap, quietly stroking the dog with one hand. As I got up to leave, she took her other hand from her pocket, drawing with it an unholstered, snub-nosed, .38-caliber revolver. I suddenly realized that the whole time we talked, she had it pointed at me. She revealed it now as a statement of trust. As an elderly woman, a widow living by herself, she made it public knowledge in her community that she kept a loaded weapon on her person. It helped protect her. "You must not be afraid to live," she later said, "and scared to die."[97]

With Nancy Hunter's help, I eventually reached Sonny Milton, a former student of hers as well as Ora Dell's nephew. When I told him about my conversations with her, he replied, "That story was true about Ora Dell coming out of the store and getting killed, but it didn't happen to her. It happened to her older sister Babe."[98] During the holdup, Milton explained, Babe's victim wrestled the gun from her, then shot her in the back of her head. Not long after, Babe and Ora Dell's brother Samuel went to Parchman prison. Within six months of Ora Dell's death in the car crash, Samuel was killed by his best friend. Milton's mother, Mary, the siblings' one remaining sister, had already left home to wander from one city to another. Through it all, Della Graham, Ora Dell's mother and Sonny Milton's grandmother, herself a child of slaves, remained a stable force in the family.

In the years between Babe's death and Ora Dell's, Sonny Milton grew close to his aunt Ora Dell, whom he called Honey. Her zest made her the most communicative of any in the family. "She would say what she wanted to say. It didn't make any difference. She would talk . . . and she would run. Mama [Della Graham] had a whole lot of problem keeping her up in the house . . . When something hit her, she left. She was gone."

Ora Dell never went to high school. In those years, Milton said, "she stayed in the street." Her mother, out of religious belief, didn't allow a record player or blues singing at home. "Only time the radio be on, it'd be a spiritual song coming out of Memphis. That's it." As a result, Ora Dell picked up music like she always had—"just go on singing it." Now, when she went out to clubs, she learned songs from jukeboxes. She sometimes sang too, either by herself or with her boyfriend, in taverns from Greenwood to Clarksdale. When she died on her way to one of those nightspots, Milton explained, "The only thing I can say is if it hadn't been that crash that killed her, it would have been something else. It was her time to go. She could have died like Babe." He shook his head again, and murmured, "She was my favorite auntie."

While Sonny Milton remembered Ora Dell's death in stark detail, he could not specify its date. The cemetery kept no records, the family belonged to no church, and Ora Dell never had steady employment that would have resulted in labor records. Finally, Anne Webster of Mississippi's state archives suggested I examine the *Ruleville Record,* the region's leading newspaper.

As I turned the microfilm, starting in January 1943, the *Record* plotted the region's turn toward modernity: mechanized farming and the spread of rural electricity, the growth of highway construction and the expansion of telephone service. With each passing week, advertisements by national corporations took increasing prominence over those by local businesses. Pictures of family automobile outings became more frequent, as did the number of highway fatalities. The *Record's* front page tabulated rising figures of black migration to northern cities, while letters to the editor urged its black veterans returning from World War II to accept the old ways. In a ten-year period beginning in 1943, the sole photograph of any black residents showed a group of women making miniature souvenir cotton bales.

Then, on Thursday, July 10, 1952, the paper ran this item:

Four Killed in Drew Crash

Four persons were killed last Friday in the state's first reported fatal accident of the holiday weekend. According to the State Highway Patrol headquarters, the accident occurred about three miles north of Drew on US Highway 49 when the car crashed into an embankment and was demolished completely. Those dead were identified as . . . Ora Bell, 24 . . . It was stated that all the victims were negroes.

Though her name was misspelled and incomplete, and her race deemed unworthy of capitalization, it becomes painfully clear that Ora Dell Graham, a little black girl from Mississippi whose singing is forever preserved in Thomas Jefferson's library, died as he did, on July 4th. A national treasure.

Christine and Katherine Shipp

In a Chromatic Light

"DO I REMEMBER WHEN CHRISTINE AND KATHERINE MADE those records?"[1] Luella Shipp's voice, already coursing with a vitality that defied her age, now leaped in volume. "Honey, I was *there*." Her radiance matched the front room where we sat, a room ablaze with dozens of Christmas cards propped up among smiling snapshots of nieces and nephews and surrounded by gift boxes still encased in holiday ribbons and bows. Together they formed a glittering, glowing domestic shrine. By contrast, a damp February cold pierced the house. We huddled around a small electric heater. Between us lay a cassette machine, and as it played the Shipp family's 1939 recording session, Luella sang along to each number. Throughout the morning, the phone rang as friends, aware of this visit, checked in to see if all was OK with her. Later someone stopped over, peering hard through the doorway for signs of danger. Though Luella lived on a near-empty street with just a few shuttered houses, her Byhalia, Mississippi, neighborhood stayed watchful on her behalf.

On May 13, 1939, Luella, together with her husband John Shipp, opened the door of this same house to other strangers also in search of musical information: New York–based folklorist Herbert Halpert and his locally appointed colleague and guide, Abbott Ferriss, a member of the Mississippi unit of the

Federal Writers' Project. Earlier that spring, Eri Douglass, state director of the project, and a former music teacher herself, had gotten in touch with Ethyl Bowen, a prominent white Byhalian who brought the Shipp family singers to her office's attention. Mrs. Bowen knew their singing from their matriarch and director Mary Shipp, who had previously been in her domestic employ. Moreover, for two years, the family sharecropped a farm that Bowen owned. The Shipps' singing at church services, anniversaries, and school events in that area prompted Douglass to tell Bowen, "We want you to give Mary Shipp a pencil and a paper to write down the names of the songs that she and her family are familiar with . . . we want all kinds of songs, not just the religious songs. Ask her to be thinking up all the old songs she learned when she was a girl."[2] Bowen submitted several lists, and Douglass added the Shipps to Halpert and Ferriss's schedule of stops.

Five days earlier the two researchers had begun working together, starting in northeastern Mississippi. They made some of their first recordings with white singer Theodocia Bonnet Long, born in 1856, who performed nearly two dozen numbers that included several centuries-old British ballads, a play-party piece she learned during the Civil War from a Confederate lieutenant, and a scathing anti-Lincoln polemic her mother had written. Set to the tune of "Barbara Allen," it sarcastically addressed "Old Honest Abe," calling him "an arrant fool, a party tool, a traitor and a Tory."[3] That same day, Halpert and Ferriss also recorded Birmah Hill Grissom, who promised—and nearly delivered—"half a wagon bed of songs."[4] Her repertoire ranged from camp meeting spirituals to ring plays, including a piece she learned from an itinerant singing master to practice the notes of the scale. That night, at a nearby African American church, song leader Lula Morris cheered her fellow choristers to "Sing, people, with nothing in front and nothing behind. Just sing from your souls."[5] Later that week, they gathered from singer Laura Clifton a holler for calling cows, followed by one for calling chickens, and finally, a song for calling husbands. They also recorded several old-time fiddlers, including John Alexander Brown. Brown, with his bony fingers encircling his violin, his flowing beard, and wisps of white hair, formed the very picture of a rustic patriarch. Indeed, Brown hurriedly quit the recording session after performing his pieces, for "he had left his oxen out in the field."[6] The following day, Halpert and Ferriss arrived at Luella's door in Byhalia.

The researchers had just come from Miller, Mississippi, a farming community near Byhalia, bringing with them five members of John Shipp's family whom they planned to record that afternoon: his mother, Mary Shipp,

forty-seven, and four of his siblings, who made up the Shipp family quartet: brothers Isaac (twenty-three) and Allison (fifteen), and their sisters Christine (twenty) and Katherine (eighteen). Luella recalled, "The gentlemen wanted to know if we had any electric or anything. John said, 'No, but I'll tell you. Our church is just right around the corner there. We have electricity and I'm the janitor.'"[7]

Nichols Chapel, the church that John and Luella pointed out to Halpert and Ferriss, still stands where it did in 1939, a few hundred yards from their house. Now clad in brick, it had originally been constructed in wood and heated with coal that John Shipp brought there by horse and wagon. Employed as the town's drayman, John hauled supplies and groceries throughout Byhalia. His duties also included caring for his church. The afternoon of the recording, John admitted his family and the researchers into the building, and with Luella beside him, stayed to watch. While Herbert Halpert set up the microphone and readied the disc cutter, Abbott Ferriss made notes of the surroundings. A few rows of hand-hewn pews faced the pulpit. Some white garments and banners hung from a railing, an organ stood behind the choir seats, and a sign facing the congregants read "Do not spit in here."[8]

FIGURE 20. Mary, Isaac, Allison, Katherine, and Christine Shipp outside the Nichols Chapel, Byhalia, Mississippi, May 13, 1939. Photo by Abbott Ferriss. Used by permission of Mississippi Department of Archives and History.

Once the singing got underway, Ferriss copied down the singers' replies to Halpert's questions along with their verses. Of the eighteen songs that Mary Shipp and her children recorded that day, most were "tune[d] by Mother," and several of the melodies she composed herself.[9] Mary also credited her lined-out version of "Amazing Grace" to her late stepfather, a former slave.

For Mary Shipp (1892–1966), who led her family's singing, music formed only one aspect of her public activity. This mother of twelve who farmed forty- and sixty-acre plots of cotton and corn, often without the help of her husband, also served as a neighborhood healer. She prepared herbs and made teas and ointments, sometimes fashioning poultices from chimney soot or the axle grease that lined a set of wagon wheels. Whether reducing a sore with an application of egg whites to insisting that her children wear a bag of asafetida around their necks in the winter months to ward off colds, Mary drew on a combination of inherited folk wisdom and personal intuition. Her son Isaac recalled their walks in the woods: "'Dig down here,' she'd say, 'there's a root down here.'"[10] Then Mary would tell him which ailment it treated. Her expertise led the town doctor to regularly send for "Aunt Mary" to administer her cures to white as well as black members of the community. Both Luella Shipp and her niece Opal Broadway (Katherine Shipp's daughter) recounted Mary's effectiveness with Katherine following a childhood accident, a fall into an open fireplace that nearly severed the youngster's ear. Mary applied a homemade balm that sealed the injury, and Katherine suffered no permanent damage for what could have brought lasting disfigurement. Isaac, too, showed me his arm, pointing to a scar left by a physician that he compared with another wound, smoothly healed by one of his mother's treatments.

Mary approached her music much as she did her healing. Soon after her marriage to Walter Shipp, a traveling Methodist minister, she began her musical activities in her community by setting the pitch for the local choir: "I can scale the songs. I calls the songs," she said.[11] Through singing syllable by syllable, sometimes very slowly, "apparently with the idea of covering a large range of notes for each word," wrote Abbott Ferriss, she "gives the hymn out."[12] As her own family grew, she noted that they "sent for a professor to teach us the songs. Then, when we learnt them, we started singing."[13] Mary Shipp saw the effect that music had on her children. "I keep mine busy," she told Abbott Ferriss. "Every night we sing. Every night before we go to bed. My home's happy all the time."[14]

"This undergrowth of children never learnt to sing by notes," Mary explained. "I'm teachin' 'em now . . . I just carry them on over the song. I learn each of 'em parts."[15] With only religious numbers permitted in the home—the Reverend Shipp's favorite was "Don't Forget the Family Prayer"—Mary formed the family quartet. She assigned her daughter Christine the alto part and Katherine soprano, while her sons Allison and Isaac took tenor and bass, respectively. It was this group she sent out to accompany Walter Shipp on his pastoring. In the past, Walter's sermons had drawn sparsely, resulting in the meager offerings of chickens and eggs that his parishioners could afford as his recompense. Once his children joined him on the pulpit, though, public interest visibly increased. "They didn't have to worry about a choir," recalled his granddaughter Gertha Mae Brooks, "or an empty chair."[16] Mary Shipp's homeschooled ensemble had succeeded.

Mary usually sat by herself at the kitchen table while arranging a song.[17] Then she would sing it aloud, and afterwards ask her family to stand with her as they rehearsed it through line by line. "There was hardly a night," Isaac remembered, "we didn't sing. She would make us sing till we got it right, like she'd want it."[18] When touring jubilee singers visited Nichols Chapel—they performed in a style rooted in part-singing—she encouraged her children to imitate them at home. Abbott Ferriss wrote: "In greater detail, this is the way the family learns a song. Mary speaks: 'My husband buys a ballad at the South Main Street Bus Station in Memphis. I'd read over it . . . If it was a good one, the tune would come to me in my sleep. I'd git up and tell my husband, 'The tune come to me last night.' I'd git out the ballad next day and sing it. Sometimes I'd be walking along with a song and don't know the tune. And hit would come to me.'"[19]

Katherine characterized her mother's compositional ideas as revelations. When music sounded in her mind, it seemed a gift from God. While Mary's melodies came unbidden and seemingly spontaneously, their recurrence also suggests how musically saturated she had become. Mary's fellow churchgoers also recognized her depth. Isaac recalled visitors steadily dropping by the house, asking if Mary would look over their verses, too. "This song is not worded right," she might counsel them. "It'll get you off on the wrong start."[20] When certain parts didn't fit, she recommended changes. "Grandmother," said Opal Broadway, "was good at raising children, although she didn't know she was [also] a psychologist, a poet, or songwriter. Instead she would say, 'I had a dream last night, or something told me.' She didn't know how to articulate things. All she could do was to be an example."[21] Yet in giving example to others, no matter how colloquially she might have expressed herself, she offered both information and judgment. Her musical wisdom, which included her ability to read shape-notes and her knowledge of its rudiments allowed her to tap what Isaac called "an invisible source, a divine intelligence."[22] "Divine intelligence," he explained, "is learning through tradition."

In documenting one of the pieces they recorded, "Sea Lion Woman," Herbert Halpert and Abbott Ferriss encountered the ambiguities of such tradition. Right from the start, when Mary's daughters, Katherine and Christine, sang it at Nichols Chapel, Ferriss noted discrepancies between their pronunciation and his transcriptions: "Words to the following songs do not follow exactly as they were sung," he wrote.[23] Though Halpert and Ferriss encountered "Sea Lion Woman" three times on their monthlong recording trip across Mississippi, beginning with the Shipp family, Ferriss spelled it variously depending on what he discerned in the singers' speech. One informant told Ferriss, "It's just a word we use."[24] When I asked Herbert Halpert what he thought the title meant, he replied, "I don't know what a 'see-lie woman' is, but I think Abbott Ferriss's 'Sea Lion Woman' is a beautiful example of folk etymology: he has tried to make sense of what is nearly nonsense. Whether she was a lying woman you were supposed to see, or what, I certainly can't say; but any linguist-phonetician-language expert will tell you that 'sea lion' is an improbability . . . the giant California seal is not likely to be part of Mississippi folk knowledge!"[25] For Halpert and Ferriss, the confusion over the title underlines a larger, more philosophical issue: the gulf between the world of books and that of oral tradition. While Halpert and Ferriss may not have known it at the time, their work that day at Nichols Chapel with Isaac Shipp (1915–2007), the oldest of Mary's singing brood, holds a key to the elusive song. Isaac showed them that sometimes sound alone provides meaning enough.[26]

***

"I see myself as an intimate of progress," Isaac Shipp smiled. In January 1998, this tall, square-shouldered man in his early eighties gestured to the bookcase behind him, its half-dozen shelves lined with college texts on physics and chemistry. He spoke with affection: "There's my university right there."[27] During Isaac's childhood, the only school open to him and other black youngsters in Byhalia met just three months a year during the agriculturally fallow period between mid-November and mid-February. With no classes offered past the primary level and a five-mile trek facing him in winter, he ended his formal education after second grade. He began working as a water boy at a levee camp. Along with helping his family do their farming, he cut battens on a crosscut saw and served a two-year stint as a butcher's helper.

CHAPTER 4

By the summer of 1939, soon after the Halpert-Ferriss recordings, he joined a railroad gang on a line running between Oklahoma City and Pensacola and spent the next four years as a gandy-dancer, riding a hand-powered track maintenance vehicle "tamping ties, dogging steel, and lining track."[28] Shortly before the end of the war, he moved to Detroit, where he sandblasted airplane parts in a defense plant. After V-J Day, he took a job as a construction laborer and eventually found employment as a building custodian. During that time, he taught himself the electrical trade and became an independent contractor. Once he married, Isaac took this skill to Chicago, later Los Angeles, and finally New York.

By early 1998, with the shadows of the Manhattan skyline spiking high across the river, he lived in an apartment house provided for the retired and elderly. As we worked through the performer's questionnaire devised for the 1939 recording trip, Isaac's voice resonated in his apartment, its walls bare save for a few pictures and his bookcase. More than once he referred to his lifelong quest for self-improvement. "I found out," he said, "I was a lover of knowledge at an early age."[29] Then he spoke of his grandfathers, two of his earliest—and most beloved—sources of knowledge.

Isaac sounded out the words "Alissyna Boukeyon," the name of his paternal grandfather, born in Ethiopia in 1818 (d. 1921).[30] As with so many aspects of his family's history, Isaac preserved this name not through written documentation but through audible memory. He outlined his grandfather's story: At age sixteen, Alissyna arrived in America, entering at New Orleans. Purchased by a slaveholder named Shipp, Alissyna became known as Allison Shipp and eventually married a full-blooded Choctaw Indian the family called Mama Judy. The couple had eleven children, the third to youngest being Isaac's father, Walter Shipp. Allison died when Isaac was six, but in the brief time they had, when the little boy climbed onto his lap and combed his grandfather's long whiskers, Allison taught him some words of his native language. "I made it my business," said Isaac, "to never forget them." They sheltered a piece of Isaac's heritage. "I wanted to know all about myself," he explained. Then he paraphrased a passage from the New Testament: "If you got faith as the grain of a mustard seed, you can move mountains."[31] For him, these echoes of Africa, each cherished word an individual grain, provided spiritual nourishment.

Isaac continued to gather such seeds. In 1935 he ran away from home. He worked first in Memphis as a circus roustabout, then traveled with the show to Baltimore. After the circus folded, he turned south to Newport News.[32] There he shipped out as a stevedore on a tramp steamer, headed on a two-week voyage for Sierra Leone on the western coast of Africa. Soon after the ship docked he recalled, "When we got through unloading, we had a short time and I taken a walk."[33] At an outdoor affair in Freetown, amid thatched roofs and people in colorful attire, Isaac learned several songs from a man he called "Sule Kamarah, a seer, a man that we would call a historian here." The encounter lasted just a few hours when Isaac was called back to his ship. The vessel proceeded to the Belgian Congo, where a tribesman taught him another piece identified only by its refrain, "Coca-coca-coke-jenny." During the 1939 recording session, Isaac briefly described these musical experiences to Halpert and Ferriss: "I didn't stay as long as I would have liked to, but I did learn a few words of their language . . . I just caught the soundings as he [one of his sources] sung them, and studied as I thought they ought to be sung—and sung it."[34]

Nearly sixty years later, as we sat in his apartment, he sang these songs again. Without listening to any of the recordings, he pitched them in the exact same key and with the same words as he had performed them in 1939. While Isaac could not translate the pieces he learned, he gleaned that the one he called "She-be-ni-away" involved a ritual bloodletting between a man and woman. He correlated certain sounds in the song with their English equivalents, gesturing with his hands the meanings as he understood them. Whatever sense the syllables might convey in their native tongue, these intonations memorialized what Isaac first began with his grandfather's words.

Isaac's maternal grandfather, Jack Rogers, also left him a legacy captured in sound. Rogers was born in Mississippi in 1837 (d. 1923) near the Watson's Crossroads community in Marshall County.[35] For much of his life, this man who Isaac called Papa Jack lived at Pigeon Roof, occupied as a farmer and fiddler. Though Rogers could neither read nor write, "he could tell you the things you plant above ground when the moon is strong from what you plant below when the moon is on the waste."[36] Just as Byhalians would someday seek out his stepdaughter Mary Shipp's counsel on medicine and music, Jack Rogers's nineteenth-century neighbors at Watson's Crossroads asked his advice on crops as well as cattle raising. From time to time, too, they stopped by just to hear him play the fiddle.

Isaac hummed "Mr. Blue," one of Jack Rogers's tunes. Its rhythm, corresponding to a simple melody, follows a pattern that Isaac reduced to a few vocables: "Skippy-hop-down, tap, tap." In this nineteenth-century dance reel, Isaac's phrasing simulates the timing steps of an old-time percussive clog, as weight from one leg shifts to the other while the foot rocks forward from heel to toe and back again. Another piece, musically akin to "Mr. Blue" that Jack Rogers sang and played on his fiddle, was "Sea Lion Woman."

Isaac recalled Rogers saying that he learned "Sea Lion Woman" as a child, nearly a quarter century before Emancipation. The fact that he played it on the fiddle was further indicative of its age. In the early 1920s when Papa Jack taught Isaac "Sea Lion Woman," the newer blues and rags had largely displaced the older country reels at the frolics and Saturday-night fish fries where he performed. When Papa Jack called out from his front porch to signal its start, "This is a play that is a song, and I plays it on my fiddle," he preserved in "Sea Lion Woman" a practice of an earlier time.[37] By May 1939, when Christine and Katherine recorded the piece, which they learned from Isaac, its place as a fiddle song had vanished.

At the start of her "Sea Lion Woman" recording, Katherine (1921–1978) tells Herbert Halpert, "Well, I learned it when I was small too, a little puppy really."[38] Her older sister, Christine (1919–1966), adds, "We sung this song when we was playing. We just say anything. . . . We didn't know much of anything to play. We just sang this song." She dismisses their movements and lyrics as nothing particularly organized: "There wasn't any action at all. We just moving around and jumping around from place to place."

But there was more to it than they let on. In the Shipps' way of doing "Sea Lion," one of them would take the center of a circle and dance, sometimes humorously, even flirtatiously. Isaac described these movements as "similar to what Chubby Checker would call 'Doing the Twist,' but instead of twisting your body, you would move your feet more often."[39] Using a combination of side steps and slides accompanied by clapping, he said, its singing participants "can add whatever you want to it. This was a game and dance you played at the same time. Each time you come to the end of a verse, you jump to another place, say 'sea lion,' and shake your booty." Isaac's sister-in-law Luella connected these movements to a hand-clapping game as well: "Get in a ring and you be holding hands when you start off. Then you take your partner and turn, skipping around sideways. And then, when you get through, you stop, and then you do that patty cake."[40]

On the recording, Christine and Katherine sing:

See lie woman,
See lie.
She drink coffee,
See lie.
She drink tea,

See lie.
And the gander lie
See lie.

Way down yonder,
See lie.
'Hind the log,
See lie.
And the rooster crowed,
See lie
And the gander lied,
See lie.
[Repeat first verse twice.][41]

With their coolly blended voices, Katherine and Christine convey intimacy. Instead of a shouted chorus of "see-lie" that arises in other recordings of this ring game, their quieter dynamics sound mournful rather than boisterous. Separated from the game and all its flurry, their lyrical performance stands on its own.

To a similar tune, Isaac sang these words in 1998 as he patted his hands:

Chop that cotton, sea lion,
Chop it good, sea lion.
If you don't chop it, sea lion,
Mama gonna whup you, sea lion.

The red-eyed rooster, sea lion,
Got no comb, sea lion.
These Tennessee boys, sea lion,
Got no home, sea lion.

Sea Lion Woman, sea lion,
She's so fine, sea lion,
Wish she was mine, sea lion.

Way down yonder, sea lion,
'Hind a log, sea lion.
Rooster crowing, sea lion,
And the gander lark, sea lion.[42]

That Isaac sang some verses other than those his sisters did, he felt made little difference. The song allowed for that freedom. Whatever one singer or another might bring to it, "It has a natural part, regardless of what you add."[43] By "natural part," he meant the refrain, whether "see lie" or "sea lion." When Katherine speaks with Halpert during the recording, she seems to say "sea

CHAPTER 4

lion woman," even though she and Christine sing "see lie woman." According to Isaac, and apparently for Katherine and Christine, these verbal distinctions never mattered so much as just calling out the phrase over the course of the game, to signal movement. As Christine explained, "We just wanted to have something to be saying."[44]

In the spring of 1942, Alan Lomax wrote to the Shipp sisters, seeking their permission to issue "Sea Lion Woman" on an album the Library planned for a South American cultural exchange program.[45] Katherine and Christine took his letter in part as a request for lyrics, and they wrote out the title as "Sea Lion Woman," same as he had spelled it. They also wrote "and the gander lion, sea lion"—while they sing "and the gander lie"—once more underlining the distance between the ear and the page. After all, they had learned the song in childhood, a time of life less affected by orthography than by the rhythm, rhyme, and sound of words. They also included two verses they had not sung during the 1939 recording:

I got a girl Sea lion
Long and tall Sea lion
She sleep in the kitchen Sea lion
And her feets in the hall Sea lion.

Down that road Sea lion
Across the street Sea lion
I can't get a letter Sea lion
But once a week Sea lion.[46]

The easy rhyming of these verses, and the comic sight of a person stretching from one room to another, a verse that appears in numerous folksongs, reiterates "Sea Lion Woman"'s primary function. For Katherine and Christine, it was something they played—no matter how they wrote it down.

At the time of the song's release on *Afro-American Blues and Game Songs,* its printed form remained uncertain. Shortly before the album came out, Harold Spivacke, Lomax's supervisor at the Library, measured the space the song would physically occupy on the surface of one of the five two-sided 78 rpm records in the set. In his production notes, he identified Christine and Katherine's song as "Selie," his spelling clearly guided by what he heard them sing.[47] While Lomax subsequently titled the song "Sea Lion" on the disc, he spelled the chorus "see-line" in the accompanying booklet, and attached a footnote to the entry, once again raising the question of the title's literal meaning. He wrote "see lyin'?"[48] In the fixedness of type, its sound did not readily translate into sense. Ever indefinable, "Sea Lion Woman" went out to the world.

Separated from its place on a schoolyard, apart from the children who sing it, and known only via an audio recording, the mysterious refrain understandably compels interest. That a woman is being portrayed seems beyond doubt. Who she is seems less clear. Is it "See [the] Lyin' Woman," a gossip in a small town, where lies spread about can have such a devastating effect? Since the accent comes on "see," could it instead have originated as "Sea [Board Coast] Line Woman," involving the southern railroad? What if a gleaming train shot by, and from behind the dining car window sat an elegant lady sipping coffee or drinking tea from a silver service? For an impoverished youngster standing outside by the tracks, that fleeting sight might suggest class issues as much as it denotes race matters. Perhaps the song reflects the point of view of a little girl whose mother, a domestic servant, works for a prosperous woman. In that moneyed home, the girl sees its finery and amenities and later turns her observations into verses. All possibilities certainly, all suggested by the words *see* and *lie,* all provoked by the silvery voices of the Shipp sisters. But as Isaac gently reproved, "We just used it as a play song."[49]

"'Sea Lion Woman' is just about people," he continued. "I don't know what it means, it's just our song."[50] He mentioned once again playing it in the front yard with his friends while Papa Jack Rogers fiddled. "The 'Sea Lion Woman,' Isaac said, "is a piece that everybody loved, that everybody enjoyed being around."[51] The purpose of any game song is, first and foremost, to provide recreation. In calling this one "our song," he expressed a sense of that gaiety, of how he and playmates took to it in their tiny Mississippi community. As for the animals within the song, Isaac put it this way: "Now, you see, you have a way of doing things. Well, the gander larks. That means he just has something he's doing." For a song where the apparent message of its refrain is to observe behavior and recognize deceit, Isaac was talking about animals that can do nothing except act true to their nature.

Yet Isaac did not reduce the refrain to a specific verbal equivalent. Though he assured me that it had nothing to do with the biblical word *selah,* he would not transform "sea lion" into "see the lie." Over the course of our seven interviews—perhaps to make me happy—he granted that the bewhiskered aquatic mammal known to coastal Californians is the same word he says in the song. But that wasn't what it signified. That was only a similarity, a linguistic coincidence. Instead, the refrain operated like his grandfather's words and like the songs he learned in Africa. Their meaning didn't matter so much as their resonance. For Isaac, those word-sounds harbored his ancestors, aural vessels that carried the customs and traditions of their living descendants. Spoken by mouth and retained by ear, these syllables inspired him, and it was in these terms that he now defined "Sea Lion Woman": "I loved it. It had a rhythm that elated me, that lifted me up. That's why I wanted to learn it. I loved the sound of the song. It had an elated sound that would lift you."[52]

———

Two weeks after the Shipp family recorded in Byhalia, Herbert Halpert and Abbott Ferriss reached Edwards, Mississippi, a small town west of Meridian in the southern half of the state. There, on May 27, 1939, twenty-six-year-old Leora Anderson told the researchers, "We're going to play a ring play from school":[53]

Oh see line,
Oh see line.
See lying girl, see line.
See lying boy, see line.
Up to the hickory,
Down to the pine.
Have all the women,
Ain't got but nine.

Old hen setting,
By the shack.
Laid one egg,
Hollered quack, quack, quack.

Ain't but oh one thing,
I dislike,
Two-faced woman,
And a quack, quack, quack.

Ain't but the one thing,
On the line,
Train went to hell,
Left me behind.[54]

While the "two-faced woman" surely signifies duplicity, the "lying boy" and "lying girl" of Anderson's first verse also touch on the issue of falseness. A recording that Halpert and Ferriss made the following day in Edwards again invokes this theme. Sarah Ann Reed, a local college student, learned "Seline" during her grade school years. Explaining that the song's action involved stealing partners, and as her companions clapped on the off-beat and sang the chorus, she chants at one point:

> My old master [to which the group answers]: "Seline"
> Promised me, Seline
> When he died, Seline
> Gonna set me free, Seline
> Lived so long, Seline
> Head got bald, Seline.[55]

This verse about a lying slave owner, dating back to the antebellum era, appears in numerous black music collections. African American folklorist Thomas Talley used it to lead off "Promises of Freedom," which he collected from black singers in Tennessee, while E. C. Perrow included it in a Mississippi manuscript he gathered from black sources there in 1909.[56] Dorothy Scarborough located it in at least five different African American songs, including "Po' Mona," a secular reading of the nineteenth-century "Mourner, You Shall Be Free."[57] Scarborough's source sang it with another much-repeated lyric that also involved a theft. No less ironic in tone, it reads, "One had a shovel and one had a hoe / And if that ain't stealin', well, I don't know!" This usage, too, reappears in "Sea Lion Woman." On the same day that Halpert and Ferriss recorded Leora Anderson, John A. Lomax recorded "Sea Lion" in Livingston, Alabama. There Joe McDonald sings, to a family member's refrain,

> I caught a preacher
> Seeline
> in my cornfield
> Seeline
> One had a bushel
> Seeline
> One had a peck
> Seeline.[58]

Once more the song alludes to deception—from the broken promises of a slave owner to foodstuffs stolen by a fleeing minister. While reading or even hearing the text cannot fully catch the intent of the singers, the recurrence of this theme and its resonance in sound is telling. Across these examples, the presence of "lie" in the refrain reverberates—completing, extending, and commenting on the verses.

Lomax's daughter, folklorist Bess Lomax Hawes, has noted that the genre of ring plays arose in the harshly segregated society that followed the Civil War.[59]

Bearing in mind that Isaac's grandfather knew "Sea Lion Woman" at least a generation earlier than the period Hawes addresses, sarcastic lyrics about stolen food and lying owners make sense in this period stained by racial poverty and apartheid. But no matter how aptly these widely distributed couplets might fit the circumstances of the day, Hawes explains that they had to meet an even larger and more timeless function as "small life dramas."[60] These childhood theatricals served as "ceremonials, small testimonies to the ongoingness of life." With rhyme and movement, young people express through their ring plays a perspective on a world they not only inhabit but will soon inherit.

In 1964 Hawes collected "Way Down Yonder, Sometimes" from Georgia Sea Island singer Bessie Jones.[61] "In this ring play," Bess Hawes writes, "an account of the doings of magical animals and the courtship feats of human beings is continually punctuated by the chorus' sardonic refrain of 'Sometimes.'"[62] Hawes found during her work with Jones that "plays," as the singer used this word, went beyond denoting an organized game. She meant an enactment.[63] No doubt Jack Rogers and Leora Anderson intended this sense by calling "Sea Lion" a play too. It offers the same dramatic potential as those Jones categorized. More to the point, "Sea Lion Woman" shares a number of specific elements with "Sometimes."

Bessie Jones opens her song with a familiar gathering of images: "Way down yonder, Sometimes, Below the log, Sometimes, Wild geese are holl'ring, Sometimes, Ganders trot, Sometimes."[64] Jones's melody echoes the "Seeline" tunes performed by Leora Anderson, Sarah Ann Reed, and Joe McDonald. So does its refrain, with Jones's "sometimes" providing a metrical equivalent for their "see line." Hawes's breakdown of the steps in "Sometimes" also corresponds to the dance descriptions given by Isaac Shipp and Abbott Ferriss. Most of all, the skeptical humor that punctuates Bessie Jones's "Sometimes" has a corollary in "Seeline" where this word similarly operates as a rhythmic, editorial counterbalance. In any era, children remain alert to the incongruities about them, and these game songs respond to those appearances. Whether or not these pieces stem from a common source, they show kindred ways in which their youthful interpreters meet an uncertain society.

Four days after *A Treasury of Library of Congress Field Recordings* was released in the fall of 1997, the children of Katherine and Christine threw a party. "Sea Lion Woman" numbers among the *Treasury*'s thirty tracks, and to celebrate its appearance on a compact disc, one of Katherine's daughters,

Opal Broadway, worked late into the night preparing pots of chicken and spare ribs. The following afternoon, family members of all ages gathered at her brother Sam's Memphis home to listen to the music and to remember their past. There was much to talk about. For one thing, not until earlier that year did they know their mothers had recorded.

Soon after "Sea Lion Woman" came out in 1943, Luella Shipp listened to "the big blue records from Washington" that arrived at Mary and Walter Shipp's new home in Memphis.[65] She rightly recalled the azure labels on the published discs. But she returned to Byhalia, and as one of the session's few witnesses, with her went some of its most enthusiastic memories. When the album disappeared from Mary and Walter's home, so too went the principal physical reminder of the recordings. Mary Shipp didn't sing secular songs, and "Sea Lion" didn't surface when Katherine and Christine raised their own families. None of their children learned it from them. Katherine found employment as a caterer at the Memphis airport, while Christine worked as a housekeeper. Mary Shipp died in January 1966, followed six weeks later by Christine. Katherine passed away in November 1978. What singing the sisters did as grownups, they confined to their churches.

Now, as the Nichols Chapel session played continually on the living room stereo, Abbott Ferriss's photographs passed from hand to hand. As the only two pictures taken of Mary, Isaac, Katherine, Christine, and Allison Shipp at that time in their lives, these images, even more than the music, captured the family's interest.

Opal Broadway looked at the photo of Mary holding her hand over her heart and said, "Her gift was sight, insight more than foresight. And a lot of that came through her music."[66] A singer in three gospel quartets and a lay preacher herself, Opal sat down at the kitchen table, and with gathering intensity spoke of this earnest woman, her grandmother, who helped set her life's course. "You need to be able to look beyond your world. You need to see further than your face. That's what she lived for." Growing up with slavery still in living memory, Mary found music to be a saving grace. In Opal's words, Mary knew that "if I could sing through, I could get through." Born in a family of ministers—six of Walter and Mary's sons became preachers—Opal's words took on a pulpit eloquence of their own as she described the genesis of her grandmother's music: "It started on a ship somewhere and went into a cotton field. Then it came out of a hungry belly, and a naked foot, and a rainy, leaky roof. That's where the music came from." When Mary Shipp died, Opal remembered, "She had a song in her mouth."

What then would Mary Shipp have thought about her daughters' singing appearing in a Hollywood movie? In June 1999, *The General's Daughter,* a film based on Nelson DeMille's military detective thriller of the same title and starring John Travolta, opened in theaters around the world. For nearly six minutes, "Sea Lion Woman" underscores the movie's opening, a flashing sequence of swamps and dust, jeeps and helicopters, epaulets and olive drab. During these scenes, Christine's and Katherine's voices ebb and flow at the center of an extended musical collage. A five-string banjo recorded in reverse, its spare notes complementing the melody opens the sequence. Their vocals come in next, soon joined by a sixty-piece studio orchestra tuned to the sisters' key note.

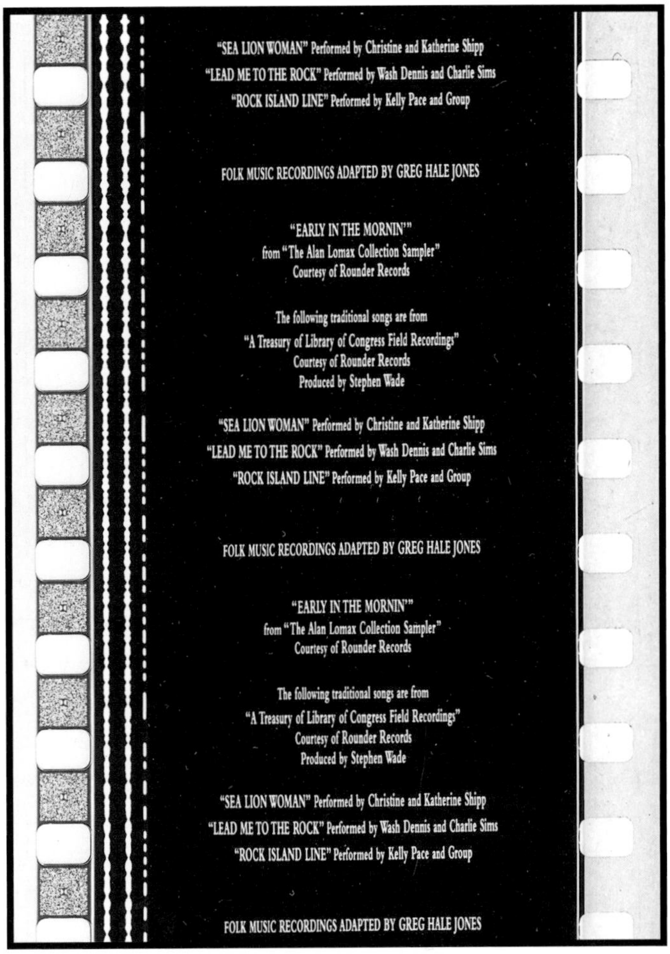

FIGURE 21. Folk music credits, *The General's Daughter,* 1999. From original celluloid. Author's collection.

Their singing drifts back, followed by passages of Japanese martial drumming and cymbals. Quieter passages of hand clapping and harmonica playing follow. Within this structure, the girls' sweet youthful voices convey an atmosphere of sorrow. At the movie's close, the song reprises during the credit roll, framing the somber story of *The General's Daughter.*

Six months earlier, during the last days of shooting, British-born movie director Simon West began piecing together his film. West, whose directing credits include a Super Bowl commercial, followed by *Con Air,* a popular action feature that brought him *The General's Daughter,* wanted some temporary music in order to make a rough cut. "Get something," West told his film editor Glen Scantlebury, "that isn't twangy steel guitar or gospel. Along the lines of some Negro spiritual stuff."[67] Scantlebury suggested a self-produced disc that a tenant in his apartment building, composer Greg Hale Jones, had recently given his neighbors as a Christmas present. Sparked by his own reawakened interest in American traditional music, and inspired by Steve Reich's 1965 "It's Gonna Rain," a seventeen-minute tape-loop composition of a San Francisco street evangelist, Jones transformed four songs he found on the *Treasury*. After downloading them to his computer, he brought the tracks' vocal pitches into alignment with standard tuning, and then reconstructed the songs, repeating certain passages, creating transitions, and adding parts that he played on instruments ranging from trap drums to electric guitar.[68]

When Simon West heard Jones's work, the director found himself particularly drawn to "Sea Lion Woman." "This is the whole tone of the film," West recalled.[69] "The little girls' voices were so evocative because the whole film is about a general's daughter who's been betrayed by her father. So it has all these connotations of children being let down by adults and losing their innocence, but it also has this great Southern back-feel to it." West played it on the set, recalling, "From John Travolta to the second assistant grip, everyone wanted to know, 'Where is that from?'" The director lamented that he hadn't heard the song earlier. "If I had this tune in my head during preproduction," he acknowledged, he would have shot the film differently. Though "Sea Lion Woman" came too late to the film to be integrated into the narrative, the voices of the Shipp sisters provided those nearest the production a musical metaphor for the story's deepest values.[70]

Shortly before the film opened, West asked if I might send him the lyrics. He was moved by a song whose words had never been entirely clear to him. But no matter what they might be, he and his staff found meaning in the Shipp sisters' voices, by their sound alone. By then, too, Greg Hale Jones titled his final remix "She Began to Lie," and since spring, bus-board advertisements for *The General's Daughter* exhorted moviegoers to "Go Behind the Lies." On all levels of the production, "Sea Lion Woman," with its uncertain words and indeterminate allusions, fit the shrouded atmosphere of this story, whose dark truths hid in army camouflage.

During these same weeks prior to the movie's premiere, a record company specializing in film soundtracks selected "She Began to Lie" to open the album.[71] The label deemed it the score's most appealing track, and with Greg Jones's help they issued two additional "trance-beat" remixes of the song, animated by synthesizers and electronic drum beats.[72] They also chose one of these remixes to close the album, and then put all three versions on a single vinyl LP sent to thousands of deejays throughout the United States and England. Inevitably, club-going children of the hip-hop generation danced to this schoolyard song of their great-grandparents' generation. When "She Began to Lie" was used to introduce John Travolta for a promotional appearance on the *Oprah Winfrey Show,* the television host recognized the Shipp sisters' song from her own childhood, and a moment later, she and the star of *Saturday Night Fever* were on their feet dancing.[73] By late summer, a message received at the Paris office of the record company advised them that the Korean censorship board had concerns about the piece. The soundtrack would not be released until the government approved the lyrics, and these the censor could not make out.[74] The Shipp family's "Sea Lion Woman" had traveled a long way from Papa Jack Rogers's front yard.

Isaac Shipp looked wearily at the cassettes, notebooks, and papers piled on his kitchen table. We finally neared the end of our day-long conversation, and after hours of taping, the bright blue sky outside his apartment window had turned magenta. He reflected on his Library of Congress recording session. "It meant to me," he said, "that I had a voice and something will happen. I didn't have the least idea that fifty years later it would be coming back, but I knew it was meant for something good."[75] He turned the *Treasury* around in his hands, and we soon began looking at the evening's train schedule. Just before I boarded a city bus to the station, Isaac handed me his card. Above his address and phone number it read, "Isaac Shipp, Free Consultant, Light Spectrum Researcher." He mentioned some books back at the apartment and that healing was involved in this work. By then, though, the bus lumbered up and it was too late to pursue the subject.

Perhaps Isaac's interest in light reached back to his years as an electrician. Maybe it allowed him to continue his mother's practice as a neighborhood healer. I can't say what drove his researches, but seeing his card brought to mind what Ralph Ellison called "the chromatic scale of American social hierarchy."[76] This metaphor, based in Ellison's musical training—a career he contemplated before turning to literature—could apply to light as well as sound. Both meanings seemed operative at that moment. Earlier that afternoon, Isaac said something that focused those elements through a single, searing prism.

We had finished our discussion about the recordings and turned to his subsequent music making. Throughout Isaac's life, his great love had been singing. Though Walter Shipp feared that his son's interest in music would make him a "dope addict and a drunk," Isaac managed to avoid those snares. "I approved of all musicians," he said, "because I wanted to be one myself." He spoke of the first

FIGURE 22.
Isaac Shipp at
home, Jersey City,
New Jersey, Janu-
ary 10, 1998. Photo
by Stephen Wade.

records he ever bought, purchased at Byhalia's mercantile store, where one could get anything from a "ten-cent comb to a wagon-and-team." Ethyl Bowen, the Byhalia matron responsible for acquainting Mississippi officials with the Shipps, had previously sold the family a wind-up record player for four dollars. When his parents weren't home, Isaac listened to his mercantile store records of Blind Lemon Jefferson's "Matchbox Blues" and the Mississippi Sheiks' "Sittin' on Top of the World." He recalled the field hollers sung by Alger "Texas" Alexander and then sang a verse of his "Levee Camp Moan Blues," citing the precise year of its release. He also described the homemade banjos, crafted from the round hoops of cheese crates that he had seen in northern Mississippi, and the cane fifes that his neighbors fashioned from bamboo to play at picnics and parties. He remembered the two-steps and waltzes that came before the "chop-out," the "camel walk," and the "mess around," contrasting the "freedom way" of dancing that took place in the country with the "stylish way" of the city.

He pointed to a picture of himself dressed up as "Two-Gun Shipp," outfitted in cowboy apparel complete with two cap pistols and singing to one of his smiling admirers. Between 1949 and 1954, Isaac led a five-piece dance band at an American Legion Hall in Detroit, and sometimes he performed there in this costume. The worksongs from his days on a railroad gang now gave way to the ballads he learned from the hit parade. His esteem for Perry Como, Bing Crosby, Vaughn Monroe, and Frank Sinatra ranked no less than his love for Cab Calloway, Count Basie, Duke Ellington, Louis Jordan, the Mills Brothers, and Lionel Hampton. His listening extended to the *Grand Ole Opry* and the *National Barn Dance,* and he spoke knowledgeably of Roy Acuff, Curly Fox, Roy Rogers, Texas Ruby, and Eddy Arnold. All these people, he explained, could "sing plain" and by "singing straight-forward, you touch people." From Nat King Cole and Arthur Prysock, Isaac traced an unbroken line back to his mother's shape-note hymns and his grandfather's fiddling. He drew freely from all these sources, for, as he said, "Just because something originated in France, doesn't mean I can't do it my own way."

[124]

CHAPTER 4

"Barriers," he added, "are only in your mind."

Suddenly his tone shifted.

"Do you like pork chops," he asked. "Well, when you eat them you don't ask if they come from a black pig or a white pig, do you?" His voice sharpened as he took this racial reasoning each inexorable step further. "It's like this. If you gonna set up and let that black cow eat green grass and give white milk, you can churn it and it gives yellow butter. You drink it. It'll give white calcium in your teeth and brown marrow in the bone. But then you gonna want to kill me because I move next door? Well, you gotta be sick."

Isaac was speaking not only vehemently but chromatically. His words rested on an old foundation, a traditional adage that explores the array of colors in nature.[77] But he goes much further. These colors, seared with lived experience, run from America's promise and diversity to its terrors and restrictions. What he said recalls what Bess Lomax Hawes detected in the ring plays as a form of African American expression. Those amusements, she noted, flourished in the Jim Crow South and the ghettos of the North, imprinted with the realities of their surroundings and the concerns of their makers. For all the fun these plays provide, for all their satire and irony, awareness runs through them. Likewise, in "Sea Lion Woman," barnyard images of ganders and roosters entwine with grown-up civilities of coffee and tea. Isaac thought of these lyrics as observations—that creatures behave according to their kind. Now, he focused on another behavior he had witnessed. The watchfulness he and his friends playfully employed in "Sea Lion Woman" forecast vigilance throughout their lives.

Isaac's story of the colors describes more than American race hatred and its madness. It also accounts for the pluralism that nourishes this society. Segregation separated the races, but it did not seal off their cultural exchange. America's musical history endlessly chronicles musicians black and white (and shades between) listening to one another, appropriating and reinterpreting their various styles, techniques, and songs. In enumerating the music and musicians he loved, from fiddle tunes to big band, Perry Como to Texas Alexander, Isaac declared his own zest to sing, drawing from all these sources while accepting their obvious differences. For him, this habit of listening began early on. His ears wide open, he sat on his grandfather's lap, taking in his elder's words. That interest had not lessened when, as a young man, he went to Africa and learned a handful of songs in languages he didn't speak.

In the same way that Isaac cherished the songs he encountered there and retained them by ear, others found rewards in Christine's and Katherine's singing that they, too, could discern only through sound. That his two sisters may have intended "Sea Lion Woman" as nothing more than a playful diversion did not dictate how these outsiders received it. In listening to the recording, beguiled by its mood, unfamiliar with its ring game, and unsure how to write out its refrain, these new listeners attached values of their own to the emotive performance. Beyond Byhalia, singers like Nina Simone in 1964 and Leslie Feist in 2007 remade the song, shaping it by their own talents and traditions. Repeating a coffee-and-tea refrain much like the Shipp sisters used, native North Carolinian Simone lifted the piece into a wholly sensuous realm of red dresses and prostitution, allure and sexuality.[78] Feist, in turn, crediting the Shipps' recording for her initial exposure to the song, combined their chorus with Simone's lyrics on her hit record.[79] For both these artists, this ring game of an earlier day became a contemporary study in sinewy rhythm and mysterious allure.

"Sea Lion Woman" affirms Ralph Ellison's belief in the "unstructured possibilities of culture in this pluralistic democracy."[80] The thirty-seven-second-long performance that Christine and Katherine Shipp recorded at Nichols Chapel fits between a slave-era fiddle song their grandfather knew and a computer-facilitated composition crafted around their voices by an Oberlin-trained film composer. Its appearance in these divergent settings reflects a larger process that Ellison found recurrent throughout American history. Long before the Revolution, new amalgams arose with each advancing settlement. Sometimes stolen, at other times shared, the appropriation went on. No matter how alien to their individual ancestries, he writes, immigrants from continents both east and west became Americans. Pilgrims took more than just maize from the Indians, while African-born slaves, unable to speak English, let alone read it, found ways through the St. James Bible, bringing new worship practices to the old stories and psalms. Then and now, Ellison observes, this nation's cultural life remains "always all-shook-up."[81] "Sea Lion Woman" provides another example of that endless unruliness. The song's resistance to the confinement of print, veiled in the possibilities of sound, has made it all the more malleable and renewable.

A story that Ralph Ellison told bears out what Isaac Shipp so wrenchingly illustrated with the colors. In 1933 Ellison entered Tuskegee Institute with the desire to become a classical composer. His program of music studies included playing the trumpet, a pursuit that obliged him to give a monthly departmental recital. Disheartened by the faculty criticism that greeted one of his performances, Ellison sought out piano teacher Hazel Harrison, a kindly disposed instructor at the school who he hoped might comfort him. Miss Harrison's response, however, took the form of advice: now that he was maturing as an artist he must always play his best. "Even if it's only in the waiting room at Chehaw Station," she counseled, "because in this country there'll always be a little man hidden behind the stove."[82] The image dumbfounded Ellison. Harrison had just described a barren, north–south railroad depot near Tuskegee, where, she maintained, someone with the fullest understanding of what an artist is doing could suddenly materialize. When she conjured up the little man at Chehaw Station, she challenged Ellison to recognize that art and its audience transcended social and political limitations. As a black music teacher in the South with a Prokofiev-signed manuscript resting on her piano lid, Hazel Harrison showed by her own commitment that culture cannot be walled off, that it cannot be confined by racial assignment. A few years later, after Ellison left Tuskegee and come to New York to pursue writing, he saw her lesson come to life in a sweltering furnace room.

Early in his employment on the Federal Writers' Project, while making the rounds of a West Side tenement with a petition, he reached the building's basement. Down the corridor he heard the sound of argument, profanities and epithets bellowed in a Southern black workingman's idiom. The unschooled voices fell on Ellison's ear, harsh audible evidence, so he thought, not only of the speakers' origins but their social station. Coming nearer, he heard something else in this clamor: the debate centered on nothing other than the relative merits of the two soprano leads then performing at the Metropolitan Opera. Amazed and entranced, Ellison knocked on the door. Immediately the shouting ceased. After another try or two, an irritated "Come in!" thundered back, and Ellison entered the close, sweaty quarters, where he began to explain his canvass to the four men gathered there, all huge, all silently watching him, and all darkly smudged with coal soot. Though skeptical, they took the petition, and slowly signed their names with a stubby pencil that one of them had scooped from his overalls. Ellison's curiosity kept him from leaving. After an awkward moment he blurted out, "Where on earth did you gentlemen learn so much about grand opera?"[83] Another silence filled the room and the men burst into laughter. Finally, one of them explained that despite their stoking a furnace by day, they worked by night as stage extras at the Met. "Strip us fellows down," he said, "and give us some costumes and we make about the finest damn bunch of Egyptians you ever seen. Hell, we been down there wearing leopard skins and carrying spears or waving things like palm leafs and ostrich-tail fans for *years!*"[84] Here was not one man crouched behind Miss Harrison's proverbial stove at Chehaw Station, but four, and all of them sitting just inches away from a blazing furnace themselves. Ellison's laughter joined their own in this wonderful realization of American possibility. He realized that no contradiction exists in being both "coal heavers *and* Met extras . . . workingmen *and* opera buffs."[85]

Isaac Shipp also embodied that truth. He resided in New York himself, not far from these others. Like them a workingman, he too had come from the South. He arrived at the city by a convoluted route that began decades earlier in rural Mississippi. Brought up on homemade music, enlarged and delighted by numerous race, hillbilly, and jazz records, he spent his life attracted to multiple musical styles. As both artist and auditor, he found that heritages existed in sound. A case in point is "Sea Lion Woman," a song he taught his younger sisters. For some listeners their recording suggested mystery and mournfulness, while for himself and his family, it remained simple and straightforward. He knew that both interpretations could be true. It depended only on how you heard it. With no musical barriers in his mind, rising up from behind the stove, Isaac Shipp offered not just warmth but light.

Nashville Washboard Band
Something Out of Nothing

D URING THE SPRING OF 1942 FISK UNIVERSITY MUSIC professor John W. Work III welcomed a quartet of street musicians called the Nashville Washboard Band into his home. This visit marked the first of two. The second took place that July when the group, bringing along a fifth player, returned to make their sole recordings. For the professor's son, John Work IV, that initial encounter remained vivid nearly six decades later. "These people," he said, "*were* their music."[1] Then ten years old, Work IV had grown up in a musical environment. His family lived in sight of Jubilee Hall, an edifice built on the success of the Fisk Jubilee Singers. His great-grandfather trained several of its founding members, his grandfather led their earliest recordings, and his father eventually directed the ensemble. Throughout his childhood, Work IV met luminaries like Duke Ellington and Jimmie Lunceford, who dropped by the house when their travels brought them to town. Many more came, too, from gospel harmonizers to classical music students, all "who wanted Professor Work to listen to them . . . to say they were good." Now Work IV sat beside his younger brother and watched these "homegrown technicians" who occupied the family living room.

The musicians faced them in a row, seated side by side, lodged between the Works' radio set on one end and their Steinway parlor grand on the

FIGURE 23.
John Work III
playing piano at
home, Nashville,
Tennessee.
Courtesy of
John Work IV.

other. One band member chorded his banjo-mandolin, and another the guitar, but Work IV fixed most on the string bass that a third member of the band had cobbled together from a length of laundry wire, a broomstick, and a lard can. Exposed since childhood to atelier-crafted instruments and steeped in classical music—piano and violin lessons, Saturday opera broadcasts, the Nashville symphony—the youngster found this contraption astounding. "Here's a guy," he recalled, "playing a bass fiddle with a damn wire coming down from a stick attached to a tub!" If that weren't enough, the band's fourth member, who was blind, sat between two washboards mounted on a sawhorse and hinged in the shape of a V. He had attached to them an assemblage of frying pans, tin plates, and a metal bell, each registering different tones. Wearing sewing thimbles on his fingers, he tapped, clocked, and hammered this clattering array of stove-top resonators and corrugated surfaces. In fall 2000, John Work IV still pictured the scene, each player wrapped around his particular instrument: "He *is* a washboard or he *is* a banjo, as opposed to separate things. Like Segovia, it's hard to separate him from his guitar. Or Duke Ellington, you couldn't separate him from his music. They could just play on and on, and the house would reverberate."

The band's visit served an informational as well as musical purpose. "It wasn't just a matter," Work IV explained, "of having them come, record, and leave." His father received them and other folk musicians in an atmosphere of respectful inquiry. That March, when fiddler Frank Patterson and street banjoist Nathan Frazier came by and made their recordings at the Works' home, "These men would have been called 'Mr. Patterson' and 'Mr. Frazier,' just as they would never have called my father anything other than 'Professor Work' or 'Dr. Work' or 'Mr. Work.'" Work would bring in some chairs from the dining room and talk with them. He didn't take notes or grill his informants. "It was quite a conversational sort of thing," his son recalled. "He was interested in the roots of music. He wanted to know, 'Where did they get these things, these songs?' He'd ask, 'Where did you get the idea for this washboard?' Those kind of questions."

Street musicians had long held Work III's interest. In his 1930 master's thesis, his earliest writing on black folksong, he discusses a washboard band he had seen on Nashville's sidewalks. This group numbered among the "novelty bands showing the originality of the players, composed of many unorthodox instruments."[2] Along with the washboardist to provide percussion, the ensemble included a player blowing on a "hand made metal instrument . . . that approximated a clarinet in character even if not in quality." Eight years later, during a speech on folk music Work gave at the Fisk Memorial Chapel, he described another group of the city's hand-to-mouth performers. "Of lower caste but no lower inspiration," they drew music from the "pieces of wood and metal they find."[3] He noted how they took a piece of iron that resounded with "good measure pulse," substituted a jug for a tuba, and employed a one-string fiddle as a violin.[4]

That spirited resourcefulness applied as much to the Nashville Washboard Band. By the time of their visits to Work's home, they had become a frequent sight in downtown Nashville, playing less than a hundred feet from the War Memorial Auditorium, where the Grand Ole Opry broadcast its weekly radio show. When not stationed there or beside the Andrew Jackson Hotel nearby, they entertained the lunchtime crowd that gathered on the south steps of the state capitol. The group's four principal members all lived within walking distance of these spots where they toted their largely climate-resistant instruments. They also offered a repertory bound to pique the attention of passersby. It ranged from Erskine Hawkins's "Tuxedo Junction" to the minstrel-era "Old Joe."[5] In addition to older fiddle tunes like "Soldier's Joy" and "Arkansas Traveler," they drew on newer media—the hit parade, commercial blues releases, and jukebox favorites—for material. Their renditions of "Tuxedo Junction" with Buddy Feyne's 1940 lyrics, the widely heard "Kokomo Blues," and the Louis Armstrong hit "I'll Be Glad When You're Dead, You Rascal You" surely found willing listeners—pleased enough with these favorites, they hoped, to loosen their coin purses.

Matters of song choice, homegrown technique, and personal background surface, albeit briefly, on the July recordings of the Nashville Washboard Band made by Alan Lomax at John Work's home. In the pages that follow, accounts of others from the community help locate these players in their idiom and environment. Particular attention falls on the band's rendition of "Soldier's Joy." Their treatment of this widely known tune identifies the creative ground they occupied. Its performance on the city's thoroughfares, let alone in the confines of the professor's living room, points to an indivisibility of art and life that their unorthodox instruments literally embodied. A year earlier at Fisk's chapel, Work assembled a program made up of some other local performers. From the pavements of Nashville, as elsewhere in America, he remarked, comes a beautiful music all around us. In the summer of 1942, the Nashville Washboard Band brought that message home.

Professor Work's papers say little about the four members of the Nashville Washboard Band. The notes he kept about them give only their home addresses and instrumentation. Beyond that, scant information survives apart from the memories of those like John Work IV who saw them play. The boardinghouses in the Gay Street neighborhood where they lived no longer stand. My efforts to find them or their families yielded names possibly theirs, but in each case these leads proved inconclusive. Alan Lomax's handwritten session notes run less than a page in a small wire-bound notebook. A fifth performer on the recordings was never even identified. He plays guitar, and according to Folk Archive listings, sings on three numbers. We may never learn anything more about him, let alone about his named companions: guitarist Frank Dalton, washboardist Theophilus Stokes, mandolinist James Kelly, and bassist Thomas James Carroll.[6] We know from a comment made between songs that they had been playing together between eight and ten years and once made a trip to Williamstown, Kentucky. The notes describe them as "two blind men and three day laborers."[7]

This anonymity mirrors their occupation. As one of a dozen Nashville street bands in those years, they followed a transient's steps across their city.[8] Police and weather permitting, in the early decades of the twentieth century combos like the Nashville Washboard Band occupied street corners throughout the South. With their lard can and washtub basses, "they were sometimes called bucket bands," writes David Evans.[9] "They might be called spasm bands because of their informal character. . . . Sometimes they were called jook bands . . . from the places and occasions where they performed." The word *skiffle* also denoted these ensembles with their ad hoc instruments and musical variety. Even without washboards and jugs, a 1929 double-sided release called

"Hometown Skiffle," performed by a variety of Paramount recording artists playing piano and guitar and singing, captures the genre's upbeat admixture of country roots and urban migration—an occasion where "all our homefolks have come to town."[10] By the 1940s, *skiffle*'s meaning had extended to another urban gathering: the rent party.[11] The money raised at these skiffles via a door charge, apart from the cost of drink and tips for the piano player, went to the landlord. With eviction and the repo man just around the corner—evoked in titles like Lil Johnson's 1929 recording "House Rent Scuffle"—this period's economic grappling, so often the experience of rural migrants and tenement dwellers, found release in good-time skiffle music.[12]

As Nashville street musician Roscoe Moore wryly remarked, "Skiffle" was just "the way they say 'skuffle' in Alabama."[13] Here Moore refers to the efforts he and his cohorts made with their music day after day. "Get your ass out on the street," said Moore, who worked in a "skuffle" band outside the Andrew Jackson Hotel in 1960. "Skuffle for some change," he counseled. "Keep your ass from starvin'." His declarations, annealing the musical genre to its surrounding social realities, made sense in the environment that these performers faced. In an increasingly industrialized America, they wrestled out their living in ways these interchangeable words suggested.

Scuffling certainly fit that particular neighborhood's history. This area astride the Tennessee state capital, once filled with businesses from burial societies to bordellos, had long teemed with outdoor tradesmen as part of its daily commerce.[14] Forty years before the Nashville Washboard Band made their trek from these blocks to John Work's campus, the *Nashville Banner* reported on a crippled handyman called Pegleg who worked this part of town. There he halted his two-wheel, mule-driven cart to blow on a cow's horn, to alert residents that he came ready to cane their broken chairs.[15] A decade later, in 1911, the paper tells of Aunt Cora, "the hominy woman," carrying on her head a bucket of the foodstuff while surrounded by youngsters eager for a taste.[16] Further references to Hominy Kate and Aunt Frances reveal them, too, engaged in this work. For all the antebellum implications of their names and the ancient call of Pegleg's horn, these alleyway vendors shouldering homemade products and subsisting on traditional handskills moved through the city's wards. Eventually the Nashville Washboard Band would trace these steps themselves. Like the earlier hawkers and walkers, street musicians equally needed to meet the interests of their sidewalk consumers. The commodity they offered was their performance, their song choices comprised their wares.

Twenty years later, that strategy still held true. Blind James Campbell, leader of Nashville's last recorded African American street band, told collector Don Hill in 1961, "I used to know a lot of songs. We used to play whatever would be the leading record around here. We'd play it all the time, then put it down and pick up another. When it come out, we'd grab it. Try to keep them all in mind."[17] Campbell's eclectic 1963 album includes blues, spirituals, a Tex Ritter song, and several old-time pieces including "John Henry" and "Buffalo Gals," variously played on five-string banjo, fiddle, tuba, trumpet, and guitar. The band additionally performed gospel, some recent pop, and sentimental numbers, though they never recorded these. They built their appeal on favorites new and old.

Campbell's group, then called the Friendly Five, remembered their predecessors in the Nashville Washboard Band. He and his bandmates, who at one time had even taken the name Nashville Washboard Band themselves and included a washboard player and lard-can bassist in their ranks, spoke with animation about the original group, especially their virtuoso blind washboardist, Theophilus Stokes.[18] They shared a connection, as well, with John Work III. One member of Campbell's group, fiddler and banjoist Beauford Clay, served as their principal song conduit. Work knew this multifaceted musician who additionally played guitar and piano and sang. Clay represented what the album's recordist Chris Strachwitz called a songster, a community musician of the generation that came of age before the blues. Songsters drew from the broad range of social music once popular in rural black communities: dance reels, ballads, hymns, and songs that included nineteenth-century hits, Tin Pan Alley rags, and Victorian parlor pieces. It became apparent to Strachwitz that Clay, "during his prime," had been an influential local songster.[19] Indeed, he turns up in Work's notes from the same period he had contact with the Nashville Washboard Band. Clay's name, listed with some fellow players in Nashville, appears above an untitled piece of music notation that one of them sang for Work, and whose words that singer had forgotten.[20] Now, in the early 1960s, Clay recalled the names of other forgotten songsters who had passed along to him a wealth of music.

One of them was a Franklin, Tennessee, fiddler named John Gibson. This may have been the fiddler George Gibson that Work documented in his 1930 master's thesis. If nothing else, this Gibson represents the kind of songster Strachwitz had in mind. Work described George Gibson as one who "knows no notes when he sees them, but knows them all when he hears them."[21] Despite the January cold piercing his shanty in south Nashville, Gibson, along with his guitar-playing partner Earl Woodard, played blues without interruption for three hours, often singing till one ran out of verses and the other took up the slack. They ended finally with the formulaic tag: "If anyone ask you who made up this song, tell 'em it was sweet papa Gibson (or Woodard), jes' gone 'long."[22] Their endless roll of verses, some improvised in the moment, anticipates the musical diversity that Beauford Clay transmitted to Blind James Campbell. For John Work, the duo's creative vitality linked to the Nashville Washboard Band.

In his thesis, Work connected Gibson and Woodard to a disappearing stratum of music as well as to contemporary forms. He characterized them as "two musicians, thoroughly steeped in the lore of the blues and other folk dance music."[23] Work observed that social folksongs and their primary medium of expression, the string bands, had largely vanished, displaced by newer music styles, dances, orchestras, and broadcast media. He expressed that thought again when he published his *American Negro Songs and Spirituals.* Along with giving the words and melodies to 230 songs, its text consists of Work's master's thesis spliced with material from his 1938 Fisk chapel speech on black folk music. Yet the book also reflected subtle changes taking place in his community. His 1930 paper noted the disappearance of the washboard bands along with the string bands, for instance, setting them in the past tense. His 1940 book refers to them in the present.[24] Work had already made this updating for his 1938 speech. Clearly, he heard that sound ringing out once more on Nashville's streets.

By the time the Nashville Washboard Band recorded at John Work's house, washboard-driven music had, in fact, found an enormous contemporary audience. In the 1930s, the Hoosier Hotshots, a Midwestern radio and recording ensemble whose catchphrase at the start of their songs, "Are you ready, Hezzie," captured their wacky ebullience, became part of the national argot. This musical slapstick reached a new height in 1942 when Spike Jones achieved one of the year's biggest hits with "Der Fuehrer's Face." The record established his career, while inventorying a whole range of the washboard's effects. Jones combined comedy with virtuosity to create an aural vaudeville that reached the entire nation. Locally, on the Grand Ole Opry, Pap's Jug Band, an offshoot group of their leading star, Roy Acuff, emitted the squeaks and honks of washboard clowning housed in a rustic framework of country music entertainment.

On July 11, 1942, four days before the Nashville Washboard Band made their recordings, Opry emcee George D. Hay introduced Acuff's jug band via their homespun persona: "We're going to call on Pap now, whose principal job is talking and fishing—that is, when he's not playing hot music and singing ditties about the countryside."[25] Then Pap's Jug Band launched into "Crawdad," setting the good-humored black folksong to modern closed-chord guitar accompaniment and contemporary country-style duet singing. They would further deck it out, Hay promised, "with trimmings."

Since the early years of World War II, in plain view of the Nashville Washboard Band playing outside, one of the Opry's perennial roles—the musically skillful hayseed—fell to Pap's Jug Band.[26] Essentially a novelty act, the jug band's consciously cornpone segments blended medicine show buffoonery with string band professionalism. To folksongs like "Froggy Went a-Courtin'" and "Oh Susannah," and later on, with hit parade items like "I'm Walkin'" and "Shot-Gun Boogie," they brought a controlled mayhem of washboard and harmonica, honking bicycle horns and loopy slide whistles. The group emerged from Acuff's days as a young performer in East Tennessee. During the summer of 1932, he worked as a fiddler and singer for Doc Hauer, appearing sometimes in blackface for the shows' "after pieces."[27] These comic skits, revived and enlarged in Pap's Jug Band, included stage routines that involved an exploding whiskey keg, a skit in which the band members wore tuxedos in various states of disrepair while playing comically reworked classical music numbers, and a sight gag in which Pap unfurled a twenty-foot-long shirttail.

Meanwhile, on the pavement nearby, the Nashville Washboard Band transmitted their own theatricality. For all the proximities of place and time that Pap's Jug Band and the Nashville Washboard Band shared, and commonalities that began with their homemade instruments, the two groups communicated different messages, just as they heeded diverse cultural sensibilities. For the Nashville Washboard Band, the fleeting transactions of the sidewalk gave them little chance to develop radio-ready characters like the taciturn "Pap" (played by guitarist Lonnie Wilson and, later, Joe Zinkan) or the trademark horse laugh of jug-blowing "Bashful Brother Oswald" (Pete Kirby). They carried no props apart from their instruments, wore no particular stage garb, and offered no scripted dialogue between songs. During their recording session, a moment arises that gives a sense of how they met the pressures of their performing milieu, a situation wholly unlike that faced by their counterparts inside the Opry.

On race records of that time, washboards found a presence in "hokum" music. This word, which combines "hocus-pocus" with "bunkum," serves as another name for the washboard and jug bands employing "fake" instruments. But hokum also identified an enormously popular, often double-entendre, light-hearted blues form. The Nashville Washboard Band invoked this kind of musical comedy in their performance of "I'll Be Glad When You're Dead, You Rascal You."[28] Previously, "Rascal"'s biggest exposure came through Louis Armstrong's performances, including his first appearance on film, wearing a leopard skin and surrounded by a sea of bubbles, and reprised in a 1932 Betty Boop cartoon. On their recording, the Nashville Washboard Band spliced two metrically similar pieces, the popular hit and the children's traditional teasing song, "You're Bound to Look Like a Monkey When You Grow Old."[29]

Following the banjo-mandolin's introduction, a husky-voiced lead, reminiscent of Armstrong, starts the title verse only to face immediate protests from a whining "rascal." This voice, feigning a woman's and filled with mock injury, goads her antagonist, "Why you be glad?" The insults and ripostes continue, and midway through the recording, after the verse in which "the monkey in the zoo / sends his best regards to you," "Rascal" segues into "You're Bound to Look Like a Monkey When You Grow Old." Again the high-pitched editorialist insists, "Don't call me no monkey," and later, "You talking about me?" This playful spate of claims and rejoinders had by then appeared on a number of recordings that included jug band renditions, featured comical call-and-response, and in one case featured a banjo-mandolin among their instruments.[30] To whatever degree these precedents influenced the Nashville Washboard Band, another inheritance also affected them.

As soon as the song ended, recordist Alan Lomax asked the band if they had made up the piece. "No," one replied, "we didn't make the tune. Started with 'Glad You Dead You Rascal You,' and we just put the other part there." Lomax then remarks, "sounds like the dozens," and the men laugh heartily. The dozens denotes an African American folk tradition of traded insults, a street-corner game of verbal one-upmanship that often turns obscene. Here, in this blending of the two playfully barbed songs, the contest remains sweetly humorous. Yet the shaping presence of the dozens remains—from the monkey stereotype to the female impersonation, from stage minstrelsy to black cabaret. That they might play the fool and play the dozens marks a cultural terrain the band negotiated as African American entertainers on the streets of Nashville.

Performer and composer Bobby Hebb knew that territory well. A native Nashvillian internationally renowned for his 1966 hit "Sunny," Hebb (1938–2010) was the sole black member of Pap's Jug Band. Before that, he grew up playing in his family's jug band (his term for it) during the same decade that the Nashville Washboard Band visited John Work. Hebb credited the formative role that street music played in his life. "The jug band . . . showed me that I should advance. . . . There was room to work there as a musician," he remembered.[31] "It said 'go with this.'" As someone who later starred as a marquee performer with the Beatles on their final stadium tour and cowrote "A Natural Man," the song that became Lou Rawls's Grammy-winning single, he brought a unique perspective to the older music, bridging its artistry of stage and street. Through his eyes the daily round of the Nashville Washboard Band draws nearer.

Bobby Hebb's parents, both blind, depended on the Hebbs' Kitchen Cabinet Orchestra as their source of income. As a young boy in the 1940s Hebb played spoons and danced with them. His oldest brother played a lard-can bass and another played washboard. One sister played triangle and "all of us would sing." His father and mother each played guitar, most often performing gospel songs, but also such nineteenth-century songster numbers as "Comin' 'round the Mountain, Charming Betsy." Hebb described his parents as "street workers," and he included in this category not just musicians, but others who took to the streets vending such items as shopping bags.[32] The Hebbs appeared throughout the week along with their fellow sidewalk entrepreneurs. In those years of urban foot traffic before suburbanization, open-air sellers, including the street bands, still seemed to be "all over the neighborhoods."[33]

In a glimmer of the Nashville Washboard Band, or at least of players living close by them, Hebb remembered that "the group over on Gay Street was Mr. Clark's, that's all I know." He also noted that jug blowers found it prudent to use a clear bottle rather than the customary earthenware containers, "so the police would know that you didn't have something that you should not have in it." He stressed the watchfulness this street work demanded, especially when it came to musicianship. Whenever someone approached, he would describe that individual to his sightless father: "I'd look around and see how the guys were dressed. I'd pass that on to Dad, and he'd know what to play." This adaptivity extended to the family's washboard, spoons, and lard-can bass. Hebb quietly remarked, "That's all the instruments one could afford at that time."

With his father's death in April 1951, the family group ended, but not Hebb's jug band career. Thirteen years old, and by then an experienced performer, he went to WSM, the Grand Ole Opry's station, where he auditioned. During a television variety show hosted by producer Owen Bradley, Hebb performed his routine playing with Bradley's orchestra. Roy Acuff, watching at home, called the studio and asked to speak with him. This began Bobby Hebb's membership in Pap's Jug Band, a job he kept until 1954, when he left for Chicago and began playing with Bo Diddley. Hebb's part in Acuff's show, like others in Pap's Jug Band, consisted of a featured turn in which he would perform two or three songs, usually with spoons and dancing, and then go offstage.

Hebb considered what they did both "legitimate music and humorous music." He singled out fiddler Howdy Forrester, who may have played "Hungarian Rhapsody" for its joke value, but "he played for real." Acuff's band, Hebb said, "used it [Pap's Jug Band] as a comedy but they wanted to prove that they could play music too." As for Acuff's past use of blackface in the medicine show and Hebb's potentially racialist place as an African American within this band, he felt that had no role in how he was presented. Without dismissing that past, and in a gentle mockery of Acuff's voice, he addressed an imaginary audience: "Now children, this is how it was. Now, this is how it is now." Hebb, the second black performer ever to appear at the Grand Ole Opry, saw Acuff as having expanded racial understanding in country music. "Roy Acuff opened up a big door, man." In that way, Acuff mirrored another change Hebb witnessed during the civil rights years: "LBJ was not who he was in 1959 that he was in 1965."

Bobby Hebb's insights speak for others who followed this occupation. It seems inescapable that Hebbs' Kitchen Cabinet Orchestra, the Nashville Washboard Band, and Blind James Campbell's group did not at some point feel "the man with the headache stick"—the name Memphis jug band musician Gus Cannon gave for that scourge of the sidewalk singer: the beat cop and his billy club.[34] Despite the constraints of segregation that circumscribed this work so steeped in race and this music so emblematic of poverty, these musicians opened themselves to influences both local and national. "When I woke up early in the morning, I woke up to bluegrass," said Hebb referring to the radio in his family's home. "When it came time to go to bed in the evenings—you know, sit down and listen to the news—we listened to Walter Winchell." Later he built his career as much on cultural sharing as on cultural distinctiveness. This breadth echoes in the Nashville Washboard Band. However marginalized by their calling, they survived the scuffle of the street by drawing on multiple sources that they translated into a distinctive musical vocabulary. None better illustrates this impulse than their coruscating performance of "Soldier's Joy." Or, as Judge Hay at the Grand Ole Opry put it only days before to introduce their counterparts in Pap's Jug Band, hot music with trimmings.

————————

On July 15, 1942, the Nashville Washboard Band returned to John Work's house to record. "The machine is running badly too," wrote Alan Lomax in his report.[35] Lomax, in charge of operating the disc cutter that evening, had come to Nashville to begin the second leg of the joint Fisk University and Library of Congress folk culture study of Coahoma County, Mississippi. The project got underway the previous summer when he traveled with John Work III to the Delta. Among their accomplishments in that brief but productive trip, the two researchers made the first recordings of McKinley Morganfield, the tractor driver and musician better known as Muddy Waters. Now in Work's home, and once again with musicians never previously recorded, they faced a different challenge: the dynamic range of the Nashville Washboard Band exceeded the recording equipment's capacities.

Lomax fed the band's several instruments into a single microphone, resulting in a sometimes muffled, overrecorded sound. Unfortunate mike placement and limited frequency response particularly obscured the lard-can bass solo, reducing it to indecipherable rumble. Of the five songs, three tunes, and six demonstrations the band performed on two discs, "Soldier's Joy" arose approximately halfway through the session.[36] Like the two breakdowns that followed it, this recording has far less distortion and much better balance than some that featured lyrics.

As the cutting arm wound out from the center of the sixteen-inch disc, thirty-nine-year-old bandleader James Kelly carried the melodic lead on his banjo-mandolin. Kelly launches into "Soldier's Joy" with biting authority, hammering and pulling the notes along the fingerboard. His strong accents at the end of phrases, fierce right-hand strumming, and constant focus on the forward part of the beat turn the dance reel into a display piece. Not only would pedestrians otherwise passing an upturned hat likely have stopped to listen to it, many would have recognized it, too.

Of all the traditional fiddle tunes to cross the Atlantic, none has found greater currency than "Soldier's Joy." Related to "Logan Waters," an Irish air from the 1680s, this widespread melody appeared in print during the late eighteenth century, including a 1778 Scottish collection of reels and minuets, and by 1780, two English fife tutors.[37] It also reached the English broadside press in the 1760s, during the years of the French and Indian War.[38] Called by one scholar "a bad old song to a good old tune," its patriotic outlook reflected fears within England itself about a possible French invasion.[39] Each stanza expands on the meaning of soldier's joy—from the conquest of foes to the pleasures after battle. The closing lines read:

Haste, haste, ye patriot friends! Advance!
And let us scourge perfidious France!
Strike all your instruments of war,
And let the sound be heard from far!
Till, level'd from their hopes on high,
Beneath your feet the victims lie;
Then love and wine each hour employ,
For such shall be the soldier's joy.[40]

Robert Burns tapped similar emotions for *The Jolly Beggars: A Cantata.* Originally titled *Love and Liberty,* his operatic poem features a troupe of imaginary mendicants that includes a fiddler, a prostitute, and a tinker. For its first piece of music, Burns chose "Soldier's Joy."[41] To this air a homeless veteran, shorn of his arm and leg from wartime wounds (bearing, too, a few scars from romantic scraps), roars out his saga to passersby. The soldier, reduced to street beggary, details his long service, first at the "heights of Abram," a reference to the battle for Quebec during the French and Indian War. Then he names figures of more current renown—"Curtis," rear admiral Sir Roger Curtis, and "Elliot," General George Augustus Eliott—both leaders in the British defense of Gibraltar. That siege ended in 1783, two years before Burns's *Cantata* appeared.

These "Soldier's Joy" songs, responding to contemporary events, relied on the tune's familiarity with listeners. It continued to circulate, and by the nineteenth century had found life throughout the British Isles as both a village and Morris dance. Novelist Thomas Hardy, who played accordion and fiddle, saluted it in *Far from the Madding Crowd:* "At the end of three-quarters of an hour of thunderous footing ["Soldier's Joy"] still possesses more stimulative properties for the heel and toe than the majority of other dances at their first opening."[42] Its appeal reached Scandinavia, too, as titles found in Denmark, Finland, and Sweden made reference to the English antecedent.[43]

By the late eighteenth century, "Soldier's Joy" had also arrived in the United States. Mentioned as one of several set dances in a 1794 Massachusetts diary, it came into print with Elias Howe's 1851 *School for the Violin.*[44] The tune spread, adapted into a breadth of regional styles—Blue Ridge and Southern Appalachian, Ozark and Western.[45] From tightly noted, arpeggiated performances based on written sources to blues-inflected mountain fiddle solos passed on by living example, "Soldier's Joy" came to figure—and still does today—in seemingly every fiddler's repertory. Some players explore it with long bowing motions that displace the beat, while others rely on its harmonic mold, using rhythmic shuffles to define it with just the barest melodic detail. This interpretative range extends to the tune's name, with titles like "French Four," "King's Head," "Rock the Cradle Lucy," "Love Somebody," and "Payday in the Army." But no matter what players might call it, whether they approach it elaborately or rudimentarily, learn it first-hand or from tune books, radio, and records, their embrace of "Soldier's Joy" has crossed all levels of skill to become a standard. Along the way it also transcended racial divides.

The Nashville Washboard Band's performance of "Soldier's Joy" reflects what the Grand Ole Opry's first African American performer, DeFord Bailey, termed "black hillbilly music."[46] Bailey (1899–1982) learned to play from his grandfather Lewis Bailey, a locally celebrated ex-slave fiddler from Smith County, Tennessee, whose barn dance selections and fiddle contest entries included such hillbilly favorites as "Fox Chase," "Old Joe Clark," "Old Hen Cackle," and "Lost John." These pieces that the elder Bailey passed on to his harmonica-playing grandson identify a repertory that blacks shared with their white neighbors. "Everybody around me grew up playin' that," DeFord Bailey recalled. "Fiddles and banjos and guitars; they weren't playin' no blues then. It was black hillbilly music."

Neighborhood accounts and regional recordings amplify Bailey's memories. Tennessee's Fentress County fiddler Cuje Bertram, an African American born at the end of the nineteenth century, recalled how his father, born in 1855, fiddled this tune for black and white dances, just as Cuje did himself.[47] In 1927, African American fiddler Jim Booker, playing in Taylor's Kentucky Boys, made the earliest commercially issued recording of "Soldier's Joy" that includes a black musician.[48] A second-generation Kentucky fiddler, Booker (b. 1872) leads "Soldier's Joy" in a fluid, hoedown style that gives no clue about his color. He recorded, too, with Doc Roberts, a white Kentucky fiddler who made scores of records in the same genre. Roberts, raised near Booker, in turn credited a mutual friend, Owen Walker, an older black fiddler as a primary source of his material.[49] These shared melodies point back to the nineteenth century and that era's social dances.[50] In Jim Booker's case this includes tunes played by his fiddling father, a former slave born in 1837, also

CHAPTER 5

named Jim Booker. Long remembered as an influential player in his community, the senior Jim Booker drew this cross-racial musical exchange even further into the past.

Closer to Nashville, Fisk University chemistry professor and song collector Thomas W. Talley gathered a "Soldier's Joy" tune and text from black sources in Middle Tennessee. He published these results in 1922, two years before any recordings of the song, white or black, appeared.[51] He did the bulk of his music collecting in Pulaski, a town located some seventy-five miles south of Nashville. With respect to the Nashville Washboard Band, Talley's efforts there have added significance. Just as James Kelly and his bandmates finished "Soldier's Joy," the disc machine still turning, Alan Lomax asked Kelly his age, and then inquired:

Lomax: "Where'd you learn to play this tune?"

Kelly: "Down in Pulaski."

"Do you play all mountain music up in there?"

"Yes I do."

"Play for dances and things?"

"Oh, yes sir."

"Do the colored and white folks up there play the same kind of music, or do each one have their own kind, or they sort of swap 'em?"

"No, they swap 'em. You see some of them playing . . . a lot at funerals—banjo players and fiddlers."

"Both colored and white, banjo players and fiddlers?"

Here a fellow band member interjects: "What he means is 'Do they play, pick on the same kind of music? Breakdowns?'"

Kelly: "Do I play that?"

Lomax: "In general."

"Oh. They plays mostly lots of breakdowns."

"Negroes and whites?"

"Yeah."

"What instruments do you know how to play?"

"Any of the stringed instruments."

"Fiddle too?"

"Yes, fiddle too."

"Well, play us 'Cotton-eyed Joe,' will you. You tuned up right to play it?"

Kelly hesitates, and Lomax suggests: "Well, play us another breakdown that you know real good."

Kelly: "All right."[52]

Here, one of the guitarists sounds a chord. Kelly strikes a note or two on his mandolin, and the band leaps into "Arkansas Traveler."

For all the terseness of this exchange, Lomax has ventured a key question about the shared repertory and the racial-cultural approaches available within it. Kelly's stumbling reply appears to have been governed more by his seeking an agreeable answer than by pondering the matter's complexity. Still, he makes clear that whites and blacks swapped "Soldier's Joy" and other square-dance tunes with one another. As for each race having its own kind of breakdown music, his band's performance brings that truth to life.

In "Soldier's Joy," as with other common-stock reels played by black folk musicians, there repeatedly surfaces a performance style bearing what Olly Wilson calls the "heterogeneous sound ideal"—"a kaleidoscopic range of dramatically contrasting qualities of sound."[53] He likens it to a mosaic: "the desirable musical sound texture is one that contains a combination of diverse timbres. . . . contrast of color—heterogeneity of sound rather than similarity of color or homogeneity of sound." Unlike a European string quartet that seamlessly blends that consort into a unified voice, this sensibility favors a composite of disparate voices.

Black vocal music correspondingly makes repeated use of differing pitches and rhythms. Along with the sudden swoops and cries heard in field hollers and the melismatic shifts that make up long-meter hymn singing, Wilson cites Duke Ellington's famous lyric "It don't mean a thing if it ain't got that swing."[54] Ellington articulated in this rhyme a core value in black music, further demonstrated by its coda: "do-*wha,* do-*wha,* do-*wha.*"[55] These compounds, each part pushing against the other, capture the tonal and rhythmic contrast that Wilson found characteristic of African and African American music.

A black string band from Campaign, Tennessee, that collector Robert S. Jamieson documented in the 1940s sets Wilson's principle in a living scene. In September 1946, using Library of Congress recording discs, Jamieson traveled to this small town on the L&N railroad eighty miles east of Nashville, where his banjo-playing grandfather's family still resided. When Jamieson first learned of banjoist Murphy Gribble, fiddler John Lusk, and guitarist Albert York, who had been performing locally since 1912, he only knew that he was going to record "the most popular band for black and white dances in six counties."[56] Not until an hour before the session did he even learn that the band was black. While this trio lived in a highly restrictive society, they reached across its racial barriers with their music. The one comment Gribble shared with Jamieson about the origins of his playing style also suggests the source of his band's appeal: "That's the way the old folks do it."[57] Much as DeFord Bailey had recalled from his younger days in a county nearby, these musicians, too, managed in an environment where dancers of both races still enjoyed the traditional reels.

For Jamieson, the significance of these old ways dramatically intensified when he heard the 1925 Gennett releases of white banjoist Homer Davenport. Davenport lived just beyond the Sequatchie Valley from Gribble, Lusk, and York, and his recordings reveal that he shared with them both repertory and technique. Unlike so many of the verbal accounts that evoke black-white musical interaction, the recordings of Gribble and Davenport provide almost without precedent "the sound of the source as well as the transferee."[58] Yet Jamieson also told me that marked stylistic differences separated these two players. Davenport hewed to the melody and filled in spaces behind his fiddler Jess Young in keeping with white string band practice. Gribble, following another aesthetic, worked his ever-varying and often intermittent lead patterns that he called "broke-legged rhythm." For Jamieson, a banjo player himself, the effect of this heterogeneous style was unlike anything he had ever experienced:

> What we heard . . . was so different it was almost disorienting. The fiddle did not always lead the melody, but passed it to the banjo, like runners passing the baton. Half the time the melody was played by the banjo, the fiddle moaning low rhythmic chords, over and over. Suddenly, at the second part of the tune, the fiddle would leap into an upper octave, with a wild cry, and take over the burden of the tune. The banjo would then play a loose and free polyphonic obbligato around a rudimentary suggestion of the melody, ranging far away melodically, omitting strong downbeats, dancing a different step rhythmically—and this was most radical of all for banjo—not hitting all the upbeats and downbeats, with sudden startling gaps and hesitations. . . . Down below all, the guitar produced steady deep heartbeats, like the throb of a great engine in the bowels of a ship, laying down the full chords that defined the threshing floor upon which fiddle and banjo leaped and soared. . . . Bach himself would have listened with delight to its wild freedom.[59]

The Nashville Washboard Band likewise brought African American musical ideals to "Soldier's Joy." Those sonic features that Stu Jamieson so cherished and Olly Wilson enumerated virtually describe their high-density playing: diverse timbres fill its musical canvas, framed by the contrasting, cross-rhythmic accents of metallic percussion. Out in the open air, playing for any who might come their way, James Kelly and his companions drew on the resources of black tradition to shape their performance of "Soldier's Joy" and enrich their music making.

Two weeks after the Nashville Washboard Band played "Soldier's Joy" into the disc machine at John Work's, fiddler Henry "Son" Sims (1890–1958), accompanist to Muddy Waters in his Mississippi Delta string band, made his Library of Congress recordings. During that session, Sims told Alan Lomax how fiddle tunes such as "Arkansas Traveler," "Turkey in the Straw," and "Leather Breeches" had once enjoyed popularity where he lived. But "by 1912 & 14, the square dances had already disappeared."[60] With their decline, the five-string banjo had also fallen away from local practice, he estimated "about 1923." The changing musical preferences of his community led Sims, a former accompanist to Charley Patton, to play music of a more modern sort, largely blues, to accompany his community's dances. With names like the "Shimmy," "Turkey Trot," and "Grizzly Bear," these vigorous steps allowed for a more intimate, yet still lively couple dancing that supplanted the shared reels of past years. Sims pursued this newer musical direction until late into his life.

John Work III found a similar shift in community taste where he lived. He made this point during his 1941 Fisk chapel concert. In presenting Nathan Frazier, Frank Patterson, and Ford Britton, he called their trio of banjo, fiddle, and guitar the "answer to a folklorist's dream."[61] He praised them as skilled keepers of the nineteenth-century rural dance reels. For Work their surfacing in Nashville brought him intense satisfactions. Eleven years earlier, in his master's thesis, he wrote about the disappearance of the five-string banjo despite its celebrated role in this once-pervasive idiom. He expanded on that sentiment in his 1938 Fisk address, commenting that he had never heard a banjo played in living tradition. Like the social dances it formerly accompanied, the instrument itself had fallen out of favor. By his 1940 book he makes no mention of the banjo at all. Now this recently discovered string band allowed him to revise his reporting, much as he had done with the city's washboard bands. Yet through all these disappearances and renewals, Work stayed constant in his belief that folk processes adapt and endure. With "Soldier's Joy," the Nashville Washboard Band proved his point.

James Kelly's banjo-mandolin coupled practices past and current. His raspy tone recalls Olly Wilson's African American sound ideal. With the banjo's inherent lack of sustain and rapid note decay, Kelly emphasizes the scraping, percussive drive that helps characterize this penchant. His instrument also met the changing repertory and social tenor of the present day. Though the five-string banjo carried the burdens of earlier blackface minstrelsy, this newer instrument, a hybrid joining of a mandolin's neck to a banjo's hoop,

CHAPTER 5

found favor in black usage. In the 1880s the mandolin became the nation's most popular fretted instrument. Black newspapers published between the late 1880s and the mid-1890s include numerous references to mandolins played by black musicians across the social spectrum: from polite gatherings to burlesque houses, from faux-Italian serenades to interludes for stage whistlers and serpentine dancers.[62] The banjo-mandolin found its most prominent place in the professional dance bands that emerged at the century's end. Possessing the volume needed to perform in those ensembles, it well served the stomps and slow drags that attracted that period's dancers leading up to World War I.[63] With its steel strings and plectrum technique, amplified by the banjo's sharp ringing, a player could focus on chord accompaniments and the short breakaway leads this music invited.

On multiple levels, James Kelly had made a deft choice. Acoustically his instrument could cut through traffic noise. Aesthetically his instrument served songs and styles currently embraced by black audiences. Equipped with a mandolin, Kelly looked ahead urbanely. At the same time, in his playing a banjo, he sustained a countryside sound and, by all appearances, offered a symbol of the instrument's past, one forever linked to black culture. A key to the Nashville Washboard Band's survival as street performers depended on their assimilation of iconic images. That awareness included their bringing recognizable melodies into their musical vernacular, and extended to their instrumental techniques and choice of instruments.

A related set of influences affected the band's bassist. With his fingers bandaged against the bite of the metal cord, Thomas James Carroll produced a sound on his "bull fiddle" then booming from big band hits to jukebox blues. In older string bands, players typically bowed their stand-up basses. By the end of the nineteenth century, however, a new technique had taken hold. "Rhythms created by plucking and slapping," musicologist Dick Spottswood has observed, made "the strings . . . more supple and energetic, and allowed a good musician to propel a band with staccato attacks on or around the beat, shaping and enhancing the new syncopations of ragtime, blues and early jazz. Plucked basses also enabled the 4/4 rhythms that would dominate popular music after the 1920s."[64] Country musicians, like Jack Taylor of the Prairie Ramblers, and Red Jones of Roy Acuff and His Crazy Tennesseans, soon copied the example set by their black colleagues, incorporating the single string and slap techniques into their repertories. Here, in "Soldier's Joy," as with his other pieces, Carroll put this propulsive finger style to use, acting as the group's central timekeeper.

That evening at John Work's, he recounted his contact with the instrument. While in El Paso working as a performer in a traveling show, he needed a portable bass. "The way I started out . . . everybody I see was playing washboard and drums. At the time . . . I met up with three sisters and a brother . . . and they didn't have any bass to go with it at all . . . I just happened to think about a lard can. If you can get a tune out of a tub, well, I'm sure I can do that with a lard can."[65] Carroll then told how he made one, first sawing down a broomstick, to which he "slapped" on a clothesline wire and rigged it to a nail. By tilting this arm back against the rim of the lard can, he found he could produce different pitches. At Lomax's request, he showed how it worked, running down the metal string with changing rhythmic combinations and pauses. The last piece he recorded that night was an instrumental duet with James Kelly. The two played "Bye Bye Blues," a big-band song written in 1930 that by 1942 had become a standard. Here Kelly plays it on his banjo-mandolin in his country ragging style, while Carroll, on the lard-can bass, adds his up-to-date drive. The session ended in a burst of percussive timbres.

Such variegated tones radiated most powerfully from the band's dominant musical personality, their blind washboardist Theophilus Stokes. Throughout the recordings, but particularly on the fiddle tunes, his bandmates provided him a harmonic and melodic amphitheater, giving him room to ornament each piece independently—from a steady roll against the washboard's surface to hitting his metal plates as if he were stirring the inside of a tin cup. His animated playing style prompted Alan Lomax to record him that night doing five washboard solos that he classified into "breakdown," "blues," and "swing" tempos.[66] Stokes takes each one at a quick pace, using off-beats, but in a regular pattern suggestive of how a buck dancer might sequence his steps. Stokes knocks his rub-boards more than he scrapes them, giving his music a marching-band, parade-drumming feel. Within this essentially old-fashioned approach, he plays tirelessly, giving the band its distinctiveness and depth.

Just as Alan Lomax had likened Carroll's bass to "the old African one string instrument," he found that Stokes's playing mirrored traditions that went beyond the local or even regional.[67] After driving the band members home that night (noting, too, that when they stopped for a beer along the way "the bartender wouldn't let me drink with them"), Lomax sketched in his notebook an overhead view of Stokes's self-styled "V-8" washboard rig.[68] Beneath the drawing, Lomax wrote, "His washboarding was as tricky as any Haitian drummer's." Around 1980, when Lomax revisited these recordings for a prospective LP release, he returned to that thought. "The washboard,"

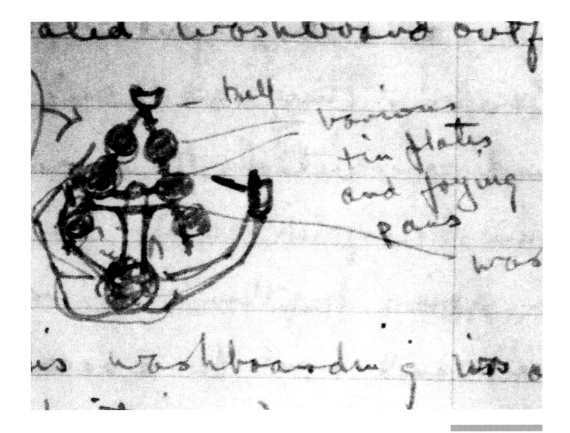

he jotted down, "with drums, bells, scrapers, rattles (similar to the steel bands of Trinidad). Outdoing the whites with [their] own music—these . . . precursors of jazz bands."[69]

In associating the washboard with the African diaspora as well as jazz origins, Lomax reveals both his own collecting experiences and his overview of the music's dissemination. Rooted in similarly scraped African and Afro-Caribbean instruments, from a sub-Saharan jawbone to the ridges of a Cuban *guiro*, the washboard had become a feature on numerous jazz, blues, and novelty recordings. Clarence Williams and Tiny Parham helped bring the washboard to recorded jazz, following its initial commercial success in 1924 with Jasper Taylor's work behind clarinetist Jimmy O'Bryant.[70] Taylor's nimble playing, more a wooden knock than a raspy scrape, occupies one end of the instrument's stylistic range. Other players stressed different potentialities. The much-recorded blues singer and composer Washboard Sam (born Robert Brown) simulated a snare drum sound on his records with Big Bill Broonzy, while choosing a quieter brush stroke, rubbing and tapping the board to accompany pieces like Bukka White's "Jitterbug Swing."[71]

FIGURE 24. Overhead drawing of Theophilus Stokes and his V-8 washboard rig, drawn by Alan Lomax, Nashville, Tennessee, July 15, 1942. Courtesy of Alan Lomax Archives.

But whatever texture these musicians favored—from the swoosh, rattle, and chug of perennially popular train imitations to the kaleidoscope of sounds made by Theophilus Stokes—the instrument never escapes its origins.

As part of a street entertainment performed by those without means, washboard playing, along with jugs, spoons, and other "found instruments," reflects, says Richard Blaustein, "the social and economic gulf which divides those who can afford the right tool for the job from those who must make do with whatever is at hand."[72] For DeFord Bailey that necessity afforded no embarrassment. He recounted a houseful of homemade instruments as expressive of invention as of indigence. The first banjo he possessed was a groundhog hide stretched over a cheese box hoop. He told how a number-two washtub worked as a bass fiddle. Corn-stalk fiddles, comb and tissue-paper kazoos, cane fifes, bamboo-cut panpipes, and animal bones all served in Bailey's childhood years as musical devices. "You know, there's some music in everything," he said.[73] "If we couldn't find nothing else, we could always blow in a jug or beat on some skillets and pans."

For others, these instruments simply reinforced the idea that blacks were irrepressibly musical and inherently juvenile. Music researcher and recordist Harold Courlander recalled going into an eastern Alabama grocery store in 1950 and watching a man choose some iron skillets intended solely for musical purposes. He tapped a number of them with his fingernail, looking for two that best emitted the tone he wanted. In a near-classic account of cultural misunderstanding, the white storekeeper remarked to Courlander, also white, "I don't know why they're always doing that. They seem to think you can tell how good a pan is by whacking it."[74] "As makeshift as these in-struments may seem," Courlander observed elsewhere, "they are anything but haphazard."[75] He explained that musical ideas can survive even without an instrument, just as various cultures can approach the same instrument differently. Scottish bagpipe music, for instance, does not sound like its Serbian counterpart. In the end, social groups heed the templates they know, no matter what lies at hand.

This adaptivity comes back to Theophilus Stokes playing his V-8 wash-boards on the streets of Nashville. For all the torrents of sound he produced and the amusement he may have provoked, he handles his instrument like a 1920s drum kit with sock, snare, and sticks. However varied his timbres and dynamics, he does not audibly pursue novelty washboarding like Pap's Jug Band or Spike Jones, who used it to make intentionally comic sounds. Using only his finger thimbles, he makes a shuffle, sometimes a slap effect, and even "buzz strokes" that simulate a drum stick's multiple bounces, staying always within the dictates of the tune.[76] In "Soldier's Joy" and other tunes, Stokes plays on the beat, but also subdivides it in various ways, hitting off-beats and inserting triplets. His effects seem reminiscent of Warren "Baby" Dodds, the famed drummer—and former washboardist—who played behind King Oliver, Jelly Roll Morton, and Louis Armstrong in the early years of recorded jazz. In a 1946 phonographic study of his style, Dodds demonstrated these ideas on a conventional drum set.[77] In a piece set to march time, he swings from cymbals to tom toms to cowbells to woodblock to rims. Dodds in effect methodically outlines how Theophilus Stokes fervidly wielded his tin plates, frying pans, and double washboards. If Stokes drew a crowd for the strangeness of his instrument and the power of his sightless musical authority—factors that might also have projected as racially characteristic and self-deprecating—he plays "Soldier's Joy" for all its worth on his washboard deluxe.

Just as James Kelly reinterpreted the tune onto his rag-influenced banjo-mandolin, Thomas Carroll's plucked bass propelled it with big-band modernity. Meanwhile, guitarist Frank Dalton kept it country, playing his first-position open chords. Filling the audible space between, Theophilus Stokes transported the reel from a mountain frolic to a New Orleans second-line parade. He summoned a black music heritage of homemade percussion and heterogeneous sound as he flew across his V-8 washboards, with his rattling, stirring, socking, beating, tapping. In bringing together these many-sided pieces of the American musical mosaic, the Nashville Washboard Band vibrantly illustrates in "Soldier's Joy" how an eighteenth-century fiddle tune from the British Isles, in Nat Hentoff's words, "leaps across the centuries in jazz time."[78]

Though Blind James Campbell's group marked the last of Nashville's traditionally based African American street ensembles, the Nashville Washboard Band that John Work documented survived into the early 1950s. "They wore no costumes," remembered veteran Nashville deejay Hugh Cherry, who first saw the band in 1950.[79] Over the next five years, Cherry watched them play on Friday and Saturday evenings outside the Andrew Jackson Hotel, where he stayed. At this spot near the capitol, the band's personnel changed from one weekend to another, sometimes adding a fiddle or a jug, while the double-washboard, rhythm guitar, lard-can bass, and banjo-mandolin remained a constant. Whatever their composition on a given night, they did not present themselves as invented personalities like Pap's Jug Band. They had to attract their physically transient audience by the sheer force of their playing. However much the Nashville Washboard Band may have animated their songs with caricature, in the end they made music their principal message.

"In Nashville," said Hugh Cherry, "the great contributors are not the performers, but the musicians." Though Cherry was speaking of the session players who appear on countless Music Row recordings, he was referring as well to the Nashville Washboard Band. Time and again he watched them fill this unheralded role. In those years when Hugh Cherry saw them play on summer weekend nights, his colleague Paul Cohen, producer for Decca records and head of the label's Nashville operations, often remarked that "someone ought to record them." Like Cherry, Cohen also stayed at the Andrew Jackson Hotel when he came to town and as a result frequently saw the group perform. But nothing happened, for, as Cherry said, "It would have been a recording for academic purposes." The group was neither smooth enough for air play nor pop enough in style to be marketable. "In the commercial end," Cherry concluded, "we didn't know anything about it."

If consigned to obscurity, the band members understood what they represented. This exchange appeared in the notes to their 1942 recording session after they performed the blues "Going Away to Make It Lonesome Here":

Q. Why do you call the blues, alley music?
A. 'Cause when our poor folks want the blues, they say "put it in the alley!"[80]

Whoever offered up this reply, his light-hearted answer spoke not only to music but to sociology. Blues played in an alley style denotes a low-down quality, a hoarse and raspy texture. It amounts to a musical correlative of the uneven pavement, discarded leavings, and crowded quarters of these enclaves. "Put it in the alley" points to a place little acknowledged and hidden from mainstream view, with values largely invisible except for those who live there. The Nashville Washboard Band produced an art from the alley, taking the barest of materials and turning that poverty into surplus. These players and others like them, who John Work called "of lower caste but no lower inspiration," attest to the creative possibilities present in everyday life. One of their peers said it well. Former Memphis Jug Band washboard player Robert Burse described an elderly neighbor, "Old Johnson," who once headed his own sidewalk string band that included a violin, a guitar, and drums. "He's a jive man," said Burse, "just like I was. Lots o' tricks, you know. Made something out of nothing."[81]

$\boxed{6}$

Vera Hall

The Life That We Live

O
N A BRITTLE, YELLOWED INDEX CARD AMONG JOHN LOMAX'S
voluminous family papers lies an account of Vera Hall singing "Another Man Done Gone." Writing in her own hand, Ruby Terrill
Lomax evokes the first time she and her husband heard Vera mention the
song, followed by their efforts to coax it from this self-effacing, thirty-eight-
year-old singer whose grandparents had been slaves:

> Mr. Lomax asked her if she knew any other blues.
> "No sir, I b'lieve not, but my husband knows some. He sings and plays the
> guitar."
> "What is his best blues?
> "I like 'Another Man Done Gone.'"
> "Would he sing it for us?"
> "He ain't home much, but I think he be home tomorrow. Maybe I can git him
> to come sing for you."
> But he didn't come home and Vera reported without him.
> "How does the song go, Vera. Can't you sing it for us?"
> "No sir, I never sing it excep' to myself.
> "You sing it for us."
> "Well le's see if I can catch it up," and after a pause she straightened herself up

in her chair and out came her beautiful tones on 'Another Man Done Gone,' six verses in all. Delighted, we recorded it at once.[1]

The discs themselves fill in the rest. On October 31, 1940, at the Livingston, Alabama, home of author, painter, and folksong collector Ruby Pickens Tartt, Vera Hall (1902–1964) sang "Another Man Done Gone" twice into Lomax's machine.[2] During the first take, the partially filled recording blank ran out of space, abruptly ending the song. The second time, however, Lomax used a fresh side, allowing Vera to include all her verses. Just as she finished, but before he lifted the cutting arm and turned off the microphone, he remarked, "That's perfect."[3] Lomax's summation, itself almost purred, saluted more than an unmarred recording.

"Another Man Done Gone" became Vera Hall's most celebrated performance. Carl Sandburg recalled listening to it more than a dozen consecutive times during a January 1944 visit to Lomax's Dallas home, later including it in his second folksong anthology and learning it himself. The poet termed it "one of the strikingly original creations of Negro singing art."[4] Of a similar mind, composer Elie Siegmeister went to Livingston, Alabama, in the early 1940s and met with Vera and her husband. He soon incorporated their music in his choral group's recitals.[5] Following his father's lead, Alan Lomax also called on Vera and by spring 1942 had selected this number for one of the Folk Archive's first releases, including it on their inaugural album series.[6] That choice led others to the song, inspiring recordings by Johnny Cash and Harry Belafonte, blues enthusiasts such as John Mayall and Jorma Kaukonen, and folk revivalists stretching from Odetta to the Carolina Chocolate Drops. These covers—and there are more—span nearly seventy years since Vera Hall first sang "Another Man Done Gone" for the disc cutter. The appeal of her recording, apparent to John Lomax from the start, turns out to be perennial.

He even tried to tell her so. In 1941, during a daylong trip to Livingston that involved no recording at all, John and Ruby Lomax called on Vera unannounced. Raised on a nearby farm, Vera now lived in town working as a domestic servant and cook. When the Lomaxes arrived at Vera's home late that afternoon, she was caring for her two grandchildren and ailing mother. By then Agnes Hall's health required her to stay with Vera. The ten-mile trek to the farm where Vera's surviving sister still lived made it difficult for doctor visits and unsafe for Agnes to remain so far away. The family had also recently suffered the loss of Vera's daughter, a passing reported in the Lomaxes' notes.

Despite these stresses, Vera received her visitors kindly. Lomax found her "gracious as hostess as in every other role. . . . Everything Vera does is done with dignity and composure."[7] In what seems painfully symptomatic of the era's racial etiquette, the Lomaxes invited Vera to Ruby Pickens Tartt's home that evening, an invitation that included her preparing their meals, washing up, and then performing for her hosts. "She readily agreed," Lomax writes, "to go home with Mrs. Tartt, cook dinner and sing for us." After finishing her kitchen duties, Vera obliged with several songs—a hymn, a lullaby, and a spiritual—pieces the Lomaxes most loved from her repertory, along with fulfilling their request for "Another Man Done Gone." Over the course of this visit, Ruby Lomax observed that Vera "listened with great interest and expressed pleasure modestly as Mr. Lomax told her how her songs are enjoyed in Washington by those who hear her records." Lomax had recently made his *Ballad Hunter* radio series, which included Vera's "Another Man Done Gone." On the program he explained it as "a blues for her work which takes her out of the kitchen. It's the blues from the chain gang, given to her by someone who had been there."[8]

When Vera Hall stepped away from the stove that evening, turning from servant to singer, she brought more than her shimmering artistry to "Another Man Done Gone." She illuminated a part of collective experience. "Those old timey songs I just heard the people sing," Vera said, was "something that just followed us."[9] By that light, community and creativity walked hand in hand.

———

Vera Hall grew up in the Black Belt. This term denotes both the region's dark arable soil and its dominant social history. Specifically, the Black Belt refers to a three-hundred-mile-long geophysical band, often described as a crescent, running through southwest Tennessee to the Mississippi Delta and including west-central Alabama, where Vera lived.[10] To the west, the Mississippi River's alluvial deposits enriched the flood plains, while closer to Vera's home the Tombigbee and Alabama river tributaries added silt to the prairie loam. This flat, fertile expanse of grasslands and forests became the center of Southern cotton cultivation. The Black Belt's other, more profound meaning came from its predominantly African American population. For over a century, living first in slave quarters and then sharecropper cabins, these inhabitants with few or no occupational choices tilled the region's cotton fields, harvested the crop, cleaned the fibers, and baled the cotton.

Until soil depletion, the boll weevil, and mechanized farming helped end the region's one-crop economy, cotton framed the lives of this workforce. By the time Vera reached adulthood, the 1930 census counted 2,803,756 black families nationwide, of whom 2,193,357 resided in the southern states, 962,401 of them in rural areas. Some 80 percent of these families lived as tenant farmers on Black Belt plantations.[11] While cotton producing stretched much farther, extending 1,600 miles from the Carolinas to Texas and three hundred miles wide, it was in the Mississippi Delta and its surrounding basins that the "plantation survives with smallest deviation from the traditional patterns."[12] Writing in his 1941 *Growing Up in the Black Belt,* Charles S. Johnson continues, "Soil conditions and historical influences have produced in other areas forms of exploitation in which many of the essential features of the plantation system appear, but nowhere else are the economic definitions and social institutions of this agricultural system so closely related." Vera and her forebears knew this system and its heritage first-hand.

At the close of the Civil War, not only did the promise of forty acres and a mule not materialize for the freedmen, but the planters of Sumter County, Alabama, had no liquid capital reserves, either. In the early 1830s, credit based on currency issued by Alabama's state-chartered banks had initially fostered the county's growth. Known as "shin-plasters," these bank notes of a size literally able to line one's shoe proved as temporary as the bandages their name implied. The Panic of 1837 created an extended national crisis of bank failures comparable to the closures of the Great Depression. While this collapse caused a number of Sumter County settlers to move away (many of them to Texas), census figures from 1840 through 1860 show the black population doubling and then tripling in proportion to a lessening number of whites.[13] Slavery allowed the planters, even with low supplies of capital, to circumvent the cost of their sole constant requirement: labor. In the war's aftermath, sharecropping offered a new means of getting return on the cotton crop. Suddenly credit and its uncertainties found a new constituency, applying now to the tenant farmers who survived by advances from "the furnish." This process of borrowing ahead, of purchasing supplies from the plantation commissary credited against the harvest, began during Reconstruction and continued into the 1950s. Garrett Williams, who grew up in the Livingston countryside in the 1930s, and who remembered Vera, told me of going to a plantation store, his family borrowing for the year in order to have food. Come picking season, they would "pay back whatever we raised."[14]

Vera herself recalled her father, Efron Hall, working all year and seemingly every day to try to avoid this kind of debt servitude. During the July and August summer "lay-by," while the cotton ripened, he took jobs elsewhere, cutting hay. In the winter months he chopped wood that he hauled by wagon and mule into town for fifty or seventy-five cents a load. While Hall's status as a renter left Vera's family better off than many of the sharecroppers around them, his unceasing efforts fit within a larger process that Charles Johnson identified in 1941. "The plantation system as it exists today," Johnson wrote, "is organized, as it was originally. . . . Essentially, the great bulk of workers must be tenants and, if the system is to continue with labor as the chief source of power and skill, they must remain tenants."[15] The squads of thirty-five or forty people working with mules and turning the fields—a scene depicted in one of the Livingston, Alabama, ex-slave narratives—persisted all across the Black Belt, even as lower export demand and higher production of rayon took hold in the mid-1930s.[16] Johnson and his research team found in their eight-county, five-state survey an "almost total absence of Negroes in the non-agricultural occupations aside from the traditional unskilled labor field, the personal and domestic service occupations, and the overcrowded and poorly paid white-collar and skilled tasks of teaching, preaching, undertaking, and carpentry."[17] Their canvass of 851 rural male youths and 1,399 rural female youths yielded only sixty-two boys who wanted to enter the farm vocation. Most of them resisted even calling this kind of work "farming," a term many felt too dignified to describe the toil of their parents and grandparents.

Related patterns of servitude extended off the farm. After the Surrender, Livingston's black town population grew rapidly. While some servants, house-men, and carriage drivers lived there before the Civil War, people now left the surrounding plantations in increasing numbers, if only to enter the static set of roles that Charles Johnson found in place decades later. Black men worked as carters, draymen, garbage collectors, lamp lighters, gardeners, and well diggers. Women took jobs as laundresses, cooks, seamstresses, and maids. A detailed 1928 history of Livingston written by a retired local physician, Dr. Robert D. Spratt, recalls the black community from a privileged and revealing perspective. He devotes only four pages at the back of the book to the 21,700 black residents in Sumter County, which according to the 1930 census had a total population of 26,929. Dr. Spratt writes of persons like Bob Witt, recently deceased, who handled express and freight for the town. While illiterate, he was "never known to make a mistake in giving change and was never known to deliver the wrong package."[18] Or: "Could any boy ever forget old Annie Mobile who roamed around picking up cigar stumps and reciting some crazy-sounding poetry?"[19] Or: "Isaiah Coleman was a mattress maker and could make more music on a mouth harp than any person I ever heard play one." Spratt sums up this chronicle from the days of Jim Crow: "As a rule, I find that our Negro people are kind and indulgent to children and that they are often patient and cheerful under conditions that would drive white people to suicide."[20]

Other cultural vestiges carried into the segregation era. As on the antebellum plantation with its area reserved for slave cabins, the town's black residential districts were called "quarters." At the time of the Lomaxes' 1941 visit, Vera lived in Nichols Quarter, named after a family for whom she worked eleven years. After W. S. Nichols died, his widow asked Vera to sleep in the twin bed next to hers. For three years, Vera came to work every evening, after spending the day at her own home nearby. Little's Quarter, named after Major W. G. Little, who built rented cabins on a former mill property, designated the largest of these black neighborhoods. The black barbershop operated on a thoroughfare locally known as Dog Street. Additional black districts developed as in-town life created housing demand—Coleman's Quarter, Hopkins Quarter, Gulley's Quarter, and Tincup's Alley that twisted through Little's Quarter. Vera mentioned two more, Factory Town and German Bottom, the latter named after Judge German, who owned and rented the houses behind his own. An older man who "used to follow the trash wagon" told Vera that Tin Cup got its name from having been a garbage dump, filled with discarded tin cups and bottles.[21] Though it eventually was cleared, with houses built over it, the name stuck. "Tin Cup," Vera said, "it's just a quarter where colored people live . . . and they call it down in Tin Cup, it's down in the bottom. They say, let's go to Tin Cup." Tin Cup and Factory Town also named cafés in those quarters. Vera frequented them, and there she and friends drank, danced, and played the jukebox. It was there, too, in the early 1940s that composer Elie Siegmeister picked her up, keeping her and her husband out late one evening as he notated some of her play party songs, spirituals, comic pieces, ballads, moans, and blues, including the near-autobiographical field holler "Black Woman."

Seven years after Charles Johnson completed his broad study of the racial position of African Americans in the South, drawing on more than a thousand personal interviews and more than two thousand questionnaires, Vera

Hall told her own story of growing up a black woman in the Black Belt. In 1948, Vera had moved from Livingston to Tuscaloosa, Alabama, where she worked as a domestic earning ten dollars a week. She sent most of her earnings home to her older sister, Estelle, who cared for Vera's grandsons, aged fourteen and eleven. While cash poor, Estelle and her husband, who had no children of their own, maintained the same farm where the Hall family had toiled for years. The youngsters, in turn, helped their partially disabled uncle with his chores. For a week or two that May, in the only out-of-state trip she ever made, Vera took leave of them all and went to New York City.

Billed as an "Alabama spiritual singer," she was appearing in a folk music concert at Columbia University, an evening presented as part of the school's contemporary American music festival.[22] The May 15 program, slotted between the Juilliard String Quartet, who played the night before, and the CBS Symphony Orchestra scheduled the night after, was titled "Ballads, Hoedowns, Spirituals (White and Negro) and Blues . . ." Its roster, set by Alan Lomax, who served as the show's narrator, more than matched this billing. Along with Vera, the concert featured Hobart Smith, Texas Gladden, Pete Seeger, Dan Burley, Jean Ritchie, and Brownie McGhee. For Vera, whose only prior public appearances had been in her church, this concert at McMillin Academic Theater marked, Lomax wrote, "the first large audience she had ever faced."[23] During that visit she stayed with Alan and Elizabeth Lomax. Her hosts interviewed her, apparently the following week.[24] Lomax had recently acquired a portable tape recorder that he put to good use with his Alabama houseguest. Their dialogue—a series of questions and answers—occupies sixteen reels of magnetized paper tape (plastic polymers still lay in the future). Several more tapes, for which there are partial transcriptions, have since gone missing. Those that survive show Vera talking warmly and at length about scenes in her life and singing such favorites as "Another Man Done Gone" into Lomax's new machine.

Vera's soft-spoken account on the tapes, her voice swaying with the mood of her stories, details intimate memories of the Black Belt. She was the youngest of three girls. Her one brother, Nemias, born a few years before her, suffered from a congenital defect, an oversized head, that led to his early death. The oldest of the three sisters, Bessie, whom Vera described as stout and big-shouldered, helped their father with the plowing on his rented farm. "He used to side cotton, and she'd split middles behind him—and she learned how to do it good."[25] Vera's middle sister, Estelle, four years her senior and whom Vera called "D-1," took after their mother, helping in the kitchen and with sewing

Columbia University
in the City of New York

FOURTH ANNUAL
FESTIVAL OF CONTEMPORARY
AMERICAN MUSIC

MAY 10, 11, 12, 13, 14, 15, AND 16, 1948

SPONSORED BY
THE ALICE M. DITSON FUND OF COLUMBIA UNIVERSITY

CONCERT OF FOLK MUSIC

SATURDAY, MAY 15, 8:30 P.M.

Ballads, Hoe-Downs, Spirituals (White and Negro),
and Blues . . .

Played and sung by:
Mrs. Texas Gladden, *Virginia ballad singer*
Hobart Smith, *Virginia Mt. fiddler*
Jean Ritchie, *Kentucky Mt. dulcimer player*
Brownie Maghee, *North Carolina blues-guitarist*
Vera Hall, *Alabama spiritual singer*
Dan Burley, *blues-pianist*
Peter Seeger, *topical ballad singer*
Alan Lomax, *narrator*

Steinway Piano

McMILLIN ACADEMIC THEATER

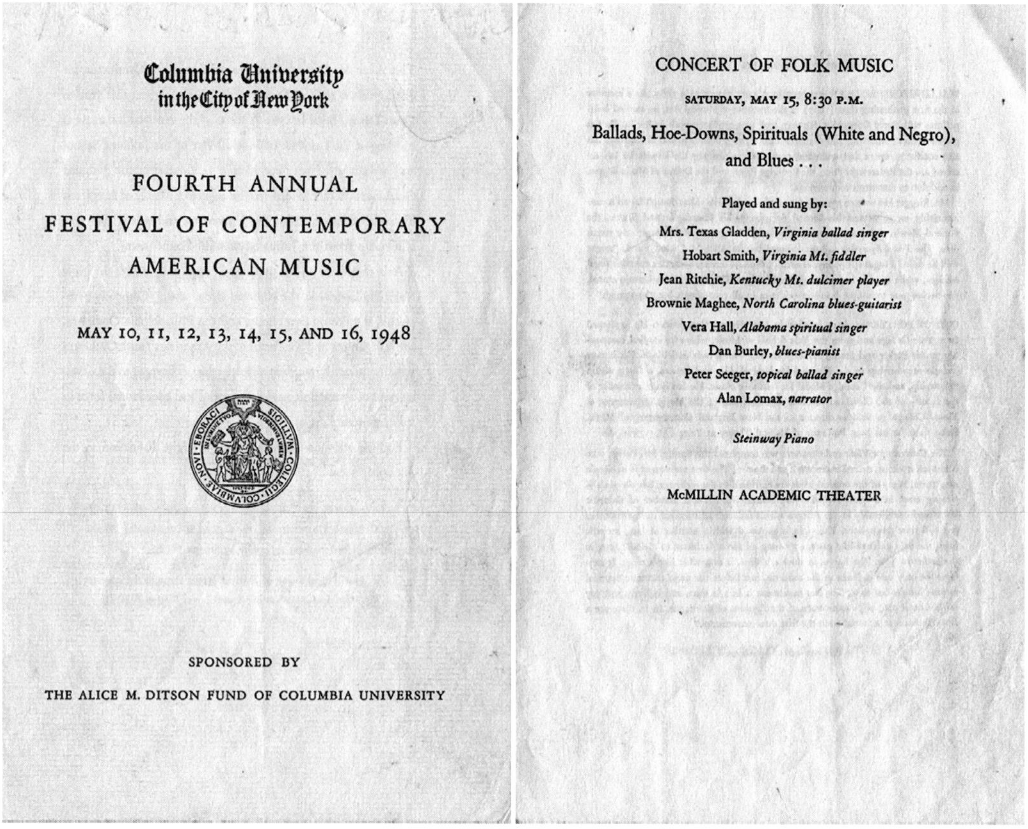

FIGURE 25. Columbia University concert program, May 15, 1948. Author's collection.

chores. On this farm, garments demanded constant patching. The children received new clothes only once a year: a pair of shoes and a bolt of homespun that their mother fashioned into dresses. In the summertime the girls went barefoot, including at church. Their friends, also shoeless on weekdays and Sundays too, dressed much as they did in some version or another of this light blue, store-bought cloth with its stripes of green, white, and red. Vera's family, like their neighbors, had almost no cash except when the cotton was ginned. Sometimes their mother would sell a rooster or some eggs, and in that way purchase supplies of kerosene, soap, and starch. Otherwise, Vera described a common upbringing in the Black Belt of homemade items and homegrown amusements.

"I just think," Vera said, "that anybody got any sense ought to be able to remember what kind of life they grew up in."[26] Like so many rural people, the Halls kept a smokehouse for their meats and used a butter churn to process their dairy. For a treat, Vera spoke of skimming back the cream and eating the clabber with her sisters. They got into trouble on one occasion, when

Vera broke the family's milk pitcher and the others did not attend to their chores. On returning home, their mother responded by grabbing a handful of peach switches that she soon put to use. Vera pictured lighter moments, too, when neighboring boys picked berries for her and the other girls.

She also told how she came to learn her music. "You catch the sounding of a song before I catch the words . . . I have to hear the words before I say them."[27] Her failing eyesight, she admitted, kept her from reading. Since childhood, she learned songs by remembering sounds, and eventually absorbing the lyrics. She recalled sitting in singer Richard Amerson's lap as a little girl and remembered her oldest sister Bessie's wry comment that Vera learned by "look[ing] right in his mouth, and when he gone, it's just another little Rich here singing."[28] Vera further recounted some of the ring plays, riddles, and courtship games that she and her friends enjoyed. One of these dances simulated a bird that "we be mocking with our hands."[29] Other singing games mixed old-time buck dancing with more recent moves like "balling the jack," the dancers just "doing everything to make that sound fit in." In the game song "All Hid," she sang verses that dated back to antebellum years, yet whose lyrics still had relevance in her time: "Cornbread rough, cornbread tough / Niggers down yonder don't never get enough."[30] While Vera explained that her father was an effective farmer—"He raised plenty hogs, corn, potatoes, syrups, peanuts, peas"—he also helped feed his neighbors. In exchange for food, they chopped his crop. "So many of them . . . didn't have anything," Vera wistfully observed, "nothing at all."[31]

Her aural autobiography, largely absent of personal complaint, carries its toll of sorrow. Vera's father, a man she described as often silent, still reminded his daughters how he went shoeless throughout the year—even in wintertime—until he reached adulthood. Vera remembers her grandfather, too, a former slave who lived on the same land he had worked before the Surrender. Toward the end of his life, he lived alone in his cabin, subsisting on a diet of milk, bread, and coffee, sometimes enjoying the pot liquor of turnip greens. When he died, he lay undiscovered for a day or two, until family members broke down his door and found him there. If his isolation gave Vera a sense of an ongoing past, so did the customary roles accorded to women, her sisters included, who lived in the country. "Woman," she exclaimed, "has a terrible lot to do on the farm!"[32]

Vera acknowledged that a man's work in the cotton fields required his hitching a mule and plowing all through the morning, afternoon, and often past sunset. But he also had a chance at noontime to stop for a meal and even nap under a tree. Unlike him, Vera says, "Now, there the wife's done went down there and chopped till eleven o'clock. And she come home, bring a turn of wood on out the field with her—got to keep on by the garden somewhere, got to get some greens—and then she just steady going all the while she's there. When she get dinner ready and they eat dinner, well, it's nearly time to go back out to the field. Now he done rested all that time."[33] The woman, she adds, must still return to the fields herself that afternoon and continue with her chopping. She also needs by the end of the day to cook supper, milk the cow, pull weeds for the hogs, and finally, wash the dishes. Vera didn't even mention child-rearing duties.

Tellingly, these multiple burdens visited on women arose in Vera's account of her oldest sister Bessie's death. Soon after Bessie married in her early twenties, during an evening game of All Hid, she fell over a tree stump in the family's yard. She hit it so hard, she thought she broke her hip. While no bruises showed outwardly, she had internal injuries, and a trickle of blood escaped from her lips. Her mother wiped her mouth clean. The next day Bessie found difficulty walking. Agnes Hall rubbed some kerosene and hog lard on her as a balm, but the eight-dollar charge for a doctor to come out from town, apart from whatever the medicine might cost, lay beyond the family's means. Bessie continued her routine as before. "She worked hard at home, but she worked harder after she got married. She still worked in the field. . . . So after she married, she had to wash and iron and cook and do everything herself. And my mother said she believed the reason her leg start to failing on her, she just had so much work to do."[34] Bessie's leg became paralyzed, and eventually she became unable to rise at all. She died within three years of the original mishap. Her decline, borne of medical inattention stemming from poverty and magnified by incessant toil, fits an all-too-typical life in the Black Belt of those, Vera said, who had "the same land, the same privilege." Her sister's accident welled up her voice with sadness. "Um-um, I hate to think about it."

More than Vera's exceptional music prompted these interviews. Part of Alan Lomax's interest in Vera arose from a recent project as well as a long-term commitment. "Early in my work in recording folk songs," Lomax wrote in his 1959 introduction to Vera's published story drawn from these tapes, "I learned that the accomplished folk singer had observed his world with an artist's eye and could talk about it with great insight. Strolling fiddlers, housewives, and mule skinners came to annotate my field recordings."[35] He cited the commentaries by Kentucky ballad singer Aunt Molly Jackson that appeared as headnotes in the Lomaxes' *Our Singing County* and Leadbelly's words framing the singer's 1936 songbook that they also assembled. Even more of a precedent, he explained, were the 1938 Jelly Roll Morton recording sessions, whose spoken-word elements eventually became the oral history *Mr. Jelly Roll.*[36] To complement that study of jazz and its makers, Lomax now sought "to record the intimate life stories of typical Negro folk singers."[37]

Apart from Vera and some inmates at the state penitentiary in Parchman, Mississippi, whom Lomax was also documenting with his tape recorder in the late 1940s, the folksingers he had foremost in mind were guitarist Big Bill Broonzy, pianist Memphis Slim, and harmonica player Sonny Boy Williamson.[38] On March 2, 1947, after performing in concert at New York's Town Hall—a series Lomax inaugurated the previous fall—this trio of Chicago-based recording artists accompanied the folklorist to Decca studios, where they engaged in a two-hour exchange about the blues and how it arose. These players, themselves natives of Mississippi and Tennessee, spoke from personal knowledge about the Delta and its past. Lomax edited their conversation for a record released in 1959, the same year he published Vera's tapes in book form.[39] He began this work eleven years earlier with "I Got the Blues," an article excerpted from the Broonzy–Slim–Sonny Boy session.[40] At one point Big Bill detailed two vigilantelike murders of entire families that went unpunished, the killers protected by that era's racial regime. With such incendiary material, he and his fellow musicians understandably insisted that Lomax preserve their anonymity, were their words to become public. Accordingly, Lomax created fictitious names. Big Bill became "Natchez," Memphis Slim "Leroy," and Sonny Boy "Sib." By concealing their real names and by obscuring places, Lomax not only protected these sources, he felt free to reconstruct the flow of their words in the article and on the album.

Similarly, a comparison of Vera's original tapes with the book *Rainbow Sign: A Southern Documentary*—there her name appears as "Nora"—reveals her interview transformed into a monologue, separated into chapters. Lomax at times added words attributed to her. He acknowledged having done this before with Jelly Roll Morton, reshaping his recorded utterances to the needs of the page: "To turn Jelly's jazzy lingo into prose without losing its color or its pace, to fill out and gently correct his great yarn, were tasks that required many months of work."[41] Lomax's outline for Vera's book evinces similar planning, and the finished product shows that he drew from throughout the tapes to fashion new narrative threads. As for Big Bill Broonzy, Memphis Slim, and

Sonny Boy Williamson, not until 1990, after these musicians had all passed away, did Lomax use their given names in a CD reissue. As before, the album includes musical interludes, with one of them, Vera's "Another Man Done Gone," set between Big Bill's accounts of the unpunished killings. "'Another Man Done Gone,'" Lomax wrote, "an Alabama chain gang chant performed by Vera Hall, reflects the bleak sorrow of these stories."[42] Clearly, Vera Hall and these three bluesmen remained associated in his mind, as they were on the album. What they all had in common, as "typical Negro folk singers," they knew from lived experience.

At the time Lomax interviewed Vera and the others, they all were community-based performers.[43] She sang in face-to-face settings with her neighbors, while the musicians played in clubs and taverns, often for fellow black migrants to the city. Just as they enjoyed applause from admirers who grew up in similar circumstances, and watched dancers sway to their jukebox hits, she received encouragement from her family and friends and praise from her fellow churchgoers. Though Big Bill, Memphis Slim, and Sonny Boy had already made hundreds of recordings enjoyed by a black record-buying public, they still fit Lomax's criterion of typicality, as did Vera Hall, who remained throughout her life a home and church singer. Lomax viewed them as localized performers, recognizing, too, that they found audiences well beyond their origins.

What brought Vera's singing and "Another Man Done Gone" to outsiders like himself and then to new communities of listeners stemmed from another outsider, albeit someone who had grown up in her hometown. Ruby Pickens Tartt (1880–1974) was a socially established white Livingston native. Born a quarter century before Vera, Tartt first met her as a little girl and lived to write her obituary. The fact that Vera came to work in her kitchen, indeed preparing dinner and washing up on the same evening she sang "Another Man Done Gone" for John and Ruby Lomax, reflects the society they both inhabited. Charles Johnson, writing at that time, sets this dynamic of custom and role in the wider view: "While the southern white traditionalist likes to believe that the race system is accepted as natural and proper, in actuality he and all other participants know that it is not. The race system in the South is preserved by legal sanctions and the threat of physical violence, quite as much as by the mutual acceptance of traditional modes of behavior."[44] On a sociological level, he framed the context of "Another Man Done Gone." On a specific level, that context becomes clearer if its focus includes Vera's benefactor and boss, Ruby Pickens Tartt.

Early in her upbringing, Tartt began listening to the black renters who worked for her father, William King Pickens. "In the horse and buggy days," wrote Tartt of this musical awakening, "I spent many Sunday afternoons with him sitting out near one of their country churches and listening to them sing. When he particularly liked a song he would make another generous contribution to the preacher and it was repeated as many times as he liked. I've kept this up through the years."[45] Schooled as a painter, college educated, the town's first female driver, and later its librarian, Tartt saw herself, as did her neighbors, as an iconoclast. "She was a woman," said Nathaniel Reed, "about whom almost no one was neutral."[46] Reed met her as a youngster visiting the library where she directed his reading (he later edited Spratt's history of Livingston, became an English professor, and served as provost of Livingston University, now the University of West Alabama), adding that she was the "most remarkable lady I've ever known."

Reed described Ruby Pickens Tartt during the voter registration efforts of the early 1960s. "She was not a 'far-out activist,' not someone who would demonstrate, but would move to quietly improve circumstances . . . and would sometimes irritate officials."[47] Reed mentioned her role as a Sumter County registrar of voters. A poll tax had been imposed along with a literacy provision that required the prospective voters to read a passage from the Constitution and then interpret it. It gave "a good deal of discretion to registrars. She thought it unfair and she achieved success despite it." Defying accepted opinion, Tartt did her part in seeing that Livingston's black voters got registered.[48]

Tartt recognized that deviance from the norm in a small town magnifies the importance of whatever has happened and threatens "the established order of society."[49] She took these limitations in stride even as her roles included being both a black music devotee and, as a result, an occasional laughingstock for Livingston's upper crust. "In a long look back," she wrote in an autobiographical entry, "I know I would not exchange my life in this small town with its ring-games and folk songs in the woods for any city life I know of."

This set of values that Ruby Pickens Tartt would not exchange led to the Livingston recordings of Vera and others of her community. In 1937, Tartt, affected by the Depression like so many Americans, accepted the one relief job open to her, a sewing project in nearby York, Alabama. Her established background notwithstanding, with scant savings in the bank she had little choice. Her husband, Pratt Tartt, had also just lost his job as the town's postmaster. While Ruby Pickens Tartt turned out to be the only white person assigned to this sewing endeavor (apart from its largely absentee manager), she encouraged her black coworkers, a number of whom she already knew, to sing away the hours. Some months into this employment, she was appointed chair of the Livingston unit of the Federal Writers' Project. That position came as a complete surprise to her—she modestly claimed that she could not even write "c-a-t" properly. In time, Tartt, a naturally gifted writer, gathered most of Sumter County's ex-slave narratives herself. The high quality ascribed to them derived not only from her respect for the actual words spoken, but also to the candor of the interviewees—a measure of the mutual trust enjoyed between herself and these subjects. Her first FWP assignment required her to send in a batch of locally gathered spirituals to the Washington office. She called on her recent experiences in York as well as her long familiarity with this body of work. In preparing her submission, she consciously set aside such well-known numbers as "Swing Low, Sweet Chariot." John Lomax's reaction to the material was both ardent and immediate. "May I come at once to see you with my recorder," he wrote. "I am not familiar with any songs you have sent in. Your area must be rich in folk music."[50]

When John and Ruby Lomax reached Livingston in July 1937, Tartt introduced them to two cousins whose singing she most admired: Doc Reed and Vera Hall.[51] They often sang together, with Reed leading and Vera seconding. Their duets evoked in miniature what took place when a whole church rose up in song, and they described their musical communion as something that congregations also found true: they would "feel together."[52] Tartt first met Doc Reed (1898–1979) after hearing him at Pilgrim's Church, a black house of worship profiled (along with herself) in Carl Carmer's best-selling *Stars Fell on Alabama*.[53] A chair and basket maker as well as farmer, Reed's emotional involvement as he sang made an indelible impression on her, and now on the Lomaxes. Reed declined to perform any "'sinful,' 'wicked,' or 'worl'ly' songs," only spirituals.[54] Lomax recognized his unswerving commitment, and developed a respect for Doc Reed that turned deeply personal. Apart from making numerous recordings of him soloing or with Vera's backing, Lomax regularly kept in touch with him via Ruby Tartt. Through her, he sent clothes and money to him, and when Doc Reed required an amputation for his leg, Lomax, ever solicitous, got in touch with the doctor. But there was more. In his 1947 autobiography Lomax sums up his feelings for the man, calling on Wordsworth's "Ode": "Dock's soul must have had intimations of immortality not given to ordinary mortals."[55] After praising Reed's voice for

CHAPTER 6

its "wonderful, tremulous tones," the folklorist ends the story of his own life's work with one of Doc Reed's spirituals.[56]

Reed shared a similar admiration in return. When he learned of Lomax's death the following year, he openly wept with Tartt.[57] As she read aloud the words that Lomax accorded him in his autobiography, he intoned the verses of that spiritual again. The bond between singer and collectors endured. In 1974, a grieving Doc Reed sang at Ruby Pickens Tartt's funeral both as a soloist and during the reading of the prayers.[58]

Tartt considered Vera the finest singer of her experience. Her initial contact came when Vera was a youngster. The Hall family raised peanuts that Tartt's father purchased for his own farming needs. "I used to drive with him in afternoons to the field to see about the work & he would have them stop early to sing spirituals for us," Tartt wrote.[59] "Vera was too small to sing but her mother had a lovely voice which Vera inherited." In the years that followed, along with the recordings she fostered, Tartt enlisted Vera's talents to perform for her visitors—compelling her at times—and at least on one occasion, had her serve as musical demonstrator. For a public lecture at the college in Livingston, or possibly the local women's club, Tartt wrote out a script for them both. As she speaks about the elements of black folksong, Vera sings in coordination with the text. At one point, Tartt explains how in a "shout" "another voice would add a second line and soon, thus spontaneously a new Negro melody would come into being. Improvisation is 2nd nature to the Negro."[60] Certain words that Tartt employs (presumably while Vera vocalizes an accompaniment)—"spontaneously," "2nd nature," and her statement about improvisation—exhibit a primitivism once commonplace in white descriptions of black folksinging, while setting a social distance superior to it. Still, Tartt touches a vital truth. These melodies, she continues, "are built to last and some have lasted for generations. It is a living art."

This living art thrives in Vera Hall's and Doc Reed's music as it does with all sixty-four of the named performers who appear on the Livingston field recordings. It animates Enoch Brown's night cries at a bridge near Tartt's home, reproducing the outdoor field calls reported from slavery times, and guides Hettie Godfrey's "Coonjine," a game song from steamboat days that required, she said, "singing, patting, and swinging when we played it."[61] Like Vera, Godfrey too worked in Tartt's household as a maid. If her job there offers a reminder of racial position in Livingston society, it also places her among the gifted singers and players that her employer so avidly sought out.

Another was blind accordionist Jesse Harris. His danceable ballads document a type of nineteenth-century black narrative song that arose before the blues. Vera credited Blind Jesse for several of her numbers, as she did Richard Amerson, a story-telling, quick-talking, harmonica-playing singer and preacher whom she knew since childhood. A true verbal artist, he became, said John Lomax to Tartt, "the prize find of all my journeyings."[62] Together these individuals, spread across Sumter County, mapped a geography of living artistry that reached back generations. Here, in "a district of worn-out farms," Lomax wrote, "covering not more than ten by twenty miles," he found himself in the fall of 1940 "surrounded by treasures."[63] Within days of that appraisal, he recorded Vera Hall at Tartt's home on Baldwin Hill. Her performance included one of Livingston's most widely acknowledged and enduring musical jewels—the song Vera called "Another Man Done Gone."

Almost six decades later, in January 1997, I had the opportunity to talk with someone in Livingston who remembered Vera singing this treasured piece. Then in her early nineties, Fannie Pickens Inglis (1906–1999) was Ruby and Pratt Tartt's only child. Age had not dimmed her memory of Vera or the song. Without pause, Inglis quoted its refrain and a verse, adding that Vera worked in their home as "our cook . . . and domestic."[64] Inglis also summarized the recording process her mother instigated. Ruby Pickens Tartt would take John Lomax "out to the Negroes' houses. He would ask them all to come to her house, and he would record them in her garden." Citing the more than three hundred recordings at Baldwin Hill or at surrounding churches and small farms, Inglis reiterated Tartt's passion for the music and its makers: "She loved it . . . [but] the [white] community wasn't interested at all. They didn't know about it." Before our brief conversation ended, Fannie Pickens Inglis brought up Vera's song again, a quiet wonder in her voice. "I just keep thinking about 'Another Man Done Gone.' Another time in our history."

Vera Hall's Library of Congress recording of "Another Man Done Gone" follows an elemental structure—a four-line repeated verse pitched in D minor that uses only a few notes in that scale. Vera keeps an unhurried pace throughout, letting her voice carry the song's pensive message in a way that sounds meditative, almost private. Part of this effect stems from the way she sustains vowels at the end of lines, a subdued vibrato that also instills her church songs. Here Vera has taken a secular theme and made it prayerful. She sings these verses:

Another man done gone,
Another man done gone,
From the county farm,
Another man done gone.

I didn't know his name,
I didn't know his name,
I didn't know his name,
I didn't know his name.

He had a long chain on,
He had a long chain on,
He had a long chain on,
He had a long chain on.

He killed another man,
He killed another man,
He killed another man,
He killed another man.

I don't know where he's gone,
I don't know where he's gone,
I don't know where he's gone,
I don't know where he's gone.

I'm going to walk your log,
I'm going to walk your log,
I'm going to walk your log,
I'm going to walk your log.[65]

Ruby Pickens Tartt described Vera's blues as "the everyday experience of an individual, a lonely man here on earth."[66] Similarly, Alan Lomax characterized this performance as "enigmatic, full of silent spaces, speaking of the night."[67] It also prompted him to suggest the song's social basis: "Like every underprivileged Negro in the South, Vera Hall knew all about the county farm and the state pen. . . . Although Vera Hall was a peaceloving cook and washerwoman and the pillar of the choir in her Baptist church, she knew about these things and she knew, as well, a song from the prison, a song about escape."

The widespread condition that Vera and others like her knowingly faced reached back to the years after the Civil War. In Sumter County, the backlash against Reconstruction that put a handful of blacks into political and judicial positions exposed white residents' intense hostility to Radical Republican rule. Part of their ardor stemmed from the establishment in 1867 of the Third Military District, which mandated locally stationed federal troops. In November 1868 Alabama redrafted its state constitution and officially rejoined the Union with representation in the U.S. Congress. Ku Klux Klan activity in Sumter County had begun that spring. A period of lynchings, shootings, whippings, house burnings, nightriding, and other mob furies intersected with coercive efforts to influence and direct the freedmen's votes. Several of the Sumter County ex-slave narratives describe not only this violence, but the political struggles between Radical Republicans and local Democrats. Stories of lost or voided votes fit with testimony heard in 1871 Congressional hearings. By 1874, Democrats regained political supremacy and enacted intimidating new county election laws that required registered blacks to vote only at polls near their homes. Should any have selected candidates on the Republican ticket, they could be identified and subjected to reprisal. This election also marked the precipitous decline of Reconstruction in Sumter County, culminating in the removal of all federal soldiers. By the mid-1870s, Sumter County, like other Southern locales in the Black Belt, entered the Redemption period, and with it began the disfranchisement of the black majority population from most legal protections. Throughout the South, harsh penalties came to be enacted for petty theft as well as capital crime, and all entailed long prison sentences. Convict leasing became a cheap source of labor and a tactic used in the period's single-crop cash economy. Punishments formerly administered by slave owners and overseers reappeared via latter-day state laws and local ordinances designed to subordinate the rights of one group to the interests of another. "Another Man Done Gone" reflected that claim on absolute power.

Vera also had a personal connection with the song that echoed lived experience. When Vera recorded "Another Man Done Gone," she told John Lomax that she learned it from her guitar-playing husband. Not long after, during his radio program, Lomax mentioned that she got the song from someone who had worked on a chain gang. Without divulging names, the folklorist spoke knowledgeably. During his May 1939 visit to Livingston, more than a year before he even heard the song, let alone made this broadcast, he learned that Vera's husband, her source for a number of her secular pieces, was currently sentenced to the penitentiary.[68] By 1943, when Elie Siegmeister met Vera at the café in Tin Cup, he also recounted that Vera's husband, who sang with her that evening, did several "chain-gang songs."[69] This man, apparently named Adair, had a history of imprisonment.[70] According to Ruby Pickens Tartt, who wrote to Alan Lomax at the time of *Rainbow Sign*'s publication, Vera's husband had been jailed "constantly" for beating her.[71] Eventually he was killed in a fight, Tartt says, "that didn't concern him." She then quotes Vera saying that he "just couldn't keep out of trouble even when it wasn't his."

This contact between Vera, the song, and the realities it invokes goes even further than the fact that Adair was the second of her husbands killed in a violent altercation. She had contact with other prisoners who sang "Another Man Done Gone." When writer-collector Harold Courlander came to Livingston in February 1950, he recorded both Vera singing "Another Man Done Gone," as well as someone she knew: Willie Turner, a twenty-seven-year-old confined at Camp Livingston.[72] With two of his fellow inmates, he recorded "Now Your Man Done Gone," a piece they otherwise sang on the county road gang.[73] Lifelong town resident Nathaniel Reed, who saw work crews like Turner's from Camp Livingston, observed that they labored under guard but not, as related in Vera's song, shackled in

FIGURE 26. Vera Hall, Livingston, Alabama, 1950. Photo by Harold Courlander. Courtesy of Michael Courlander.

chains. Reed also heard that the song arose from events at this camp. "Supposedly," he said, "someone escaped from there more than twenty years ago."[74] While that story should not be taken as evidence of the song's origin, it does resonate with local circumstances.

Yet a philosophical difference separates Willie Turner's interpretation from Vera's. While he sings a melody that closely resembles hers, and his lyrics follow the same pattern, he expresses a different sentiment. If Vera's performance seems more reflective, Turner's sounds more declarative. His personalized approach suggests a greater blues influence, while hers, in its stillness and abstraction, inclines toward the spirituals. These styles correspond with the singers' respective performance environments. Turner sang this piece outdoors with an all-male road gang, and his text echoes the larger body of worksongs and their usual content. Vera, meanwhile, has taken whatever she heard her convict husband play on the guitar, and fitted it stylistically into her domestic and church house repertory. Turner makes a statement of masculine loss, while Vera conveys a message akin to a civil rights anthem. In essence, Willie Turner's "Now Your Man Done Gone" transforms Vera's prison lament into a lover's plea:

Now your man done gone (3x),
To the county farm,
Now your man done gone.

Baby please don't go (3x),
Back to Baltimore,
Baby please don't go.

Turn your lamp down low (3x),
And baby please don't go,
Baby please don't go.

You know I love you so (3x),
And baby please don't go,
Baby please don't go.

I beg you all night long (3x),
And night before,
Baby please don't go.

Now your man done come (3x),
From the county farm,
Now your man done come.

Baby please don't go (3x),
Back to Baltimore,
Baby please don't go.

I'm goin' to walk your log (2x),
and if you throw me off,
I'm goin' to walk your log.[75]

With verses that range from begging to enticement, from distrust to revenge, most recorded versions of the song—there are more than fifty—follow the direction that Willie Turner took.[76] They fix on personal desire more than the social condition that frames their stories. The song becomes an emotional monologue of a jailed man addressing his lover. "Among the gnawing fears and anxieties of the long term prisoners," writes Harold Courlander about this piece, "is the thought that when they return home they may find that their women are no longer waiting."[77]

Two days before Courlander recorded Willie Turner at Camp Livingston, he stopped forty miles away in Marion, Mississippi. There he recorded a singer identified in his notes only as Cora, who sang "Baby Please Don't Go." It is the same song, but with some variance in the lyrics:

Baby please don't go (3x),
Back to New Orleans,
You know I love you so,
Baby please don't go.

Got me way down here (3x),
By the Rolling Fork,
Treat me like a dog,
Baby please don't go.

Repeat first verse.

Oh I be your dog (2x),
Get you way down here,
Make you walk your log (2x).

Baby please don't go (3x),
Back to New Orleans,
Get you cold ice cream,
Baby please don't go.

Repeat second verse.

Repeat first verse.

Got me way down here (2x),
Treat me like a dog,
Baby please don't go.[78]

Courlander sets Cora's rendition alongside Willie Turner's as an example of how a single folksong can alter within a narrow geographic area. "Sometimes a singing leader may remember only the melody and a few lines of a song he had heard, but that is usually enough; out of these elements new variants are born."[79] While true enough, something more has happened here. Cora drew from a recording that she either heard herself, or she got from someone who did. Her choice of song title, its chorus about returning to New Orleans and its reference to "cold ice cream," followed by her verses about the south Mississippi town of Rolling Fork, and of suffering "like a dog," appear in nearly the same form on Big Joe Williams's 1935 hit record, "Baby Please Don't Go."[80] Should this have not been her precise source, by the time Cora sang it in February 1950, Williams had recorded it twice more, once in 1941 and again in 1947.[81] These, too, found play on regional jukeboxes and thus afforded even more opportunity for Cora, and those around her, to learn it. Cora's rendition principally differs from Willie Turner's by drawing from an identifiable, commercially released sound recording. Though less clear his source, Willie Turner's performance audibly suggests, as well, his indebtedness to one or another of Big Joe Williams's releases.[82]

For Joe Williams (ca. 1903–1982), "Baby Please Don't Go" became his signature piece, his "trademark," his "theme song."[83] Over his long career, he continued to perform and interpret it. His 1935 recording features a fiddle played in an old-time style, while on his next two recordings he engaged Sonny Boy Williamson on harmonica, playing the very instrument that displaced the violin as the black string band matured into the more modern blues ensemble.[84] Electrification was making its way across America, and in the noisy confines of a roadhouse or tavern, amplification became part of this music. As players found that a harmonica pumped through a microphone worked more effectively than a fiddle, it took over that function, occupying the same bandwidth in that musical consort.[85] By 1947, Big Joe Williams continued to fit the song into the present day by adding drums, emphasizing its danceable beat, and enhancing its jukebox appeal. No wonder it became so influential.

In December 1964, just months after two of Harold Courlander's books based on his Alabama and Mississippi recording trip first appeared, a Belfast-based rock band, Them, led by singer Van Morrison, recorded a supercharged version of "Baby Please Don't Go."[86] They credited it to Big Joe Williams, and with it, the band netted their first hit. "In a way," said scholar Paul Oliver, playing this song to open a BBC broadcast in 1967, "the story of this song summarizes the development of the blues, from work songs to a new folk music to international popularization."[87] In that sequence, Oliver cited Willie Turner's worksong performance. But Oliver also admitted that he didn't know whether it came to Turner via Joe Williams's recording. For that reason, he added that this song "summarizes a few of the problems about the music, too," citing gaps in its history and raising questions about its origin.

A closer look shows that the song's four-line verse pattern appeared before the blues found its basic form. It corresponds better to the formats of older dance reels, church songs, and preblues pieces like "Crawdad Song" and "K. C. Moan." Songs recorded in Livingston like "Little Bitty Man," a children's rhyme sung by Mary McDonald, or "I'm Chopping Cotton" by Sim

Tartt and his group, also have verse patterns comparable to "Another Man Done Gone."[88] Even though their melodies differ, their structures parallel. "Another Man Done Gone" stands on an old foundation.

Scholars on both sides of the Atlantic have shown that "Another Man Done Gone"/"Baby Please Don't Go" fits within a larger family of songs that include "I'm Alabama Bound," "Don't Ease Me In," "Don't Leave Me Here," and "Elder Greene's in Town."[89] This network of songs that arises by the late nineteenth century uses a consistent verse pattern and, largely, a recurring subject matter.[90] Longing for another place, desiring a different circumstance, and wishing not to be left behind figures in many of these pieces. Sometimes a piece of melody transfers from one title to another. In fact, one who brought both those aspects together was Joe Williams. In 1947 he recorded "Baby Please Don't Go" and, to the same tune, "Don't Leave Me Here."[91] He preserves the same themes in both, reworking the lyrics from one and using them in the other. If his past success prompted this additional product with the proven formula, his lyrics still reflected the larger historical lineage.

The fact that this complex of songs variously split off and amalgamated not only underlines its collective longevity, but suggests how its components remained individually alive in tradition. When the Lomaxes first published "Alabama Bound," they didn't categorize it solely as blues. They also labeled it a "barrelhouse conversation" played by both races.[92] Specifying that locale, a recreational setting where songs of all sorts got performed, freed the piece from serving just one function or limiting it to one genre. In Livingston, for instance, Rich Brown sang "Alabama Bound" for John Lomax, and explained he usually did it while chopping cotton.[93] Yet Lomax's earliest recorded source for the song, a prisoner at Parchman called Bowlegs, associated it with the levee camp.[94] Jelly Roll Morton, who told Alan Lomax he wrote the song, played it in Mobile's turn-of-the-century sporting clubs.[95] Such range also applies to "Another Man Done Gone." As Harold Courlander's recording of Willie Turner shows, "Now Your Man Done Gone" served as a worksong. But it could also make an effective holler and, as later blues revival recordings show, a rousing stomp. The "Baby Please Don't Go" rock formulations that emerged in the mid-1960s, offered a vehicle for riff-driven jamming. While Big Joe Williams's version has become the one most often credited, Vera shows through her performance that still other stylistic models could shape the song. By this means "Another Man Done Gone" has endured and regenerated.

"You got to know where you been before you know where you're going."[96]
Veteran blues performer Willie "Big Eyes" Smith, who started out in 1960 as
Muddy Waters's drummer, now leads his own Chicago-based blues band. A
native of the Arkansas delta, born in Helena in 1936, he has heard "Baby Please
Don't Go" nearly all his life. He sets its lasting popularity within the larger
workings of folk tradition. "It's one of those standard songs that go on for years
. . . come all the way up through history, but the meaning's still the same."

Yet one verse that he often performs no longer signifies what it did to
Vera and her contemporaries. For Willie Smith, "walking the log" shows
the narrator beseeching, remonstrating for his woman. He does it to show
"something he didn't want to do, but he was doing it for her." Likewise, Big
Jack Johnson, a Clarksdale, Mississippi, bluesman (1940–2011), who sang
"Baby Please Don't Go" throughout the Delta, characterized the song in
familial terms. He described a man out plowing with his mule, whose wife
leaves him to go North, seeking a better life for herself. If he's "way down here
in Rolling Fork," like the verse says, then "'I walk a log' for her [means] he'll
do anything for her," to keep them together.[97] For both players, the song and
this verse express an old story of the blues—a response to abandonment, a
heartfelt shout of "don't leave me here."

In Vera's community, however, "walking the log" meant something else.
She told Harold Courlander straight out: if the convict's girl didn't meet
him after his escape, he would kill her.[98] As the fugitive plans his break he
demands cooperation from one of his own. Unlike Willie Smith's suitor risk-
ing personal safety in pursuit of love, and Jack Johnson's field hand going the
distance to keep his mate, this man fleeing confinement makes steely clear
the pressures of chain gang escape. He brings the coercion from the social
environment to bear upon the personal.

In his liner notes that accompanied Vera's 1940 recording, Lomax ques-
tioned how this verse fit the logic of the song. While he comprehended these
closing lines as a reproach, the tense domestic scene that Vera envisioned
lay outside his vernacular. Yet that elusiveness makes his point all the more
persuasive. In a dialogue between the singer and an outsider, "the singer if
she knows anything about the runaway prisoner, certainly will tell you nothing."[99] When Vera sang the piece again in Lomax's home in 1948, she varied
the shadowy ending: "I'm gonna walk your log / You don't meet me at the
waterfall / I'm gonna walk your log." Two years later she reprised the threat
in her three recordings for Harold Courlander: "You better be sure to meet
me right now."

By then commercial media had also played a role in disseminating the verse. In June 1940 Leonard "Baby Doo" Caston recorded his own version of "Another Man Done Gone"/"Baby Please Don't Go" as "I'm Gonna Walk Your Log."[100] Singing with his guitar, using a simple repeating melodic figure and backed by a percussive washboard (an effect that Joe Williams also used on his first recording), he tells a story of faithlessness and vengeance. Caston, who claimed to write this version, gives no hint of the song's penal context, and like Joe Williams before him, he locates the girl down in New Orleans with the cold ice cream. Just as Caston seems to be responding to Williams's record with his version, the following year, when Big Joe Williams rerecorded the song, he now included a stanza about "walking the log." The verse cycled forward once again, its intent inevitably revising over these transfers.

Eventually the song's original references to imprisonment at the county farm shifted, like this verse, to a more accessible theme embraced by a wider audience. Latter-day interpreters like Willie Smith and Jack Johnson have emphasized its musical appeal, especially its danceable rhythm. With vocals supported by harmonica, drums, bass, guitars, and piano, it fits an amplified era that Willie Smith calls "band time."[101] That drive, coupled with its romantic pleas against abandonment, has turned "Baby Please Don't Go" into a blues standard. "Every man that's been born can relate to that song," Smith opined. "Like the Bible. Everybody might interpret it differently. When it all boils down, it's a true song that everybody can relate to and understand."

Indeed, in 2008 "Baby Please Don't Go" surfaced in that most omnipresent of venues, *American Idol*.[102] There the musicians looked to Van Morrison and Them for inspiration, just as other singers and players have drawn upon the precedents that suited their needs. Willie Smith carries forward the legacy of Muddy Waters, who in turn credited Big Joe Williams for the song. Art goes on, re-creating old materials anew. Culture copies and builds on itself. To whatever extent Big Joe Williams's 1935 recording may have affected Vera Hall in the fall of 1940—his song was recorded five years to the day before she recorded it herself—she set it into a creative idiom that worked best for her. She invested this blues with the solemnity of a psalm, grounded in a recurrent local reality that she knew painfully well.

Less than two months after Vera recorded "Another Man Done Gone," her performance found a hearing during the seventy-fifth anniversary of the ratification of the Thirteenth Amendment to the United States Constitution held that winter at the Library of Congress. The four-day affair celebrating "the contribution of the American Negro to American culture" offered, along with an exhibition of art, books, and sound recordings, a recital by Roland Hayes and a performance by the Budapest String Quartet doing works of black composers.[103] Events included a folk music concert. On the evening of December 20, 1940, in the Library's Coolidge Auditorium, the Golden Gate Quartet performed with Josh White. The program began with spirituals, followed by blues and ballads, and finally, reels and worksongs. Each part had separate presenters with Alain Locke, Sterling Brown, and Alan Lomax commenting on their respective portions. Just after the Golden Gate Quartet opened the show with a close harmony rendition of "Freedom," Locke briefly characterized the spirituals as "the tap root of our folk music."[104] He pointed out that these songs represent more than simply black life in America. In expressing "the body and soul-suffering slavery," they convey "for the race, for the nation, for the world the spiritual fruitage of that hard experience." While originating as a regional and idiomatic art form, the spirituals "belong to a common heritage . . . [that] can be, should be, will be a part of the cultural tie that binds." The same applies to Vera's hard-experience blues, broadcast during the anniversary celebration. This glimpse of involuntary suffering now belongs to a common heritage, a cultural tie that binds.

Her song could also have served Charles Johnson's 1941 study of Black Belt life. In the post-Emancipation society he so methodically portrays, Vera's plaint finds its place. His work ends prophetically: "If one cannot safely predict progress in race relations, he can at least predict change."[105] We need only picture Vera that same year singing "Another Man Done Gone" after first cooking dinner and then washing her listeners' dishes. When she said "Any song that we sing have reference to the life that we live," she told the story not only of "Another Man Done Gone," but of her people, too.[106]

Bozie Sturdivant

A Song That Went with Him

L EWIS W. JONES, A FISK UNIVERSITY SOCIOLOGIST, TOOK ON A
research-and-recording project with the Library of Congress in September 1941 to study how music functioned in the lives of Coahoma
County, Mississippi, black residents. In the county seat of Clarksdale and
its outlying communities, Jones and his colleagues documented a cotton-
growing region shifting from manual labor to modern mechanization. Just
as the tractor vied with the hoe, the music touched both older forms and
what he called "the world of the outside."[1] His first evening in town, Jones
dropped by the segregated nightspots near Clarksdale's downtown business
district. At Messenger's Café, the Dipsy Doodle, the Chicken Shack, Lucky's,
and New Africa he surveyed 108 songs listed on their five jukeboxes.[2] Along
with a handful of country blues and even fewer gospel items, most of the
titles featured big band and swing numbers, emphasizing artists such as
Count Basie and Louis Jordan. Jones anticipated that his jukebox researches
might help to reveal "the temper of the place," a temper that in 1941 clearly
gravitated to the cosmopolitan.[3] While his subsequent interviews with the
area's oldest inhabitants summoned a frontier of wetlands and wilderness
and a musical liturgy of "Dr. Watts" and "rock Daniels," Jones also found in
this community that "the new has as much place as the old."[4]

When Jones returned to Coahoma County in May 1942, he identified a number of candidates to record later that summer with the Library's Alan Lomax.[5] His contacts included "Union Jubilee Gospel," a vocal quartet founded four years earlier, whose main lead singer was thirty-seven-year-old domestic worker Bozie Sturdivant. That July, during a service at Clarksdale's Silent Grove Baptist Church, Bozie made nine recordings with this group including a spiritual called "Ain't No Grave Can Hold My Body Down."[6] Bozie's approach to the song reflected a traditional style of religious singing and an emerging sound in quartet performance. Like the jukeboxes that Lewis Jones cataloged, Bozie's impassioned performance brought together the local with the national and the personal with the manufactured. Life in the Delta, as elsewhere in rural America, was changing. Bozie Sturdivant's song captured the complexity of that change. It also preserved what he held most dear.

On July 25, 1942, as Lewis Jones and Alan Lomax operated the disc machine they had set up near the altar of Silent Grove's one-story frame church, the Union Jubilee second tenor Bozie Sturdivant led on "Please Don't Drive Me Away" and "When I've Done the Best I Can, I Want My Crown." In "I Want My Crown," with a melody nearly identical to "Ain't No Grave," Bozie showed his voice as capable of steep falsetto flights as of a buzzing growl. Earlier he displayed this soaring range during both takes of "Ain't No Grave," soloing while the group chanted a quiet, harmonic backdrop. Fifty-five years later, Appolonia Cotton, a former musician at Silent Grove who remembered Bozie's singing with the Union Jubilee Quartet, placed these songs in context. "Their music really wasn't printed in a book," Cotton explained. "They would get together and make up songs that had a different rhythm."[7]

Appolonia Cotton understood music transmitted both through oral tradition and according to written method. For twenty-five years she served as Silent Grove's principal pianist and organist. She inherited this role from her older sister, whose early tutelage of "five-finger exercises," followed by a mail-order instruction manual, provided her first keyboard lessons.[8] After her sister got sick in the late 1940s, Cotton took her place at Silent Grove, playing as she said "by music and by memory." Moreover, in 1983 Cotton wrote the congregation's history in celebration of its 112th anniversary, an effort that gave her detailed knowledge of its past membership.[9]

Now in the hush of her Clarksdale apartment, its windows shut tight against the heat and its walls overwhelmed by dark burnished furniture and brittle antique glassware, she bent over a list of the 1942 Silent Grove recordings. Through the thick ovals of her eyeglasses, she studied each detail on the page, deciphering the sequence of songs and singers. Though marred by misspellings and names garbled by ear, all of the information she examined—from street addresses to the performers' ages—was familiar to her. Cotton found her sister's name among them: Savannah Galmore, age twelve, playing and singing a piano-accompanied hymn.[10] For a ten-cent price of admission, the afternoon's program included the reading of a Paul Laurence Dunbar poem, the singing of the church's junior choir, and the performances of two local gospel quartets.[11] Of the latter, most of the recordings featured the Union Jubilee Quartet, a group that Cotton remembered well.

Founded by long-time Silent Grove member John Skipper, the group kept busy that 1942 summer with weekend performances and twice-weekly rehearsals. "Skipper was an overseer for some of the quartets," said Cotton. "He couldn't read notes, but he'd teach that kind of music, the quartet style."[12] As owner of the Big Six barbershop, a gathering place for local quartets, and in later years the host of a weekly WROX broadcast that featured many of the groups he trained, Skipper affected generations of Clarksdale singers. At the time of the recording, four of the community's leading quartets, the Union Jubilees among them, were in the process of forming a membership organization that assured them of a place to practice along with a scheduled time to compete against one another.[13] Skipper had lately cut back on the number of churches where his own group appeared. Nevertheless, he reserved the third Sunday of every month for their programs at Silent Grove.

Cotton listened intently to a tape of Bozie singing "Ain't No Grave." Years earlier, she had seen him perform this piece, her first exposure to the song. But he never joined her church and they had little contact outside of his appearances there with John Skipper. Subsequently, she heard the song performed by other quartets until the mid-1950s, at which point it seemed to drop from active repertory. Now, as the recording played, she responded to Bozie's manner as much as to his message. "It sounds like a preacher," she remarked. "I've heard ministers say, 'No grave could hold His body down.'" She likened it to a verse in Corinthians: "O Death where is thy sting? O grave where is thy victory," a passage still repeated at countless funerals.[14] Cotton explained that the song's wording was an unschooled way of expressing the same idea.

"There was a time," Cotton continued, "when people didn't read the Bible . . . and preachers didn't study." She linked the spiritual to an era when few in her community were literate and the music most people had to accompany their church services came from "patting their feet." That "Ain't No Grave" had become a quartet song only added to its common origins. "People didn't think too highly of quartet music then," she remarked, recalling how some of her fellow church members felt it prolonged a heritage they wanted to move beyond. Cotton viewed Bozie Sturdivant's rendition as "a song being sung by someone who was himself unlearned." To make her point that there were two texts by which to understand "Ain't No Grave"—the Scripture's and the song's, one written and literary, the other oral and idiomatic—Cotton reached for her Bible.

"The song comes from rolling the stone to the door," Cotton said, "and when they went back, the stone had rolled away." She read aloud from the book of Mark: "And he saith unto them, Be not affrighted: Ye seek Jesus of Nazareth, which was crucified: he is risen; he is not here: behold the place where they laid him."[15] Even though the Bible specifies a tomb and not a grave—again she drew a distinction between the Bible's language and the song's—she added, "The grave is in the Bible." Cotton turned to the gospel of St. John: "For the hour is coming, in which all that are in the graves shall hear his voice."[16] Then she repeated the story of Lazarus brought back to life. He, too, had lain in a cave with a stone for its entrance.[17]

Several months earlier, Clarksdale minister and quartet singer Willie Morganfield made a similar connection. "Ain't No Grave," he said, "comes from Jesus saying He would rise in three days. All that died in Him would be like Him."[18] For the Reverend Morganfield, first cousin of blues singer Muddy Waters and a former member of Clarksdale's Four Star Quartet, the song inspired several of his sermons. It revealed "God dressed up in human clothes," he explained. "He's a man and he's also God. One hundred percent either way."

The passage that both Willie Morganfield and Appolonia Cotton identified as the dramatic premise of "Ain't No Grave" appears in its earliest known publication, a 1933 Church of God in Christ hymnal, published by a church elder in Arkansas and sold by mail.[19] This pocket-sized paperback cites Isaiah 12 on the cover, a verse that fits with Pentecostal fervency: "Sing unto the Lord . . . cry out and shout." The absence of musical notation indicates that buyers would have known the tune to which the words were set. All evidence suggests that "Can't No Grave Hold My Body Down" circulated before this appearance in print.[20]

It was early one morning,
Just about the break of day.
The angel came from glory
And rolled the stone away.
But when the women came along,
And found that their Savior was gone,
Couldn't no grave hold His body down.

> Chorus:
> Can't no grave hold my body down,
> Can't no grave hold my body down.
> When the first trumpet sound,
> I'm going to get up out of the ground,
> Can't no grave hold my body down.

Go yonder, Gabriel,
And just stand on the land and sea,
But don't you blow that trumpet, Gabriel,
Until you've an order from me.
Because can't no grave hold my people down.

How well can I remember,
The day He sanctified me Holy,
And fill me with the Holy Ghost,
Now if you ride this train,
You got to call on Jesus name.
Then Can't no grave hold your body down.[21]

Like the sermons that the Reverend Morganfield modeled after "Ain't No Grave," the text entwines Jesus' message with human experience. The song moves from no grave holding "His body down" to "my body down," followed by "my people down" to "your body down." By shifting pronouns and their objects, the song spans a range of meanings from personal to political that even its earliest recordings reveal.

Five days before Jones and Lomax recorded Bozie Sturdivant at Silent Grove, the two researchers made their first trip to Friars Point, Mississippi, a river town twenty-two miles north of Clarksdale. That evening at a nearby roadhouse, they watched young people jitterbug to jukebox records of Duke Ellington, while earlier that afternoon they had listened to bluesman David Edwards captivate a downtown crowd with his guitar playing. Meanwhile, in a vacant lot across the street, they found a Holiness group holding a musical service for a few listeners. Lomax's field notes include the reminiscences of Fannie McCottrell, born a slave in 1851, who described to him brush arbor meetings of a bygone day, and a conversation he had with Miss Chapman, the town's first music teacher, who recalled the serenades and cotillions played by black musicians in the days of her youth. Now, with the aid of a local druggist named Mason, Lomax and Jones began to make recordings that included a Baptist quartet called the Friendly Five Harmony Singers. Formed in 1939, the five-man group consisted of a truck driver, a carpenter's helper, a millwright, a farmer, and an ice packer. The quartet (in African American usage, *quartet* refers to musical style and not to the number of singers) had secured a regular slot on KFFA, a radio station in nearby Helena. Their recordings included introductory patter much like a radio broadcast.[22] While they noted that some of their pieces came from hymnals and others from "ballets"—cheaply printed sheets sold on the street—four of their numbers they identified as "hallies." Short for *hallelujah*, these were "the old spirituals," which Jones noted "were used as collection and revival songs."[23] One of those hallies was "There's No Grave Can Hold My Body Down."

The Friendly Five's performance marks the first time the song was ever recorded.[24] Their lead's subdued but earnest voice begins with a personal testimony. "I know I've got religion," he sings. "I know I'm not ashamed. . . . My mother she died and left me. My father, he stole away too. I don't have no friends and kindred to depend upon," leaving the final verse to convey the underlying story: "It was on one Sunday morning, just about the break of day. When the angel came from heaven, just to roll the stone away." The other singers enter on the chorus. The group's arrangement involves none of the repeated syllables under an improvised lead that marked a popular style at that time or the head tones that characterized the university-trained quartets. Instead, the group presented what gospel experts today call a community-based jubilee style.

With the exception of Bozie Sturdivant's performance, the Friendly Five's version anticipated all of the song's 1940s-era recordings, verbally similar though musically diverse, including an unpublished New England field recording by the daughter of a former slave.[25] In 1947, "Ain't No Grave" was released on two commercial recordings. In the first of these by the Two Gospel Keys, a female duet from Atlanta, Emma Daniels and Mother Sally Jones, both members of the Church of God in Christ, accompanied themselves on guitar and tambourine. Sister Rosetta Tharpe, who was raised in the same Pentecostal denomination and who learned the song from her mother (and later sang it at her funeral), played it in her signature style using single-string guitar leads over a jukebox-friendly combo of bass, piano, and drums.[26]

Of the decade's recordings, only Bozie Sturdivant's substantively expanded the lyrics via several New Testament scenes:

> Ain't no grave can hold my body down,
> Ain't no grave can hold my body down, my body down
> When the first trumpet sound,
> I'll be getting up, walking around,
> Ain't no grave can hold my body down.
>
> Ain't no grave can hold my body down,
> Ain't no grave can hold my body down, my body down.
> Now when that first trumpet sound,
> I'll be getting up, walking around,
> Ain't no grave can hold my body down.

When I heard of a beautiful city,
The street was paved with gold.
Then I had not been to Heaven,
Oh, Lord, I've been told.
Then I found this throne of grace,
It's gonna appoint my soul a place.
Ain't no grave can hold my body down.

> Ain't no grave can hold my body down,
> Ain't no grave can hold my body down,
> When the first trumpet sound,
> I'll be getting up, walking around,
> Ain't no grave can hold my body down.

When Jesus was hanging on the cross,
It made poor Mary moan.
He looked down on His disciples,
"They've taken my mother home."
Ain't that a pity and Lord a shame,
How they crucified the Lamb.
Ain't no grave can hold my body down.

> Ain't no grave can hold my body down,
> Ain't no grave can hold my body down.
> When the first trumpet sound,
> I'll be getting up, walking around,
> Ain't no grave can hold my body down.[27]

According to Appolonia Cotton, the refrain originates in 1 Corinthians: "Behold, I shew you a mystery; We shall not all sleep, but we shall all be changed. In a moment, in the twinkling of an eye, at the last trump: for the trumpet shall sound, and the dead shall be raised incorruptible, and we shall be changed."[28] The song's first thematic element, the beautiful city, limns the new, heavenly Jerusalem depicted in Revelation. The city is where the redeemed come to live, an altered reality with twelve gates, walls of jasper and pearl, and streets that glow "as it were transparent glass."[29] Bozie's verse sequence suggests that the grave is a door into the ascension sounded by the trumpet and signaling a new mode of being in the heavenly City. In Revelation, the enthroned recording angel blots out the sins written in each person's history. "And I saw a great white throne," writes St. John the Divine, "the dead, small and great, stand before God; and the books were opened: . . . and the dead were judged out of those things which were written in the books, according to their works."[30] The song's last image, the crucifixion that Mary witnesses, echoes the Gospel of John. In a compound of poetic rhyme and casual speech, Bozie intones "Ain't that a pity and Lord a shame, How they crucified the Lamb."[31] Bozie ends this Easter story with a startling, falsetto turn.

A year before this recording was made, Lewis Jones, along with Alan Lomax and John Work III of Fisk's music department, recorded the Reverend C. H. Savage, a preacher from Hollendale, Mississippi, who led a revival service at the 14,000-acre King and Anderson plantation, a sixteen-mile-long tract on the outskirts of Clarksdale. When asked for some "story songs," the Reverend Savage replied, "Oh yeah, that's what we call hallies, sung when we took up collection."[32] If *hallie* was understood as a story, it was not necessarily one built on a chronological sequence of episodes. Bozie's "Ain't No Grave" also forms a story song, tracing a course from the grave to the heavenly city to the throne where humankind is judged to the sorrow that surrounds Jesus' death. His entombment and ascension are implicit. In Bozie's extended treatment, "Ain't No Grave" did not need the usual image of the cave that the more abbreviated versions required.

Appolonia Cotton sensed that Bozie's song mirrored a sermon.[33] Her experience showed her that "Ain't No Grave" worked like a pulpit oration, rendered in language she had heard preachers use and threaded by an associative unity of images they employed.[34] Like a hallie, a sermon does not have to keep strict chronology to make sense to its listeners, but it does need to draw upon a common fund of references to be successful. "The minister," she cheerfully noted, "is the one who makes it clear." The story's kernel, as the recordings show, was the cave where Christ's body lay. Cotton knew that this "Ain't No Grave," straddling the two traditions, operated as an oral telling of a written parable. It was not unlike her own experience in learning the piano, an instrument she practiced, in her words, "by music and by memory." Admittedly, Cotton lived in a social sphere that prized the written over the oral, one that favored printed hymns over unwritten arrangements. But she also recognized that a number of the spirituals her older sister taught her at Silent Grove derived from an oral basis, given by example and retained by ear.

With our visit nearing its end, Cotton drew a phonograph record from her closet. In 1986 she wrote a song about the *Challenger* disaster called "The Shuttle and the Crew of Seven." The LP she held up featured a postcard view of a church set in a mountain cove. Her song appeared first among a selection of twelve compositions, each by a different songwriter. Published in Nashville, the album was marketed to the country music trade in the hope that one or another of its pieces might be picked up by a name performer seeking new material. The team who issued the record took credit in a process described in the sleeve notes: "Every song in the album . . . started first with you the co-writer with the lyrics then a little polish and a wholesome melody."[35] Cotton's song noted how the accident "startled little boys and girls" who watched the ship explode with schoolteacher Christa McAuliffe aboard and acknowledged the *Challenger* astronauts' sacrifice, which "proved their love for God and country." By depicting a recent event in sentimental verse, Cotton drew upon a rhetoric that hearkened back to sidewalk broadsides and ballet-card dramas. "The Shuttle and the Crew of Seven," marketed to Nashville's recording stars, extended that venerable process into the present day with its space-age theme, modern country music setting, and recording studio technology.

Cotton tucked the record under my arm and gave me one last counsel: I might have better success in tracking down those who knew Bozie Sturdivant if I ran an ad in the Clarksdale paper. By then I had already spoken during a Sunday morning service at Silent Grove Baptist Church describing the Fisk-LC-Coahoma project and Bozie's recording. Contacts there led to a number of Clarksdale's older quartet singers and musically knowledge-able persons, including Cotton.[36] But none brought any positive leads about Bozie himself. Clarksdale's city directories also proved limited, last listing his residence in 1939.[37] Earlier I mentioned to Cotton that files at the Folk Archive had also yielded little, despite efforts over the years to locate him. Bozie's last communication with the Library took place in 1943 when he corrected the printed text planned to accompany publication of "Ain't No Grave Can Hold My Body Down." At that time he lived nearby in Helena, Arkansas, but my search of that city's records, an interview with a longtime KFFA radio broadcaster where Bozie's group had possibly performed, and a visit to a local photographer who had documented singers of that era also failed.[38] The celebrated Early Wright, the first black disc jockey in the Delta, kindly invited me onto his long-running WROX Sunday morning radio show, where he enlisted his listeners' help in this search. While Wright had comanaged Clarksdale's Four Star Quartet in 1942 and served as a contact named in Lewis Jones's fieldnotes, he, too, had known Bozie only in passing. Consequently, I followed Cotton's advice and placed a notice in the newspaper's classified section, set up a local telephone number with voice mail, and wrote a brief message that rolled continuously for a month on the local TV cable channel. In 1942, Lewis Jones saw Coahoma County balancing the folk culture of a time past with present-day technology. His observation still applied a half century later. Appolonia Cotton was right, too.

For twenty-two days my Clarksdale phone never rang. Its recorded message, asking callers for whatever information they might have about Bozie Sturdivant, went unheard. Then, a week before the service expired and the notice in the *Clarksdale Press Register* was to cease, four calls came within an hour's time. An elderly woman spoke in a quivering but assertive voice: "My name is Georgia Wicks, W-I-C-K-S. I live in Clarksdale, Mississippi, and Bozie Sturdivant was my cousin. Please call me at once. Thank you. God bless you."[39]

Although nearly six decades had passed since Georgia Wicks last saw Bozie Sturdivant—they grew up on the same plantation outside of Clarksdale—and almost twenty years since she learned of his death, her memories of him have remained evergreen. When she first saw the classified notice in the paper followed by the TV cable roll, she admitted that in the passage of years, "he had nearly gone out of my mind."[40] But Wicks recognized her cousin's name, and coupled with the mention of "Ain't No Grave," his self-professed favorite song, she found herself as curious about the unexpected inquiry as she was certain of its subject. A lithe figure blessed with a keen knowledge of her family's history, she spoke of him with animation. "The more I talk about him," she later reflected, "the better I remember him."[41] Tenderness instilled her memories: "Bozie and I were on the same scale. If I can help anyone anywhere, my living won't be in vain, even if it's just to speak an encouraging word."[42]

Bozie Sturdivant was born May 12, 1905, on a small farm thirty-one miles south of Clarksdale in Swan Lake, Mississippi, the only child of Miles and Fannie Parker Sturdivant.[43] His mother died soon after his birth, and he was raised by his father's second wife, Mary. After Miles and Mary divorced, she and Bozie moved away to live with her sister in Farrell, a community adjacent to the Sherard plantation, a 6,000-acre cotton and pecan farm. There she met her second husband, Eugene Coleman, Georgia Wicks's uncle. Eugene's parents had come from Livingston, Alabama, in 1874 with John Sherard Sr., the property's founder. In 1920, Bozie Sturdivant moved with Mary and Eugene to Sherard, where the family lived as sharecroppers. Like many of their fellow tenants, they occupied a three-room house, fitted with plank floors and shingle-board siding, without indoor plumbing or electricity. A hand-cranked pump stood in the yard. They farmed "on the halves," giving half their crop to the Sherards in exchange for land and housing, while Wicks's father, Howard Coleman, who owned his own wagon, plow tools, and mules, worked "on the two-thirds," keeping that portion for his family and allotting the final third to the landlord.[44] Either way, Wicks recalled, both families worked from "sun to sun," toiling from daylight to dark.[45] Because a deformity in Bozie's right hand limited his capacity as a field laborer, the foreman installed him as caretaker and groundskeeper. Following the death of Eugene Coleman, and unable to get along with Mary's third husband, Bozie quit Sherard for Clarksdale, where the 1936 city directory described his employment as "yard boy."[46] The following year he took a job in Memphis at a salvage company, then in 1939 moved back to Clarksdale, where the directory now termed him "houseboy."[47] By that time, too, Mary returned to Swan Lake, where she reunited with Miles Sturdivant and remained for the rest of her life.

At Sherard, Bozie Sturdivant made religious music his calling. "He hadn't passed the play stage when he was singing church songs," said Wicks.[48] The plantation provided four churches for its residents, three Baptist and one Methodist, and Bozie sang at all of them. The only time Wicks ever saw her cousin perform nonsacred material was in an end-of-year program at the one-room Methodist church, which doubled as a school. Bozie sang the replies in "Charming Billy," a courting song of English origin that asks, "Oh where have you been, Billy Boy, Billy Boy, / Oh where have you been, charming Billy?" Beyond this episode, however, he evinced little or no interest in singing nonreligious material. When Sherard tenants gathered for "a Saturday night fling," partying in their cabins by the light of their kerosene lamps, Bozie Sturdivant would not have numbered among the revelers. As Wicks explained, "He wasn't a worldly person."[49] She remembers him turning instead to his mother's well-worn Methodist hymnal.

"I used to aggravate him so much," Wicks giggled. "Whenever I saw him, I'd say, 'You sure can't sing.'" Her teasing, she knew, did nothing to deter Bozie's passion for spiritual song. "When he started to sing, it'd go all through him. He'd start walking. He had to do something." Of all his pieces, "Ain't No Grave Can Hold My Body Down" became the number his Sherard neighbors most often requested. "After a program concluded," Wicks recalled, "he'd have to sing this song."[50] It remained his signature piece. Not long after January 22, 1978, Bozie's wife Stella contacted Wicks to say that he sat up in his bed that day and sang "Ain't No Grave Can Hold My Body Down," his final act before he died.

Though Wicks saw him only twice after he left Sherard, a memory from the late 1940s remained with her. In 1947 or 1948, Bozie posted from Texas an eight-by-ten-inch photograph that shows him dressed in a tuxedo with three other male singers similarly attired. The group stands in single file with Bozie heading the line, each touching the shoulder of the one before. Wicks thought the ensemble was the Soul Stirrers of Houston. While the picture in fact portrays another quartet that her cousin had joined, Wicks's connecting Bozie to the Soul Stirrers reflects a notion of modernity that has surrounded him since "Ain't No Grave" first appeared on record.

Within a year of Bozie's recording at the Silent Grove Baptist Church, the Library of Congress released *Negro Religious Songs and Services,* a fifteen-song album edited by Benjamin Botkin.[51] This collection, which includes "The Man of Calvary," a 1934 Easter-day sermon by Texas minister "Sin-Killer" Griffin that also tells of the dead rising from the grave, marks the initial publication of "Ain't No Grave Can Hold My Body Down."[52] In the album notes, Botkin wrote that Bozie's piece "illustrates the new kind of gospel song growing out of the union of jazz and religion." While not jazz in the usual sense, Bozie's performance does stand out for its elaborate manipulation of the melody and its foregrounding of his work as a virtuoso soloist. No matter, by using this label Botkin emphasized the novel features that marked the recording.

That same year, Fisk musicologist John Work III made some related observations about the song and its style. In a manuscript provisionally titled "In the Bottoms" (a regional name for the Delta), he included a list of locally made, newly created spirituals.[53] Among them he placed Bozie's "Ain't No Grave," which he also transcribed and notated. Work called the piece a "solo-spiritual" that "undeniably borrows its more sophisticated verse style and its extended musical-phrase structure from the gospel songs, without the easy performance of the latter. The congregation finding these songs too difficult to sing usually surrenders the melody and verse to a leader while it hums or listens."[54] Though Work classified the song as of

FIGURE 27. John W. Work III's notation for "Ain't No Grave Can Hold My Body Down." Courtesy of Special Collections, Fisk University Franklin Library.

local origin, he also considered other sources for the solo-spirituals, citing in particular "the easy access to Memphis, where Mississippians can learn new songs."[55] Just as Lewis Jones described in his report how Coahoma's rural dwellers readily moved between the countryside and Clarksdale and increasingly felt the sway of the city, Work acknowledged a similar role of urban influence: "Thus the disappearance of some songs, the continued life of others, as well as the appearance of new songs could be explained."[56]

Wherever "Ain't No Grave" in its solo-spiritual form may have originated, its modernity was apparent.

Throughout the Fisk-Coahoma fieldwork—whether conducted by John Work, Lewis Jones, Alan Lomax, or other members of the research team—performers were queried about their listening habits. Asked whether they owned radios and record players and if the latter, which records comprised their collection, respondents disclosed how popular taste and technology played a role in the music they admired. Muddy Waters, for instance, mentioned "Chattanooga Choo-Choo" and "Deep in the Heart of Texas" as songs that he heard and enjoyed via mass media. Though the Fisk researchers pointed out that jukebox records and radio broadcasts imposed "standardization" on regional creativity, John Work realized years before that widely heard performances also stimulated folk usage: "The phonograph recording of these songs does not destroy the 'folkness' of them."[57] Now he cited the Golden Gate Quartet, whose effect was that "They regularly supply songs through their recordings to their rural counterparts who imitate and vary them."[58] Among those that Work named so supplied with songs were Bozie's group, the Union Jubilees, and the Friendly [Five] Harmony Singers. For them and other local singers and instrumentalists such media-generated products resulted in "new virtuosic melodic idioms . . . being introduced into their play and harmony . . . being enriched."[59] Consequently, when Bozie recorded "Ain't No Grave" at Silent Grove Baptist Church, even though the particular song had never been previously released, the unique singing style he employed had already made its way via records, broadcasts, and personal appearances.

In July 1942, "the talk of the quartet community," said music historian Tony Heilbut, centered on the Chicago-based Soul Stirrers.[60] Founded in Houston in 1927, this five-man group demonstrated a new approach to quartet performance with their 1940 recording of "Walk Around."[61] On it, tenor singer Rebert Harris uses his pliant, emotive voice, his self-styled "delayed time"—singing behind the beat—and natural falsetto to create what soon became a much-imitated vocal style.[62] Pivoting against the choruses of his fellow Soul Stirrers, Harris focuses on certain words and passages, selectively dwelling on notes, inflecting them with a contained but palpable clarity. His soloing technique set him apart from other singers of the era, singers of whom he later said, "They don't read, don't define, don't insert themselves into the composer's condition and bring the thing to a picture."[63] Under Harris's direction, the Soul Stirrers traced a new vision, innovating the "swing lead" in which the melody passes from one singer to another. This trading of parts, occurring over a continuous four-part harmony, had the effect of magnifying a song's dramatic impact. Whether the second singer leaps into a higher pitch or hunches down into a huskier register, the structure recast the close harmony workings of the traditional jubilee ensemble into the soloist-centered gospel quartet. Harris's style set a precedent that Sam Cooke, who replaced him in the group, eventually translated into his own pop success, and that foretold the gospel blues of Ray Charles and Otis Redding.

Bozie's approach to "Ain't No Grave" bore such similarities to Harris's mannerisms that despite the difference of their voices (Harris's registered lighter and higher than Bozie's), Heilbut could assert, "He's singing Harris."[64] However distantly Bozie lived from the music's recording and publishing hub, he still managed in an environment in which records, radio, and motor highways spread ideas and idioms. By these means, local quartet singers like Bozie regularly found new material. That the song had not numbered among the Soul Stirrers' repertoire only underscores the degree to which Bozie had assimilated Harris's influence. Bozie took a folk spiritual that he had known since his youth, a song that had both entered Holiness usage (shown by the 1933 paperback songster) and made its way into Baptist-style jubilee (reflected by the Friendly Five's recording), and recast it according to Harris's example. By doing so, Bozie confirmed what John Work had seen among Nashville's street musicians: "Tricks of embellishment," transmitted on records, "originally the property of one player, once exhibited, become the property of all the players in his vicinity if they be of sufficient merit to catch their interest."[65]

In a 1970 interview, Harris named Bozie Sturdivant as one of his acolytes. When Bozie sang "Ain't No Grave," a piece he purportedly dramatized with shoveling gestures, Harris said that the performance inspired Chicago churchgoers to cry out, "Sing Harris, dig that grave, R. H."[66] Harris used this anecdote to show the impact he had made not only on this individual whom he remembered, but on an entire genre. The image of Bozie digging, however, does not fit other accounts of Bozie's stage demeanor. Nor do city records show any sign of his residence in Chicago.[67] Heilbut acknowledges that Harris may have been mistaken in certain respects about Bozie, but he also says that "there's always some validity to his memories."[68] Indeed, another connection between the two singers confirming Harris's influence surfaced when Bozie Sturdivant first came to Denison, Texas, in 1946.

Ralph Dawson held up the framed photograph that he keeps beside his easy chair. The eight-by-ten image, the same one Georgia Wicks saw at Sherard in the late 1940s, shows the Friendship Spirituals, a Denison-based quartet comprised of Dawson, his brother Joe, their friend Arthur Blanton, and Bozie Sturdivant. A few weeks earlier, when I first contacted him by phone, I asked the Reverend Dawson, a former construction laborer and still-active minister, whether he ever heard of a singer named Bozie

FIGURE 28.
From Bozie Sturdivant's funeral program. Courtesy of Ralph Dawson.

Sturdivant.[69] He answered with electrifying directness: "I'm looking at his picture right now."[70]

Dawson propped the picture next to his chair and fed some scrap wood into a small cast-iron stove whitened with ash. It quickly filled the windowless rooms with heat. In the back, a blanket curtained off the bedroom from the kitchen, where along the walls hung a jumble of calendars, promotional giveaways from local businesses, the most recent advertising a funeral parlor where Dawson still worked part-time. Outside, discarded auto parts and broken-down washing machines congested his front yard, each waiting to be repaired or salvaged. Earlier that day we stopped at Bozie's house a few blocks away. The bare, shotgun-style dwelling sagged with age, its emptiness fixed by the rough planks hammered over its back door and window.

Dawson looked again at the likeness of his old musical partner, recalling how Bozie used to walk into Denison's business district and serenade passers-by with unaccompanied hymns. "We called him 'Singin' Bozie,'" mused Dawson. "He was dedicated all the way down." Dawson removed Bozie's funeral program that he kept tucked behind the photo. It specified that his brother Joe Dawson would solo on "Ain't No Grave Can Hold My Body Down." Not only had this been the one musical piece chosen to commemorate Bozie's life, it was the first number his friends in Denison ever heard him do. Dawson gently remarked, "It was a song that went with him."

During the summer of 1946, a touring gospel quartet calling themselves the Five Soul Stirrers of Denver, Colorado, stood at the pulpit of Denison's Antioch Baptist Church. While not the same Soul Stirrers from Chicago that featured Rebert Harris, they knew the original group's repertoire and had just sung "I'll Never Turn Back" and "Don't Wonder about Him," two songs the famous ensemble had issued only a few months earlier.[71] Suddenly, a high voice from the back of the church launched into "Ain't No Grave Can Hold My Body Down." Until then, Bozie Sturdivant had been sitting quietly in a pew near the door. Now Bozie walked to the front as he led the song, while the rest of the group carried its refrain of "hold my body down." Ralph Dawson, who was in attendance, remembers the wonder that spread through the room. All heads turned as if to ask, "Where'd he come from?"[72] For Dawson, a young quartet singer who had recently moved to Denison from the Oklahoma countryside to work as a section hand for the Katy (nickname for the Missouri, Kansas & Texas railroad), Bozie's entrance compared to only one other singing experience he had known.

Three years earlier, a quartet called the Detroiters founded by Denison native Oliver Green had come from Michigan to appear at the Mt. Zion Baptist Church, bringing with them Joe Louis's mother, an added attraction who packed the house. During the service, and again without announcement, singer Leroy Barnes, acting under what Dawson called "the anointing of the spirit," stood balanced on the back of a chair and sang. Barnes's unforeseen display of conviction so moved Dawson that when he and his brother returned to their home town of Hendrix, Oklahoma, some twenty miles distant, they started their own quartet. Though Dawson had previously sung, following the example of his father and uncles (who supplied quartet music at family picnics in addition to playing mandolins, harmonicas, and guitars for dances), and while he already knew the Golden Gate Quartet and the Five Blind Boys of Mississippi through their recordings and had long made it a habit to listen to the weekly CBS radio broadcasts of the Wings over Jordan choir, he found Barnes's spiritual candor that evening overwhelming. Before then, Dawson admitted, "I was singing, but I was seeing in my mind a Seagram's bottle. You can't serve both."

Bozie's performance captured Dawson with comparable force. He followed "Ain't No Grave" with "I Want My Crown," a melodically similar piece also set to a four-part harmony.[73] Bozie next joined the group for one or two up-tempo jubilee numbers, his agile voice allowing him to serve as the group's utility man. Although the Five Soul Stirrers of Denver, Colorado, had come for the one-night engagement at Antioch Baptist, playing the date as an "open-door offering"—a term Dawson used to indicate no set admission charge—they stayed on for the remainder of the week. The group came back twice more in succeeding years, but they no longer brought Bozie with them. Nor did they need to. In 1947, shortly after that first appearance in Denison, Bozie made this city his permanent home, having met Stella Harris, the woman who eventually became his wife.[74] Early on as a Denison resident he also became friends with Ralph Dawson.

Dawson remembers Bozie saying that the Five Soul Stirrers of Denver, Colorado, formed at a barbershop in St. Louis, Missouri. Both the group's leader, Frank Kemp, who sang bass and the first tenor, Cumby (Dawson couldn't recollect his first name), worked as railroad porters. The group met at the shop between their out-of-town runs. Other members included lead singer Walter Thomas, who shined shoes there, and a native of Muskogee, Oklahoma, named Osborne who sang baritone. Bozie usually took the role of second tenor or else switched parts with Osborne and Thomas, depending on a given song's requirements. The Denver name the group adopted had less to do with any member's residency out west than with establishing themselves in the Soul Stirrers' mold. Between 1945 and 1955, gospel quartet singing enjoyed a peak decade of popularity with the Soul Stirrers at the genre's forefront.[75] By adopting this name, the St. Louis–based ensemble both honored the original group's artistry and defined themselves as a branch of their style. Dawson recalls Bozie's mentioning that he had sung with Rebert Harris and that he knew James Medlock and Jesse Farley, two of the group's most celebrated baritone and bass singers.

We know little about the extent of Bozie's contact with the Chicago Soul Stirrers, let alone about the Denver Soul Stirrers. One clue to those years, between his last known address in Helena, Arkansas, in 1943, and his moving to Denison in 1947, lay with his half-sister Zora. Born at Sherard, Zora lived with her daughter Estella in St. Louis.[76] Both Georgia Wicks and Ralph Dawson feel sure this family presence impelled him there. Throughout the years of their friendship, Dawson found Bozie responsive to any subject that might arise in conversation. But he also accepted that his friend did not volunteer information. Dawson quietly reflected, "He was a loner and he wasn't a loner. . . . I took what I caught from him."[77]

Though Bozie's singing career eluded any known commercial recordings or full-time membership in the era's most celebrated groups, he remained professionally active until 1950.[78] As late as 1949 the Denison directory listed his occupation as "singer," after which he became a city maintenance worker along with seasonally operating a two-wheeled handcart at the local cotton compress.[79] Before he shifted vocations, Bozie traveled during the late 1940s as a quartet performer. "When groups come through town," Dawson remembers, "and if they needed a first tenor man . . . and they were up in Kansas City, [they'd say] 'Old Sturdivant's down there in Denison and we need him up here in Kansas City. Call him.'"[80] Bozie's strength as a lead singer in addition to his facility with tenor and baritone parts made him useful as a substitute vocalist, and his contact with the various groups and their recordings contributed to his knowledge of the idiom. All of this expertise came into play when he and Ralph Dawson began singing together.

"Bozie and Cumby enlisted me and my brother to sing," Dawson reported. "They came here to look for us."[81] In early 1947, Bozie and one of his partners from the Five Soul Stirrers of Denver, Colorado, needed two more singers for a nearby engagement. Dawson and his brother had become known from their appearances as the Calvary Gospel Singers, the quartet the siblings launched after seeing the Detroiters several years earlier. More than a half century later, Dawson could still reconstruct Bozie's gusto when he first approached them. "Well, boys," he said, "let's see what we can do about some *harmony*."

Dawson now took the phrase "I found a horseshoe" and explained, "Even if there are more than four people, you have four parts of music, that's the order of the music. You have your bass and then graduate up." He then sang "horseshoe" in four pitches, demonstrating bass, baritone, lead, and tenor parts. Similarly, in the 1950s, Dawson and his brother opened their programs with each man in their quartet singing his name according to his vocal assignment: "Good morning, how are you? My name is. . . . I'm doing fine. How do you do."[82] The greeting not only introduced the singers to their audiences but showed their command of the music's four parts. When Bozie first asked the Dawson brothers, "Did we know what we were singing?" they could give him no reply beyond their tacit understanding of its rudiments. "We were singing the style of the music," Dawson said, "but he knew the name of it."

Bozie began to instruct the younger men, giving them a grammar by which to shape their arrangements. He spoke of "up-ratcheting," modulating one step higher.[83] "Double-stackatory time" referred to the process of starting a song at one rate and then quickening it to twice the tempo, all the while keeping the vocal parts dispersed in parallel lines, as if they stacked up vertically by pitch. His tutoring further extended to time signatures. While Dawson formerly classified songs simply as "slow beat," "fast beat," and, quickest of all, "jubilistic," with its "full-time beat," he now began to work according to a more precise formula that Bozie provided. "Four-four" meant that "every beat you're saying something, you sing every beat." If a song were in "three-quarter time" (which Dawson said included "Ain't No Grave"), "you take one beat out," which meant observing a rest before starting the next verse. While Bozie used a nonstandard nomenclature, younger singers like Ralph Dawson found his onomatopoetic terms both practical and lucid.

Bozie also counseled them on performing. "When you get on a stage to sing, you do your job the way you're supposed to do it. You're supposed to know how it's done before you get there. I don't want you up there talking about 'I forgot.' I don't want you talking 'I don't know my tune,' because you're gonna know your tune."[84] By emphasizing professionalism, Bozie acknowledged there would come nights when, as Dawson said, "they sang flat-footed and didn't move." When that happens, Bozie stressed, "You don't get up and tell them 'I ain't got no spirit.'" Dawson later added, "If you did, you'd look like a double fool."[85]

Within months, the contact between the veteran performer and the Dawson brothers led to their founding the Friendship Spirituals. It was a four-man group with Joe Dawson singing first tenor, Bozie, second tenor, Arthur Blanton, baritone, and Ralph Dawson, bass. Joe Dawson and Bozie alternated leads, their voices fluidly reaching across their chosen ranges: "First tenor goes all the way up and back down to baritone," said Dawson. "Second tenor can take the baritone part and baritone goes to the bass."[86] Bozie's job as second tenor best suited his talents, Dawson explained, in being "the voice that's totally related between all of them. It'll melody off from one to the last one." The group traveled for the next two years within a fifty-mile radius of Denison, playing at churches and school auditoriums. Except for Bozie, the others kept their day jobs, pursuing their singing largely on weekends.

While Bozie "didn't like a whole lot of funny stuff. He was kind of more or less 'the subtle guy,'" helping the group arrange pieces that included sound effects and choreography, like "This Train."[87] To start the number, Dawson vocally hooted the distant-sounding blast of a train whistle, a long "wah," followed by a short, resonate "wah-wah," an effect based on the Golden

Gate Quartet's handling of "Gospel Train," their first recording.[88] Bozie then launched an "oom-ma-lank-a-lank-a-lank" chorus (a background riff heard on numerous quartet records) and called out "All aboard." For the rest of the song, the foursome interlocked their arms and cranked like the axles of a moving locomotive. With these visual effects, "This Train" was a crowd-pleaser, but for members of the group, the dramatization met only one part of their purpose. "'You are not just entertainers,' Bozie told the others, 'you are spiritual singers.'"[89]

Bozie warned his younger colleagues against any feigned displays of enthusiasm. "Don't put on a form and a fashion," he said.[90] At the same time, as Dawson cautioned, "If you say a show is dynamite, you have to remember that dynamite destroys."[91] Ever the Baptist, even when dealing with Pentecostal songs, Bozie insisted that his younger colleagues keep their attention on their work: to meet the needs of the audience and to observe the solemnity of their material. As performers, their burden lay in making the program succeed no matter how they might feel while simultaneously being a conduit

FIGURE 29. The Friendship Spirituals, Denison, Texas, 1948 or 1949. *Left to right:* Bozie Sturdivant, Arthur Blanton, Ralph Dawson, Joe Dawson. Courtesy of Ralph Dawson.

for the songs. To achieve those ends, Dawson explained, they had to be "neither free nor bonded." A fuller quotation from St. Paul reads: "Where there is neither Greek nor Jew . . . bond nor free: but Christ is all, and in all."[92] This credo pertained to performance strategy as well as to the unity underlying differences of origin and caste. Focusing on the essential motive for their singing—"I'm only an instrument and it ain't me"—gave Bozie and his companions a means to shape their programs. The artifices of stagecraft, whether taking the angular poses of a gospel train or marching up the aisle doing "Ain't No Grave," served a greater purpose. All became legitimate ways of expressing religious content. "We didn't have to turn the church out by shouting," Dawson added. "But if this happens we can rejoice in it."[93]

The Friendship Spirituals found a corresponding freedom to craft their arrangements. Though Dawson demurred that they were just "local, country boys," he spoke assuredly of their capacity to master new material. "We did it from recordings or natural, if they came around singing."[94] In the late 1940s, numerous quartets rode the "gospel highway," stopping at the churches that dotted Dawson and Bozie's Denison neighborhood. The two singers found that many of the pieces these groups offered followed such a uniform pattern that "the only thing that was missing was the words." As a result, the Friendship Spirituals consistently reshaped the material they heard. Dawson mentioned as an example the Pilgrim Travelers' baritone Jesse Whitaker: "We would take a song not that he did, but arrange it as he might have." Just as Bozie had adapted Rebert Harris's trademark flourishes for "Ain't No Grave," Dawson said, "Maybe we might turn around and say 'we'll sing this song in the tune of so-and-so.'"[95] By this kind of synthesis the Friendship Spirituals made the music their own. "We were prepared to do whatever we needed to," Dawson maintained. "If anybody else could do it, we could do it. That was our attitude about it. We learn what we want to learn. We learn what we need."[96]

The Friendship Spirituals' creative confidence, a corollary to John Work's view that an individual's technique could become "the property of all," girded Dawson's analysis of "Ain't No Grave." As a tape of Bozie's 1942 recordings played through his headphones, he connected the performance to its historical sources. He began with his old friend's voice. "He's singing solo, but it's still on the style of a quartet." Dawson explained that when the Friendship Spirituals performed the song, Bozie kept his vocal moving at a similar pace, but instead of the Union Jubilee Quartet's chanting behind him, Dawson and the others quietly refrained the chorus of "hold my body down" just as the Five Soul Stirrers of Denver, Colorado, had done. As the tape continued to play,

Dawson compared the song's two recordings, noting that the first, taken at a lower pitch, "didn't have a balanced harmony. He mis-keyed it." Dawson found the second performance more fluid, allowing Bozie to better vary his volume and tone. "Without the right key," Dawson explained, "he's not getting the response he wants out of himself." In saying this, Dawson linked Bozie's vocal expressiveness to his situating the song at the right place during a program. "You learn the emotion of the people," he continued. "The preacher does the same thing. People tired, want to sit down and soothe themselves, and that's when Bozie come up with this. He's going through that slow motion." "That slow motion," he added, "was the purpose of the song."[97]

Dawson began to define "Ain't No Grave." He called it a "slow-beat, spiritual number," one of the "'Old One Hundred' songs," his name for the church's congregational hymns. Keeping to a stately eight-syllable-per-line stanzaic pattern, "Old Hundred," a psalm tune with sixteenth-century roots, appears in most contemporary Protestant hymnals as "Doxology."[98] A more common term for slow beat, "long-meter" pieces like "Old Hundred" invokes "Dr. Watts," a reference to English divine Isaac Watts (1674–1748), whose psalms, spirituals, and hymns have been part of black services since colonial times. This usage has become so popular it extends beyond the man and his works to describe an entire form of spiritual singing. A "Dr. Watts" piece involves a slow, ornamented vocal practice with slurs, turns, quavers, glides, falsetto, portamento, melisma, and blues notes.[99] For Ralph Dawson, this same lingering, elongated, buzzing, and by turns roaring style audible in Bozie Sturdivant's "Ain't No Grave Can Hold My Body Down" derives from Dr. Watts and "Old Hundred" singing. What he and his fellow churchgoers heard when Bozie performed the song was not simply a popular quartet style indebted to Rebert Harris, but also a slow-beat sound that resonated with the earliest forms of musical worship in America.

Dawson recognized this heritage: "When the pastor gives out the hymn, he's a director. Basically the quartet does the same."[100] Likewise, Mahalia Jackson set her modern gospel solos such as "Amazing Grace" on the foundation of Dr. Watts singing and what Dawson called its "slow motion."[101] When Rebert Harris described his plaintive, solo cries in relation to Dr. Watts, he also echoed the link that Jackson and Dawson had made: "I was the first quartet singer to bring out the old hymns; that's my meat, a sad slow minor song."[102] In these ambitious words, Harris expressed how a musical heritage moves forward.

In January 1997, while sitting in a corner of the Delta Blues Museum, only a short distance from the Silent Grove Baptist Church, Mississippi quartet singer Marvin Myles listened to Bozie Sturdivant and the Friendly Five sing "Ain't No Grave." Raised in Friars Point and Clarksdale, the Reverend Myles's musical background closely ties with these two recordings. Though he never saw Bozie, Myles had known the Reverend McGhee, longtime leader of the Friendly Five, and as a youngster, his quartet instructor had been John Skipper, founder of Bozie's original group, the Union Jubilee Quartet. For Myles, who grew up singing with his brothers in their family quartet, Skipper was an especially important presence. After Myles and his brothers sang on one of his local radio programs, Skipper became "our guide and manager."[103] Eventually Skipper left his barbershop, a place where so much of this community's singing had gone on, to Myles's proprietorship.

"Sturdivant is way back," said Myles after listening to the tape. "He's a solo singer." In contrast to the Friendly Five's handling of "Ain't No Grave," Myles thought Bozie's approach older, its lineage revealed by its "emptiness between the lines." A more modern quartet, he explained, would have filled in those gaps. Bozie's approach reminded him of a blind singer he had seen years earlier in Cleveland, Mississippi. The elderly musician played his guitar "in Spanish," an old-time, open G tuning, and sustained his notes with a pocket knife. Players working in this mode can take their slider—be it pocketknife, bottleneck, or metal tube—and glide over the strings, making the notes dwell and linger as they vary in pitch. A 1967 field recording of Delta musician Robert "Nighthawk" Johnson provides a nearby example of what Myles remembered.[104] Here Johnson uses an alternative tuning and plays "Ain't No Grave" with a bottleneck. The correspondence of the guitarist's microtonal bottlenecking to Bozie's singing fits a broader performance style that spans a solitary farmhand projecting a field holler to a meetinghouse of churchgoers embellishing a lined-out hymn. Bearing in mind Rebert Harris's affinity for Dr. Watts hymns, I asked the Reverend Myles if he sensed any relationship between Bozie's "Ain't No Grave" and Harris's soloing in the Soul Stirrers. With memorable conciseness, Myles replied, "Sturdivant and Harris are looking back and bringing it up into the music. It's a way of keeping alive the old music and the old style."

Myles had identified what the Fisk researchers found in Coahoma County back in 1942. Coahoma's youths, wrote Lewis Jones, "sing the songs currently popular on the radio and the juke boxes and learn others as they hear them sung by older people at home and in the fields. Theirs is the task of discov-

ering a pattern of living in confor-
mity with their opportunities and
the varied inheritance which their
elders have handed on to them."[105]
Muddy Waters, the most renowned
of the many musicians and singers recorded during the 1941–42
Coahoma study, epitomized this
equilibrium of influences and
forces. Commenting on the Delta
blues he amplified in the smoky
neighborhood taverns of Chicago's
South Side and eventually shared
with the world, he said, "I took the
old-time music and brought it up
to date—you've got to stay alive
with it."[106]

In the balance between old-time and up-to-date, past practice and present technology, receding inheritance and emerging opportunity, lies Bozie
Sturdivant's "Ain't No Grave Can Hold My Body Down." The Friendship
Spirituals drew from the records, broadcasts, and performances available to
them to make their own choices within the music. As Ralph Dawson said,
the group prided themselves most "on the merits of their abilities." Despite
the many times I pressed him, he never conceded that Bozie's performance
simply mirrored Rebert Harris's influence. While granting Harris's place in
Bozie's life—after all, it was under the Soul Stirrers' banner that Bozie came
to Denison—Dawson contends that in this song "what Bozie did was his
own."[107] He described a particular quality that set Bozie's "Ain't No Grave"
apart: "To me it was just . . . a personal invention to a song, a personal way of
accompanying it."[108] It wasn't simply that the Soul Stirrers didn't do the song
that made it Bozie's or that he had spliced a long-meter style to Harris's quartet
approach. Bozie and Dawson operated by an aesthetic—as much a competitive
instinct—that they could match whatever the full-time singers did, reserving
a freedom to shape the music themselves. John Work witnessed this same
impulse in Nashville as street musicians incorporated the latest recordings and
broadcasts into their performances, bringing the newest licks into their musical
vocabularies. Like Dawson, he did not find modernity an irredeemable threat
to folklore's process. Understandably then, when touring groups like the Soul

Stirrers came to Denison, and Dawson and his partners served as the local act, he explained, "It won't have made sense for me to open up their program imitating them and their songs. So I have to give them something of my own that maybe they never heard. When they leave here, they leave with a new song."[109] In this way, Dawson and his group relied on their own resources—not only "we learn what we want," but also "we find a way." Then he added, "We were blessed to be able to do that."

Given the importance the Friendship Spirituals invested in their artistic autonomy, I asked Dawson, "Would this capacity to learn what you want and to perform what you will extend to competency, to life as a whole?" He nodded affirmatively and cited a shoeshine boy "popping the rag." A well-placed snap of the cloth, he pointed out, could coax a tip that otherwise might never have been offered. His image of a youth crouched over a man's shoes evoked not only a scene weighted with American social history, it also supplied a principle of survival. The creativity manifested in that task, displaying its own percussive and visual artistry, exemplified folk tradition itself: constant and supremely supple at the same time, with custom and wisdom adapting to changing circumstances, not through formal means such as laws and regulations, but through observing and doing and responding and venturing, ready for anything and everything that may come along. As Dawson summed up his quartet days with Bozie and what they represented, his voice husky with the gravity of personal experience: "We learned to cope with what we needed to cope with." This resolve found expression in "Ain't No Grave," a piece he aptly called a "sermonic song":

> "No Grave" could serve a similar purpose as "Steal Away": to get out of the situation where you are. The meaning of the song is 'You can't keep me down, I will not be confined.' God said, 'I'm forever alive,' so when you go from this life, physical life into spiritual life, you're still alive. . . . They put Him in the grave, then He got up. You all can't kill me, you think you can. But I have overcome the power of death. It's the same story told over and over: Jesus and his crucifixion, burial and resurrection. The whole sermon, the whole message in song. . . . "No Grave" is about an impossible move that's going to be done and it was done. . . . It's a true saying. It says, 'I'm yet alive.' My soul is going back to who give me, so you can put my body where you want to.[110]

Ralph Dawson encompassed the song's social and spiritual dimensions, its historical and political overtones, theology and practice. In the end, what he said comes back to Bozie Sturdivant himself. In January 1978, Bozie contracted pneumonia after changing a tire in inclement weather. Earlier that day, he visited with Dawson. As Bozie had done of late, he mentioned wanting to "go down home to Mississippi." But Bozie never made that trip. He and Dawson never saw one another again. Bozie died in Denison a few days later. Now, on a gray February afternoon in 1998, Dawson and I stood in the cemetery where twenty years before he had led the funeral procession to Bozie's burial. In this part of the graveyard, many of the plots had sunk, leaving only gaping holes. All around us, headstones had collapsed while others were swallowed whole into the ground. Dawson walked back and forth through the area, increasingly agitated, looking for Bozie Sturdivant's grave. His marker was nowhere to be found. Then it came to us: no grave could hold his body down.

Pete Steele

It's What Folks Do

PETE STEELE HAD DECIDED TO PACK UP HIS FAMILY AND START over. Afflicted with black lung disease after seventeen years as an East Kentucky coal miner, he planned now, a few months short of the Great Depression, to begin sharecropping in Bismarck, Illinois.[1] Born Simon Peter Steele (1891–1985) in Woodbine, Kentucky, Pete spent his youth in White Oak, a rural community in adjacent Laurel County. There he attended a one-room school where he met his future wife of seventy-three years, Lillie Mae Swanner (1895–1986), herself raised in Sinking Creek, a mile from his home. At school Pete assumed the role of class cut-up and never learned to read or write. Starting at age six he did learn banjo playing from his father, a gregarious mountain fiddler, and, later, carpentry from his father-in-law. After marrying in 1912, Pete began in the mines, erecting bulkheads and braces in addition to digging coal. He worked seasonally, going to the Harlan coal fields in the fall and moving back to Laurel County in the warmer months to raise a crop. There were horses on the Illinois farm where he currently set his sights, which, his oldest daughter remembers, especially drew his interest. In May 1929, he hired a truck and driver to go north, taking himself, his wife, their five children, and all the household possessions the Chevrolet could bear.

Along a one-lane bridge on the Shelbyville pike outside of Louisville, a seventeen-year-old trucker, ignoring the right of way, rammed head-first into the Steeles' vehicle. Up front, Pete's wife Lillie carried their three-month-old son in her arms. Next to her, by the driver, sat their thirteen-year-old daughter, Pearl. Pete rode in the back with their three older sons, along with the family sewing machine, cook stove, table, and bedding. The impact sent them off the roadway, veering down an embankment inches short of the water. Its force, said Pearl Steele Dickman, "broke my mother in two."[2] Lillie's pelvis was split open. Traffic came to a halt and rescue efforts began.

FIGURE 31. Samuel and Sarah Baker Steele, Pete's parents, at their home on Sinking Creek, Laurel County, Kentucky, ca. 1920. Courtesy of Leona Steele Gabbard.

Onlookers carried Lillie to the nearest home and laid her on the porch. Sylvia Jane Thomson, one of the travelers stopped on the bridge, left her chauffeured car and came to Lillie's aid. Mrs. Thomson had been riding with her husband, Logan G. Thomson, an executive (and future president) of his family-owned Champion Coated Paper Company, the world's largest manufacturer of this product, located in Hamilton, Ohio. The Thomsons were coming from Chicago, where they had attended some horse races and were presently en route to Louisville, less than twenty miles away, where Mrs. Thomson had relatives.

Observing that Lillie, trembling from her injuries, was going into shock, Mrs. Thomson asked the people at the house, "Do you have any whiskey?"[3] They didn't, but they had some wine that she administered to this teetotaler. Mrs. Thomson further told them to get blankets, stressing that "this woman needs help." Pearl Dickman recalled the intensity of those moments: "She had some wine poured into a glass, got a blanket. . . . Mom didn't drink. The baby was three months old and on the breast. I had to ride in the ambulance to the hospital, and they had to keep him there 'till they got a formula that would agree with him. I was only a kid. I didn't know where my dad was and tried to console my brother. I didn't know if my mother would live or die."

Lillie, the sole person injured in the wreck, survived and made a full recovery. But something else arose from that scene of twisted metal and shattered glass: a friendship between herself and Sylvia Thomson that continued for the next three decades. Following her surgery, Lillie

stayed in Louisville with her sister, her body mending in a cast that reached from her breast to her buttocks.[4] In the ensuing months, Mrs. Thomson sent her relatives to check in with Lillie. Aware that Pete found work at a nearby lard plant and then moved to a factory in Indianapolis, Mrs. Thomson extended the Steeles a more permanent offer of employment. She promised that, along with Pete, any of them could have a job at Champion Paper once they reached the age of eighteen. Within two years of the accident, Pete Steele took up Mrs. Thomson's offer, working first in the loading dock, and later in the box shop, building platforms and skids. Eventually all nine of Pete and Lillie's children—the last four of whom Lillie named for members of the Thomson family or else for close friends of Sylvia Thomson—came to work at Champion.[5]

Seventy-nine years after the crash, Bob Steele, the three-month-old boy his mother had shielded from the impact, recounted, "That wreck was the best thing ever happened to me. There's no telling where our family would be today if an angel had not appeared that day. That angel was Sylvia Thomson, and from that day on, it was as though she had adopted our whole family."[6] His brother Dwight, named after Logan Thomson's older brother (the Steeles' last-born is named Logan), called it a "godsend," acknowledging Mrs. Thomson's intercession.[7] He guesses that without the accident he would have labored—and languished—in a Kentucky coal mine instead of having a forty-four-year career at Champion. His sister, Leona Steele Gabbard, adds, "If it [the crash] hadn't happened, we'd have starved to death. It was just hard times. Having that many children, I don't know how we'd ever have made it."[8] Recalling the Thomsons' unexpected kindness, Leona softly noted, "For their class of people, they were humble and caring people."

Over the years, the Steeles have recounted the serendipitous appearance of Sylvia Thomson in their lives, even as a comparable story began to unfold after they came to Hamilton. Thanks to his 1938 Library of Congress recordings, Pete Steele later achieved prominence during the urban folk music revival, especially for "Coal Creek March," his most famous banjo solo. Once again the family found hands reaching across class and cultural divides, hands literally knocking on Pete Steele's door, hands seeking the knowledge that resided in his own. Like that narrow highway bridge near Louisville, within the rippling arpeggios of "Coal Creek March" lies a crossing in American society—requiring watchfulness to steer, by turns open to all, and sometimes completely surprising.

On March 29, 1938, at his company-owned home on Rhea Avenue a few blocks from the Champion paper mills, Pete Steele first recorded "Coal Creek March" along with twenty-six other songs and tunes. Pete's facility with multiple tunings, combined with his various right-hand picking styles, demonstrates a technical range unsurpassed on the Folk Archive's numerous other disc-era banjo recordings. Surrounded by his wife and children, Pete applied these skills either solo or to accompany Lillie, who additionally sang four numbers by herself. Their son Craig joined them on three pieces, playing guitar and sometimes adding his voice to theirs. These performances, which range from balladry to blues, church songs to hoedowns, took place two days after Pete played Cincinnati's Music Hall, site of the Ohio Valley Folk

FIGURE 33. The Steele family band at home on Rhea Avenue, Hamilton, Ohio, in 1942. *Left to right:* Pete Steele, Fred Steele, Craig Steele, Lee Hamlin, and Ed Steele. Courtesy of Leona Steele Gabbard.

Festival.[9] At this event attended by some fifteen hundred listeners, Alan and Elizabeth Lomax first heard Pete doing the banjo song "Little Birdie" for his brief turn at the microphone. Lomax took an interest in several of Pete's fellow performers as well, and recorded that day a version of "Coal Creek March" by Jesse Spencer, a Cincinnati-based banjoist and string band member.

Lomax, however, little enjoyed the festival, terming it "largely hill-billy and very little folk."[10] His negativity focused on its partiality for songs that he considered less than authentic, terming it "a caterwauling of 'Little Rosewood Caskets,' 'Maples on the Hill,' etc." While these titles reflected genuine folk taste and long-time folk use, he preferred a repertory of presumably older numbers that circulated via noncommercial channels. He writes: "No question that 'hill-billy' music is following a vigorous development of its own, more or less apart from folk music, and this group of performers thoroughly vindicated its independence with tremendous vigor; but it was obvious that these people knew a great deal of folk material, too, and there was no excuse for a gathering called Folk Festival, that did not give this material a chance to speak for itself as well." For Alan Lomax, Pete Steele offered the desired strain, even though he, too, drew from these same disputed sources. While Lomax's own views on hillbilly records and their folkloric value soon enlarged, he recognized Pete as a homegrown virtuoso and seized this opportunity to document his music in depth. A year earlier Lomax repeatedly heard how a number of Kentucky-bred musicians had migrated to Hamilton to work in its factories. Two days after the festival in Cincinnati, Pete Steele became Alan Lomax's first stop in this community.

Right off Lomax considered Pete's version of "Pretty Polly," the first title they committed to disc, "certainly one of the finest recorded performances in American folk song."[11] Lomax both recorded and filmed it, and in 1941, chose it as one of only two examples of Anglo American music for the sampler that launched the Folk Music of the United States record series.[12] Yet with his appreciation for Pete Steele's music, Lomax expressed in Hamilton, as he had in Cincinnati, judgments that indicated his distance from the milieu he entered. "Pete himself is middle aged, a sweet and rather ineffective little blue eyed man," Lomax observes in his report, "extremely sure of himself as a musician but obviously somewhat bewildered by the rest of life. His wife and numerous children have the mountaineer candor, shyness and hospitality."[13] Commentaries of a similar nature surfaced decades earlier as the musical prototypes for "Coal Creek March" came into print.

In 1838, James Ballard, a New York City "professor of the guitar, singing and flute," published two music books for his principal instrument.[14] The first was *The Elements of Guitar-Playing,* a sixty-eight-page method subsequently recognized as the most substantial American guitar tutor to appear prior to the Civil War.[15] It highlights an eleven-part system of harmony and chord construction obtainable along the instrument's fingerboard. Ballard acted on the principle that formal musical knowledge has greater value for the student than just providing simplified harmonizations of classical works or accessible arrangements of popular numbers. He cited Fernando Sor, the instrument's leading composer, performer, and author, who eight years earlier had written in his native Spanish that "examples tell me clearly enough *what* I am to do; but the text should tell me *how* I am to do it."[16] Toward the end of the book, he promises a less analytical volume soon to follow, a work that would provide a "Series of Lessons, Exercises, and pleasing Pieces."[17]

Ballard's Guitar Preceptor delivered on that promise. The manual features twenty-three pages of music "intended for the use of commencing students."[18] Along with starter arrangements of "Oft in the Stilly Night" and "The Bride's Farewell," he includes another pleasing piece titled "Fandango."[19] Its place here marks the tune's earliest known publication.[20] "If you could have gathered all the guitarists in America together a century ago," classical guitar authority

Peter Danner writes, "chances are the one piece they all knew would be a frivolous little number called 'Spanish Fandango.'"[21] While some musicians disparaged it as elementary and lowering the dignity of the instrument—one calling it "the guitarist's version of 'Chopsticks'"—it appeared repeatedly in nineteenth-century method books and sheet music for banjo and guitar.[22] It even reached internationally, an achievement that instrument maker and music publisher S. S. Stewart recorded in his 1889 historical poem, "The Banjo":

> For some titled Nabob over the sea
> Introduced the Banjo at an afternoon Tea.
>
> . . .
>
> So over the seas
> It became quite the cheese
> To play the Spanish Fandango.[23]

Critics of the "Fandango," writing in the late nineteenth and early twentieth centuries, faulted it for musical and social simplicity. These commentators, themselves banjo and guitar players, judged it inferior to the more challenging pieces they labored to present. In 1889, one reader of *S. S. Stewart's Banjo and Guitar Journal* wrote in from rural Virginia, wanting "to learn . . . the better class of music; it is all 'Run Nigger, Run,' and 'Fandango' here."[24] The magazine, a forerunner in the effort to elevate the banjo above its common origins, reprinted the letter, adding the encouragement that "soil that has been used only for the cultivation of weeds requires time to become fit for the rearing of plants." In 1891, the *Journal* responded to another who wanted a list of "*easy, showy* pieces."[25] Advice came in the article's headline: "Try the Spanish Fandango." A year later, a guitarist noted: "In conclusion I would say that in my opinion the guitar is a very much abused instrument, owing to there being so few who know how to play it properly. The extent of the many (so-called) guitarists reaches to playing a few chords, Spanish Fandango, etc."[26] Another music periodical of that time recommended its readers attempt a particular setting from the opera *Il Trovatore*: "Guitarists who aspire to something higher than the Spanish Fandango style of music will find in this arrangement a good beginning toward the study of the guitar as an art."[27]

While anathema to some, the tune held understandable appeal for beginners. Ballard presented "Fandango" as an "Example of Peculiar Tuning."[28] "The peculiarity of tuning," he wrote in *The Elements of Guitar-Playing,* "which is by many considered as a great imperfection, is, to the amateur of the guitar, a matter of congratulation; for it adds to the variety of guitar effects; and by its means, passages which sound very difficult to the ear, are often rendered exceedingly easy for the hand."[29] An open-tuned number like "Fandango," with its principal notes rising up the highest string (the one easiest to play), its gentle fills—the notes that surround the melody falling in uncomplicated right-hand sequences—and its fully formed major chords made by a single finger barring the neck, achieves for the listener a potentially impressive effect. In short, "Fandango" afforded amateur players an accomplished-sounding piece with a minimum of practice. If its performance could inspire the congratulations of one's friends, one means to this success, Ballard recognized, stemmed from its peculiar tuning.

From my own experience of playing thirty-one versions of the "Fandango" that appeared in sheet music between 1838 and 1903 for both guitar and banjo, I found an array of interpretations spanning the lyrical to the dramatic.[30] Arrangers took the tune's basic parts and variously emphasized their dynamic, decorative, and melodic elements. In his 1856 setting, the celebrated African American guitarist Justin Holland, for instance, employs a series of six-note clusters instead of the usual four, forming sensitive combinations of right-hand arpeggios and harmonics.[31] The lilting melody in his second section even seems to anticipate "Bicycle Built for Two," the 1896 popular song. Pursuing a different course, Frank B. Converse's 1887 banjo variant evokes a Chopinesque polonaise, employing triplet flourishes, slides, "rascondo and hammer movements," double sharps, and two-count grand chords for the finale.[32] Albrecht's 1890 arrangement goes from a disarmingly simple opening to a nearly baroque movement by the end, the final patterns suggestive of an Alberti bass.[33] Franklin Eaton's 1898 gentle banjo arrangement mirrors its title, "Fantasie on the Spanish Fandango," while his 1903 guitar setting introduces two additional sections in 2/4 time—a gallop and then a polka—original tunes reworking "Fandango"'s melodic and rhythmic components.[34] At the end of his 1887 arrangement, S. S. Stewart caught the thread that joins them all: "The Fandango should be played in Waltz time and with expression. The Variations possible to construct from this melody are boundless."[35]

Rural American folk musicians like Pete Steele found similar diversity in their ear-based settings of the tune. At his 1938 recording session, Pete performed "Spanish Fandango" as well as "Coal Creek March" and "Last Payday at Coal Creek." Despite their different tunings and textures, these pieces all share the "Fandango"'s musical structure. For the very reason that some commentators railed against the "Fandango"—"It is simply a succession of chords in arpeggio form, and so simple in construction," warned Vahdah Olcott-Bickford, "that a person not knowing a note of music could learn to play the entire number with variations in an hour's time"—the tune lent itself to continual reinterpretation.[36] Uncle Dave Macon recorded the piece twice, varying it each time. In 1925 he used it as an instrumental preface to a black gospel number. A year later, in "Uncle Dave's Beloved Solo," he announced the sound effects that follow: "Now, soldier boys, listen for that lonesome bugle call."[37] Subsequent recordings further express "Spanish Fandango"'s variety: Frank Jenkins's "Baptist Shout" and Kirk McGee's "Snowdrop," Wade Mainer's "Trickling Water," and Frank Hutchison's "Logan County Blues," to name a few.[38] Each performance reflects a unique approach to the essential melody, yet different enough that the players presented these tunes as works wholly apart from the original.

Hillbilly recording artist Wade Mainer told me he took his inspiration from nothing more than the sound of droplets. "We was out there by a little puddle of water, rain dripping off my motor home in a pan, making a kind of clinging noise. . . . A tune came into my mind and I went and got my banjo . . . that sounded like that and I named it 'Trickling Water.'"[39] Similarly, Etta Baker, a revered African American guitarist and banjoist, viewed her banjo piece "Marching Jaybird" on its own terms without ever connecting it to "Spanish Fandango," which it mirrors.[40] She had learned "Jaybird" from her brother-in-law, who got it from his father. In Etta's North Carolina community it functioned as "an old dance, sixteen hands-up, circle-to-the-right. That was a very special piece played with violins."[41] Perhaps like the social dances in the American southwest also called fandangos, Etta Baker described hearing it at "a happy gathering that the older people had, like corn shuckings and a big dinner at night . . . and this tune would be played at an old mountain entertainment." When I asked her if she thought it similar to "Spanish Fandango," which she played on the guitar, she paused. "I would think so, yes. I hadn't really thought of that. . . . The chords in there are so much alike, it keeps you kindly on the go to keep them separated."

This accommodating informality inflamed the "Fandango" critics all over again when they reckoned with another widely popular guitar piece from the mid-nineteenth century. This, too, has bearing on Pete Steele's "Coal Creek March." The 1856 instrumental "descriptive fantasie" called "Sebastopol" commemorated the 349-day siege of the Russian seaport that had recently gained the world's attention during the Crimean War.[42] Guitarist Henry Worrall (1825–1902) composed "Sebastopol" soon after the siege, finishing his piece at the bedside of an infirm Cincinnati friend. Worrall intended his piece as "an imitation of military music. The Harmonics in single notes imitate the Bugle. The Harmonics in chords imitate a Full Military Band at a distance."[43] Here, as in a number of Worrall's other compositions, his performance directions play a part, detailing rising and falling volume, dynamics that often figured in such "characteristic pieces."[44] It soon went through multiple editions, in arrangements for piano, banjo, and brass instruments as well as guitar. By Worrall's death, "Sebastopol"'s sheet music sales exceeded $200,000, making it "the favorite piece of guitar players through the world."[45]

Like "Fandango," "Sebastopol" employs an open tuning (a D major chord, guitar strings tuned lowest to highest DADF♯AD), its melody principally carries on the outside string, and most strikingly, it follows the same chord structure as "Fandango." In their corresponding arpeggio sections, the two pieces differ only in their key. Yet that is not to say "Sebastopol" is a remake of "Fandango," so much as a creative by-product. The two pieces follow different melodies and they operate to different ends. The "Fandango" provides an essentially gentle, melodic waltz, while "Sebastopol," set in 2/4, emphasizes the martial and theatrical. Both tunes sometimes use harmonics, but unlike "Fandango," which employs this chiming effect simply as an alternative for otherwise barred notes, in "Sebastopol" they sound the troops to battle.

Yet Vahdah Olcott-Bickford, one the nation's leading guitarists, termed "Sebastopol" a "musical atrocity."[46] She ranked it alongside "Spanish Fandango," which she deemed "its twin in music crime." Expressing similar disenchantment more than twenty years earlier—during Worrall's lifetime—European-trained American guitarist C. D. Schettler lambasted stateside teachers who "know nothing whatever of exercises and have for their complete repertoire the 'Spanish Fandango' and sometime 'Sebastopol' . . . wrong impressions are engendered in the public mind and the guitar is looked upon as a mere plaything."[47] Apart from these critiques, guitarists addressed the two tunes side-by-side purely on their level of technique. In 1902, writing about the practicality of standard versus open-chord tunings, Richard M. Tyrell allows "yet for some solos as 'Sebastopol,' 'Spanish Fandango,' etc. they are effective."[48] Specialists realized that however much these tunes might color public opinion of the instrument, the pieces shared musical properties. Indeed, for Worrall these tunes entwined not only in "Sebastopol"'s early drafts, but in the public record.[49] On June 29, 1860, Worrall's sheet music editions of "Sebastopol" and "Spanish Fandango" were registered for copyright.[50] The cover page for "Sebastopol" identifies him as the "Author of . . . The Original Spanish Fandango."[51]

However much Vahdah Olcott-Bickford and others of her persuasion might have shuddered at the tunes' pervasiveness, both of these works came to mass circulate under Worrall's name, published in method books sold with mail-order guitars. By the appearance of the 1894 Sears catalogue, terms like "the Spanish key," drawn from "Spanish Fandango," carried clear meaning for those who wanted to play in the open G tuning, whether they read music or not.[52] "Sebastopol" similarly came to represent not just Worrall's wartime commemorative but also its particular tuning. The term, like the music, passed from printed page to word of mouth, with pronunciations spanning "Sevestapol" and "Paskapool" to "Vestibule" and "Sylvesterpool." Worrall's dissemination of the interrelated pieces, "Spanish Fandango" and "Sebastopol," transformed them into templates. In turn, new works emerged from them, including a march connected with recent events in Coal Creek, Tennessee.

When Pete Steele recorded "Coal Creek March," he explained to Alan Lomax that this tune and its companion piece, "Pay Day at Coal Creek," concerned two mine explosions that took place in Tennessee before he was born. "I don't know the date when the 'March' was composed but it was made from another explosion at Coal Creek. . . . the first explosion . . . 600 men were killed . . . I wasn't there, but they would tell me there were a band there, come there to play it over the dead men that were laying out at the drift mouth of the mine. . . . That's where it started from there, from the brass band."[53] Numerical errors notwithstanding, Pete had the historical outlines of these man-made disasters right.

On May 19, 1902, at 7:30 A.M., an explosion occurred at the Fraterville mine, a few miles from Coal Creek itself. The blast of gas and coal dust killed 184, making it one of the worst accidents in U.S. mining history. A grand jury found that Fraterville's coal operators and mine inspectors had neglected to check air circulation over the weekend. The flow became blocked, and the pent-up gases ignited once the day's work began. While most of the miners died from the initial impact, others escaped as far as the headings and entries, where they died from heat suffocation and afterdamp. Some survived as long as eight hours, long enough to write the farewell notes found with their bodies. Jacob Vowell, who perished with his brother and four nephews, wrote to his wife Ellen, "We are shut up in the head of the entry . . . and the bad air is closing in on us fast."[54] His words, as well as those of several others, would appear in the community memorial service program, and later surfaced in a ballad that commemorated the explosion.[55]

For Coal Creek native Della Tuttle, whose father worked at that mine but had not gone in that Monday, it was not the music she remembered so much as the train that ran from the minehead: "At that time there wasn't any funeral parlors here in Lake City, and there was a man down there that sold coffins. They transferred the bodies back down to Coal Creek for burial on the flatcars of the trains; flatcars of the trains hauled and the bell tolled and made such an awful, dreadful, mournful sound a-comin' up the holler and a-going back down, that even to this day I can't hardly stand to hear the train bell toll because it brings so much of that back."[56] Throughout her community's history, no single event equaled the devastation of Fraterville.

But that wasn't the last of the troubles. In a twenty-year period between 1891 and 1911, Della Tuttle and her neighbors endured a series of uprisings, strikes, shootings, and natural disasters all connected with coal mining. Alvin Vowell, who worked fifteen years underground, including a stint at the Slatestone mine, which lay two miles from Fraterville and exploded nine years later, summed up these ordeals:

> I've thought about the tragedies we've had here through the years. [People] build their homes, started their families here. Men were looking forward to a complete life. All at once this tragedy came along and blasted the lives of 184 men in Fraterville. Left a lot of mourning and sadness for years. The place never did overcome it. Then in 1911 along comes the Slatestone explosion. Eighty-four men were snatched out the same way. There was another tragedy. The dreams and expectations were shattered . . . Then we've came along with strikes and labor troubles and hardships as miners. Through the years this place has had its toll of misery, it really has. But there's been some brave souls here, there's been some people that stood it and rejoiced in their poverty and in their estates of life. . . . It was a human tragedy. It was a human experience, whatever you can make out of it. . . . And when you weigh it all up, it's like going back and looking at Job's experience. It's just another human experience.[57]

The earliest of these human tragedies reaches back to 1876, seven years after the town's first mine opened, rich with seams of bituminous coal. A strike occurred when a leading operator lowered the value of a load to two and half cents from five cents a bushel. Miners also worked in conditions with water up to their knees and faced repeated threats of job loss. The following year, when the company replaced them with unpaid convicts leased to the operators, the free miners set off three kegs of dynamite (effecting little damage) under the convict quarters on the day of their arrival. Pressures concerning convict labor did not end there. In 1881, the giant Tennessee Coal, Iron, and Railroad Company brought in 160 prisoners to work in the Coal Creek Company mine. The situation worsened a decade later when TCI acquired the state's contract for all its convict labor.

In April 1891, with the expiration of the local Knights of Labor contract, a Coal Creek mine operator signed a five-year deal with TCI and announced that all current employees must sign a nonstrike, nonunion agreement. The operator also dismissed the checkweighman, who independently verified each miner's tonnage. This new plan limited individual earnings to 2,200 pounds of loaded coal per car, and compensated only in scrip tokens, redeemable at the company store and discounted as much as 20 percent elsewhere. Not surprisingly, the miners struck. On July 4, 1891, the company brought in forty convicts assigned to raze the miners' quarters and reuse that wood to erect a stockade. In response, on Bastille Day, July 14, several hundred armed miners surrounded the new enclosure, sending the guards and their one hundred and fifty convict miners away on a train back to Knoxville. Their telegram to Governor John P. Buchanan explained their need to take these steps to support their families and thwart starvation.

The governor resisted and ordered in three companies of militia while hardening state penalties for obstructing the work of convict lessees. Over the next year, free white and black miners, coming from Coal Creek and surrounding regions, repeatedly marched the troops and convicts back to the train station. Without exacting any loss of life, the popularly supported rebels burnt the newly built stockades at the various mines. However, the situation continued to heat up, with increased reinforcements, mercenary reward monies, imposition of martial law, and finally, lethal force, including the lynching of an opposing miner. By the end of August 1892, a corps of ten thousand heavily armed state militia overpowered the resistance of some three thousand miners. Facing Gatling guns and small-bore cannon as well as the debilitating threat of federal troops being dispatched to Coal Creek, the miners gave up. Mass arrests ensued, although only two convictions resulted. Governor Buchanan lost his reelection bid, and the state legislature outlawed convict leasing with the expiration of the TCI contract. A standing militia force remained in the community through October 1894.[58]

To these events—the Coal Creek War, the other strikes, and the two mine explosions—some residents responded with music and tales. Della Tuttle remembered Cal Luallen, the owner of a nearby grocery, who wrote a ballad about Fraterville. Locals sang his piece to the melody of "Claude Allen," a ballad of a rebellious local hero in southwest Virginia. Others learned "The Minery Boys," written about the 1911 Cross Mountain explosion, set to the tune of "Home Sweet Home." Alvin Vowell sang a couplet to the air of "Charles Guiteau" for a ballad about the Coal Creek War that his father had known (his father's cousin, G. D. Vowell, recorded it for the Library in 1937). In meticulous detail it reported the events of the strike and argued the justness of the miners' cause.[59] The mournful "Shut Up in the Mines of Coal Creek" had its tune rooted in the British-derived "Girl in the Blue Velvet Band," while its lyrics drew from the dying miners' farewells written at Fraterville. "Hearsay stories" also circulated and these, too, followed older forms.[60] These narratives, whether spoken or sung, relied on models familiar to all. Just such a ready-made framework also supported the "Coal Creek March."

Pete Steele, who never performed professionally, or even much outside his home, did not conceive of the march as a military contest of competing forces, nor did he play it with bugle calls and drumming. Instead, it evoked for him a funeral ceremony. "Women couldn't identify their husbands," he added. "They was all burnt and parched."[61] He vividly limned the grisly scene even though the death counts were, in truth, lower than what he imagined. Nor did these accidents, which occurred during his lifetime, shut down the mines as he thought they had. In fact, the Fraterville mine operation awarded the heirs $325 per miner killed, and at Cross Mountain, widows received $200 each, with children under five years old getting $50, and those between ten to fifteen, $25. No families in either misfortune took the mine owners to court. Similarly, Pete thought that "last pay day at Coal Creek" meant that the mines had closed down from the damage suits, while in Coal Creek itself, both stayed in business for years to come. The "last pay day" phrase simply meant no income during a strike. Miners there only received their pay in three-month increments anyway.[62]

The fact that Pete Steele thought otherwise reveals his priorities, his understanding of events. His sense of this tune and "Payday"'s significance ultimately have to do with the human costs this community endured. Indeed, at the Circle Cemetery near Lake City, the 184 Fraterville victims are buried together in three concentric circles around a memorial obelisk inscribed with their names. When Pete later said, "They played a march around the dead miners," he may have known about this circular memorial—set high on a hillside, reached only by a one-way road, each grave footed by a plain marker.[63] This haunting image gives a telling clue about his banjo arrangement.

After taking a long time to tune up and even more to practice before he first recorded "Coal Creek March," Pete informed Alan Lomax that he did it in a "different key than any other key."[64] Now, as he readied to play the "March," he tuned his banjo not in "the Spanish key," in G, as most others did, but in D, the "Sebastopol" key (fellow musician Roscoe Holcomb played it in both tunings).[65] Players of Pete's generation shared an idea about "Sebastopol" that reflected how that piece had come to be known. "That's a regular band piece," Kentucky banjoist Forrest Lewis said, just before recording it. "There's more music in that stuff than just a common song."[66] His banjo performance uses Worrall's melody and the usual "Fandango"–"Sebastopol" chords along with drumming on the head and harmonics, as well as some moveable, and even dissonant chord melodies—"getting runs in there," he says of those parts.

What this suggests in relation to Pete Steele, who learned "Coal Creek March" in about 1910 from a Laurel County neighbor named Andy Whittaker, was that he, too, used the "Sebastopol" setting to connote a brass band. He divided the piece into sections, saying to one banjo student, "Some parts are easy, some parts pretty hard."[67] The low-note run that he plays on the bass string has its equivalent in Worrall's "Sebastopol," a piece that he may never have heard himself. But even without adopting that composition's other special effects, the form served his purpose. Via the time-tested vehicle of "Sebastopol," he could re-create a brass band piece to play a farewell to his brothers in the mines.

Pete Steele took "Coal Creek March" personally. When he performed it for Alan Lomax and others, he told his one story about it—the dark picture of the corpses by "the drift mouth," wives unable to identify their husbands who had been burnt beyond recognition. But at a 1965 concert at Indiana University he went even further, describing not just the event as he knew it, but the process of how an explosion gets touched off in a mine.[68] For nearly seven minutes he described the passageways, the air courses, and the ways that mine gas turns into fire, traveling through the tunnel, headings, and breaks like a rolling tornado. With a tremor in his voice, he spoke of government inspectors making air tests a mile and a quarter underground, of how he and his coworkers nearly smothered with so little air pumped in by a single fan, and of the brattices, the cloth barriers hung between tunnels to regulate the ventilation currents. "In the Harlan fields," he said, he had worked under a foreman who came from Coal Creek and who knew about the explosions. Pete didn't say so at this concert, but he had once saved his oldest son's life in a Harlan mine, pulling debris off him during a rock fall. The next day, the cleanup crew said it took three men to move the same piece of slate that Pete had lifted. He told his daughter, "When it's your own child, and he's saying 'Daddy, save me,' well, what else could you do?"[69] No wonder he spoke so emotionally as he talked about this tune.

Once he had finished with his explanation, and just before starting the march itself, Pete's tone lightened. "I have got it like I learned it fifty-five years ago."[70] Musing over the many decades he had played the banjo showpiece, he added, "I'd like for the boys to learn it that-a-way and carry it on out." Earlier that evening, a young banjoist in the audience had stopped by, interested in "Coal Creek March." Pete vowed on stage that he'd teach him how to play the tune before he left the next morning. "I'm going get him right on that thing," he laughed, "like it ought to be."

One admirer who took up Pete Steele's offer to get right with this tune was folklorist Ed Kahn (1938–2002). During the summer of 1960 and continuing the following year, while enrolled as a folklore student at UCLA, Ed visited Lake City, Tennessee (the name given to Coal Creek following construction of the Norris Dam), seeking out residents like Della Tuttle and Alvin Vowell, who remembered the songs and legends associated with these events. "I interviewed everyone who knew about it," Ed explained, "even a woman who saw it [the Cold Creek War]. Nell Raines watched the battle from her front porch."[71] Ed's interest in Coal Creek began with Pete Steele's 1938 Library of Congress recording of "Coal Creek March." That led him in 1957 to twice visit Pete in Hamilton, Ohio, and return in 1958 to finish recording Pete's one solo album.[72] This interest also inspired him between 1957 and 1962 to locate and record at least eight more versions of the march, all from traditional players raised in Kentucky, Tennessee, and North Carolina. Though Ed did not write the Coal Creek book that he sometimes contemplated, he never wavered from the premise he expressed in his earliest student paper: Connections existed proportionally between the historical events that took place in Coal Creek and the folklore that ensued.[73] For "Coal Creek March," Ed recalled from his fieldwork, "The closer you got to the center, the more historical evidence you found."[74] Similarly, as players got further away from the scene, it became "just an instrumental tune."

In Lake City, Ed recorded the march three times, all set in the "Spanish key." Consistently the basic sequence of descending notes, the open tuning, and the chord structure that Ed documented echoed the "Spanish Fandango," while the decorative effects—the percussive tapping and string harmonics serving as metaphoric drums, parade steps, and bugle calls—fit the precedent established in "Sebastopol."[75] These two well-known instrumental pieces, not requiring sight-reading skills to master and absent of particularly developed melodies of their own, provided the essential musical and dramatic materials. The march became its own "descriptive fantasie," fitting an already popular affinity for program music. The various strains of the march, sometimes played with different picking styles in a further show of skill, could act interchangeably. Just as some performers emphasized sound effects and then returned to the "Fandango" pattern, others introduced singing, an addition that easily entered this flexible and multifaceted number. In traveling farther from Lake City, Ed came in contact with even more complex march performances. As the musicians' knowledge of the Coal Creek events lessened with the distance, their musical content widened. Experiences beyond the mine war affected these players. They felt other influences, played to different audiences, and conveyed additional meanings in performing the piece. Away from Coal Creek, the march found new steps.

Two months after Ed first visited Pete Steele in June 1957, he called on banjo player Sam Gaston of Junction City, Kentucky.[76] Gaston had toured for several years with blackface comedian, banjoist, and singer Frank Lewis (1874–?).[77] Calling him "one of the best to ever travel the road," Gaston affectionately recalled his old friend: "We had a lot of downs and ups. . . . I never had a brother, but if I would have had a brother, I couldn't have thought any more of him."[78] Lewis, he marveled, could "juggle the banjo, twist it around and under his legs and over his head . . . and never miss a note." Sam Gaston learned "Coal Creek March" from Frank Lewis. "This tune," Gaston explained, "is about the miners come out on strike and the governor had to send a standing army in there. They had a little battle, and oh, I don't know, several days before they got it all settled."

Even if Sam Gaston possessed a less than complete history of the Coal Creek War, he fills the march with an expanse of musical knowledge. He starts low on the neck, setting up a finger-drumming pattern on the banjo head that corresponds with an equal number of picked notes. One effect rhythmically completes the other. After these introductory measures, he plays a sequence based around a minor chord, running the shape assertively up the fretboard. To do so, Gaston reproduces the staccato finger picking of such ragtime banjo artists as Vess L. Ossman. He was not alone among rural banjoists to enjoy the virtuoso marches, rags, and cakewalks that early recording artists like Ossman, Fred Van Eps, and Ruby Brooks placed on turn-of-the-century cylinders and discs. These plentiful pieces found audiences in that era's emerging vaudeville, with the newest of them created by ragtime composers as well as Tin Pan Alley songsmiths. Banjoists like Ossman drew from printed scores while Gaston and his peers played by ear. But when Gaston brought moves like Ossman's to "Coal Creek March," he did more than signal his command of the instrument. He reset the piece from its "Spanish Fandango" basis. Even when he plays its most characteristic part with the tell-tale chord structure and the descending notes down the outside string, he does so with a propulsive drive indicative of the classical and ragtime banjo arrangements. While Sam Gaston's highly punctuated three-finger picking keeps a Southern rural sound, his rendition of the march moves beyond the old and familiar. He allies it with this new body of marches transmitted in the popular culture. In piloting the tune through the contrasting strains, he regales his listeners with something more modern, more dynamic than the graces of the old "Fandango." For a road performer like Sam Gaston, that made sense.

The credit Sam Gaston accorded Frank Lewis points to a convergence of country and city influences that variously met in the "Coal Creek March." Lewis, of rural background himself, affected a number of Kentucky folk performers playing this piece. Country music historian Charles Wolfe detailed Lewis's role with those players he inspired.[79] One of the most prominent, at least to today's audiences, was Dock Boggs from southwest Virginia. Boggs credited his initial exposure to the "Coal Creek March" to two players Wolfe believes were Frank Lewis and his playing partner (and brother-in-law) Bailey Briscoe. Briscoe and Lewis played banjo and banjourine duets as part of Dakota Jack's medicine show that traveled in eastern Kentucky from the early years of the century through the 1920s. Calling the march "one of the first chording pieces that I learned," Boggs told of a duo exactly like them appearing near the decade's end at a land sale in Mayking, Kentucky.[80] By then the duet had become, said fiddler and banjoist Ernie Hodges who played with them in the mid-1920s, "the two most famous banjo players ever in Kentucky."[81] Other performers, like Dick Burnett of Monticello, Kentucky, a pioneering hillbilly recording artist himself, learned the march from them, crediting especially Frank Lewis. Though Burnett never recorded it, he told

Wolfe that his fellow banjoist Marion Underwood also learned "Coal Creek March" from Lewis. In May 1927, Underwood, who lived near Berea, Kentucky, made the first recording of the march.[82] Underwood's masterpiece, assertive and virtuosic, assembles the piece's various parts into a forceful musical statement. The way Sam Gaston worked the banjo head's drumming into the tune reproduces the same passage Underwood plays on his record. Frank Lewis clearly emerges as a central figure in the march's dissemination, influencing, among others, Dock Boggs, Dick Burnett, Sam Gaston, and Marion Underwood. Another Kentucky native, and in his youth, a Hamilton, Ohio, resident, "Doin' My Time" composer Jimmie Skinner also credited Underwood, whom he saw in person, for the version he recorded for Gennett in the early 1930s.[83] Younger Kentucky banjoists David "Stringbean" Akeman, who called the piece the "Dead March," and Red Belcher, with his "Coleman's March," had likely heard Underwood's recording, too, thereby extending the Lewis and Briscoe legacy, a musical lineage audible in Jesse Spencer's recording from the 1938 Ohio Valley Folk Festival.[84] Fortunately, in the summer of 1957, Sam Gaston pointed Ed Kahn to the person closest to Frank Lewis, his son Forrest Lewis of Parksville, Kentucky.

The following August, three days after completing the last of his recordings with Pete Steele, Ed Kahn visited Forrest Lewis. Like Gaston, Lewis had a thorough knowledge of the banjo fingerboard, playing across its length with right-hand triplets, single-string bass runs, and double-time accompaniments transforming otherwise straightforward songs into set pieces. When Ed mentioned something Gaston had played for him, Lewis replied, "Sam's a pretty good old banjo picker. He plays a whole lot in the chords, but he don't go straight through it."[85] Lewis was not content with just keeping accompaniment, no matter how many places a chord might be located on the neck. He wanted an unbroken stream of melody. Lewis then demonstrated this aesthetic with an elaborate version of "Over the Waves." He carries this waltz down the entire fingerboard with all the flourishes of the classical banjo style, his notes cascading at times, its melody set within constantly shifting chord positions and textures.

Ernie Hodges recalled the singular phrase Frank Lewis and Bailey Briscoe used to characterize their music: "They called it scientific playing. They'd heard some classical players in the past I think. While they didn't read, they did play good music—so far ahead of the ordinary playing around."[86] "Scientific playing" is the precise term that S. S. Stewart repeatedly used in the 1880s to describe the cultivated method he advocated for the five-string banjo.

This kind of agile, musically literate approach meant to sever the banjo from its slave era and minstrel show past. Scientific playing also fit the aspirations of later fretted-instrument commentators like Vahdah Olcott-Bickford, who wanted the guitar to receive equal stature with the symphony and chamber music ensemble.[87] For Frank Lewis and Bailey Briscoe to adopt this phrase as their credo, too, suggests that they applied it to "Coal Creek March," their most famous and most requested showpiece. Clearly, "Coal Creek March" can trace its beginnings to the humbler "Spanish Fandango" and "Sebastopol." At the next level, if Forrest Lewis's rendition approximates what his father and his father-in-law actually achieved, then he illustrates a level of scientific technique, well ahead of the ordinary playing around.

When Lewis starts the piece, he tells (incorrectly) of hundreds dying in the Coal Creek war and gives Teddy Roosevelt credit for ending the hostilities. "You see, the National Guards over here tried to stop them, and they went out like this," he says, seamlessly launching a long harmonics passage of bugle calls placed in different locations on the neck.[88] From there he goes into the drumming and note section that Gaston and Underwood also played. All the while his foot thumps like a bass drum against his lighter hand-tapping cadences. He introduces then a new melody, a song with verses adapted from "A Fight for Home and Honor." Written about the 1892 Homestead steel strike near Pittsburgh, this piece depicts a confrontation that paralleled the Coal Creek experience.[89] Both conflicts involved the use of state militia, the breaking of a union, and the killing and injuring of strikers. "Trouble down in Coal Creek," Forrest Lewis sings, "come up all about this / A lot of disorganized men come to take away their work."[90] Following the song, Lewis returns to the minor run that Gaston also used and repeats the drumming and melody passage. He executes a single-string triplet on the high string hurtling from one end of the fingerboard to the other, then pivots between major and minor chords, and ends the piece with a ritard.

Ed Kahn felt Forrest Lewis played the most technically advanced version of "Coal Creek March" he had heard, while his verses cemented a crucial historical link. They "definitely put the march in the context of the 1891 incident."[91] His visit with Forrest Lewis led him to contact his father's former music partner Bailey Briscoe (1888–1965). By spring 1961, Briscoe supplied Ed with two more verses of the Homestead-based song. Briscoe dated them to approximately 1895, recalling that he had recorded them himself on a never-released master of "Coal Creek March" that he made for Columbia in October 1928.[92] Ed stayed in touch with Briscoe, and in August 1961 he wrote that he had recently met an old friend of his, one who called him "the master banjo player of 'em all. He is Doc Hopkins who worked with Dakota Jack after you. He remembered some of your songs and sang them to me."[93]

Ed Kahn had located Doc Hopkins (1900–1988) near his own home in southern California.[94] After twenty-two years of country music broadcasting that started in 1930, best known for his appearances on the WLS *National Barn Dance,* Doc had taken work as a machinist. He knew that after his live radio career ended, he would need a pension to supplement the few dollars he received as a World War I veteran. While his family stayed on in Chicago, Doc took the California sheet metal job that offered that security. The four reels of Doc's taped interviews in 1961 and 1962 mark the last of Ed Kahn's recordings of "Coal Creek March."[95]

Born in Harlan County, Kentucky, and raised in Rockcastle County, Doc Hopkins first heard Bailey Briscoe and Frank Lewis perform at the Brodhead fair, which he attended as a boy. They arrived with medicine show doctor Dakota Jack Pearsley, a native of Louisville and former cowpuncher and immigration ranger. The troupe set up a platform, and on two-by-fours around the stage they attached gasoline torches for nighttime lighting. On the stage they put a card table, two chairs, and the trunk that held Jack's medicines. Then Lewis and Briscoe came out playing. "They were both very good," Doc recalled.[96] "They had no mikes nor amplifiers in those days, and you could hear Bailey Briscoe sing so loud all over the fairground. To me, it was the main attraction of the fair." Doc remembered their tenor voices on "Home Sweet Home," sung while they waltzed with their instruments as if they were dance partners. It was here too, in about 1909, that he heard Dick Burnett perform the "Coal Creek March." He credited the song principally to Burnett.[97]

Doc Hopkins called the piece "Trouble at the Coal Creek Mines." It alternates talking, singing, and instrumental passages with a remarkable inventory of comic sounds: He frails the banjo loudly, then mutes it as the train "goes into a tunnel."[98] He pauses for a moment, then starts playing again, exclaiming, "She come out on the other side!" By drumming a parade tattoo on the banjo's head, Doc calls up an image of soldiers marching. Octave harmonics simulate bugle calls: first, parade assembly, then "Officer's Call." The troop train pulls into the Coal Creek station and Doc whooshes the sound of air brakes. Soldiers leave the train and the town's dogs begin to bark. Little dogs on the second string, midsized dogs on the third string, and great big dogs on the fourth string. Another bugle call, and the soldiers form up for assembly.

"Unexpected to them," a distant miner's bugle call is "answering 'em back." Doc's finger slips on the neck and he chuckles, "Wasn't a very good bugler that time." Doc puffs out his cheeks and makes a tuba sound as the band begins to play. Neither this melody nor his sung lyrics resemble Briscoe and Lewis's Homestead-based ballad. Instead, Doc's verses trace the movement of the combatants, from the troop train entering town, to its being "a dark day in Coal Creek," to the white flag of surrender finally raised by the defeated miners. The song flows in and out of the "Fandango" pattern, with the usual instrumental parts played along the high string. Doc alternately up-picks, frails, and three-finger picks the various sections, one of which includes "Yankee Doodle" as part of the military theme of "Coal Creek March."

It seems possible that after Doc first absorbed the march at the Brodhead fair—an intent nine-year-old musician drawn both to Dick Burnett's playing and to Briscoe and Lewis's showmanship—he found in 1919, and by then a performer himself, that certain of its elements had receded into the past. The verses he chose to sing, while less topical than the "Homestead-based" ballad, likely had more dramatic relevance for a newer audience. Doc's extended rendition, the longest of those Ed Kahn recorded, offers no trenchant commentary on labor relations or any mention of convict leasing. Instead, it is a program piece—in truth, a miniature musical comedy. Under the flickering lights of a makeshift stage in a rural backwater of early 1920s Kentucky, a talking banjo song like Doc's "Trouble at the Coal Creek Mines," concerning a recognizable if distant event from thirty years before, might well have appealed to those who gathered for Dakota Jack's medicine show where Doc, like Briscoe and Lewis before him, had performed. This theatricality sets "Trouble at the Coal Creek Mines" into a larger framework. Virtuoso effects characteristic of turn-of-the-century ragtime banjo and the multi-part nature of popular marches got refashioned by country entertainers. Doc joined his fellow Kentuckians who had found ways to translate the new body of music into their own sensibility.

Doc Hopkins spent years trying to teach me "Coal Creek"'s grand confection of music and stagecraft. Toward the end of his life, when his hands became too cold to play, he would place my fingers along the fretboard to show me the fingering of a particular passage. On my trips to Chicago, we met at his small north-side apartment where he lived in retirement. We sat next to each other on furniture covered with sticky plastic, with aluminum television tray-tables in front of us. On my table I would put my cassette recorder while his supported the sagging flesh of his frail, thinning arms. Near the end, when he became short of breath and hard of hearing, he whistled his tunes, fighting against time, struggling to reconstruct this vestige of bygone entertainment. He also wrote numerous letters. First he typed them, and when that became too painful to manage, he reverted to his spidery script, doing all he could to bring this piece and others from his medicine show past into the present. He made tapes at his bedside when songs and stage patter came to him. Doc's tireless efforts on my behalf echo Pete Steele's as he welcomed other aspiring players into his home who had come there to learn "Coal Creek March."

FIGURE 34.
Doc Hopkins
songbook, 1945.
Author's collection.

During the summer of 1985, at the Ohio State Fair, Pete Seeger opened his concert saying, "This is something I learned from the best banjo player I ever knew, Pete Steele of Hamilton, Ohio."[99] Then he played "Coal Creek March." Since 1939 when he first heard it, the renowned singer-activist has praised Pete Steele's "Coal Creek March," celebrating it on records, in writings, and at concerts. The two banjoists finally met in 1957 when Seeger came to Hamilton. Two years later he returned to film Pete Steele playing the march. Since then, the families have stayed in touch. Pete's daughter, Leona Steele Gabbard, has preserved years of Seeger's letters and cards, all reflecting his affection for Pete Steele and his admiration for the number he has called "my favorite banjo piece."[100] In 2008, in his late eighties himself, Seeger wrote to Leona, "I still play 'Coal Creek March,' but your father Pete Steele played it *best!*"[101]

In August 1984, a year before Pete Steele died, Seeger visited the family for the last time. Pete's wife, Lillie, by then nearly ninety, was bedridden, with Pete, a few years older, watching over her. Many of their children and grandchildren gathered for the occasion. Seeger arrived a few minutes late. Peggy Kriemer, a journalist present that day, remembered that Pete Steele had gotten up to eat when "Seeger walked into the kitchen and sat down at the table. Pete Steele looked up and years drained away—his eyes brightened, and he said, 'Pete, I didn't think you was coming,' and he reached out his hand with the sandwich. 'You want some sausage?' Steele and Seeger ate sausage and biscuits. And they started to talk about the first time they met."[102]

Music followed, as Pete Seeger took out his banjo and twelve-string guitar. One of Pete Steele's grandchildren taped the visit, and several of them, musicians themselves, played with Seeger. At one point Pete Steele sang a verse or two of "East Virginia," and Seeger responded by playing his own version back to him. Then, in reference to "Coal Creek March," he asserted, "Pete, believe me. Music is going to go on. There'll be young people wanting to pick a banjo, and they are going to listen to that record and say, 'How did that man Pete Steele ever play that?' 'What tuning did you use?' And they'll be figuring it out."[103] Pete's granddaughter chimed in, "That'll be hard to do!" Pete Steele quietly laughed, evidently pleased about this tune so closely identified with his skills, and one that he had shared with so many.

FIGURE 35. Pete and Lillie Steele celebrating their sixty-sixth wedding anniversary at home, Hamilton, Ohio, 1978. Photo by Myron Gabbard. Courtesy of Leona Steele Gabbard.

Some came from Hamilton itself. One of them was Paul Pell, the sheriff's son, who found the Steeles' hospitality endlessly welcoming—"like we were family from the time we walked in."[104] Over the years, Paul not only came to make two banjos for Pete Steele, but as a student at Indiana University arranged for Pete's 1965 concert there. Tom Loughead, who also lived in Hamilton, was a Pete Seeger fan before he knew about Pete Steele. When a guitar-picking electrician at the high school mentioned that someone in town played the banjo, Tom called on Pete to try to absorb some of his playing. In 1959 he even drove Pete to a Seeger concert in Cincinnati. Once there, Pete offered to take him backstage despite Tom's apprehensions over meeting his musical hero. The older man assured him, "He's just as common as you and me."[105] Banjoist Lew Cisle, also a Seeger devotee and a visual artist, came by and taped Pete and Lillie reminiscing about their lives. Later, when Lillie Steele passed away, he sent the family a flower stand shaped around a banjo and inscribed with the words to "Uncloudy Day," a gospel number she and Pete performed together.[106] Cisle, like these other locally raised, college-educated musicians, numbered in a stream of grateful visitors who came to learn from Pete Steele.

By the late 1950s, tens of thousands of suburban, middle-class college students had been caught up in the "folk boom" ignited by the Kingston Trio's 1958 hit "Tom Dooley." In this piece the Trio took a banjo ballad from the North Carolina–Virginia borders and supercharged it with catchy, calypso-inspired syncopation. For the next several years, "folk music" of this sort followed the bell curve typical of most popular music fads in the United States. It arced upward to the top of the sales charts and then gradually declined as rock and other genres replaced it. But popular folk music did inspire a number of banjo players to learn the old tunes in traditional versions. For them, playing "Coal Creek March" exactly as Pete Steele rendered it on his Library of Congress recording was requisite. It became a unit of currency in the economy of the folk revival.

Some of the fascination with authentic traditional banjo styles actually preceded the period of folk music's commercial popularity. In 1953, Tom Paley, a young, Yale-educated, New York–born college math instructor, released a recording of himself playing the "Coal Creek March" on a ten-inch Elektra LP titled *Folk Songs from the Southern Appalachian Mountains.*[107] Since the late 1940s, he and other musicians had been gathering in Greenwich Village for weekly "hootenannies." At these parties the guests would take turns playing along with such luminaries as Pete Seeger and Woody Guthrie. At one get-together, Paley played Wade Ward's "Old Joe Clark" just as he had learned it from the Library of Congress's AFS L2, *Anglo-American Shanties, Lyric Songs, Dance Tunes, and Spirituals.* Another participant observed disdainfully that Paley sounded just like the Library's recording. "I do?!" Paley exclaimed.[108] He felt he had made it. That same Library album contained "Coal Creek March," the source from which he learned Pete Steele's "Coal Creek March."

In a penetrating essay titled "'An Icy Mountain Brook': Revival, Aesthetics, and the 'Coal Creek March,'" Neil Rosenberg traces the movement of this banjo showpiece out of the mountains to its new constituency.[109] Here in barest outline is the story: By late 1957 Pete Seeger was performing the "Coal Creek March" (whose tuning he learned from Tom Paley) in concert.[110]

Over the next couple of years Seeger worked up a presentation in which he advised his listeners—among them Ed Kahn—to go to Ohio and learn the song directly from Pete Steele. Moreover, he prepared them for the experience of doing their own field research with a discourse covering the history of mine rebellions, the convict-lease system, and, in particular, the 1891 miners' strike at Coal Creek.[111]

In the headnotes to "Coal Creek March" that appear in his 1962 songbook *The Goofing-Off Suite* (there was also an earlier LP recording of the same name), Seeger writes, "A famous banjo solo was composed at that time [of the 1891 mine rebellion], a program piece, which included imitations of bugle calls, barking dogs, and rifle shots. One high section of the piece was taken over by Pete Steele, a carpenter and fine banjo player now living in Hamilton, Ohio. The rather pretentious virtuoso sound effects he abandoned, leaving this fine folk fragment, clean and high, reminding one of the waters of an icy mountain brook."[112] It was Fleming Brown's 1949 home recording of Doc Hopkins's "Trouble at the Coal Creek Mines" to which Pete Seeger made uncomplimentary reference.

Neil Rosenberg contemplates how the kind of idealism expressed in Seeger's aesthetics evolved in the folk revival. Years later, Seeger told Judith Tick about his parents' musical modernism, which he also adopted: "Father and Ruth [Crawford Seeger, his stepmother] didn't like the Romantic aesthetic. Once you started off with one rhythm, you held it to the end. And if a song was in a certain key, you didn't suddenly make it louder in one place and softer in another. A typical Romantic trick."[113] Seeger told me also that he didn't think Doc's performance made good music. "Steele," by contrast, "played it as a great tune. It's what folks do with fancy music. Boiling it down."[114] In reality, of course, folks make fancy music as well as austere. Think of the electrifying impact bluegrass banjo first had on country audiences—emcee George D. Hay on the Grand Ole Opry introducing Earl Scruggs "playing his fancy banjo" and the people there going completely wild. Or the demanding versions of the "Coal Creek March" that Ed Kahn collected from Sam Gaston and Forrest Lewis.

Nor was Pete Steele devoid of program pieces himself. His self-professed favorite was "The Train a-Pullin' the Crooked Hill" (also called the "Heavy Loaded Freight Train"), a banjo showpiece he learned from Andy Whittaker, his same source for "Coal Creek March." In this piece, he slows down and then speeds up like a train, simulating its driving wheels slipping and then catching on the rails. Back in East Bernstadt, Kentucky, Pete had watched neighborhood kids soap up the tracks and confound the locomotive engineers with this caper. His "Scoldin' Wife," a fiddle tune his father played, is also programmatic, an instrumental likeness of a couple arguing. "Just pay attention," Pete said, "how much ahead that woman is of the old man."[115] During his 1984 visit to the Steeles, Pete Seeger himself generously performed his remake of May Irwin's 1907 "Frog Song," a cante fable, a story with song and here with all sorts of sound effects, volume dynamics, and audience participation.

Traditional musicians know that dramatic pieces have their place no less than straightforward tunes. Pete Seeger's uncompromising love for Pete Steele's "Coal Creek March" lies in a purely musical realm. While Seeger often performed the tune in connection with the mine war, he gravitated toward the piece itself for its sparkling, pinpoint qualities of sound. It makes abiding sense that when Seeger wrote to the Steeles after this final visit, he ended, "Who knows, I may even learn how to play the Spanish fandango by the time I see you again."[116]

After leaving the Harlan coal fields in the spring of 1929 and hoping to start over, Pete and Lillie Steele found the course of their lives changed on the highway bridge outside Louisville. Sylvia Thomson's concern for Lillie Steele's well-being moments after the wreck, followed by the job offers, and her staying in touch with Lillie's family in the years to come, finds later echoes with Pete Seeger, who likewise championed Pete Steele. Just as the two women shared warmth and understanding, the two Petes found their own common ground. Pete Steele inspired Pete Seeger, which Seeger reciprocated with his own kindness, from sending him cash to contacting a publisher for his "Coal Creek March." He made Pete Steele a sought-out musician during the folk music revival and encouraged audiences to seek out other tradition bearers like him. When Pete Steele died in November 1985 at the age of ninety-four, a saddened Pete Seeger wrote to Leona Gabbard, "Every time I play the banjo, I think of him."[117]

Ed Steele, the eldest of Pete's surviving sons, summed up these separate but sometimes intersecting trajectories. "Pete Seeger, you know, he goes all over for that folk music. He said that my Dad was the best banjo player in the world."[118] With these words, Ed, a steel guitarist himself, delineated both what his family held in common with Pete Seeger and what set them apart. By "that folk music," Ed meant something other than what he, his brothers, and their father played together. Homemade tapes from the mid-1980s show them doing songs not in the Seeger canon, but from Marty Robbins, Bob Wills, the Louvin Brothers, Lefty Frizzell, Johnny Cash, the Statler Brothers, Hank Williams, Flatt and Scruggs, Carl Story, Buck Owens, Porter Wagoner, and the Stanley Brothers—latter-day equivalents of the hillbilly repertory Alan Lomax struggled with the day he met Pete Steele. Among the oldest numbers they ran through were "Billie in the Lowground" and "Whistling Rufus," while the newest was John Prine's "Paradise." Ed himself credited Leon McAuliffe's "Steel Guitar Rag" with sparking his interest in that instrument. The tune, which he knew as a western swing classic, has roots in "Spanish Fandango."

This repertory of country music, jukebox hits, and bluegrass appeared earlier too, in 1958, when Ed Kahn recorded Pete Steele. Near the end of their last session, Pete picked the banjo behind his daughter Sue leading on "Why Baby Why," "Uncle Pen," and "If Teardrops Were Pennies."[119] Ten years before that, Pete wrote to Alan Lomax at the Library in a similar vein. Set down in Lillie's hand, he notes, "I still play the 5 string banjo. One Son plays the harmonica, one Plays the Steel Guitar, and one Plays the Electric guitar. One is learning the Base Fiddle and one is learning the Violin. You see I soon will have a band of my own, ha ha."[120] That band, which gathered annually at Pete and Lillie's on Christmas day, nearly knocked the house off its brick foundations. As the rest of the family danced away and the neighbors came by to watch, Pete and his sons played music worthy of a roadhouse. In later years, Pete and Lillie loved to watch *The Dukes of Hazzard* on television. With a soundtrack evocative of Nashville, it offered a vision of folk music distant from the urbane variety presented on the *Hootenanny* TV show that so many of their young student visitors just as eagerly absorbed in years past. When Pete Seeger played "Union Maid" for the family in 1984, everyone recognized its old-time source, "Redwing," not its Woody Guthrie lyrics.

For as much as that meeting on the highway bridge or effusions from the stage have meant to this family—both have mattered profoundly—they still lived within their own culture. While Pete Seeger used the "Coal Creek March" in a set piece with other Coal Creek songs to express the valor in unionism, the cause of social justice, and his sense of an unencumbered folk aesthetic, Leona Steele Gabbard spoke with gratitude for having worked at Champion Paper, of getting "a good-paying job, you know, without college degrees."[121] She had little use for unions or "radicals" at this family-run company that hired whole families, like hers. A lot of social history lies in her older sister Pearl's statement "Kentucky people were good workers."[122] A forty-five-year shop floor veteran, she spoke on behalf of her family as well as the company's attitude. She said it with pride and she said it more than once.

Complex experiences have shaped "Coal Creek March," a tune-song-ballad based on traditional precedents that reflects with varying degrees of literalism a community's wrenching history. Just as the earlier development of "Spanish Fandango" and "Sebastopol" tracks disparate creative processes for both schooled and home musicians, "Coal Creek March" resists portrayal by a single aesthetic measure. For rural and revivalist banjoists alike, the march summons different influences and desires, which they, in turn, invest in it and take away from it. In the name of "what the folk do," when Pete Steele performed the "Coal Creek March," he described more than a brass band and he played more than a mountain brook of rippling notes. He also saw disfigured, immolated miners. In sharing this tune with all who asked, Pete Steele brought an emblem of that dark world into ours.

Texas Gladden
From Here to the Mississippi

J IM GLADDEN STOOD IN HIS CANNING SHED LOOKING OVER his neatly stacked shelves of jams, jellies, and pickles. Each fall Jim made preserves for the winter months. Now, with Thanksgiving just two days away, he took a quick inventory. Along one shelf he kept several rows of homegrown tomatoes. Packed into wide-mouthed jars, their lids made tight with spring-loaded clamps, the largest of the produce looked faintly orange while the rest resembled grayish plums. In narrow glass cylinders fastened with rubber seals, peppers suspended in a vinegary solution splayed like branches across some miniature forest. He began to pick out an assortment, asking whether my family might prefer this item or that. With so many provisions at hand, Jim Gladden's larder appeared ready not only for the holiday, but for the longer cold times ahead.

Years before, his mother, Virginia ballad singer Texas Gladden, first showed him how to prepare and store foodstuffs. "We lived like pioneers, you know," said Jim of the early 1930s when he, his eight brothers and sisters, and their parents, James and Texas Gladden, occupied a nearby log cabin five miles outside of Salem. Wagon tracks rutted the one sloping lane to their home, surrounded by woods, that perched at the furthest end of Mangrum's Holler. A large family with little cash, the Gladdens had to grow their own food and put up what they needed for the frigid months. Even so, Jim recalled, "In the fall, harvest time, that was my mother's favorite time of year. With the canning and preserving and putting things away, you could see what you was accomplishing."[1]

Just then, a motor kicked on and he pointed to a pump that operates from the same enclosure. In this part of Virginia's Roanoke Valley, water runs in seams of such irregularity that while Jim's well extends 54 feet deep, his next-door neighbor had to drill 300 feet. When survey teams came to locate a potential site for a dam, they found a widespread underground network of limestone caverns. One test drilling alone required some 2,500 bags of cement to fill the narrow hole. Not only could no reservoir be built, as the land could not have supported such a weight, but the drillers detected by sound a submerged river rolling through many of the jagged tunnels. A surveyor told Jim that "This country is so cavernous, it would be possible to travel from here to the Mississippi, if you could find your way."[2] That such a complex might exist and that one could follow it, however fancifully, to the nation's central tributary suggested another meandering, too: the course of a ballad his mother used to sing, the piece she called "One Morning in May."

This mournful story of a girl gone wrong offers a feminine retelling of "The Unfortunate Rake," an Anglo-Irish broadside of the eighteenth century that conveys the last words of a young soldier dying of venereal disease. With its famous set of funeral instructions, the ballad has achieved abiding life in two of America's most popular songs: "Streets of Laredo" and "St. James Infirmary Blues." It has appeared under various titles and on myriad recordings—from Louis Armstrong and his Savoy Ballroom Five to the Norman Luboff Choir; from Blind Willie McTell's guitar-accompanied eulogy titled the "Dying Crapshooter's Blues" to cowboy singer Dick Devall's tale of a fallen wrangler in "Tom Sherman's Barroom." So popular has been the "Rake" that it has given rise to numerous parodies as well, parodies that span the troubles besetting a downhill skier to the trials of being a fan of the Chicago Cubs.[3] Contemporary interpreters of the ballad include a hard rocker, a mystery novelist, and a Pulitzer prize–winning poet.[4] Over the years the song has operated as a kind of public property, a created work whose artistic responsibility many have borne.

Texas Gladden took this most supple of ballads and made it her own. Just as she came to be presented as an exemplary Appalachian singer, "One Morning in May" has come to represent a folksong that continues to live through a dazzling variety of forms. Together their histories map an artistic process defined as much by its diversity as by its continuity. The underground tunnels that Jim Gladden envisioned from Mangrum's Holler to the Mississippi may be fragmented and dark, unmapped and irregular, but if you could find your way, their paths would reach across a nation.

Texas Anna Smith Gladden (1895–1966) was the third of eight children born to Alexander King Smith (1868–1958) and Sarah Louvenia Hammonds Smith (1868–1949).[5] Alexander and Sarah, whom their Saltville neighbors called King and Louvine—and sometimes, playing on the rhyme between his name and hers, King and Queen—were second cousins, descendants of Irish immigrants who first reached this part of southwestern Virginia in the mid-eighteenth century. According to family legend, Francis Smith, the earliest of their ancestors to behold the Rich Valley of Smyth and Washington counties, was a surveyor. The same story reports that he held a chain for another young surveyor from Virginia, one George Washington.[6] Apocryphal or not, this image of Francis Smith assisting the nation's future leader sets him within a wider social history. A related set of circumstances surrounds Texas's name.

"Texas" was not the singer's nickname, but her given name, taken from one of her aunts. Likewise, Texas's sisters, Kansas and Virginia, as well as their first cousin, Tennessee, were named after older relatives. Apart from honoring family members, their names clearly saluted public entities—some of them relatively recent additions—on the American map. The optimism that the Smiths associated with these burgeoning symbols of the Union and conferred onto their children extended to some of the era's most celebrated persons. In January 1897, William McKinley took office as the twenty-fifth president of the United States, with Garret A. Hobart as vice president. That May, Texas's parents had a boy whom they named after these two officials—Hobart McKinley Smith. Two years younger than Texas, Hobart (1897–1965) remained throughout her life her closest musical companion. Their attachment carried over to the families they raised. Texas named her oldest son Hobart, and Hobart gave his second daughter Texas's name. The commemorating of political figures also continued. In August 1933, during her final pregnancy, while singing at Virginia's Whitetop Mountain folk festival, Texas met Mrs. Franklin D. Roosevelt. Come December, Texas named her newborn daughter Eleanor Wilma Jean.[7]

When Wilma Jean mentioned this connection between her name and her mother's experience with the first lady, the three of us—she, her older brother

Jim Gladden, and I—were sitting in her home, a dark log house striped with white mortar that their parents built in the late thirties after fire destroyed the family's first cabin farther up the holler. In this very room in September 1941, Wilma Jean, then seven years old, watched her mother sing more than a dozen songs into a Library of Congress disc machine.[8] "One Morning in May" Wilma Jean knew intimately. "It was a pretty song," she said, recalling how Texas used to sing it to her and her siblings at bedtime. "Mama," Wilma Jean added, "had all the talent in the family."

In November 1997 this seemed a fitting place to listen to it again. *A Treasury of Library of Congress Field Recordings* had just gone into national release, and it includes this song, marking its first transfer to compact disc.[9] As "One Morning in May" played, Jim evoked that evening fifty-six years before, when he, along with Wilma Jean and others in the family, watched their mother record. Jim's attention had fixed on certain mechanical aspects of the recording process. He told us how Alan Lomax changed one bamboo recording needle for another still sharper. Then Jim recalled his own concerns whether the crickets and birds chirping near the house might intrude on the discs being cut. Over the years he found those noises on the record (which might have included inherent scratchiness) spoiling his enjoyment of his mother's singing. Now, with the signal remastered and the scratches reduced, Jim was relieved that the katydids and other sounds of Mangrum's Holler had finally been dispelled. "He's fine-tuned it," Jim declared. "It's clear as a bell. No background noise."[10]

The song finished, but our attention stayed on Texas. "Mama," Wilma Jean remarked, "could sit and tell jokes all day long and never tell the same one twice."

"Remember any?" I asked.

"None fit to tell," came her answer.

Jim brought up a fable Texas used to repeat about the preacher and the bear, where "prayer is all right, but it ain't worth a damn in a bear fight." He laughed easily. The relaxed setting at Wilma Jean's that evening, with no tape recorder running or lists of questions to pursue, freed up his memories and his conversation.

Earlier that day, however, Jim's spirits had taken a different turn. I had peppered him with a questionnaire used during the 1942 Fisk University–Library of Congress Coahoma County folk culture study.[11] Its schedule of questions originated with Fisk's sociology and music departments along with the Archive's earlier surveys (such as the one collector Herbert Halpert used in 1939) and Alan Lomax's own song-collecting experiences. Designed to elicit quick responses from a wide sampling of musicians, it centered on identifying the singers' sources, their musical preferences, and other traditional practices present in their homes and community.

In September 1941, when Alan and Elizabeth Lomax recorded Texas in this room, the questionnaire was nearly complete. At the time the Lomaxes were returning to Washington from the Coahoma project's initial recording expedition in Mississippi. Their homeward swing into southwest Virginia included a limited number of ballad singers with whom they had previous contact. Based on what songs were recorded and what notes exist from those sessions, no evidence suggests they exposed Texas to the questionnaire. Still, it offered a handy set of queries that I thought might be worth using again. On a more practical level, this continuity with the past also held the possibility of helping him recall certain experiences of so long ago. As it turned out, it revealed something else instead.

That morning, soon after we started going through the survey, Jim removed from his bedroom wall three framed photographs. The first, taken in December 1912, was Texas and James Gladden's wedding portrait. Mounted beside it was a photo taken in 1926 in Henrytown, Virginia, that section of Saltville where Texas's family lived. It shows four generations, thirty-four persons in all, arranged along a hillside. At the top, Texas stands between her husband, James, and her brother Hobart, who clasps a guitar. Jim, still a toddler, sits a few rows lower near his cousins and beside his maternal great-grandmother. The third picture, taken the year before in Roanoke, features James Gladden's family. At one end, Texas holds their infant daughter Mary, with James standing beside them. On his other side, he leans closely to his sister, also named Mary. Altogether, sixteen persons look deep into the camera, dressed as if for a formal occasion.

So that I could copy these images, we broke from our taping and drove to Salem's Super K-Mart. As the pictures streamed from its photo processor, Jim named everyone, explaining how each was related to the other. He also acknowledged that he was the last in his family to hold them in living memory, and possibly the last to even possess this information.

Jim's knowledge of the pictures proved every bit as sharp as the questions specified on the Coahoma form. Yet for all the information he shared that day—from which old-time cures the Gladdens used to the homemade games they played, from the superstitions they observed to the records they owned (they had only one recording for their cylinder player, "The Little Old

FIGURE 36.
Smith-Gladden
family, Henrytown,
Virginia, 1926.
Courtesy of Jim
Gladden.

Log Cabin in the Lane")—this specificity, in fact, inhibited him. Again, his handling of the photographs was telling. Once we got back to his house, Jim strode into his bedroom to rehang the pictures. Centering them with care, he studied each one for a long moment. Clearly much more attended these images than what he had enumerated beside the copying machine. His effortless listing of names barely touched their significance. Now he returned to the kitchen, where the cassette recorder and microphone lay in readiness. He paused, steeling himself for the next round of questions. Jim Gladden's patience exceeded his frustration that day, but the survey soon put him in touch with something he found wholly painful.

For Jim, as well as for his brothers and sisters, Texas's singing had been an everyday affair, not something they gave much thought to during their younger days. "She sang when she worked," he recalled, "when she washed clothes, when she cooked." Texas's voice even served as factory whistle for the family, her mealtime call carrying into the woods where her husband and

FIGURE 37.
Gladden family,
Roanoke, Virginia,
1925. Courtesy of
Jim Gladden.

sons worked as loggers and sawyers. "She'd come to the back door and give the yell, you know. . . . We knew what it was. Come back to the house." Yet for all of Texas's music making, neither Jim nor the others took up playing and singing themselves. Nor did the Gladdens acknowledge or necessarily even realize her gathering reputation as a source of Appalachian song. Despite the appreciations penned by an occasional journalist or the interest taken by those devotees of Virginia folk music who championed her, Jim explained, "We had things on our mind besides old country songs. We didn't care about those mountain ballads." His voice tightened. In the parlous days of the Great Depression, "Everybody was wrapped up in just trying to live."

In those years Jim, along with his siblings, still dwelled at home. Texas understandably saw her role there not as a singer but as the mother of nine. When asked why she didn't pursue a musical career at a time when recognition of her singing was mounting, she admitted, "Been too busy raising babies."[12] Lullabies—which included ballads such as "One Morning in

May"—were what her brood most often required of her talents. In effect, her music, however much she shared it with her family, became invisible to them. Likening it to a treasure hidden in plain sight, Jim now remarked sadly, "You can't dig it up anymore."

Jim most readily communicated by letting things unfold as they did that evening at Wilma Jean's, by recalling events that freely associated one incident to another. The stories that he and others in his family chose to tell, like the photographs he cherished on his bedroom's walls, captured memorable experiences. That's not to suggest that a tool like the Coahoma questionnaire, designed to elicit rapid-fire responses under limited time and resources, did not in its day accomplish its purpose. It's just that for those nearest to Texas herself, it didn't play into their strengths as witnesses able to identify meaningful events in her life, intimately recall her singing, and evoke telling aspects of her character. What Jim and the others had to say, coupled with more formal historical resources as might be found—newspaper articles, family papers, recordings, institutional correspondence—mapped a course, however much it might twist and stray, that could perhaps lead one across that subterranean route from Mangrum's Holler to the Mississippi.

Yet for all the virtues of family storytelling, despite its spontaneity, insight, and intricacy, Jim also cautioned, as D. K. Wilgus once sagely advised an audience of trained folklorists, that "'folk explanations' . . . furnish truths but not always facts."[13] Soon after Jim brought up the preacher and the bear story at Wilma Jean's, he recalled another, of the "kid that said his 'dad had a gold mine, which really was a coal mine, that turns out to be a coal yard where . . . [in truth] he drove a coal truck.'"[14] Jim laughed and added, "That's the way some of these tales are when you boil it down. They [the tellers] tell it so much they get to believing it themselves." Jim was referring to the exaggerations that some of his family members were prone to relate, to their "telling wild stories." Still, one they all told—Jim included—and with striking consistency, involved a particular event in Texas's life. Pivotal in her life's course, it also marks the direction she found in her music.

At Wilma Jean's that night, conversation soon turned to Texas's father, King Smith. Wilma Jean said that "King never did trust Pap."[15] After a two-week courtship in December 1912, James Gladden, then twenty-six, eloped with seventeen-year-old Texas Smith. Speaking of King's displeasure over this turn of events, Jim noted, "He always thought if he'd [James Gladden] steal his daughter, he'd steal his geese," referring to King's affection for these birds.[16] In his youth King Smith roamed Saltville's countryside for their nests, watching them hatch, sometimes protecting the eggs from bears, and always caring for some at home. "Father said his greatest delight used to be to hunt a goose's nest when he was a boy," Texas recalled in a 1946 interview, when "Henrytown was all in big tall timbers, big hemlocks and pines."[17] The peace King Smith found in his gentle pursuit contrasted with his fierce resistance to Texas's marriage. Even in 1946, thirty-four years after her elopement, Texas still called his marital opposition "a bad affair."

The most often repeated of the many family stories about Texas told of her eloping with James Gladden. I heard it from Jim almost as soon as I met him, and the same from Wilma Jean. Hobart's daughter and son (Texas's niece and nephew) as well as Texas's grandson, also spoke of it within minutes of our first meeting.[18] Moreover, the experience never lost its force on Texas herself. She took over ten minutes to tell it in a 1946 interview, and in 1952, she began her book of poems with it:

> Of all the obstacles we overcame,
> As we were running away.
> . . .
> Now it is forty years later,
> And we still talk of our wedding day;
> And the same old pines are still whispering,
> About a boy and girl who ran away.[19]

Ten years later, it rang out again as the centerpiece for the couple's fiftieth wedding anniversary. At a banquet styled after the television program *This Is Your Life*, Texas and James listened to her cousin Leonard Smith detail the day's events, followed by a surprise appearance of Hobart Smith singing a composition about the minister who married them.[20]

Although the extent of detail varies from one teller to another, Texas's version largely goes like this: While visiting relatives in Saltville in December 1912, James Gladden of Roanoke met Texas Smith. The two "fell desperately in love with each other."[21] After accepting James's proposal, which he made in the town drugstore, Texas decided they must elope, as she knew her father would oppose the match. By all accounts a severe man, King Smith made it clear that he preferred that none of his daughters marry. "He wanted to keep us always if it could be possible," Texas explained. Nevertheless, on the appointed day, Texas used the pretext of getting a new shuttle for her mother's sewing machine in order to leave the house. While waiting for a train to take her to Glade Springs, a community ten miles from Saltville, where the two planned to meet, word got out that she was fleeing home. "Oh my goodness," Texas said. "The fat was in the fire." Though she made it to Glade Springs, she didn't get far along the town's main street before being arrested. King Smith had by then already contacted the local authorities. The policeman who escorted her back to the station for the return train, acknowledged his own past: "I've had the same row to weed." At that point James made a last appeal to King Smith from the depot telephone. King again denied his daughter's hand. "I'm going to have her if it takes me twenty-five years," James countered, and then hung up on King.

Not to be dissuaded either, Texas asked the police officer if she could use the ladies' lounge. There she unpacked her suitcase and put on several sets of clothes, one over the other. She then escaped through the freight room, jumping off the platform and making her getaway on what she recalled was an icy, wet, and snowy December day. James, dragging their bags behind him, met her at a private coal wharf where they continued to elude capture. With her cousin Leonard Smith's help, they hired an open hackney, the first of two, to take them to Abingdon. As the second carriage was a single buggy, its driver, Leonard, and James occupied the same bench seat. That meant that Texas had to sit on James's lap for the ride, a circumstance she found to be an "an awful disgrace . . . I tried to sit so light." They reached Abingdon after dark but stayed out of sight by going to a movie before catching their next train. Knowing that her father would again contact someone to intercept her at the Bristol station, Texas disguised herself on the train with a different overcoat and scarf. Although spotted on their way to the minister's chapel, just before midnight on December 28, 1912, they finally married.

This incident provides a touchstone to Texas's personality. On one side comes the pressure of tradition—her father's will—while on the other, her act of declaring independence. Even though signs of modernity appear throughout this coming-of-age story—horse-drawn carriages and Victorian decorum set alongside moving-picture shows and trunk-line telephones—these mark the times in which she lived, not the direction to which she was turning. She found pain in severing from her father, in going against his resolve. Nor did she wed James Gladden to effect an unconventional life. As she explained, "Marriage was a sacred responsibility. . . . It was something that I studied thoroughly before I took the jump. I made up my mind thoroughly before I married that I would never separate from my husband. . . . He was the boss, you see . . . he's ten years older than I. And he more or less just raised me to his own notion. And I felt that that was as it should be."[22] Texas decided to wed James Gladden over her father's wishes not so much to break with her upbringing as to chart her own course through it.

This holding her own to claim the circumstances around her appears time and again in the stories that Texas and her family told about themselves. Her maternal grandmother, for example, described Saltville's settlement entirely in terms of their own experiences, a saga Hobart repeated years later.[23] A similar personalizing instills the Smith family legend that ties young George Washington to surveyor Francis Smith. It also runs through the family's penchant for taking public figures for their names.

Two anecdotes from widely separated times in Texas's own life reveal how she kept her habitual bearings. In 1909, at age fourteen, Texas went to work at Mathieson Alkali Works, a 12,500-acre facility that launched full-scale operations in Saltville the year she was born. Her job there involved packing the company's Eagle Thistle brand of bicarbonate of soda, a full-time occupation she kept until she met James Gladden. In addition to singing with her coworkers to while away the hours, she and the others relieved the day's tedium by stuffing handwritten notes with their names and addresses into the baking soda boxes.[24] Sometimes they did receive return mail to these latter-day messages-in-a-bottle. Embedding a small town's chatter in an assembly line's drone brought handmade qualities to a machine-dominated workplace. This immediacy reappears in a jest Texas told in 1946 that resounds with provincial wit. "Did you ever hear about the old lady who made her first trip to New York? That's kind of like me now. She looked up on the side of one of these tall buildings and she saw 'Smith Manufacturing Company.' She said, 'There now, I've just found out where all these Smiths is coming from.'"[25]

FIGURE 38. Texas and James Gladden's wedding photo, December 1912. Courtesy of Jim Gladden.

Whether Texas spoke of her elopement, the boxes she and her coworkers stuffed with notes, or even Manhattan's Smith Manufacturing Company, these incidents all contrast personal resolve with established order. A comparable process took place in her music. There, too, Texas relied on her own sensibilities to navigate an inherited tradition. Jim Gladden described this balancing during a phone call—our last conversation—on what would have been Texas's 110th birthday. "It was a fortune in history in those old songs," he began, "and having my mother's name connected to it adds to the history of it."[26] He weighed Texas's singing against other mountain performers he had heard at Salem's fiddler's conventions, high school events, and church fund-raisers. "What was different," he explained, "was they didn't know how to turn a song like my mother did." By this craftsman's term, indebted as much to his years as a carpenter as to the embellishments by which a singer shapes a song, he framed his mother's artistry.

Texas's musical aptitude surfaced at an early age. In 1900, King Smith began building his family a new home after fire destroyed their cabin in Henrytown, one of Saltville's mountainside communities that flourished with the opening of the Mathieson Alkali Works. Texas, then five, spotted her father's nail keg, hid inside it, and found herself sealed in. Her father finally freed her from the barrel. "I was a monkey," Texas conceded, "did everything I saw everyone else do."[27] Like the children's game of monkey, she mirrored the activity around her. This talent extended to reproducing the speech she overheard. Texas's two older sisters called her "mouthy," warning that her aptitude for imitation was bound to get her into mischief. Whether further troubles in that realm befell her, Texas left no account, but she continued to employ her talents for mimicry. Early on she also found that she could hear a song once and retain its words and tune complete.

At home she had plenty of opportunities to cultivate these gifts. Both her parents played the banjo and both her grandfathers were fiddlers. A violin tied in a black "poke" bag hung beside the family's parlor organ. Texas learned the keyboard by ear at an early age, as did her brother Hobart, who began playing it standing up, since he was too small to stay seated and still reach the pedals. In the evenings, King and Louvine Smith gathered their eight children by the fireplace to sing. "Your legs would be burning up," Hobart recalled, "and your back a chillin'"[28] As the youngsters squirmed to get closer to the heat, both Texas and Hobart recalled their father leading them on hymns such as "I'm

Bound for the Promised Land." Afterward, King would reach for his banjo to play more worldly pieces like "John Henry," "Walking Boss," and "Hawkins County Jail." "Old love songs"—the name their mother gave to the ballads that Texas later became famous for singing—followed. Texas drew from these songs what she called "a perfect mental picture," seeing in her imagination their unfolding drama and color. Song by song, she detailed a vision of the characters and their doings as they moved across the "casements . . . and gallows."[29] This stock of personal images grew as neighboring aunts, uncles, and cousins came over in the evenings, singing still more songs and playing often until midnight. Texas fell asleep to their voices, finally going to bed when she lost her place by the fire and the cold compelled her to reach for warmer covers. At least twice a week, square dances took place in Texas's home or at a neighbor's. "Just like a prayer meeting," Hobart said, "catch it around from house to house."[30] Once their cabin floorboards collapsed from the dancing, and the snow underneath came up through the cracks and settled on the bed. Texas concluded that you could never give the Smiths too much music.

She recalled that period as rich in "packing" songs away.[31] Words and music fixed themselves indelibly in her mind. "Like a closed book," Texas said, "but I never forgot what was in the book." She contrasted that permanence with her experiences with the hit parade. She still absorbed songs, hearing them on the radio, but most, she found, fell away after a day or two: "I want to tell you very frankly that all the things that you ever remember that amounts to anything in this life you learn it when you're young."

In Texas's youth, phonographs and radio—then new inventions—had not made their way to the family's home, just as sheet music and paperback songsters, the primary commercial means of song distribution in the nineteenth century, also exerted no direct presence there. Among her earliest musical memories she included her paternal grandfather, Civil War veteran Samuel George Smith, who arose at four every morning to tend to Old Ned, "an old, flea-bitten gray horse he had."[32] At those times, Sam, with his white beard lapping down his chest, but whose hair stayed "black as a raven's wing," would whistle and sometimes sing "Wildwood Flower." By then over a generation old, this 1860 composition, originally titled "I'll Twine 'mid the Ringlets," imparts the words of a frail, spurned lover in verses dense with Latinate floral names. With lyrics written by stage performer Maud Irving and music credited to composer J. P. Webster, the song came to be known as "Wildwood Flower." The 1928 Carter Family recording secured its national prominence. Here, however, Texas speaks of an encounter at least two decades before the record's release. In recalling her grandfather singing in the barn, she conveyed a pastoral scene suggestive more of a nineteenth-century genre painting than a secondary effect of that era's mass media: a patriarchal man currying Old Ned by lantern light, while a fascinated little girl with a musical aptitude takes it all in. By whatever means "Wildwood Flower" had been transmitted to Sam Smith, by the time it reached his granddaughter, Texas said, "It was the prettiest thing I thought I ever heard."

Texas's exposure to song inevitably went beyond her family circle. She credited her rendition of "Old Kimball," originally an Anglo-Irish ballad of the early nineteenth century, to listening to a black work gang operating near the Smiths' home in Henrytown. She also spoke knowingly of blues being played in Saltville several years before she wed, predating its earliest appearance on sheet music or recordings. As a teen employed at the Mathieson plant, she picked up songs from her coworkers. "Every evening when I went home from work, I had a new song to sing."[33] In those years, Texas also began to develop a number of her duets with Hobart that drew upon these nearby resources. Their joint version of "Poor Ellen Smith," for example, demonstrates Hobart playing the banjo in an approach radically differently from their father's.[34] Hobart follows John Greer's example, a West Virginia native who lived near the Smiths. Unlike King Smith's hearth-side style that Hobart called "old-time long rapping" for its slow, sustained lope, Hobart harnesses Greer's "double-noting" attack, an insistent, pulsating foundation over which rides Texas's keening vocal.[35] The siblings achieved a similar melodic density in "The Devil and the Farmer's Wife." With Texas singing lead, Hobart plays guitar, an instrument whose technique he first absorbed from an itinerant African American guitarist known to locals as Blind Lemon. In 1913 or so, Blind Lemon stayed with the alkali workers, providing afternoon entertainment for listeners that included Hobart and his cousins. In this piece, a comic ballad that Louvenia Smith sang at home, Hobart seconds Texas's vocal line on the strings of his guitar in near syllabic unison. Hobart follows this pattern as well in "Rose Connelly," a mountain song of Irish origin, that again closely complements Texas's vocal. Here Hobart plays it on fiddle, an instrument he first learned from ex-slave Jim Spencer. Spencer, who chopped wood in the neighboring hollows in exchange for an evening's meal, made the Smiths' cabin one of his regular stops. After supper, with his back to the fire, he often played till bedtime. Eventually he gave Hobart his fiddle. Years later, Texas and Hobart's guitar-playing cousin John Galliher said about these encounters, "We'd foller the music. We'd hunt up everybody we could find."[36]

FIGURE 39.
Hobart Smith and
Texas Gladden
at her home in
Salem, Virginia,
1950s. In 1941
Texas recorded
"One Morning in
May" in this room.
Courtesy of Jim
Gladden.

For Texas, this thirst for songs continued with her move to Salem. Soon after her marriage to James Gladden, she began learning ballads from her neighbors. She got "Mary of the Wild Moor" from "Mrs. Morse who lives on Back Creek," who passed it along soon after they met.[37] Texas especially credited her father-in-law, English born William Langstaff Gladden (1842–?). From "Papa Gladden," who lived with Texas, and her new family she learned such British music hall numbers as "Villikens and his Dinah" and "Sweet Julia Flanagan."[38] She acquired the ballad that became her most influential recording, "Mary Hamilton," from Alfreda Peel, a Salem schoolteacher and

Virginia Folklore Society collector who first met her in the winter of 1916. The song had already passed through generations of Peel's own family, reaching back to the time of Mary, Queen of Scots.

Peel shared "Mary Hamilton" with Texas, who recorded it along with "One Morning in May" at the 1941 session that Jim and Wilma Jean witnessed.[39] Two years later it appeared on the Library's second volume of Anglo-American ballads. The first volume had inaugurated the Library's folk music series. It opened with Texas's "The House Carpenter" and included her versions of "One Morning in May," "Old Kimball," and "The Devil's Nine Questions," the last of which she also learned from Alfreda Peel. As for "Mary Hamilton," nearly twenty years after Texas's performance was first issued, Joan Baez echoed her melody with variant words to form what became a staple of her early concerts.[40] In turn, it was Baez's "Mary Hamilton" that inspired Emmylou Harris to learn her first chords on the guitar. Though Texas's name does not appear, her presence figures in an omnipresent outlet of contemporary American life: Emmylou pays tribute to Baez's "Mary Hamilton" on a 2004 CD anthology marketed at Starbucks.[41]

This winding stream of influences likewise animates the song list that Texas brought to her 1946 interview with Alan Lomax. Typed out on eight double-spaced pages by one of her daughters, it names 194 entries.[42] While undoubtedly incomplete—it lists just two religious numbers—it brings together Texas's public repertory, which spans published songs of the nineteenth century to children's play parties, old-time dance breakdowns to bad man ballads. None of these is overtly political, and only one concerns industrial change—"Peg and Awl"—a plaintive song portraying the shift from hand-pegged shoes to their machine-made successors. Despite Texas's fame as a singer of traditional British ballads, here she names but eleven titles that appear in Francis James Child's collection. At least fifty-five of her songs, like "Wildwood Flower," have known authors, with the earliest published in 1850 and the newest dated 1919. Nearly all of them reflect an era in American songwriting that stressed sentimental themes.

Texas's repertory illustrates a widespread tendency among performers of her generation. Folklorist Bill Ellis writes that "the dominant folk tradition *was* sentimentality."[43] Ellis points out a common thread that unites these more recent products with the older narrative ballads. Though rhetorical strategies and poetic diction distinguish nineteenth-century parlor ballads from those earlier works that appear in Child's canon, they both maintain an "emotional core" as the vital spark of their appeal.[44]

Certainly deep emotion permeates Texas's choice of songs. With repeated images of personal loss, sorrow, and melancholy, her 1946 list overwhelmingly fixes on childhood death, aged parents, homeless orphans, broken hearts, unstable love, curtailed courtship, lovers' deaths, marriage laments, the effects of drink on home life, and death-bed farewells.[45] Nearly all the "native American ballads" and those "American ballads based on British broadsides"—recognized scholarly categories—that she names take on related themes of murdered girls, outlaws, and prison stays.[46] Still others look back yearningly to plantation life, while some, like "John Henry," have more direct roots in African American sources. Yet these, too, largely bear mournful themes. A few, like "Redwing," convey ethnic subjects, calling on the kindred emotion of nostalgia to lament times gone by. Texas does include some humorous pieces that she called "jolly songs." But these also dwell in familial relationships, depicting either comical bachelors or grumpy husbands and their hellion mates. All in all, the central dramatic condition that she evokes—from Child ballads to Victorian parlor songs—involves domestic scenes filled with longing and sadness.[47]

Texas freely acknowledged this focus. In a 1939 interview printed just a fortnight before she came to Washington to sing at the sixth National Folk Festival, she names "Too Late" as her favorite number.[48] By then, this lyric piece, a popular nineteenth-century sentimental song, had found its way onto nearly a dozen hillbilly recordings. It tells of a woman betrayed by her suitor who faces him once more. After many years' absence he has returned, seeking her renewed affections. Without apparent anger but with the resolve of age, she replies to him in song, "Oh no, you cannot touch my hand / God never gives us back our youth."[49] The reporter marvels that Texas knew so many ballads and folksongs, when Child's entire collection comprised only 305 ballads. But she also contrasts his choice of canon with Texas's affinity for "Too Late." The article suggests it a lesser work, "a folksong and not a ballad, which discredits it somewhat in her [Texas's] eyes."[50] However, until Texas began being visited by folksong collectors and later by journalists deferential to such published studies, she and her family had never made such a distinction. As she told Alan Lomax, "'course we didn't know that they were ballads in those days. . . . We just called them love songs."[51] Here, in spring 1939, despite these pressures, Texas was not shaken by this hierarchy of song, calling "Too Late" the "prettiest tune of them all."[52]

Texas still maintained that opinion in 1946, when Alan Lomax asked her to name her favorite old-time songs from childhood.[53] She replied with three titles similar to "Too Late": "Drowsy Sleepers," "Cold Mountains," and "Love's Worse than Sickness." The first tells of a double suicide by thwarted lovers; the second, of a person dreaming of her loved one who awakens to find herself alone and bereft; and the last, where the title conveys a meaning more fully developed in its lyrics—"Love's worse than sickness / Ten thousand times." Afterward, Texas calls them "old love songs. That is why," she explains, "they were my favorites."

Lomax, struck by this interest, repeatedly queries Texas about their appeal. His questions fix on the psychological motive of these songs, seeking their basis in lived experience. At first, Texas tells him that as early as she can remember she found them to be "very beautiful, very romantic. . . . I just used to revel in those stories when mother would sing these songs."[54] By adolescence, she and her friends shared "get-together songs." These took courtship for their principal theme, and excepting the comical pieces they otherwise enjoyed, these, too, were "romantic and sad." One number she describes as "very dreary" so matter-of-factly it seems like a common enough occurrence. She also notes a dissonance between certain pictures formed in her mind and the realities she sometimes found. From "Gypsy Davy," a Child ballad she learned as a girl, she had "built up the most beautiful thoughts" about the hero. But when in the summer of 1945 she met some actual gypsies, "I was never so disappointed in all my life."

Undeterred, Lomax's questioning stays focused on what he terms "old-time love."[55] "Why," he asks Texas, "are people always so sad about love?" "I guess they just didn't have anything else for recreation," she replies. Then, growing more serious, she mentions the incidence of divorce and speculates how this trend contrasts with her own upbringing. "I don't know what it [old-time love] was made up of," she says, "but whatever it was, it was the real McCoy. . . . And these songs, you know, that was the best way that they could find to express it, don't you think?" She notes her complexity of emotion as a youth, and reasons that in the aftermath of a break-up "these old mournful love songs" came to be made and provided some relief. Moments later she tells her own love story. This comes when Hobart mentions the song "Broken Hearts," with its "sad affair." Texas chimes with in "bad affair"—her words noted earlier—and then recounts her elopement on that wintry day back in December 1912.

Just as Texas's marital story reveals her acting independently in a socially rigid situation, she found a related autonomy in her approach to songs. She traces this freedom to her greatest influence. "All that I am or ever hope to be I owe to my mother. She taught me everything I know."[56] The way Louvenia pitched her songs would "raise the hair on your head . . . she seemed to have a knack at making them sad. Now, Dad would stick to the tune. He would stick to the words and all, straight through. He tried to make it sound just like he had heard it all the time, like he knew it. But my mother . . . [she'd] give it a little twist at the end of a note that no one on earth can do." Louvenia's vocal ornamenting inspired Texas to "put something to it, it didn't have." When Lomax later asked Texas, "Was it your idea to reproduce the song just the way that you heard it," Texas replied, "Oh yes, except I felt like that I could do something with the song that no one else could do, and that I cannot explain."

Coupled with this freedom to interpret, both Texas and Hobart believed that songs at their core possessed an ideal form. This belief remained consistent throughout their lives. Hobart remarked to Lomax that Texas's version of "I Never Will Marry" "got all the notes in," unlike others he had heard.[57] He was referring to the 1933 recording by the Carter Family, who, he said, "got it wrong." Speaking about the song years later, as Arkansas singer Almeda Riddle did it at the urban folk festivals where they were appearing together, Hobart asserted that she "ain't got the tune."[58] In both instances, he insisted, "They didn't have it all." Both he and Texas thought of songs in terms of possession. In having it all, he meant not a choice of lyrics, but what he felt constituted the fullness of the song.

This ideal revealed itself in certain prized, individual performances. Take, for instance, Hobart's account of "Railroad Bill," a blues ballad that in the 1950s and early 1960s became his most famous showpiece among urban aficionados. Though years earlier Saltville musicians of both races played the song, none, Hobart told Fleming Brown, could match Bob Campbell's version. Campbell, an albino guitarist of Caucasian descent who lived in a mixed-race section of town called Smoky Row—the neighborhood took its name from the trains that gusted past on their way to the alkali plant—was adept at six- and twelve-string guitar, blues and ragtime. "Of all my traveling since, of all the colored people I've heard play it, of all the men I ever heard play it," Hobart declared, "I've never heard a man could beat Bob Campbell playing 'Railroad Bill.' Ah, he was wonderful." With Campbell's thumb holding a bass pattern on the low strings and his forefinger playing the melody on the outside strings, he brought together tune and technique in a performance that inspired Hobart and his cousin John Galliher to practice the piece repeatedly. Echoing this account, Galliher told Hobart's son Wiley that "there ain't nobody got that 'Railroad Bill' the way me and Hobe did."[59]

Texas crafted her songs also according to this aesthetic, as others came to realize. In the midthirties, she had become a celebrated performer at the White Top Festival in her native Smyth County. When the festival's founder, Virginia composer John Powell, commented on her artistry, he pointed out how she varied her pieces. At first, she took this to be an admonition. "He said, 'Now you don't stick to the same notes every time, I noticed, when you sing a song.' 'Well,' I said, 'if you will show me where I don't, I will try to stick to it.' He said, 'For God's sakes, don't. Keep doing it just like you always do.'"[60] A musician himself, Powell readily understood that Texas filled each song's performance anew. These variations only confirmed her fluency and, in his view, her place as a preeminent traditional singer.

Powell's view fits with a distinctly modern understanding that had emerged in folksong scholarship.[61] Earlier commentators typically gave scant recognition to individual performers and their creativity, focusing instead on the songs themselves. By Powell's time another perspective came to supplant it.[62] In spring 1945, Professor Bertrand H. Bronson wrote about a celebrated eighteenth-century ballad singer whose variations anticipated Texas's. Anna Gordon Brown (1747–1810) of Aberdeen, Scotland, became one of Francis James Child's primary sources, providing nearly three dozen ballad texts in his landmark collection. Like Texas, Mrs. Brown exercised a liberty in her singing. "What was it she had carried in her memory," Bronson asks. "Not a *text* but a *ballad:* a fluid entity soluble in the mind, to be concretely realized at will in words and music . . . a melodic idea, not a note-for-note record."[63] This perception of a ballad as an idea variously interpreted from one singer to another draws on the work of New England scholar Phillips Barry. Beginning in 1903, Barry explored the notion of a song as something fluid rather than fixed, and credited the role of individual performers in shaping given songs. He was also the first American scholar to study "The Unfortunate Rake" in its musical and textual variety—a variety that includes "One Morning in May." How his insights correspond with Texas's experiences, and how that scholarship bears upon this ballad remains for the following section. For now, Texas has the last word on her musical upbringing.

Texas Gladden's command of her idiom reaches back to those chilly nights she spent before the hearth when her family sang together in their Henrytown cabin. "I made it my business," Texas told Lomax, "when I was just a child, to try to sing those songs just as perfect as I could . . . sound as beautiful and romantic as I could. I put all these little twists, little grace notes, I call them."[64] By firelight, Texas coupled her pliant technique and aesthetic purposefulness with the beautiful mental pictures she found in the songs. She kept that approach her whole life. In the final moment of their 1946 conversation, Lomax turns from the social milieu of the love songs to their musical interpretation: "You were telling me," he says, "about how you thought these songs should be sung." To which Texas replies: "They should be sung just [with] the unlearned or uneducated voice. . . . I don't think a person who sings operetta should toy with these mountain songs."

From Louvenia Smith's knack for those old mountain songs to the twists she brought to them—these "unlearned and uneducated," ever-changing, individually shaped elements guided Texas's decidedly nonoperatic style. She applied these techniques to a body of works that registered along an emotionally charged series of scenes she saw in her mind, "One Morning in May" among them. Though no interviews, field notes, or letters record Texas's thoughts on this particular song, her family recalls its effect in ways that match so much else of her repertory and style. When I asked Jim Gladden about his mother's singing it, I wondered aloud, too, if she ever alluded to its subject being a prostitute and her death from venereal disease. He shook his head emphatically. That was never a meaning, he said, that she communicated either to him or to his siblings. Instead, in her "One Morning in May," with its cadences of a funeral march, they heard a mournful plaint, an expression of sympathy for a young girl dying. It was for them, and I believe for Texas herself, another affectingly sad mountain love song. Wilma Jean remembered that "it just made them weep."[65] Then she added to her indelible memory of those times, when Texas sang the ballad to her own granddaughter: "Every time she'd sing it, Melanie would just cry. It was so melancholy and sad sounding. She'd lay her head down and sob."

Deposited in the files of the Virginia Folklore Society under the category "white religious songs," and then subgrouped with eighteen other pieces designated as "temperance songs," are two ballads about prostitution. Most listeners, however, have come to know them by names other than the titles found there. One, called "New Orleans," turns out to be a version of the "House of the Rising Sun," in this instance collected in 1932 from a Virginia singer in Alleghany County. Filed beside it is a piece titled "When I Was a Young Girl." Dated April 28, 1934, when collector Alfreda Peel copied it down from the singing of Texas Gladden, it represents the earliest documentation of what Texas later recorded as "One Morning in May." Whether Texas purposely changed the title or a misunderstanding arose during the 1941 recording session is unknown. But by 1946 she, too, included "One Morning in May" in her song list that she brought to New York, leaving no further mention of the earlier name. Be that as it may, its placement in these files, together with "New Orleans" and its kindred tale of wasted lives, provides a framework for interpreting Texas's song.

"One Morning in May" appears within a larger family of ballads known as "The Unfortunate Rake." *Rake* stems from *rakehell,* a now obsolete word that flourished roughly between 1550 and 1725, when broadsides like "The Unfortunate Rake" began finding their way into print. The *Oxford English Dictionary* further discloses *rakehell,* along with *rake* as its abbreviated form, as a "debauchee . . . a dissolute person [with] loose habits . . . and immoral character."[66] Moreover, a rake need not only be male, as Oliver Goldsmith illustrates in 1777: "Cruel Iris, pretty rake, Dear mercenary beauty." Indeed, this monetary allusion brings to mind numerous versions of the song that specify the sexual trade. Their place references often name the St. James Hospital or the St. James Infirmary, medical facilities in London and possibly Dublin, that provided treatment for syphilis. Drawing on local architectural and hospital histories, D. K. Wilgus points out that St. James Palace, built in London in 1532 during the reign of Henry VIII, stood on the site of the old St. James Hospital. From Henry's time until well into the nineteenth century, this area remained a center of illicit activity, teeming with bawdy houses.[67]

Likewise, the song's oldest known imprint, a broadside called "The Buck's Elegy," circa 1800, portrays two male friends who have consorted with the same woman. The narrator laments: "Had I but known what his disorder was, / Had I but known it, and took it in time, / I'd took pila cotia, all sorts of white mercury, / But now I'm cut off in the height of my prime."[68] Here, "pila cotia" refers to "*pill of cochcia,* colocinth, an early remedy for venereal disease."[69] In a subsequent printing of the song, circa 1850, the protagonist tells of "Pills and salts of white mercury," another outpatient means that offered a cure.

Texas's 1941 recording expresses these matters from a female point of view. She sings "My body's salivated," a condition that carries with it physical and moral consequences. "And I'm bound to die" completes the line. In the succeeding verse she again tells of her body's salivation. Now, "Hell is my doom." Being "salivated" refers to the effects of mercury, the earliest means used to treat syphilis. Mercury induced the production of saliva, whose flow, it was believed until the development of Salvarsan in 1910, and later, penicillin, afforded the best means for the body to rid itself of the disease. During this process, after the mercury was rubbed on as an ointment, ingested as a pill, or inhaled, patients were wrapped in absorbent materials such as flannel or linen. Wilgus observes, too, that in none of the song's "male-victim" renditions does the word *salivated* appear.[70] This suggests to him, along with certain verbal elements indebted to an ancient type of Irish nature poetry, that versions centered on the "female-victim"—such as Texas's—represent the "Rake's" oldest form.[71] In spring 1934 when Alfreda Peel transcribed "When I Was a Young Girl" from Texas's singing, she was unfamiliar with this feminine adaptation. Though thirteen years earlier she had collected "The Dying Cowboy" from another Virginia singer, that text lacked any reference to salivation, let alone venereal disease.[72] Instead, drinking and card playing dictated that buckaroo's doom. With Texas's version, Peel was less certain. After "salivated," she twice put a question mark on the manuscript, not convinced of what she heard. Here are the verses as Texas sang them:

One Morning, one morning,
one morning in May
I spied a young lady all wrapped in white linen
and cold as the clay.

When I was a young lady
I used to see pleasure
When I was a young girl
I used to drink ale

Out of the ale house
into a jail house
Out of a jail house and
into my grave.

Come papa, come mama
and sit you down by me
Come sit you down by me,
and pity my case.

My poor head is aching,
My sad heart is breaking
My body's salivated, (?)
And I am bound to die.

Send for the preacher
To come and pray for me
Send for the doctor
to heal up my wounds.

My poor head is aching
My sad heart is breaking.
My body is salivated, (?)
And hell is my doom.

I want four young ladies,
To bear up my coffin
I want six young ladies
To carry me on.

And each of them carry
A bunch of wild roses
To keep me from smelling
As I pass along.[73]

At the time Alfreda Peel copied down Texas's words, the Roanoke school-teacher could already look back on decades as a ballad collector. Her forays began in 1911, fully two years before the forming of the Virginia Folklore Society. Along with an interest in her family's established British ancestry, Peel (1890–1953) credited her attraction to folksong and folktale to her childhood reading of lords and ladies, Robin Hood and King Arthur.[74] In her subsequent song and tale collecting, she found equally romantic stories expressed by neighboring mountaineers of Roanoke County.[75] That romance transferred to the research itself, despite the muddy roads and sometimes hazardous travel she endured.[76] Driven by a preservationist's wonder, she gathered her "quota of song" from those who included "a grave-digger, a boot-legger, a night watchman, a scrubwoman in an insane asylum, and an old woman whose chief duty seemed to be 'to set up with the dead.'"[77] By her dogged efforts, she retrieved a body of literature that made her one of the Virginia Folklore Society's leading fieldworkers.

Of all the singers whose folkways Peel gathered, none affected her as much as Texas Gladden. In November 1916, Peel first copied down Texas's lyrics on a Schoolcraft tablet. Then twenty-one years old, Texas began with a popular nineteenth-century sentimental number called "The Blind Girl." Next came ten romantic pieces that included two Child ballads, as well as "Poor Ellen Smith," which she later recorded with Hobart on banjo.[78] Two years earlier, the Virginia Folklore Society had launched a statewide effort to find in every county living examples of the Child ballads. A number of the pieces the singers offered did not meet this criterion, with Texas's no exception. Society officials deemed only two of Peel's submissions worthy of consideration. The rest they set aside or rejected outright.[79] Given this ranking of songs with

CHAPTER 9

lesser pedigree, it seems not surprising to find Peel's introduction in her forty-seven-page notebook brushed with a certain paternalism. Identifying her main informants in the Roanoke County regions as Sis Sears and Texas Gladden, she saw them as stereotypical mountain women, unschooled, who entertained friends and family with a hand-me-down repertory.[80]

In the ensuing years, however, the distance between Peel and Texas narrowed. The two became close, sharing songs with one another and finding mutual support in their roles as singer and collector, which, as noted earlier with "Mary Hamilton" and "The Devil's Nine Questions," sometimes reversed. If some from Peel's social sphere might occasionally regard her as Texas's mentor, Texas found in Peel an ardent supporter.[81] Jim Gladden spoke of Alfreda Peel as his mother's good friend, "a part of the family," he said, "who considered Mama on the same level as herself."[82] Unquestionably, Peel's esteem for Texas grew well beyond her 1916 letter to the Virginia Folklore Society that set her lyrics among the oddities and eccentricities of mountain culture.[83]

Peel's embrace, in fact, led to Texas's subsequent fame. While preparing the Library of Congress album that originally included "One Morning in May" as well as three more of Texas's ballads, Alan Lomax wrote to Peel, "I don't remember whether or not I have ever thanked you for your kind offers in introducing me to Mrs. Gladden. . . . It was generous and comradely of you to do what you did. . . . We are going to release four of Mrs. Gladden's ballads in a series of records."[84] Nine years earlier, Peel's admiration for Texas also fostered her first recordings. In 1932, the Virginia Folklore Society's archivist, Arthur Kyle Davis Jr., equipped with a disc-cutting machine, called on a number of informants who had contributed to the landmark 1929 volume he edited of locally sung Child ballads. Texas's rendition of "The Maid Freed from the Gallows" (Child 95), which she called "Hangerman Tree," appeared in this book, along with a page-long version of "Barbara Ellen" (Child 84) complete with music.[85] A photo that Peel took shows Texas standing outdoors with a baby in her arms. Other Virginia singers appear similarly arrayed in front of log cabins and dense foliage. Now, following a spate of letters from Peel urging Davis to come to this part of Virginia to meet "his" singers, Davis recorded Texas. The six numbers she sang into his microphone reflected the book's orientation toward older ballads of British descent.[86] On the eve of this encounter, Peel raved about Texas Gladden, dirt-poor and surrounded by children in mean circumstances, yet alert and smart. Peel, whose enthusiasm radiated from her letter, accorded Texas top honors for the integrity of her singing and the range of songs at her command.[87]

Peel's correspondence in the Virginia Folklore Society files—she writes almost always to Arthur Kyle Davis Jr.—reveals Texas performing for local events as well as larger venues sponsored by organizations closer to Peel's and Davis's circles. One letter describes a poultry and cat show where Texas won a five-dollar prize for her singing. In another, Peel expresses frustration that people at a local fiddlers' contest did not accord ballad singing the respect she thought it was due.[88] The most pivotal of Texas's appearances also took place in Smyth County, where she had been raised. In August 1933, Peel took Texas to the third White Top Festival in Marion, Virginia, where an audience of twenty thousand had gathered. Though Peel expressed a reluctance to share her ballad singing discovery in such a public forum seemingly overrun with competing collectors, Texas prevailed upon her to make the trip from Salem. They struck a deal in advance: Texas promised to limit her song choices to those already in the Virginia Folklore Society collection. With Peel's anxieties allayed, at the event Texas and her mother, Louvenia, met Mrs. Roosevelt and also Virginia composer John Powell and festival director Annabel Morris Buchanan. Texas took second prize in the ballad singing competition with her performance of "The Three Babes."

Come 1934, Peel's letters reflect the increasing demand for Texas's performances. In the wake of the first lady's presence at the White Top Festival, Peel received a letter that January from John Powell asking if Texas might appear on the inaugural program for a seven-part NBC shortwave broadcast to Britain. With Eleanor Roosevelt introducing the show, he was desperate to have Texas sing "Mary Hamilton" and "The Three Babes."[89] Two months later, in March, Texas performed at Salem's town festival before an audience of 900 singing "Come All You Fair and Tender Ladies" and "John Henry." Along with her brothers Hobart and Ed, who won the festival's string band competition, Texas received for her ballad singing a prize of five dollars, a corsage, a bag of flour, and hair tonic for her husband.[90]

Now, on April 28, 1934, Peel wrote down the words for a batch of songs no less varied than those gathered during her first visit with Texas eighteen years earlier. Peel collected "When I Was a Young Girl" and ten other texts in a decidedly primitive setting, in the chicken coop where Texas and her many children had moved following a devastating house fire. After dinner they settled beside a roaring creek under trees in spring bloom, and Texas regaled Peel with wild stories of the supernatural. The day's heady experience confirmed Peel's judgment of Texas as the best singer she ever knew.[91] A month later, Texas repeated her batch of new ballads for Peel's colleague

Kathleen Kelly Coxe, who notated their melodies.[92] She also told a ghost story from her local Mormon church, about the "witch of Colliersville," a woman with a capacity for foretelling death, and whose burden is lifted by her church members' prayers.[93]

However unique "When I Was a Young Girl" may have seemed to Peel, and possibly to Coxe, by then the song had long come under scholarly scrutiny. Within a year of the Virginia Folklore Society's founding, in April 1913, field collectors throughout the state began recovering it in some form or another. In March 1914, Peel's collecting counterpart, Juliet Fauntleroy, transcribed it from Mrs. John Maxi of Altavista. Mrs. Maxi's singing of "Catherine's Bar Room," a western song of regret for a dissipated life, reflects the long reach of "The Cowboy's Lament," which cattle drover F. H. Maynard composed on the Wichita trail in 1876. He based his version on what he called "one of the favorite songs of the cowboys in those days . . . 'The Dying Girl's Lament.'"[94] Maynard wrote the poem so that it could be sung to this tune, consciously changing the locale from a hospital ward where the dying girl lay to a well-known saloon belonging to a legendary proprietor of that time, Tom Sherman. Once the song traveled to Mrs. Maxi in south-central Virginia, certain details had shifted in transmission, but its message stayed intact.

The ballad's transatlantic roots come into higher relief during this period, too, beginning with the activities of British folksong collector Cecil Sharp. In 1918, during his second American tour, Sharp collected two versions in Virginia. In one, a soldier or sailor tells his woes, while in the other, a cowboy speaks of his impending death.[95] The song was not new to Sharp. Between 1904 and 1909, soon after he commenced his folksong research, he notated the ballad from four different singers in England. The last of these, taken down from an eighty-three-year-old man in Oxfordshire, tells of a female victim, akin to Texas's, although told from a male perspective. He sings of his "own comely maiden / Wrapped in some flannel, so cold blowed the wind."[96] By then, three different versions of "The Young Girl Cut Down in Her Prime" had appeared in the *Journal of the Folk-Song Society*. In 1909, Irish music scholar Patrick W. Joyce disclosed a telling indicator of the ballad's age. Joyce collected a single verse in 1848 from a Dublin singer who recalled learning it in 1790 as "My Jewel, My Joy." It kept to the familiar poetic pattern. On the musical side, the air to "The Unfortunate Rake" first found publication in 1808 in *Crosby's Irish Musical Repository,* further evidence of the song's dispersal.

In the United States, academic discussion of the ballad also began in 1909, when the *Journal of American Folklore* printed another of the cowboy texts and referred to its English antecedents.[97] Two years later, Phillips Barry began his multiple studies of the ballad in an article on Irish song.[98] He finds "The Unfortunate Rake" an exception to the rule in which most imported Irish songs in the U.S. have retained their original references. Instead, the "Rake" represents what he earlier called the workings of "individual invention plus communal re-creation."[99] This concept appears throughout his many writings to describe an inevitable artistic operation: while folksongs are themselves products of individual authorship, over the course of their transfer, succeeding singers reshape them, guided by their own traditions and inclinations. Communal re-creation, Barry writes, involves "an indefinite number of authors of poetry and composers of music . . . interpreters. . . . whose right consists in every possible form and degree of collaboration with the individual author and composer."[100] Barry concluded his longest study of "The Unfortunate Rake," completed in 1934, with the assertion that *Every folk singer is a folk composer.*[101]

Barry explained this re-creative process through a German aphorism, "mündliche Überlieferung macht zersingen," which translates roughly as "oral transmission makes for variation."[102] Its imagery revolves around *Mund,* or mouth, and *mündlich,* by mouth. Delivering something orally creates variation or *zersingen*—literally, singing something to pieces. *Zersingen* captures what Barry considered the paradoxical nature of folksong, that "there are texts, but no *text;* tunes, but no *tune.*"[103] Here Barry echoes what Texas and Hobart meant about "having a song," possessing their vision of a given work. When Texas spoke of her mother fluttering a note "that no one on earth can do," and for herself, mentioning "all these little twists" by which she turned a phrase; or when Hobart talked about Bob Campbell's unbeatable version of "Railroad Bill," and when he promised to play the banjo "for everything that's in it," both of them saw beyond matters of vocal inflection and instrumental technique.[104] They pictured songs as fully elaborated forms, singular melodies that they tried to capture in their performances. No wonder Phillips Barry wrote in an essay for the White Top Festival folk music conference in 1936, to which Texas was also invited, that "the folk singer, however much he be keeper of a tradition, is never for a single moment dominated by it."[105]

For Texas, who offered so much by way of varied repertory, no ballad she sang better illustrates this artistic malleability than "One Morning in May." As of March 2007, the same British folksong organization that Cecil Sharp fostered a century earlier listed 317 entries for the "Unfortunate Rake" in its online folksong index. That number continued to increase as singers and musicians have claimed this piece for their own. One need only listen to Louis Armstrong, who brought his New Orleans ensemble sound to "St. James Infirmary," and contrast that to Dick Devall's modal evocation in "Tom Sherman's Barroom." Blind Willie McTell recollects in ragtime an old friend's fate in "Dying Crapshooter's Blues." With a song still so alive, there are always countless examples. Cast in such profusion of styles and heard in so many accents, its vitality, indeed its *zersingen,* brings to mind Jim Gladden's subterranean passages that run, if only in the imagination, from Salem, Virginia, to the Mississippi River.

The same morning Jim Gladden described these caverns, he also talked about a tree in his front yard. He had just closed the door to his canning shed, and for some reason we both looked up at a sycamore that towered several stories in the air. "If it fell," Jim whispered, motioning to his home a few yards away, "it would break our house in two."[106] The tree was over fifty years old, and Jim had grown it from a sprout. Initially the tips kept poking up, despite Jim's attempts to mow them away. The sapling would not be deterred. "Finally, I told Marvel, my wife, that it wanted to grow so bad, I decided to let it grow and see what happens." Now he opened his hands, spreading his fingers like a flower in bloom. Suddenly the twin images of this great sycamore and Jim's sunken river system—one visible, the other hidden—suggested something more. For Texas and her family, "One Morning in May," a favorite of her old love songs, marked a familiar part of their lives. Whether she sang it as a lullaby at home or into a recording machine for others, it remained rooted in their memories, a story of intemperance and heartbreak. At the same time, the song intersects a much wider river, a system of musical tributaries and channels that flow to the present day. Like the character of folksong itself, it thrives majestic and compelling, pliable and tenacious, mercurial and enduring.

Luther Strong
Way behind His Time

A FEW FEET FROM FAYE SANDLIN'S DOOR, AT THE NEXT house trailer over, a nine- or ten-year-old girl stands outside playing a violin. Coming closer up the walkway, we make out "Old Joe Clark." I can't help but smile at Faye, conscious that her father, mountain fiddler Luther Strong, once knew this piece himself. It's hard to imagine a more appropriate, if unintentional, greeting. Faye thinks so too. When she was younger than this girl, she used to dance as he played the tune outside their home in rural Kentucky.

Faye's neighbor keeps at her music and we step inside the mobile home. A large colorized photograph of a navy seaman, Faye's son, dominates a front room wall. A smaller picture of him, taken a few years later in his civilian clothes, hangs beside it. On the other side of the big portrait, Faye has framed a cover torn from an issue of *Time* magazine. Captioned "20th Century Blues," it features Edward Hopper's 1927 painting *Automat*.[1] The solitary image pictures a woman alone at nighttime, nursing a cup of coffee at the New York eatery. She hasn't removed her hat or coat and still has a glove on one hand. Sadness seems to dim her eyes. Faye says it reminds her of her mother. Faye's only photo of her, kept in a scrapbook, shows her weary, slumped on the porch behind their house, next to the wringer washer. The Hopper painting has, in

effect, become her mother's portrait. Faye also mentions that the blues in the cover story's headline makes her think of music, like something her father played. With so few mementoes of her parents, Faye's putting this magazine cover on her wall makes perfect sense.

Just below the *Time* cover, Faye has hung an even more familiar image, the official photograph of President Kennedy. Balancing this, on the other side of her son's portrait, she displays its counterpart, Jacqueline Kennedy at the White House. Why exhibit these here? I wondered. Are the Kennedys personal heroes? Is this an homage to an era, to Camelot? The popular 1960 Lerner and Loewe musical of that title expressed for so many of Faye's generation the young couples' elegance and attractiveness, their erudition and promise. Faye's explanation came as a surprise. Shortly after PT-109 went down, and Lieutenant (j.g.) "Jack" Kennedy was hospitalized, Faye's ex-husband, also in the navy and injured during the war, briefly came to know him as they recovered at the same facility. Later, Kennedy sent him a card, and Faye named one of her daughters after the First Lady. No wonder on Faye's other wall, near her own Jackie's photo, along with snapshots of children and grandchildren, hangs another portrait of the presidential couple. Clearly, the first family is also part of this family.

A mixture of public and private images, legends and facts, memories and documents likewise surrounds her father's performance of "Glory in the

Meetinghouse." In 1937 Luther Strong recorded "Glory" as one of over two dozen fiddle tunes for the Library of Congress. His playing, long admired in his community, became revered nationally through these recordings, with "Glory" among them still regarded as a masterpiece of this idiom. When Luther played it for his neighbors, Faye said, "Everybody was wild about it. It had such get up and go."[2] "Glory" functioned not as a dance number, but as a virtuoso piece for listening. This was music made for music's sake. It required, he said, the skills that "make a fiddler."[3] Like the pictures on Faye's walls, Luther's "Glory in the Meetinghouse" brings together the personal and the historical.

When Faye finally sits down, she begins to talk about this music she knew from more than sixty years ago. Sometimes melancholy, always lovingly, she recalls her father and his fiddle: "He'd get up early in the morning and play them old sad, tunes. He'd have such a faraway look when he'd play them." Then she adds wistfully, "We just thought his music was all there was."[4] Now Faye and I struggle to fix the sequence of his life to these deeply felt experiences. Matters of time thread our conversation. Here in southern Indiana, Faye's house trailer stands near a border of Eastern and Central time zones. Simply crossing that line can make an hour's difference. Faye's sister-in-law, for instance, speaks of towns east of there as being on "fast time."[5] To commute to work, cross into Kentucky, catch a bus, or make a flight, you need to stay aware of this clock. Like the progress of "Glory in the Meetinghouse" from the frontier to modernity and back again, it shifts forward or backward depending on which direction you go. Meanwhile, the girl outside hasn't stopped playing her fiddle.

When Luther Strong (1892–1962) awoke on October 18, 1937, he was in jail. Arrested on a charge of public drunkenness, he had spent the night in the Hazard, Kentucky, lockup. He didn't know it yet, but in a few hours and with a borrowed fiddle, he would record his Library of Congress discs, the most celebrated documents he made in his lifetime. For many younger players drawn to these recordings, he serves as a model of Kentucky mountain fiddling, hailed for his masterful bowing, authoritative arrangements, and resonant tone. For now, though, the circumstances in which he found himself reflected other patterns, his repeated bouts of drinking and incarceration.

At that time, Luther, his wife, and six of their nine children lived some thirty miles from Hazard in the tiny mountain community of Buckhorn.[6]

All eight occupied a house he had recently built, consisting of three small rooms. Because he hadn't yet completed the work, they were without water, indoor plumbing, or electricity, though they had a wood stove for cooking and heating. The nearest well was a mile away. When I asked Faye about this home, she spurned that word to describe it. Instead, she explained, it was just a place where they lived for a while. The family moved with Luther's employment. Depending on opportunity, he variously farmed, logged, coal mined, worked as a WPA blacksmith, put in two stints as a factory hand at the Champion paper mill in Hamilton, Ohio, did stone masonry and carpentry, and ended his wage-earning years at a vegetable-packing plant in southern Indiana.[7] His periods of unemployment and his repeated absences from home also uprooted the family. Unable to make the rent, they sometimes had to skip out on their landlords, leaving dishes on the table. Luther's son Jim recalls attending seventeen different schools, "from one railroad town to another," before graduating high school.[8] They lived mostly in southeastern Kentucky, where Luther himself had grown up on a farm outside Jackson before moving to Perry County. The string of towns where Luther took his brood—Typo, Napfor, Krypton, Buckhorn, Miller's Branch, Dalesburg, Buffalo, and Beattyville, the last two of these in neighboring Owsley and Lee counties, respectively—reflected what Faye called his "restlessness," which she associated with his drinking. As his son Jim also said, "He'd work a while and then drink a while."[9]

Jim continues: "He'd stay drunk two or three weeks at a time. Then, when he sobered up, he'd go right back to work. That's the way I was raised up. Just about as hard as a little boy could be raised. We'd move from one place to another. Go hungry. Get run off from the house. I'm not blaming my Pap. He was the greatest man that ever lived when he was sober. But then he'd get hateful and mean when he was drinking. And then, when he'd get so drunk he'd start jumping on my mother, calling her every you-know-what. She'd get scared and she'd get the young'uns and take off with us and go to some neighbor's house and stay until he sobered up."[10]

Luther also made moonshine whiskey. When uninvited strangers came by, they received from his children his standing directive: "If anyone comes looking for me, tell them you don't know where I'm at."[11] Come the fall of 1937, Faye, then ten years old, already had experience deflecting revenue officers. When three sheriffs showed up in Buckhorn to bring Luther in and break up his still, she had this exchange after telling them he wasn't home:

CHAPTER 10

"Where's he gone to."

"I don't know."

"Little girl, if you'll tell us, we'll give you a quarter."

"You give me a quarter first, 'cause you're not a-coming back."

They apparently stomped away, with one of them muttering, "Did you hear that!"[12]

Faye may not have known that she was repeating a folktale. She told this story not with humor so much as defiance. She ardently protected her father. With a disabled mother bedridden since the birth of a younger brother, Faye and her siblings depended on Luther. For one thing, he cooked for them. "We always wanted hot biscuits of a morning. 'If you leave,' she said to him, 'who'll bake our biscuits?'"[13] When he did leave, his departures sometimes gave the children no choice but to steal food. She recalls taking a clawhammer to pry open a local grocery's front door and with one of her brothers stealing candy and Spam that they hid in their attic. The next day the candy melted, and Faye and the others ate it with a spoon. She spoke, too, of once grabbing a platter of meat off a neighbor's table to take home. Yet despite these deprivations, which included, at their worst, Luther's domestic violence, his throwing rocks at the family as they fled his inebriated rages—obliging them to carry, even drag their immobile mother away—both Faye and Jim spoke of him with intense devotion. His kindness when sober did not go unappreciated. Just as Jim regarded him as "no man I loved more or hated more," Faye said, "To me, he was always an angel."[14] These elements converged in a premonition:

In my childhood, I was a very disturbed child. I worried about my dad all the time. He was gone a lot playing music. This one time . . . we lived near Typo, Kentucky, and I was awful disturbed about knowing our dad was going to leave the next morning. He was going to build us a house in a little town called Buckhorn in Perry County near Hazard. So I didn't want him to go. . . . I would panic, go into shock if he wasn't home right at the time that he would tell us.

Well, he come out on the porch that night and call for me to come in [Faye was outside playing ball with the other children] and I started in, and right on the steps there was a man appeared to me and he fired a pistol. I can still see that man. And I began screaming. My dad come out and he said, "What on earth is the matter with you." And I said, "Oh Dad, did you not hear that gun?" He said "No." I said, "Daddy, there was a man right on our steps and he fired that gun and he just went away." He said, "Alright, I'm gonna get the lights and look. And if I don't find anybody I'm gonna give you a whipping." . . .

I told him, "I don't want you to leave in the morning." . . . I didn't want to go to sleep and him be gone . . . So [the next morning] I got up and he got up. And he said, "Faye, you don't look like you slept any all night." I said, "I didn't." I said, "Please don't leave today. Forget about the house." He said "Why." I said, "If you go, you're going to be shot." And I vapor down yet when I think about it.

"Well," he said, "I don't know what I'm going to do with you." Well, I couldn't talk him out of going, and I made him come back three times. I said, "Come back and let me kiss you before you go." He said, "I'm gonna come back this time and you're gonna cause me to miss the train." Well, he went on and he did get shot. He got his eye put out in Perry County at a square dance. He tried to break up a fight and they said he accidentally got shot. And when we heard from him he was in the hospital. He knew everybody in the little town of Hazard . . . So Mr. Gross [Sheriff A. M. Gross] came to the house.[15]

"Does Luther have a little girl here by the name of Faye?"
My mother said, "Yes. There she is."
My mother was in bed. I was eight year old, just a little girl trying to do dishes.
"Well, Luther sent me after her and wants me to bring her to the hospital."
So he took me to the hospital to see my dad. And my dad went to crying when we walked in. He said, "If I'd only listened to this little girl, I wouldn't be laying here with my eye put out."[16]

It was Luther's own brother who shot him. As family historian and cousin Lowell Morris explained the brawl, Luther and his brother, known as Jim-bug, had been drinking and arguing.[17] Jim-bug fired his pistol and the bullet that wounded Luther went through a door closed between them. By the time the doctor arrived, blood covered Luther's fiddle, which he kept on playing. Years later Luther's son, Green Strong, in a fit of alcohol-fueled retaliation, shot his uncle to avenge this injury to his father.

For now, though, on October 18, 1937, three years after Luther lost his eye, a man previously unknown to the family arrived at the house in Buckhorn. Faye answered the door, and when the stranger asked for Luther, she hesitated. Beyond her usual disavowal regarding his whereabouts, she felt embarrassed about his confinement. Recalling that moment sixty-one years later, Faye confessed, "I didn't want to say that he was in jail."[18]

The visitor detected the youngster's hesitation. "You must tell me," she recalled him saying.

Faye called to her mother for help. "I'm talking to a man and I don't know who he is and he wants to know where Daddy is. Do you want me to tell him?" Lillie Abner, Luther's wife, replied, "Ask him what he wants."

"I want him to play the violin for me," said the stranger.

With Lillie assenting from the other room, Faye now gave him the answer: he was jailed in Hazard. At this point, the man left.

The stranger was Alan Lomax, who, along with his wife, Elizabeth, was in the final weeks of a two-month trip to eastern Kentucky collecting songs and tunes for the Library of Congress. On this same trip, eight days later, he recorded fiddler Bill Stepp, whose "Bonaparte's Retreat" became so widely heard via Aaron Copland's arrangement. That episode marks the trip's best-known product. Its other most influential finding was Georgia Turner's "Rising Sun Blues," which the Middlesboro singer, Lomax noted, "learned from records."[19] By then two recordings of the song had appeared: a 1934 Tom Ashley and Gwen Foster version and a release two years later by Homer Callahan. The subsequent appearance of her rendition in the Lomaxes' *Our Singing Country* introduced the song to city players, who then propelled "House of the Rising Sun" into a pop hit.[20]

In addition to these success stories, the ten-county expedition yielded hundreds more recorded items.[21] Shortly before the Lomaxes met Luther Strong in Hazard, they arrived in Hyden, Kentucky, where they recorded various old-time fiddlers, banjoists, guitarists, and ballad singers. Included among them was Eliza Pace, who, in 1917, had sung for Cecil Sharp, the celebrated British folksong collector, during his second American foray.[22] They found her now eighty-four years old and living in a log cabin with her daughter, where "she gave us 'some of the good songs I forgot to sing fer that English feller . . . that come over the mountain years ago.'"[23] Shortly after recording Pace, they documented miner and UMW organizer George Davis with his self-penned labor songs. The eras these two performers represent frame the trip as a whole.

By the fall of 1937, America's modern mass media had reached into eastern Kentucky. Mountain families who might have gathered at hearthside to sing for an evening's entertainment found themselves increasingly drawn to country music records and to broadcasts available on home receivers. Since 1925, Kentucky folk musicians entering both radio and commercial record studios had created a dazzling body of work, from B. F. Shelton's brooding banjo pieces to the close harmony singing of Karl and Harty, from Cliff Carlisle's Hawaiian-inflected blues to the Prairie Ramblers exploring old-time tunes to a jazz-derived plucked bass, from the sweet-voiced ballads of Bradley Kincaid to the vivacity of the Coon Creek Girls, who launched their group in 1937. Here in eastern Kentucky, contemporary hillbilly performers presented musical dramas of the sort Eliza Pace still sang, but cast in newer guises. Likewise, George Davis's mining songs, responding to industrial practices and reflecting current experiences, extended an established form of social commentary to the accompaniment of a steel-string guitar, itself a recent addition to the Appalachian sound. "Commercial music," Lomax wrote in his final report, "via the radio, the movies and the slot phonograph is usurping the place of traditional and homemade music, but that their case is not entirely hopeless I shall have occasion to point out later on."[24] Even the process Lomax went through to reach Luther Strong makes that cultural continuity clear.

In an undated letter from Hazard, likely written the day he met Luther Strong, Lomax alludes to both George Davis and Eliza Pace. After tallying the recorded discs, 156 so far, Lomax describes his recent song-collecting encounters. Apart from specific finds, he characterizes the ongoing trip, ranging from purely convivial moments—the hours spent socializing with contacts—to the life-threatening. He humorously details a misunderstanding that arose when he helped a portly woman down a hillside. That good deed almost got him stabbed, if not shot, by her jealous husband. Elsewhere, in an effort to quiet down some noisy youths disturbing a recording session, after getting no help from the hotel keeper, Lomax made veiled threats about being a Library of Congress officer, hinting at what weaponry such governmental agents concealed. While quieting the crowd, Lomax admitted being uneasy were push come to shove. In the course of these forays, his Studebaker, too, felt the effects of the mountain roads that "devour its entrails and fret its extremities."[25] Clearly, legacies of the past reached into conditions of the present.

It appears from Lomax's notes jotted on the sleeves of several recording discs that on October 14, 1937, Hyden barber, fiddler, and banjoist Theophilus Hoskins pointed Lomax toward Luther Strong. When he recorded, Lomax often used these brown paper jackets to write down biographical information and potential song sources. Over the course of this particular session, he lists Luther on several sleeves along with three other musicians. Hoskins, thirteen years Luther's senior, played a number of old-time mountain tunes and songs including a fiddle solo he called "Glory in the Meetinghouse." While his melody markedly differs from the "Glory" that Luther recorded a few days later, it denotes the first recording ever made with that title.[26] Another of the fiddlers named on the Hoskins record sleeves was Boyd Asher, also of Hyden. The next day, October 15, 1937, Asher performed his version of "Glory in the Meetinghouse" for the disc machine.

Whatever Hoskins, and perhaps Asher, may have said about Luther, it also seems possible that Lomax might have heard still more about him two days later from banjoist Justus Begley, whom he recorded soon after arriving in

Hazard. Begley (1881–1956), an impressive instrumentalist and singer, lived only a few miles from Luther in Buckhorn at Gays Creek. Faye identified Begley as a neighboring banjoist who often played with Luther, and she recalled his bid at that time for public office. In August 1937, Begley won the Republican primary for sheriff of Perry County, later winning the general election and serving for four years beginning in January 1938. Lomax was also conscious of Begley's ambitions, and in his summary of the trip completed a few months later, he names several contacts who especially contributed to the trip's success, writing "a collector of folksong lives and works by the kindness of the people in the localities to which he goes."[27] There he cites Begley, mentioning his run for sheriff, followed by Luther Strong, whom he calls "lanky and shy and our favorite fiddler."[28] In making these thanks, Lomax tacitly acknowledged he had come upon a community of players interacting with one another. Luther's own lineage makes this musical network all the more evident.

Luther's full name was Luther Callahan Strong. While his first name came from an uncle killed in the Civil War, as well as from his father's brother, his middle name bore a musical legacy. Luther's mother, a Callahan by birth, had a grandfather named Isaac Callahan. A story told by Luther's cousin, Lowell Morris, and affirmed by Jim Strong and Faye Sandlin, concerns the family's connection with a fiddle tune Luther played called "The Last of Callahan." According to Morris, in the 1820s or '30s in Clay County, Kentucky, this same Isaac Callahan was hanged for the murder of a man named Newberry. "He was on the scaffold and was supposed to have had the fiddle brought up there and challenged anybody in the crowd to play the tune. Nobody had never heard it. . . . That was the first time he had ever played it in public, I reckon. . . . There's all kinds of tales about this, but this, now, is the man who really played the tune. This is Luther Strong's great grandfather. . . . He just played the tune and [later] they called that tune 'The Last of Callahan.'"[29]

Morris's account conforms with a number of stories centered in southeastern Kentucky that accompany this tune. In the mid-1940s, Mrs. Herman R. Santen, another Kentucky descendant of Isaac Callahan, wrote to the Folk Archive about the piece. Her recollections, drawn from her father, himself a fiddler, and from her great-grandmother's daughter, fit in the same time span and locale and name Isaac as the hanged fiddler.[30] Further research by D. K. Wilgus into that correspondence, along with other versions of the story, point to the hanging of Scotsman James MacPherson in 1700, who, according to oral tradition, first issued this musical challenge at his execution. When the setting shifted to America, MacPherson's name largely fell away, and that form of the ballad was not recovered until 1961. But scholars working in Kentucky as early as 1909 witnessed the singing of Callahan's farewell and made the connection. Wilgus goes on to cite Alan Lomax's 1938 interview with former Kentuckian Oscar Parks. Parks told of a John Callahan hanged in the course of a feud that took place around the turn of the century. The incident, Wilgus opines, possibly occurred during one of the Callahan-Deaton feuds in Breathitt County, Kentucky. This, too, fits with Lowell Morris recalling that Luther's uncle, Ned Callahan, killed Jim Deaton over some rafted timber. Their dispute resulted in a trial and sentencing in Hyden. While that affair, as Morris described it, did not involve music, it fits with Parks's time, place, and protagonists. Wilgus points out that "people have a habit of living up to their legends."[31] Even if "The Last of Callahan" originated as a musical tale with transatlantic roots, certain events connected with the Callahan family in this part of Kentucky came to mirror the old story.

Another musical continuity accompanies this legend. Lowell Morris told how a fiddler witnessed Isaac Callahan's hanging: "'Black' Bob Baker of Upper Buffalo was supposed to be in the crowd.... They [fiddlers like himself] remembered the sound of the tune, the notes, and so on. There was good fiddlers there and they remembered how the tune sounded and went, and Luther does a magnificent job of playing it on the fiddle."[32] Indeed, fiddlers held the tune in memory, passing it on by ear, and playing it for one another. Oscar Parks, for example, told of his learning it from fiddler and singer Bob Lehr, who said he witnessed the hanging in Jackson County. The fact that "The Last of Callahan" appears in three of the twenty-two fiddle tune lists compiled in March 1915 by adult students at Kentucky's Berea College attests to its oral circulation.[33] If this were the same piece, which seems likely, it was heard by these students in their home counties as early as the late nineteenth century. Between 1919 and 1928, the college also sponsored a series of old-time fiddle contests whose participants often included "Callahan" as an entry. A clipping from the first Berea festival shows it played there by three contestants, antedating its earliest commercial recording by five years.[34] Like so much in older tradition, this piece was making the rounds entirely by informal means.

The experiences of Kentucky fiddler Hiram Stamper (1893–1991), a friend of Luther's and his contemporary, who lived in nearby Knott County, echo this contact among players. Stamper repeatedly credited learning much of his repertory from players alive during the Civil War. Hiram's son, fiddler Art Stamper, told me that "People like my dad, [Bill] Stepp, Bev Baker, [Boyd] Asher, Luther Strong, Alvy Green, John Saylers, and Clarence Hay—all those people [older players before them] like A. B. Stamper, Joe Stamper, Billy Gore, Shade Sloan, Daniel and Dete Triplett—they had no way of listening to music like we have today. They had to learn it from one another and it had to be passed from generation to generation. There was no radios, no transportation except a horse and buggy, or a mule, or walk. How far could they go in a day's time to listen to a concert? They'd have little house parties and people would come and gather to listen to the fiddle players play. That's the way it was."[35] Information on all six of the Kentucky players, including Luther, who recorded "Callahan" for the Library in 1937, confirms their learning it via direct, oral transmission.[36] A year later, traveling in the Midwest, Lomax recorded it three more times. Pete Steele of Hamilton, Ohio, for instance, who recorded his version on the banjo in 1938, learned it from his father, a Kentucky fiddler. He told a story, varied yet again, of Callahan handing off his fiddle before the noose.

Luther's early learning fits this larger pattern of transmission. He began playing as a little boy, his grandfather sometimes finding him in the barn at age eight practicing on a violin slipped from the house. Though neither of Luther's parents played, his brother, Lewis, did, on harmonica. With him, Luther played "the old blues, old tunes like that."[37] In his youth Luther traveled to local dances, "howdy-dos," in Jackson and Breathitt counties, where if he didn't play alone, he typically teamed up with a banjo player. At these events, no less than contests or jam sessions, he learned from his fellow musicians. He possessed neither radio nor phonograph, let alone knowledge of written music. Nor did he keep a radio or record player in the years he raised his own family. At home Luther either played by himself, or with neighboring fiddlers and banjoists when they dropped by. "Pickers would come to Pap's house," Jim Strong said.[38] "A banjo picker, and once in a while, someone would whittle out two sticks and beat on the fiddle while Pa played it." Luther's good timing, Jim observed, made him easy to accompany. "He'd just tap one foot."

One of those visitors was Big Hiram Begley, another name listed along with Luther and Boyd Asher on Lomax's 1937 record sleeves.[39] Begley, from southern Leslie County, also appeared in August 1919 at the first of the Berea College fiddle contests. Jim Strong recalled him in later years visiting his father and remarking on his facility with waltzes. A lesser-known early influence on Luther that Lowell Morris named was fiddler Bill Harrell, who lived "on the Middlefork River close to Crockettsville."[40] But whoever Luther may have come in contact with, be it these nearby musicians or others, like banjo player Scott Hacker or guitarist Hiram Couch, frequent accompanists that

Jim Strong named, one constant applied: "This was the only stuff he knowed. Just what he heard other fiddle players play. That's all he knowed."[41] Of all these players, Luther stayed closest to the one who called himself his teacher, fiddler Bev Baker.

Bev Baker (1872–?) lived in Chavies, Kentucky, thirteen miles from Buckhorn.[42] It's unclear just how Baker was related to Luther. Jim, Faye, and Lowell Morris identified him as a second cousin to Luther's mother. All of them rejected Hiram Stamper's claim that Bev Baker was Luther's father-in-law. Both Jim and Faye spoke of his frequent overnight visits. "Bev," Jim said, "would always come to our house, and him and Pap would stay up till late in the night fiddling. . . . They'd get drunk and they'd fiddle till they got so drunk they couldn't play and then they'd go to bed."[43] Jim and Faye also remember Bev as considerably overweight, with Faye telling how he once had a heart attack at their home. Luther revived him with whiskey, asking him repeatedly till he recovered, "Who am I?"[44] Other memories center on his music. The two regularly fiddled at political rallies. "They'd have a fire, standing around, and when he'd see Luther coming, Bev would just quit playing and just reach the fiddle to Luther."[45] That Luther had surpassed his teacher came out, too. "Bev stayed with us a lot," Jim Strong related. "He was a good fiddler. And him and Pap got into a fiddling contest at Hazard. There was a twenty-dollar gold piece for the prize. Pap won the prize and Bev got kind of teed off. He said, 'Well, I guess I taught you a little too much, didn't I, Luther?'"[46]

On the day Luther made his Library of Congress recordings, Bev Baker participated in the same session. In Alan and Elizabeth Lomax's hotel room, playing either by himself or, on one number, with guitarist Norman Combs accompanying him, Bev recorded six pieces. While no information survives to tell who contacted Bev that day, this much can be reconstructed: After seeing Faye at the door of Luther's home, Lomax drove from Buckhorn back into Hazard, where he bailed Luther out of jail. Luther then sent Lomax out for a pint of whiskey to get the session underway. Jim recalled his father's oft-repeated words: "Pap said, 'The only way I can record any tunes is I'm gonna have to have a drink.'"[47] As his hangover lessened, Luther played twenty-nine tunes, a virtuoso survey of Southern fiddle repertory, all in the presence of his teacher.

Sometimes in the background, near the microphone, Bev Baker's craggy voice comments while Luther plays. During "Callahan," which in Luther's hands sounds like several instruments at once, with the adjacent strings echoing and amplifying its piping drive, Bev approves, "That's a good tune."

Further back from the microphone, cars go by, a door closes, and someone comes into the room. Then a woman, presumably Elizabeth Lomax, utters a syllable before catching herself. All the while the fiddle plows through uninterrupted. On "Ways of the World," a tune that Hiram Begley and Bev Baker both played at Berea, Bev again talks in the background, but this time his comments are harder to make out. The tune flows more quietly than "Callahan," its plaintive phrases crossing back and forth as if they wordlessly repeat its title. In "Glory in the Meetinghouse," Luther has already gotten underway when the recording needle drops. Here no one talks at all. A car drives past, and then perhaps, a truck. Over its one-minute-and-forty-two-seconds' duration, Luther structures the dynamic, dark instrumental in three parts: a low passage, the one most often repeated, generating the tune's essential rhythm; a higher-pitched strain that completes the tune's musical thought; and a third section leaping up the fingerboard to mark a singularly wailing coda. Right afterward, on the same disc, Bev Baker follows with his own version. He plays "Glory" in truncated form, only seconds long, intruded upon by a car horn. Even then, the similarity between the two interpretations is unmistakable.

Within months of the session, Luther wrote to the Folk Archive about the disposition of the recordings and wanted copies on behalf of Bev and himself.[48] He also offered, on both their parts, to record more pieces. The letter apparently got lost at the Library. Lomax replied a year later, promising to make duplicates for them, and professing, "I still can say with assurance that I like your fiddling better than anyone I have heard."[49] There's no record that the duplicates ever got made. In 1942, when Lomax prepared three of Luther's tunes for release, "Callahan," "Ways of the World," and "Glory in the Meetinghouse," scheduled for the Library's second full-length album, Luther wrote back twice in a month's time hoping to receive them soon.[50] For Luther and Bev, "Glory in the Meetinghouse," in particular, reached into their mutual past. Bev had entered it at the August 1919 Berea College fiddle contest, a performance that marks the tune's earliest mention in print. Moreover, it was Bev Baker, says Jim Strong, who taught "Glory in the Meetinghouse" to Luther.

Like "The Last of Callahan," "Glory in the Meetinghouse" also circulated locally and crossed generations, eventually passing from Bev Baker to Luther Strong to Jim Strong. Hiram Stamper, who played it in contests beside his friend Luther Strong, learned "Glory" from Bev Baker and acknowledged hearing it from local fiddlers Hiram Begley and Shade Sloan, the latter born in the 1840s. Hiram Stamper later introduced it to his son, Art Stamper, and the tune moved through them to other performers.[51] Hiram Stamper taught it to Marion Sumner, and Art Stamper brought it to the Goins Brothers. At the Appalachian Center Sound Archive at Berea College, all the versions on file have a direct connection with one another.

The Berea files also include younger players like Bruce Greene, drawn to playing the fiddle in no small measure because of Luther's recorded performance of "Glory," and later learning it in person from Hiram Stamper.[52] Other holdings name the Hurricane Ridgerunners, a Seattle-based old-time band who credited Luther's Library of Congress recording for their version released in 1985. Since then, fiddlers James Leva and Bruce Molsky drew from Luther for their renditions, while Laurie Lewis acknowledges both Luther and the Hurricane Ridgerunners as her source.[53] While these urban-raised players grew up in a radically different cultural environment than the eastern Kentucky life Luther had experienced, they also learned mainly by ear, apprenticed themselves to older musicians, and taught others by example. These bonds give continuing evidence, as Alan Lomax wrote of this 1937 trip, of "the tenacity of the tradition of homemade music."[54] At the very least their interest underscores the appeal of Luther's performance, a point that he observed himself. Right after Luther played "Glory in the Meetinghouse" in that Hazard hotel room, he speaks for the one and only time on the recordings, saying, "I've won five hundred dollars on that tune."[55]

―――――――――――

"I don't believe," said Jim Strong of "Glory," "that if you got half-drunk, that you'd get up and try to dance to it. You'd be all out of shape to get your feet going with the tune."[56] The undanceable piece his father entered at contests served a different purpose: a piece of art to be listened to and appreciated. The fact that Luther accumulated winnings so consistently with this fiddle tune—back then no single purse amounted to five hundred dollars—speaks not only to his skills, but to his listeners' preferences. While related tunes exist elsewhere, neither this piece nor its title has been collected outside of Luther's region in southeastern Kentucky. How "Glory in the Meetinghouse" fared locally gives a key to its understanding.

Throughout "Glory's" documented history, from 1919 when Bev Baker entered it at the Berea old-time fiddler's contest through the 1970s when the Kentucky-based Goins Brothers performed it in their shows, the tune represented for many a sense of the past. Guitarist and singer Melvin Goins recalls his audiences' reaction. "It reminded the old timers of what they growed up with . . . a good lonesome mountain tune."[57] Art Stamper introduced it to the

Goins Brothers. They did it as a fiddle showpiece with no other instrumental breaks. It communicated, Goins said, "that sound he put in it. It's pure. It's a pure mountain tune. . . . It's a tune that will make you listen because you wonder what's coming next and you wonder how it's going to go and how it's going to flow . . . Because it's not an ordinary number that ordinary people play, ordinary fiddle tunes. . . . It's more or less like an orchestra playing or bagpipes . . . its got its own sound, its got its own potentials." Yet for all this depth, Goins also found that Art Stamper's performance of "Glory" carried a lesser resonance for their younger bluegrass fans. "Young people," he said, "wouldn't know what it is."

For the Goins Brothers' older audience, part of their acceptance may also have come from knowing the tune's titles. As Melvin Goins explained, "'Glory to the Meeting House' reminds you of an old-time church meeting, brush arbor . . . a gospel meeting-and-preaching in a church back years ago."[58] Camp meetings marked a major public phenomenon in Kentucky beginning in 1800 with the Great Awakening, which attracted massive crowds and much singing. Listeners who heard the Goins Brothers introduce "Glory" not only got to hear an instrumental that calls on sounds that lie at the roots of bluegrass, but a title that summoned a time of traveling preachers and outdoor revivals. When I mentioned to Goins how the fervor of the tune's third part summoned for me a Holiness service at its peak, he said "you're on the right trail." The compilers of a 2004 three-CD gospel anthology marketed to country listeners evidently thought along similar lines.[59] To better-known offerings of the Carter Family, the Blackwood Brothers, and the Oak Ridge Boys, they added "Glory to the Meeting House," the 1972 Goins Brothers recording. The homespun title doubtlessly played a role in its selection.

Kentucky fiddle music scholar Jeff Todd Titon has found "Glory" not melodically indebted to any local hymns. But he also observes that its high-pitched third strain evokes a sense of "getting happy, feeling the Spirit."[60] A verse that Luther's son Green Strong remembered in 1986 points even more directly to this religious legacy: "Glory in the meeting house, / Glory in the hall, / Glory in the meeting house, / Glory to us all."[61] Green Strong's verse, which reads like a vocal refrain, brings a spiritual dimension that some, including his father, might have sung to accompany the piece. For Luther himself, Holiness religion entered his life, but not until his last two years, when illness had set in and he had stopped playing the fiddle. Whatever he may have felt about the tune's religious dimension, what comes through is the art of old-time mountain fiddling.

From the start, a listener to Luther's "Glory in the Meetinghouse" confronts the sheer sound of his fiddle. All through the recording the notes ring out, strident, enriched, and lingering.[62] This reverberation stems in part from the tuning. Luther's "Glory," the other 1937 performances, and the later versions including Art Stamper's, all depart from the violin's standard configuration of fifths, GDAE (lowest string to highest). Instead, Luther and his fellow players have shifted the bass string down from G to E, to reinforce the tune's underlying tonal center. With the violin now set at EDAE, the sympathetic strings support the melody. This "cross-keying" or "cross-tuning" boosts a violin's overall volume. The matching notes and reverberating strings proved an especially useful device when fiddlers played alone and without amplification. The notes echo and answer one another, giving a sense of multiple instruments playing in unison. With the fiddle strings doubled and sometimes tripled, all tuned to a given chord, the resulting drones and harmonies allow for resonances not available in standard tuning. When Art Stamper listened to Luther's "Glory" (after first playing it himself), he repeated what he had said about Luther's "Last of Callahan." It, too, drew upon a cross-tuning, or positioning what he called "closed strings against open notes": "He's really getting a lot of sound there that really you don't hear today. . . . All that noise out of one box. Sounds like such a force . . . That's the old way of playing."[63]

Art Stamper, himself a veteran bluegrass musician, liked to point out that an unbroken artistic thread joins the country music of Jimmie Rodgers's day to the country music of Garth Brooks's era. Similar development, he said, applies to the fiddle. "Look at the progression. Every generation takes the same music and puts some different feeling to it."[64] In the older style that his father and Luther Strong played, fiddlers kept more to melody than to accompaniments or spontaneous breaks. Art cited Posey Rorer, who played behind Charlie Poole in the 1920s. Rorer and others of that time played "the same thing in the back as they did up front." The Poole band's interlocking banjo, guitar, and fiddle parts, with each instrument filling a discrete role during a vocal number, keep a continuous stream of fiddle-led melody running through it all. That method, Art explained, contrasted with present-day practice. "Now what we'll do playing after a singer, we'll listen to him sing, get a feeling from the front man . . . [then] back up, fill in empty lines, accent, help bring his singing out." He named leading fiddlers of the 1940s and '50s—Dale Potter, Tommy Jackson, Howdy Forrester, Spade Cooley, and Tex Williams—as pioneers of this modern, antiphonal style. For all of them, popular music, especially swing jazz and blues, played a role in their artistic development. These players developed breakaway leads and traded hot, often improvised choruses with their fellow bandmembers. They "won't play till there's a place open, for fear of interfering with the singer." "But Luther," Art continued, as we sat listening to his version of "Sally Goodin," "this man here plays it just like it's sung." "The reason behind this musical evolution?" I asked. "It's just change in times is all I can tell you."

Jim Strong agreed. After high school, a hitch in the air force, and a career as a barber, he became a professional country music fiddler, working with Jimmie Skinner and Carl and Pearl Butler. Later, Jim spent a decade playing nightly in a hillbilly bar in southern Indiana. Like Art, he spoke of providing close musical support to whoever led a song. At the same time, he noted that over the years a division of labor had arisen in country music. In a telling image of compartmentalization, he described himself along with his fellow bandmembers all going separately to a recording studio, adding their own tracks for a single number—hardly the model of simultaneously played melodies that characterized his father's old-time music.

Jim reflected on the modern use of commonplaces. Instead of a "shave and a haircut" button to end a tune, Luther finished as he began, or as Jim said, "on the note."[65] Luther and his peers typically stuck to the melody itself. "They didn't play fill licks," Jim continued, identifying a change in the music from solo playing to part playing. Just as modern bluegrass banjoists build up an inventory of chord-centered phrases, patterns that can be dropped in to accompany a tune, latter-day fiddlers have developed, along with their ending tags, an adaptable series of shuffles and turn-arounds. These fit a breadth of musical situations, varied according to the chord changes. Jim, however, adopted the practice he first learned at home, skipping the customary tag to end a tune. Whenever anyone played with him, Jim made clear to them: "I don't end my tunes. I end it where the guys in the band know where I'm going to end it." That meant they had to know the tune, and not just its structure, for them to finish together.

Now Jim picked up his violin and began to play an old-time breakdown, crafting his bowing around the melody, as his father had done in years past. "He just played the whole tune plumb through by himself."[66] His voice softened as he recounted the allure of his father's music. "I've heard him play them tunes a thousand times when I was little. They just sank right in your mind. I wanted to play the fiddle so bad. Wasn't no way I was going to play as good as Pap."

A hallmark of Luther's unforgettable fiddling lies in his use of alternative intonations. Along with "Glory in the Meetinghouse," Luther's "Hog-Eyed Man" illustrates this distinctive method. Fiddler Suzy Rothfield Thompson shows how he variously and deliberately sets certain notes in this tune microtonally higher than their standard positioning.[67] Thompson finds that other Appalachian fiddlers did the same. Along with "Hog-Eyed Man" she notates "Hannah at the Springhouse," an old-time tune that West Virginia's Melvin Wine learned from his father. There, too, Wine shifts the intonation of certain notes, using "two different thirds, and a sharp flat seventh. . . . He also occasionally plays a slightly sharp second scale degree."[68] Jeff Titon found these nuances in the fiddling of Luther's fellow Kentucky players as well. Along with Luther he names Hiram Stamper, Manon Campbell, and John Salyer, the last of whom evocatively termed them "'wild' notes."[69]

Here Luther's "Glory" is set in the E Dorian mode. Transcriber Liberty Rucker, a fiddler who spent her early years in north central Kentucky, studied Luther's recording both at performance speed and slowed down electronically. Though the tune holds E at its tonal center, she found that the D key signature best frames the intervals he used. "The rules of the tune," she said, guided her setting.[70] His style also stretches the rules of standard notation. As in "Hog-Eyed Man," Luther brings microtonal variations to "Glory in the Meetinghouse." The G notes in the lower register consistently keep perfect intonation, while those on the high E string fluctuate in pitch. Sometimes Luther leans slightly sharp, but in the third part—the section that dramatically swoops up the fingerboard—he hits a true G natural. Upward arrows highlight those notes that Luther altered.

Luther persisted with these intonational effects. On a 1955 home recording of "Glory in the Meetinghouse" that he made with his friend Arthur Francis, the same dissonant notes ring out over an accompanying guitar.[71] Francis, who often seconded Luther during his last years in southern Indiana, holds down an E major chord throughout the tune. The two musicians play at an even faster clip than the Library's version. They follow a more organized sequence than Luther's solo recording, with the third part recurring at set points. Yet even in this more modern and structured framework, the pairing of the guitar monophonically driving against the fiddle only intensifies Luther's biting, modal rendition.

This contrast reflects a wider sensibility at work, one not necessarily conforming to music-school conventions. When Earl Scruggs played "Foggy Mountain Breakdown," the famous 1949 recording used in the *Bonnie and*

Glory in the Meetinghouse

Luther Strong
AFS 1536 A2

Tuning: EDAE

EXAMPLE 1.

"Glory in the Meetinghouse." Transcription by Liberty Rucker.

Clyde soundtrack, and went to E minor on the banjo, his guitar-playing partner Lester Flatt used an E major chord. A similarly structured though more harmonious blend marks Uncle Dave Macon's "The Death of John Henry." For that 1926 release (in G tuning, capoed up three frets) he played an E minor during the song's chorus while Sam McGee held a C major on his guitar. Wade Mainer and Zeke Morris's 1937 recording of "Down in the Willow Garden," also set in G, brings a strident fusion of banjo and guitar to the fiddle-led ballad. Here they use an E major chord in the verses instead of the expected E minor. A "borrowed chord" in musical parlance, the substituted chord appears in a parallel key sharing the same tonic. This deliberate dissonance extends to vocal tradition as well. The major accompaniments to Ralph Stanley's minor melodies, for instance, heighten the power and appeal of what he calls his "old-time mountain music." In all these examples, the play of major against minor creates an artful tension, an ambiguity that Luther employs in his double stops of E against G. There he plays neither a true G natural nor a full G sharp. In making these intonation adjustments to "Glory in the Meetinghouse," as he did elsewhere in his repertory, by hovering sometimes above or below the note, Luther brought an ear-catching uncertainty to his fiddle tunes. Years later, he kept these variant microtones during his duet with Arthur Francis, just as other musicians, playing their clashing chords, found ways to uphold this musical ideal themselves.

Luther's 1955 taping, heard alongside his earlier solo recording of "Glory," confirms a broader issue raised by Alan Lomax in his final report on the 1937 Kentucky trip. As the collector watched residents there eschewing their homemade resources for professional entertainments, he expressed the hope that the old music would somehow endure. In his words, "there is a gradual trend toward the absorption of more of the traditional styles into the 'hillbilly' broadcasts and this may be one of the important channels through which the homemade music of the mountains can reassert itself."[72] Indeed, long after 1937, players from this region (and points beyond) have continued to draw from a traditional aesthetic. By integrating old styles into new settings, they reassert the homemade music of the mountains.[73]

From the fiddle tunes to the hymns, most of the 859 tracks that comprise the Library's 1937 Kentucky field recordings consist of solo performances sung at home or played at small social gatherings.[74] The keening tones, metrical irregularities, and modal scales shared by these fiddlers and singers attest to long-standing regional preferences. Even the more recent pieces in the collection—a scattering of disaster and mining songs, mountain blues, and some redactions of hillbilly recordings—these, too, extended that style, even if their subject matter did not reach as far back in time. One way or another, the focus stayed on what Alan Lomax called "the tradition of ballad singing and that which is associated with it."[75]

Alan and Elizabeth Lomax roamed the Kentucky countryside in the fall of 1937 much as collectors before them had. Howard Brockway and Loraine Wyman, for instance, in spring 1916 responded to what Brockway called "the quest of the lonesome tunes."[76] Both couples found in this region myriad pieces fitting that description, a music of "haunting and pathetic beauty," kept alive by youngsters and old people, even nursing mothers singing their babies to sleep.[77] Guided by the ballad canon established by Harvard professor Francis James Child and set on a mission to "harvest before the killing blight" of modern communications and transport, Brockway and Wyman traversed southeastern Kentucky first by horse and then by foot.[78] Trekking some three hundred miles, Wyman took down lyrics by hand as Brockway wrote out tunes, prizing a preindustrial music whose "melodic intervals . . . frequently of an unusual and curious character" survived in the memories of singers they often found unable to read or write.[79] The Lomaxes documented many of the same songs, coaxing their automobile along the steep terrain, while bearing a more recent technology that permitted them to make "instantaneous acetates."[80] Both sets of researchers located their center of gravity in gifted community musicians like Luther Strong who drew upon what many still call "that high lonesome sound."[81]

The Lomaxes' 1937 Library recordings of Luther Strong, Bill Stepp, Bev Baker, Boyd Asher, T. G. Hoskins, and the others capture an otherwise largely undocumented style. Memories of senior players and studies of their repertories show that solo fiddling flourished in the mountains long before the advent of recorded sound and prior to the introduction of the guitar, or even the banjo.[82] Since the 1920s, a prodigious amount of Kentucky fiddling had appeared on commercial releases. Indeed, these store-bought records constitute an extraordinary gathering of players, performances, and historical styles. They highlight more often than not mountain string bands over solo playing, just as they feature accompanied rather than a capella singing.[83] To create appeal to the public these country music records emphasized newer interpretations of the old music as well as more recent rags and blues. Put another way, when I asked Art Stamper to differentiate his rendition of "Glory

in the Meetinghouse" from his father's, he replied: "Dad puts some things in there that I don't, and I put some things in it that he doesn't. . . . [each of us] according to the time he played it."[84] The strength of the Library's Kentucky recordings is that they documented players like Luther, who didn't just respond to present-day influences but, like Art's dad, put things in there "way behind his time."

"Glory in the Meetinghouse" had much to offer a soloist like Luther on the fiddle contest stage. It allowed him to call upon the prized dissonance of the high lonesome sound, an ideal signified by Howard Brockway's "melodic intervals . . . of an unusual and curious character." That "Glory" worked for Luther and his southeastern Kentucky audiences, his five hundred dollars in winnings furnishes proof. The tune's range from the lowered E string to its soaring third part, which reaches the highest note available in first-position violin playing, gave him a wide platform on which to exhibit his command of the instrument. And with his skills, he could draw from his fiddle all the thunder suggested by its title.

James Leva, who plays Luther's "Glory in the Meetinghouse," spoke of it and pieces like it as "multi-dimensional" as opposed to the "linear" fiddling that succeeded it.[85] Effects like bowed triplets and trills had less place and became buried in the audio mixture when other instruments joined in. "The fiddle," James said, gave "parts away," passing along formerly self-sufficient functions in rhythm and ornamentation. By the advent of the bluegrass ensemble in the postwar years, with the guitar playing chords, the bass setting a beat, the mandolin contributing its rhythm, and the three-finger banjo dividing up the phrases, fiddlers like Chubby Wise and Benny Martin found themselves exploring a new vocabulary of swing chords and double stops. "It [the music] became more of a chromatic, harmonic left-hand thing," James continued, "rather than the old right-hand dominance of the old-time fiddle."

In the words of both Jim Strong and Art Stamper, Luther "pulled the long bow." During a single stroke he might fit in several notes, his left-hand finger positions moving with the glide of his bow. Art Stamper explained that old-time fiddlers like Luther "get all their rhythm in that bow . . . it's got kind of a roll to it, almost a windmill."[86] Within this movement, and given Luther's typically fast pace, he often achieved, Art said, "three or four notes on the bow, two notes in the other stroke." This slurring of notes aided his speed, harnessing his control while unleashing his expressiveness. In "Glory," for instance, Luther sometimes plays two successive E notes on the same stroke by changing the bow's pressure and adjusting his speed, moving the bow faster or slower, creating accents. His fellow players recognized the skill involved. Jim remembered his father's reproof that he "didn't think I'd make a fiddler until I learned to put more than one note on a bow."[87]

Fiddler Bruce Greene, who met and learned from a number of Kentucky fiddlers of Luther's generation, noted Luther's "amazing wildness" and the momentum he built by alternating short, saw strokes with long, drawn-out strokes.[88] Luther might stop the bow, then "break the notes up into little phrases, hesitate, then shove it ahead . . . and explode into the next phrase. . . . Most fiddlers get their emphasis and beat on the down bow, but he gets his emphasis in the pushing."

The opening section of Luther's "Glory" reveals this vivid combination of push, pull, and long-bow techniques. In the pickup and first three full measures, lasting all of six seconds, he changes direction twenty times.[89] The rest of the piece demonstrates a similar complexity of movement.

Until a stroke late in life stilled his arm, Luther remained a community musician who played largely for dances and sometimes for contests. Though he finally got a radio and listened to the *Grand Ole Opry,* he was part of the last generation to grow up without having contact with records and radio, as well as the first to reckon with these media. Later developments in fiddle music, such as his son's bluegrass, held little interest. Jim Strong still remembers how his father dismissed it, in the way others might scorn rock and roll. Luther's passion for those unusual and curious melodic intervals would not seem to answer the implicit question posed by Alan Lomax's 1937 collecting trip: how can the homemade music of the mountains reassert itself in a modern era? Luther looked to the past for models, and later, as his music got more widely known, came to serve as an invaluable resource of that past. For that very reason, it turns out, his performance of "Glory in the Meetinghouse" holds a portent to the music's future.

In the fall of 1961 or early 1962, less than a year before Luther died, a talented family bluegrass band from central Illinois made a home recording of "Glory in the Meetinghouse." The group was the Bray Brothers: mandolinist Nate, banjoist Harley, and bassist Francis, along with guitarist Red Cravens. Often during this period they lived together in Urbana, Illinois, renting the second floor of an old house divided into apartments. There they gathered around two microphones set up in their combination living room–bedroom. With one mike reserved for the string bass and the other for everything else, Harley Bray recalled, "Red would fire the old tape recorder up."[90] The tapes were used for noontime country music broadcasts on a radio station some thirty-five miles away. That recording of "Glory," led by their fiddler friend John Hartford, who had taught them the tune, marked the only time they ever played it. It never entered their performing repertory, and for many years it simply lay unheard on a roll of magnetic tape.

In 1960, Hartford, the future composer of "Gentle on My Mind," was working as a Nashville record promoter. On one of his sales trips he came to station WHOW in Clinton, Illinois, where Uncle Johnny Barton, host of *Cornbelt Country Style,* introduced him to the Bray Brothers. The Bray Brothers had already become the house band at Bill Monroe's country music park at Bean Blossom, Indiana, and they had much to share. "He was a good fiddler," Harley recalled, "and good fiddlers were very rare around Champaign. So every time he'd come around promoting records, he'd give us a call . . . and we'd do a few numbers." One of the tunes Hartford played for them was "Glory in the Meetinghouse." "We wanted a fiddle tune, so he played that one and we really liked it and so we recorded it. . . . We put it together right there." Harley made up a tuning to go with it on the banjo, an unusual and effective E minor tuning.

Thirty years later Harley asked John Hartford about his source for "Glory." Hartford "thought it might be the Library of Congress." When I called Hartford in 1995 to talk about the tune, he said again that the Library of Congress performance was the one source he knew for it. I took that to mean Luther Strong's recording, since those by Bev Baker and Boyd Asher had never been released. By way of John Hartford, then, Luther's tune went out to a group of traditional musicians—the Bray Brothers' father, born in 1893, and their grandfather, born in 1861, were both rural fiddlers—who recast it into a bluegrass format. But it may have gone even further than that, into the whole genre of bluegrass music, via an instrumental called "Jerusalem Ridge."

In 1972 the Bray Brothers' first LP was released.[91] Titled *419 West Main* after their apartment where they made their recordings, and produced by John Hartford, it included their one-time performance of "Glory in the Meetinghouse." Another LP followed in 1976, also culled from the tapes made at their Urbana apartment. Between these two release dates, Kentucky fiddler Kenny Baker, a long-time bandmate to Bill Monroe, "played at a little teacher's college in Bloomington, Illinois," Harley recalled, "and a bunch of us filled in. They were playing those records a lot and I always wondered if it ["Glory in the Meetinghouse"] started running through Kenny's head, and he went back and he played something like that for Bill. They changed the key, they played it in A minor, and they shifted the parts around and wrote a really nice tune." Here Harley refers to "Jerusalem Ridge."

In the 1990s Kenny Baker told more about the tune's development: "According to Kenny Baker," writes bluegrass journalist Joe Cline, "the band was staying in a motel in (I believe) Ashland, Kentucky, back in the early to mid-70s, and Bill asked Kenny to come down to Bill's room with his fiddle. Bill would play (on mandolin) a phrase of this new tune he was working on, and have Kenny play it back on the fiddle. Bill would then ask Kenny to modify what he played. This went back and forth for several hours until the two of them had worked out the tune. Kenny claims to have made a major contribution, but insists that the composition was all Bill's."[92]

Bill Monroe explained that the title "Jerusalem Ridge" referred to a rise by that name overlooking his home in Rosine, Kentucky. "That's where we fox-hunted when I was growing up. I have loved that area ever since I was a kid. I wanted to write a song about it, and I wanted to go back in time with the music to reflect the Scottish and Irish sounds."[93] He wrote this piece in 1973. After mentioning that it had four parts, he added, "I think it is one of my best numbers." He recorded it with the Blue Grass Boys including

Kenny Baker in 1975, and again a year later for Baker's own album. By then "Jerusalem Ridge" had become a Kenny Baker showpiece.

Harley Bray makes no claim that the recording that he and his brothers taped in the early 1960s necessarily made an impression on Kenny Baker or Bill Monroe. He just knows that the two pieces are similar and that Baker heard their version of "Glory in the Meetinghouse" around the time the newer tune got written. As an eastern Kentuckian, Baker may also have heard "Glory" from other players, including Marion Sumner, whose place he took in Don Gibson's western swing band before joining Monroe, or the Goins Brothers with Art Stamper. Likewise, Kentuckian Bill Monroe could have been acquainted with some version of "Glory." Bill was also fond of the Bray Brothers, and he, too, owned their albums. When Harley visited Bill at his home in 1960, he remembers Bill pointing to Jerusalem Ridge, calling it a place that stirred him.

Other sources may have also played a role in the tune's creation. A related number, set in the same tuning and mining the same tonal core, "Say Old Man Can You Play the Fiddle" had long circulated by then. Prominent fiddlers familiar to Kenny Baker and Bill Monroe, players such as Bob Wills with his 1936 release of "Crippled Turkey," and performances of "Say Old Man" by Eck Robertson, Benny Thomasson, Howdy Forrester, and Robert Rutland (whose version shares a strain strikingly similar to Luther's low part) all helped establish it as a contest showpiece.[94] Further afield, its design branches into other tunes. Just as "Say Old Man" became established as a Texas contest favorite, the memorable minor-chord-to-major-chord shift surfaces, for example, in Nebraska radio fiddler Uncle Bob Walters's "Drunken Wagoner."[95] There the idea carries on, though not in Luther's style with his cross-key drones and alternative intonations. Closer to home, the telltale pattern surfaces in "Snowbird in the Ashbank" played by Kentucky fiddler Jim Woodward.[96] Set in E minor, its tune evocative of "Say Old Man," Woodward's "Snowbird" forms a middle ground in that its overall contour closely follows "Glory." Woodward credited Jim Booker, an African American fiddler, as his source. Previously, Booker appeared on more than a half-dozen of the celebrated 1927 hoedown recordings of Taylor's Kentucky Boys. Booker's presence here, tied to a fragment of "Glory's" heritage, highlights the cultural cauldron that produced the region's fiddle music.

That Luther Strong's performance of "Glory in the Meetinghouse" may have made its way to the Bray Brothers, whose own recording of it may then have figured in the making of "Jerusalem Ridge," dwells heavily in speculation. But fiddle tunes do get extended and reworked and musicians do listen to records and to each other. By this process they create new pieces and vary old ones. It seems unlikely that Monroe and Baker were thinking of Luther Strong when they wrote "Jerusalem Ridge." But the sound of "Glory in the Meetinghouse," a knowledge of its motifs and patterns, was implicitly present as the two veteran musicians crafted something new from those old and curious intervals Bill Monroe liked to call "ancient tones." Sitting together in a motel room, passing back and forth a tune based on old sonorities, finding a form that could be remembered and repeated, eventually creating a piece both surprising and familiar, Bill Monroe and Kenny Baker had a conversation with the past. The quest of the lonesome tunes turns out to inspire not only their collectors but also their creators.

FIGURE 42. Luther Strong, Austin, Indiana, ca. 1955. Photo by Faye Strong Sandlin. Courtesy of Faye Sandlin.

Behind "Jerusalem Ridge" lies a kinship, a set of musical values cherished and shaped by players over the generations. A related kinship applies to the pictures that hang on Faye Sandlin's house trailer walls. Some of the images she set there represented persons born in her family, while others, the woman in the Hopper painting and the Kennedys, she adopted. Like this lineage of "Glory in the Meetinghouse" and "Jerusalem Ridge," they tell a history both tangible and imagined.

So it is, too, for Luther's own history. When folklorist Ralph Rinzler became Bill Monroe's manager in 1963, he reported that Luther attended Monroe's Bean Blossom festival.[97] But in truth that was Jim Strong who came there. Luther was gone by then, and even before that time, he never attended this

event. Rinzler's sighting of Luther was wishful thinking. Whatever Ralph Rinzler's agenda in asserting Luther's legitimizing presence at Monroe's festival, Rinzler deeply loved the three issued Library of Congress tracks of "Last of Callahan," "Ways of the World," and "Glory in the Meetinghouse." By bringing up Luther's name in connection with Bill Monroe, he accorded him an honored, even legendary status.

Local fiddlers that Bruce Greene met in Kentucky in the 1970s and 1980s also remembered Luther in fabled terms. One said that he used a larger bow than normal. Others told of Luther's efforts to enhance his tone during a contest, or simply to get his fiddle to work better by raising the strings off the fingerboard, putting pennies under the bridge "to get a keener sound."[98] While Jim Strong made no mention of that fix or the unusual bow in our conversations, he did say that Luther never kept any fiddle for too long. At most, he held on to one for six months, perhaps a year. Then he would trade it off for whiskey. Sometimes for even longer periods he had no fiddle at all. Ultimately these stories matter less about Luther's instruments than about his mastery of them. This is a man who, without practice or forewarning, on a borrowed fiddle, just bailed out of jail and with a hangover, made recordings that have meant so much to so many committed to this art form.

For Luther's daughter Faye, his music stirred more than just her reverence for his artistry. It recalled memories marked with varying degrees of happiness and sadness. She spoke contentedly about his coming home after dances. His dance income was always a welcome answer to the family's needs, earnings that he would typically tuck inside his felt hat band. "Take care of Pap's hat," he said as he handed it to her. "You be careful with it and don't you be looking around it too much."[99]

"I danced my leg off at many dances with my dad," Faye reminisced. "He'd say, 'Faye girl, we're going to go to a party tonight. Get your dancing shoes on.' We'd go way up a hollow. They moved all their furniture out so everybody could dance, and I really had a good time that night. And when we left it was getting daylight." On another occasion, he merrily announced to her, "'We're gonna play for the school. We're going to play in the gym. A dance in the gym for the school.' If he got drunk, there was always somebody there to take us home." She continued:

> Everyone here in this town knew he played the violin. One day the mail truck came by and he [the postman] come and knocked on the door. And I went to the door and he said, "I've got a nice big package out here for you." . . . And I ran for the van and he opened the back doors, and there was my dad. He had picked up my dad somewhere passed out. I said, "Oh no." And he said "Well," he said, "Ain't it a nice big package?" And I said, "Yes it is." He helped me get my dad in the house. He said "Now I do have a package for you. I've got his violin out here." So I went back out and got his violin. I asked him, "Where did you find him?" "I think he was trying to walk home. He'd been playing music with somebody in a store. He just had too much. I just come by and got him up and brought him home."[100]

"I've thought about that many times," Faye added quietly. "My dad was laying in there and not even knowing where he was."

Of all these memories, one in particular brings together Luther, his music, the community, and Faye herself. She mentioned an annual Memorial Day visit to a cemetery five miles from Buckhorn. Dinner was served on the grounds, and those that gathered there would "play music to the dead," she remembered.[101] "Like they'd raise the dead." Her dad played all day long. "Preachers we never knew, they threw money at him to keep him playing close to dark." So there was Luther at the Loose Angel Cemetery. Faye called him an angel while he was alive, and maybe that's what he became—Luther Callahan Strong fiddling "Glory in the Meetinghouse," an angel on the loose.

Charlie Butler

Call Me to Home

P AUL OLIVER'S MASSIVE 1997 *ENCYCLOPEDIA OF VERNACULAR Architecture of the World* surveys an estimated 800 million dwellings. Their occupants include nomads, urban dwellers, pastoralists, and peasants, living under pointed thatch in Indonesia, makeshift huts in the Scottish outlands, and wooden farmhouses across Pennsylvania's country-side. They have constructed with palm date grasses in North Africa and sun-dried brick in Pakistan, finished shelters with mud plaster and ceramic tile, created hygiene systems that range from sweatlodges to bathhouses, channeled ventilation through courtyards or sometimes wind catchers, and funneled water via cisterns and wheels. "All forms of vernacular architecture," Oliver observes, "are built to meet specific needs, accommodating the values, economies and ways of living of the cultures that produce them."[1]

Oliver, an Oxford professor in architecture, is also a pioneering chronicler of the African American blues. Since 1952, he has written nearly a dozen books and hundreds of articles on the blues, exploring this vernacular genre as he has the other: by situating the music and its practitioners within their cultural settings.[2] While his interests have centered on commercially released blues recordings, his knowledge extends to the Library of Congress field trips of the 1930s and 1940s. So it came as no surprise in early 1998 when I sent him a copy of the *Treasury* that Paul Oliver was already familiar with "Diamond Joe" and its singer, Charlie Butler, just as he knew many of the CD's other selections.

Oliver wrote back a most encouraging note. He saw this book, then embryonic, as a way of learning about the artists included on the *Treasury*. Unlike a number of their counterparts in the blues, only a few of these performers had been extensively researched. Largely home musicians and lacking much renown beyond their families and communities, their anonymity paralleled so many of the vernacular builders whose work Oliver included in his *Encyclopedia*. If individually unknown to historians—despite their voices etched onto discs and their names entered in card catalogs—their songs represent collective products as well as personal achievements. Just as a dwelling can disclose the slope of a site, the demands of a climate, the resources available to its makers, the components of its construction, and the needs of its occupants, folksong bears a like set of traits. The words Oliver used to describe vernacular architecture, with its basis in local values, economies, and ways of living, apply here, too, as individuals craft the cultural vessels of song with the tools of their traditions and the capacities of their talents.

Charlie Butler, convict number 10636, recorded "Diamond Joe" at the Mississippi State Penitentiary at Parchman, Mississippi, in the spring of 1937. Two years later, he sang it again into John Lomax's disc machine. At the time, he left only the barest account of how he learned "Diamond Joe," and none at all concerning how he came to sing. Vanished, too, are most details about his life. Though he appears in the 1920 state census that positively identifies him and his wife, later searches have proven less conclusive. For one thing, he took aliases. For another, he could not write, leaving only an "X" on the signature line of his commitment papers. This elusiveness reaches back to the Library's files: a January 1943 letter from the Folk Archive seeking his permission to issue "Diamond Joe" was returned unopened. He had been pardoned six months earlier. The prison's mailman wrote prophetic words on the envelope: "Gone free left no address."

Whatever course his life took from that point on, let alone so much of what came before his captivity in this hard place, I cannot say. Here at Parchman, where Charlie Butler sang "Diamond Joe" across its flat, rutted landscape whose turnrows he once walked, he left behind a work of art that speaks to a process of creation—a process, as Paul Oliver reminds us in the *Encyclopedia of Vernacular Architecture*, that goes on the world over.

FIGURE 44. Charlie Butler, 1936. Courtesy of Mississippi Department of Corrections.

On March 8, 1937, the day he recorded "Diamond Joe," Charlie Butler, age forty, had nearly completed his first year of imprisonment for attempted murder. Apprehended after escaping from the county penal farm in Tunica, he was now serving a ten-year sentence, his second term, at the state penitentiary. He had been there before, imprisoned in 1918, under another name, but convicted of the same crime and given the same penalty, for which he was pardoned in 1920. This most recent incarceration stemmed from an assault he made on Booker T. Robinson, who, like Charlie, lived in Tunica, a Delta community forty-one miles south of Memphis. One night, as Robinson's houseguest, and after Robinson had gone to bed, Charlie attacked him with an axe, cutting his head severely and causing him, according to circuit court records, near-fatal wounds. Following this summary, the document turns personal: "Bad case and one of BEAL STREETS bad boys. Take good care of him in the LINE."[3] However habitual Charlie Butler's criminality, this sarcastic evaluation by District Attorney Greek P. Rice evokes a system in which informal understanding played as telling a role as written statute. Rice's knowledge of Charlie Butler, the company he kept, and the punishment he would soon receive, while expressed euphemistically, left little to his keepers' imagination.

Read more closely, Greek Rice's words also capture a basic truth of that period, a reality magnified by his later contact with the Library. Between 1932 and 1941, the Rosedale, Mississippi, native served as district attorney before assuming the role of Coahoma County sheriff.[4] On August 29, 1941, a few months into his new job, he met with Alan Lomax, then on the first leg of the joint Library of Congress and Fisk University folk culture study, centered in that county. Rice opened the meeting with a thinly veiled threat: "Well, if you begin any labor trouble," the sheriff vowed, "we'll finish it."[5] Lomax realized that local planters felt "an acute shortage of labor here, the boys running off to the defense jobs." Plantation owners, farm managers, and absentee landlords all had an interest in maintaining cotton productivity. With mechanical farming still a few years away, the crop required large-scale physical labor in its planting and harvesting.[6]

But Rice had an even more specific concern in mind when he spoke to Lomax. Beginning in 1939, the Southern Tenant Farmers Union started organizing on the Arkansas side of the river, near enough to home that Coahoma County planters opposed those efforts to the point of physically threatening the union leaders. Firsthand reports circulated in the local political establishment of how the organizers championed messages of "social equality" and "intermarriage."[7] Such explosive ideas, wrote one infiltrator, fell under a broader category still: "abusive, vindictive and profane denunciations of plantation . . . and commercial agriculture." If allowed to come to pass, these upheavals threatened the stability that Greek Rice intended to preserve.

Mississippi, as Sheriff Rice and the others knew, was losing its African American work force, a trend that only spiraled in the coming years. Between 1940 and 1947, the *Ruleville Record,* the local newspaper that ran a weekly column on Parchman, reported that 4.7 percent of the state's population, approximately 102,000 persons and nearly all of them black, had migrated north.[8] The field hands—those boys running off to the defense jobs—were heeding the North's call of better wages and greater freedom. No wonder, as the LC-Fisk folk culture study wore on, that Lomax repeatedly heard from irritated farm managers, let alone this early warning from the sheriff, of their fear that music recordings might prove a distraction to the cotton hands, and possibly furnish another enticement to leave. "Delta lands without labor," wrote Coahoma political leader Walter Sillers Jr. in 1927, "are as useless as an automobile without an engine."[9] That engine—the laborers who worked the Delta's crop—served a social, political, legal, and economic system reflected in Greek Rice's "clear hard blue eyes."[10]

Even in the smallest encounters, such as this meeting at Rice's office, the economy of cotton pervaded. After Lomax heard out the sheriff's caution, he and Rice's deputy began making a list of his Fisk colleagues.[11] The two struggled over whether the title "Mister" was appropriate in designating these African American social scientists participating in the documentation project. While prevailing racial etiquette dictated that blacks not receive the same verbal respect as whites, the issue unavoidably came back to labor management. Another black resident had told Lomax that Sheriff Rice recently "closed all the dance halls & whore houses & gambling games & and nobody could have no fun no more."[12] Additional ordinances banned the playing of jukeboxes in Clarksdale's cafés on Sundays, and included periodic arrests of guitar-playing musicians at harvest time when all available hands were needed in the fields. Singer and storyteller Will Starks subsequently described these weekend prohibitions to Lomax: "He [Sheriff Rice] say, they voted the law to put the lid on, so 'Let's put it on good and tight.'"[13] If outwardly a crusade for moral uplift, these mandates, Starks explained, concealed a more utilitarian motive: they strove to keep the workers ready, "so the folks wouldn't be too tired to go to work on Monday morning."[14]

The folks Will Starks had in mind lived in the Yazoo Delta, the nation's epicenter for the production of cotton. A soil-enriched flood plain, the Delta borders the lower Mississippi River, running two hundred miles from Memphis south to Vicksburg, while eastward it extends seventy-five miles to the hill country. Parchman is located near its center, a place that William Faulkner realistically described as "The vast flat alluvial swamp of cypress and gum and brake and thicket lurked with bear and deer and panthers and snakes . . . rich ragged fields in which cotton stalks grew ranker and taller than a man on a horse."[15] Faulkner's character Mink Snopes, a hill country native seeing the penitentiary for the first time, tells the deputy in charge of transporting him there, "This here's all swamp. . . . It don't look healthy." His keeper replies, "It ain't healthy. . . . It ain't intended to be."

During the second half of the nineteenth century, the Delta's malaria-filled wilderness was turned to cultivation, and, by the 1880s, its products reached markets across the country via rail. The clearing and draining of the land, productivity of its farms, and building of its railroad beds had depended on the labor of folks like those Will Starks described and Greek Rice policed. The Civil War had left Mississippi planters with arable land and little means to pay for labor, while its former slaves found themselves jobless and impoverished. "All these circumstances," noted the state's unit of the Federal Writers' Project, "led naturally to an arrangement whereby the labor undertook to work the land for the privilege of living on it and sharing in its product, while the landowner supervised the labor and marketed the cotton."[16] In 1930, just a few years before Charlie Butler returned to Parchman for the second time, the state census counted nearly 400,000 residents in the Delta, 297,000 of whom were black. Forty-seven of every one hundred persons in the state worked as tenant farmers, and "in ten of the most densely populated cotton counties, about 94% of the farm population were tenants."[17]

The Delta tenant farmers, most of them sharecroppers, lived on credit the greater part of the year, receiving their food and necessities called "furnishings," which they paid for with interest from their share of the crop at the season's end. Numerous stories recall planters giving them short counts and debt servitude that left these field hands with little recourse and no legal redress. The principal means they had of asserting their autonomy, says historian James Cobb, lay in vacating one plantation for another, often in the stealth of a Sunday night.[18] This, in turn, fueled the planters' anxieties about keeping the labor force intact, as Greek Rice communicated to Alan Lomax. Throughout this time, specifically the six years that Charlie Butler remained at Parchman—sentenced July 12, 1936, and pardoned on July 3, 1942, exactly one day before Rice himself enlisted for the army and his wife took over his sheriff's job—a fundamental rule prevailed in the Delta: Both inside the prison's wire and beyond, the force of the state lay with the planters, as it did with the powers at Parchman.

Delta writer David Cohn recounted a moment that crystallized this common plight for black Mississippians. At a local courthouse sometime around 1935, he observed a woman in the process of being transported to Parchman, which also housed the state's female offenders. Manacled with some other prisoners, she kept smiling even though she faced a two-year sentence. Cohn asked her how she could stay so lighthearted at such a time, and then he understood the lesson in her laughter. "It ain't no diffunce, white folks," she replied. "I'm got to work wherever I'm is."[19]

She faced at Parchman, as Charlie Butler would soon himself, a constant round of toil. The penitentiary's female prisoners, all of them black, lived in a separate camp located between Camp Two, which held infirm black male convicts unable to sustain long physical labor, and Front Camp, which housed white prisoners only, selected for their mechanical skills and employed at the prison's cotton gin, machine, and shoe shops. Here at the Women's Camp, the inmates sewed the prison's clothing (the ubiquitous "ring-arounds," the striped black and white uniforms worn by the male prisoners), made the bedding (sheets, mattresses, and pillows), and ran the cannery. The prison had its own peach and apple orchards, and the women peeled, processed, and canned those items. A verse Cohn collected in the mid-1930s at this camp translates their daily tasks into song: "You talkin bout trouble / You don't know what trouble means (repeat) / What I call trouble / is a Singer Sewing Machine."[20] Just as the incoming female prisoner had told Cohn that Parchman echoed the economic system around it, Charlie Butler's first assignment at the penitentiary matched outside conditions as well.

Throughout Charlie's incarceration he lived a mile or so from the women's compound at Camp One, one of the sixteen racially segregated camps then spread over the facility's 15,497 acres that housed 1,989 convicts.[21] Camp One was located near the prison's front entrance in sight of the highway, the warden's home, and the train station that crossed the property. One of only two units enclosed by a fence, Camp One consisted of several small shelters adjacent to its long one-floor barracks. A shed holding the day's farm tools and the trusties' rifles stood inside the compound along with an outbuilding called a "tonk" or "red house" set aside for conjugal visits. The sergeant, C. B. Boleu, the prison official most involved with Camp One's inmates at that time, lived just outside the fence in a small two-bedroom house.[22] Charlie stayed with 120 other convicts in a brick dormitory they rebuilt during those years to replace its wooden predecessor. This "cage," the space into which they were locked at night, was divided into two areas separated by bars. One side was reserved for the trusties. These included the trusty-shooters, convicts themselves, charged with guarding the other convicts. When Charlie later became the camp's gateman trusty, he also lived on that wing. Before then, he, like the majority of inmates, lived in the general quarters. In Parchman parlance, they were known as gunmen.

Six days a week, from dawn to sunset, with twenty minutes out for lunch, marshaled into columns a hundred men wide, the gunmen worked under the supervision of the armed trusty-shooters. This was "the line" that Greek Rice mentioned at Charlie's commitment. If a gunman came within twenty feet of a trusty-shooter and wasn't "hollered out" in advance, he would be shot. Confined to each day's gun line, a marked point they crossed only at mortal peril, the gunmen planted, hoed, and plowed the 222 acres of cotton assigned to Camp One. They also raised a plot of vegetables and corn for their camp's personal consumption as well as silage for the animals. Little relieved this daily exertion except the "mercy man," the convict who came

FIGURE 45.
One of the last
cages at Parch-
man, January 1997.
Photo by
Stephen Wade.

by with water, set in a barrel on a cart. Convicts made their own soap, built their own plywood coffins, raised their own chickens, and fed their own hogs. While prisoners' meal portions may have equaled, if not exceeded, what black Mississippians consumed on average in civilian life, at least one old story suggesting something else made the rounds at Parchman. It concerned "the fellow who complained about a weevil being in the beans. 'Quit complaining,' said another. 'That's the meat.'"[23]

With a sawmill, brick factory, and ice plant on the grounds, Parchman provided for nearly all the material needs of its prisoners and employees. Fire Marshal Charles Winters, who had grown up at Parchman—his father and grandfather were both camp sergeants there—told me that salt was the only item that the state bought from outside sources. "Every unit," he said, "was self-supporting."[24] The warden's secretary, Marilyn Corbin, who also resided there for twenty-one years beginning in the 1970s, described herself as "institutionalized," pointing out how convicts and some staff lived apart from what they all called "the free world"—the society beyond Parchman.[25] Back then Corbin's family paid almost no rent or utilities. A convict they called Hoppin' Bob regularly gathered the broccoli, turnips, and watermelon from their garden, for which they paid him a quarter. Then, on a pretend phone, fist to his ear, he'd check in. "Boss, I'm leaving the Corbins' house," and go to his next stop. As a staff family living at Parchman they received seven and a half pounds of beef and pork a month, paying fifteen cents a pound. Now, Corbin said, "It's a rude awakening to go back out. You spend what you make." "Parchman," observed still another staffer raised there, "was a small town."[26]

Parchman paralleled, as penologist William McWhorter has pointed out, an antebellum plantation. In particular, it followed a hierarchy of masters (the warden), overseers (the sergeants), slave drivers (the trusties), and slaves (the gunmen).[27] Its twentieth-century inmates received privileges according to an ascending level of cooperation in the same way nineteenth-century slaves might progress from the fields, perhaps to someday serve in the master's house. Both hoped for freedom, a freedom at Parchman delivered in the form of a pardon. In the years of Charlie's incarceration, a sizable if varying percentage of inmates received pardons yearly—parole wasn't established in Mississippi until 1944—thus creating a major incentive for compliant behavior. Charlie's own elevation to trusty gateman contributed to the reduction of his sentence. His file bears five slips signed by Sergeant Boleu recommending credit for time served. Willing to work on Sundays and holidays, Charlie received his pardon six years into his ten-year sentence.

During Charlie's tenure, the penitentiary ran according to an informal system of rewards and punishments. No specific criteria dictated the elevation of a gunman to trusty, just the instinct of the sergeant. Moreover, if a gunman on the line turned "rabbit" and a trusty-shooter killed him in that escape attempt, the shooter, even if previously convicted of murder, could earn a pardon. Lesser rewards ranged from weekly visits with prostitutes at the various tonks, family visits on the fifth Sunday of a given month, tolerance of cash gambling, and the distribution of home brew, to Christmas furloughs instituted in the mid-1940s. Discipline of the gunmen ranged from denial of water on the line to corporal punishment the sergeant administered from Black Annie, a leather strap four feet long and six inches wide attached to a wooden handle. Policy dictated that the sergeant sign a slip informing the warden whenever he had used Black Annie. Charlie's file contains no such slips, and his record lists no infractions.

In 1997, twenty-five years after the federal court reorganized Parchman, citing it for violations of the eighth amendment—"cruel and unusual punishment"—retired sergeant J. B. Burchfield and I drove the prison's sixteen-mile-long central road and looked over its largely barren fields. In 1954, he noted, some eighty employees monitored 1,500 inmates on these nearly 22,000 acres. They picked by hand that year some 7,200 bales of cotton. We stopped at the dog pens once run by convict trusties to apprehend escapees and then visited the graveyard. At one end, a stack of plain metal crosses rusted away in the dirt. I took a picture or two as the sergeant talked, his eyes scanning the distant tree line. He viewed the 1972 ruling by Judge William C. Keady as an abandonment of a quieter and better operated facility. He, too, had grown up near one of the cages. His father had also been a Parchman sergeant. "Everyone," he said, "knew their place."[28] The incentive system of rewards and punishments worked, and even though the prison operated as a segregated facility, inmates had less strife among themselves. After all, he observed, it was a time when "The whole world was segregated." While he kept his distance from prisoners as a matter of course, he also found a level of contact with them that was not faceless. Sometimes, he recalled, he got Christmas cards from former inmates. As for Black Annie, he simply remarked, "Back then, they had no kind of disciplinary problems."

Nor economic ones. By Charlie Butler's second term at Parchman, between July 1, 1936, and June 30, 1940, the penitentiary reported a $400,000 surplus, making it, in the words of warden Jim Thames, "the only profit-making prison in the country."[29] Warden Thames, like many who had come before him in that role, represented a management approach not based in penology, but experienced in farming. A half century later, Parchman warden Donald Cabana, who had been schooled in criminal justice, looked back on this era: "After all, the mission of the penitentiary had always been primarily economic: to be frugal with state funds; to be self supporting . . . and to make a profit growing cotton. Good security, public safety, and humane treatment of prisoners were all subordinated to economic efficiency—the penitentiary was just one more large plantation."[30] In specifying "plantation" and "efficiency," Cabana highlights an economic strategy that mirrored free-world black experience in Mississippi. The historical conditions that marked the Delta and its primary enterprise, reverberating in Parchman's cotton rows that spread across forty-six square miles, created an environment to which inmates like Charlie Butler responded through the medium of their music and the content of their songs.

"The steel heads of a hundred axes describe parabolas of radiance in the bright November sun as they rise from the ground, mount high into the air, and descend with deep bite into logs of wood."[31] This scene at Parchman, witnessed by David Cohn in 1935, pictures a line of gunmen amid the ash and oak that ringed the penitentiary's perimeter. The logs the prisoners were cutting furnished the fuel to heat the various camp cages. Now, a singer, probably tenor voiced and therefore able to carry above the outdoor sounds (unlike the basso profundo prisoners depicted on stage and screen), leads his companions in a centuries-old British folksong.[32] Cohn transcribed the verses as its leader calls out, "Who's gwine to buy my high-heeled shoes."[33] A hundred voices respond, "Who's gwine kiss my ruby-red lips / Who's gwine be my man." With allusions to fidelity and allure heating their thematic core, the lyrics suggest understandable concerns for gunmen and trusties alike. Both had to cope with years of imprisonment, isolated from home, and, in the words of another of their songs, with being "a long-time man." Presently the song trails off and the chopping continues. Group singing coordinated the fall of axes and the crush of hoes, and in a little while, another singer begins a number also timed to the day's task. "A tall column of song," Cohn concludes, "trembles on the air. For crime in Mississippi is expiated to music, and these Negro convicts on the state prison penal farm at Parchman sing at their work until they are released or die."[34]

At Parchman, and at other Southern penal farms of that era—Cummins and Tucker in Arkansas, the series of prisons set along the Brazos and Trinity rivers in Texas, and Angola in Louisiana—observers found a body of outdoor songs that African American convicts used to accompany their work. Like the military cadence chants heard in today's boot camps, many moved like fast-ticking clocks as four-man teams felled a tree, axes striking in strictly phased intervals. The clear pulsing rhymes of these songs were critical in regulating movement and so insuring the men's safety. Likewise, the songs that emerged with slower, solo tasks such as picking cotton allowed more ornate melodies and afforded singers a chance to develop them thematically. At whatever level the songs' narrative complexities and whatever speed they paced the work, their subjects ranged from the religious to the worldly. A number of them commented on the condition of imprisonment, the absence of companionship and warmth, and the presence of the captain overseeing their labors.

Fantasy and lived experience play out in the prisoners' songs. If one or another lyric tells of certain blue-eyed children, a wry indictment of the overseers in their miscegenations, others make trenchant observations on the economic and social system that surrounded the inmates' lives. During

August 1933, when John Lomax first came to Parchman for these "jumped-up pieces and sinful tunes," he recorded "Rosie," which the men sang while they hoed the fields.[35] In later years, both John and his son Alan documented the song at various prisons at least a dozen more times. While thoroughly a part of penal tradition, it might also speak for the Jim Crow South as a whole, given in the words of those who endured it: "Ain't but de one thing I done wrong," begins one verse, "Stayed in Mis'sippi jes' a day too long."[36] Other lyrics evoke the endless arc of blazing sun as the men worked from "can to can't." Recordings caught the sounds of axes and hoes punctuating "John Henry," the saga of a steel-driving hero, "Lost John," the celebration of a fleet-footed convict who eludes capture, and "Stewball," a reworking of an Anglo Irish racehorse ballad. Often localized and reset to the needs of the work pace, these songs offered, writes folklorist Harry Oster, who recorded at Louisiana's Angola prison, "a kind of control over the harsh world that he's [the convict] a part of . . . to convert it into something sharp and witty and clever."[37] A longtime prisoner at Angola pointed up that harshness in a guard's dismissive suggestion that in lieu of a drink from the water boy the convicts could draw the moisture lodged in the handles of their axes and hoes. "They mean," Roosevelt Charles told Oster, "by gettin' water outa the tools you'd hafta drink the sweat from yo' top lip."[38]

On March 8, 1937, John Lomax returned to Parchman for his third visit. Over the course of a single day, he recorded twenty-five songs. The numbers included two more renditions of "Rosie," a version of "Makes a Long Time Man Feel Sad," as well as "Stewball," "John Henry," and "Midnight Special." Other titles like "I Will Be So Glad When I Get Home" unambiguously addressed the prisoners' desire for freedom. Nearly all the songs were un-accompanied vocals, either solo or ensemble, but the session also featured three numbers accompanied with guitar, and two instrumentals, one of a train, another of a fox chase, played by a convict on harmonica. One of the performers, Jim Henry, had recorded for Lomax the previous spring. His evocative singing took place at Camp One, where Charlie Butler resided. Charlie himself recorded three songs that day: two solos, "You Don't Seem to Care" and "Diamond Joe," and one group number called "Have You Ever Been to Nashville." Apart from "Diamond Joe," and like his later session in 1939 when he again recorded "Diamond Joe" along with "It's Better to Be Born Lucky," all these pieces were identified as field hollers.

Sometimes called arhoolies, shouts, or whooping, the hollers are solo musi-cal plaints, typically sung by an individual engaged in a solitary task—a field hand following a mule in the blistering heat. Considered the foundation for the blues, the hollers provide opportunity to "play" with the voice. Flattened intervals, wavering tones, and vocal slides characterize these unaccompanied songs. Often improvised on the moment, sounding minor or modal, many hollers open with a steep call and then trace an elongated, jagged melodic descent. Within this pattern, arhoolie singers will linger on certain notes, then leap whole registers. In 1960, while recollecting his own field holler that he later set to a stinging electric slide guitar and thumping string bass and that became his first hit, Muddy Waters told Paul Oliver, "You might call them blues but they was just made-up things."[39]

This vibrato-rich, dwelling, moaning, twisting vocal style takes its place beside "the old Dr. Watts," an early type of highly individualized congregational singing that invested the slow hymns with such variation. Yet the vocal ornamentations of the hollers also look forward to the bottleneck guitar, its droning bass strings and bent treble notes that came to be played by bluesmen like Muddy Waters. Eddie "Son" House, once a Parchman inmate himself—and blues guitar exemplar to a young Muddy Waters—located the hollers historically in both the church and the field: "We'd call them old corn songs, old long meter songs."[40] Drawing from this tradition steeped in a rural experience that they themselves knew, Son House, Muddy Waters, and others used the field holler to evoke themes of individual longing and pervasive loneliness.[41]

These elements also appear in Charlie Butler's recordings. In "You Don't Seem to Care," he sings mournfully of a man in trouble. The song's narrator, confined to prison, laments that his woman possibly doesn't even know that he's there. "I'm getting along," he intones, but "next time I'm in trouble, long way from home, I just can't help it, I'll go ahead on." The song ends with, "There ain't but one thing I done wrong, I hung out in the Delta, Captain, one day too long." The worksong "Have You Ever Been to Nashville" draws on lyrics found in the "Midnight Special," in which the prisoner's woman comes up to the sergeant, "paper in her hand," seeking his pardon: "I wants my man." In May 1939, Charlie recorded one more solo field holler called "It's Better to Be Born Lucky." Here, a prisoner "troubled in mind" and weighted by hard fortune, knowing it's "better to be born lucky than be born blind," thinks about his woman, Sal. And when he does he "can't keep from crying."

The narrator in "Diamond Joe" likewise cries out for companionship. Just as the disc begins, Lomax says, "Now hit it this time hard," and Charlie begins to sing:

Refrain:
Diamond Joe, come-a git me,
Diamond Joe, come-a git me,
Diamond Joe, come-a git me,
Diamond Joe.

Went up on that mountain,
Give my horn a blow.
Thought I heard Miss Maybelle say,
"Yonder come my beau."

    Refrain

Spoken by another inmate: Talk it, man.

Ain't goin' work in the country,
And neith'r on Forrest's Farm.
I'm goin' stay till my Maybelle come,
And she goin' call-a me t'home.

    Refrain

Spoken: Sing it, boy. You can do it!

Ain't goin' tell you no story,
Neither would I lie.
Wonder did my Maybelle stay?
Did she keep on by?

    Refrain

Spoken: Sing "Joe," boy.

Diamond Joe, where'd you find him?
Diamond Joe, where'd you find him?
Diamond Joe, where'd you find him?
Diamond Joe.

    Refrain
Spoken: Talk it. Talk it.

Ain't goin' work in the country,
And neith'r on Forrest's farm.
I'm goin' stay 'til my Maybelle come,
And she gonna call-a me t'home.
Diamond Joe, come-a git me,
Diamond Joe, come-a git me,
Diamond Joe, my black Joe.[42]

Charlie shaped his sound—a rich, lyric baritone—with artistry. He moved fluidly from chest to head tones, through several timbres and vocal jumps,

Diamond Joe

Charlie Butler
AFS 941 B1

Dia - mond Joe___, come - a git me, Dia - mond Joe, come - a

git me, Dia-mond Joe, come - a git me, Dia-mond Joe___

Ain't goin' work in the coun-try___ and neith'r on For - rest's farm

I'm goin' stay till my May-belle come, and she goin' call - a me t'home, Dia-mond

Joe___, come a git me, Dia - mond Joe, come - a git me, Dia - mond

Joe___, come - a git me, Dia - mond Joe___

EXAMPLE 2. "Diamond Joe." Transcription by Mike Craver.

with confidant authority. No surprise, really, that a fellow inmate spurs him on during the recording, finally telling him to "talk it." That's an old-time way of saying that he'd hit his stride and his performance brimmed with life's truth. No wonder, too, that Alan Lomax wrote in the notes that accompanied the song's first issuing, referring here to Charlie, that "the singer was known in the whole prison as the man who could sing 'Diamond Joe.'"[43]

That the song has a specific, repeatable form Charlie reaffirms in his 1939 recording. Though bothered with a cough, he performs "Diamond Joe" much as he did two years earlier, the difference residing largely in its duration. After two choruses and verses of this May 24, 1939, performance, John A. Lomax interrupts him, telling him to "sing it again, but louder." Charlie responds, but not by raising his volume so much as by singing more deliberately. By leaning into specific words and shaping certain vowels in this performance and by raising and lowering pitch when he chooses, he steers the song with control and dynamics.

According to Ruby Lomax's notes, Charlie sang "Diamond Joe" twice that day. She also copied down an additional verse that Charlie sang with "Diamond Joe": "De woman I'm loving, took de train an' gone / (Oh, my heart is lovin') / I jes' can't help it, Capt'n, can't stand it long, / I can't be contented pardner, my doney done gone."[44] This verse adds another layer to the song's richness. "Captain" comes from prison lingo for the camp sergeant, and "doney" is an antiquated term, originally Spanish, for a sweetheart. In his 1942 notes for "Diamond Joe"'s first release, Alan Lomax stated that this song, as well as two hollers he sequenced it with, had been "colored by the thoughts of the convict."[45] Leaving aside that the recordings preserve traditional lines that have appeared in other songs, they do situate "Diamond Joe" in the prison experience.

Just before the 1939 recording John Lomax tried to pin down the nature of the piece.

> "What are you going to sing for me, Charlie?"
> "Sing anything," [Charlie replies], "An old field holler, boss . . ."
> [Then an indistinct remark, off mike, and Lomax asks:] "What are you going to sing now?"
> "Diamond Joe."
> "Where'd you learn it, Charlie?"
> "Out in the field."
> "Make it up?"
> "Yes sir. Learned it here."
> "All right, sing 'Diamond Joe.'"[46]

Charlie could have been giving Lomax a convenient answer in calling the song a field holler. Lomax made no secret that he found great interest in the field hollers and worksongs. However, if "Diamond Joe" was something Charlie sang in the fields and had learned at Parchman, it did not share certain features of his other field hollers. Alan Lomax noted this difference, too: "The melody of this song marks a departure from the ordinary 'holler.'"[47] "Diamond Joe" took neither an elongated solo form like other hollers nor did it operate as an antiphonal chant sung as the gunmen advanced the long line through the fields. Instead, "Diamond Joe" stands as a melodically compact piece indebted in form to the dance reels and social songs that antedated the blues. If the extra verse that Ruby Lomax transcribed underscores Alan

Lomax's perception of how localized these songs were to the prison experience, the opening verse that Charlie sang in 1937 helps set "Diamond Joe" within the larger tradition outside the walls.

"Went up on that mountain, / Give my horn a blow. / Thought I heard Miss Maybelle say, / 'Yonder come my beau.'"[48] Charlie's verse, admitting some variation, appears in numerous old-time songs, part of a common store of images. If the horn he has in mind carries associations of slavery times, appearing in songs that mention dinner horns or Gabriel's, the call to gather corn, the master's signal from the house to assemble, and even announcements of emancipation, it also carries associations of the hunt and the invitation to frolic. Either way, the horn beckons, and in this verse it hails, with a term drawn from the French language, someone's boyfriend. This happy sentiment runs a gamut of nineteenth-century secular folksongs both black and white. Banjo pieces, dance breakdowns, lyric songs, and ballads have all used this verse. No doubt Charlie Butler, or whoever showed Charlie Butler the song, came upon this verse earlier. Here the lines introduce a romantic element, a sentiment soon amplified by Maybelle's calling Charlie home. Similarly, other singers drew from a wide range of verses to shape their versions of "Diamond Joe."

The first scholar to document "Diamond Joe," North Carolina sociologist Howard Odum, made the point that any of the songs he gathered might shift in their usage. "Thus 'coon songs,' 'rag-times,' 'knife-songs,' 'devil-songs,' 'corn-songs,' 'work-songs,'—all alike may become love-songs or dancing 'breakdowns.'"[49] "Diamond Joe" was "a love-song," Odum wrote, "sung by a woman."[50] He collected it in Newton County, Georgia, between 1905 and 1908. Its first verse also functions as its chorus: "Diamon' Joe, you better come an' git me: / Don't you see my man done quit? / Diamon' Joe come'n git me." Diamond Joe serves as both the singer's companion who abandons her and someone she asks to comfort her. This ambiguity—perhaps ambivalence figures here, too—suggests a complexity of emotion housed in its three short verses.

As a sociologist, Odum found that the "study of the social songs [in which he included "Diamond Joe"] current among Southern negroes shows that they have arisen from every-day life, and that they portray many of the common traits and social tendencies."[51] Odum likened "Diamond Joe" to another song in his collection in which the protagonist escapes from both the police and his woman. He considered both numbers emblematic of domestic instability in the present-day black community. A version that he subsequently published, which includes a verse typically associated with "Goodnight Irene," addresses the realities of work, the need for food, and the doggedness of Diamond Joe to "drive on."[52] It leaves suicide the one other available option: "To jump in de river an' drown."[53]

Soon after Odum's initial publication of the song, E. C. Perrow reported a version collected from black informants in Mississippi in 1909. Here the refrain reads "Diamond Joe, Diamond Joe, / Run get me Diamond Joe."[54] This song does not concern romance, whether lost or found. Instead, it portrays a dice game, and in each verse the narrator calculates his increasingly higher throws. Finally, if he makes a nine, "then yo money will be mine."[55] With that stake in his pocket, he's able to eat. The song ends with "Then I'll buy me a bar'l o' flour / Cook and eat it every hour / Yes; an buy me a middlin' o' meat / Cook and eat it twict a week."[56]

The theme of gambling associated with "Diamond Joe" extends further with Dorothy Scarborough's 1925 printing of the African American blues ballad "Duncan and Brady," in which Diamond Joe appears fleetingly. With music hall gaiety, the song tells of Brady, a bullying policeman, shot by Duncan the bartender. Scarborough received the song from a local collector in Waco, Texas, who wrote her, clearly tongue in cheek: "It is easy to see that Diamond Joe had the ladies with him in the unfortunate affair."[57]

> Twinkle, twinkle little star,
> Brady come down on—Gabriel car,
> Kickin' out windows and knockin' out doors,
> Tryin' to play even with Diamond Joe!
> Been on a jolly so long![58]

If in the Perrow text Diamond Joe is called on to give luck to a laborer throwing dice, here he operates as a rakish figure with a moll on each arm. Varying images of Diamond Joe increase with each collected version, and this view of him as a gambler numbers among those that took hold. In spring 1926, Robert Winslow Gordon, who two years later founded the Archive of American Folk Song at the Library of Congress, made the first recordings of "Diamond Joe." The next year, launching a series of articles for the *New York Times Magazine,* he grouped it with "[Duncan and] Brady." Both, he said, fell in a category of "underworld or 'outlaw' songs," which often had their basis in actual events and concerned real figures.[59] While historians have confirmed Gordon's claim for Duncan and Brady, Diamond Joe still eludes factual identification. Whatever his historical basis, he had by then become an expansive character able to fill various roles. In these songs, he is part of the demimonde, someone special, someone with extraordinary powers. Gordon also pointed out that traditional singers call on a storehouse of verses, with the "ability to sew or patch them together as occasion demanded," much like the process of piecing a quilt.[60] Old lines form new wholes to create new sense. "Diamond Joe"'s changing texts attest to this compositional process, just as its melodic contour helps to define the song and its continuities.

In the tidewater community of Darien, Georgia, Gordon located two black solo singers who knew "Diamond Joe." He recorded the first, identified as A. Wilson, on April 15, 1926. Wilson sang, as did Perrow's sources, of buying a ham and a "middlin' of meat."[61] His basic story centered on the fact that "my honey sure done quit me." In the chorus, he asks that "Diamond Joe come get me, Diamond Joe." Gordon's second cylinder recording, made with an unidentified singer on May 3, 1926, suffers from much greater audio dropout, but the refrain is clearly the same as Wilson's. As an alternate refrain, the performer sings at the end "Diamond Joe, Diamond Joe, Diamond Joe," distinctively drawing out the vowels. The melodies of the songs Gordon received not only resemble one another, they show a kinship with Charlie Butler's. Like Charlie, in the chorus Wilson brings a two-note slur to the words "Diamond Joe."

"Diamond Joe"'s distinctive melody made itself heard again the following year. In March 1927, a young white string band calling themselves the Georgia Crackers, comprised of two brothers and their friend, waxed the song's first commercial recording. Their lyrics, too, celebrate the joys of the Southern diet: a sack of flour to make hoecake every hour, a peck of meal, a slice of meat once a week, and even a jug of whiskey "to make my baby frisky."[62] They framed the song's motive in the chorus: "Diamond Joe come and get me / My wife now done quit me / Diamond Joe, you better come get me / Diamond Joe."

Native Georgians Leon and Paul Cofer grew up in Hancock, a largely black county, some twelve miles from Sparta. Close in age to Charlie Butler, they learned not only from their father, a gospel hymn writer and singing school-teacher, but also from local black musicians—their neighbors, playmates, visitors, and employees of their father's sawmill plant. Among them, their younger brother, P.A., Jr., recalled "a bunch that lived about a mile from us . . . two boys about the age of Paul and Leon. . . . Paul and Leon would sing the same songs."[63] Music historian Gene Wiggins described these visits: "On some rainy days mill operations had to stop, and the workers, black and white, would spend the day on the Cofer porch, according to Jewell [the boys' sister], 'singing and carrying on.' . . . When night fell the workers would ride away still singing."[64] Of those voices moving into the distance, Jewell added, "Paul and Leon loved them." The result, audible in their recordings, led country music discographer Tony Russell to call their body of work "one of the most extensive and interesting repositories of black style and repertoire in recorded old-time music."[65]

Russell asked, "Did the brothers hear them [the songs] that way, or shape them according to their own musical standards?" At least with respect to "Diamond Joe," they used a melody similar to what Robert Winslow Gordon had recorded the year before in Darien, nearly two hundred miles away, and their text corresponds with verses found in black use. As for their own artistry, with their banjo and fiddle, and guitar accompaniment by their friend Ben Evans, they recorded "Diamond Joe" in the manner of a rough-hewn old-time ensemble. Their down-beat heavy pulse, plangent singing, and gritty fiddling made their music, as their sister affectionately observed, "not very aristocratic."[66] Her comment applies as much to their sound as to their sources.

It was that theme and this recording of the Georgia Crackers that Benjamin "Tex" Logan drew upon when he rewrote "Diamond Joe." In 1944 or '45, as an undergraduate at Texas Tech, he first came in contact with the song. A friend down the hall played the Georgia Crackers recording continuously, as it was his favorite. Tex reacted to its uniqueness: "You don't hear much of that in West Texas."[67] It stayed with him, and in 1956 he wrote new words to the Georgia Crackers' "Diamond Joe." "I started from that old record," Tex recalled, "and I wondered 'how did this all happen?'" He explained further:

> I got this idea, what I felt like it ought to be. To me, the story in it was that these two guys, Diamond Joe and the guy singing, were buddies, old buddies from way back. When they were single, they were tearing up the town like Boston, where I was living at the time.
>
> Well, the other guy finally got married and Diamond Joe probably went on his merry way. And this other fellow, his wife left him, like the verse says. And for good reason I suppose. . . . That line, "Diamond Joe, don't you know / She should have left me long ago," that's his concession right there. She'd been complaining 'cause he was a no-good-son-of-a-gun.
>
> So he started dreaming about the old days, "wouldn't things be great if we could go and do that again." So he says to Diamond Joe "come and get me." But really in his heart he knows it's not going to happen and he's trying to make out like he

CHAPTER 11

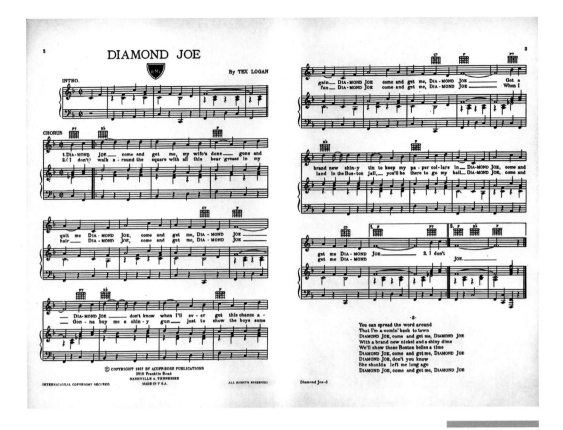

FIGURE 46.
Tex Logan's "Diamond Joe." Sheet music reproduced with Permission. Diamond Joe. Words and Music by Tex Logan. Copyright © 1957 Sony/ATV Music Publishing LLC, 8 Music Square West, Nashville, TN 37203. International Copyright Secured. All Rights Reserved.

can relive that past, "let's do it again." But that's just not possible. . . . He knows it's all over and too late.[68]

Tex wrote "Diamond Joe" on the fiddle, keeping the same tune as the Georgia Crackers but setting his new text to a special tuning (BF#BE). This allowed him to play harmony simultaneously with the melody, an effect he described as "a sorrowful sound in contrast to the lyrics."

He sent a tape he recorded of himself doing "Diamond Joe" to Wilma Lee and Stoney Cooper. He had met them in 1948 at radio station WWVA and later accompanied them on the road. Their 1957 recording with banjo and steel guitar made his song public. Tex himself never recorded the song for release but he did play it in a group with Peter Rowan in the late 1970s. That exposure led former Rowan bandmate David Grisman to introduce it to Jerry Garcia, who recorded it with his acoustic band in 1987. Other bluegrass musicians took it up, including Boston bandleader and mandolinist Joe Val.[69] Summing up the several forms it has taken, Tex said Wilma Lee did it "mountain style," while he considered his own version "bluegrass style."[70]

When Tex listened to Charlie Butler's "Diamond Joe" on the *Treasury,* he made only a "vague connection" between that and what he had heard from the Georgia Crackers. The thread that led from them to their neighbors, and the larger thread that includes the Gordon recordings, the texts in Odum and Perrow, and even Tex's own composition, forms a musical and verbal continuity. Across them all the image of Diamond Joe remains an independent spirit, someone one could turn to, someone able to improve one's lot. But in contrast to what the Georgia Crackers expressed on their record, Tex said, "Charlie is singing to a different purpose."

No doubt Tex Logan is right. As his live performances show, he treated the song as a driving virtuoso fiddle showpiece played in an entirely different musical context, to a wholly different audience, and telling a vastly different story than does Charlie. Still, a point Tex made about songwriting spans all these differences and runs through all these versions: "I like a song," said Tex Logan, "that's got a simple, obvious meaning but a deeper meaning at the same time."[71] He caught the spirit of "Diamond Joe" perfectly.

—————

For the first release of Charlie Butler's "Diamond Joe," Alan Lomax wrote that it "refers to a character mentioned often in American folksong; but so far as my questioning has gone, no one has yet explained who he was."[72] In 1961, singer Bessie Jones gave Lomax an answer. As a child she had "pranced" to it with her playmates. She says:

> It's a person in trouble. You know, an' he calls for somebody to come an' git 'im. Jist like you off from home? You know, you can't git nothin' an' can't git back. They say, that's what the song—They off, ya know, 'way off, an' so they say, "You better come an' git me."
>
> AL: Well, who was Diamond Joe?
>
> BJ: I don't know. I guess Diamond Joe was just the one who got some money. See, like I'd send back to you to tell ya to come an' git me. Or send back to my parents, you know. Hit *mean* money. 'Cause Diamond Joe jus' natchully mean money, ya know. But for somebody to sell a diamon', ya know, is money, that what they meant then. But the Joe, I reckon, that was just some*body* sayin' to come an' git me. Any-anyone that got money come an' git me. 'Cause Diamond Joe, I need to come home![73]

In a separate file, presumably intended for a songbook or record notes, Lomax refers to Perrow's "Diamond Joe" text as "one of the songs a gambler on a losing streak sings." Before integration in the South, he adds, "a Negro depended for survival and personal safety on the protection and friendship of some white man."[74] He then tells a story based on his 1947 interviews with Big Bill Broonzy, Memphis Slim, and Sonny Boy Williamson about an Arkansas labor contractor who had this power and sense of justice.[75] His account fits in its own way with the social environment of the song and the economic structures that surrounded it—a core that Bessie Jones identified.

The song's association with money appears in another of its settings, one that Lomax's father knew. In November 1935, John A. Lomax recorded J. D. Dillingham, a former train conductor from Texas. Dillingham worked for many years on the Houston and Texas Central Railroad, keeping his home in Austin. He was a skilled banjo player with an articulate knowledge of black banjo styles that he demonstrated on other recordings. Here he sings "Diamond Joe" in a gentle voice without accompaniment.[76] "Diamond Joe," Dillingham says in the introductory note printed in *Our Singing Country,* "was a Texas cattleman, the story goes, so rich that he was said to wear diamonds for his vest buttons. I learned this song years ago."[77] John Lomax's third edition of *Cowboy Songs* (1938) makes that date more specific. There Dillingham points to the song's popularity in central Texas some sixty years earlier. Assuming his remark also dates from then, that would put the song in circulation by 1875.[78]

In it a young cowboy speaks about his work. Early in the song we learn about Diamond Joe: "He's a rich old jay with lots of cowboys in his pay." The cowboy narrator explains his background with images familiar to the black versions of the song. "I left my gal in a Texas shack, / And told her I was a-coming back; / But I lost at cards, then got in jail, / Then found myself on the Chisholm Trail."[79] He has few prospects beyond going from one job to another, and admits not being especially moved to work for someone as well off as Diamond Joe. In a verse that didn't fit on the 1935 recording but was included in the printed texts, the song concludes with a touch of good riddance: "When my summons come to leave this world, / I'll say good-by to my little girl; / I'll fold my hands when I have to go / And say farewell to Diamond Joe."

This theme of economic protest reappears in the version first recorded by Cisco Houston in 1952 for an album of western songs.[80] Here "Diamond Joe" finds its basis in "State of Arkansas," a traditional song that spoofs the rugged conditions of the Ozark frontier. Historian Guy Logsdon, citing Lomax's *Cowboy Songs,* which contained both the Dillingham "Diamond Joe" and "State of Arkansas," speculates that either Houston or, more likely, singer and songwriter Lee Hays made the unattributed adaptation.[81] At that time, the most widely known version of "State of Arkansas" had been recorded by Lee Hays for the 1947 album *Sod Buster Ballads,* which he made with Woody Guthrie, Pete Seeger, and Millard Lampell.[82] Hays included there a spoken interlude about working in Arkansas. With that piece's success in integrating humor with music, it does not seem a stretch that Hays, a creative songwriter with traditional materials (including partial responsibility for "If I Had a Hammer"), gravitated to this model to fashion a new song. *Sing Out!* magazine, a publication closely allied with both Cisco Houston and Lee Hays, called it "Cisco Houston's version," implying its traditionality, and attributed the verse with "his bread it was corn dodger and his meat I could not chaw" to the "State of Arkansas" ballad as the song's source for both words and music, mentioning, too, the Lee Hays performance.[83] So it was that this traditional-sounding song based on an older folk model has gone into circulation veiled as traditional in origin. Ramblin' Jack Elliott recorded it at least three times, and Bob Dylan covered it, too (as well as recording separately the Georgia Crackers version of "Diamond Joe").[84] The notes to Elliott's 1960 Monitor recording suggest that Diamond Joe "whose original identity is now lost, epitomizes the old time cattle baron."[85]

Another theory about "Diamond Joe"'s meaning has more lately emerged. One person who happened upon the Charlie Butler recording was Art Thieme, a professional folksinger who in the late 1980s spent three years performing for sightseers aboard the Illinois River steamboat *Julia Belle Swain.* "The job," he wrote to the Archive, "has given me a fine reason to do research into river songs and lore. One of the things I uncovered was a ton of great information on Joseph Reynolds and his Diamond Jo Steamboat Line."[86] Reynolds's fleet plied the upper Mississippi from 1862 to 1911. High up on the side of each boat appeared his company emblem, "a large diamond with the name 'JO' in the middle of it." From this Thieme speculated that the subject of Charlie Butler's song may not have been a person but a steamboat.

This attractive idea has taken on a life of its own. What Art Thieme called a "gut feeling" about the song and the Diamond Jo line acquired the weight of printed authority, appearing with the song listing in *Country Music Sources,* a major scholarly work. In the headnote to "Diamond Joe" the editors repeat, without attribution to Thieme, his surmise about the steamboat.[87] They further mention the years the company stayed in business and how each boat bore the diamond-shaped trademark. Art Thieme's research, now dislodged from its creator—his idea also appears in Web discussions of the song—has increasingly gained public acceptance.

To be sure, a summons to a steamboat with its implicit promise of freedom might well have appealed to Parchman's Charlie Butler. The weight of evidence, however, does not show that this poetic image inspired his folksong. For one thing, the Diamond Jo line did not operate in the South.[88] Though certainly prominent in its day, it ran from St. Paul on the upper Mississippi no farther than St. Louis, its southern terminus. Moreover, a number of boats working this portion of the river had a different hull design that better suited northern waters than those below. *Way's Packet Directory* accordingly lists few Diamond Jo craft sold to companies that plied the lower portion of the river, and those firms invariably repainted Reynolds's distinctive diamond-shaped logo. Possibly some riders received from their passenger agents steamboat passes that sported the emblem. The Diamond Jo railroad line that Reynolds also owned did come closer to Charlie's location, but that was a small venture, with two locomotives on a narrow gauge line running between Malvern and Hot Springs, Arkansas, twice a day.[89] In full operation for just over a decade, by 1902 it changed hands and again the trademark disappeared. Given these conditions, Reynolds's southern ventures on rail and river, locally remote and largely unknown, would have made little sense to Charlie's prison mates.

I have found but two musical references to Diamond Joe as the name of a boat. One appears in a version of "John Henry" sung in Charleston, West Virginia. The singer reported that in the 1880s a boat called the Diamond Joe worked the Kanawha: "John Henry sent for his shaker, / But he didn't want to go; / John Henry says, 'Just one more round before going down, / I'm shipping on the Diamond Joe.'"[90] Indeed, West Virginia coal district records and boat listings for the Diamond Coal Company of Pittsburgh and the Diamond Transportation Company of Charleston, West Virginia, show that both used steam-powered, stern-wheel towboats. *Way's Steam Towboat Directory* names three, all of them called "Diamond," though not "Diamond Joe." Two were licensed solely for the Ohio River, leaving only one boat that actually navigated the lower river. She burned in April 1894.[91]

The other musical use arises in the third verse of W. C. Handy's 1914 hit "St. Louis Blues." Handy created his songs from the folklife and traditional music around him. The Diamond Jo steamboat line was well known in St. Louis, where its fleet reversed course to go back up the river. In his song, the Diamond Jo allusion amplifies the first verse with its "St. Louis woman, wid her diamon' rings, / Pulls dat man roun' by her apron strings."[92] The third verse continues this line of glittering imagery. Here Diamond Joe cuts the figure of the gambler rake, akin to the one in "Duncan and Brady": "You ought to see dat stovepipe brown of mine, / Lak he owns de Dimon Joseph line." The verse goes on about his striking appearance, his skill at craps, his punctuality at work, and his being a good touch for a ten-dollar loan. Hale and hearty he might well be, but not the answer to Charlie Butler's pleas.

Given the details we have, it seems unlikely that Charlie's song was, as Art Thieme wrote in his initial letter to the Archive, "a plea to a boat to come and take the singer away."[93] Since then he has come to feel it was probably wishful thinking on his part, a point he has since made on both internet postings and in his notes to a recent album: "I am possibly wrong about my steamboat connection idea as expressed on this CD—but the romantic side of me wants my theory to, somehow, some day, prove true."[94]

Still, Thieme's theory takes its place within a larger network of ideas. His excavation of the Diamond Jo emblem as the object of Charlie Butler's metaphor makes sense. Here, as we make our way deeper into the world of the song, mystery man Diamond Joe recedes and a riverboat comes forward. To those who lived within range of its whistle, the steamboat was like the railroad that succeeded it—a symbol of freedom and power for those who had no freedom and power. In the American historical landscape it provided a lyric embodiment of the hopes and dreams of many in its time. What is so interesting here is that the idea of a rescuing vessel *already* had a place in Parchman lore.

The 1938 WPA state guide to Mississippi's entry on Parchman pointed out it was best seen on visitor's day, scheduled in months that had five Sabbaths. On that fifth Sunday, "a train called the Midnight Special brings the visitors to the farm, arriving about dawn and leaving at dusk. The Negro prisoners have made up ballads about the train which they sing and chant while they work, waiting for the fifth Sunday. One song is: 'Heah comes yo' woman, a pardon in her han' / Gonna say to de boss, I wants mah man / Let the Midnight Special shine its light on me.'"[95] In 1932, Mississippi Governor Mike Conner established at Parchman what he called the "mercy court," essentially parole hearings that he attended with two colleagues.[96] William Banks Taylor traced its history into the 1940s, illustrating it with a verse taken from the "Midnight Special." As in the song, families did come, usually women arguing for pardons on behalf of their "forgotten men," the term Governor Conner used for these inmates. The connection with the song finds another local basis in that from 1920 on the Midnight Special train left Jackson at 12:05 on Sunday mornings to begin its trip to the Parchman Station, arriving there at dawn for the recently established family visitation day. Taylor adds that the belief had gone around that those bathed in its light would get their pardon.

Former warden Donald Cabana (once a guard there himself) encountered the same legend but, in the way of folklore, with some difference. Cabana recalled that the inmate who first *saw* the train's headlight would be freed.[97] Either way, at Parchman that train was visible to only one camp, and that was Camp One, where Charlie Butler lived.

While "Midnight Special" was known and recorded at Parchman, it made the rounds of other penitentiaries. Singers there, too, localized it to their circumstances. We saw that in "Have You Ever Been to Nashville" Charlie Butler himself sang a core verse of "Midnight Special," his woman coming for a pardon, piece of paper in her hand. The song shifts with the locale just as the song shifts in locating itself in other songs. This same process applies to "Diamond Joe."

Unconfined to any one setting, Diamond Joe's identity dodges a single answer. In recent years, music historians and folk enthusiasts have embraced the thought of Diamond Joe as a steamboat. Even if not found in regional folk use, this reading reflects habits of mind of these observers. Certainly there is precedence for vehicles like the Midnight Special offering deliverance in folksong and story. Other accounts, no less rooted in their cultural environments, make different sense of the title. Marilyn Corbin, who served under eleven superintendents at Parchman as administrative assistant, drew on her years at the prison when she first heard Charlie Butler's lyrics. Her reaction to "Diamond Joe"'s refrain of "come and get me" made her wonder if it weren't an inmate's call to a future employer. Parole boards at Parchman, she explained, tended to look favorably on those prisoners, hard put to create new lives after captivity, who had work promised them on release: "It was advantageous to have someone write."[98] Parchman's files brim with such letters, offered as a kind of insurance policy, a stopgap against a parolee's return to crime (Kelly Pace, lead singer of "Rock Island Line," had similar letters in his Arkansas state file). Ultimately, Marilyn Corbin's impression of Charlie's song doesn't stray that far from Bessie Jones's view. Bessie also thought of Diamond Joe as a person with money, a figure empowered to aid someone in trouble. All of these interpreters—a veteran prison official versed in parole board hearings, a traditional singer raised on the Georgia Sea Islands, or a coffeehouse performer filled with historical curiosity—respond to different social circumstances and frame their thoughts according to their experiences. While the Diamond Joe image consistently conveys yearning, an answer to a prayer, the fact that it speaks to us in so many ways brings to mind what Paul Oliver found to be as true of recorded blues as of vernacular architecture.

"Diamond Joe" in its variety reflects a view from the ground, a sense of the local, the feel of a place. Whatever Charlie Butler may have thought about the song, all we have is less than twenty seconds of his commentary. As a subject of study "Diamond Joe" offers a limited number of texts and even fewer recordings. Yet each fragment of the song's history, its settings, its concerns—the transactions surrounding food, the instability of home life, the gambling and the swells, the desire for freedom, and a prisoner's need for love from inside a Mississippi penitentiary that mirrored the longings of those on the outside—each testimony tells us something about the era to which this song bears witness. "The subject clearly demands more research," writes Paul Oliver, referring to "the songster's involvement in his material as he adapted it to suit his chosen context."[99] At least we have the effervescent insights of Bessie Jones and the thoughtful reflections of Tex Logan. Like the countless buildings in Oliver's encyclopedia, the song adapted to local conditions, cultures, and economies, its meanings altering with its audiences and the discernment of its singers.

Nowadays, a traveler moving through the ink-black darkness along Mississippi's Highway 49 finds that the amber horizon glowing in the distance will eventually reveal a searing battery of sodium vapor lamps staring down on the maximum security units at Parchman. When I visited there in January 1997, the separated camps where Charlie and his fellow inmates once lived had been dismantled. Prisoners still wore the ring-arounds, but they had different colors now, denoting their assigned levels of custodial classification. Only those with green and white stripes could spend time away from their cells. Black and white stripes indicated a greater security risk. Inmates obliged to wear red stripes had no privileges at all. They could leave their cells an hour a day, but only to spend time in another caged area. Parchman has become a place of fences and cellblocks, no longer fields and turnrows.

Virtually all the outdoor music is also gone. Sergeant Burchfield still remembered the work chants in the days of the long line. "They made their own songs," he said. "Most were about 'a two-timing woman' or a religious song." By the late 1960s, those songs had stopped. "When it integrated," he said, "it quieted down."[100] Black and white prisoners did not share the songs of outdoor labor. In April 1960, Wendell Cannon, a musician and former campaign manager for Governor Ross Barnett, came to Parchman as its first music director. Given the authority to relieve convicts from their work, he had two professional bands established by November, touring the state in a bus. One was the white band, the Insiders, and the other their black counterpart, the Stardusters. "Up until then," his daughter Dede Cannon told me, "the music was out in the fields."[101]

At first, for two afternoons a week, the bands rehearsed, the black one playing rhythm and blues, and the white one, country. They rehearsed in the same room, which allowed the players to learn from one another. In the early 1970s, the bands desegregated and the two groups became one. Wendell Cannon, who also ran the prison's baseball leagues, said that "sports and music are the most efficient tools of integration, racially as well as culturally."[102] By the 1980s, the band had rehearsals throughout the week, with dancers coming from the women's prison to augment its enlarged line-up of drums, horns, and guitars. Dede, who worked for the parole service then, listed their styles like an index of the American pop songbook: country, blues, fifties rock, reggae, disco, funk, and sentimental all made it on their set list. "From Kenny Rogers, Lionel Ritchie," she said, "to Conway Twitty."[103] They had become "a stage band" and they recorded three albums. Dede herself sang with them and wrote several songs the group performed. They finally disbanded with her father's death in 1996.[104]

The Library's recordings at Parchman came as a surprise to Dede. She had no idea "that records got made of those men singing outdoors like that."[105] The music that she, her father, and the Parchman band made reflected another time and a different professionalism. Still, the band gave the prisoners a chance to get off the line, and while they played, some said that for a time they didn't think about being imprisoned. They appeared at the Mississippi state fair, some rodeos, and whatever events involved the Department of Corrections and its efforts at public outreach. For the musicians, the band let them out into the world, even if a trusty-shooter stood nearby. In the end, how different is what they sought from Charlie Butler's singing to Diamond Joe? No one wants to go to Parchman and nobody wants to stay there. Maybe that's why the envelope addressed to Charlie came back the way it did: "Gone free left no address." Diamond Joe had come and got him.

Jess Morris

Boiled Shirt and Cowboy Boots

T O OPEN THE JESS MORRIS "CORPORATE SUBJECT" FILE at the Archive of Folk Culture is to release a veritable flood of clippings, letters, and postcards brimming with the Texas fiddler and singer's picturesque experiences and expansive personality. Other collections harbor the same unsinkable spirit, from the autographed sheet music he sent the Wyoming State Archives to the musical autobiography he provided the *Amarillo Sunday News and Globe,* from an update he returned to his college alumni office to heated moments he shared with the Texas Folklore Society. In one 1940 letter to the *Fort Worth Star-Telegram* he acknowledges with mock biblical solemnity that "I have learned, that: 'He that tooteth not his own horn, the same shall not be tooted.'"[1] A year earlier, writing to John A. Lomax, and dismayed over a proposed recording session in which he could not participate because of the distance to Washington, D.C., Jess (1878–1953) ruefully observes, "I guess that they will get some 'pretty boy' from Hollywood that don't know a cow from a giraffe, to sing their cowboy songs." Lomax responds to this sentiment on the letter's margin, "This is probably true."[2]

Nor has the Folk Archive been able to confine Jess to a single file cabinet. Once, while researching a totally unrelated subject, I happened upon a folder labeled "Johnson, Lyndon." The future president had forwarded to the

Archive a 1952 letter from "a constituent of mine, Mr. Jess Morris."[3] Duncan Emrich, then head of the Folk Archive, wrote back to Senator Johnson about the forthcoming release of what Jess called a "large record," a point Emrich explained as "his interpretation of the fact we are issuing his 'Goodbye, Old Paint' on a 'long-playing record' later this fall."[4] Shortly before this exchange, in another of his typed postcards to Emrich, Jess implored, "I wrote you . . . last . . . Saturday, and told you to use the Ol' Paint, anyway you saw fit. Mr. Emrich, can't you get The Hon. Lyndon Johnson and The Hon. Tom Connally, to write the proper Authorities, in Austin, Texas, to let me hang my picture alongside of Jean Autry, in their 'Hall of Fame' in the Capitol Building in Austin? I can't see that 'JEAN,' has anything on me, unless it's his beautiful teeth. Sincerely, Ol' JESS."[5]

Ol' Jess lived many of the realities that Gene Autry portrayed on the movie screen. Like the wide open spaces Autry traversed by projectionist's lamp, Jess knew firsthand the unbroken range of the Texas Panhandle, the last of the long-distance cattle drives, and the all-night ranch dances reachable only by horse-drawn wagon. He also embodied a cultural breadth that exceeds cinematic stereotype. On the day Jess died, his hometown Dalhart newspaper observed that "Morris was a genuine son of the Old West. He was as much at home in a tuxedo, boiled shirt and bow tie playing classical music on a violin, as he was in levis, loud shirt, big hat, and cowboy boots playing the lilting tunes of the Old West on his fiddle."[6] Schooled as a sight reader and knowledgeable as an ear player, Jess's expertise gave him ease, the obituary continued, at both "cowboy dances and high-falutin' formal balls."

His community remembered him especially for "Goodbye, Old Paint," a song he learned in childhood. It became his signature number, one that he copyrighted and published. His contribution to the piece mattered to him to the end of his life as he waited anxiously for its release on a Library of Congress album of cattle calls and cowboy songs. Conscious of its place in folk tradition, Jess wrote detailed, even notarized accounts of how he made this song his own. With "Goodbye, Old Paint," he grappled with questions of culture and ownership, and by extension, of what is ours, individually and collectively. Fully able to tell a giraffe from a cow, Jess's penetrating combination of horse sense and refinement not only fit his own past, it underlies his gift to America.

"Each generation," Vera Skelton Morris writes in her 1983 genealogy centered on Jess's parents, his brothers and sisters, and their families, "seems to be confronted with their own 'Red Sea—you can't go over it or under it or around, So you go through it.'"[7] In her handwritten manuscript that she keeps in a large three-ring binder, the looseleaf pages left unnumbered to incorporate new information as it arises, Vera traces the journey the Morrises made from the mid-Atlantic to the Texas Panhandle. She credits the biographical efforts that one of Jess's sisters began years before. By 1910, Lulah Lee Morris Frederick (1881–1930) had started scribbling notes on envelopes, her husband's business stationery, and old bills—whatever lay handy—to compile the family's story. Vera built upon these memos by researching the Morris name, locating deeds and land grants, gathering cemetery listings, tax rolls, military records, census data, photographs, and family poetry. Interested in the wider social environments that the Morrises faced along their westward trek, she also read county histories and looked up local mortality schedules. She correlated those reports of cholera, dysentery, flux, scarlet fever, and consumption—common diseases in pioneer times—with Morris family deaths. "I tried, above all else, to be accurate," Vera explains, "in case of family disputes and bets are settled on the contents herein."[8]

The earliest of Vera's documents reaches back to the family's patriarch, Ezekiel Morris (1744–ca. 1823), a Pennsylvanian who fought as a private second class in the colonial army. In the war's aftermath Ezekiel took advantage of newly opened public lands, and in 1804 moved from Washington County, Pennsylvania, to Pickaway Township in southern Ohio, near the town of Circleville, five years before the county officially formed. President Thomas Jefferson signed his land grant, with Secretary of State James Madison adding his authority to the certificate. Other Morrises, coming from Pennsylvania and New Jersey, joined Ezekiel there, and for the next three generations, this part of Ohio was the family's primary home.

"Wide awake [and] well to do," comments one nineteenth-century recollection of Ezekiel's nephew John Morris, a judgment that could apply to all his kinsmen in Pickaway County.[9] Biographical histories from this period repeatedly characterize the Morrises as early pioneers who rose to social and civic prominence. They typically had families of eight to fifteen children, and without the benefit of inherited wealth, thrived as independent farmers and stock raisers. Their properties ranged from eighty to a thousand acres. With no known convicts or criminals to tarnish their name, various Morrises served as county commissioners, justices of the peace, and township trustees. Ezekiel, for one, sat on the first jury trial held in Pickaway Township. In his 1820 will, he describes himself as a "yeoman," leaving his acreage, house, furniture, cash, horses, and cows to his wife and ten children. Another Morris property inventory from 1839 highlights the era's requirements, listing such everyday items as a plow, skillet, tin ware, saddle and bridle, log chain, a pair of pocket pistols, scythe, and a red calf. The Ohio-based Morrises, Vera found, approached this frontier much as the one they settled out west: "They don't wait for fate or divine intervention. . . . If they don't like a situation or circumstance, they change it by one means or another."[10]

In 1820, Jess's paternal grandfather, John Atchison Morris, moved to west-central Indiana. There he purchased eighty acres of public land, recorded in a transfer signed by Andrew Jackson. Along with members of his wife's family, John soon joined the Christian Church (also called the Disciples of Christ) founded by Alexander Campbell following the Second Great Awakening. As a believer in adult baptism, Morris received this rite in the Wabash River near Covington, Indiana. By then he had relocated to Fountain County, where his first child, Edward James Morris, was born in 1834 (d. 1921). John uprooted his family three more times, first to Danville, Illinois, and then to two different locales in Missouri. He died in 1848 outside of Springfield, leaving fifteen-year-old Edward (E.J.) to head the household. Sometime during the intervening years John Morris's maternal uncle, John King, moved to Texas. King's daughters and their husbands settled in Denton County and along the Trinity River. They all brought with them their Campbellite belief. Whether for reasons of family, faith, or personal future, E. J. Morris likewise led his widowed mother and seven brothers and sisters to Texas in 1849. E.J. became a circuit-riding lay preacher in his father's denomination, a calling he followed for the rest of his life. (In 1884 the *Texas Gazetteer and Business Directory* listed E.J. as a "Christian minister in Bartlett."[11]) For now, the Morrises traveled by oxcart, joining a wagon train making its way from Missouri to the dark soil of Williamson County.

E.J. and his family arrived with the last wave of statehood-era settlers who chose this part of central Texas, a blackland prairie, to both farm and raise cattle. The Morrises alighted at Donahoe Creek, a small community a mile and a half from what thirty years later became the town of Bartlett. Its attractions included the creek's lively running-water supply and land that sold for five dollars an acre. That property value markedly increased during the years E.J. lived in this area, an upsurge from which he materially benefited.[12] By 1854 he was working as a freighter. His trips to the ports of Houston and Galveston, made by ox team, usually took between four and six months. The length of these journeys varied with Brazos River flood levels and the progress his animals made lumbering across stretches of mud and quicksand. E.J. transported locally produced items that probably included ground corn, animal hides, and pecans, and returned home with supplies of calico, wheat flour, sugar, salt, tobacco, ammunition, and firearms.[13] The 1860 census enumerated E.J. as a laborer residing in neighboring Bell County with a land value of $250 and a personal estate of $200. It listed his local post office as Belton, a stagecoach stop and the newly established county seat.[14] Three years earlier he wed Mary S. Allison. This short-lived marriage produced two sons. He owned no slaves.

In June 1862, E.J. joined the First Texas Mounted Rifles, a Confederate cavalry unit assembling in Belton. With a total county population of just over four thousand, eleven hundred Bell County men joined the Confederate army (with three hundred more volunteering for the Union). Only a third of them returned. The regimental records, which include his picture, describe him as a farmer, six feet tall with blue eyes and auburn hair. Holding the rank of private throughout his service, he was detailed as a provost guard. By then E.J.'s two brothers closest to him in age had also enlisted. One of them, William, joined the same company with E.J., attaining the rank of fourth corporal. After serving along the lower Rio Grande and the San Bernard rivers, E.J. and William saw action in Louisiana and Arkansas. Their brother John, attached to a separate unit, suffered battle wounds and died days before his twenty-first birthday, while William was taken prisoner and placed in a Union stockade in New Orleans. Jess's nephew Bob Morris told me that E.J.'s brothers both had been shot in the war, with one wounded on the left side and the other on the right. Nearly a century after this traumatic event in his family's and the nation's life, Jess wrote to Duncan Emrich that his father, though wearing a Confederate uniform, "really did not want to fight against the Government."[15]

While stationed at a camp 250 miles from Belton, E.J. received word from his mother, who urgently sought his help. With her older sons away at the war, she had become unable to keep enough provisions for herself and the three youngest of E.J.'s five siblings still living with her. "She has rode," E.J. noted, "in search of corn some three or four days and had procured but a very small quantity."[16] Concerned for their welfare, E.J. wrote to his captain, James Swan Bingham: "I love both my mother and my country but the love for my mother predominates over that for my country in this instance, and if you can feasibly give the leave of absence for which I have asked you, you shall have the prayers of a widowed mother and a fatherless son." In a warmly phrased reply, Bingham granted E.J. furlough home, allowing him to help with the crops and livestock.

The war also affected E.J.'s second wife, Lucy Lee Hughes (1842–1915), a native Tennessean who came to Bell County via Arkansas in 1859. Her first husband, Andrew Jackson Felton, died soldiering for the Confederacy, a victim of pneumonia following a case of measles. At the time of A. J. Felton's death—he numbered among the last volunteers in that community to enlist—he and Lucy Lee had two sons, one two years old and the other only eight months. Family writings allude to both their vulnerability and the hardship Lucy Lee faced as solitary head of her household. Though a state tax to provide assistance to families of Confederate soldiers passed in 1862, within two years the worsening economic climate reduced that aid by two-thirds. In 1868, still in perilous times, she and E. J. Morris married. Together they had seven more children, with their fifth, Jess, born ten years after they wed.

Jess's few available comments about his upbringing in Williamson and Bell counties focus largely on music. Apart from their value in documenting "Goodbye, Old Paint," his words offer a glimpse into his early home life. As a preacher's son, Jess said his father "didn't want any fiddlers in the family."[17] E.J.'s resistance echoed his church's rejection of instrumental music in their liturgy. Some believers felt strongly that musical accompaniment to psalms, hymns, and spiritual songs signified human vanity and contradicted scripture. Tensions over appropriate worship practices coupled with debate about the role of missionary work led the church to split. E.J., however, remained with the Disciples of Christ.

In 1890, E.J. and Lucy Lee relocated their family (minus her two sons by her first marriage, who by then had established themselves locally and would soon affiliate with the new church) to a ranch thirty miles west of Amarillo, near the future site of Vega, Texas.[18] "It wasn't even settled then," Bob Morris explained.[19] "They wanted something new. New country." For the next six years E.J. raised free-range horses and sheep there, his last major undertaking before retirement. He also continued his circuit-riding ministry, keeping intact his suspicions about fiddle music and its frivolity. As Jess launched his ranch dance ensemble and traveled all around Amarillo and Dalhart, he recalled his father in those years "watching me pretty close."[20]

E.J. maintained a tightly disciplined regime with a zeal, he later admitted, that he regretted. Al Morris, E.J.'s first-born child with Lucy Lee, remembered how his father insisted that he and his siblings must unfailingly attend church services. No matter how wet or snowy the day, Al found himself on horseback behind his father, aware that once he got there, his work had just begun. "Inside the warm church," Al knew "he had better not go to sleep during the sermon or he'd catch hell!"[21] But apart from that one regular public outing, "Paw never wanted us to go anywhere. He said if 'we wanted entertainment we could stay at home and read the Bible.' All we wanted to do was to go to play-parties and eat tea cakes."[22] Vera, Al's daughter-in-law, described how E.J.'s domestic rule affected Jess, too, prompting him to follow his siblings' example: "Jess preferred music to being a cowboy. Nothing wrong with that—except to his father, who didn't allow his children to dance, gamble, smoke, drink, cuss—They did it all, as most PK's do (Preacher's Kids)."[23] E.J.'s granddaughter Elizabeth Morris Roberts also recalled their response to him: "Their father was a minister. . . . He was one of those ministers that traveled. He was a Campbellite . . . like Church of Christ but a little different. All those children were bought up with very strict upbringing. So that when they did get away from home, boy, they didn't even go to church. But they could quote the Bible. . . . My father [Sam Morris] he knew the Bible in and out. . . . But he would [also] read that Gautama Buddha and Confucius—all of them. He just thought one was as good as the other. He was very much a Christian, but he was just a free thinker actually."[24] A second later she added, "Uncle Jess claimed that he did not believe in God, or didn't believe in an afterlife . . . that he was an atheist. And we use to laugh at him about it. But I think [this came about] because they [he] had a very strict upbringing, just so strict." Though Jess's obituary names him a member of Dalhart's Church of Christ, according to Bob Morris, Jess neither attended church nor for that matter played hymns on his fiddle.

"They each had minds of their own," said Elizabeth about Jess and his brothers and sisters. "My God," she exclaimed, "I think all that family did." If their father's religious resolve affected their choices about faith, so, too, did his embrace of the written word. Elizabeth's father, Sam, for example, wrote poetry throughout his life, penning hundreds of verses, often on western themes and the region's development. While some poems, largely humorous, stayed within the family, others made their way into publication, and even marked the dedication of public buildings.[25] Though Sam's brothers and sisters—specifically Jess—didn't write poems themselves, Elizabeth recalled that "the entire family, they were all well read. I think their father insisted on it, that they read books. And not just the Bible. They read literature. . . . I remember when my father would say, 'I don't want to go to school today. I don't feel good.' And he [E.J.] would say 'All right. Sit down and read. You'll

Jess Morris

FIGURE 47.
The Morris family,
Amarillo (or pos-
sibly Dalhart),
Texas, ca. 1905.
*Left to right,
standing:* John, Al,
Sally, Sam, Jess;
seated: Lulah, E.J.,
Lucy Lee, Annie.
Courtesy of
Vera Morris.

learn more here anyway.'"[26] Early in those years, Jess's literacy extended to his chosen instrument.

Jess played classical violin. He took lessons in Bartlett with a "Professor Kuler," who had studied violin in Milan, Italy.[27] "He was quite a musician," Jess remembered. John R. Kuler (1835–1903), a Norwegian emigrant, and identified in Bell County annals as a musician, wallpaper hanger, and house painter, came from Texas's Brazoria County to Bartlett, where he "engaged in the mercantile business."[28] By the time of Jess's boyhood studies with Kuler, which ended at age twelve when his family moved to the Panhandle, Bartlett and its surrounding communities resounded with formal musical activity. The 1884 Texas business directory reports that the former stagecoach stop of Belton, close to the Morris home, presently supported two music stores and an opera house. Eleven years later the community built a second hall, still more opulent than the first, to accommodate the traveling theatricals that now made it a regular stop on their tours. These signs of Gilded Age grandeur came only forty years after the earliest report of Bell County music instruction: a shape-note singing school that met in a log cabin.[29]

On his family's nearby ranch, Jess received another kind of musical instruction as well. In 1885, at age seven, he first heard "Goodbye, Old Paint" sung and played to him on a Jew's harp by Charley Willis, a seventeen-year-old former slave who E.J. hired as a horse breaker shortly after the war.[30] To supplement his work for the Morrises, Jess recalled, Charley "had gone up the trail to Wyoming, the neighborhood of Cheyenne."[31] There he rode for the Snyder Brothers, also of Williamson County. After previously delivering cattle for the Confederate Army's commissary service, their company soon ranked among Texas's leading beef herders to the Wyoming and Kansas railheads.[32] Charley learned "Old Paint" on one of the Snyder Brothers' cattle drives, and in 1885, with Charley still in the Morris employ and now working in Bell County, where the family had moved, he sang the piece for Jess. "It was on this jews-harp," Jess writes, "that I learned to play Ol' Paint at the age of seven. . . . In later years I learned to play the fiddle, and played Ol' Paint on the fiddle, in my own special arrangement—tuning the fiddle accordingly."[33] The first fiddler he heard also worked for the family, a black horse breaker named Jerry Neely. During Jess's youth, Neely worked for E. J. Morris on their Williamson County ranch. There he gave Jess his earliest lessons. Over the ensuing decades, Jess evidently kept tabs on him. He mentioned Neely in a January 1940 *Fort Worth Star-Telegram* article and again during his 1942 Library of Congress recordings as living in Milam County.[34] Jess, however, didn't pursue that style until after his family moved to the Panhandle in 1890.

Nor did Jess's youthful interest in classical violin abate in adulthood. Though he worked as a semiprofessional fiddler throughout his teens, playing for Panhandle ranch dances and cowboy balls, in 1900 he traveled to Austin, fifty-six miles south of Bartlett (where he had moved back, joining his older half brothers who still lived there) to begin instruction under "Professor Klotz."[35] Henry A. Klotz, who taught violin, piano, and voice from his home, enjoyed a long career teaching music at the Texas School for the Blind in Austin. The city directories issued between 1881 to 1907 show him giving private lessons while also teaching for the state. Perhaps a sign of what Klotz, and Kuler before him, had fostered appears in two formal portraits taken of Jess in 1907. They show him garbed in formal wear, and in one, posed elegantly in profile with his violin. Four years later he enrolled in the music program at Indiana's Valparaiso University.

Jess attended Valparaiso, "the Poor Man's Harvard," from 1911 to 1913.[36] With a student body of six thousand and an expansive curriculum, comparable, school officials said, to Harvard's academic breadth, Valparaiso offered flexibility in both cost and course requirements. It allowed undergraduates to pay according to a sliding tuition scale and to design their own study programs. "Whatever was needed was provided" became a watchword of Henry Baker Brown, the school president from 1873 to 1925. This accommodating principle advanced Valparaiso's diversity: coeducational, nonsectarian, with many foreign students, and a secondary school for those with remedial needs. It also welcomed adult learners. Jess was thirty-three when he enrolled, one of seven hundred in the university's Conservatory of Music. He named E. J. Morris as his

FIGURE 48.
Jess in classical mode, 1907.
Courtesy of Vera Morris.

parent/sponsor and gave Bartlett as his home address.

Jess took advantage of the school's opportunities. Valparaiso's music students had access to all departmental offerings at no additional cost. Jess's transcript, dated September and December 1911, shows that in addition to studying harmony (for which he received a grade of 95), he signed up for a course in rhetoric (achieving an 84) and one in law (82). After these two terms his school records become bare. By then he had launched into private studies with members of the music faculty. A February 1912 handbill shows Jess appearing as a soloist in an all-student recital. Listed there as a pupil of Professor Fritz Ingersoll, head of the violin department, he played Raff's "Cavatina," a popular solo by this prolific Swiss-born nineteenth-century composer. Years later, both family accounts and newspaper articles noted Jess's admiration for the Berlin-trained Ingersoll as a notable and accomplished teacher.

CHAPTER 12

Yet he did not stay long enough to graduate. Contrary to accounts that his Valparaiso instructors discouraged him, Jess made this hard choice himself. He left the university after two years. "I thought I was a fiddler," he said, "and heard a few good ones, and decided I couldn't play the fiddle, that is, the violin. And so then I decided I'd just make a fiddler out of myself."[37] Even though Jess continued to play at formal affairs around home—usually weddings that called for violin-style favorites and occasional classical airs—he concentrated on fiddling and folksong. "But I went on," Jess continued, "and I'd play for dances."[38] In 1933 he replied to an inquiry from the university alumni office that he "sings old cowboy songs and plays the violin" on station WDAG in Amarillo.[39] He listed his occupation as "radio entertainer."

Five years earlier, during Amarillo's first "All-Panhandle Old Fiddlers' Contest," Jess told how he became a fiddler. His remarks originated in a letter sent to the newspaper following a request that every contestant furnish his own biography. While the paper noted, seemingly in reference to Jess, that "many of the fiddlers who will play in the contest also are artists in handling classical numbers," the contest allowed only "old fashioned music, preferably quadrilles, as this is more closely associated with the old breakdown dance."[40] The event coincided with the opening of the Amarillo cattleman's convention—sponsored by the same organization—and its promotional thrust drew on local history just as the trade fair celebrated the local economy. "Every person who is interested in the development of this great Panhandle country," remarked contest director O. H. Loyd, "should . . . make it a point to attend the old fiddlers' contest."[41]

The musicians' stories that Jess and his compatriots shared from their younger days evoke the region's hardscrabble heritage. One player recalled his log schoolhouse with its chimney made of sticks and dirt, while Jess and another fiddler spoke of playing music in solitary dugouts, cellarlike shelters hewn from the prairie itself and propped up with a few pieces of lumber. Under this earthen roof, Jess said, "I learned all my old fiddling tunes," including "Goodbye, Old Paint."[42] That effort took place, he explained, out on the Tumbling Two, the Morris family's Panhandle ranch. There he learned the song from "an Oklahoma cow puncher in 1892," who played it for him on a harmonica. Years later he informed the same paper that he composed it in 1893 at the Tascosa ranch of his friend Theodore Briggs, an Oldham County luminary who fought in the Indian battle of Adobe Walls.[43] Either way, during those years Jess began his apprenticeship to the fiddle, developed his interpretation of "Goodbye, Old Paint," and furnished music for neighboring ranch dances. Now in March 1928, while acknowledging his current residence at Dalhart, Jess reaffirmed his local allegiance. "When I make some 'fiddling' records soon," he promised, "I intend saying 'I'm an old Oldham county fiddler.'"[44] To the audience of over two thousand that assembled at Amarillo's municipal auditorium Jess's music summoned the town's leathery past. "Tell the world," he vowed, "that I intend 'Pulling the Bridle off of Old Paint' in the song: Goodbye Old Paint, I'm Leaving Cheyenne."[45] While Jess did not win that year (he took second place in 1931), he did coax an unbridled response from his listeners. As he sang and fiddled his song, the "audience forgot all dignity and joined in a hearty lusty yell on the chorus."[46]

Jess spent his initial years as a fiddler traveling across the Panhandle and adjacent states with his "five-piece orchestra" of flute, violin, string bass, guitar, and banjo.[47] He went preferably in the company of Mexican musicians like Pancho, a monte dealer from San Angelo, who, Jess said, "could do everything with a guitar except make it talk."[48] Their trips together generated their own adventures, and Jess gleefully recounted tales of runaway coaches careening down canyons and arroyos, the bass fiddle all the while hanging precariously to the roof by a strap. He recalled one of the Amarillo-area cowboy Christmas balls they worked back then: "At this particular dance we played plenty of Mexican music, and the old folk songs, for old Pancho knew them all. You should have seen the orchestra and the dancers wade into 'Masubiana,' and there was one little senorita, Pauline Sanchez her name was, who would call for 'Sobre las Olas' (Over the Waves), again and again."[49]

Jess and Pancho's musical bond epitomized an intercultural milieu long present in their region. In October 1935, Elijah Cox (1842–1940), a free-born black Civil War veteran also living in San Angelo, recorded three songs for John A. Lomax.[50] Cox's music reaches deep into the nineteenth century. For his second piece, "Whoa Mule," Cox set down his guitar and picked up his fiddle.[51] Lyrically "Whoa Mule" draws from the body of verses that Leadbelly summoned in his steamboat-era worksong "Old Man."[52] Musically it suggests the playing (and employs certain intervals) that African American fiddler Frank Patterson used in his 1942 performance of the folk and minstrel piece "Old Joe."[53] Based on his age, "Old Cox" appears to be the oldest fiddler ever recorded, black or white.[54] He had by then become a well-known figure in this community where he settled after his army discharge in 1871. He busked in saloons, gambled like his neighbor Pancho at monte, and "played for many Mexican dances that lasted all night. After midnight the musicians received extra pay for their work, and with their tips they made a good living."[55] He also fiddled for dances at Fort Concho, a local garrison that served as regimental headquarters for two companies of Buffalo Soldiers, black cavalry troops assigned to control Indian uprisings. Black string bands, whose members included soldiers posted there, or else Mexican ensembles enlisted from the surrounding settlements, played for these affairs. "'There wasn't none of them turkey trots in that day,' said the old fiddler. 'Folks danced the schottische, the polka, the square dance, and the quadrille. We had real music in them days, too. I'll bet I can play 300 waltzes, all different without stopping.'"[56] His staggering number of waltzes speaks to their popularity in the late nineteenth century. Moreover, these waltzes, like other dances he names, appealed to a diverse audience. In the Southwest, blacks, whites, and browns all danced to these rhythms. Jess Morris knew this too and acted accordingly.

When Jess's audiences waltzed to "Goodbye, Old Paint," they were responding to a piece he learned to sing and, on a fundamental level, to play from African Americans. He avidly shared this and other numbers with Spanish-speaking musicians like Pancho. Nor did Jess limit himself to playing only for Anglo-American dances. He performed for Mexican gatherings as far away as Clayton, New Mexico, and Trinidad, Colorado. When he entered the first Amarillo fiddle contest he advertised his interest in Mexican accompanists. "Mr. Morris, like several of the other musicians, is seeking some local musicians for seconds. He wants some of the Mexican guitar or cello players in Amarillo for his aides, saying they know how to put real life into old cowboy and Spanish music."[57] Newspaper mentions of Jess's later appearances at ranch reunions and other dances, a bill for his band's musical services, and the memories of Elizabeth Morris Roberts and Vera Morris put him continually in company of Mexican musicians. "Why did Jess prefer Mexican guitar players?" I asked Bob Morris. "I don't know," Bob answered. "He said 'they added a little something to it.'"[58]

Jess brought this artistic surfeit to his own compositions, works that simultaneously made use of his academic background. In June 1940 he registered with the U.S. Copyright Office two pieces of music he wrote for fiddle and piano: "El Rancho Grande XIT Schottische" and "XIT Ranch Cowboy Polka."[59] The schottische, which he composed that April, reflects a classical affinity, for all its traditional structure and familiar-sounding melody. Unlike the less-exacting bass figures usually played behind this traditional dance form, here the piano harmonizes with the fiddle's melody, evoking Chopin or Percy Grainger. The polka, which he had written some forty-five years earlier sounds similar as well, with the two instruments alternating solos.

Jess had learned how to splice informal tradition with what he gleaned from his formal education.

Now, in July 1940, Jess wrote to the Pioneer editor of the *Fort Worth Star-Telegram*, explaining the background of the two pieces. They commemorated, he said, the "Old XIT cowhands," who had worked on the famed Panhandle ranch in bygone years.[60] He mentioned a Mexican quadrille that he recently directed and for which he played the fiddle. In citing these aspects of his musical life to introduce "XIT Schottische," Jess called attention to both a newly composed work and a vanishing history. Many of his fellow cowboys had died by then, and he recognized his own advancing age. "It's 'Custers last stand' with me," he admits, "and it's people like you people down there, that help get us places."[61]

From seeking a write-up to soon thanking both the editor and the publisher for the features they obligingly ran after getting his letters, he remarked, "I believe that those two numbers will stand the 'GAFF,' and one reason why I think that they will go over, is the fact that Dr. Chaffe, of Valparaiso University, would have told me, because he is getting to the age, when he don't have to 'string a fellow.'"[62] Indeed, Dr. Edmund W. Chaffee (1862–1945), whom Jess identified as the head of harmony in the music department, was old enough to be secure in his opinions. He had evidently received from Jess a copy of the handwritten sheet music submitted for copyright registration. Jess could count on his old teacher Dr. Chaffee for comments and criticisms.

Two years later Jess had "XIT Schottische" commercially published as sheet music. The cover features one of his 1907 classical music portraits ("Jess Morris in the Gay Nineties"), and a banner identifies him as "Texas Panhandle Cowboy Fiddler and Singer."[63] Just beneath the "Schottische" title, in large italic type, appears an inscription jarringly different from most cowboy songs: "Dedicated to the Glory of ADOLPH—Napoleon Bonaparte Alexander the Great—HITLER."

In the last half of 1942, the Battle of Stalingrad raged on the Russian front. Jess responded with four verses and a chorus, all topically driven, historically informed, and utterly sarcastic. Copyrighted that October, the following lines, occurring midway through the song, can speak for the whole:

So it's here to you ol' funny face with spinach
On your lip, and remember Bonapart's retreat,
The Russians you can't whip.
You will have to fill our baggy pants, and plenty

Limburg eat, and the Cossacks they will call
Your hand and you defeat.[64]

On multiple levels the song captures Jess's creative disposition. Musically, the piece calls on his classical training and his knowledge of fiddling. Using the "XIT Schottische" to address Hitler's invasion and the hubris of fallen conquerors underlines the choice he made decades earlier at Valparaiso when he set aside the violin for the fiddle. No matter how unusual such a topical theme might seem in the setting of a Southwestern ranch dance, Jess relies on this form to carry his message. Like so many of his letters and anecdotes, the lyrics cackle with humor and slang, his passionate directness and fluid grasp of stereotypes. Its subject matter affirms his involvement with his times.

As a Texas Panhandle cowboy singer and fiddler, Jess found his medium and his inspiration. He recognized that Old West song repertory and technique better suited his abilities as musician, bandleader, and composer. Given where he lived, the fiddler's calling also offered him more reasonable prospects of a livelihood than what might await him as a purely classical interpreter. Above all, in embracing the role of cowboy musician, he not only chose a style, he chose a subject. Jess had witnessed an extraordinary set of events: the closing of the Texas trail, the cattle boom of the 1880s, and the settlement of the range. To the *Fort Worth Star-Telegram* he spoke for more than just his own past, summoning a heritage his whole community understood: "I, Jess Morris, was a cowhand, on the famous 3,000,000 Acre XIT Ranch."[65]

From 1893 to 1898 Jess roved the largest fenced ranch in the world, tracking and killing predatory wolves that attacked the herd. Sometimes called "Ten in Texas," the XIT crossed ten counties and stretched two hundred miles from the state's northern border with Oklahoma to its southern boundary due west of Lubbock. It required fifteen hundred miles of barbed wire to enclose. If reduced to a single strand, that wire would have measured six thousand miles in length.[66] XIT management understandably split the immense ranch into eight geographical divisions, each assigned a different role in the husbandry of the 150,000 head of cattle raised there. A team of 150 cowboys ran the ranch's ninety-four pastures. Faced with prairie fires, rustlers, and drought, they also had to manage animal predators. Jess's job as a wolfer kept him in the northernmost Panhandle division called Buffalo Springs. He began the job when still a teen, and with one assistant patrolled this 470,000 acre ranch, divided into nine smaller pastures where some 35,000 steers grazed. He also worked as a wolfer at two other Panhandle ranches in that decade, accumulating eleven or twelve sections of land in the XIT's Agua Frio Pasture adjoining Buffalo Springs that he eventually sold for a profit.

In the wintertime Jess captured and killed wolves and their pups, while hunting their dens in the warmer months. "He's controlling the predator population," said Bob Morris, a lifelong cowboy and ranch foreman himself. He spoke knowledgeably about the wolfer's job:

> They're raising cattle on XIT, a cow and calf operation. Them old wolves teach the young ones how to catch a calf or a yearling. They'd bite 'em on the hamstring right behind the leg. If they didn't get them down and kill them right then, they [the cows and yearlings] would take blood poisoning and die. So they'd get around a watering place where there's a lot of them, and the cattle would follow them, trying to hook 'em or something. . . . Wolfer got a little more money than a cowboy. They'd have to know where one [a wolf] was. Then they'd kill the old one. They might crawl in there and get all them young ones. . . . Sandy country, you know, and when they'd dig in there, it can cave in on you.[67]

Smaller than any of his male siblings, Jess's lithe frame suited him for this work. An experience he had in 1894 on the LS ranch, adjacent to the XIT, reinforces what Bob Morris described: "With Pedro [Baca's] lasso around his waist, Jess crawled into the big den, shined a candle into the old wolf's eyes and shot her. The explosion caused the sand to cave in behind him. Pedro tied the lariat to his saddle horn and pulled Jess out."[68]

For Jess such adventures could translate into art, both musical and narrative. In a freewheeling ten-minute monologue, recorded in 1942 and filling two sides with spoken-word reminiscences, he unleashes a comic litany of bartenders, cowhands, herders, cooks, book-writing ranchers, and old soldiers who made up the Panhandle in its woollier days. Hispanic ranch hands figure most often in Jess's anecdotes (he ably imitates their accents), but Chinese laborers are deemed expendable, and eccentric Anglo-American cowpunchers receive comic portraiture, too. He tells, for instance, about a cowboy called Spider, who Jess says "never took a bath in his life." Once, at an Amarillo drinking hole where he and his fellow cowboys made a game of asking the bartender to guess their age and weight, Spider begged for a personal appraisal. Finally he got his estimate: "From the standpoint of intelligence," the saloon keeper dryly observed, "you don't look like you're over three years old. But from the standpoint of filth, you look like you're over fifty."[69] Barely pausing for this retort to settle on the ear, Jess recounts another amusing incident as the recording continues. Just as the last disc breaks off, he asks, "Did I tell you about [the] three-million-acre ranch I worked on up there, the XIT?" The reverence in Jess's voice for that bygone place was as palpable as the pungency of his stories.

He approached "Goodbye, Old Paint" in like spirit. Jess's niece Elizabeth, who, at age twelve in 1931, lived with Jess and his piano-playing sister Anne in Dalhart, attended a number of fiddle contests with him in those years. "He always played 'Old Paint,'" she remembered.

> To me it was sad and nostalgic . . . that day and time I'm talking about, far re-moved. There was always that mystery and stuff about the Old West that was very interesting and very sad. I could sympathize and empathize with the tremendous hardships that the women of that day and time had to go through. It was pretty much a man's world, really, to live out. . . .
>
> Wherever he would go, whenever he came to a fiddlers' contest, they always wanted him to play "Old Paint." . . . I think it affected them in kind of a nostalgic way. . . . It was not like "Sallie Gooden" or "Turkey in the Straw" and some of those things that they played when people felt like beating their feet to or clapping. But I think that Jess always wanted to do it. For him it was a throwback in his mind to the days when he cowboyed, you know.[70]

Jess invested this song with the varied musical resources at his disposal. He shifted his fiddle strings from the standard configuration of EADG (high-est string to lowest) to DADD, which rural players in Texas and across the South sometimes used to accompany traditional hymns, marches, and set pieces. They found its reverberant octaves, spilling out like an unstopped reed organ, especially accommodating for slower melodies and tunes. While Jess often performed "Goodbye, Old Paint" purely as an instrumental waltz (and according to Bob Morris did not use it to close an evening's dance), his tuning rested on a time-tested foundation that supported his needs for both an unhurried danceable piece and an evocative lyric song.

More than just folk tradition figures here. On his 1942 recording Jess harmonizes the fiddle to his vocal, playing fifths as he sings. He also plays harmonies during instrumental passages by holding intervals on the lower notes while he executes the melody on the treble strings. Although he never sounds like a classical musician in accomplishing these effects, he uses schooled techniques to perform them. He notes certain drones instead of playing them as open strings. For a descending bass figure, he employs closed-position, left-hand fingerings that reflect music-school more than traditional playing methods. Several ornamental trills, his vibrato, and certain nomenclature he used when he wrote out the notes—"interlude," to identify the instrumental part of the piece—again point to his formal training. Classical music may even have affected his tonal choices. Long after metal wire became available, Jess continued to use catgut for his two treble strings. "I guess," Bob Morris ventured, that Jess thought "them steel strings is too loud or something."[71] Jess's comment on "Goodbye, Old Paint" applies as much to his own rendition as it does to others: "Most every cowpoke who sang it added something."[72]

_____

Jess had long asserted his unique approach to "Goodbye, Old Paint." At least twenty-nine years before he made his final recording of the song, he made his first, a four-minute fiddle-and-piano performance preserved on an Edison cylinder. No files at the Edison Laboratories show that he produced it under their auspices, nor do other labels of that time list the piece among their authorized releases. It appears, instead, that Jess made home recordings of "Goodbye, Old Paint."[73] Today that recording survives only in the form of a promotional notice, a postcard offering customers the completed cylinder, postage and shipping included, for seventy-five cents. One of these shop-printed mailers, postmarked December 1913, Jess sent to someone in Dalhart and later recovered. It quotes a verse from the song, followed by Jess's claim to be "the only one who knows how to play the old cowboy tune."[74] What this announcement doesn't say is that Jess may well have made the first recording, commercial or otherwise, of a traditional cowboy song.[75]

This cylinder brought together a prestigious modern technology epitomized by the Edison brand name and a treasured past commemorated in the song. By using a detachable "recorder" accessory, consumers could adapt their phonographs to make home recordings.[76] Prior to 1912, Edison offered only two-minute recording blanks, which would have accommodated only half of Jess's full performance of "Goodbye, Old Paint." The new extended recording blanks marked an exciting development, and on the postcard Jess made sure to call attention to "Old Paint's" four-minute length. That he played the piece on fiddle with piano accompaniment appealed to living practice. Pianos, common in homes and schoolhouses, occupied a place in ranch dance tradition as well as in popular music. Jess often performed with pianists, including his younger sister, who in later years played in his band. Likewise, he wrote "XIT Ranch Cowboy Polka" and "El Rancho Grande XIT Schottische" for piano and fiddle.

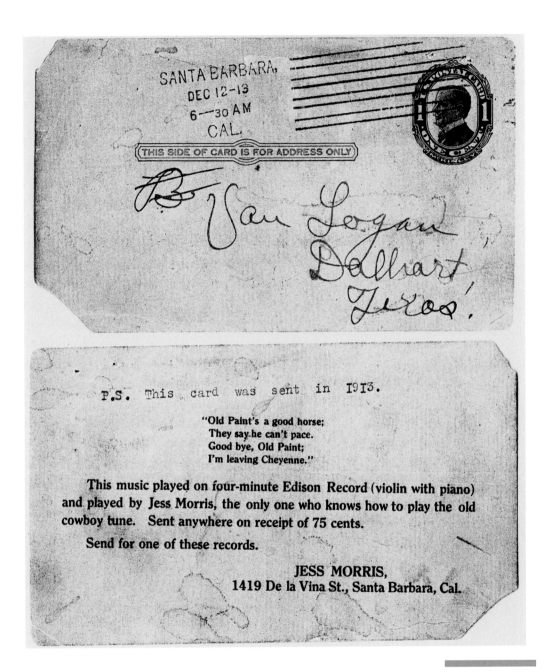

Curiously, Jess never mentions this recording in his later letters and interviews. Presumably it garnered him little tangible benefit. In 1913 he was still enrolled at Valparaiso University, and on the postcard he gives a Santa Barbara, California, home address. Lost to time is why he came that far west, let alone how he juggled his schedule between the two locales. His parents received letters from him, Vera Morris remembers, not only from points

FIGURE 49.
The 1913 postcard announcement of Jess's recording. From Jess Morris's Archive of Folk Culture file.

across the West where he performed, but also from Cuba and Mexico. These last came during the heyday of Pancho Villa, around the time Jess cut the cylinder. Whatever guided his movements back then, with this landmark if unheralded recording he asserted his commitment to the song and put his stamp upon it.

Jess played "Old Paint," he maintained, like no one else, and by 1893, had devised a setting he could call his own. John A. Lomax, who had met Jess near the time of the Edison recording, recognized this particularity. Decades later he wrote to him, "As you know, I think you have the best tune that exists to 'Goodbye Old Paint.'"[77] In the same January 1941 letter he invited Jess to record the song. Soon after doing so, Jess pursued this subject with him further. "There might have been some kind of a tune floating around the country," Jess wrote back, "similar to my tune, all of which I can't of course know anything about. I can get affidavits by the hundreds, from people of all walks of life, who would I'm sure, swear that I'm the only human who could do the tune right, at least I have been told."[78] Likewise, for "XIT Ranch Polka," "I can't say that I ever heard anyone else play it, but there might be tunes that sounded like it." Finally, in the letter, he writes that "'El Rancho Grande XIT Schottische' was not a community tune." Jess knew that however much this piece and his others echoed older waltzes, polkas, and schottisches, they still possessed their own individuality. "We will come closer to understanding such songs," Edward Ives has written of songmakers like Jess, "if we look for the artistry in the skillful adaptation of traditional elements . . . rather than in novelty and experimentation."[79]

In March 1941 Jess presented Lomax with his Amarillo recording of "Goodbye, Old Paint."[80] That spring he also copyrighted "Ridin' Ol' Paint an' Leadin' Ol' Ball," following Lomax's suggestion that he find his own name for the song in order to set it apart from other versions previously registered. "I wish I had the money," he mused to Lomax, "I have made in fiddlin' contests."[81] Jess made this remark not with an eye toward accumulating more revenue, but to inform him of the respect local audiences accorded his performances of "Goodbye, Old Paint."

Around home, Bob Morris said, "Everybody thought it was his song."[82] Seth Woods, a retired ranch manager who grew up in Dalhart in the XIT era, recalled a cowboy dance that included Jess, well-known to him through "Goodbye, Old Paint." "So they had this song stuck on these pieces of paper, you know, with different verses, and they passed them around to everybody."[83]

The crowd joined Jess as he performed the song, everybody singing along and dancing. "Oh boy," Woods chuckled, relishing the memory, "they like to never got that stopped." Implicit in this gentle recollection, Jess had taken an old song widely known, played it his own way, and given it back to a community that, in turn, identified it with him.

For now, Jess included a letter with the 1941 disc, and in a handwritten note at the bottom of that page, Lomax added to Jess's correspondence: "The tune of 'Goodbye Old Paint' was first written out for me by Jess Morris in 1915. Oscar Fox of San Antonio combined my singing of the song (as I first learned it in Cheyenne, Wyoming, in 1910) with the rough notes of Jess Morris['s] version. The resultant sheet music of Mr. Fox introduced the song to the public."[84] Lomax solemnized this statement by setting down the date, his home address, and signing his name.

Lomax's deposition enumerates a set of personal contacts that led to the song's national prominence. By then, he had written a story of "Goodbye, Old Paint" that he reprised in two songbooks, his radio series, and his autobiography, though he did not mention Jess in this narrative until the last of these publications.[85] The first account appeared in February 1934 in a pulp magazine, Street and Smith's *Wild West Weekly*, aimed for cowboy aficionados. The publishers had launched a feature on "the old cowboy songs and frontier ballads that have come down to us by word of mouth from our grandfathers," and Lomax's article marked his first contribution to "Fiddlin' Joe's Song Corral."[86] For Lomax, "Goodbye, Old Paint" arrived at a pivotal moment in his life. During the August 1910 frontier celebration in Cheyenne, Wyoming, he met with President Theodore Roosevelt, who wrote out for him the endorsement that graced Lomax's *Cowboy Songs*, then on the verge of publication.[87] Apparently later that day, the collector ran into a former University of Texas classmate, Boothe Merrill, coming out of a saloon just as Lomax was going in. The two friends retired back to a table where Merrill told Lomax, "I live in the western part of Oklahoma where they still have the old-style cowboy dances . . . a universal custom, when the last dance is called, is to stop the music—usually a fiddle and a guitar—and everybody sings, to a slow waltz time, the cowboy song known as 'Good-by, Old Paint, I'm a leavin' Cheyenne.' It is a favorite with us in Oklahoma."[88] That story made such an impression on Lomax that he reported it from then on, affecting others, like Fox (1879–1961), who repeated it in their own notes. Here, at the Cheyenne saloon, Lomax had Merrill go through the song until he learned it by rote. Once he had it under command, "I sang this tune to Oscar J. Fox, a musician, of San Antonio, Texas, who had it issued as sheet music. It was thus scattered over the United States."

Wherever it went, Oscar Fox's sheet music bore the unmistakable though largely unacknowledged imprint of Jess Morris. While Fox credits John Lomax as the song's collector and cites his *Cowboy Songs and Other Frontier Ballads*, Fox used Jess's melody for the verses and begins his arrangement with one of Jess's stanzas: "My feet are in the stirrups, / My bridle's in my hand; / Goodbye, my little dony, / My pony won't stand."[89] These lines do not appear in Lomax's *Cowboy Songs*.[90] Their inclusion in the sheet music confirms what Jess later recounted to Duncan Emrich. When Jess wrote down his tune for Lomax, which he rightly remembered as "some time prior to 1927," he also included "some of the words" that eventually got passed along to Oscar Fox.[91] It certainly makes sense for an arranger like Fox to start out with Jess's wording, given its natural fit with the melody. He chose its four remaining stanzas from Lomax's collection, and then moved into the arrangement's central feature, the chorus that Merrill taught Lomax at the Cheyenne saloon. By incorporating this part, simpler than Jess's own chorus, Fox hit a winning combination of sources. In December 1927, six months after registering his initial arrangement, Carl Fischer Inc. copyrighted Fox's setting of "Old Paint" as a quartet for men's voices. The conjoined melodies remained, despite their well-scrubbed glee club sound far removed from the song's rawhide roots.

Into this setting steps Woodward Maurice "Tex" Ritter (1905–1974), whose live appearances and cowboy films nearly rivaled Gene Autry's in popularity. Earlier, Ritter had been enrolled at the University of Texas law school. He also pursued there the study of folksong with three campus experts: his voice teacher Oscar J. Fox, song collector John A. Lomax, and chronicler of Southwestern lore J. Frank Dobie. "I had the benefit of association at the University," Ritter recalled, "with three men who encouraged me to sing and they helped direct my career."[92] Historian Douglas Green writes, "He learned vocal and guitar technique from Fox, discussed folklore with Lomax, and collected folk songs like 'Rye Whiskey' with Dobie, who [Ritter said] 'played a large part in making me what I am today.'"[93]

As a member of the glee club, Ritter worked under Oscar Fox. On July 1, 1927, Fox presented a combined lecture and concert at the school that featured Ritter in one of his earliest public appearances. The handbill accompanying this open-air presentation of "Cowboy Songs of the Southwest" reads, "These songs, which will be sung by Mr. Ritter, accompanied by Mr. Fox, during the lecture, were collected by John A. Lomax, formerly of Austin and now residing in Dallas. The music was arranged by Mr. Fox."[94] The evening's program of twelve songs ended with "Old Paint."

The song stayed with him, and in January 1931, twenty-six-year-old Woodward Ritter, his stage name before he adopted his famous sobriquet, performed it as part of his featured role in the New York premiere of Linn Riggs's *Green Grow the Lilacs*. This Pulitzer Prize–nominated play became the basis of the acclaimed Rodgers and Hammerstein musical *Oklahoma!* While lead actor Franchot Tone sang "A Ridin' Old Paint" in the play—a different song—Ritter sang "Goodbye, Old Paint," though the script does not include its text or specify when he performed it. The script does, however, credit its arrangement to Oscar J. Fox.[95]

The prominence of *Green Grow the Lilacs* led to Ritter's professional record and film career, which he launched in March 1933, with "Goodbye, Old Paint," backed by the musically interrelated "Rye Whiskey" (Jess himself paired the two songs on both of his Library of Congress recordings). He saw this record issued on at least twelve different labels. His rendition of "Goodbye, Old Paint" shows him precisely repeating Fox's music and words. Ritter also heeded his teacher's prompting to fade the ending, singing "softer and softer" as directed—a musical simulation of a cowboy ball winding down.[96] Perhaps with related theatrical if not solely ethnographic impulse, Ritter added some yips and calls on the recording that simulate a cowboy at work with his herd. His recording of the song, more than any other, spurred the transmission of Jess's tune. In a melodic trail that picks up with Boothe Merrill and Jess Morris, then gets relayed from John Lomax to Oscar Fox, and passed onto Tex Ritter, the song traveled from their voices to the printed page to broadcast recordings and radio transmissions to the national consciousness.

On one of those stops, Oscar Fox's sheet music reached Aaron Copland. The composer used this arrangement, later discovered stitched inside another songbook in his library, for his 1938 score of the ballet *Billy the Kid*.[97] In that piece, he explores the refrain more than he does Jess's verse, bringing new harmonizations to the plain chords of the original. Still, Jess's passage appears twice in the composition, rendered first with violins and cellos, and then with a lone woodwind. These quicksilver moments filled with Jess's thoroughly recognizable melody anticipates a role that Bill Stepp's "Bonaparte's Retreat" occupied in Copland's 1942 *Rodeo*. Both players created singular versions of traditional works, subsequently transcribed in print, which Copland took and transformed. Moreover, both used the same fiddle tuning. Not to be forgotten in this admixture, either, Agnes de Mille not only choreographed *Rodeo* in 1942, but a year later did the same for *Oklahoma!* Copland and his circle wove their own lines of artistic descent into "Goodbye, Old Paint," as they did other melodies from American folk tradition.

On May 3, 1942, a month shy of his sixty-fourth birthday, Jess recorded "Goodbye, Old Paint" for the last time. The recording took place in conjunction with the annual meeting of the Texas Folklore Society held in Denton. *Life* magazine covered the event, and for the June 1, 1942, issue with Hedy Lamarr gracing the cover, ran an article titled "*Life* Goes to a Tall Tales Session in Texas."[98] The magazine anchored the piece around a highly atmospheric and entirely staged photograph. Jess, wearing "boots bearing name" (as he soon noted about the *Life* appearance on his sheet music editions of "Ridin' Ol' Paint an' Leadin' Ol' Ball" and the "XIT Schottische") and holding his fiddle and bow, sits next to author-professor J. Frank Dobie. Campfire listeners, characterized by the copywriter as "folklore lovers," look upon Dobie, who, in borrowed hat and bandana, is purportedly telling them old-time stories.

A related artifice seemed, at first, to haunt the recording session. Though Jess had sung "Goodbye, Old Paint" into a disc cutter at an Amarillo music store the year before, neither he nor John Lomax liked the results. Jess had misgivings about the performance that he subsequently shared with Vera. He didn't like its sound. Poor microphone placement had obscured the vocals, he sang fewer verses than he normally used, and some of his fiddle parts meandered. Not only that, but Lomax, he recalled in a separate letter, had "bellyached" about the 1941 performance and suggested an improved rendition might ensue if Jess took "a snort or two of Scotch."[99]

Here on the eve of the session in Dallas, Jess and Lomax, who already vacillated between being cordial and competitive with one another, fell into a new round of chafing. As Lomax biographer Nolan Porterfield artfully recounts, the friction began with the folklorist passing off a dinner check to his houseguest Jess, and by the end of the evening fevers escalated to Jess's threatening to leave Lomax's home altogether for the next train to Dalhart. While they got through the recording unscathed—Jess performed with ardent, declamatory force—more hurt lay ahead. Lomax had vowed that the public recognition Jess desired for himself and his song would surely follow from this effort. The collector further promised that he would take every opportunity to talk up Jess's "Goodbye, Old Paint" in his interviews. That notice failed to materialize, as Lomax mentioned neither in a widely distributed 1945 *Readers' Digest* feature. Jess volubly shared his dismay with the Texas Folklore Society and evidently also with the Secretary of the XIT Cowboy's Association, who in turn passed the complaint on to a shocked and rattled Lomax. This final tempest between these strong-willed but thin-skinned Texans barely strays from their earlier relationship. That they could simultaneously irritate and support one another becomes evident when Jess sent Lomax his April 1941 *Amarillo Daily News* article about his initial Library of Congress recording.[100] At the bottom of Jess's cover letter, Lomax added a note to his son Alan that captures the relationship's underlying tenor: "You ought to write to the old coot."[101]

Age was hardly a factor in the Dallas recording. At times Jess sounds operatic, projecting his voice in arcs and turns that could penetrate a dance hall. At other points he almost talks, a recitative style suggestive of a nineteenth-century stump speaker. Either way, the performance recalls an era before amplification and the whispered intimacy that marks so many of Jess's twenty-first-century counterparts.

After a hesitant start, edited out from the final, issued performance, he sings:

Farewell, fair ladies, I'm a-leaving Cheyenne,
Farewell, fair ladies, I'm a-leaving Cheyenne,
Goodbye, my little doney, my pony won't stand.

> Chorus:
> Old Paint, Old Paint, I'm a-leaving Cheyenne,
> Goodbye, Old Paint, I'm leaving Cheyenne,
> Old Paint's a good pony, and she paces when she can.

In the middle of the ocean may grow a green tree,
But I'll never prove false to the girl that loves me.

> Chorus

Oh, we spread down our blankets on the green grassy ground,
And the horses and cattle were a-grazing all around.

> Chorus

Oh, the last time I saw her, it was late in the fall,
She was riding Ol' Paint and a-leadin' Ol' Ball.

> Chorus

Old Paint had a colt down on the Rio Grande,
And the colt couldn't pace and they named it Cheyenne.

Jess Morris

Chorus

Oh my feet's in my stirrups, and my bridle's in my hand,
Goodbye, my little doney, my pony won't stand.

Farewell, fair ladies, I'm a-leaving Cheyenne,
Farewell, fair ladies, I'm a-leaving Cheyenne,
Goodbye, my little doney, my pony won't stand.[102]

For all its Old West subject matter and scenery, Jess's text of "Goodbye, Old Paint" echoes the "Wagoner's Lad," a widely sung lament of British origin.[103] The theme of movement that the older song embodied in horses and wagons provided an available repository of symbolism and poesy for "Old Paint." "Wagoner's Lad" and its commingled pieces that include "The Rebel Prisoner," "The Forsaken Girl," "The Cuckoo," "An Inconstant Lover," and "On Top of Old Smoky," writes Missouri-based collector Henry M. Belden, fall under a category of "folk-lyric" songs. Though they do not present a single narrative, they largely share a common emotion, employing "a number of images, symbols, tropes that somehow convey . . . mood or feeling."[104] Belden identified "Wagoner's Lad's" precursors in Ireland, Scotland, and England. In turn, their metaphors and commonplaces "combine, resolve and recombine," spreading across Appalachia, the Adirondacks, and the Ozarks.

One image that many of them shared came in "the warning not to set one's affections on a sycamore (or green willow, or other) tree, for its leaves will wither and die." "The willow" Belden reminded his readers, "is an ancient symbol of unrequited love."[105] Yet that line in Jess's song goes beyond the unrelieved sorrow and uncertainty that permeates the "Wagoner's Lad." In leaving a loved one behind with long travel ahead, the narrator in "Old Paint" pledges fidelity. He bids goodbye to his doney, derived from the Spanish *doña*, for lady. He may not see her again, but he does not abandon her in perfidy. The green growing tree that in the "Wagoner's Lad" and its related songs symbolizes a young man who cannot be restricted and must not be trusted, here becomes a foil. However impossible for a tree to sprout from the ocean, even more impossible for him to scorn his beloved.

Another folk-lyric stream had fed into "Goodbye, Old Paint," as a penny broadside printed circa 1849 in Glasgow called "The American Stranger" documented, well before Jess or Charley Willis ever heard their cowboy song. Unlike most emigration ballads, "The American Stranger" tells of a man leaving the New World to retrieve his darling in the old country. He vows: "The moon shall be in darkness, the stars shall give no light / If ever I prove false to my own heart's delight. / In the middle of the ocean there will grow a plum tree / If ever I prove false to the girl that loves me."[106]

These lines, in turn, recall the perennial "Storms Are on the Ocean." There, long absence, distant travel, and personal fidelity all combine in symbolic expression of love's constancy. While this song, sometimes called "The False True Lover," gives no promise of a requited ending—the singer may never see his loved one again and harbors constant fear of infidelities—his faithfulness knows no end: "The storms are on the ocean / And the heavens may cease to be. / This world may lose its motion, love / If I prove false to thee."[107] As consistently as "Goodbye, Old Paint" draws from the "Wagoner's Lad"—time and again its singers reiterate the old stanza "My horses ain't hungry / They won't eat your hay / My wagon is loaded / And rolling away"—the cowboy song calls upon an equally traditional but separate lyrical pattern: the promise of fidelity in the face of departure.[108] Vera Morris characterized Jess's juxtaposition of the tree and ocean as a symbol of "truth in a sea of lies."[109] Eleven years earlier, she said much the same, the message being "There is always hope."[110]

Something else, too. "Goodbye, Old Paint" not only bids an affectionate farewell to a woman left behind, it warmly salutes a horse and the companionship this helpmeet gives the cowboy. "There was actually an 'Old Paint,'" Jess told the *Amarillo Daily News* shortly after he made his first Library of Congress recording. "I have ridden him many miles and he has taken many a drink of water out of the red-maned Canadian in the vicinity of Old Tascosa."[111]

Amid this ceaseless transit of literary and musical materials available to "Old Paint," Jess located his place in the song. During the 1942 recording session, after recalling his decision to become a fiddler and leave a career in classical violin behind, Jess addressed the social creativity of folksong and its correspondence to individual composition. Speaking of "Goodbye, Old Paint," he remarked, "I took parts of it and I heard something. It's an old, old tune, you know. I don't know where it did originate from, the original 'Old Paint,' but I did compose a tune called 'Ridin' Ol' Paint an' Leadin' Ol' Ball,' and got it copyrighted."[112] While Jess saw his copyright as an official imprimatur to his personal, creative contribution, he recognized that in the end the song really has no owner. A moment earlier he crystallized the folk process: "I thought I composed 'Old Paint,' but I don't know, I think it just grew up."

Throughout the last years of his life, Jess kept close stock of "Goodbye, Old Paint." "I had slept on my rights, and was a little late rounding up the old maverick."[113] So he wrote in December 1949 to the Library of Congress. Jess had learned of the American Folklore Society meeting then taking place at the Library, and he took the occasion to send a copy of John Lomax's letter from eight years earlier that saluted his tune and invited him to record. Jess also enclosed his published sheet music, which, he explains, "is none other than "good-bye-ol' paint." After mentioning where he composed the piece, he reflects how his father first came to that part of Texas in 1849, "100 years ago." By the following week, Duncan Emrich warmly responded, marking the beginning of their correspondence.

Jess's contact with the Folk Archive between December 1949 and March 1953—his last communication with them—as well as with local newspapers, ranch journals, and radio broadcasters marked his final telling of "Old Paint's" story. On January 10, 1950, he wrote to Emrich, "If you care to have me do so, I shall be glad to write you, a more detailed History of the song: 'ol' Paint,' and how I came about composing same. My inspiration was gotten from an old ex slave, who broke horses for my father, from 1867 on up until . . . 1888."[114] Here Jess clearly differentiates his version from his source. That same day—exactly nine years after John Lomax invited him to record "Goodbye, Old Paint"—Jess wrote out his detailed account of the song. This history subsequently became the primary source for information on Jess's performance.[115]

Part of that history that Jess relayed went beyond his personal contact with Charley Willis or his family past. Two years earlier, on August 1, 1948, three Wyoming communities dedicated public memorials to the great trail drives of the 1870s and 1880s, the last of which (in 1897) the XIT led. Jess, aware of these ceremonies, sent a published edition of his "Ridin' Ol' Paint an' Leadin' Ol' Ball" to Catherine E. Phelan, the assistant state historian of Wyoming. On the sheet music he wrote "the original, composed in 1885."[116] This date again matched his contact with the song from Charley at age seven. A few weeks later he sent her the pivotal 1941 Lomax letter. Jess now appended to it a note that he also had notarized. At the bottom, half typed and half hand-written, he swears, "I, Jess Morris, hereby make affidavit that the above letter, was received from the late John A. Lomax, while he was in Washington. I also swear that I played the above song, on violin, and sang same for Forty-Eight years previous to receiving the above letter. John A. Lomax searched thru Texas; Oklahoma; Nevada; Montana; N. M., and Arizona for 48 years, before coming to the above decision, that I had the original and only 'Goodbye Ol' Paint.'"[117]

The Wyoming state histori- cal society soon published an article in their journal on the trail dedications as well as separately listing the acces- sioning of Jess's materials. What spoke most to Jess in the article was a letter from a former Texas cattle drover who tells of being hired out in 1871 by the Snyder Broth- ers. In just a few sentences the cowboy catalogs the hard- ships he and his team faced during their three-month- long, thousand-mile journey to Cheyenne. Parts of the route still required clearing and Indian attacks remained a constant threat. On reach- ing Kansas and Nebraska, they found themselves amidst thousands of buffalo, which at any moment could rout the cattle. Compounding these pressures, "they were driving ten herds with about 1,500

FIGURE 50. Jess Morris fiddling, Dalhart, Texas, late 1940s. Courtesy of Vera Morris.

head to the herd."[118] Apparently this image stirred a memory, for Jess incor- porated the statement into his 1950 song history, almost verbatim. He added, "it was one of these herds, that Charley took the trail, and on one of these trips, Charley, learned to sing Ol' Paint."[119] Jess accordingly titled his page-long, single-spaced, typewritten account "History of Ridin' Ol' Paint & Leadin' Ol' Ball, An old cowboy song, the history dating back to: 1871."

Soon Jess asked Emrich for photostats of his history that he could send to journalists, archivists, and politicians. In a note of thanks for the first of these copies, Jess pointed the folklorist to the Wyoming journal. "You will see much history about the Texas Trail Drivers," he writes. "The names of the famous Snyder Bros . . . the monument erected at Pine Bluffs . . . with all the old trail drivers, and their brands."[120] He further promised, "if they don't send you one, then Ol' JESS will send you HIS—I'll do this in appreciation for what you've done for me."

He saw no reason, he told Emrich, "in hiding one's 'light under a bushel.'"[121] He especially wanted notice in his region's major newspapers, and expressed little shyness in getting public officials, like the Texas-born governor of Colorado, or Jess's senator, Lyndon Johnson, to read his song history. Emrich supported Jess in his efforts to reach media outlets and these highly placed personages. He made copies and forwarded items whenever asked. Jess explained: "You see Mr. Emrich, I'm kinda in the category of the old home talent boy, whom they spoke of in the Bible, and times haven't changed much in the last 2,000 yrs. Here's the passage: St. Matthew 13, 57 'a prophet is not without honour, save in his own country, and in his own house.'"[122]

Emrich also understood Jess's creative claim. The place of the individual in folksong, and in particular this folksong, occupied Emrich's attention before he ever heard from Jess Morris. In 1947, Emrich included Oklahoma singer Dick Devall's version of "Goodbye, Old Paint" in an album he compiled of Folk Archive recordings. "The freedom with which Devall treats music and text," Emrich wrote about that performance, "is characteristic of many folk singers and accounts, of course, for the wide differences to be found in the many versions of a single song."[123] By the time Jess's "Goodbye, Old Paint" neared release, Emrich wrote again on this freedom to recreate, focusing now on Jess alone: "Morris's brand on 'Ol' Paint' is clear and unmistakable: he has the oldest known version; he traces it to what may be its point of origin, Charley; he made his own 'special arrangement' for the fiddle; and he has, in the folk tradition, his own song."[124]

These words, however, came late for Jess to long savor. In March 1952, plans for release of "Goodbye, Old Paint" moved forward when Jess gave permission for the Library to issue his performance. The album on which it would appear was originally scheduled for release that fall. Delays ensued, and the date shifted to December. During this wait, Jess sent postcards and letters to Emrich, sometimes teasing and other times troubled, about the production lags. With the election of Dwight Eisenhower, he pondered whether federal support for cultural ventures like this LP might vanish under a new administration. "If the Republicans get in, that it will be 'goodbye ol' Paint.'"[125] Finally, on May 5, 1953, the Library announced the album's publication, and Jess received his copy soon thereafter. With only weeks before his death, "He notified the General XIT Reunion committee," the *Dalhart Texan* reported, "that he wanted to present the record to them as a gift from him to old XIT hands and everyone else interested in the XIT Reunion."[126] Plans called for newspaper and magazine coverage, and the committee's head made several appointments to come over for the presentation. Each time, however, Jess's rapidly declining health prevented it. Jess died June 22, 1953, days earlier having turned seventy-five. In the same Dalhart obituary that recounted his final effort to tie this song to the XIT, the writer calls Jess a "gallant Old Westerner" who has "become nationally known; and his voice, his fiddle and violin music, and his songs have been preserved for all time through original records that now repose in the archives of the Library of Congress in Washington, D. C."

His songs, while preserved, have not reposed. Since then, Jess's grand-nephew, David "Rooster" Morris, the son of Bob and Vera Morris, began performing the song with the fiddle.[127] Rooster, a former working cowboy and ranch manager, heard both his father and his Uncle Red, Vera's fiddling brother, play "Old Paint" at home, but he was too young to have heard Jess. "I didn't know Uncle Jess existed," Rooster said.[128] He credited his awakening to three sources. First was the family history that Vera assembled in the early 1980s that included Jess. Then, two friends: "I got acquainted with Buck Ramsey, and he and Hal Cannon were in love with that song. So it really brightened my interest a lot then." The late Buck Ramsey, a cowboy singer and poet, who in 1996 recorded the song with Rooster's fiddling, linked Jess's performance to Cannon, founder of the National Cowboy Poetry Gathering.[129] "Hal Cannon," Ramsey relates, "considered an album of cowboy songs collected by John Lomax, including Jess Morris' 'Leaving Cheyenne,' ['Goodbye, Old Paint'] to be the prime inspiration behind his wish to organize a gathering which would inspire a revival of cowboy song and poetry, a revival of American West oral traditions. Hal's favorite song on the album was 'Leaving Cheyenne.'"[130] Since 1985, the Cowboy Poetry Gathering has become a major annual celebration, precipitating like events across the West. As its touchstone, Jess's performance of "Goodbye, Old Paint" achieves here what he had hoped at the end of his own life his recording would accomplish: to commemorate his companions at the XIT and encourage the XIT Reunion's efforts to value their lives and works. The Cowboy Poetry Gathering carries forward the spark Jess ignited.

Jess also lives on in classical music. In June 2000, John Steinmetz, a California-based bassoonist, composer, and teacher completed a setting for bassoon and piano based on Jess's 1942 recording of "Goodbye, Old Paint."[131]

Having previously arranged "Streets of Laredo," Steinmetz received a commission from fellow bassoonist Jeffrey Lyman, chair of the winds and percussion department at the University of Michigan's music school, to create a recital piece for a cowboy number. Lyman sent him a cassette of several western numbers including Jess's song, drawn from the performance he discovered on *A Treasury of Library of Congress Field Recordings.*[132] Steinmetz embraced Jess's intensity, moved by "affection for his singing," likening it to a bursting out of emotion. "His singing," he said, "has more feeling than a human voice can contain."[133] He kept that intensity in mind when he wrote performance cues on the notation, telling players to be "forceful," "urgent," and "exuberant."[134] With these words Steinmetz approximated Jess's presence on the recording, translating his vocal subtleties with the suppleness of bassoon technique. The piano, meanwhile, takes the role of Jess's fiddle, and near the end, with bassoon dropping back, it reprises Jess's instrumental interlude. Then the bassoon returns and the duet gradually quiets to silence, "as though the song is riding off into the sunset."[135] With poetic grace, John Steinmetz united the two strands of Jess's musical life, as a fiddler and a violinist.

Jess Morris, whose obituary recognized that he wore a tuxedo as easily as he did denim, depending on which music he played, and was "as much at home in a saddle, astride a good horse, as he was sitting . . . on his front porch," had a life "packed with adventure and interesting experiences."[136] He grew up to be cantankerous and exuberant, garrulous and impassioned, determined and sharp. His ebullient singing sounds like his letter writing, and his letters sound like him talking. He was, Vera Morris said, "a completely honest man. No guile about him. Just himself."[137] He could also be, as Elizabeth Morris Roberts knew from living under the same roof with him, "quite a sourpuss . . . kind of cynical, and yet could make you laugh."[138] She chuckled at how her father and Jess would endlessly argue for the sheer joy of it. Bob Morris remembered how, even when Jess knew the answer, "He'd ask you some question just to see what you thought about it."[139] Bob also said, "He was a pretty cranky feller. He knew what *he* was going to do, you know." No wonder when I asked why he thought Jess never married, Bob ventured, "Too ornery, I guess." One final question put to Bob: "How would Jess like to be remembered?" A moment later he replied, "I imagine as a musician. That was about all he ever talked about."

From Jess's tireless talk of music radiates a microcosm of this nation. His family's journey across successive frontiers follows a familiar tune. It starts with a veteran of the Revolutionary War and a deed signed by Thomas Jefferson. That soldier's path to the Western Reserve leads to his grandfather, now bearing a note from Andrew Jackson as he built his home further inland. Eventually Jess's parents made their way to Texas, where they endured the Civil War, to finally settle amidst the arroyos and rises of the Panhandle. Along with his brothers and sisters, Jess engaged in the mercantilism that prospered their region. He went from a cowboy's job on the world's largest fenced-in ranch to singing on Dalhart's first radio station, whose call letters surely trumpeted a boom town's dreams: "WDAG—Where the Dollars Always Grow."

"Goodbye, Old Paint" follows a migration no less panoramic or unstoppable. It begins in a heritage of British song imported to the Appalachians and spread beyond, to reach a trail-herding former slave on his way to Wyoming. Barely an adult himself, he sang it to young Jess, who later refined it on his fiddle beneath a dugout's makeshift roof. From an old fiddler's convention to a cavatina recital in a concert hall, from the tutelage of European-trained professors in Bartlett, Austin, and Valparaiso to decades of performing with Hispanic Americans at *bailes* and cotillions, from pioneering sound recordings to the committed interest of John A. Lomax, from Oscar Fox to Tex Ritter to Aaron Copland, Jess Morris and "Goodbye, Old Paint" have come a good long way from a blackland farm in Williamson County, Texas. All these interconnecting lives bring Ben Botkin's words to mind: "Culture, like love, laughs at locksmiths."[140] The piece of art Jess wanted us to remember him by was born of a creative process as irrepressible as his own indomitable spirit. In that beloved song he left behind, he gave not only of himself, but something of America too, and its promise.

Throughout this book I have used the following citation practice: Within each paragraph the note number appears after the first sentence of the source cited. The reader may assume that any subsequent quotations within that paragraph come from the same source. Quotations from other sources are indicated by note numbers after the first sentence of the material quoted. Full information on interviews is found in the Works Cited list. Explanations of abbreviations used in the notes appear at the beginning of the Works Cited list.

PREFACE

Thanks to Etta Moten Barnett, Timuel Black, Margaret Burroughs, Ted Gray, Margaret Stewart Joyner, Archie Motley, and Dempsey Travis, who generously shared their memories of Casey Jones. Additional thanks to Michael Flug, archivist of the Vivian G. Harsh Research Collection of Afro-American History and Literature, Carter G. Woodson Regional Library, Chicago Public Library; Frank Francis Jr., director of the Thomas Winston Cole Library in Marshall, Texas; and to Genell Barclay of the Harrison County Museum, who assisted me during my visit there, March 1, 1994, and afterward, to learn more about Casey and his upbringing.

1. Burroughs, "Casey Jones, and Lady Baby," 3.
2. Ibid., 4.
3. Ibid., 5.
4. See the Casey Jones file at the Chicago Historical Society; Archibald J. Motley, Jr.'s 1948 painting *Casey and Mae in the Street*; and *Lizard Music,* a 1992 stage play in which Casey became the model for a lead character. Casey graces the cover of a book about the Maxwell Street market where he often performed, and appears in Mike Shea's documentary noted below. For years, Casey also participated in Chicago's Bud Billiken parade, one of the largest black community spectacles in the country.
5. *Chicago Defender,* June 15, 1974.
6. Black interview.
7. Travis interview.
8. Casey Jones in Mike Shea's 1965 Maxwell Street film *And This Is Free*, Shanachie VHS 1403. This scene can also be accessed on the Web at YouTube under "Casey Jones, Chicken Man."
9. Botkin, "We Called It 'Living Lore,'" 190.

10. B. A. Botkin described the "Living Lore" part of the Federal Writers' Project in ibid., 193–94.

11. "Shad Song," AFS 3654 A2. See Clyde "Kingfish" Smith's twenty-one other recordings housed at the Archive of Folk Culture, AFS 3654 A1 to 3656 A6.

12. Banks, *First-Person America,* 238.

13. Ibid., 239.

14. See Benjamin Filene's analytical account of "Hoochie Coochie Man" in *Romancing the Folk,* 97–109, and Zora Neale Hurston's poetical essay, "High John de Conquer."

15. Botkin, "We Called It 'Living Lore,'" 191.

16. Wade, "Fleming Brown," 9.

17. See Wade, *Catching the Music.*

INTRODUCTION

Thanks to Senior Warden John D. Netherland and Capt. Dick Taylor Jr., both of State Farm penitentiary, as well as Cindy Collins in Central Criminal Records, Virginia Department of Corrections. Warden Netherland had great interest in the history of his institution and was enormously supportive during my visits there. He also had a reputation as the best man-hunting dog-tracker in the state. Further thanks to Texas's Warden Morris Jones at Huntsville Walls, Warden Mike Wilson at Wynne Farm, Assistant Warden Brian K. Horn at Clemens Unit, Sergeant Ken Palombo at Clemens, Sergeant Jesus Peralto at Walls, Michael W. Countz, assistant director of Classification and Records, and especially Simon Beardsley of the Texas Department of Criminal Justice—all generous with their time, guidance, and memories. "Tradition," one sergeant told me, "is what we do everyday."

1. J. Work III, "Typescript of Address," 1.

2. Ibid.

3. See J. Lomax, "Field Experiences with Recording Machines."

4. For more on the establishment of the Archive of American Folk Song, see Wade, *Treasury.* For its ideological roots and historical background, see Archie Green, "The Archive's Shores," in *Torching the Fink Books,* 134–50.

5. "The Library of Congress Is Ready to Begin the Distribution of Albums of Records from the Archive of American Folk Song," Library of Congress Press Release, Office of the Secretary, Feb. 28, 1943, no. 106, p. 1.

6. A listing of the week's events at Fisk used this alternate title. I'm indebted to Fisk University's special collections librarian Beth M. Howse for this information.

7. J. Work IV interview, Nov. 6, 2000.

8. See Gilpin, "Charles S. Johnson." See also Gilpin and Gasman, *Charles S. Johnson.*

9. Charles Johnson's pivotal role during the Fisk/LC project included not only his shaping its research methodology, but also choosing where it took place. In Work to Lomax, July 24, 1941, Work acknowledges that Johnson would select "an area or areas previously studied by him for the recording to be done." In "Now What a Time": Blues, Gospel and the Fort Valley Music Festivals, 1938–1943. LOC American Memory, online collection.

10. C. Johnson, "Chapel Talk," 3.

11. Ibid., 4.
12. Ibid., 14.
13. Ibid.
14. Ibid., 16.
15. Ibid., 15.
16. C. Johnson, "Jazz Poetry and Blues," 18.
17. Ibid., 19.
18. C. Johnson, "Chapel Talk," 12. See also his "Spiritual Autobiography," "Some Notes on a Personal Philosophy of Life," and "Some Suggestions for a New Pragmatic Philosophy," where he repeats this thought. For these sources I'm indebted to George Hutchinson's superb *Harlem Renaissance in Black and White.*
19. C. Johnson, "Spiritual Autobiography," 8.
20. C. Johnson, "Some Notes on a Personal Philosophy of Life," 13.
21. C. Johnson, "Spiritual Autobiography," 8.
22. J. Work III, "Typescript of Address," 3.
23. Ibid., 4.
24. Ibid. John Work III's March 1942 recordings of Frazier and Patterson appear on *Altamont: Black Stringband Music,* Rounder CD 0238 (1989). Other tracks appear on *Black Fiddlers,* Document Records DOCD-5631 (1999). More recently, Joe Dan Boyd's study *Judge Jackson* explores the background of Work III's first field recordings.
25. John Work III's uncle, Frederick J. Work, also played a significant role in the collection and dissemination of black folksong. See his "Search for a Song." For more on the Work family, see Garcia, "Life and Choral Music of John Wesley Work," and Seroff, *Gospel Arts Day.* See also Seroff's notes to *There Breathes a Hope: The Legacy of John Work II and His Fisk Jubilee Quartet, 1909–1916,* Archeophone 5020 (2010).
26. See DuBois, "Of the Sorrow Songs," chapter 14 in *Souls of Black Folk.*
27. See John Wesley Work, "Negro Folk Song."
28. J. Work III, "Typescript of Address," 3.
29. Bruce Nemerov and Robert Gordon discuss Work's thwarted Natchez fire study in Work et al., *Lost Delta Found,* 1–14 and 291–93.
30. Lomax training session lecture notes, undated, but used Sept. 20–22, 1941. LC/Fisk.
31. Handy, *Father of the Blues,* 76–77.
32. For more on functionalism, see Filene, *Romancing the Folk,* 137–51.
33. For George Herzog's 1935 letter to Work III, see Work et al., *Lost Delta Found,* 3–4.
34. Herzog, "Study of Folksong in America," 62–63.
35. A. Lomax, "Functional Aspects of Folklore," 507. At the 1942 conference, Herbert Halpert followed Lomax, further exploring the functionalist approach, 510–512.
36. See A. Lomax's and Spivacke's handwritten notes on prospective album selections such as AFS 1415 B, 1725 B1, and 896 A1. AFC.
37. Botkin, "Folk-Song Record Albums."
38. Botkin, "Applied Folklore," 36.

39. That was Flying Fish Records, then run by Jim Netter. Following the label's sale to Rounder, the album, eventually called *A Treasury of Library of Congress Field Recordings,* became Rounder CD 1500 (1997), the lead title in the Rounder Library of Congress series.

40. For a transcription of Belo Cozad's "Kiowa Story of the Flute," see Willard Rhodes, notes to *Plains: Comanche, Cheyenne, Kiowa, Caddo, Witchita, Pawnee,* AFS L39.

41. Hull, *Addresses and Statements,* 87. See also Hull on cultural isolation, 6.

42. See the reports from the Library of Congress's 1939 and 1940 meetings, *Conference on Inter-American Relations in the Field of Music.* The second of the two includes Alan Lomax's checklist of 350 commercially recorded race and hillbilly songs. His grading system there anticipated the evaluative formula he used at times with selections considered for the Library's folksong albums that soon followed.

    Articles such as Charles Seeger's "Inter-American Relations" and his address "Importance to Cultural Understanding" give larger context to the international goals surrounding the Library's album series. For a historical view of the era's commercial forces that combined with fine arts music initiatives, see Donald Meyer, "Toscanini and the Good Neighbor Policy." Thanks also to John Cowley for sharing his extensive newspaper research and insights on Leopold Stokowski's youth concert tour, the stateside popularity of Brazilian music, and that country's strategic importance to U.S. interests.

43. A. Lomax to Shipp, Apr. 24, 1942. AFC.

44. Parsons to author, ca. Jan. 1995, quoted in Wade, *Treasury.*

45. Parsons to author, ca. Jan. 1995.

46. Quoted in Ives, "Teamster in Jack MacDonald's Crew," 76.

47. From Abbott Ferriss's field notes, May 10, 1939, "Folk Music Recordings Made in Mississippi by Herbert Halpert." AFS.

48. Fletcher Stokes, "Personal History of Informant," Folk Music Survey Files, RG 60 Series 439. See also Folklore, RG 60 Series 438. MDAH.

49. See Cowley's "Collecting the Treasury" for an analysis of the album's contents.

50. J. Lomax and A. Lomax, *Our Singing Country,* xiv.

51. A. Lomax, "Field Notes."

52. The 1941–42 Fisk/LC Coahoma recordings were made on sixteen-inch blanks recorded at 33⅓ rpm, allowing them to record more material per disc. Thanks to Dick Spottswood for this information.

53. Ware, *Cultural Approach to History,* 15. See also Fitzpatrick, "Caroline F. Ware." For more on the shift from item to biography in folklore collecting, see N. Rosenberg, "Icy Mountain Brook," 181.

54. C. Seeger, "Music in America," 411.

55. State Farm, Virginia, is the location as well as the former name for this penal institution, founded in 1896.

56. My NPR *All Things Considered* piece on Learned Hand and his music first aired on Oct. 5, 1999. It includes the multiplication table song. The segment can be accessed on the NPR Web site.

57. Boudreaux interview, Feb. 6, 1997. Ella died in Nov. 2008. For more examples of her family's music, including this track (listed on the *Treasury,* following the

Lomaxes' title, as "Sept ans sur mer"), see *Cajun and Creole Music 1934/1937: The Classic Louisiana Recordings,* Rounder 1842 (1999).

58. Boudreaux interview, Feb. 21, 1999.
59. Ibid.
60. Boudreaux interview, Dec. 17, 1996.
61. Boudreaux interview, Feb. 21, 1999.
62. Archie Green conversation, Sept. 22, 1996.
63. Archie Green conversation, Jan. 4, 1999.
64. A. Green, *Torching the Fink Books,* 211.
65. Archie Green conversation, Jan. 4, 1999.
66. Archie Green conversation, Oct. 3, 2004.
67. E. C. Ball interview with Lornell and Owen, *E. C. Ball and Orna.* Ball used nearly these same words, quoted in Bruce Kaplan's notes to *E. C. Ball with Orna Ball,* Rounder CD 11577 (1996). His relatives and playing partners Blair and Kathryn Reedy showed me that language again from another interview with Ball during my first visit to their home in Nov. 1996.
68. Henderson interview, Nov. 18, 1996.
69. Parsons to author, ca. Jan. 1995, quoted in Wade, *Treasury.*
70. Botkin, "We Called It 'Living Lore,'" 195.
71. Dewey, "Americanism and Localism," 685.
72. Ibid., 684.
73. Ibid., 687.

CHAPTER 1. BILL STEPP

An earlier version of this chapter appeared in *American Music* 18, no. 4, Winter 2000. I feel fortunate to have been welcomed at two Stepp family reunions, one in Kentucky and another in Indiana, where many of Fiddler Bill's grandchildren told me stories about him. At the center of those gatherings stood Becky Arnett. Becky spent years seeking out her grandfather's past, and she eagerly shared the documents and images that she had so painstakingly gathered. Ever available, she and her husband, John Arnett, also took me to places where Bill lived, worked, and eventually raised his family. Other family members, including Becky's mother, Nannie Howard, as well as Dorothy Allen and Elsie Risner, along with Peggy Howard, whose mother played guitar to Bill Stepp's fiddle, furnished priceless photographs in addition to their memories. Bill's Magoffin County neighbors, such as Arnold McFarland of Lakeville, Kentucky, and Ollie Barnett at Stinson Creek, brought to life the joyous role he played in their communities so long ago. Additional thanks to Elizabeth Lyttleton Sturz (and to her daughter, Anna Lomax Wood), who accompanied Alan Lomax on the 1937 collecting trip. Bess Lomax Hawes described the process that led from Bill Stepp's recording to Ruth Crawford Seeger's transcription. Herbert Haufrecht kindly recalled Aaron Copland, the Composers' Collective, and the heady times that inspired their work.

1. The National Cattlemen's Beef Association and Cattlemen's Beef Board sponsored the TV ad first broadcast in spring 1992. As late as summer 2000 the commercial had returned to national television, but with a new announcer (leathery-voiced actor Sam Elliott), and a sped-up arrangement of the "Hoedown" movement from *Rodeo.* According to the Wikipedia entry for "Beef.

It's What's for Dinner," accessed Dec. 14, 2010, both the musical theme and motto continue to air on radio in the "Powerful Beefscapes" ad campaign.

2. Becky Arnett, personal communication, May 1998.

3. Bill Stepp's recording of "Bonaparte's Retreat," AFS 1568 A2, occurred on Oct. 26, 1937, and was first issued in 1971 on *American Fiddle Tunes,* AFS L62.

4. Emerson, Lake and Palmer, "Hoedown" *Trilogy,* Cotillion SD-9903 (1972). In 1972 "Hoedown" reached number 5 on *Billboard's* LP charts. From Rockwell, "Art Rock," 352.

5. Becky Arnett to author, June 12, 1997.

6. Eunice Arnett interview, Aug. 4, 1997. A woods colt is a traditional term for an illegitimate child.

7. From photocopies of Lee County Circuit Court records, dated Oct. 1876, Apr. 1877, and Apr. 1878. Lizzie Seale interviewed by Becky Arnett and Lucy Noe Gay; Gay to author, June 12, 1997.

8. Dorothy Allen interview, Jan. 16, 1997. Lucy Noe Gay and Becky Arnett's sources for this information included Oma Ross, Morning Stepp's granddaughter, and local resident Georgia Lands.

9. Clayton Congleton, son of Bill's sister, Kate Congleton, recalled this scene in a discussion with Lucy Noe Gay and Becky Arnett. Impressions of Stepp's showmanship also came from my interviews with Ollie Barnett, Richard Whitley, and Arnold McFarland, all of whom had seen Stepp perform once he had moved to Magoffin County.

10. Dorothy Allen interview, Jan. 28, 1997.

11. Nannie Howard interview, Jan. 10, 1997. Nannie, born May 5, 1919, died Christmas Day, 2006.

12. William Stepp interview, Aug. 3, 1997.

13. Sam Stepp interview, Oct. 1, 1999.

14. Nannie Howard interview, Jan. 10, 1997.

15. William Stepp interview, Aug. 3, 1997. Interviews with other grandchildren of Bill Stepp included Elsie Risner, Jan. 3 and Aug. 3, 1997; Sonny Stepp, Aug. 3, 1997; Sam Stepp, Aug. 3, 1997, and Oct. 2 and 3, 1999; Gentry Stepp, Aug. 3, 1997; Richard Stepp, Aug. 3, 1997, and Oct. 2, 1999; and Francis Wayne, Jan. 14, 1997.

16. Dorothy Allen interview, Jan. 28, 1997.

17. This popular traditional program piece is called the "Drunken Hiccups." Stepp recorded it for the Library of Congress in 1937.

18. The Archive's card entry for "I'm Gonna Feast at the Welcome Table," AFS 1573 A2, indicates that Stepp is on fiddle, although the recording has no fiddle on it, only a female vocal.

19. See Fuson, *Ballads of the Kentucky Highlands,* and J. Lomax and A. Lomax, *American Ballads and Folk Songs.*

20. H. H. Fuson, letter to Library of Congress, June 28, 1937, Folk Archive correspondence files, AFC.

21. Alan Lomax, letter to the Acting-Chief of the Music Division, Aug. 14, 1937. Lomax Kentucky. Lomax to Harold Spivacke, from Hazard, Ky., n.d., but likely Oct. 18, 1937. Lomax Kentucky.

22. Ova Haney, Superintendent of Morgan County Schools, West Liberty, Ky., to Lomax, Sept. 22, 1937. See also Lomax to Haney, Sept. 8, 1937. Lomax Kentucky.

23. Sturz interview, Jan. 2, 1996.

24. See Lomax Kentucky.

25. Becky Arnett used the term "in good mind" when she began telephoning possible contacts.

26. Barnett interview, Aug. 4, 1997.

27. Roscoe McFarland's name is misspelled in the Archive listings.

28. Lydie McFarland interview, Oct. 2, 1999.

29. Arnold McFarland interview, Oct. 2, 1999.

30. Roscoe McFarland, recorded on Oct. 25, 1937, sang: AFS 1567 A, "The Ship Carpenter"; B1, "Pearl Bryant"; B2, "Fare You Well, My Pretty Little Miss."

31. Clay Walters recorded on Oct. 27, 1934, AFS numbers 1574 B through 1584 B. Many of the twenty-nine pieces he played were songs with his own fiddle accompaniment.

32. Peggy Howard interview, Oct. 8, 1999.

33. Bill Stepp and Mae Puckett recorded together on Oct. 26, 1937, beginning with AFS 1572 B2, "Pretty Little Widow"; B3, "Old Hen She Cackled"; and AFS 1573 B1, "Old Ship of Zion" with Nell Hampton singing. Eula Cooper was recorded on Oct. 27, 1937, AFS 1586 A1, "My Son Johnny O"; A2 "Poor Robin Is Dead"; and 1586 B1, "If I Were Some Little Bird." Basil May recorded on this same day AFS 1587 B, "The Lady of Carlisle." Harvey Porter, recorded on Oct. 24, 1937, appears on AFS 1554 B1, "The Covington Burglar"; and 1554 A, "The Lonesome Scenes of Winter."

34. Arnold McFarland interview, Oct. 9, 1999. See J. Lomax and A. Lomax, *Our Singing Country*: "Vance Song" appears on 322–23 and "Lady of Carlisle" on 162–63. Walter Williams, recorded on Oct. 28, 1937, appears on AFS 1599 B, "Mississippi Sawyer"; 1600 A, "John Hardy"; B1, "The Wild Horse," with Bill Stepp; B2, "The Mud Fence," with Bill Stepp; 1601 A, "East Virginia"; B, "Pass Around the Bottle."

35. A. Lomax, "Field Trips Eastern Kentucky," 57.

36. Two additional performers are ascribed to the Salyersville location. However, these are errors in the Archive log. Banjoist J. M. Mullins came from Floress, Ky., where his recordings were made, and Monroe Gevedon and family are listed as recording in both West Liberty and Salyersville. However, Gevedon came from Grassy Creek, Ky., and was recorded there, prior to the sessions held in Salyersville.

37. Whitely interview, Oct. 8, 1999.

38. Lomax to Spivacke, Oct. 26, 1937. Lomax Kentucky.

39. Kay Starr (vocal), with orchestra. Recorded in 1950 on Capital 1652. Rereleased on LP DT 415. *Hits of Kay Starr.*

40. In June 1998 numerous exchanges concerning both "Bonaparte's Retreat" and the "historians differ" story appeared in the internet discussion group called "rec.music.country.old-time."

41. A. Eaton, *Handicrafts*, 204–5.

42. See Lomax to Eaton, Dec. 9, 1939; Eaton's reply, Dec. 15, 1939; and Lomax's answer, Dec. 18, 1939. Folk Archive correspondence files. AFC.

43. Lomax to Eaton, Dec. 9, 1939. Folk Archive correspondence files.

44. Lomax recorded this story along with many others of Aunt Molly Jackson's in New York City in 1939. For a study of Aunt Molly Jackson, see Romalis, *Pistol Packin' Mama.*

45. J. Lomax and A. Lomax, *Our Singing Country,* 54–55.

46. This quotation appears in a typed headnote for Bill Stepp's "Bonaparte's Retreat." It adjoins the quote from Aunt Molly Jackson that appeared in *Our Singing Country,* 54–55. However, here Lomax attributes those words to Stepp himself. Page marked "S-61." ALC.

47. Gammon, "Grand Conversation."

48. Bayard, *Hill Country Tunes,* No. 87, "Bonaparte's Retreat," n.p. Whistled by F. P. Provance at Point Marion, Pa., Sept. 1943.

49. Burman-Hall, "Southern American Folk Fiddling," 107.

50. Frank Ferrel, "The Eagle's Whistle," *Yankee Dreams,* Flying Fish CD 70572 (1991).

51. J. Lomax and A. Lomax, *Our Singing Country,* 54.

52. Bascom Lunsford, AFS 1834 A3, "Bonaparte's Retreat," recorded in Mar. 1935. Crockett's Kentucky Mountaineers, Brunswick 353, "Bonaparte's Retreat," released in Nov. 1929. Unnamed old-timer quoted in C. Wolfe, *Kentucky Country,* 75.

53. A. A. Gray, Okeh 40110, "Bonaparte's Retreat," released in Aug. 1924. Four years earlier Gray had won third place with this tune in the Georgia Old Time Fiddler's Contest in Atlanta. Gid Tanner and the Skillet Lickers, with Riley Puckett and Clayton McMichen, Columbia 15485-D, "Bonaparte's Retreat," released in Oct. 1929. Smoky Mountain Fiddler Trio with Arthur Smith, Bluebird B6387, "Bonaparte's Retreat," released in July 1936. George Nicholson, AFS 1502 A, recorded at Laurel County, Ky. Boyd Asher, AFS 1528 B1, recorded at Hyden, Ky., and Luther Strong, AFS 1538, recorded at Hazard, Ky.

54. Alan Jabbour, personal communication, Oct. 1994. Jabbour's own writings on Bill Stepp's "Bonaparte's Retreat" include his notes to *American Fiddle Tunes,* which first published this performance, and his article "Copland's Kentucky Muse." See also the four folders on AFS L62, which detail how the album was assembled. Administrative files, AFC.

55. De Mille, quoted in Pollack, *Aaron Copland,* 365.

56. Pollack, *Aaron Copland,* 365.

57. See "Ballads of Lover's Disguises and Tricks," in Laws, *American Balladry from British Broadsides,* 201–25.

58. De Mille's interest in folk music continued beyond "Rodeo." In the 1950s de Mille asked Copland to write a ballet using sea shanties. See her interview in Copland and Perlis, *Copland: 1900 through 1942,* 362.

59. Copland and Perlis, *Copland: 1900 through 1942,* 357.

60. Sandburg, *Good Morning, America,* 15–18.

61. Haufrecht interview, May 8, 1996.

62. See Warren-Findley, "Passports to Change."

63. Haufrecht interview, May 8, 1996.

64. Pollack, *Aaron Copland,* 468.

65. Copland and Perlis, *Copland: 1900 through 1942,* 279.

66. "Sis Joe" appears in J. Lomax and A. Lomax, *Our Singing Country,* on 262; "If He'd Be a Buckaroo" on 249–50; and "Bonyparte" on 54–55. Bess Lomax Hawes recalled playing field recordings for Copland at the Archive around that time, which may have included these selections. See her "SEM Lecture."

67. See chapter 12 for more on Copland and "Goodbye, Old Paint."

68. Tick, *Ruth Crawford Seeger,* 265. See also Tick, "Ruth Crawford, Charles Seeger, and 'The Music of American Folk Songs.'"

69. R. Seeger, *Music of American Folk Song,* 13.

70. Hawes, "SEM Lecture," 2–3.

71. R. Seeger, *Music of American Folk Song,* 23.

72. This is true with the exception of "The Sporting Cowboy," by Watts & Wilson, 241–42, and "Down on Penny's Farm" (called "Po' Farmer" here), 280–81, by the Bentley Boys, both of which were taken from commercial sources. No recordings were cited for "Cotton Eyed Joe," 99; "Old Banghum," 149–50; "Old King Cole," 204–5; "The High Barbaree," 212–13; "Down Down Down," 273; "Bugger Burns," 331; "I Got to Roll," 390; and "Godamighty Drag," 398.

73. Tick, *Ruth Crawford Seeger,* 279.

74. J. Lomax and A. Lomax, *Our Singing Country,* xviii.

75. Ibid., 57.

76. Pollack, *Aaron Copland,* 367. Pollack notes that Copland's source for these three tunes came from I. Ford, *Traditional Music of America.* See also Pollack, 635, n.28.

77. Tick, *Ruth Crawford Seeger,* 272.

78. Nannie Howard interview, Jan. 10, 1997.

79. Becky Arnett interview, Jan. 10, 1997.

80. Dorothy Allen interview, Jan. 28, 1997.

81. R. Seeger, *Music of American Folk Song,* 29.

CHAPTER 2. KELLY PACE

Archie Green had the confidence that before any recordings of this song ever came to be made, some railroader somewhere had commented on "Rock Island Line." It would just take some searching. Charles Wright of the University of Maryland's interlibrary loan department helped put that destination within reach. Others, too, patiently guided this journey: the family of Kelly Pace that included his brother Lawrence and wife Ruby, and their daughter Bobbie Ann Wade; Kelly's sister Lorine Pace Strong; and Kelly's cousin Otis Sams. Deepest thanks to Bob Cochran for introducing me to this wonderful family. Thanks as well to Marcia White of the Arkansas Department of Corrections. On the railroading side, I'm grateful to Gail and William Withuhn. Even from a hospital bed, Bill, the Smithsonian's expert on steam railroads, explained timetable arcana and railroad procedures. Jack Carson and his fellow members of the Rock Island Technical Society generously shared their knowledge of this bygone line. In Little Rock, thanks to Sara Thompson and Charles Rodgers at the Butler Center of Arkansas Studies, and to the Central Delta Depot Museum in Brinkley, Arkansas, where the train daily passed. Thanks also to Kip Lornell's gospel quartet research housed at the McWherter Library of the University of Memphis, under Edwin G. Frank, curator of special collections. Finally, lasting gratitude to Ralph Dawson, who recognized both the medium and the message behind this fabled song.

1. J. Lomax to Ruby T. Lomax, Oct. 1, 1934, box 3D150, folder 3, LFP.
2. J. Lomax to Ruby T. Lomax, Oct. 2, 1934, box 3D150, folder 3, LFP.
3. J. Lomax, *Adventures of a Ballad Hunter,* 147.
4. Field notes, May 21, 1939, from "John and Ruby Lomax Southern Recording Trip," AFC.
5. "Rock Island Line," AFS 2671 A1.
6. J. Lomax, *Adventures of a Ballad Hunter,* 147. Lomax's spoken account of the 1934 Arkansas recordings appears on *The Ballad Hunter,* AAFS L 50, side B.
7. See Oliver, "Rock Island Line"; Cohen, *Long Steel Rail,* 472–77; and Cochran, "Ride It Like You're Flyin'."
8. These officials were, respectively, O. J. Page, C. H. Horton, and R. L. Griffin.
9. The text appears in small type for a monthly feature, called More or Less Personal, about the local divisions. This entry on the Biddle Car Department was reported by Wilhelmina Schultz, *Rock Island Magazine* 25, no. 1 (Jan. 1930): 34. Hereafter cited in these notes as *RIM.*
10. "Modern 'Casey Jones' Blows a Musical Whistle" first appeared in the *Little Rock Democrat* and was reprinted in *RIM* 21, no. 1 (Jan. 1926): 40.
11. "Eight Dead at Rail Crossing Near Carlisle," *Arkansas Gazette,* Oct. 22, 1945.
12. "What Is Pep?" *RIM* 16, no. 10 (Oct. 1921): 37.
13. "What It Means to Be a Rock Island Man," *RIM* 15, no. 1 (Jan. 1920): 7.
14. "How Each Man May Do His Bit for Rock Island," *RIM* 15, no. 5 (May 1920): 13.
15. "The Rock Island—A 100 Per Cent Railroad," *RIM* 15, no. 9 (Sept. 1920): 1.
16. "Getting the Business," *RIM* 17, no. 6 (June 1922): 18.
17. "Trenton Shop Band Puts "Pep" in Meeting," *RIM* 20, no. 12 (Dec. 1925): 42.
18. "Station KTHS Offers Prize!" *RIM* 22, no. 3 (Mar. 1927): 15.
19. "Rock Island Magazine Staff Invades Arkansas," *RIM* 20, no. 7 (July 1925): 12.
20. *RIM* 27, nos. 3–4 (Mar.–Apr. 1932): 15.
21. Under "More or Less Personal, Arkansas-Louisiana Division," *RIM* 27, nos. 5–6 (May–June 1932): 24.
22. Additional songs include "Page Mr. Dempsey, Please," *RIM* 15, no. 11 (Nov. 1920): 30; "Rock Island Song," *RIM* 17, no. 3 (Mar. 1922): 22; "Rock Island Railway" appears on page 31 in *Story of the Rock Island's Seventieth Anniversary Celebration, October 10, 1922,* a booklet published by the magazine. Nelson reprints it under "Colorado-Nebraska Honors Road" in *October, 1922 Rock Island Magazine.* "Our Day Is Marching On," *RIM* 17, no. 11 (Nov. 1922): 42; "A Song of the Great R.I.," *RIM* 18, no. 2 (Feb. 1923): 33; "The Old Rock Island Line," *RIM* 18, no. 4 (Apr. 1923): 55.

   See also Norm Cohen's study of "The Wabash Cannonball" in *Long Steel Rail,* 374–75. He compares it to its 1882 antecedent, "The Great Rock Island Route," written and composed by J. A. Roff. In 1883 Roff followed his original anthem with "A Famous Railroad Line!" For that text, see *RIM* 26, no. 1 (Jan. 1931): 37.
23. "The Golden State," *RIM* 21, no. 7 (July 1926): 39.
24. "The Rock Island Line," *RIM* 26, no. 11 (Nov. 1931): 11.

25. "Add-a-Link to the Rock Island Friendship Chain," *RIM* 26, no. 6 (June 1931): 48.

26. J. Lomax and A. Lomax, *Negro Folk Songs as Sung by Lead Belly,* 35.

27. J. Lomax, "Some Types of American Folk Song," 3.

28. J. Lomax, "Hunting Negro Songs in the Prisons."

29. H. G. McCall, private secretary to Governor J. M. Futrell, wrote to S. L. Tod-hunter, the Superintendent of the Arkansas Penitentiary in a letter dated Sept. 25, 1934, file 3D171, LFP.

30. J. Lomax to Ruby T. Lomax, Sept. 28, 1934, file 3D150, folder 3, LFP.

31. Although the Library's card catalog says it occurred in Little Rock, Lomax's correspondence shows he was in Tucker at the time. On September 28 he directs his wife to send her letters to a postal box in Little Rock, during the time he would be 35 miles south at Tucker.

32. J. Lomax to Ruby T. Lomax, 3D150, folder 3, Sept. 30, 1934, LFP.

33. "Rock Island Line," AFS 236 A1.

34. AFS 236 A1. Author's transcription. See also musical notation in Cochran, "Ride It Like You're Flyin'," 212–13.

35. See Wood, "Development of Arkansas Railroads." The October 1922 issue of the *Rock Island Magazine* also recounts this early history in detail.

36. "Wreck of the Rock Island," *Time,* Mar. 31, 1975, 72. *Time* quoted the familiar Leadbelly version.

37. See Seroff, *Gospel Arts Day,* for Fisk University's teacher training and voice-culture influence on rural schoolteachers and their students. See also J. W. Johnson and J. R. Johnson, *Book of American Negro Spirituals,* 35, and Abbott, "Play that Barbershop Chord."

38. Sams interview, Oct. 23, 1997.

39. "Rock Island Line," AFS 248 A1. Author's transcription.

40. Dawson interview, Sept. 8, 1998.

41. Lornell's and McCallum's separate researches have resulted in a number of works including Lornell's *"Happy in the Service of the Lord,"* and McCallum's "Songs of Work and Songs of Worship." Recorded anthologies, radio broad-casts, liner notes, and other writings also emerged from their efforts.

42. Will Rodgers interview, June 9, 1982, tape 26/14 A, CL.

43. Willie Neal interview, Apr. 14, 1981, transcript, CL.

44. McCallum, "Songs of Work and Songs of Worship," 53, 55.

45. Ibid., 56.

46. Dawson interview, Sept. 8, 1998.

47. Levine, *Black Culture and Black Consciousness,* 262.

48. For a fuller account see Wade, "Tom Paley Interview," 18.

49. "Rock Island Line," AFS 995 B2.

50. See Cochran's "Ride It Like You're Flyin'," 223, n. 24.

51. For Leadbelly's sequence of recordings, see Norm Cohen's chapter on "Rock Island Line" in *Long Steel Rail,* 472–77.

52. "Beatles' George Harrison Dies," *Washington Post,* Dec. 1, 2001.

53. Oliver, "Rock Island Line," 6. I'm grateful to John Cowley for sharing this early account.

54. Ibid., 8.

55. Bickal, "Rock Island Line."
56. West interview, June 4, 1999.
57. Sams interview, Oct. 23, 1997.
58. "Field Holler," AFS 6978 A.
59. "Oh I'm So Sleepy," AFS 244 A1.
60. "Guard Talking to Convict," AFS 244 A2.
61. Sams interview, Oct. 23, 1997.
62. Pace interview, Oct. 24, 1997.
63. From my interview with Kelly's younger sister, Lorine Pace Strong, Aug. 1, 1999.
64. "Samson," AFS 6980 B.
65. "Will You Marry Me, My Pretty Little Miss," AFS 6976 A2.
66. "Story by Kelly Pace," AFS 6975 A.
67. "Pick a Bale o' Cotton," AFS 6975 A.
68. "Samson," AFS 6980 B 1.
69. "Bad Laz'us," AFS 6979 A.
70. "Kelly Pace Speaks," AFS 6983 B.
71. Lomax's letter, dated Sept. 22, 1944, is in the Kelly Pace file, Arkansas Department of Corrections, Pine Bluff, Ark.
72. W. E. B. DuBois, *Souls of Black Folk,* 17.

CHAPTER 3. ORA DELL GRAHAM

Deepest thanks to Leon Milton. Ever since our first conversation in January 1998, he has patiently shared his memories of his much-loved aunt Ora Dell Graham. The day we met he entrusted me with his sole photograph of her, and I'm grateful for his faith that it would return safely home. Thanks as well to Ron Terrell of the Sunflower County Department of Education, who opened the department's files to me and let me borrow three large ring binders of original prints from John Phay's notable 1949 photographic study of Sunflower County's segregated schools. Over the years Nancy Hunter granted me a series of enormously reflective conversations about her life in the Delta, especially in the wartime and postwar periods. Anne Webster of the Mississippi Department of Archives and History generously contacted Mississippi State University for their microfilms of the *Ruleville Record.* Additional thanks to Helen Marie Rowe for her intimate knowledge of folktale, riddle, and recipe. Our talks became a seasonal fixture and I miss those calls. Marie and Bernice Taylor, daughters of Henrietta Taylor, gave their help, too, when it was needed. Tom Rankin, Kathleen Milton, Emma Deal, Isaac Shipp, and Marvin Flemmons all contributed to this study with their insight and experience.

1. Leon "Sonny" Milton interview, Jan. 31, 1998.
2. *Afro-American Blues and Game Songs,* as AAFS L4 (1942), reissued on Rounder CD 1513 (1999). In addition to AFS 4017 A2, "Pullin' the Skiff," and 4017 B2, "Shortenin' Bread," Ora Dell Graham led "Little Girl," 4017 A1.
3. Leon Milton interview, Jan. 31, 1998.
4. "Canons of Selection," published Nov. 15, 1940, appeared in the Librarian's Annual Report. John Cole cites them in *For Congress and the Nation,* 106.
5. Beginning Oct. 23, 1940, the Lomaxes called on Irene Williams, recording her on AFS 4011, 4014, 4015, 4016. Her handwritten (and typed) manuscript is included with the field notes.

6. AFS 4012 and 4013 document several of these singers, including Walter White-head, along with John Lomax himself. AFS 4015 includes Albert and Myrtle Lee Williams and Wash Davidson.

7. While John A. Lomax refers to it as the Drew Colored High School in his field notes, it was called the Drew Colored School from the time of its establishment in 1921. Emma Deal also called it by that name. In addition to my interviews about the school with Emma Deal, Sonny Milton, and Nancy Hunter, who attended it, I'm indebted to Patricia Johnson at Drew City Hall, Leslie Downing from Drew Public Library, and Mrs. Jimmy Langdon, wife of the former superintendent of the Drew school district for additional information on its past.

8. Phay, *Report of a Study of the Education for Negroes in Sunflower County, Mississippi*, 29. Exact numbers of educable children in 1940–41 totaled at 22,754 school-age children, of whom 4,803 (21 percent) were white and 17,951 (79 percent) black. Attendance figures reflected similar proportions, but by half: a total of 11,388 children were enrolled, with 2,177 white (19 percent) and 9,211 (81 percent) black.

9. Phay, *Report of a Study of the Education for Negroes in Sunflower County, Mississippi*, 101. For pupil instructional costs, see table 45, p. 139. Comparative per capita instruction expenditures for white and black students appear in table 33, p. 123.

10. The Phay study showed that for those courses that required fewer individual study materials such as spelling and arithmetic, which could be presented on a blackboard, these same pupils ranked above average.

11. This phrase appears in the field notes on a page titled "Drew Colored High School" in J. Lomax, "Southern Recording Trip."

12. John Grant, AFS 4011 B.

13. Recordings of "All Hid," on AFS 4013 B1, include Ostella Redmond, Jessie MacIntyre, and Perry Redding. Other recordings made at the Drew School include AFS 4014, featuring "Chariot Gambler," "Satisfied," "Hey Pretty One," "John the Rabbit," "Mazoo," "Hoodi-Cat," "Shoo-Fly," "Goin' Over the Mountain," "Old Speckled Lady," and AFS 4017, with "Little Girl," "Pullin' the Skiff," "Rock Candy," and "Shortenin' Bread."

14. Ora Dell Graham, AFS 4017 A2.

15. Deal interview, Oct. 11, 2000.

16. Isaac Shipp interview, Jan. 10, 1998.

17. Quoted in connection with Eva Grace Boone's "Pullin' the Skip" (crossed out and handwritten as "Ship"), AFS 3051, May 25, 1939, in Halpert, "Folk Music Recordings," 330.

18. Sarah Ann Reed, AFS 3070, B2, May 28, 1939.

19. Isaac Shipp interview, Jan. 10, 1998.

20. Ibid. Isaac Shipp sang two verses that day. This is the second of the two. The first verse included the line "I use my hands just like I'm a man / that's pullin' the skiff."

21. John Grant, AFS 4011 B.

22. Sarah Ann Reed, AFS 3070 B2. She sings her first verse: "Saw cow saw / Back your leg / Gimme some milk / Go with my bread / If you don't / Gonna kill you dead."

23. Sandburg quote from *The People, Yes,* 88.

24. Randolph, *Ozark Folksongs,* 3:202. See also "Nottingham Fair," sung by Charles Ingenthron, *Anglo-American Songs and Ballads,* AAFS L20 (1947).

25. Opie and Opie, *Lore and Language of Schoolchildren,* 24.

26. Rammel, *Nowhere in America,* 11. See also Babcock, *Reversible World.*

27. Ora Dell Graham, AFS 4017, A2.

28. J. Lomax, "Southern Recording Trip"; Irene Williams manuscript, 2.

29. See A. Green, *Wobblies, Pile Butts, and Other Heroes,* 322–27. See also McKnight, "Charivaris," and Cockrell, "Jim Crow."

30. Taylor interview, July 6, 1997.

31. Eva Grace Boone, AFS 3051.

32. Parchman women prisoners, AFS 3084 A2.

33. Halpert, "Folk Music Recordings," 453. While Abbott Ferriss took the notes, he acknowledged in our interviews that they reflected Halpert's conclusions.

34. This handwritten text, its contents communicated to Alan Lomax by Fisk student Margaret Wormley, appears in one of his 1942 Library of Congress field notebooks that by November 1996 had found its way to a display case at the Rock and Roll Hall of Fame Museum in Cleveland. On July 26, 1942, Lomax recorded a version of "Pullin' the Skiff" from Emma Jane Davis and her group in Friars Point. However, it did not have these words, nor did he indicate whether these were the same singers.

35. A. Lomax, 1942 field notebooks.

36. The "Pullin' the Skiff" recordings are AFS 3051, Eva Grace Boone, May 25, 1939, Brandon, Miss.; AFS 3070 B2, Sarah Ann Reed, May 28, 1939, Edwards, Miss.; AFS 3084 A2, Parchman women prisoners, May 31, 1939, Parchman, Miss.; John Grant, AFS 4011 B, Oct. 23, 1940, Drew, Miss.; AFS 4017 A2, Ora Dell Graham, Oct. 24, 1940, Drew, Miss.; AFS 6644 A5, Emma Jane Davis, July 26, 1942, Friars Point, Miss. Davis's lyrics also depict the truculent cow.

37. Mullen, *Man Who Adores the Negro,* 175. See also Gaunt, *Games Black Girls Play,* especially her discussion of "Ballin' the Jack," 99–102.

38. Kathleen Milton interview, Jan. 31, 1998.

39. Deal interview, Oct. 11, 2000.

40. Nulton, "Jump Rope Rhymes as Folk Literature," 58. See also Ainsworth, "Jump Rope Verses," 186.

41. The Texas citation comes from Roger Abrahams, "Some Jump-Rope Rimes from Texas," 200; Indiana, from Buckley, "Jump Rope Rhymes," 101; New York, from Knapp and Knapp, *One Potato, Two Potato,* 136; New Zealand, from Sutton-Smith, *Games of New Zealand Children,* 78.

42. M. Brown, *Amen, Brother Ben,* 22, 26.

43. Valin, "Landing on Their Feet."

44. J. Cohen, *Back Roads to Cold Mountain,* 27.

45. Its first reading occurred in 1984 for the National Playwrights Conference at the Eugene O'Neill Theater Center, its Yale Repertory staging in 1986. The production opened at Arena Stage in 1987, and the play was published in 1988, the year of its Broadway opening. Thanks to Amy Saltz, William Partlan, Zelda Fichandler, and Guy Bergquist for the production history and for helping my efforts to reach August Wilson.

46. See T. Harris, "August Wilson's Folk Traditions."

47. A. Wilson, *Joe Turner's Come and Gone*, 26–27.

48. Hay, "Joe Turner's Come and Gone," 98.

49. Rammel, quoted in *Nowhere in America*, 141.

50. AFS 4029 A2. It can be heard on *Alabama, From Lullabies to Blues*, Rounder 1829 (2001).

51. The principal musical differences, both melodic and rhythmic, lie in the first line of the verse and the first line of the chorus. The rhythm depends on the number of syllables in those lines. The York students go up to the subdominant on their chorus, while Ora Dell stays with the tonic and uses the blue note instead.

52. Ruby Smith, AFS 6657, Aug. 11, 1942.

53. AFS 6656 B. The AFS card identifies her as Billie James Levi, but on the recording she tells Alan Lomax her name is Bobbie Mae Brown.

54. Emma Jane Davis, AFS 6644A, July 26, 1942.

55. Celina Lewis, recorded May 26, 1939, AFS 2699 B3; Tom McKinney, recorded Apr. 10, 1936, AFS 617 A1. Though not indicated on the Library card, he accompanied himself with guitar. Henry Truvillion recorded on May 18, 1939, AFS 2664 A1; George James recorded Mar. 14, 1937, AFS 943 A3.

56. Rowe interview, July 27, 2001.

57. Helen Marie Rowe was born in June 1933 and died in August 2006. "Lead Me to the Rock," performed by Wash Dennis and Charlie Sims, AFS 739A, first appeared on AAFS L3, *Afro American Spirituals, Work Songs, and Ballads*, and appears on *A Treasury of Library of Congress Field Recordings*, track 20.

58. See Cussler and De Give, *'Twixt the Cup and the Lip*, 112, 115, and 248–49. See also "Manner of Living of the Inhabitants of Virginia," 215–16.

59. See "hoecake" in Cassidy and Hall, *Dictionary of American Regional English*, 1032–33. Hundley, *Social Relations in Our Southern States*, 343–44. Also, C[harles]White, "De Old Roast Possum," in *My Old Dad's Woolly Headed Screamer*, 8–9; Kinnard, "Who Are Our National Poets?" 339; and Genovese, *Roll, Jordan, Roll*, 549. Kinnard also appears in Jackson, *Negro and His Folklore*.

60. Rowe interview, July 27, 2001. I am indebted to researcher Doug Seroff, who found no reports of the song in his newspaper searches of minstrelsy through vaudeville, or in black stage repertory, Seroff to author, Nov. 23, 2008. Thanks to Tim Brooks for his extensive knowledge of early black music recording, telephone interview, Nov. 16, 2008, and email, Jan. 15, 2009.

61. Thomas, "South Texas Negro Work-Songs."

62. Ibid., 154.

63. Ibid., 162.

64. Lunsford mentions these experiences on his two AFS recordings of "Shortenin' Bread," AFS 1799 B2, and "Shortning Bread," 9491 A1.

65. Bascom Lunsford, AFS 9491 A1. Author's transcription.

66. "Wild Horse (Short'nin' Bread)" from Lunsford and Stringfield, *30 and 1 Folksongs*, 55.

67. See Alan Jabbour, notes to "Old Dad," on *American Fiddle Tunes*, 37–40.

68. Riley, "A Short'nin' Bread Song," *Complete Works*, 7:1957–59.

69. Although his name has been variously spelled in historical accounts, Reese

DuPree signed his name this way on his February 28, 1941, Social Security application. Copy in author's collection.

70. Campbell, "Blues," 118. "Blues are the Negroes' Lament" first appeared in *Esquire,* Dec. 1939.

71. Bobbie Leecan's Need-More Band, "Shortnin' Bread," Victor 20853, recorded Apr. 5, 1927. They sang DuPree's third, seventh, and ninth verses.

72. Oliver, notes to *Bobbie Leecan and Robert Cooksey 1926–27.*

73. This Sept. 1927 version is actually DuPree's second registering of the song. His first, for words and melody registered Feb. 12, 1925, was copyrighted by musician and publisher Clarence Williams. Both times DuPree is named as composer and lyricist.

74. Henry Whitter, Okeh 40064.

75. Perrow, "Songs and Rhymes from the South," 28:142. His rendition of "Shortened Bread" is musically echoed in Dorothy Scarborough's 1925 transcription of a Lynchburg, Va., version in *On the Trail of Negro Folk-Songs,* 151. A similar tune marks the piece Vance Randolph collected in Missouri in 1919. His other version, collected in Missouri in 1941, reflects the popular song's lyrics and, based on its chorus, that tune as well. Randolph's entry on "Shortenin' Bread" appears in *Ozark Folksongs,* 2:328–30.

76. Talley, *Negro Folk Rhymes,* 71–72, 147.

77. Ibid., 158.

78. Botkin, *Treasury of Southern Folklore,* 551.

79. R. W. Gordon quote from "Old Songs That Men Have Sung," 192. Spaeth calls it a folk tune in "Dixie, Harlem, and Tin Pan Alley," 25. His arrangement of a mountain version of "Shortenin' Bread" appears in Richardson, *American Mountain Songs,* 81.

80. White, *American Negro Folk-Songs,* 193.

81. See White, "White Man in the Woodpile," 212.

82. In "Put On the Skillet," Scarborough, *On the Trail of Negro Folk-Songs,* 152–53, which she calls "a slightly different version," a distinctive interval appears in the chorus, the leap of a sixth, which resounds in the Skillet Lickers' 1926 recording, the 1927 release by Earl Johnson's Clodhoppers, and in the earlier cited field recordings of Henry Truvillion and Celina Lewis. May Kennedy McCord sings it on AFS 5302 A1. It also appears in Reese DuPree's handwritten notation that he submitted for copyright. Absent any notation but apparent from its poetic meter, Robert W. Gordon's version in "Fiddle Songs," 75, suggests this pattern, as do Frank C. Brown's versions F and H, and Newman Ivey White's first version. See F. Brown, *Frank C. Brown Collection of North Carolina Folklore,* 535–38, and White, *American Negro Folk-Songs,* 193. Finally, Gates Thomas's "Don't Love-a Nobody," noted previously, uses a different interval in the same part of its chorus, but to similar effect.

83. Scarborough, *On the Trail of Negro Folk-Songs,* 149.

84. Ibid., 149–51.

85. Jacques Wolfe, "Short'nin' Bread," 1928 sheet music edition.

86. From Wolfe's "Short'nin' Bread" copyright registration card, Apr. 15, 1935, Library of Congress.

87. Spaeth, *History of Popular Music in America,* 471.

88. See Hughes and Meltzer, *Black Magic,* 310.

89. Spaeth, "Dixie, Harlem, and Tin Pan Alley," 23.

90. Cohen, notes to *Minstrels and Tunesmiths,* 2.

91. In turn, Ora Dell's interpretation caught the attention of Linda Tillery and the Cultural Heritage Choir, who recorded Ora Dell's version on their *Shakin' a Tailfeather* CD, Music for Little People R2 72940 (1997).

92. See Rammel, *Nowhere in America,* 37–38, 42.

93. Ora Dell at age seven, for instance, appears along with her enrolled siblings on the 1935 "List of Educable Children" in the Drew school district. That form, issued by the state, names the students, their parents or guardians, race, gender, school, possible disabilities, and status as full or part-time attendees. Ora Dell does not appear on the 1937 list. Department of Education papers (series 21), MDAH.

94. Alan Lomax to Ora Dell Graham, Mar. 19, 1942, and her signed release dated Mar. 22, 1942, in Ora Dell Graham correspondence file, AFC.

95. Evans, *Big Road Blues,* 167–264. Robert Palmer discusses Dockery's importance in *Deep Blues,* 54–57, as does Evans, *Big Road Blues,* 174–78.

96. Hunter interview, Jan. 31, 1997.

97. Hunter interview, Mar. 8, 1999.

98. Leon Milton interview, Jan. 31, 1998.

CHAPTER 4. CHRISTINE AND KATHERINE SHIPP

Many persons contributed with open hearts to this story of "Sea Lion Woman," beginning with Delta native Abbott Ferriss. Fifty-eight years after Abbott guided folklorist Herbert Halpert down Mississippi's dusty highways in the spring of 1939, he provided a home base in my search for the Shipp family. In Byhalia itself, thanks begin with Joseph Travis. It took a couple of trips to prove that I wasn't, as he said, "an ax murderer." Then he pointed the way to Luella Shipp's just up the road. Her flood of recollections led to her family in Memphis, where children of Christine and Katherine Shipp lived. To Gertha Mae Brooks, Opal Broadway, Thadis Cosby, and Sam Baker, deepest thanks for their passion, knowledge, and support. They in turn led me to Isaac Shipp, a truly amazing man who sang on some of the 1939 Library of Congress recordings. Isaac and I talked time and again, and I will always remain in awe of him. Since his death, I've had the good fortune to converse with his daughter LaVern Shipp Baldwin. Thanks are also due *The General's Daughter* film director Simon West; Kevin Koloff and Jayne Edwards at Paramount Pictures; the late Greg Hale Jones; Russell Ziecker and Jodi Tack of Milan Records; and Jake Guralnick of Rounder Records. Each played a crucial role as this song made its way from the *Treasury* to the screen. Finally, thanks to Herbert Halpert and his wife, Nettie, who so warmly passed along their memories of this song and the remarkable Shipp family singers.

1. Luella Shipp interview, Feb. 8, 1997. Luella, born in Nov. 1919, died in Oct. 2000.

2. Eri Douglass to Ethel Bowen, Apr. 6, 1939. Other correspondence includes Bowen's postcard reply, Apr. 8, 1939, a letter from state music director Jane T.

Browne to Bowen, Apr. 21, 1939, a list titled "Songs sung at Mrs. Bowen's by the Shipp Spiritual Club," and a separate list of songs, informants, and addresses provided by Mrs. Bowen. MDAH.

3. "Song to President Lincoln" in Halpert, "Folk Music Recordings," 24–25.
4. Halpert, "Folk Music Recordings," 40.
5. Ibid., 64.
6. Ibid., 190.
7. Luella Shipp interview, Feb. 8, 1997.
8. Abbott Ferriss, longhand field notes, later included in Halpert, "Folk Music Recordings," notebook 3, RG 60, MO 671, MDAH. Also available as thirteen pages of typescript in the field notes, titled "Negro Folk-Songs and Spirituals—Shipp Family" in "Folk Music Recordings," 193–211. AFC.
9. Halpert, "Folk Music Recordings," Shipp Family field notes, 201. See also 195.
10. Quoted in Isaac Shipp interview, Jan. 10, 1998. Other taped interviews with Isaac Shipp occurred Dec. 21, 1997, Feb. 6 and 7, 1998, Apr. 8, 1998, July 5 and 7, 2002. On Apr. 3, 2007, Isaac died at home. He was ninety-one.
11. Halpert, "Folk Music Recordings," 194.
12. Ibid., 195.
13. Ibid., 194.
14. Ibid., 195.
15. Ibid., 194.
16. Brooks interview, May 28, 1997.
17. Luella Shipp described this repeated scene.
18. Isaac Shipp interview, Jan. 10, 1998.
19. Halpert, "Folk Music Recordings," 195–96.
20. Quoted in Isaac Shipp interview, Jan. 10, 1998.
21. Broadway interview, June 5, 1997.
22. Isaac Shipp interview, Jan. 10, 1998.
23. Halpert, "Folk Music Recordings," 196.
24. Sarah Ann Reed, in Halpert, "Folk Music Recordings," 404. Reed with "young people's group" recorded "Seline" on May 28, 1939, AFS 3069 B2.
25. Halpert to author, Feb. 10, 1997.
26. I explored this theme in my NPR *All Things Considered* piece "The Shipp Family Singers," which aired July 10, 1998.
27. Isaac Shipp interview, Jan. 10, 1998.
28. Ibid.
29. Ibid.
30. Isaac provided these dates.
31. Matthew 17.20 (Authorized Version): "If ye have faith as a grain of mustard seed, ye shall say unto this mountain, Remove hence to yonder place; and it shall remove; and nothing shall be impossible unto you."
32. Though Isaac told Halpert and Ferriss during the recording session that he left from New York, that wasn't the case. For personal reasons, he didn't want his mother to know his true place of departure.
33. Isaac Shipp interview, Jan. 10, 1998.
34. Halpert, "Folk Music Recordings," 211.
35. Isaac Shipp provided these dates. Shipp interview, Feb. 6, 1998.

36. Isaac Shipp interview, Feb. 7, 1998.

37. Isaac Shipp interview, July 7, 2002.

38. AFS 3008 B3.

39. Isaac Shipp interview, July 7, 2002.

40. Luella Shipp interview, Feb. 8, 1997.

41. AFS 3008 B3. Author's transcription.

42. Isaac Shipp interview, Jan. 10, 1998.

43. Ibid.

44. AFS 3008 B3.

45. Alan Lomax to Katherine and Christine Shipp, Apr. 24, 1942. The Shipps' reply is dated Apr. 27, 1942. Lomax sent a follow-up letter, May 1, 1942, along with an authorization form. AFC.

46. Katherine and Christine Shipp to Alan Lomax, Apr. 27, 1942. AFC.

47. Spivacke's unsigned, handwritten notes are in an administrative file for the published recordings at the Archive of Folk Culture.

48. Footnote 6 to "Sea Lion Woman" on AFS L4, *Afro-American Blues and Game Songs,* reissued as Rounder CD 1513 (1999). On Aug. 12, 1942, Alan Lomax recorded Anne Williams singing what he by then titled "Sea Lion" in Dundee, Miss., AFS 6669 B4. Unfortunately, at the time of this writing, its reference tape could not be found.

49. Isaac Shipp interview, July 7, 2002.

50. Isaac Shipp interview, Jan. 10, 1998.

51. Isaac Shipp interview, July 7, 2002.

52. Ibid.

53. AFS 3067 B1.

54. AFS 3067 B1. Author's transcription. Where Abbott Ferriss wrote "sea lion" in his notes, I have transcribed this as "see lying."

55. "Seline," recorded on May 28, 1939, AFS 3069 B2, by Sarah Ann Reed and "young people's group." Author's transcription. Ferriss wrote her first name as "Sara" in his handwritten notes.

56. Talley, *Negro Folk Rhymes,* 21. Perrow, "Songs and Rhymes from the South," 138. In addition to Odum and Johnson in their 1926 *Negro Workaday Songs,* White discusses this verse in *American Negro Folk-Songs,* 151–52, citing its multiple appearances in minstrel songsters.

57. Scarborough, *On the Trail of Negro Folk-Songs,* 224–25.

58. AFS 2689 B1. Author's transcription.

59. Hawes makes this point in B. Jones and Hawes, *Step It Down,* 117, unnumbered note.

60. B. Jones and Hawes, *Step It Down,* xv.

61. "Way Down Yonder, Sometimes" appears in ibid., 100–101. Bessie Jones sings "Sometimes" on *American Folk Songs for Children,* reissued as part of *Sounds of the South,* Atlantic 7 82496-2 (1993).

62. B. Jones and Hawes, *Step It Down,* 100.

63. Bess Hawes explores the distinction Bessie Jones made between plays and games in B. Jones and Hawes, *Step It Down,* xiv–xv.

64. B. Jones and Hawes, *Step It Down,* 100.

65. Luella Shipp interview, Feb. 8, 1997.

66. Broadway interview, Oct. 25, 1997.

67. West interview, June 4, 1999. More of his thoughts on the movie's music appear in his liner notes to the film soundtrack.

68. The four songs were "Sea Lion Woman," "Rock Island Line," "Lead Me to the Rock," and "Sept ans sur mer." All but the last appeared in the completed film. Greg Hale Jones and I corresponded about the songs, and I interviewed him by phone on June 3 and 4, 1999.

69. West interview, June 4, 1999.

70. That's not to say national film reviewers caught this connection or found any particular significance in the folk music tracks. Music purchasers, however, did respond positively to "Sea Lion Woman," with "She Began to Lie" taken as the film's highlight. A number of these reactions have been posted on the Amazon.com Web site for *The General's Daughter*.

71. *Music from the Motion Picture: The General's Daughter*, Milan 73138 35885-2 (1999).

72. The term *trance-beat* appeared on the packaging of both the soundtrack CD and the disc LP.

73. John Travolta appeared on the *Oprah Winfrey Show* on June 11, 1999. Thanks to Jayne Edwards at Paramount Pictures who saw that appearance and reported it to me.

74. On Aug. 12, 1999, I sent the lyrics to the label, which then forwarded them to the Korean officials.

75. Isaac Shipp interview, Jan. 10, 1998.

76. Ellison, "Little Man at Chehaw Station," 28.

77. Motif J1291.1.1, "Why is it that a black cow eats green grass, gives white milk and yellow butter? For the same reason that blackberries are red when they're green." Baughman, *Type and Motif-Index*, 303.

78. Unfortunately, my efforts in May 1998 to contact Nina Simone, who lived in France, about her evolution of the song did not succeed. Thanks to her manager Rusty Michael in Nashville for the help he did provide.

79. Feist's popular recording of "Sealion" appears on *The Reminder*, Cherrytree/Interscope Records B0008822-02 (2007). As of Nov. 7, 2007, *Billboard* reported U.S. album sales of 333,000. Thanks to Julian Kerbis for passing along this figure. Email to author, Nov. 19, 2007. Feist discussed her contact with the song on CBC, posted at Radio 2 Blog, "See Line/Sea Lion Woman," by Li Robbins, May 30, 2008.

80. Ellison, "Little Man at Chehaw Station," 43.

81. Ibid., 44.

82. Ibid., 26.

83. Ibid., 47.

84. Ibid., 48. Original emphasis.

85. Ibid. Original emphasis.

CHAPTER 5. NASHVILLE WASHBOARD BAND

On October 22, 1997, the day after *A Treasury of Library of Congress Field Recordings* went into national release, a piece that I titled "The Beautiful Music All Around Us: Washboards, Street Music, and John W. Work III" aired on National Public Radio's

All Things Considered. To write that report and eventually this chapter, I am indebted to the late scholar Charles K. Wolfe. He was a longtime and dear friend. In May 1997, on a trip to Nashville to learn more about the Nashville Washboard Band, Charles showed me where they lived and where they performed. Without him, too, I would have not contacted Hugh Cherry. Charles Wolfe was generous in so many ways and he is missed.

A personal thanks as well to Bruce Nemerov, who freely shared his continuing research on John Work III at the Center for Popular Music, Middle Tennessee State University, Murfreesboro. Thanks to Bobby Hebb and his archivist, Joe Viglione, for making our conversation possible. As Joe said, Bobby Hebb was an American treasure. At Fisk, Beth M. Howse has been an endless help, even to the point of recording on audio tape a piece of microfilm text that could not otherwise reproduce. Finally, I'm indebted to John Work IV, who alerted me to the signal importance that Charles S. Johnson played in his father's life. From that point on so much else became clear.

1. John Work IV interview, Nov. 6, 2000.
2. J. Work III, "Folk Songs of the American Negro," 33.
3. J. Work III, "Negro Folk Music." Work repeated this phrasing in *American Negro Songs and Spirituals*, 44.
4. J. Work III, "Negro Folk Music."
5. "Tuxedo Junction" is listed in AFC logs as "Deary, Don't Be Angry." AFS 6109 A1.
6. Here I rely on this more conventional spelling of his name based on John Work's notes. Lomax spelled his name "Theopolis."
7. Alan Lomax, from his handwritten field notebook from the 1942 Coahoma trip. ALC.
8. Charles Wolfe suggested this number of street bands during one of our 1996–97 conversations about the Nashville Washboard Band. He is later quoted with this figure in *Too Late, Too Late. Vol. 10 (1926–1951)*, Document Records DOCD-5601 (1998).
9. Evans, notes to *Good Time Blues*, 5. See also Oliver, "Tub, Jug, Washboard Bands."
10. Paramount All Stars, "Hometown Skiffle, Parts One and Two," Paramount 12886 (1929). See Dixon, Godrich, and Rye, *Blues and Gospel Records*, 703–4.
11. See *skiffle* in Hall, *Dictionary of American Regional English*, 992.
12. Vocalion 1401. Thanks to Dick Spottswood for this reference as well as to the Paramount All Stars recording noted above.
13. Joe Wilson, notes to *Beat It, Blow It, Strum It, Hum It!* See also Sam Charters, notes to *American Skiffle Bands* and his writings about jug bands in *Country Blues*, 70–89.
14. See Robbins, "A World-Within-a-World."
15. Huddleston, *Big Wheels and Little Wagons*, 52.
16. Ibid., 63.
17. James Campbell, unissued tape made by collector Don Hill in April 1961. Hill's work with this group alerted producer Chris Strachwitz, which led to the Arhoolie LP *Blind James Campbell and His Nashville Street Band*, Arhoolie F1015 (1963), and reissued as CD 438 (1995). Great thanks to Don Hill for sharing his research.

18. Chris Strachwitz recalled in a June 1, 2009, conversation how Campbell and his bandmates kept referring to the earlier Nashville Washboard Band because of their unforgettable percussionist.

19. Strachwitz, notes to *Blind James Campbell.*

20. Work papers, box 3, folder 8, Fisk. Part of this page is reproduced in the liner notes to *John Work III, Recording Black Culture,* SFR-104 (2007). See also Nemerov, "John Wesley Work III."

21. J. Work III, "Folk Songs of the American Negro," 27. Thanks to David W. Ment, Head, Special Collections at Milbank Library, Teachers College, Columbia University, for making this thesis available. Work repeats this story in abridged form in *American Negro Songs and Spirituals,* 35–36.

22. J. Work III, "Folk Songs of the American Negro," 28.

23. Ibid., 27.

24. Compare ibid., 33, "Then there were . . ." with J. Work III, *American Negro Songs and Spirituals,* 44, "There is another group . . ."

25. George D. Hay, Prince Albert Grand Ole Opry broadcast, July 11, 1942. Thanks to Alan Stoker and the Country Music Foundation Library for this air check.

26. For more on the Grand Ole Opry's expression of performance values and country virtues, see Bill Malone, *Don't Get above Your Raisin'.* See also Charles Wolfe, *Good-Natured Riot,* for insight into the Opry's early years.

27. For this term that Roy Acuff used, as well as for several of the examples cited, I'm indebted to his biographer, Elizabeth Schlappi. See also her *Roy Acuff,* 21. Thanks also to Grand Ole Opry music collector and musician Dick Hill. Our March 2003 conversations and correspondence led to Dick's generously sending along his air checks of Pap's Jug Band Prince Albert Show appearances from Feb. 14 and July 26, 1942. See also Hill, "The Grand Ole Opry, 1944–45." Joe Bussard provided tapes of two later shows from Luray, Va., Sept. 27, 1959, and a WSM broadcast of Oct. 12, 1957.

28. AFS 6109 A3.

29. Christine and Katherine Shipp recorded it as a childhood song for the Library of Congress, AFS 3008 B2.

30. A wealth of recorded precedents may have contributed to the band's conjoining of the two songs. Among them see Sam Theard's 1929 "You Rascal You," accompanied by Charles "Cow Cow" Davenport, soon followed by others on the Vocalion label. Tampa Red's July 1930 version includes side comments and a female-sounding voice much like the Nashville Washboard Band's rendition. In 1928 Stump Johnson recorded "Monkey." Clarence Williams recorded it soon thereafter and then "Rascal" a month later. In 1932 Ben Curry recorded "Rascal" on a banjo-mandolin and harmonica.

31. Hebb interview, Apr. 9, 2009.

32. While Hebb remembered shopping-bag salesmen, he did not specifically remember blind Nashville street singer Cortelia Clark, who sold them from his spot on Nashville's Fifth Avenue North. Clark's *Blues in the Street,* RCA LPM 3568 (1966), received that year's Grammy for best folk recording. Thanks to Tennessee folklorist Roby Cogswell for his memories of Cortelia Clark during our May 23, 1997, conversation.

33. Hebb interview, Apr. 9, 2009.

34. See Cannon's Jug Stompers, "Madison Street Rag," *Gus Cannon Complete Recorded Works, Volume One,* Document Records DOCD-5032 (1990). Cannon, who recorded it twice, uses this line in his 1928 recording.

35. From typewritten page titled "6109 Lomax-Fisk (1)" in 1942 Coahoma/Fisk folksong expedition files. LC/Fisk.

36. I base this count on the session's contents rather than the AFC card catalog. In the last of the demonstrations, Thomas Carroll leads a rendition of "Bye Bye Blues." The recordings are listed as AFS 6109 A1 through B4 and continue on a separate disc, 6604 A1 through A7. Also see Groom, "Nashville Washboard Band," for his summary of the session.

37. Guthrie Meade cites this seventeenth-century date with his "Soldier's Joy" listings in *Country Music Sources,* 713–14. For more on "Soldier's Joy," see Burman-Hall, "American Traditional Fiddling," "Southern American Folk Fiddle Styles," and "Southern American Folk Fiddling"; Jabbour, notes to *American Fiddle Tunes,* to Leizime Brusoe's 1940 performance of "French Four"; "The King's Head," no. 21 in Bayard, *Hill Country Tunes,* n.p., and Bayard, *Dance to the Fiddle,* 303–10, 571–72; Titon, *Old-Time Kentucky Fiddle Tunes,* 178–79; and Andrew Kuntz, "The Fiddler's Companion" (www.ibiblio.org/fiddlers/), an internet site that includes "Soldier's Joy."

38. The late William Bruce Olson noted that a ca. 1760 single-sheet song, with music and bearing the title "The Soldier's Joy," survives in the British Library. "Soldier's Joy" file, AFC.

39. The scholar was Bruce Olson; see http://www.csufresno.edu/folklore/Olson/.

40. "Soldier's Joy," Vocal Music, or the Songster's Companion (London, ca. 1778), 240. Bruce Olson located this printing of the song, with music, but without a title, in the Folger Shakespeare Library. "Soldier's Joy" file, AFC.

41. See Robert Crawford, *The Bard,* 199–200, and Burns, *Burns: Poems and Songs,* which includes "Soldier's Joy" in musical notation, 158.

42. The full Thomas Hardy quotation appears with "Soldier's Joy" at Kuntz, "Fiddler's Companion."

43. See "The King's Head" in Bayard, *Hill Country Tunes.* See also Edwin Johnson Trio, "Polska from Boda/Soldier's Joy" on *Dance Music: Breakdowns & Waltzes,* Folk Music in America series, LBC 3 (1976).

44. Cited in Titon, *Old-Time Kentucky Fiddle Tunes,* 178.

45. Burman-Hall classified the tune according to these regions.

46. C. Wolfe, quoted in "Rural Black String Band Music," 32.

47. See Fulcher, "Cuje Bertram," 60. See also *Black Fiddlers,* Document Records DOCD-5631 (1999), for Bertram's 1970 home recordings.

48. "Soldier's Joy," Taylor's Kentucky Boys, Gennett 6205. For additional recordings, see *Kentucky Mountain Music,* Yazoo 2200 (2003); for discographical information see Russell, *Country Music Records,* 894–95; and Dixon, Godrich, and Rye, *Blues and Gospel Records,* 93, 758–59. During the session that included Doc Roberts, Booker also recorded with his family band as the Booker Orchestra.

49. For information about Jim Booker and Taylor's Kentucky Boys, see Nevins, notes to *Kentucky Mountain Music,* and Meade and Nevins, notes to *Wink the Other Eye.*

50. For more on common-stock repertory see Russell, *Blacks, Whites and Blues,* 31.

51. Talley, *Negro Folk Rhymes,* 45. The tune transcribed there is "Soldier's Joy." The tune referred to in the headnote and which appears on the two commercial recordings cited is different and often called "Too Young to Marry."

52. AFS 6109 B2.

53. See O. Wilson, "Heterogeneous Sound Ideal," 329. I'm indebted to Travis A. Jackson for bringing up Wilson's work in relation to the Nashville Washboard Band's sound in his review of *Black Appalachia.*

54. O. Wilson, "Heterogeneous Sound Ideal," 327–28.

55. Ibid., 338.

56. Jamieson interview, Mar. 3, 1998.

57. Quoted in Jamieson interview, Mar. 3, 1998.

58. Jamieson interview, Mar. 3, 1998.

59. Jamieson, "Gribble, Lusk and York," 49. I've also written about Jamieson and these recordings in "New Photos, Old Daguerreotypes" and in my notes to *Black Appalachia.*

60. Alan Lomax, notes from July 25, 1942, during his visit with Henry Sims and Muddy Waters at the Stovall plantation. I examined this notebook in Nov. 1996 at the Rock and Roll Hall of Fame and Museum in Cleveland. See also Wardlow, "Henry 'Son' Sims."

61. J. Work III, "Typescript of Address," 4.

62. See Abbott and Seroff, *Out of Sight,* 247–51.

63. See Linn, *That Half-Barbaric Twang,* 91.

64. Spottswood, notes to *How Low Can You Go,* 6–7.

65. The "bull fiddle—cord-can—one-string tuning and interview" (as Lomax labeled it) appears on AFS 6604 A6.

66. Washboard solos are AFS 6604 A1, 2, 3, 4, and 5.

67. Alan Lomax notebook entry. From one of his three handwritten notebooks used during the 1942 Fisk/LC Coahoma trip. ALC.

68. Ibid.

69. A. Lomax's notes, essentially preliminary thoughts, were intended for what eventually became the CD *Black Appalachia.* ALC.

70. "Red Hot Mama" and "Drunk Man's Strut," Jimmy O'Bryant's Washboard Band, Paramount 12246 (1924).

71. Actually titled "Bukka's Jitterbug Swing," Okeh 05625 (1940).

72. Blaustein, "Jugs, Washboards and Spoons," 79.

73. Morton, *DeFord Bailey,* 21.

74. Courlander, *Negro Folk Music,* 209. See also Blaustein commenting on Courlander's thoughts in "Jugs, Washboards and Spoons," 78.

75. Courlander, *Negro Folk Music,* 206.

76. I'm indebted to drummer and teacher Steve Larrance for his analysis of Theophilus Stokes's recordings.

77. "Spooky Drums No. 1," *Baby Dodds Talking and Drum Solos,* Folkways FJ-2290. Dodds played washboard with his brother, clarinetist Johnny Dodds, in the Chicago Footwarmers.

78. Nat Hentoff's comments on "Soldier's Joy" first appeared in his review of *A Treasury of Library of Congress Field Recordings,* "American Folk Songs, Direct from the Field." He subsequently reprinted this review in *American Music Is,* 243–46.

79. Cherry interview, May 30, 1997.
80. From typewritten page titled "6109 Lomax-Fisk (1)" in 1942 Coahoma/Fisk folksong expedition files. LC/Fisk.
81. Olsson, *Memphis Blues and Jug Bands,* 34.

CHAPTER 6. VERA HALL

This study of "Another Man Done Gone" began in western Alabama in January 1997 with the aid of Hank Willett and the Alabama Center for Traditional Culture. He kindly led me to Alan Brown of the University of West Alabama and thence to Gregor Smith, kin to Ruby Pickens Tartt and caretaker of her collection at the Julia Tutwiler Library in Livingston. Apart from her own memories of Doc Reed, Enoch Brown, and Ruby Tartt, Gregor introduced me to Tartt's friend Nathaniel Reed, to Tartt's daughter, Fannie Pickins Inglis, and to Vera Hall's neighbor Garrett Williams. A decade later Michael Courlander, with his wife, Phyllis, opened his home and shared his father's files of this music he loved so much. Roger Misiewicz generously sent copies of the song's older commercial recordings, and Lynn Abbott provided early sheet music renditions of "I'm Alabama Bound" from the Hogan Jazz Archive at Tulane University. Eugenia Ho, in turn, brought the music to life as she played these piano scores. Thanks also to Michael Frank and to Pat Morgan for helping me reach blues musicians Jack Johnson and Willie Smith, who continued to bring this song to neighborhood audiences everywhere.

1. Cards in box 3D 198. LFP. This account, rewritten in the first person and presented with slightly less detail, appears in John A. Lomax, *Adventures of a Ballad Hunter,* 202–3.
2. Ruby Pickens Tartt acknowledged that Vera herself was not wholly sure when she was born. Tartt, along with John A. Lomax (box 3D 198, LFP), and Alan Lomax (in his July 1964 *Sing Out!* obituary), and Laurella Owens (*Totin' the Lead Row*) gave Vera's birthdate as 1906. More recent scholarship, including the *Encyclopedia of Alabama,* cites 1902 as her year of birth. We know Vera married in 1918. Her parents' encouragement of the union makes much more sense for a girl of sixteen than for a girl of twelve.

    Vera's maiden name was Hall. Later she married Willie Ward, making her Vera Hall Ward (though some have written this as Vera Ward Hall). An Alabama probate court decision on her estate gives her name as "Adell Ward." Researcher Gabriel Greenberg found "Adele" on the 1920 census, but "Vera" ten years later. She called herself Vera in all her meetings with Tartt and the Lomaxes, and said her parents did the same.
3. AFS 4049 A4 and 4049 B1.
4. Sandburg, *New American Songbag,* 84. Sandburg's Jan. 1944 visit is recounted in box 3D 198, LFP.
5. Siegmeister describes this visit in "Letter from Alabama."
6. Alan Lomax wrote to Vera Hall on Mar. 20, 1942, for her permission to issue "Another Man Done Gone." AFC. It appeared on *Afro-American Blues and Game Songs,* AAFS L4.
7. John Lomax, box 3D 198, LFP.
8. John A. Lomax, "Blues and Hollers: 'Being Lonesome' Songs," *The Ballad Hunter, Part II,* AFS L49.

9. Alan Lomax Collection, tape 812, AFC.

10. See McDearman, "Black Belt."

11. Figures in C. Johnson, *Growing Up in the Black Belt,* xviii.

12. Ibid., 44.

13. See L. Smith, "History of Sumter County."

14. Garrett Williams interview, Jan. 24, 1997.

15. C. Johnson, *Growing Up in the Black Belt,* 46.

16. See "Reckon You Might Say I's Jes Faithful," ex-slave Charlie Johnson's account in A. Brown and Taylor, *Gabr'l Blow Sof',* 80.

17. C. Johnson, *Growing Up in the Black Belt,* 194.

18. Spratt, *History of the Town of Livingston,* 130.

19. Ibid., 129.

20. Ibid., 130.

21. Vera Hall Interview Transcription for Reel Two (missing tape), 1–2. Alan Lomax Collection. AFC.

22. Program notes, "Concert of Folk Music," Fourth Annual Festival of Contemporary American Music, May 10–16, 1948, Columbia University.

23. A. Lomax, *Rainbow Sign,* 22.

24. The notation "Sunday, May 23" in Lomax's hand on a piece of paper left in tape box 819 provides a possible date for the recording. Alan Lomax Collection, AFC.

25. Alan Lomax Collection, tape 807, AFC.

26. Ibid., tape 815.

27. Ibid.

28. Ibid., tape 814.

29. Ibid., tape 805.

30. Ibid., tape 807.

31. Ibid., tape 811.

32. Ibid., tape 807.

33. Ibid.

34. Ibid.

35. A. Lomax, *Rainbow Sign,* 3.

36. J. Lomax and A. Lomax, *Negro Folk Songs as Sung by Lead Belly,* and A. Lomax, *Mister Jelly Roll.*

37. A. Lomax, *Rainbow Sign,* 4.

38. Selected recordings of those prisoners and some of their talk can be heard on *Prison Songs,* vol. 1, *Murderous Home,* Rounder CD 1714 (1997), and *Vol. 2: Dont'cha Hear Poor Mother Calling?* Rounder CD 1715 (1997). Lomax made these recordings in Dec. 1947 and Jan. 1948.

39. Thanks to Matthew Barton, who helped produce and wrote the artist biographies for the 2003 *Blues in the Mississippi Night* release on Rounder Records.

40. A. Lomax, "I Got the Blues," 38–52.

41. A. Lomax, *Rainbow Sign,* 3–4.

42. A. Lomax, notes to *Blues in the Mississippi Night,* reprints his 1990 notes from the Rykodisc reissue, RCD-90155, of an album originally released in 1959 as United Artists UAL 4027.

43. On Vera as a "community-based singer," see Jerrilyn McGregory's "Living-

ston, Alabama, Blues." See also her notes to *Alabama, from Lullabies to Blues,* Rounder CD 1829 (2001).

44. C. Johnson, *Growing Up in the Black Belt,* 326–27.

45. Ruby Pickens Tartt to Alan Lomax, Nov. 5, 1941. Series 4A, folder FF, box 24, item 4, RPT.

46. Reed interview, May 10, 1997. Reed also recorded in 1961, with Tartt present, the singer and storyteller Richard Amerson, available on the CD *Rich Amerson, Selected Songs and Stories,* annotated by Alan Brown (no named publisher, but available through the Alabama Center for Traditional Culture).

47. Reed interview, May 10, 1997.

48. V. Brown and Owens go into greater detail on Tartt's thoughts and experiences as a registrar in *Toting the Lead Row,* 52–53.

49. Series 2, folder B, box 1, item 1, RPT. Internal evidence shows that this undated typescript would have been written in the summer of 1955.

50. From Ruby Pickens Tartt's letter cited in V. Brown and Owens, *Toting the Lead Row,* 13.

51. Tartt spelled Doc Reed's nickname without the "k," as it sometimes appears. Zebediah was his given name. He himself didn't read or write, leaving this matter up to others.

52. Quoted in "Handwritten Papers by Ruby P. Tartt about Negro Folk Music," series 7, folder I-1, box 3, item 16. RPT.

53. Carmer called Pilgrim's Church "Bethel Hill," and Ruby Pickens Tartt is "Mary Louise" in the book. See *Stars Fell on Alabama,* 189–92.

54. Quoted in "Handwritten Papers by Ruby P. Tartt about Negro Folk Music."

55. J. Lomax, *Adventures of a Ballad Hunter,* 203, and also cited in V. Brown and Owens, *Toting the Lead Row,* 47. Wordsworth's "Ode" is fully titled "Intimations of Immortality from Recollections of Early Childhood."

56. J. Lomax, *Adventures of a Ballad Hunter,* 301.

57. V. Brown and Owens explore this relationship between Lomax and Reed in *Toting the Lead Row,* 46–52. Lomax's biographer Nolan Porterfield draws from this same account to close his *Last Cavalier,* 485–86.

58. Reed interview, May 10, 1997.

59. Series 7, folder I-1, box 3, item 18, RPT.

60. Series 7, folder I-1, box 3, item 6, RPT.

61. Hettie Godfrey, "Coonjine," AFS 4049 B4.

62. J. Lomax to Ruby Pickens Tartt, Apr. 27, 1943. Series 4A, folder FF-3, box 24, item 35, RPT.

63. John Lomax letter to Sandburg quoted in Sandburg, *New American Songbag,* 84; John A. Lomax to Alan Lomax, possibly Oct. 24, 1940, "Southern Recording Trip, 1940," AFC.

64. Inglis interview, Jan. 24, 1997.

65. AFS 4049 B1. Author's transcription.

66. Handwritten note. RPT.

67. J. Lomax and A. Lomax, *Folk Song: U.S.A.,* 295.

68. See the field note entry marked "Vera Hall" in J. Lomax and R. Lomax, "John and Ruby Lomax 1939 Southern Recording Trip."

69. Siegmeister, "Letter from Alabama," 24.

70. According to the biographical note in V. Brown and Owens, *Toting the Lead Row,* 162, "Adair" is one of Vera's three husbands. During her 1948 interview with Alan Lomax, Vera goes into detail about Nels Riddle, her first husband (not "Nash," as Owens had it), whom she married at sixteen, as well as her then-current courtship with Willie Ward, whom she eventually married. Adair, of whom she makes no mention, would have fit between these two in this chronology.

71. Series 2, folder B, box 1, item 2, RPT. Internal evidence indicates this letter dates from 1959. It is also reprinted in Tartt, *Dim Roads and Dark Nights,* 170–71.

72. Ruby Pickens Tartt, who aided Courlander on this trip, noted Vera's connection to Turner. RPT.

73. Willie Turner's Feb. 28, 1950, performance is available on *Negro Folk Music of Alabama,* vol. 1, *Secular Music,* Smithsonian Folkways FWO4417 (1951). Other reissues vary the release number and date. Based on his field notebook, Courlander recorded Vera singing "Another Man Done Gone," possibly on Feb. 22, 1950. Her three takes, never issued, appear on OT 6810, ATM.

74. Reed interview, May 10, 1997.

75. Willie Turner, recorded by Harold Courlander "Alabama and Mississippi, 1950." Tape OT 6809b, ATM. Author's transcription.

76. See Garon, "Baby Please Don't Go."

77. Courlander, *Negro Folk Music,* 108. He also explores this song and this meaning in his ethnographic novel, *The Big Old World of Richard Creeks,* 37–39.

78. Cora, tape OT 6813b, ATM. Author's transcription.

79. Courlander, *Negro Folk Music,* 110.

80. Big Joe Williams, "Baby Please Don't Go," Bluebird B6200, recorded Oct. 31, 1935. This has been reissued numerous times, e.g., on *Big Joe Williams, Complete Recorded Works in Chronological Order,* vol. 1, *1935–1941,* Document Records BDCD-6003 (1991).

81. "Please Don't Go," Bluebird B8969, recorded Dec. 12, 1941, was also reissued on *Big Joe Williams,* vol. 1, Document Records BDCD-6003. For "Baby Please Don't Go," Columbia Co 37945, recorded July 22, 1947, see *Big Joe Williams, Complete Recorded Works in Chronological Order, Volume 2, 1945–1949,* Document Records BDCD-6004 (1991).

82. See Courlander, *Negro Songs from Alabama,* 2nd ed., 83 n.

83. See Garon, "Williams, Big Joe Lee."

84. Though fiddler "Dad" Tracy is credited with playing a most archaic, one-string model, it's aurally evident that he played a fiddle with multiple strings on Williams's 1935 recording.

85. See *The Chicago String Band,* Testament Records TCD 5006 (1994, originally recorded in 1966). In the liner notes, producer Pete Welding writes, "Another consideration was that of testing the theory that the harmonica had taken over the functional role formerly held by the fiddle in blues ensembles, an assumption I feel has been fairly well validated by these recordings."

86. Thanks to Michael Courlander for sharing his father's correspondence from May 1964 about his then-recent books.

87. Paul Oliver first read these words on Jan. 29, 1967. They appear as "Introduction: The Development of the Blues" in *Broadcasting the Blues,* 2.

88. Both of these songs appear on *Alabama: From Lullabies to Blues,* Rounder CD 1829 (2001).

89. Bob Groom's excellent summary of this song complex appears with *Jack O' Diamonds: 1934 Field Recordings from Texas.* Paul Oliver also explores "Alabama Bound" in *Songsters and Saints,* 115–17.

90. I arrived at this approximate date by working backward from the two earliest sheet music editions of "Alabama Bound" in 1909, to Jelly Roll Morton's claim of its authorship in 1905, to the inquiries made by steamboat song collector Mary Wheeler. From her correspondence in the early 1930s with a steamboat company manager, she learned that the building and operation of the Stacker Lee steamboat began in the 1890s. Her version of "Alabama Bound" names this boat. Her source for the song would have been one of the elderly roustabouts she knew in the Paducah area, and who worked on this boat in that time period.

91. It can be heard on *Big Joe Williams, Complete Recorded Works,* vol. 2, *1945–1949,* Document Records BDCD-6004 (1991). He also recorded it for his 1962 Folkways LP.

92. See J. Lomax and A. Lomax, *American Ballads and Folk Songs,* 206–9. Thanks also to John Cowley, email and telephone conversation, Apr. 17, 2008.

93. It appears on *Alabama,* Rounder 1829.

94. John Lomax first mentions "Don't Leave Me Here" and "Alabama Bound" in "Self-Pity in Negro Folk-Song," 142, 144.

95. A. Lomax, *Mister Jelly Roll,* 111–12.

96. Willie Smith interview, Apr. 28, 2008.

97. Jack Johnson interview, Apr. 28, 2008.

98. Vera Hall, "Alabama and Mississippi, 1950," tape OT 6810, ATM. See also Courlander, *Negro Folk Music,* 108.

99. Alan Lomax, notes to "Another Man Done Gone," *Afro-American Blues and Game Songs,* AAFS L4. These are reprinted with Rounder CD 1513 (1999).

100. Leonard "Baby Doo" Caston, "I'm Gonna Walk Your Log," Decca 7773, recorded June 4, 1940. Available on *Chicago Blues,* vol. 2, *1939–1944,* Document Records DOCD-5444 (1996). See also Titon's *From Blues to Pop,* 14, where Caston discusses the song.

101. Willie Smith interview, Apr. 28, 2008.

102. Singer Amanda Overmyer performed "Baby Please Don't Go" on *American Idol* using Them's arrangement on Feb. 20, 2008.

103. Cited in McLean, notes to *Freedom at the Library of Congress,* 5.

104. Alain Locke speaking on track two of McLean, *Freedom at the Library of Congress.*

105. C. Johnson, *Growing Up in the Black Belt,* 327.

106. Tape 816, Alan Lomax Collection, AFC.

CHAPTER 7. BOZIE STURDIVANT

My interest in Bozie Sturdivant and "Ain't No Grave Can Hold My Body Down" began in 1994 when I asked Joe Hickerson, Alan Jabbour, and Gerry Parsons of the Folk Archive to name their favorite song issued on any of the Library of Congress folk music albums. Without knowing the others' replies, each singled out Bozie Sturdivant's performance of "Ain't No Grave." Archie Green sparked the search that soon followed. One morning in my home, he looked over a radio script I'd written about Bozie, filled with mystery more than knowledge. Archie shook his head. "People do not vanish," he said. "You have to look for him." That dictum proved true, and many wonderful individuals helped along the way. These include former Mississippi quartet singer Reverend Flem Bronner, who said from the start, "You're gonna have to walk it down"; and Memphis singer Brenda Patterson, who kindly shared her earliest experiences with this song, and whose classic 1970 recording wails it into the spirit of another day. Helena, Arkansas, jukebox record distributor Morse Gist, told marvelous accounts of local music choices guided by his patrons' taste more than the national hit parade. He recalled those times while standing before an enormous wooden rack where he and his father once sorted those records before delivering them to roadhouses, cafés, and groceries throughout Phillips County. Remembering Bozie best is the Reverend Ralph Dawson, whose affection for his old friend and profound understanding of this music has guided this chapter. Another whose support has mattered so much throughout is Virginia Johnson. I am indebted to her, and to her late husband, the Reverend E. L. Johnson, who pastored the Silent Grove Baptist Church for forty years. Happily, our visits by phone, letter, and in person continue.

1. Lewis Jones, "Mississippi Delta," 49.
2. These lists reside at the Archive of Folk Culture in the LC/Fisk files. Early discussion of them appears in Tony Russell, "Clarksdale Piccolo Blues." Alan Lomax refers to the lists in *The Land Where the Blues Began,* as does Robert Gordon in the notes to his Muddy Waters biography, *Can't Be Satisfied.* They also framed my own essay on "Ain't No Grave Can Hold My Body Down" that first aired on National Public Radio's *All Things Considered* on Nov. 26, 1996. Via personal correspondence in 1998, British music historian John Cowley sent me his unpublished discographical analysis of these items, a detailed chronology that includes their release dates, record labels, and titles. More recently, Elijah Wald discusses and reprints these lists in his *Escaping the Delta.* The lists again appear in Work, Jones, and Adams, *Lost Delta Found,* 311–14.
3. Lewis Jones to Lomax, Sept. 9, 1941. LC/Fisk.
4. Lewis Jones, "Mississippi Delta," 7.
5. Lewis Jones's memorandum to Fisk's Charles S. Johnson and the Library's Alan Lomax, "Field Trip to Coahoma County, Mississippi in Connection with the Folk Culture Study," is undated. But a personal letter from Jones to Lomax on May 31, 1942, indicates this date for the memorandum. "Plans for the July Trip." LC/Fisk, 6–7.
6. AFS 6638 A2, "My Lawd So High You Can't Go Over Him"; A3, "Please Don't Drive Me Away"; B1, "Christ My Lord Is Coming Soon"; 6639 A3, "The Holy Baby"; B1, "Ain't No Grave Can Hold My Body Down"; B2, "When I've Done the Best I Can, I Want My Crown"; 6640 A2, "A Charge to Keep I Have"; A3, "I'm Tolling [Toiling], Lord." Sturdivant recorded "Ain't No Grave Can Hold My Body Down" twice that day, with 6639 B1(a) being issued on AAFS 47, one of five 78 rpm records included in the 1943 compilation *Negro Religious Songs and Services.* The song's slightly longer second take, 6639 B1(b), was issued when the Library's published series converted to LPs. In 1994 the Archive's reference librarian Gerry Parsons told me that he thought the substitution of one for the other resulted not by conscious design but simply from a confusion

of the two takes when the format changed. The latter version also appears on *A Treasury of Library of Congress Field Recordings* as well as the reissue of the Library's compilation, Rounder CD 1514 (1999). Both versions can be heard on *Negro Religious Field Recordings 1934–1942,* Document Records DOCD-5312 (1994).

7. Cotton interview, Oct. 26, 1997.

8. Ibid.

9. Cotton, "Silent Grove Baptist Church."

10. It is unclear why Galmore's age is given as twelve in Alan Lomax's typed notes, when other evidence indicates she would have been older at the time. The typescript is a list of recordings made during the 1942 Coahoma expedition. LC/Fisk.

11. The Silent Grove Baptist Church recordings begin on AFS 6604, A8 through B5, and continue on 6637 B2 through 6639 B2.

12. Cotton interview, Oct. 26, 1997. Virginia Johnson, the Reverend E. L. Johnson, and the Reverend Marvin Myles provided further information on John Skipper's role in the quartet community.

13. In addition to Jones's observations and Lomax's field notes, recollections of the Clarksdale quartet union came from their original manager, Early Wright, in our interview, and from the Reverend Marvin Myles interview, May 12, 1997.

14. 1 Corinthians 15.55, Authorized Version. Thanks as well to Martha Sheppard (interview, June 8, 1998). Sheppard, an inveterate Bible reader and church member in Washington, D.C., also knows the song, its social uses, and its textual basis in the New Testament. Both she and Cotton highlighted the same Bible passages pertinent to "Ain't No Grave Can Hold My Body Down."

15. Mark 16.6.

16. John 5.28.

17. John 11.38.

18. Morganfield interview, Jan. 26, 1997.

19. Mitchell, *Select Pentecostal Songs of the Kingdom.* I'm indebted to Georgia folksong researcher John Garst for sharing this treasure.

20. Many familiar with this song will associate these words with Brother Claude Ely, a white Holiness pastor and evangelist from southwestern Virginia. Ely's influential 1953 radio station recording of "There Ain't No Grave Gonna Hold My Body Down," King 1311 and 5616, is presently available on *Satan, Get Back!* Ace CDCHD 456 (1993), a compilation devoted to his work, and on *Goodbye, Babylon,* Dust-to-Digital DTD 01 (2003). Ely's great-nephew Macel Ely II's assertion that Claude Ely composed the song in ca. 1934 was picked up by NPR's *All Things Considered,* May 5, 2011, "A Nephew's Quest: Who Was Brother Claude Ely?" See also Ely, *Ain't No Grave,* 99–109. Other artists indebted to Ely's version include the Caudill Family, Champion 902-A (1954) and reissued on *The Early Days of Bluegrass,* vol. 5, Rounder 1017 (1974); Jimmie Williams, Starday SLP 165 (1962); *The Singing Cookes Live,* TSRC-9851 (1990); E. C. Ball, *E. C. Ball with Orna Ball and the Friendly Gospel Singers,* Rounder 0026 (1973); Russ Taff, *The Way Home,* Myrrh Records 701 6880 613 (1989), and featured in Robert Duvall's 1998 film *The Apostle;* and Tim and Molly O'Brien's rendition on *Away Out on the Mountain,* Sugar Hill SC-CD 3825 (1994). Brother Ely also

influenced a "music minus one" version on Daywind Soundtracks 3012 (n.d.), used with smaller churches. The Fisk Jubilee Singers, who performed "Ain't No Grave" at the Ryman Auditorium for Johnny Cash's memorial service, November 2003, learned the song from a home tape sung by Cash himself, which they rearranged to fit their style. For that setting, see *Voice of the Spirit: The Gospel of the South,* Dualtone 80302-01228-2 (2006). Cash's own studio recording appears on *American VI: Ain't No Grave,* American B0013954-02 (2010). Thanks to Paul T. Kwami, director of the Fisk Jubilee Singers, and to Lane Connor, musician at the Assembly of God, Aberdeen, Mississippi.

21. Mitchell, *Select Pentecostal Songs of the Kingdom.*

22. The Friendly Five Harmony Singers appear on AFS 6612 B4 through 6613 A5. Along with Lomax's field notes, additional information on the Friendly Five comes from the Reverend Edgar Marshall (interview, May 12, 1997). Marshall, a Clarksdale quartet singer, first pastored under the Reverend John McGhee, who sang bass on these recordings and led the group for decades more.

23. Lewis Jones, Memorandum to Charles S. Johnson, 7.

24. AFS 6613 A1.

25. Jessie Anthony, "Can't No Grave Hold My Body Down," Helen Hartness Flanders Ballad Collection, D53A02, Middlebury College, Middlebury, Vt. Thanks to Flanders's granddaughter and biographer, Nancy-Jean Siegel, for duplicating a copy of this recording and its related documentary material.

26. Two Gospel Keys, "Can't No Grave Hold My Body Down," C-2080 B-Ap 137, recorded in Feb. 1947 and reisssued on *Country Gospel,* Document Records DOCD-5221 (1993). Sister Rosetta Tharpe, "Cain't No Grave Hold My Body Down," 74170-A-De 48154, recorded Nov. 1947 and reissued on *Sister Rosetta Tharpe,* vol. 3, Document Records DOCD-5607 (1998). See also Marion Williams's 1974 "Can't No Grave Hold My Body Down," available on *My Soul Looks Back,* Shanachie 6011 (1994).

27. AFS 6639 B1(b). Author's transcription.

28. 1 Corinthians 15.51–52.

29. Revelation 21.21.

30. Revelation 20.11–12.

31. John 19.25–27.

32. This quote appears in one of Alan Lomax's 1941–42 field notebooks. ALC. The Reverend Savage can be heard on *Mississippi: Saints and Sinners,* Rounder CD 1824 (1999).

33. See Ong, *Orality and Literacy,* 165. For a similar concept, folklorist D. K. Wilgus coined the term "blues ballad": a song that tells a story without an explicit narrative. See Wilgus and Long, "Blues Ballad." "The narrative coherence of the song," they wrote, "is provided by community knowledge of the events" (446).

34. See B. Rosenberg, *Can These Bones Live?* which explores the imagery and aesthetics of African American preaching.

35. Unattributed quote, *There Is a Rose in the Garden,* Nashco Music Service NR 17184 (1987).

36. Some of the persons I interviewed locally in connection with Bozie Sturdivant, but not otherwise mentioned in this text, include Robert Banks, Herman

Brown, Jessie Dobbins, Benny Gooden, James Shelby, and Wade Walton. They provided their memories not only of Bozie, but of Clarksdale in the early 1940s, its musicians, nightlife, and institutions.

37. The Clarksdale Public Library has city directories for 1936 and 1939. According to the library's reference specialist Missy Craig, none was published between 1940 and 1945. Bozie Sturdivant was not listed in 1933 or 1946.

38. In Helena, Ark., thanks to reference librarian Carolyn Cunningham for her tireless efforts with city records, and to photographer Ivy Gladdin, who searched his invaluable archive of images. In Jan. 1997 I spoke via telephone with local quartet singer the Reverend Percell Perkins, who had been a member of the Original Five Blind Boys of Mississippi in 1944. He recalled only Bozie Sturdivant's name. But Sonny Payne, veteran announcer at radio station KFFA, contacted his former engineer J. Warren, who believes that Bozie appeared with the Union Jubilee Quartet on a KFFA gospel show sponsored by the Turner Drug Company. These broadcasts featured the Delta Rhythm Boys for four weeks in 1943. Payne interview, Oct. 27, 1997.

39. Wicks called on May 17, 1997.

40. Wicks interview, May 18, 1997.

41. Wicks interview, Oct. 27, 1997.

42. Wicks interview, May 18, 1997.

43. Though Bozie Sturdivant's funeral program names Glendora, Miss., an adjacent community, as his birthplace, his Social Security application, which he signed, names Swan Lake. Georgia Wicks confirmed Swan Lake as his birthplace. Documents in author's collection.

44. Wicks interview, May 19, 1997.

45. Wicks interview, Oct. 27, 1997.

46. *Baldwin and Register,* 1936, 182.

47. *Baldwin and Register,* 1939, 291.

48. Wicks interview, Oct. 27, 1997.

49. Wicks interview, May 18, 1997.

50. Wicks interview, Oct. 27, 1997.

51. AAFS L-10.

52. "Sin-Killer" Griffin, "The Man of Calvary," AFS 187A.

53. Thanks to Beth Howse, Fisk reference librarian, for this title, by which the manuscript had become known. Its inspiration possibly came from Work's report that singer Will Starks "has been living in the 'Bottoms'—his name for the Delta—all of his life" (89).

54. J. Work III, "In the Bottoms," 16. Elsewhere in the manuscript, he notates the Union Jubilee's recorded performance of "A Charge to Keep I Have," AFS 6640 A2.

55. J. Work III, "In the Bottoms," 13.

56. J. Work III to Thomas E. Jones, July 20, 1943. Thomas E. Jones Collection, box 44, folder 18, Fisk.

57. Lewis Jones, "Memorandum," 12. LC/Fisk. J. Work III, "Folk Songs of the American Negro," 20.

58. J. Work III, "In the Bottoms," 26.

59. Ibid., 40.

60. Heilbut interview, Dec. 7, 1996.
61. Soul Stirrers, "Walk Around," Bronze BR 102. Thanks to Chris Smith for his help in determining the July 1942 release date. Personal correspondence, Dec. 14, 2003.
62. Heilbut, *Gospel Sound*, 79.
63. Ibid., 81.
64. Heilbut interview, Dec. 7, 1996.
65. J. Work III, "Folk Songs of the American Negro," 32.
66. Quoted in Heilbut, *Gospel Sound*, 84.
67. In May 1997, Diana Haskell of the Newberry Library kindly checked the Chicago city directories from 1943 to 1970. None listed Bozie Sturdivant as a resident during those years.
68. Heilbut interview, Dec. 21, 1996.
69. Thanks to Laura Haworth, reference librarian of the Denison Public Library. During our Dec. 1997 communications, a coworker of hers recognized Bozie's name and mentioned his singing with Ralph Dawson.
70. Dawson interview, Jan. 7, 1998.
71. The Five Soul Stirrers' "I'll Never Turn Back" and "Don't Wonder about Him" appear on Bronze 126. Chris Smith indicates this record was released in 1945 but suggests it may have been recorded in 1940, along with four previously released sides on this label. Personal communication, Dec. 14, 2003.
72. Dawson interview, Feb. 16, 1998.
73. As previously noted, Bozie also recorded this song after singing "Ain't No Grave" for the Library in 1942. It can be heard on Document Records DOCD-5312.
74. The 1949 Denison city directory lists Bozie Sturdivant with Stella as his wife at the same address. Bozie's funeral program, though, says they were not wed until 1955. Either way, they remained together in that home until his death. They had no children.
75. Boyer, *How Sweet the Sound*, 50.
76. Bozie Sturdivant does not appear in any of the three St. Louis city directories covering the years 1943 through 1947 (1944, 1946, and 1947–48). Thanks to Adele Heagney of the St. Louis Public Library, local history, for her efforts.
77. Dawson interview, Feb. 17, 1998.
78. Dawson believes that Bozie's voice appears without credit on a few commercially issued sides. He named as possibilities the gospel quartet records made for the Peacock label or, less likely, Specialty, which recorded the Soul Stirrers in the 1950s. Gospel discographer Bob Laughton has been helpful in providing names of the various labels during that period. Thanks again to Chris Smith for helping me contact Laughton, whose discographies I showed to Dawson during my visit to Denison.
79. *Denison City Directory*, n.p. Denison librarian Laura Haworth checked all the city directories from 1940 through 1984, tracking Bozie's occupation, address, and wife.
80. Dawson interview, Dec. 27, 1998.
81. Dawson interview, Feb. 16, 1998.
82. Dawson credited the introduction piece to the Kansas City Gospel Singers.
83. Dawson interview, Feb. 17, 1998.

84. Dawson interview, Feb. 16, 1998.

85. Dawson interview, Apr. 25, 1998.

86. Dawson interview, May 8, 2003.

87. Dawson interview, Feb. 16, 1998.

88. Golden Gate Jubilee Quartet, "Golden Gate Gospel Train," Bluebird BB B7126. This was their first recording, issued in 1937, and reissued on *Train 45: Railroad Songs of the Early 1900's*, Rounder CD 1143 (1998).

89. Quoted in Dawson interview, June 9, 2003.

90. Quoted in Dawson interview, May 14, 2003.

91. Dawson interview, May 14, 2003.

92. Colossians 3.11 and Galatians 3.28.

93. Dawson interview, May 14, 2003.

94. Dawson interview, Jan. 8, 1998.

95. Dawson interview, Feb. 16, 1998.

96. Dawson interview, May 8, 2003.

97. Dawson interview, Apr. 25, 1998.

98. See Richard Crawford, *America's Musical Life*, 22–23.

99. Raichelson, "Black Religious Folksong," 357, 359.

100. Dawson interview, Feb. 17, 1998.

101. Tallmadge, "Dr. Watts and Mahalia Jackson."

102. Heilbut, *Gospel Sound*, 81.

103. Myles interview, Jan. 28, 1997.

104. In 1967, folklorist David Evans recorded Mississippi Delta guitarist Robert "Nighthawk" Johnson performing "Can't No Grave Hold My Body Down." See *Sorrow Come Pass Me Around: A Survey of Black Religious Music.* Advent 2805 (1975). Rereleased by Blues Interactions in 1989. Thanks to the album's coproducer, Frank Scott, for generously sharing this recording with me.

105. Jones, "Mississippi Delta," 8.

106. Muddy Waters, quoted in Rooney, *Bossmen*, 120.

107. Dawson interview, June 9, 2003.

108. Dawson interview, Apr. 25, 1998.

109. Dawson interview, Feb. 16, 1998.

110. Dawson interview, Apr. 25, 1998.

CHAPTER 8. PETE STEELE

Many individuals have contributed to this story of "Coal Creek March." Apart from those named in the notes below, let me recognize the following for their kindness: guitarists Peter Danner, John Renbourn, and John Stropes; Jill Winchell of the Guitar Foundation of America; Steve Weiss, Matthew Turi, and John Loy of the Southern Folklife Collection; and Susan K. Forbes of the Kansas State Historical Society. This chapter draws deeply upon the invaluable efforts of folklorist Ed Kahn. In September 2000, he sent me all of his written research on Coal Creek, including printed artifacts, original ballets, local newspaper accounts, and letters. Heartfelt thanks go to his daughter, Autumn Kruse, and wife, Peggy Moore, for their support in the face of his loss. Still more thanks go to Peggy Kreimer, Paul Pell, Jack McKart, Lewis Cisle, Tom Loughead, and David Brose, who visited Pete Steele and freely offered their recollections. Patrick Mullen checked Ohio folklife archives, and Pete Seeger shared his thoughts on "Coal Creek March" and Pete Steele, whose music has meant so much to him for so long. Above all, thanks to Pete Steele's family, in particular his daughter Leona Steele Gabbard. Ever available, she even gathered her brothers and sisters to share stories of their musical parents one evening as we passed around Pete Steele's banjo. Leona's son Myron Gabbard has been equally warm. He continues to play, sing, and write songs with the same leathery strength his beloved grandfather exemplified. I'm grateful for friendship with this family. Finally, loving thanks to Doc Hopkins, who first taught me this piece and wanted so much for its story to be told once more.

1. At his Feb. 6, 1965, concert at Indiana University, Pete Steele mentioned having worked as a miner for twenty-four years. His son, Ed Steele, recalled it as eighteen years, which corresponds more closely with the timing of these events. Either way, Pete contracted silicosis from this work, a condition diagnosed during World War II when he worked at a turret factory in Hamilton, Ohio. He later received compensation through the federal black lung pension program.

2. Dickman interview, Dec. 13, 1997.

3. Ibid.

4. Alan Lomax reports in his entry for Mar. 29, 1938, Ohio and Indiana field notes, that the Thomsons helped pay for the surgery. AFC.

5. Over the course of their marriage, the Steeles had fifteen children, of whom nine survived infancy.

6. Bob Steele to author, Feb. 15, 2008.

7. Dwight Steele interview, Feb. 15, 2008.

8. Leona Steele Gabbard interview, Feb. 15, 2008.

9. For more on this festival, see M. Williams, *Staging Tradition*, 53–55. According to Steele family memory, a young Bill Monroe was there also and approached Pete about joining his band to play banjo.

10. A. Lomax, field notes, "Ohio and Indiana," entry for Mar. 27, 1938, AFC.

11. Ibid., entry for Mar. 29, 1938.

12. Pete Steele's "Pretty Polly" appeared on the Library of Congress's 1941 *Friends of Music* album. Alan Lomax again included it with the other three selections from this sampler on AAFS L1, *Anglo-American Ballads* (1942). It can also be heard on *Anglo-American Ballads, Volume One*, Rounder CD 1511 (1999), whose cover art pictures Pete Steele and his family at the time of the 1938 recordings. Two moments from Lomax's silent filming of Pete's "Pretty Polly" appear in the opening segment of Wade, *Catching the Music*.

13. Alan Lomax, Ohio and Indiana field notes, Mar. 29, 1938.

14. This description comes from an 1845 advertisement that Peter Danner reprinted in "Noteworthy Early American Guitar Treatise," 270. I'm indebted to Peter Danner for our many conversations and communications in Feb. and Mar. 2008 and for his guidance in matters of guitar history.

15. For appraisals of Ballard, *Elements of Guitar-Playing*, see Gura, *C. F. Martin and His Guitars*, 24–28, and Danner, "Noteworthy Early American Guitar Treatise." Thanks to the Newberry Library and Alison Hinderliter for providing a copy of this rare sixty-eight-page book. In 1838 (or possibly later than that copyright date), Ballard also published an expanded edition, "88 folio size

pages," which is the one Peter Danner explored and which, unlike the shorter edition, included "Fandango," along with all the other *Preceptor's* titles.

16. Ballard, *Elements of Guitar-Playing,* 2. Original emphasis.

17. Ibid., 44.

18. Cited in Danner, "Noteworthy Early American Guitar Treatise," 271.

19. For more on the *Preceptor's* publishing background see Danner, "Noteworthy Early American Guitar Treatise," and Cox, "Classic Guitar Technique and Its Evolution," 187.

20. The circa 1812 "Spanish Fandango," a piano rondo by B. Carr and sold from Carr's Baltimore music store, offers a very different, somber-sounding classical piece set in A minor, shifting to C, and ending in A major. Call number box 037, item 046, Lester S. Levy Sheet Music Collection.

21. Danner, "Bolero," 31.

22. Olcott-Bickford, quoted in Danner, "Bolero," 31.

23. S. S. Stewart, "The Banjo, An Extemporaneous Poem," *S. S. Stewart's Banjo and Guitar Journal* 6:2 (June–July 1889): 6.

24. Daniel Fitler, letter to the editor, *S. S. Stewart's Banjo and Guitar Journal* 6:1 (Apr.–May 1889): 3.

25. *S. S. Stewart's Banjo and Guitar Journal* 7:6 (Feb.–Mar. 1891): 2. Original emphasis.

26. E. H. Frey, letter to the editor, *S. S. Stewart's Banjo and Guitar Journal* 9:5 (Dec. 1892–Jan. 1893): 9.

27. J. E. Henning, *J. E. Henning's Elite Banjoist and Guitar and Mandolin News* 1:2 (Jan.–Feb. 1891): 1. Quoted in Noonan, "Guitar in America," 464.

28. Thanks to Peter Danner for passing along this page (62) from the enlarged edition of Ballard, *Elements of Guitar-Playing.*

29. Ballard, *Elements of Guitar-Playing,* 16.

30. I'm indebted to Clarke Buehling for sharing his extensive files of nineteenth-century banjo and guitar music as well as Paul Wells at the Center for Popular Music, Middle Tennessee State University, Murfreesboro, for relevant copies from that collection. Elias Kaufman generously shared his knowledge of music from this era. Finally, I'm indebted to Mike Craver for demonstrating these pieces on the piano and commenting on them.

31. Justin Holland, "Spanish Fandango," from *Winter Evenings, Six Arrangements for the Guitar* (Cleveland, Ohio: S. Brainard, 1857). Sheet music courtesy of the Center for Popular Music.

32. Converse, "Spanish Fandango," in *Analytical Banjo Method,* 119–20.

33. Albrecht, "Spanish Fandango," in Albrecht, *Progressive Studies for the Banjo,* 12.

34. F. Eaton, *Up to Date Method for the Banjo,* 49, and *Up to Date Method for the Guitar,* 58.

35. Stewart, "Spanish Fandango," in *Complete American School,* 89–90.

36. Olcott-Bickford, "Guitarist," 24.

37. Uncle Dave Macon's "Spanish Fandango" variations appear in "Station Will Be Changed after a While," recorded Apr. 13, 1925, Vocalion 15341; and closer to "Coal Creek March" itself, in "Uncle Dave's Beloved Solo," recorded Sept. 8,

1926, Vocalion 15439. Both have been reissued on Uncle Dave Macon, *Keep My Skillet Good and Greasy,* Bear Family BCD 15978 JM (2004).

38. Frank Jenkins's 1927 "Baptist Shout" has been reissued on *Old-Time Mountain Banjo,* County 3533 (2005); Kirk McGee's "Snowdrop" appears on McGee Brothers and Arthur Smith, *Old Timers of the Grand Ole Opry,* Folkways FA-2379 (1964); Wade Mainer's "Trickling Water" appears on his *Live for Collectors,* Old Homestead OHCD-4032 (2000); and Frank Hutchison's 1927 "Logan County Blues" appears on *Old-Time Mountain Guitar,* County 3512 (1998).

39. Mainer interview.

40. Etta Baker plays both "Marching Jaybird" and "Spanish Fandango" on *One-Dime Blues,* Rounder CD 2112 (1991).

41. Baker interview.

42. These words appear at least by 1860 on the sheet-music edition published by A. C. and J. L. Peters. Pianist Charles Grobe's "The Fall of Sebastopol, Op. 606" appeared before Worrall's, registered for copyright on Nov. 17, 1855, only two months after the city's fall. Grobe called this a "descriptive fantasie," complete with piano-simulated sound effects, a funeral march, and during the finale, "God Save the Queen." See the highly annotated score at the Library of Congress's American Memory Web site, Music for the Nation: American Sheet Music.

43. Worrall, *Eclectic Guitar Instructor,* 50–51.

44. C. L. Partee used this term specifically in connection with "Sebastopol" in "Practical Hints on Modern Guitar Playing." Quoted in Noonan, "Guitar in America," 496.

45. From "Henry Worrall Dead," *Topeka State Journal,* June 21, 1902, 5. Thanks to Michael A. Church of the Kansas State Historical Society for additional information on Worrall.

46. Olcott-Bickford, "Guitarist," 25.

47. Schettler, "Guitarist of European Training," 14. Quoted in Noonan, "Guitar in America," 490–91.

48. Tyrell, *F. O. G.* 2, no. 6 (Sept.–Oct. 1902): 2. Quoted in Noonan, "Guitar in America," 566.

49. Surviving pieces of Worrall's handwritten notation for both the "Violet Waltz" and "Sebastopol" reveal passages and rhythmic patterns redolent of "Spanish Fandango." Henry Worrall Collection, series 2, KSHS.

50. Handwritten on both editions, published by A. C. and J. L. Peters, Cincinnati. Reproductions appear in Renbourn, "American Steel-String Guitar." I'm grateful to John Renbourn for sharing his work.

51. *Sebastopol, a Descriptive Fantasie for the Guitar,* Cincinnati, Ohio: A. C. & J. L. Peters, 1860.

52. "Spanish Key" appears in the title in J. W. Herrington's 1910 *Self Instructor for the Guitar.* As Peter Danner writes, "the very first piece in the folio is our old friend 'Spanish Fandango.'" Danner to author, Mar. 18, 2008.

53. AFS 1703 A.

54. "Program for Memorial Services in Memory of Those Who Lost Their Lives in Fraterville Mine Explosion," n.d. (likely late May 1902). A later program, held at Fraterville Missionary Baptist Church, and sponsored by locals of the

United Mine Workers, reprinted all these accounts plus similar notes found after the 1911 Cross Mountain explosion. Copies and an original reside in Kahn/Wade. Loyal Jones reprints the Fraterville notes in *Faith and Meaning in the Southern Uplands*, 1–3.

55. One of the ballads that commemorated the Fraterville explosion is Green Bailey, "Shut Up in the Mines of Coal Creek," Challenge 425-B (1929). Meade, *Country Music Sources*, 47, connects this recording to the 1911 Cross Mountain explosion, which inspired a separate ballad and tune.

56. Tuttle interview, Aug. 22, 1960.

57. Vowell interview. Archie Green, also present on this occasion, refers to Vowell in *Only a Miner*, 184–85.

58. Much more extensive accounts of the Coal Creek rebellion can be found in A. Green, *Only a Miner*; Foner, *History of the Labor Movement in the United States*, vol. 2; and Korson, *Coal Dust on the Fiddle*.

59. A. Green explores this song in *Only a Miner*, 175–93.

60. "Hearsay stories" was the term Ed Kahn and his Coal Creek informants used in telling these tales in 1960 and 1961.

61. AFS 1703 A.

62. Ballad singer Leon Polston provided this information. Tape FT-12567. Kahn.

63. Tape FT-12595. Kahn.

64. AFS 1703 A.

65. In Seattle, sometime during the early to mid-1970s, Roscoe Holcomb played the "March" in both keys for banjoist Irwin Nash (Nash to author, email, Apr. 18, 2001). The D tuning version is available on Roscoe Holcomb, *An Untamed Sense of Control*, Smithsonian Folkways SFW CD 40144 (2003). Great thanks to Irwin for sharing copies of these invaluable performances, taped by Phil Williams.

66. Tape FT-12602. Kahn.

67. Quoted in Rosenbaum, *Old-Time Mountain Banjo*, 31. In his writings and recordings, Art Rosenbaum has continued to champion Pete Steele's artistry.

68. Pete and Lillie Steele concert, Feb. 6, 1965, tape ATL 19159, ATM. Thanks to Neil Rosenberg and to Marilyn Graf, ATM archivist, for their help with this recording.

69. Dickman interview, Dec. 13, 1997.

70. Steele concert.

71. Kahn interview, Sept. 22, 2000.

72. Pete Steele, *Banjo Tunes and Songs*, Folkways FS 3828 (1958).

73. See also Kahn, "Ballad of Coal Creek."

74. Kahn interview, Sept. 22, 2000.

75. Sherman Campbell, Aug. 18, 1960, FT-12572; Charles Frederick Braden, Aug. 23, 1960, FT-12570; and Maynard Braden, Aug. 21, 1961, FT-12569. The Maynard Braden date comes from the actual recording, and the finding aid date is incorrect. Kahn.

76. Ed Kahn, with banjoist Art Rosenbaum, first visited Pete Steele in Hamilton, Ohio, on June 9, 1957, where they made a tape. Ed returned to Pete Steele's to record the Folkways album on Aug. 27, 1957, and finished this work on Aug. 17, 1958. He visited Sam Gaston on Aug. 2 and 3, 1957.

77. This birthdate comes from John Garst's research notes with Ernie Hodges, communicated to Archie Green by letter, Mar. 9, 1973. Copy in Kahn/Wade.
78. Sam Gaston, tape FT-12594. Kahn.
79. C. Wolfe, "New Light on 'The Coal Creek March.'"
80. *Excerpts from Interviews with Dock Boggs,* Folkways FH 5458 (1965). He plays the "Coal Creek March" on *Dock Boggs: His Folkways Years 1963–1968,* Smithsonian Folkways SF 40108 (1998).
81. Ernie Hodges, quoted in John F. Garst to Archie Green, Mar. 9, 1973. Copy in Kahn/Wade.
82. Marion Underwood, "Coal Creek March," Gennett 6240 (issued three more times as by Floyd Russell), and reissued on *Old-Time Mountain Banjo,* County CD-3533 (2005).
83. See Tribe, "Jimmie Skinner."
84. On Aug. 31, 1961, while visiting with Stringbean at his home outside Nashville, Ed Kahn and Archie Green met Bob Akeman, the performer's father. The elder Akeman, who hailed from Annville, Ky., taught String the piece, calling it "Old Death March." Kahn/Wade. Stringbean announces "Dead March" during "Stringbean and His Banjo" on *Hee Haw Corn Shucker,* Gusto GT7-0878-2 (1971). Also see C. Wolfe, "String," for additional information on his recording of "Cold Creek March" for the Cullman label. Another enthralling possibility lies in the fact that Stringbean sometimes visited Pete Steele in Hamilton, Ohio. In Dec. 1997 Leona Gabbard first told me how the Steeles lived just a block away from Stringbean's sister, whom the entertainer would come and see in the late 1930s and early 1940s. Finally, Red Belcher recorded "Coleman's March" on Page Record Co. 501 (1948). More information on Belcher appears in Spottswood, notes to "Old Grey Goose."
85. Tape FT-12602. Kahn.
86. C. Wolfe, *Devil's Box,* 211.
87. See Karen Linn's valuable discussions of "scientific playing" in *That Half-Barbaric Twang.*
88. Tape FT-12602. Kahn. Author's transcription.
89. See Archie Green's case study of the Homestead ballad, including the verses that Ed Kahn collected from Forrest Lewis, in *Wobblies, Pile Butts, and Other Heroes.* He summarizes recent "Coal Creek March" scholarship on 251–54.
90. Tape FT-12602. Kahn.
91. Kahn, "Ballad of Coal Creek."
92. Ed Kahn's notes in Kahn/Wade, based on Briscoe's memories, say the recording was made for Victor, but Tony Russell in *Country Music Records* specifies Columbia. Either way, scarce information surrounds Briscoe's unreleased session.
93. Kahn to Briscoe, July 12, 1961. Kahn/Wade.
94. Doc Hopkins was not born in 1899 as elsewhere reported. He falsified his papers in order to enlist in the army, which became the source of the date confusion.
95. During his visit to Forrest Lewis, Ed Kahn also recorded "Coal Creek March" from another banjoist, the highly accomplished Sam Davis. Two days later, he taped early hillbilly recording artist Clarence Greene playing it. Both offered accomplished banjo versions in the "Fandango" mode, while expressing no particular knowledge of the tune's historical background.

96. Hopkins to author, Sept. 22, 1986. In an earlier conversation he enumerated the physical stage settings detailed in the text above.

97. Doc additionally credited his Marine buddy from Manchester, Ky., Jesse Ball, for the tune—they served together between 1921 and 1924—but reserved most credit and accorded most influence to the version played by "Blind Burdette," who was Dick Burnett.

98. "Trouble at the Coal Creek Mines" appears on *Doc Hopkins,* Birch 1945 (1965).

99. "Pete Steele, Clay County Native, Banjo Player and Folk Musician," *Kentucky Post,* Nov. 23, 1985.

100. Seeger to Gabbard, June 1997. Courtesy of Leona Gabbard.

101. Seeger to Gabbard, Jan. 25, 2008. Original emphasis. Courtesy of Leona Gabbard.

102. Kreimer to author, email, Mar. 7, 2008.

103. Steele family tape of Pete Seeger's visit, Aug. 1984. Personal collection of Myron Gabbard.

104. Pell interview, Feb. 17, 2008.

105. Loughead interview, Mar. 4, 2008.

106. Leona Gabbard has preserved Lew Cisle's piece, kept forever in bloom with artificial flowers.

107. Tom Paley, *Folk Songs from the Southern Appalachian Mountains,* Elektra EKL-12 (1953).

108. Paley interview, Dec. 1, 1994. This anecdote appears in greater detail in Wade, "Tom Paley Interview," 17.

109. Rosenberg, "Icy Mountain Brook."

110. "Coal Creek March/Pay Day at Coal Creek/Roll Down the Line," recorded Dec. 27, 1957, appears on *Pete Seeger and Sonny Terry at Carnegie Hall,* Folkways FA 2412 (1958).

111. See Rosenberg's discussion in "Icy Mountain Brook."

112. P. Seeger, *Goofing-Off Suite,* 18.

113. Tick, *Ruth Crawford Seeger,* 274–75.

114. Seeger interview, Jan. 6, 1997.

115. "The Scoldin' Wife" first appears on tape FT-12596, recorded Aug. 27, 1957, Kahn, and later appears on Pete Steele, *Banjo Tunes and Songs,* Folkways FS 3828 (1958).

116. Seeger to Steele, Aug. 14, 1984. Courtesy of Leona Gabbard.

117. Seeger to Gabbard, Dec. 23, 1985. Courtesy of Leona Gabbard.

118. Ed Steele interview, Dec. 12, 1997.

119. Tape FT-12597, recorded Aug. 17, 1958. Kahn.

120. Steele to Lomax, Feb. 2, 1948. Pete Steele correspondence file, AFC.

121. Leona Gabbard interview, Feb. 14, 2008.

122. Dickman interview, Dec. 13, 1997.

CHAPTER 9. TEXAS GLADDEN

My life would have taken a very different direction without Texas Gladden and Hobart Smith. Their remarkable duets, first issued on *Texas Gladden Sings Blue Ridge Ballads* (1948), inspired my teacher Fleming Brown to learn the five-string banjo. His love for their music, and especially his 1963 recordings of Hobart Smith, shaped my own course in music. Years later, without the kindness of the Gladden and Smith families, I could not have written this chapter. Over several decades two of Hobart's children, Wiley J. Smith and Charlotte Texas Smith Fields, summoned memories as powerful as their father's astounding musicianship. Two of Texas's children, Jim Gladden and his sister Wilma Jean, readily shared their rich recollections of her life in Salem, Virginia. Jim has gone on now, and I join his family in their admiration of him—a temperate man, thoughtful, candid, and graceful.

Thanks, too, to the late Helen Barbrow and the Museum of the Middle Appalachians in Saltville, Virginia, which she served so well. Through her an exhibition about Hobart Smith and Texas Gladden has now found a permanent place in their community.

1. Jim Gladden interview, Nov. 25, 1997. Jim Gladden's given name was James Clayton Gladden. Born Nov. 2, 1921, he died Oct. 16, 2007. His father was James Thomas Gladden (1881–1968). In this chapter, "Jim" refers to Jim Gladden, and "James" to his father.

2. Quoted in Jim Gladden interview, Nov. 25, 1997.

3. See Lodewick, "'The Unfortunate Rake' and His Descendants." See also Goldstein, *Unfortunate Rake,* a phonographic study that includes a downhill skier's parody. Finally, Steve Goodman's "A Dying Cub Fan's Last Request," first issued on *Affordable Art,* Red Pajamas RPJ 002 (1983), extends the telltale pattern.

4. The White Stripes recorded "St. James Infirmary Blues" on *The White Stripes,* Sympathy For The Record Industry SFTRI 577 (1999). David Fulmer wrote a mystery novel, *The Dying Crapshooter's Blues,* the title (and one of its characters) based on Blind Willie McTell and his recording. "Blackwatertown," by Paul Muldoon, is an original poem based on "The Unfortunate Rake."

5. Alexander King Smith's dates, actually Feb. 26, 1868, to May 26, 1958, come from the family Bible, family genealogy records, and his gravestone as well as Hobart Smith's interview with Studs Terkel, in which he discusses his father's ninety-year life span. Different information in the U.S. Census gives the less reliable birth date. Similarly, although reported elsewhere as 1967, Texas died on May 23, 1966, in Salem, Va.

6. Fields interview, June 19, 2002, and Margaret Smith et al., "Abraham Smith Family."

7. Her full name is Eleanor Wilma Jean Gladden Vandergrift.

8. Texas Gladden's fifteen Library of Congress recordings made in Salem are AFS 5230 A1 "One Morning in May," and A2 "The Two Brothers"; AFS 5231 A1 "The Devil's Nine Questions," A2 "The Scolding Wife," B1 "The Three Babes," and B2 "The House Carpenter"; AFS 5232 A1 "Barbara Allen," A2 "The Scolding Wife," and B1, B2, B3 "Lord Thomas"; AFS 5233 A1 "The Gypsy Davy," A2 "My Lovin' Old Husband," A3 "Kind Sir, I See You've Come Again," A4 "Hush, Baby, Don't You Cry," A5 "The Four Marys," and B1 "Old Kimball."

9. For a recent compilation of Texas's recordings on compact disc see *Texas Gladden: Ballad Legacy,* Rounder CD 1800 (2001). She also appears in the Southern Journey series of the Alan Lomax Collection on Rounder as well as his *Sounds of the South,* Atlantic 7 82496-2 (1993).

10. Jim Gladden interview, Nov. 24, 1997.

11. For copies of this questionnaire, list of training recordings, Alan Lomax's hand-

written notes, and administrative memos regarding its development, see LC/
Fisk and ALC. At Jim Gladden's, I also used the earlier Joint Committee on
Folk Arts, WPA, "Folksong Questionnaire."

12. Texas Gladden interview, Spring 1946.

13. Wilgus, "Text Is the Thing," 251. Wilgus first made this statement during his
presidential address at the annual meeting of the American Folklore Society
in Nov. 1972.

14. Jim Gladden interview, Nov. 24, 1997.

15. Wilma Jean Vandergrift interview, Nov. 24, 1997.

16. Jim Gladden interview, Nov. 24, 1997.

17. Texas Gladden interview, Spring 1946.

18. Charlotte Texas Smith Fields and Wiley Johnson Smith are the niece and
nephew mentioned here. Her grandson referred to here is Chris Gladden.

19. Gladden, "Our Honeymoon," in *Along Life's Highway.*

20. I'm grateful to Jim Gladden for giving me his original audiotape of this event.
The song Hobart performed, "Parson Burr," available on *Southern Journey,*
vol. 2, *Ballads and Breakdowns,* Rounder CD 1702 (1997), was also recorded by
the Carter Family as "It'll Aggravate Your Soul," Bluebird B-5817 (1934). Both
songs concern the "Marrying Parson," the Reverend Alfred H. Burroughs, who
officiated at the weddings of some five thousand couples in the first decades
of the twentieth century, making Bristol the leading matrimonial spot in the
South. The parson's customers included not only Texas and James, but in Nov.
1917, Hobart Smith and his bride, Pearl Malinda Smith.

21. Texas Gladden interview, Spring 1946.

22. Ibid.

23. Hobart Smith (with Texas Gladden) interview, Spring 1946.

24. I'm indebted to Charlotte Fields for this anecdote.

25. Texas Gladden interview, Spring 1946.

26. Jim Gladden interview, Mar. 14, 2004.

27. Texas Gladden interview, Spring 1946.

28. Hobart Smith interview, Oct. 2, 1963.

29. Texas Gladden interview, Spring 1946.

30. Hobart Smith interview, Oct. 2, 1963.

31. Texas Gladden interview, Spring 1946.

32. Ibid.

33. Ibid.

34. "Poor Ellen Smith" and the two songs that follow, "The Devil and the Farmer's
Wife" and "Rose Connelly," originally appeared on *Texas Gladden Sings Blue
Ridge Ballads,* Disc 737 (1948). As of 2001, they can be heard again on *Texas
Gladden: Ballad Legacy,* Rounder CD 1800.

35. These interactions reach even further back. In 1963, when Fleming Brown
asked who might be John Greer's stylistic model, Hobart named Henry Hays,
an African American banjoist from that area. John Galliher, in his 1972 interview with Wiley Smith, also discussed Hays and his influence. For more on
these relationships, see my notes to Hobart Smith, *In Sacred Trust.*

36. Galliher interview, Jan. 24, 1972.

37. Texas Gladden interview, Spring 1946.

38. These titles appear at the end of Texas's book of poems, *Along Life's Highway*. In our conversations, Jim Gladden also spoke of William Gladden's musical role in their home.

39. Alan Lomax listed it as "The Four Marys," and under this title it subsequently appeared on AAFS L7 (1943).

40. "Mary Hamilton" appears on Joan Baez's first album (1960) and a 2001 reissue, Vanguard 79554-2.

41. See Emmylou Harris, notes to *Artist's Choice*. Country music historian Bill Malone also cites the formative influence that Texas Gladden's "One Morning in May" had on singer-songwriter Alice Gerrard. See Dickens and Malone, *Working Girl Blues*, 12.

42. Actually, 196 titles are listed, but two are likely repetitions. Texas's earlier list of 150 titles, also compiled with her daughter's help, was lost in a Feb. 1937 house fire.

43. Ellis, "Sentimental Mother Song," 97, original emphasis. See also Ellis, "Blind Girl." I'm also indebted to Norm Cohen for sharing his and Anne Cohen's "Sentimental Ballad." More recently, Malone, *Don't Get above Your Raisin'*, explores this sensibility.

44. Here Ellis echoes Tristram Coffin's phrasing in "'Mary Hamilton' and the Anglo-American Ballad as an Art Form."

45. See Meade's categories in *Country Music Sources*.

46. G. Malcolm Laws Jr. explores these divisions in *Native American Balladry* and *American Balladry from British Broadsides*.

47. Roger D. Abrahams discusses song choice in "the most common dramatic circumstance" in "Creativity, Individuality, and the Traditional Singer," 30. See also Riddle, *A Singer and Her Songs*, 155.

48. "Mrs. Texas Gladden, Mother of Nine Children and Well Known Ballad Singer, Invited to Appear at National Folk Festival," *Roanoke World-News*, Apr. 12, 1939. See Meade, *Country Music Sources*, 181–82, for a list of recordings.

49. See Spaeth's discussion of "Too Late" in *Weep Some More, My Lady*, 33–34.

50. "Mrs. Texas Gladden," *Roanoke World-News*.

51. Texas Gladden interview, Spring 1946.

52. Quoted in "Mrs. Texas Gladden."

53. Texas Gladden interview, Spring 1946.

54. Ibid.

55. Ibid.

56. Ibid.

57. Hobart Smith (with Texas Gladden) interview, Spring 1946.

58. Hobart Smith interview with Fleming Brown, Oct. 4 or 5, 1963.

59. Galliher interview, Jan. 24, 1972. In 1948, when Hobart Smith recorded "Railroad Bill," it became a standard of excellence all over again. See Wade, notes to Hobart Smith, *In Sacred Trust*.

60. Texas Gladden interview, Spring 1946.

61. For John Powell's role in the formation of the White Top Festival, see Whisnant, *All That Is Native and Fine*, 181–252. On Jan. 21, 1934, Powell wrote to Peel requesting Texas's participation in a contemplated series of national radio broadcasts featuring accomplished traditional musicians. He foresaw the

positive benefits to the performers and their communities stemming from this public presentation. Alfreda Peel correspondence, acquisition 9829, box 8, AKD.

62. A detailed exploration of this era in folksong study appears in Wilgus, *Anglo-American Folksong Scholarship*, 3–122.

63. Bronson, "Mrs. Brown and the Ballad," 135.

64. Texas Gladden interview, Spring 1946.

65. Wilma Jean Vandergrift interview, Nov. 24, 1997.

66. *Oxford English Dictionary*, compact edition (Oxford: Oxford University Press, 1981), 2,409–10.

67. Wilgus, "*Aisling* and the Cowboy."

68. Holloway and Black, *Later English Broadside Ballads*, 48.

69. Ibid., 49. I'm indebted to ballad scholar W. Bruce Olson for this information. From March 1999, when I came to know him, until shortly before his death in October 2003, our conversations about this song and other selections from *A Treasury of Library of Congress Field Recordings* benefited from his rigorous studies of primary materials.

70. Wilgus, "*Aisling* and the Cowboy," 298.

71. Wayland D. Hand called attention to its nature-poetry introduction in "Cowboy's Lament." The following year, Kenneth Goldstein and Jan Brunvand published items pertaining to the song, "Still More of 'The Unfortunate Rake' and His Family." Lodewick's "'The Unfortunate Rake' and His Descendants" inspired these and other commentaries, which end with Goldstein's 1960 recorded study. In 1985, D. K. Wilgus renewed this discussion with "*Aisling* and the Cowboy."

72. Alfreda Peel collected "The Dying Cowboy" from a Mr. Parker of Vinton, Va., in June 1921. Peel to C. Alphonso Smith, box 10, acquisition 9829, AKD.

73. Accession 9936, box 13, folder 15 E, VFS.

74. See "Alfreda Peel, the Lady of Legends," *Richmond Times-Dispatch*, Sunday Magazine section, Aug. 30, 1936.

75. See Peel, *Witch in the Mill*, a collection of folktales she gathered during her researches.

76. See Peel to Arthur Kyle Davis Jr., July 26, 1932, Alfreda Peel correspondence, acquisition 9829, box 8, AKD. See also in the same box, Peel to Davis, Apr. 9, 1935. Peel further discusses her folksong adventures in "On the Trail of Virginia Folk Lore."

77. Davis, *Traditional Ballads of Virginia*, 48.

78. Texas's remaining titles collected on Nov. 5, 1916, are "An Orphan Girl," "Samuel Moore and Johnny Dyer," "A Neat Young Lady," "Beauty Bright," "A Little Miss Down in the Garden," "Young Charlotte," "Poor Ellen Smith," "Blue Eyed Daisy," "Poor Willy," and "Ships on the Sea." Alfreda Peel notebook, accession 9936, box 25, folder 1, VFS.

79. Evaluation by F. Stringfellow Barr, Nov. 15, 1916, accession 9936, box 25, folder 1, VFS.

80. See first page of Peel's notebook, accession 9936, box 25, folder 1, VFS.

81. Annabel Morris Buchanan to Peel, Aug. 10, 1935, Alfreda Peel correspondence, accession 9829, box 8, AKD.

82. Jim Gladden interview, Jan. 6, 1998.

83. Peel to C. Alphonso Smith, Nov. 5, 1916, accession 9936, box 25, folder 1, VFS.

84. Lomax to Peel, Apr. 24, 1942, accession 9829, box 24, AKD.

85. Davis, *Traditional Ballads of Virginia*. The text of Texas's "Barbara Ellen" appears on 318–19, and its music on 578. "Hangerman Tree" is on 373. Alfreda Peel's photograph of Texas appears on 117.

86. Arthur Kyle Davis Jr., recorded Texas on Aug. 7, 1932. The songs were "Barbara Allen," "Two Little Devils," "Jessel Town," "The House Carpenter," "Broken Hearts," and "Samuel Moore and Johnny Doyle." Virginia Folklore Society.

87. Peel to Davis, July 26, 1932, Alfreda Peel correspondence, accession 9829, box 8, AKD.

88. Peel to Davis, Sept. 20, 1932, ibid.

89. John Powell to Peel, Jan. 21, 1934, ibid.

90. Peel to Davis, Mar. 30, 1934, ibid.

91. Peel to Davis, May 7, 1934, ibid.

92. Coxe's notation of "When I Was a Young Girl" is in "Sheet Music, Alfreda Peel," accession 9936, box 23, folder 21, VFS.

93. The tale about the Colliersville witch is in accession 9936, box 25, folder 11, VFS.

94. Cited in Hoy, "F. H. Maynard, Author of 'The Cowboy's Lament.'" See also Tinsley, *He Was Singin' This Song*, 77–79.

95. Sharp, *English Folk Songs from the Southern Appalachians*, 2:164–65.

96. Sharp, *Cecil Sharp's Collection of English Folk Songs*, 2:123.

97. Will, "Songs of the Western Cowboys."

98. Barry, "Irish Folk-Song." He continued his studies of the ballad in "Some Aspects of Folk-Song." Here he includes a Nova Scotia text called "The Maiden's Lament." He makes the point (contrary to Wilgus's mentioned earlier) that the cowboy and maiden's versions necessarily grow from the soldier's version by virtue of the military funeral verse. He explores the song in still greater detail in nos. 7, 8, and 11 of the *Bulletin of the Folk-Song Society of the Northeast*.

99. Barry, "Folk-Music in America," 76.

100. Barry, "American Folk Music," 44.

101. Barry, "'Lake Chemo' and 'The Cowboy's Lament,'" 18, original emphasis.

102. Barry, "American Folk Music," 31.

103. Barry, "Part of the Folk Singer," original emphasis. Barry's declining health prevented his delivering this August 1936 essay at the White Top Festival conference. He gifted it to Annabel Morris Buchanan to disseminate as she pleased. In accordance with Robert Winslow Gordon's suggestion, she made copies for attendees and later provided it to Leach and Coffin for publication. Folder 149 contains the original typescript, and Buchanan to Barry, Sept. 4, 1936, box 15, folder 329, describes this experience. AMB.

    Barry's correspondence with Buchanan also reveals that Barry knew of Texas Gladden. In a letter dated Dec. 26, 1936, he queries Buchanan about how Texas handled a particular Child ballad that Buchanan had heard her sing. Box 15, folder 329. AMB.

104. Hobart Smith interview by Fleming Brown, Oct. 4 or 5, 1963.

105. Barry, "Part of the Folk Singer," 61. See also Peel to Davis, July 25 and 30, 1936, Alfreda Peel correspondence, accession 9829, box 8, AKD.

106. Jim Gladden interview, Nov. 25, 1997.

CHAPTER 10. LUTHER STRONG

Faye Sandlin sometimes drove fifty miles to her nearest family member's telephone to talk with me about Luther Strong's music. She also welcomed me at home. I'm grateful to her and her daughter Jackie Johnson. Faye's brother Jim Strong and his wife, Polly, deserve thanks as well. They, too, cherish Luther's memory, and Jim's own fiddling preserves his father's passion. Lowell Morris stayed in touch by phone and mail, ever conscious of Luther's legendary skill. Other gifted musicians have contributed to this story: Harley Bray (reached through his friend Michael Melford), my friend and musical partner James Leva, and Melvin Goins, one of bluegrass music's great witnesses (reached through Kerry Hay of Hay Holler Records). Over the years Stephen Green and Bruce Greene shared their insights, historical research, and firsthand experience as players. Liberty Rucker created "Glory's" meticulous transcription. Finally, I'm grateful to Kentucky fiddler Art Stamper and his wife, Kay. As we sat in his living room talking of persistence and change, he bounded across eras, at home as much in bluegrass as in the old-time music his father and foreparents knew so well.

1. *Time,* Aug. 28, 1995.

2. Sandlin interview, Sept. 9, 1998.

3. Quoted in Jim Strong interview, Sept. 10, 1998.

4. Sandlin interview, Dec. 16, 1994.

5. Polly Strong interview, Sept. 10, 1998. Since this interview, Indiana adopted Daylight Savings Time statewide. Further legislation moved most counties into the Eastern Time Zone, while the others are in the Central Time Zone.

6. By 1942, when three of Luther's recordings including "Glory in the Meetinghouse" were released on *Anglo-American Shanties, Lyric Songs, Dance Tunes, and Spirituals,* AAFS L2, Luther and his family had moved to Dalesburg, Ky., which is where the record notes identify him as living.

7. It is tantalizing to imagine that when Luther worked at the Champion Paper Company, in Hamilton, Ohio, in 1940, he may have encountered another Kentucky-born, old-time-music-playing employee, Pete Steele.

8. Jim Strong interview by Guthrie Meade, undated.

9. Jim Strong interview, Sept. 10, 1998.

10. Ibid.

11. Quoted in Sandlin interview, July 10, 1998.

12. Ibid. Faye told me this story on another occasion as well.

13. Sandlin interview, Sept. 9, 1998.

14. Sandlin interview, July 10, 1998.

15. Elsewhere Faye identified him as Sheriff Lloyd Gross. The sheriff at the time was Dr. A. M. Gross, in office from 1930 to 1934.

16. Sandlin interview, July 8, 1998. She told this story in nearly the same words in an earlier interview, Dec. 16, 1994.

17. Lowell Morris interview, Sept. 28, 1998. Luther's son Jim Strong also confirmed these details.

18. Sandlin interview, July 10, 1998.

19. Disc sleeve note for Georgia Turner's recording, AFS 1401 A1.

20. Ted Anthony explores this process in *Chasing the Rising Sun*.

21. Other items from this trip that made their way into the greater exposure of the folk revival include Monroe Gevedon's "Two Soldiers," recorded by Mike Seeger, Hazel Dickens and Alice Gerrard, Jerry Garcia, and Bob Dylan; and Walter Williams's "East Virginia," recorded and performed by Pete Seeger.

22. Along with making sound recordings, Lomax also took some color film footage of Eliza Pace.

23. A. Lomax, "Field Trips Eastern Kentucky," 57.

24. Ibid., 54.

25. Lomax to Harold Spivacke, n.d., but internal evidence in coordination with the recording log indicates that it was written on Oct. 18, 1937. AFC.

26. Kentucky fiddle historian and musician Bruce Greene likened Hoskins's "Glory" to Hiram Stamper's "Hog-Eyed Man." Greene to author, Jan. 14, 1996.

27. A. Lomax, "Field Trips Eastern Kentucky," 56.

28. Ibid., 57. In an unpublished song headnote about Luther's "Callahan," Lomax connects the two, citing Begley as sheriff at the time of Luther's jailing. When this recording was made, however, Begley was still running for office. ALC.

29. Lowell Morris interview, Sept. 28, 1998.

30. Mrs. Herman R. Santen of Paris, Ky., wrote to the Folk Archive on Mar. 6, 1944, and again on that same day three years later. D. K. Wilgus discusses this correspondence in "Hanged Fiddler," 125.

31. Wilgus, "Hanged Fiddler," 120.

32. Lowell Morris interview, Sept. 28, 1998.

33. See Stephen Green, "Berea Tune Lists," which includes the tune sometimes spelled with a single l, "Calahan," and sometimes titled simply "Callahan."

34. "Old Time Fiddlers Meeting," *Citizen*, Berea, Ky., Aug. 14, 1919. Thanks to Stephen Green for this invaluable clipping. See also Jeff Titon's transcription and discussion of the tune in *Old-Time Kentucky Fiddle Tunes*, 114–15. The earliest issued recording was "Callahan's Reel" by Fiddlin' Powers and Family in 1924.

35. Art Stamper interview, July 7, 1998.

36. The four fiddlers that recorded "Callahan" on this trip in 1937 were George C. Nicholson, Boyd Asher, Luther Strong, and Bill Stepp. McKinley Asher and Winnie Prater also recorded it on the banjo. Ruth Crawford Seeger provides a detailed notation of Luther's "Callahan" in *Our Singing Country*, 56–57. The unattributed headnote there transcribes Oscar Parks's story. Seeger also began a transcription of Luther's "Glory," pictured in *Music of American Folk Song*, 73.

37. Sandlin interview, Dec. 16, 1994.

38. Jim Strong interview, Sept. 10, 1998.

39. Art Stamper called him "Black Hiram Begley." Stamper interviews, June 25 and July 6, 1998.

40. Lowell Morris interview, Sept. 28, 1998.

41. Jim Strong interview, Sept. 9, 1998.

42. Guthrie Meade found Bev Baker's year of birth listed in the 1900 Clay County census. This date precisely corresponds with the recollections of both Jim Strong and Faye Sandlin, who described him as being twenty years older than Luther. A different and younger Bev Baker from another part of Kentucky appears in the Social Security Death Index.

43. Jim Strong interview, Sept. 10, 1998.

44. Sandlin interview, Sept. 9, 1998.

45. Lowell Morris interview, Sept. 28, 1998.

46. Jim Strong interview, Sept. 9, 1998. Jim previously told this story to Guthrie Meade, May 1, 1981, with Baker purportedly saying, "I think I taught him too much."

47. Jim Strong interview, Sept. 10, 1998.

48. Strong to Lomax, Jan. 11, 1938. AFC.

49. Lomax to Strong, Jan. 17, 1939. AFC.

50. *Anglo-American Shanties, Lyric Songs, Dance Tunes, and Spirituals,* AAFS L2. Letters are Strong to Lomax, Oct. 13, 1942, and Nov. 16, 1942. AFC.

51. Another Stamper name, Richman Stamper, connected with the tune appears with notation in John Jacob Niles's handwritten "Field Notebook Eastern Kentucky," ca. 1932, "Glory at [?] the Meeting House," 100. University of Kentucky, Lexington, photocopy courtesy of Stephen Green.

52. See Mary Larsen, "Bruce Greene," preceded in that issue by Greene, "Romance of the Kentucky Fiddler."

53. The Hurricane Ridgerunners' rendition of "Glory" appears on *The Young Fogies,* Heritage 056 (1985). Bruce Molsky's appears on *Contented Must Be,* Rounder 0534 (2004); James Leva's on *Winkin' Eye,* Copper Creek CCCD 0241 (2007); and Laurie Lewis's on *Guest House,* Hightone HCD 8167 (2004).

54. A. Lomax, "Field Trips Eastern Kentucky," 55.

55. AFS 1536 A2.

56. Jim Strong interview, Sept. 9, 1998.

57. Goins interview, Oct. 23, 2007.

58. Ibid.

59. *More Southern Gospel Classics,* Madacy Christian Music Group MC2-50737 (2004). The Goins Brothers recording of "Glory" originally appeared on *In the Head of the Holler,* Jessup Records MB121 (1972).

60. See Titon, *Old-Time Kentucky Fiddle Tunes,* 80–81. What I call here the third strain, Titon identifies as B^1 in his transcription.

61. Quoted in Bob Butler to Guthrie Meade, Dec. 15, 1986. Meade.

62. I'm indebted to Marion Unger Thede's description of cross-tuning in "Traditional Fiddling," 19.

63. Art Stamper interview, July 6, 1998.

64. Ibid.

65. Jim Strong interview, Sept. 10, 1998.

66. Ibid.

67. Thompson, "Time Traveling." For "Hog-Eyed Man" see *The Music of Kentucky,* vol. 2, Yazoo YA 2014 (1995).

68. Thompson, "Time Traveling," 47.

69. Titon, *Old-Time Kentucky Fiddle Tunes,* 154.

70. Liberty Rucker interview, Oct. 16, 2009.

71. Arthur Francis, a guitarist and banjoist, also recorded Luther playing "Katy Hill," which Francis accompanies on banjo. Thanks to Jim Strong and Polly Strong for sharing this revealing homemade audiotape.

72. A. Lomax, "Field Trips Eastern Kentucky," 55.

73. See also Wilgus, "Country-Western Music and the Urban Hillbilly," especially 143–44.

74. This count is slightly higher than the actual number of songs and tunes, for in some instances longer ballads required more than one side of a recording disc. A few in this count also include several spoken recitations, including one track of traditional hog and other farmyard calls.

75. Lomax, "Field Trips Eastern Kentucky," 54.

76. Brockway, "Quest of the Lonesome Tunes." I'm indebted to Jeff Todd Titon's study of Kentucky fiddling that alerted me to this source.

77. Ibid., 229.

78. Ibid., 230.

79. Ibid., 229.

80. *Instantaneous acetates* was a term used at the Library for these recordings made in the field.

81. For more on this concept, see N. Rosenberg, *Bluegrass,* 173–74 and 357.

82. See Carter, notes to *Emmett W. Lundy* and "I Never Could Play Alone."

83. A sampling of these recordings is available in the seven-CD set *Kentucky Mountain Music,* Yazoo YA 2200 (2003).

84. Art Stamper interview, July 6, 1998.

85. James Leva interview, Aug. 16, 2007.

86. Art Stamper interview, July 6, 1998.

87. Jim Strong interview, Sept. 10, 1998.

88. Bruce Greene interview, Dec. 15, 1995.

89. Twenty-two, counting the midbow speed fluctuations.

90. Harley Bray interview, Oct. 17, 2007.

91. Red Cravens and the Bray Brothers, *419 West Main,* Rounder 0015 (1997) and *Prairie Bluegrass,* Rounder 1011 (2000).

92. Posting by Joe Cline on the Internet listserv rec.music.country.old-time. Oct. 29, 2001, based on an IBMA oral history session.

93. C. Wolfe, notes to *Bill Monroe: Bluegrass 1970–1979,* 16. The same passage, from a 1978 Bill Monroe interview, also appears in Rosenberg and Wolfe, *Music of Bill Monroe,* 197.

94. A 1935 performance recorded in Austin, Tex., called "Fiddle Tune," played by A. J. Miers with J. D. Dillingham seconding on banjo, AFS 537 B1, marks the Library's earliest field recording of "Say Old Man." Bob Wills also recorded in 1967 a variation on this motif called "Comanche Hit and Run." Bobby Hicks has recorded it on *Fiddle Patch,* Rounder 0416 (1998). See also Robert "Georgia Slim" Rutland, *Raw Fiddle,* Tri-Agle Far Records (2004).

95. R. P. Christeson includes fiddler Red Williams's version of "Oh Say Old Man, Can You Play the Fiddle" in *Old-Time Fiddler's Repertory,* 75. Williams was

born in Texas and resided in Lincoln, Neb. A cassette of Uncle Bob Walters performing "Drunken Wagoner" is available on Missouri State Old Time Fiddlers Association MSOTFA 106 (1993). I've also recorded it on *Dancing Home,* Flying Fish FF 70543 (1990).

96. Jim Woodward's recording from Sept. 1979 resides with Guthrie Meade's materials in the Southern Folklife Collection. My copy was supplied through the kindness of Stephen Green. Thanks also to John Harrod, who participated in this recording with Meade, and discussed it and other matters pertaining to Luther Strong with me on Dec. 9, 1995. See also Meade, *Country Music Sources,* 711.

97. R. Smith, *Can't You Hear Me Callin',* 182.

98. Greene heard the pennies account from Lloyd Rader of Clay County, and added this in a postscript to his handwritten essay on Luther Strong and Bill Stepp (courtesy of Stephen Green). He heard both the large bow and pennies story from Donald Goodman of Booneville, as Greene reported in "Romance of the Kentucky Fiddler," 7.

99. Sandlin interview, Sept. 9, 1998.

100. Ibid.

101. Ibid.

CHAPTER 11. CHARLIE BUTLER

Rarely in the study of folksong does one get to speak with a sole creator responsible for changing a song's course in tradition. I count myself more than fortunate to have explored with Tex Logan the new life he gave to "Diamond Joe." Tex's delight in fiddlers past, let alone his reflections about this song, have yielded many wonderful conversations. As a musician, songwriter, and disseminator, Tex is one of bluegrass music's great figures.

I'm grateful as well to the Mississippi Department of Corrections for its support. Since my initial contact with this agency in December 1996, many individuals there have abetted this work, beginning with Ken Jones in Jackson and superintendent James Anderson at Parchman. Fire marshal Charles Winters and sergeant J. B. Burchfield spent hours driving me across the penitentiary's expanse, sharing stories about their lives within its barren confines. Barbara Bailey in records was warm and welcoming, as was Robbie Venable in photos. I'll never forget the old camera he used. It lasted so long, he explained, for it only ever had to take two poses: face front and profile. Equally unforgettable was his studio—the handcuff clamp that held his subjects, the file cabinets bursting with forgotten negatives, and the mug shot he displayed of former Parchman inmate Vernon Presley, Elvis's father. Above all, thanks to Marilyn Corbin for her keen observations and continued help years after our initial meetings, and to Dede Cannon for sharing her family's legacy. Together we discovered that the Cannons brought music not only to Parchman, but to Mississippi and beyond.

1. Oliver, *Encyclopedia of Vernacular Architecture,* xxiii.

2. See R. Ford, "Paul Oliver: A Selective Bibliography, 1952–2005," and Oliver, *Barrelhouse Blues.*

3. Circuit Court, July 16, 1936, with Charlie Butler's arrest and imprisonment records, at the Mississippi State Penitentiary (Parchman).

4. When a predecessor died in office, Greek P. Rice became sheriff in Mar. 1941. Rice was elected sheriff again in 1947 and later was appointed County Judge. See list of Coahoma sheriffs in Weeks, *Clarksdale and Coahoma County,* 216. I'm also indebted to Missy Craig of the Carnegie Public Library in Clarksdale for providing Greek Rice's obituary from the *Clarksdale Press Register,* Aug. 4, 1979.

5. Alan Lomax, 1941 field notes. ALC.

6. Nicholas Lemann sets Oct. 2, 1944, for the successful test in Clarksdale of the mechanical cotton picker, precipitant of the post-1940 migration. Lemann, *Promised Land,* 3.

7. Quoted in Cobb, *Most Southern Place on Earth,* 201.

8. "Mississippi Has Lost Population," *Ruleville Record,* Aug. 28, 1947; "Mississippi Negroes Migrating North," *Ruleville Record,* Oct. 9, 1947.

9. Cobb, *Most Southern Place on Earth,* 185.

10. Alan Lomax, 1941 field notes. ALC.

11. In *Land Where the Blues Began,* 24, Lomax elides this moment with Rice and his deputy into the same person.

12. Alan Lomax, 1941 field notes. ALC.

13. Will Starks, AFS 6654 A4. "Mr. Greek Rice Stops Music" interview, Aug. 9, 1942, and quoted in A. Lomax, *Land Where the Blues Began,* 210. There's another recording about Greek Rice made with Asa Ware, AFS 6734 B4, at whose home Starks's interview occurred.

14. Quoted in A. Lomax, *Land Where the Blues Began,* 210.

15. Faulkner, *Mansion,* 48.

16. Federal Writers' Project, *Mississippi,* 99.

17. Ibid., 101.

18. Cobb, *Most Southern Place on Earth,* 107.

19. Cohn, *Where I Was Born and Raised,* 110.

20. Quoted in Oshinsky, *"Worse than Slavery,"* 173.

21. At the time I visited Parchman in Jan. 1997, it covered 21,640 acres.

22. This name appears on a dim microfilm in the prison's files. As best I can make out, the spelling is "Boleu." Unfortunately, the board minutes that list Parchman employees from 1933 to 1944 are missing from the prison's files transferred to the Mississippi Department of Archives and History. Neither the budget reports from that period nor the 1942-era biennial report listed staff by name. The 1930 census also proved inconclusive. Thanks to Anne Webster at MDAH for her many efforts to help track down this sergeant's elusive identity.

23. Retired Parchman sergeant J. B. Burchfield told me this story on Jan. 27, 1997. In 1947, Memphis Slim told the joke in expanded form, available on "Levee Camp and Prison Songs/Conversation Continues," track 7, *Blues in the Mississippi Night,* Rounder CD 1860-2 (2003).

24. Winters interview, Jan. 27, 1997.

25. Corbin interview, Jan. 6, 1997.

26. Cannon interview, Jan. 27, 1997.

27. McWhorter, *Inmate Society*, 37–38.

28. Burchfield interview, Jan. 27, 1997.

29. Quoted in Taylor, *Down on Parchman Farm*, 81.

30. Cabana, *Death at Midnight*, 90.

31. Cohn, *Where I Was Born and Raised*, 102. Cohn uses *parabola* loosely.

32. Higher voices actually reached farther and more clearly in this setting. Bruce Jackson makes this point in his landmark book *Wake Up Dead Man* as well as his album of the same name, Rounder CD 2013 (1994). In the mid-1960s he recorded the last vestiges of these songs in active use at comparable Texas prison farms.

33. Cohn, *Where I Was Born and Raised*, 102.

34. Ibid., 103.

35. John A. Lomax cites this phrase in his first published article following the expedition, "Hunting Negro Songs in the Prisons."

36. J. Lomax and A. Lomax, *American Ballads and Folk Songs*, 63.

37. Oster, notes to *Prison Worksongs*, 23.

38. Ibid., 2.

39. Quoted in Oliver, *Conversation with the Blues*, 26. See also Frederick Law Olmsted's 1853 description of a South Carolina field holler in Courlander, *Negro Folk Music*, 81–82. Epstein also cites this quote in *Sinful Tunes and Spirituals*, 182. My history of "I Can't Be Satisfied" was aired on NPR's *All Things Considered*, Aug. 28, 2001.

40. Quoted in Evans, *Big Road Blues*, 43.

41. In 1941, Son House recorded some hollers for the Library, one of which is available on *Negro Blues and Hollers*, Rounder CD 1501 (1997).

42. Alan Lomax and David Evans have heard these lyrics differently than I have written here. See their transcriptions in Lomax, notes to *Afro-American Blues and Game Songs*, and Evans, notes to *Mississippi*.

43. Alan Lomax, notes to *Afro-American Blues and Game Songs*.

44. John Lomax and Ruby Lomax, "1939 Southern Recording Trip" notes. AFC. Archive records indicate that Charlie sang "Diamond Joe" on AFS 3557 A.

45. A. Lomax, notes to *Afro-American Blues and Game Songs*.

46. AFS 2681 A1. Author's transcription.

47. Alan Lomax, notes to *Afro-American Blues and Game Songs*.

48. "Diamond Joe," AFS 941 B1.

49. Odum, "Folk-Song and Folk-Poetry," 260.

50. Ibid., 280.

51. Ibid., 262.

52. Odum and Johnson, *Negro Workaday Songs*, 130. Earlier, a reprint of Odum's original "Diamond Joe" text appeared with added comment in Odum and Johnson, *The Negro and His Songs*, 184–85.

53. Odum and Johnson, *Negro Workaday Songs*, 130.

54. Perrow, "Songs and Rhymes from the South," 28:133.

55. Perrow, "Songs and Rhymes from the South," 28:134. See McCormick, who connects Perrow's nine toss to Mance Lipscomb's "Jack of Diamonds." "Mance Lipscomb, Texas Sharecropper," 66. See also Groom, notes to *Jack O' Diamonds*.

56. Perrow, "Songs and Rhymes from the South," 28:134.

57. Scarborough, *On the Trail of Negro Folk-Songs*, 86. "Duncan and Brady" receives a thorough, historically based exploration in John Russell David, "Tragedy in Ragtime," 95–148.

58. Scarborough, *On the Trail of Negro Folk-Songs*, 86.

59. R. W. Gordon, "Folk-Songs of America," 3.

60. R. W. Gordon, "Negro Chants," 39.

61. A. Wilson, "Diamond Joe," A-375 (GA-143), AFC.

62. Georgia Crackers, Okeh 45098, available on *Georgia Stringbands*, vol. 1, Document Records DOCD-8021 (1998).

63. Wiggins, "Not Very Aristocratic," 6.

64. Ibid., 7.

65. Russell, notes to *Georgia Stringbands*.

66. Wiggins, "Not Very Aristocratic," 5.

67. Logan interview, Sept. 28, 2001. For an overview of Tex Logan's background, see Carr and Munde, *Prairie Nights to Neon Lights*, 104–10, as well as Kochman, "Tex Logan," and Talbot, "Tex Logan."

68. Logan interview, Sept. 28, 2001.

69. Joe Val's recording, however, was the version that Cisco Houston originally popularized. See his compilation, *Diamond Joe*, Rounder CD 11537 (1995).

70. Wilma Lee and Stoney Cooper's 1957 recording can be heard on *Big Midnight Special*, Bear Family 16751 DK (2007). Jerry Garcia Acoustic Band's recording of "Diamond Joe" appears on *Almost Acoustic*, Grateful Dead Records GDDLP LP5.00036 M (1989).

71. Logan interview, Oct. 4, 2001.

72. A. Lomax, notes to *Afro-American Blues and Game Songs*.

73. Bessie Jones, interview with Alan Lomax, tape 10, 6. ALC.

74. Alan Lomax, NE-167, two-page typescript. ALC.

75. See "Conversation continues," track 16, *Blues in the Mississippi Night*, Rounder CD 1860-2 (2003). See also Alan Lomax, "I Got the Blues." For a detailed overview, see John Cowley, "Shack Bullies and Levee Contractors."

76. AFS 537 A.

77. J. Lomax and A. Lomax, *Our Singing Country*, 247. There Dillingham's middle initial was incorrectly given as B.

78. John Lomax told the Texas Folklore Society that he placed the song at the time of the Civil War. See Nye, *Texas Folk Songs*. See also John A. Lomax, "Old Trail Driver Sings Sad Song in Lyric Ballad of Diamond Joe," *Dallas Morning News*, Apr. 12, 1936. Here Lomax credits his friend and old trail driver Ed Nicholls, from Texas's Bosque County, for the song. Though the words there replicate the earlier Dillingham text, Lomax avers, "And then Ed sang me a cowboy song, the best cowboy song I have heard in many a day."

79. J. Lomax, *Cowboy Songs and Other Frontier Ballads*, rev. ed., 66.

80. It appears on Cisco Houston, *Cowboy Ballads*, Folkways FA 2022 (1952).

81. See Guy Logsdon's notes to *Cisco Houston, the Folkways Years 1944–1961*.

82. *Sod Buster Ballads, Folk Songs of the Early West*, Commodore Records CR-10 (1947). The recordings were actually made in 1941.

83. "Diamond Joe."

84. Bob Dylan recorded the Cisco Houston–Lee Hays–Ramblin' Jack Elliott version of "Diamond Joe" on his *Good As I Been to You,* Columbia CT 53200 (1992). He recorded the Georgia Crackers version on *Masked and Anonymous,* Columbia C2K 90618 (2003).

85. Notes (unsigned) to *Ramblin' Jack Elliott Sings Woody Guthrie and Jimmie Rodgers and Cowboy Songs.*

86. Art Thieme to Joseph Hickerson, Nov. 29, 1988. AFC.

87. Meade, *Country Music Sources,* 502.

88. See William J. Petersen's extensive articles in *Palimpsest,* for example "Diamond Jo Line." See also George B. Merrick, "Joseph Reynolds and the Diamond Jo Line Steamers." I'm indebted to the staff of the Mississippi River Museum in Dubuque, who sent clippings that detailed the line's history locally and alerted me to Jack and Sandy Custer, Louisville-based publishers of the *Egregious Steamboat Journal.* They, in turn, explored old issues of the *Waterways Journal* for the period of Reynolds's operation. The Custers, who gave generously of their time and knowledge, also referred me to Delores Jan Meyer, "Excursion Steamboating on the Mississippi," with information on the Streckfus line, which acquired a number of the Diamond Jo boats.

89. Construction of the twenty-five-mile-long Hot Springs Railroad took place between 1875 and 1889, followed by conversion to standard gauge. In 1902, Joe Reynolds sold the branch to the Choctaw, Oklahoma, and Gulf Railroad, subsequently acquired by the Rock Island.

90. Chappell, *John Henry,* 106.

91. Way, *Way's Steam Towboat Directory,* 56.

92. Handy, *Blues,* 82–85.

93. Art Thieme to Joseph Hickerson, Nov. 29, 1988. AFC.

94. Thieme, notes to "Diamond Joe," *Chicago Town and Points West.* Thieme's reflections on "Diamond Joe" can be found in the discussion forum at www:// mudcat.org under "Diamond Joe."

95. Federal Writers' Project, *Mississippi,* 408.

96. Quoted in Taylor, *Down on Parchman Farm,* 54.

97. Taylor, *Down on Parchman Farm,* 59; Cabana, *Death at Midnight,* 130.

98. Corbin interview, Sept. 22, 2009.

99. Oliver, *Songsters and Saints,* 68.

100. Burchfield interview, Jan. 27, 1997.

101. Cannon interview, Jan. 27, 1997.

102. Quoted in Danchin, "Chanter le blues," 24. Thanks to Kathy James for her translation from the French.

103. Quoted in Danchin, "Chanter le blues," 25.

104. His grandsons Ryan and Spencer Medders continue his music. Wendell Cannon himself had extended the family tradition. Both his father, Grady Cannon, and his uncle, Alfonzo Cannon, played guitar and sang. Fonzo brought these talents to Freeny's Barn Dance Band, who in Dec. 1930 recorded some of the most celebrated sides in old-time music.

105. Cannon interview, Jan. 27, 1997.

CHAPTER 12. JESS MORRIS

The last song in this book, "Goodbye, Old Paint," was the first song I thought to include on *A Treasury of Library of Congress Field Recordings.* It's also the last song that Bob and Vera Morris ever danced to. In early March 1998, as their son, David "Rooster" Morris, rehearsed for a recording, they waltzed to him playing and singing it in Bob's old elementary schoolhouse. Located on a property where his parents raised him, and before that, where his grandparents once lived, this is the same schoolhouse where Jess Morris performed this song in years past. Vera remembered how tired Bob looked in those days just before his death at age eighty-five. "Do you want to go today," she would ask him. "As long as they're fiddling, I'll go," Bob replied.

I could not have written this chapter without Bob's help, Rooster's support, and above all, the presence of Vera Morris. For thirteen years she has sent me letters detailing family history, western life, cowboy music, and happenings around home. A writer, visual artist, and former fiddle contest judge, Vera Morris gives living proof that in the middle of the ocean may grow a green tree.

In addition to the many people acknowledged in the notes below, I wish to thank the following: Lisa Shiota, reference specialist at the Library of Congress music division; musicians Mike Craver and Liberty Rucker; record collectors Joe Bussard and Cary Ginell; Stephen Green and Charlie Seemann of the Western Folklife Center; Nicky Olson of the XIT Museum; Frank Scott of Roots and Rhythm and the British Archive of Country Music; attorney Michael Melford and ethnomusicologist Anthony Seeger for their counsel on traditional music and copyright law.

1. Morris to Pioneer editor, *Fort Worth Star-Telegram,* July 18, 1940. Thanks to Joe Carr for sharing copies of this correspondence, Jess Morris file, TT.
2. Morris to Lomax, May 10, 1939, in correspondence file for the "John A. Lomax and Ruby T. Lomax Southern States Collecting Tour, March 31–June 14, 1939." AFC.
3. Johnson to Emrich, May 13, 1952. I found this letter in the Lyndon Johnson file at AFC and later placed a copy in the Jess Morris file at AFC.
4. Emrich to Johnson, May 18, 1952. Jess Morris file, AFC.
5. Morris to Emrich, Apr. 5, 1952. Jess Morris file, AFC.
6. "Jess Morris," galley proof for obituary that appeared in the *Dalhart Texan,* June 22, 1953. Thanks to Zelda Beth Lang, editor of the paper, who knew Jess when she was a girl living up the street from him and his sister. Zelda shared her memories as well as opened her newspaper's files during our interview, Feb. 20, 1998.
7. V. Morris, "Bell County" and "Civil War" sections, in "Descendants."
8. V. Morris, "Credits" section, in ibid.
9. "John Morris," photocopied from "Portrait and Biographical Record," Pickaway County, Ohio, 849. In V. Morris, "Descendants."
10. V. Morris, "Greetings to the Morris Family," 5, in "Descendants."
11. Limmer, "James Felton," in *Story of Bell County,* 1:517.
12. One resident from the early 1880s described Belton's land values as increasing 500 percent with the coming of the railroad. Limmer, *Story of Bell County,* 1:95.
13. Limmer, "Bell County before the Civil War," in *Story of Bell County,* 1:41, and "Anglos Begin Settlement (1830–1849)," in *Story of Bell County,* 1:6–7, in addition to Bob Morris interview, Feb. 18, 1998.

14. According to Jess's Jan. 10, 1950, song history, his father didn't settle in Bell County until 1879, although the 1860 census showed him already there. In 1880 the census identified E. J. Morris as a Bell County farmer.

15. J. Morris, "History."

16. A copy of E. J. Morris's partially reproduced, undated handwritten letter and his captain's response resides in V. Morris, "Descendants."

17. Jess Morris, "Unfortunate Dog, or Stony Point, with parts of Old Cacklin' Hen (Fiddle Tune, and Conversation about Being a Fiddler)" AFS 5648 A.

18. See Limmer, "Church of Christ—Bartlett," in *Story of Bell County,* 1:122.

19. Bob Morris interview, Feb. 18, 1998.

20. Jess Morris, AFS 5648 A.

21. Vera Morris, paraphrasing her late father-in-law, Al Morris, "Edward James Morris," 2, in "Descendants."

22. Al Morris, quoted in V. Morris, "Children of Lucy Lee & E. J. Morris," in "Descendants."

23. Vera Morris to author, May 15, 2001.

24. Roberts interview, Mar. 9, 1998.

25. Vera Morris, "Descendants," contains six of Sam Morris's poems. Bob Morris recited still another one, a humorous and slightly off-color couplet, during our Feb. 18, 1998, interview.

26. Roberts interview, Mar. 9, 1998.

27. Jess Morris, "Dalhart Fiddler Tells of Playing for Ranch Dances during Days of Frontier," *Fort Worth Star-Telegram,* Jan. 3, 1940. With some abridgment this article was later reprinted as "'After the Ball Was Over' Several Days Had Slipped Away," *XIT Brand,* Aug. 1940, 17–18. It also appeared in the *Bartlett Tribune* and, as late as 1996, in the *Dalhart Daily Texan.*

28. Limmer, "John R. Kuler," in *Story of Bell County,* 2:671.

29. Berneta Peeples, "White Settlers Return to Area," ch. 4 in Limmer, *Story of Bell County,* 1:24–25.

30. Jim Chilcote puts Charley Willis's birth in Milam County at 1850, see "Charley Willis," 174.

31. J. Morris, "History." Subsequent typewritten copies of Jess's "History" bear slight differences in punctuation, subtitle, and spelling.

32. See Anderson, "Snyder." See also Sharpe, "Experiences."

33. J. Morris, "History."

34. "Dalhart Fiddler Tells of Playing for Ranch Dances during Days of Frontier." Jess's accounts sometimes varied about his upbringing in Williamson and Bell counties, which adjoined and actually divide Bartlett itself. Here the journalist, if not Jess, may have elided Neely's location relative to Jess and his family's history.

35. Jess Morris, AFS 5648 A. Klotz also appears in Hunter, *Book of Years,* 111–12. That article, in turn, synthesizes several earlier newspaper articles, drawing particularly on Jess's interview about ranch dances, "They Came from 50 Miles Around and Danced from Sun to Sun," that originally appeared in *XIT Brand,* Aug. 1939, 76–77.

With respect to Jess's return to Bartlett, the *Bartlett Tribune* reports that Jess and his half-brother Jack Felton went together to visit their mother (Jan. 22,

1915), and later took a camping trip with their friends (Aug. 13, 1915). A published death notice, dated Nov. 23, 1912, also reports that Jess's oldest half-brother (from his father's first marriage), Edward J. Morris Jr. (b. 1857), died at Jack Felton's home in Bartlett. Thanks to Valerie Bartlett at the Tienert Memorial Public Library in Bartlett, Tex.

36. I'm indebted to Judith K. Miller, special collections librarian and professor at Valparaiso University, for this quotation and the next. Thanks to Robert Vega for suggesting I get in touch with her.

37. Jess Morris, AFS 5648 A.

38. Ibid.

39. "Alumni Record, Mr. Jesse Morris." Valparaiso University Archives.

40. "Inferiority Complex Was Unknown When Panhandle Fiddlers Learned to Play," *Amarillo Daily News,* Mar. 18, 1928; "Best Fiddlers of Nation to Compete in Program Here," *Amarillo Sunday News and Globe,* Mar. 18, 1928.

41. "Old Fiddlers Contest Here Will Be Great," *Amarillo Daily News,* Mar. 13, 1928. See also Carr, "'Hardy Pioneers' and Amarillo's Panhandle Fiddle Contests."

42. "Hardy Pioneers of Panhandle Compete as Old Fiddlers," *Amarillo Sunday News and Globe,* Mar. 18, 1928.

43. "Ridin Ol' Paint: Famed Dalhart 'Fiddler' Has Song Recorded," *Amarillo Daily News,* Apr. 16, 1941.

44. "Hardy Pioneers of Panhandle Compete as Old Fiddlers."

45. "Inferiority Complex Was Unknown When Panhandle Fiddlers Learned to Play."

46. "Louis Franklin of Wilbarger Wins Old Fiddlers Contest," *Amarillo Daily News,* Mar. 21, 1928. Thanks to Warren Stricker, director of the Research Center at the Panhandle-Plains Historical Museum in Canyon, Texas, for providing articles about Amarillo fiddlers contests.

47. Jess Morris, "Stories of Frontier Cattle Days," AFS 5648 B.

48. "Dalhart Fiddler Tells of Playing for Ranch Dances during Days of Frontier."

49. Ibid.

50. The LC card catalog lists him as "Elisha Cox." Elijah Cox's three titles appear as AFS 547 A1, A2, and B1. I'm grateful to Dr. William E. Green, past curator of history at the Panhandle-Plains Historical Museum in Canyon, Texas. In 1998 Bill first told me about Cox, having written about him in *The Dancing Was Lively.* Further information on Cox comes from Wynn, "Old Cox." A terrific 1880s-era photograph of Cox with his fiddle appears in Carr and Munde, *Prairie Nights to Neon Lights,* 19, along with discussion of him, 12–13.

51. Elijah Cox, "Whoa Mule," AFS 547 A2.

52. Archie Green and I collaborated on a song study of "Old Man." Our Aug. 23, 2006, radio broadcast, "Leadbelly's 'Old Man,'" and a brief essay I wrote about our work, "Byways of a River Song," can be found at the NPR Web site.

53. Nathan Frazier and Frank Patterson, "Old Joe," AFS 6679 B2.

54. I base this statement largely on Charles Wolfe, "Oldest Recorded Fiddling Styles." His list of birthdates cites Uncle Jimmie Thompson, born in 1848, as the oldest (6). Stephen Green's research, quoted in the notes to *Old-Time Texas String Bands,* County 3525 (2001), goes even earlier to Texas fiddlers

(and Confederate veterans) M. J. Bronner, born in 1847, and Henry Gilliland, 1845. Scottish fiddler J. Scott Skinner was born in 1843.

55. Sanders, "Honor the Fiddler!" 83. Sanders drew on "Old Cox Charms with Fiddle Yet," *San Angelo Standard,* May 3, 1924. Unfortunately, this article is now unavailable, as only an incomplete issue of the paper survives on microfilm at the Panhandle-Plains Historical Museum.

56. W. Green, *Dancing Was Lively,* 110. Green drew this quote from the same missing article described in the preceding note.

57. "Hardy Pioneers of Panhandle Compete as Old Fiddlers."

58. Bob Morris interview, Feb. 18, 1998.

59. Both tunes, taken directly from Jess's sheet music, can be heard on the CD *Ridin' Old Paint: Documenting the Canadian River Breaks Fiddle Tradition,* Grey Horse (2000).

60. J. Morris to Pioneer editor, *Fort Worth Star-Telegram,* July 13, 1940. Jess Morris file, TT.

61. J. Morris to James R. Record, managing editor, *Fort Worth Star-Telegram,* July 24, 1940. Jess Morris file, TT.

62. J. Morris to Pioneer editor, *Fort Worth Star-Telegram.* July 18, 1940. Jess Morris file, TT.

63. Jess writes in his July 16, 1940, letter to the *Fort Worth Star-Telegram* that its companion picture, clearly from the same session, was taken in 1907.

64. "El Rancho Grande XIT Schottische" (Song for voice and piano). Words and music by Jess Morris, registered under Ep 1120000, Oct. 31, 1942. Published by G. Schirmer, Inc.

65. J. Morris to Pioneer editor, *Fort Worth Star-Telegram,* July 13, 1940. Jess Morris file, TT.

66. See Duke and Frantz, *6000 Miles.* See also Haley, *XIT Ranch,* and Sullivan, *LS Brand.*

67. Bob Morris interview, Feb. 18, 1998.

68. Hunter, *Book of Years,* 112.

69. Jess Morris, AFS 5648 B.

70. Roberts interview, Mar. 9, 1998.

71. Bob Morris interview, Feb. 18, 1998.

72. "Jess Morris," galley proof.

73. I'm indebted to Tim Brooks for sharing his knowledge of early commercial cylinder recordings, and for leading me in Nov. 2009 to Gerald Fabris, museum curator, Thomas Edison National Historical Park, and to its archivist, Leonard DeGraaf. Thanks to them for searching their files and kindly sharing their immense knowledge of this company and its recording procedures.

74. From Jess Morris's postcard, dated Dec. 12, 1913. Jess Morris file, AFC.

75. For an overview on cowboy song recording history, see Norm Cohen, notes to *Minstrels and Tunesmiths,* 14–16. See also Porterfield, *Last Cavalier,* 147 and 149, regarding John Lomax's early cowboy recording recollections. Nolan Porterfield's insights into Lomax's activities remain unsurpassed.

76. Fabris to author, email, Nov. 16, 2009.

77. Lomax to Morris, Jan. 10, 1941. Jess Morris file, AFC.

78. Morris to Lomax, Apr. 22, 1941. Jess Morris file, AFC.

79. Ives, "A Man and His Song," 80. See also Ives, *Joe Scott,* for a book-length study of this kind of creativity.

80. Jess's Jan. 31, 1941, Library of Congress Amarillo recordings are AFS 6108 A, "Old Paint," and 6108 B, "Jack O' Diamonds." The card catalog entries combine his place of residence, Dalhart, with the place of recording, Amarillo. John Lomax did not make these recordings, though he arranged for them to take place. Jess's first registration of "Ridin' Ol' Paint an' Leadin' Ol' Ball" is listed at the Office of Copyright as E unpub 251907.

81. Morris to Lomax, Apr. 22, 1941. AFC.

82. Bob Morris interview, Feb. 21, 1998.

83. Seth Woods, an oral history done by Elizabeth Shrank, May 1980, TT. Thanks to Amy Salit and Diana Martinez at WHYY in Philadelphia and to Gilbert Padilla in Lubbock.

84. At the bottom of Jess's Mar. 31, 1941, letter to him, Lomax wrote this comment and dated it Apr. 9, 1941. Jess Morris file, AFC.

85. J. Lomax and A. Lomax, *American Ballads and Folk Songs,* 383–84; John A. Lomax, *The Ballad Hunter,* AAFS L49 (1941); J. Lomax and A. Lomax, *Folk Song: U.S.A.,* 254; J. Lomax, *Adventures of a Ballad Hunter,* 70–71.

86. Lomax, "The Story of 'Good-by, Old Paint,'" 132.

87. See Porterfield, *Last Cavalier,* 150–52.

88. J. Lomax, "Story of 'Good-by, Old Paint,'" 134.

89. Fox, "Old Paint," 2.

90. While Lomax first published "Old Paint" in the 1916 edition of *Cowboy Songs,* he did not print any music for this piece until 1934.

91. Morris to Emrich, Jan. 29, 1950. Jess Morris file, AFC.

92. Quoted in D. Green, *Singing in the Saddle,* 160.

93. Ibid., 161, 164.

94. A. Green, "Dobie's Cowboy Friends," 28.

95. See Riggs, *Green Grow the Lilacs.* See also Braunlich, *Haunted by Home,* and Riggs, *Cherokee Night.* D. Green, *Singing in the Saddle,* discusses Tex Ritter's role, 164.

96. Fox, "Old Paint," 5.

97. See Pollack, *Aaron Copland,* 320, 628 n16.

98. McNutt has described the *Life* article as a "pseudo-event." See "*Life* Goes to a Tall Tales Session," *Life,* June 1, 1942, 78–82, and McNutt, "Beyond Regionalism," 239–40.

99. Porterfield, *Last Cavalier,* 448.

100. Ibid., 449. The *Amarillo Daily News* article appeared on Apr. 16, 1941.

101. See Morris to J. Lomax, Apr. 16, 1941. John Lomax's handwritten note appears at the bottom of the page. Jess Morris file, AFC.

102. Jess Morris, "Goodbye, Old Paint," AFS 6108 A. In his copyright submission Jess used the spelling "dony" instead of "doney." He also wrote down and sang here "*may grow* a green tree" instead of what Emrich and others originally heard as "*there grows* a green tree."

103. See the Digital Tradition Web site entries by Robert Waltz and Paul Stamler, respectively, on "Wagoner's Lad" and "Goodbye, Old Paint." Earlier, Fife and

Fife, in *Cowboy and Western Songs,* made this connection in "Old Paint," 226. For "Wagoner's Lad," see Kittredge, "Ballads and Rhymes from Kentucky," 268–69, and "Ballads and Songs," 344–46 and 349–52; Belden, *Ballads and Songs,* 473–76; and Perrow, "Songs and Rhymes from the South," 28(108): 177.

104. Belden, *Ballads and Songs,* 473.
105. Ibid., 482.
106. "Broadside ballad entitled 'The American Stranger'" from "The Word on the Street," National Library of Scotland Web site.
107. Carter Family, "Storms Are on the Ocean," Victor 20937 (1927).
108. See Fife and Fife, *Cowboy and Western Songs,* 226–28.
109. Vera Morris interview, Aug. 21, 2009.
110. Vera Morris interview, Mar. 7, 1998.
111. "Ridin Ol' Paint, Famed Dalhart 'Fiddler' Has Song Recorded."
112. Jess Morris, AFS 5648 A.
113. Morris to LC, Dec. 30, 1949. Jess Morris file, AFC.
114. Morris to Emrich, Jan. 10, 1950. Jess Morris file, AFC. In Jess's first letter to Emrich, however, written Dec. 30, 1949, he says "I composed my tune 'ridin' ol' paint, in Bartlett, Bell County, Texas in 1884–85." AFC.
115. Scholarly entries on Jess's "Goodbye, Old Paint" include Emrich, *Folklore on the American Land,* 489–92; Lingenfelter et al., *Songs of the American West,* 380–81; Tinsley, *He Was Singin' This Song,* 122–25; Carr and Munde, *Prairie Nights to Neon Lights,* 17–18. N. Cohen discusses Jess's performance both in *American Folk Songs,* 2:572–73, and in his *Traditional Anglo-American Folk Music,* 223. Chilcote, "Charley Willis," draws on Jess's song history also, via Tinsley and Emrich.

   Early popular articles that drew on Jess's history, and which Jess knew about, include Albert Law in his *Dalhart Texan* column, "Fare," May 23, 1952, reprinted in the *New Mexico Stockman,* Sept. 1952, 75, as "Ridin' Ol' Paint and Leadin' Old Ball." Law earlier referred to the history in his Jan. 12, 1950, "Fare" column in the *Dalhart Texan.* Lewis Nordyke also utilized it in his "Random Thoughts," *Amarillo Daily News,* Feb. 21, 1950.
116. Cited as "Song 'Ridin Ol' Paint and Leadin Ol' Ball' Together with Letters Regarding the Song, August 20, 1948," *Annals of Wyoming* 21, no. 1 (Jan. 1949): 102. Wyoming State Archives. Thanks to Curtis Greubel and Cindy Brown at the Wyoming State Archives.
117. Jess dated this account Sept. 12, 1948, and in the presence of a notary, swore to its contents the following day. Jess Morris file, AFC.
118. Love, "Dedication of Texas Trail Monuments," 99.
119. J. Morris, "History."
120. Morris to Emrich, Feb. 13, 1950. Jess Morris file, AFC. Emrich replies on Feb. 17, 1950. Jess again mentions his appearance in the magazine on Feb. 24, 1950. Jess never precisely names the magazine, but it is *Annals of Wyoming* 21, no. 1 (Jan. 1949).
121. J. Morris to Emrich, Jan. 10, 1950. Jess Morris file, AFC.
122. J. Morris to Emrich, Mar. 29, 1952. Jess Morris file, AFC.
123. Emrich, notes to "My Sweetheart's a Cowboy" on *Anglo-American Songs and Ballads,* AFS L20 (1947).

124. Duncan Emrich, notes to "Goodbye, Old Paint (I)" on *Cowboy Songs, Ballads, and Cattle Calls from Texas.* See also Jess's final interview, "'Ridin Ol' Paint' 87 Years Old, Music Writer Says," *Fort Worth Star-Telegram,* June 1, 1952: "People got the idea I wrote the song . . . but I didn't. I learned to play it on a jew's harp when I was 7 and later worked out a fiddle arrangement."

125. Morris to Emrich, Sept. 7, 1952. Jess Morris file, AFC. Jess may have meant "then" rather than "that."

126. "Jess Morris," galley proof.

127. Rooster Morris sings and plays the song on *Ridin' Old Paint: Documenting the Canadian River Breaks Fiddle Tradition,* Grey Horse (2000).

128. Rooster Morris, during Bob Morris interview, Feb. 18, 1998.

129. See Ramsey, *Hittin' the Trail,* Smithsonian Folkways SFW CD 50002 (2003).

130. Ramsey, "Revival Meeting and Its Missionaries," 42.

131. Steinmetz, "Goodbye, Old Paint." Thanks to Jeffrey Lyman for sharing his recording, to John Steinmetz for providing the background of his bassoon and piano setting, and to Eugenia Ho for playing it.

132. Lyman email to author, Jan. 21, 2010.

133. Steinmetz interview, Jan. 20, 2010.

134. Steinmetz, "Goodbye, Old Paint."

135. Performance note in ibid.

136. "Jess Morris," galley proof.

137. Vera Morris interview, Aug. 21, 2009.

138. Roberts interview, Mar. 9, 1998.

139. Bob Morris interview, Feb. 21, 1998.

140. Botkin, "The Folk and the Individual," 8.

ABBREVIATIONS AND ARCHIVAL COLLECTIONS

AFC	Archive of Folk Culture, American Folklife Center, Library of Congress, Washington, D.C.
AKD	Arthur Kyle Davis Jr. Papers, Alderman Library, University of Virginia, Charlottesville, Va.
ALC	Alan Lomax Collection. Materials formerly at Hunter College, N.Y., and now at AFC.
AMB	Annabel Morris Buchanan Collection, SFC.
ATM	Archives of Traditional Music, Indiana University, Bloomington, Ind.
CL	Christopher Lornell Memphis Black Gospel Quartet Singers Oral History Collection, Mississippi Valley Collection, University Library, University of Memphis, Memphis, Tenn.
Fisk	Special Collections, Franklin Library, Fisk University, Nashville, Tenn.
Kahn	Ed Kahn Collection, SFC.
Kahn/Wade	Ed Kahn, Coal Creek Papers. Manuscripts, correspondence, and ephemeral publications sent by Kahn to Stephen Wade, Sept. 2000, for eventual deposit in Kahn.
KSHS	Kansas State Historical Society, Topeka, Kans.
LC/Fisk	Library of Congress/Fisk University Mississippi Delta Collection, AFC.
LFP	Lomax Family Papers, Eugene C. Barker Texas History Center, Research and Collections Division, Briscoe Center for American History, University of Texas, Austin, Tex.
Lomax Kentucky	Alan and Elizabeth Lomax Kentucky Collection, AFC.
MDAH	Mississippi Department of Archives and History, Jackson, Miss.
Meade	Guthrie Meade Collection, SFC.
RPT	Ruby Pickens Tartt Collection, Julia S. Tutwiler Library, University of West Alabama, Livingston, Ala.
SFC	Southern Folklife Collection, Southern Historical Collection, Manuscripts Department, Wilson Library, University of North Carolina, Chapel Hill, N.C.

TT	Southwest Collection, Special Collections Library, Texas Tech University, Lubbock, Tex.
VFS	Virginia Folklore Society, Special Collections, Alderman Library, University of Virginia, Charlottesville, Va.

INTERVIEWS

Unless otherwise indicated, I conducted and tape-recorded the following interviews.

Allen, Dorothy. Telephone interview, Jan. 16, 1997, Ft. Myers, Fla. Handwritten notes.
———. Telephone interview, Jan. 28, 1997, Ft. Myers, Fla.
Arnett, Becky. Jan. 10, 1997, Winter Garden, Fla.
Arnett, Eunice. Aug. 4, 1997, Salyersville, Ky. Handwritten notes.
Baker, Etta. Telephone interview, Sept. 10, 2001, Morganton, N.C.
Barnett, Ollie. Aug. 4, 1997, Stinson Creek, Ky.
Barton, Matthew. Telephone interview, May 14, 2008, Washington, D.C. Handwritten notes.
Black, Timuel. Telephone interview, Jan. 25, 1994, Chicago, Ill. Handwritten notes.
Boudreaux, Ella Hoffpauir. Telephone interview, Dec. 17, 1996, St. Martinsville, La. Handwritten notes.
———. Feb. 6, 1997, St. Martinsville, La.
———. Feb. 21, 1999, St. Martinsville, La.
Bray, Harley. Telephone interview, Oct. 17, 2007, Edmonds, Wash.
Broadway, Opal. Telephone interview, June 5, 1997, Memphis, Tenn. Handwritten notes.
———. Oct. 25, 1997, Memphis, Tenn.
Bronner, the Reverend Flem. Telephone interview, Jan. 13, 1997, St. Louis, Mo. Handwritten notes.
Brooks, Gertha Mae. Telephone interview, May 28, 1997, Memphis, Tenn. Handwritten notes.
Burchfield, J. B. Jan. 27, 1997, Parchman, Miss. Handwritten notes.
Cannon, Dede. Jan. 27, 1997, Parchman, Miss. Handwritten notes.
Cherry, Hugh. Telephone interview, May 30, 1997, Houston, Tex. Handwritten notes.
Corbin, Marilyn. Telephone interview, Jan. 6, 1997, Parchman, Miss. Handwritten notes.
———. Telephone interview, Sept. 22, 2009, Cleveland, Miss. Handwritten notes.
Cotton, Appolonia. Oct. 26, 1997, Clarksdale, Miss.
Dawson, Ralph. Telephone interview, Jan. 7 and 8, 1998, Denison, Tex. Handwritten notes.
———. Feb. 16 and 17, 1998, Denison, Tex.
———. Telephone interview, Apr. 25, 1998, Denison, Tex.
———. Telephone interview, Sept. 8, 1998, Denison, Tex.
———. Telephone interview, Dec. 27, 1998, Denison, Tex.
———. Telephone interview, May 8, 2003, Denison, Tex.
———. Telephone interview, May 14, 2003, Denison, Tex.
———. Telephone interview, June 9, 2003, Denison, Tex.
Deal, Emma. Telephone interview, Oct. 11, 2000, Drew, Miss.
Dickman, Pearl Steele. Dec. 13, 1997, Hamilton, Ohio.

Fields, Charlotte Smith (with Wiley Smith). June 19, 2002, Saltville, Va.

Gabbard, Leona Steele. Telephone interview, Feb. 14 and 15, 2008, Hamilton, Ohio. Handwritten notes.

Galliher, John. Tape-recorded interview by Wiley Smith, Jan. 24, 1972, Saltville, Va.

Gladden, Chris. Nov. 25, 1997, Salem, Va. Handwritten notes.

Gladden, Jim. Nov. 24 and 25, 1997, Salem, Va. Tape-recorded interview and handwritten notes.

——. Telephone interview, Jan. 6, 1998, Salem, Va. Handwritten notes.

——. Telephone interview, Mar. 14, 2004, Salem, Va. Handwritten notes.

Gladden, Texas (with Hobart Smith). Phonographically recorded interview by Alan Lomax, Spring 1946, New York, N.Y.

Goins, Melvin. Telephone interview, Oct. 23, 2007, Catlettsburg, Ky.

Greene, Bruce. Telephone interview, Dec. 15, 1995, Burnsville, N.C. Handwritten notes.

Haufrecht, Herbert. Telephone interview, May 8, 1996, Shady, N.Y. Handwritten notes.

Hebb, Bobby. Telephone interview, Apr. 9, 2009, Nashville, Tenn.

Heilbut, Anthony. Dec. 7, 1996, New York, N.Y.

——. Telephone interview, Dec. 21, 1996, New York, N.Y. Handwritten notes.

Henderson, Sylvia. Nov. 18, 1996, Rugby, Va. Handwritten notes.

Hill, Don. Telephone interview, Jan. 25, 2000, Oneonta, N.Y. Handwritten notes.

Howard, Nannie. Jan. 10, 1997, Winter Garden, Fla.

Howard, Peggy. Telephone interview, Oct. 8, 1999, Salyersville, Ky.

Hunter, Nancy. Jan. 31, 1997, Ruleville, Miss. Handwritten notes.

——. Mar. 8, 1999, Ruleville, Miss. Handwritten notes.

Inglis, Fannie Pickens Tartt. Telephone interview, Jan. 24, 1997, Livingston, Ala. Handwritten notes.

Jamieson, Robert S. Telephone interview, Mar. 3, 1998, Longwood, Fla.

Johnson, Jack. Telephone interview, Apr. 28, 2008, Clarksdale, Miss.

Kahn, Ed. Telephone interview, Sept. 22, 2000, Pinole, Calif. Handwritten notes.

Kreimer, Peggy. Email correspondence, Mar. 7, 2008, Cincinnati, Ohio.

Larrance, Steve. Oct. 29, 1999, Hyattsville, Md. Handwritten notes.

Leva, James. Aug. 16, 2007, Hyattsville, Md.

Logan, Benjamin. Telephone interview, Sept. 28, 2001, Madison, N.J.

——. Telephone interview, Oct. 4, 2001, Madison, N.J.

Loughead, Tom. Telephone interview, Mar. 4, 2008, Huntsville, Ala. Handwritten notes.

Mainer, Wade. Telephone interview, July 30, 2001, Flint, Mich.

Marshall, the Reverend Edgar. Telephone interview, May 12, 1997, Clarksdale, Miss. Handwritten notes.

McFarland, Arnold. Oct. 2, 1999, Lakeville, Ky. Handwritten notes.

——. Telephone interview, Oct. 9, 1999, Lakeville, Ky.

McFarland, Lydie. Oct. 2, 1999, Lakeville, Ky. Handwritten notes.

Miller, Judith. Telephone interview, Dec. 18, 2009, Valparaiso, Ind. Handwritten notes.

Milton, Kathleen. Jan. 31, 1998, East St. Louis, Ill.

Milton, Leon "Sonny." Jan. 31, 1998, East St. Louis, Ill.

Morganfield, the Reverend Willie. Telephone interview, Jan. 26, 1997, Clarksdale, Miss. Handwritten notes.

Morris, Bob. Feb. 18, 1998, Channing, Tex.

———. Feb. 21, 1998, Channing, Tex.

Morris, Lowell. Telephone interview, Sept. 28, 1998, Booneville, Ky.

Morris, Vera. Telephone interview, Mar. 7, 1998, Channing, Tex. Handwritten notes.

———. Telephone interview, Aug. 21, 2009, Channing, Tex. Handwritten notes.

Myles, the Reverend Marvin. Jan. 28, 1997, Clarksdale, Miss.

———. Telephone interview, May 12, 1997, Lyon, Miss. Handwritten notes.

Pace, Lawrence. Oct. 24, 1997, Bradley, Ark.

Paley, Tom. Dec. 1, 1994, Bethesda, Md.

Payne, Sonny. Oct. 27, 1997, Helena, Ark.

Pell, Paul. Telephone interview, Feb. 17, 2008, Nashville, Ind.

Reed, Nathaniel. Telephone interview, May 10, 1997, Livingston, Ala. Handwritten notes.

Reedy, Kathryn. Nov. 18, 1996, Rugby, Va.

Roberts, Elizabeth Morris. Telephone interview, Mar. 9, 1998, Redlands, Calif.

Rowe, Helen Marie. Telephone interview, July 27, 2001, Okolona, Miss.

Rucker, Liberty. Oct. 16, 2009, Hyattsville, Md. Handwritten notes.

Sams, Otis. Oct. 23, 1997, Stephens, Ark.

Sandlin, Faye Strong. Telephone interview, Dec. 16, 1994, Scottsburg, Ind. Handwritten notes.

———. Telephone interview, July 8 and 10, 1998, Austin, Ind.

———. Sept. 9, 1998, Austin, Ind.

Schlappi, Elizabeth. Telephone interview, Mar. 7 and 10, 2003, San Diego, Calif. Handwritten notes.

Seeger, Pete. Telephone interview, Jan. 6, 1997, Beacon, N.Y. Handwritten notes.

Sheppard, Martha. June 8, 1998, Washington, D.C. Handwritten notes.

Shipp, Isaac. Jan. 10, 1998, Jersey City, N.J.

———. Telephone interview, Feb. 7, 1998, Jersey City, N.J.

———. Telephone interview, July 7, 2002. Jersey City, N.J.

Shipp, Luella. Feb. 8, 1997, Byhalia, Miss.

Smith, Hobart. Radio interview by Studs Terkel, "The Studs Terkel Wax Museum," WFMT, Oct. 2, 1963, Chicago, Ill.

———. Tape-recorded interview by Fleming Brown, Oct. 4 or 5, 1963, Chicago, Ill.

Smith, Hobart (with Texas Gladden). Phonographically recorded interview by Alan Lomax. Spring 1946, New York, N.Y.

Smith, Wiley (with Charlotte Fields). June 19, 2002, Saltville, Va.

Smith, Willie. Telephone interview, Apr. 28, 2008, Chicago, Ill.

Stamper, Art. Telephone interview, June 25, 1998.

———. July 6 and 7, 1998, Shepherdsville, Ky.

Steele, Dwight. Telephone interview, Feb.15, 2008, Hamilton, Ohio. Handwritten notes.

Steele, Ed. Dec. 12, 1997, Hamilton, Ohio.

Steinmetz, John. Telephone interview, Jan. 20, 2010, Altadena, Calif. Handwritten notes.

Stepp, Sam. Oct. 1, 1999, Slade, Ky. Handwritten notes.

Stepp, William. Aug. 3, 1997, San Pierre, Ind.

Strong, Jim. Tape-recorded interviews by Guthrie Meade, May 1, 1981, and undated [ca. 1981], Austin, Ind. Meade.

WORKS CITED

———. Sept. 9 and 10, 1998, Austin, Ind.

Strong, Lorine Pace. Telephone interview, Aug. 1, 1999, Spring Hill, La.

Strong, Polly. Sept. 10, 1998, Austin, Ind.

Sturz, Elizabeth Lyttleton. Telephone interview, Jan. 2, 1996, New York, N.Y. Handwritten notes.

Taylor, Henrietta. July 6, 1997, Washington, D.C.

Travis, Dempsey. Telephone interview, Jan. 14, 1994, Chicago, Ill. Handwritten notes.

Tuttle, Della. Tape-recorded interview by Ed Kahn, Aug. 22, 1960 [date incorrect on shelflist]. Coal Creek, Tenn. FT-12565, Kahn.

Vandergrift, Wilma Jean. Nov. 24, 1997, Salem, Va. Handwritten notes.

Vowell, Alvin. Tape-recorded interview by Ed Kahn, Aug. 29, 1961, Briceville, Tenn. FT-12568, Kahn.

West, Simon. Telephone interview, June 4, 1999, Los Angeles, Calif.

Whitley, Richard. Telephone interview, Oct. 8, 1999, Jeffersonville, Ky.

Wicks, Georgia. Telephone interview, May 18 and 19, 1997, Clarksdale, Miss. Handwritten notes.

———. Oct. 27, 1997, Clarksdale, Miss.

Williams, Garrett. Jan. 24, 1997, Livingston, Ala.

Winters, Charles. Jan. 27, 1997, Parchman, Miss. Handwritten notes.

Work, John, IV. Telephone interview, Nov. 6, 2000, New York, N.Y.

Wright, Early. Jan. 26, 1997, Clarksdale, Miss. Handwritten notes.

OTHER SOURCES

Abbott, Lynn. "'Play That Barbershop Chord': A Case for the African-American Origin of Barbershop Harmony." *American Music* 10 (Fall 1992): 289–325.

Abbott, Lynn, and Doug Seroff. *Out of Sight: The Rise of African American Popular Music, 1889–1895.* Jackson: University Press of Mississippi, 2002.

Abrahams, Roger D. "Creativity, Individuality, and the Traditional Singer." *Studies in the Literary Imagination* 3, no. 1 (Apr. 1970): 5–36.

———. "Some Jump-Rope Rimes from Texas." *Southern Folklore Quarterly* 27, no. 3 (Sept. 1963): 196–213.

Ainsworth, Catherine Harris. "Jump Rope Verses around the United States." *Western Folklore* 20, no. 3 (July 1961): 179–99.

Albrecht, Otto H. *Albrecht's Progressive Studies for the Banjo.* Philadelphia, Pa.: N.p., 1890.

Anderson, H. Allen. "Snyder, John Wesley." In *The New Handbook of Texas,* 5:1128–29. Austin: Texas State Historical Association, 1996.

Anthony, Ted. *Chasing the Rising Sun: The Journey of an American Song.* New York: Simon and Schuster, 2007.

Babcock, Barbara A., ed., *The Reversible World: Forms of Symbolic Inversion in Art and Society.* Ithaca, N.Y.: Cornell University Press, 1978.

The Baldwin and Register Clarksdale City Directory. Vol. 2, 1939, ABCD no. 82. Columbus, Ohio: Mullin-Kille.

The Baldwin and Register Clarksdale, Mississippi City Directory. Vol. 1, 1936, ABCD no. 32. Columbus, Ohio: Mullin-Kille.

Ballard, James. *The Elements of Guitar-Playing.* New York: Geib and Walker, 1838.

Banks, Ann. *First-Person America.* New York: Alfred A. Knopf, 1980.

Barry, Phillips. "American Folk Music." *Southern Folklore Quarterly* 1, no. 2 (June 1937): 29–47.

———. "The Cowboy's Lament." *Bulletin of the Folk-Song Society of the Northeast,* no. 8 (1934): 16–17.

———. "The Cowboy's Lament." *Bulletin of the Folk-Song Society of the Northeast,* no. 11 (1936): 18.

———. "Folk-Music in America." *Journal of American Folklore* 22, no. 83 (Jan.–Mar. 1909): 72–81.

———. "Irish Folk-Song." *Journal of American Folklore* 24, no. 93 (Jul.–Sept. 1911): 332–43.

———. "'Lake Chemo' and 'The Cowboy's Lament.'" *Bulletin of the Folk-Song Society of the Northeast,* no. 7 (1934): 14–18.

———. "The Part of the Folk Singer in the Making of Folk Balladry." In *The Critics and The Ballad,* edited by MacEdward Leach and Tristram P. Coffin, 59–76. Carbondale: Southern Illinois University Press, 1961.

———. "Some Aspects of Folk-Song." *Journal of American Folklore* 25, no. 97 (Jul.–Sept. 1912): 274–83.

Baughman, Ernest W. *Type and Motif-Index of the Folktales of England and North America.* Indiana University Folklore Series, no. 20. The Hague, Netherlands: Mouton, 1966.

Bayard, Samuel P. *Dance to the Fiddle, March to the Fife.* University Park: Pennsylvania State University Press, 1982.

———. *Hill Country Tunes: Instrumental Folk Music of Southwestern Pennsylvania.* Philadelphia, Pa.: Memoirs of the American Folklore Society 39, 1944.

Belden, H. M. *Ballads and Songs Collected by the Missouri Folk-Lore Society.* University of Missouri Studies 15, no. 1. Columbia, Jan. 1940.

Bickal, Jim. "The Rock Island Line: A Mighty Good Road." Minnesota Public Radio broadcast, Oct. 10, 2002.

Blaustein, Richard. "Jugs, Washboards and Spoons: Why Improvised Musical Instruments Make Us Laugh." *Tennessee Folklore Society Bulletin* 47, no. 2 (June 1981): 76–79.

Botkin, B. A. "Applied Folklore: A Semantic-Dynamic Approach." Typescript, 1967. AFC.

———. "The Folk and the Individual: Their Creative Reciprocity." Typescript. Published in *English Journal* 27 (Feb. 1938): 121–35.

———. "Folk-Song Record Albums." *Music Educators Journal* 29, no. 5 (Apr. 1943): 21.

———. *A Treasury of Southern Folklore.* New York: Crown, 1949.

———. "We Called It 'Living Lore.'" *New York Folklore Quarterly* 14, no. 3 (Fall 1958): 189–201.

Boyd, Joe Dan. *Judge Jackson and the Colored Sacred Harp.* Montgomery: Alabama Folklife Association, 2002.

Boyer, Horace. *How Sweet the Sound: The Golden Age of Gospel.* Washington, D.C.: Elliott and Clark, 1995.

Braunlich, Phyllis Cole. *Haunted by Home: The Life and Letters of Lynn Riggs.* Norman: University of Oklahoma Press, 1988.

Brockway, Howard. "The Quest of the Lonesome Tunes." *Art World* 2 (June 1917): 227–30.

Bronson, Bertrand H. "Mrs. Brown and the Ballad." *California Folklore Quarterly* 4, no. 2 (Apr. 1945): 129–40.

Brown, Alan, and David Taylor, eds. *Gabr'l Blow Sof': Sumter County, Alabama Slave Narratives*. Livingston: Livingston Press, University of West Alabama, 1997.

Brown, Frank C. *Frank C. Brown Collection of North Carolina Folklore*. Vol. 3, *Folk Songs from North Carolina*. Edited by Henry M. Belden and Arthur Palmer Hudson. Durham, N.C.: Duke University Press, 1952.

Brown, Marice C. *Amen, Brother Ben: A Mississippi Collection of Children's Rhymes*. Jackson: University Press of Mississippi, 1979.

Brown, Virginia Pounds, and Laurella Owens. *Toting the Lead Row: Ruby Pickens Tartt, Alabama Folklorist*. Tuscaloosa: University of Alabama Press, 1981.

Buckley, Bruce R. "Jump Rope Rhymes: Suggestions for Classification and Study." *Keystone Folklore Quarterly* 11 (Summer 1966): 99–111.

Burman-Hall, Linda C. "American Traditional Fiddling: Performance Contexts and Techniques." In *Performance Practice: Ethnomusicological Perspectives*, edited by Gerard Béhague, 149–221. Westport, Conn.: Greenwood Press, 1984.

———. "Southern American Folk Fiddle Styles." *Ethnomusicology* 19, no. 1 (Jan. 1975): 47–65.

———. "Southern American Folk Fiddling: Context and Style." Ph.D. diss., Princeton University, 1974.

Burns, Robert. *Burns: Poems and Songs*. Edited by James Kinsley. London: Oxford University Press, 1969.

Burroughs, Margaret. "Casey Jones, and Lady Baby, Street Jesters: The Last of a Species Indigenous to Chicago's Fast Disappearing Black Belt." Unpublished manuscript, ca. 1950s. Eleven pages. Author's collection.

Cabana, Donald A. *Death at Midnight: The Confession of an Executioner*. Boston: Northeastern University Press, 1996.

Campbell, E. Simms. "Blues." In *Jazzmen*, edited by Frederic Ramsey Jr. and Charles Edward Smith, 101–18. New York: Harcourt, Brace, 1939.

Carmer, Carl. *Stars Fell on Alabama*. 1934. Rpt., Tuscaloosa: University of Alabama Press, 1985.

Carr, Joe. "'Hardy Pioneers' and Amarillo's Panhandle Fiddle Contests." *Journal of Texas Music History* 1, no. 1 (2001). Posted online at eCommons@Texas State University.

Carr, Joe, and Alan Munde. *Prairie Nights to Neon Lights: The Story of Country Music in West Texas*. Lubbock: Texas Tech University Press, 1995.

Carter, Thomas. Notes to *Emmett W. Lundy, Fiddle Tunes from Grayson County, Virginia*. String Records STR 802 (1977).

Carter, Thomas, with Thomas Sauber. "'I Never Could Play Alone': The Emergence of the New River Valley String Band, 1875–1915." In *Arts in Earnest: North Carolina Folklife*, edited by Daniel W. Patterson and Charles G. Zug III, 47–74. Durham, N.C.: Duke University Press, 1990.

Cassidy, Frederic G., and Joan Houston Hall, eds. *Dictionary of American Regional English*. Vol. 2. Cambridge, Mass.: Belknap Press/Harvard University Press, 1991.

Chappell, Louis W. *John Henry: A Folk-Lore Study*. 1933. Rpt., Port Washington, N.Y.: Kennikat Press, 1968.

Charters, Samuel. *The Country Blues.* New York: Rinehart, 1959.

———. Notes to *American Skiffle Bands.* Folkways FA 2610 (1957).

Chilcote, Jim. "Charley Willis, a Singing Cowboy." In *Black Cowboys of Texas,* edited by Sara R. Massey, 172–78. College Station: Texas A&M University Press, 2000.

Christeson, R. P. *The Old-Time Fiddler's Repertory.* Columbia: University of Missouri Press, 1973.

Cobb, James C. *The Most Southern Place on Earth: The Mississippi Delta and the Roots of Regional Identity.* New York: Oxford University Press, 1992.

Cochran, Robert. "'Ride It Like You're Flyin'': The Story of the 'The Rock Island Line.'" *Arkansas Historical Quarterly* 61 (Summer 1997): 201–29.

Cockrell, Dale. "Jim Crow: Demon of Disorder." *American Music* 14, no. 2 (Summer 1996): 161–84.

Coffin, Tristram P. "'Mary Hamilton' and the Anglo-American Ballad as an Art Form." *Journal of American Folklore* 70, no. 277 (July 1957): 208–14.

Cohen, John. Notes to *Back Roads to Cold Mountain.* Smithsonian Folkways SFW CD 40149 (2004).

Cohen, Norm. *American Folk Songs: A Regional Encyclopedia.* 2 vols. Westport, Conn.: Greenwood Press, 2008.

———. *Long Steel Rail: The Railroad in American Folksong.* 2nd ed. Urbana: University of Illinois Press, 2000.

———. Notes to *Minstrels and Tunesmiths: The Commercial Roots of Early Country Music.* John Edward Memorial Foundation LP-109 (1981).

———. *Traditional Anglo-American Folk Music: An Annotated Discography of Published Sound Recordings.* New York: Garland, 1994.

Cohen, Norm, and Anne Cohen. "The Sentimental Ballad: A Neglected Folk Song Category." Unpublished paper, [1974].

Cohn, David L. *Where I Was Born and Raised.* 1935 (as *God Shakes Creation*). Rpt., Notre Dame, Ind.: University of Notre Dame Press, 1967.

Cole, John Y. *For Congress and the Nation: A Chronological History of the Library of Congress.* Washington, D.C.: Library of Congress, 1979.

Conference on Inter-American Relations in the Field of Music. Digest of Proceedings. Principal Addresses. Washington, D.C.: Division of Cultural Relations, Department of State, January 1940.

Converse, Frank B. *Analytical Banjo Method.* New York: S. T. Gordon and Son, 1887.

Copland, Aaron, and Vivian Perlis. *Copland: 1900 through 1942.* New York: St. Martin's Press, 1984.

Cotton, Appolonia. "Silent Grove Baptist Church, 1871–1983, May 22, 1983." Church leaflet, Clarksdale, Miss. Appolonia Cotton's personal collection.

Courlander, Harold. *The Big Old World of Richard Creeks.* Philadelphia, Pa.: Chilton, 1962.

———. *Negro Folk Music, U.S.A.* New York: Columbia University Press, 1963.

———. *Negro Songs from Alabama.* Rev. and enl. 2nd ed. New York: Oak Publications, 1963.

Cowley, John. "Collecting the Treasury: Rounder's Recent Releases of Field Recordings on CD." Musical Traditions Web site, www.mustrad.org.uk/reviews/treasury. Posted March 1998.

———. "Shack Bullies and Levee Contractors: Bluesmen as Ethnographers." In A. Green, *Songs about Work,* 134–62.

Cox, Paul. "Classic Guitar Technique and Its Evolution as Reflected in the Method Books ca. 1770–1850." Ph.D. diss., Indiana University, 1978.

Crawford, Richard. *America's Musical Life: A History.* New York: W. W. Norton, 2001.

Crawford, Robert. *The Bard: Robert Burns, A Biography.* Princeton, N.J.: Princeton University Press, 2009.

Cussler, Margaret, and Mary L. De Give. *'Twixt the Cup and the Lip: Psychological and Socio-Cultural Factors Affecting Food Habits.* New York: Twayne Publishers, 1952.

Danchin, Sebastian. "Chanter le blues: Le prix de l'inspiration." *Soulbag,* no. 143 (Summer 1996): 22–25.

Danner, Peter. "'Bolero,' Op. 46 by Luigi Castellacci." *Soundboard,* Summer 1999, 31–36.

———. "A Noteworthy Early American Guitar Treatise: James Ballard's 'Elements' of 1838." *Soundboard,* Nov. 1981, 270–76.

David, John Russell. "Tragedy in Ragtime: Black Folktales from St. Louis." Ph.D. diss., Saint Louis University, 1976.

Davis, Arthur Kyle, Jr. *Traditional Ballads of Virginia.* Cambridge, Mass.: Harvard University Press, 1929.

Denison City Directory. Vol. 15. Dallas, Tex.: John F. Worley, 1949.

Dewey, John. "Americanism and Localism." *Dial* 68 (June 1920): 684–88.

"Diamond Joe." Unsigned article, *Sing Out!* 4, no. 4 (Mar. 1954): 8–9.

Dickens, Hazel, and Bill C. Malone. *Working Girl Blues: The Life and Music of Hazel Dickens.* Urbana: University of Illinois Press, 2008.

Dixon, Robert M. W., John Godrich, and Howard Rye. *Blues and Gospel Records 1890–1943.* 4th ed. Oxford: Oxford University Press, 1997.

DuBois, W. E. B. *The Souls of Black Folk.* 1903. Rpt., New York: Fawcett, 1961.

Duke, Cordia Sloan, and Joe B. Frantz. *6000 Miles of Fence: Life on the XIT Ranch of Texas.* Austin: University of Texas Press, 1961.

Eaton, Allen H. *Handicrafts of the Southern Highlands.* New York: Russell Sage Foundation, 1937.

Eaton, Franklin. *Up to Date Method for the Banjo.* Cincinnati, Ohio: John Church, 1898 [possibly 1896].

———. *Up to Date Method for the Guitar.* Cincinnati, Ohio: John Church, 1903.

Ellis, Bill. "The 'Blind Girl' and the Rhetoric of Sentimental Heroism." *Journal of American Folklore* 91, no. 360 (Apr.–June 1978): 657–74.

Ellis, William Carson [Bill Ellis]. "The Sentimental Mother Song in American Country Music, 1923–45." Ph.D. diss., Ohio State University, 1978.

Ellison, Ralph. "The Little Man at Chehaw Station." *American Scholar* 47 (Winter 1977–78): 25–48.

Ely, Macel, II. *Ain't No Grave: The Life and Legacy of Brother Claude Ely.* Atlanta, Ga.: Dust-to-Digital, 2010.

Emrich, Duncan. *Folklore on the American Land.* Boston: Little, Brown, 1972.

———. Notes to *Cowboy Songs, Ballads, and Cattle Calls from Texas.* AFS L28 (1952), reissued as Rounder CD 1512 (1999).

Epstein, Dena J. *Sinful Tunes and Spirituals.* Urbana: University of Illinois Press, 1977.

Evans, David. *Big Road Blues: Tradition and Creativity in the Folk Blues.* 1982. Rpt., New York: Da Capo, 1987.

———. Notes to *Good Time Blues: Harmonicas, Kazoos, Washboards and Cow-bells.* Columbia/Legacy CK 46780 (1991).

———. Notes to *Mississippi: Saints and Sinners.* Rounder CD 1824 (1999).

Faulkner, William. *The Mansion.* 1955. Rpt., New York: Vintage, 1965.

Federal Writers' Project. *Mississippi: A Guide to the Magnolia State.* New York: Hastings House, 1938.

Fife, Austin E., and Alta S. Fife. *Cowboy and Western Songs: A Comprehensive Anthology.* New York: Clarkson N. Potter, 1969.

Filene, Benjamin. *Romancing the Folk: Public Memory and American Roots Music.* Chapel Hill: University of North Carolina Press, 2000.

Fitzpatrick, Ellen. "Caroline F. Ware and the Cultural Approach to History." *American Quarterly* 43, no. 2 (June 1991): 173–98.

Foner, Philip S. *History of the Labor Movement in the United States.* Vol. 2. New York: International Publishers, 1955.

Ford, Ira. *Traditional Music of America.* New York: E. P. Dutton, 1940.

Ford, Rob. "Paul Oliver: A Selective Bibliography, 1952–2005." *Popular Music* 26, no. 1 (Jan. 2007): 157–86.

Fox, Oscar. "Old Paint, Sheet Music Edition." New York: Carl Fischer, 1927.

Fulcher, Bobby. "Cuje Bertram: Excerpts from an Interview." *Tennessee Folklore Society Bulletin* 53, no. 2 (Summer 1987): 58–70.

Fulmer, David. *The Dying Crapshooter's Blues.* San Diego, Calif.: Harcourt, 2006.

Fuson, Henry Harvey. *Ballads of the Kentucky Highlands.* London: Mitre Press, 1931.

Gammon, Vic. "The Grand Conversation: Napoleon and British Popular Balladry." *RSA Journal* 137, no. 5398 (Sept. 1989). Rpt. Musical Traditions Web site, article MT 033.

Garcia, William. "The Life and Choral Music of John Wesley Work (1901–1967)." Ph.D. diss., University of Iowa, 1973.

Garon, Paul. "Baby Please Don't Go/Don't You Leave Me Here." In *Encyclopedia of the Blues,* edited by Edward Komara, 1:39–40. New York: Routledge, 2006.

———. "Williams, Big Joe Lee." In *Encyclopedia of the Blues,* edited by Edward Komara, 2:1076–77. New York: Routledge, 2006.

Gaunt, Kyra D. *The Games Black Girls Play: Learning the Ropes from Double-Dutch to Hip-Hop.* New York: New York University Press, 2006.

Genovese, Eugene D. *Roll, Jordan, Roll: The World the Slaves Made.* New York: Vintage Books, 1976.

Gilpin, Patrick Joseph. "Charles S. Johnson: An Intellectual Biography." Ph.D. diss., Vanderbilt University, 1973.

Gilpin, Patrick Joseph, and Marybeth Gasman. *Charles S. Johnson: Leadership beyond the Veil in the Age of Jim Crow.* Albany: State University Press of New York, 2003.

Gladden, Texas. *Along Life's Highway: Poems by Texas Anna Smith Gladden.* Privately published, 1952.

Goldstein, Kenneth S. Notes to *The Unfortunate Rake: A Study in the Evolution of a Ballad.* Folkways FA 3805 (1960).

Goldstein, Kenneth S., and Jan Brunvand. "Still More of 'The Unfortunate Rake' and His Family." *Western Folklore* 18, no. 1 (Jan. 1959): 35–38.

Gordon, Robert. *Can't Be Satisfied: The Life and Times of Muddy Waters.* Boston: Little, Brown, 2002.

Gordon, Robert W. "Fiddle Songs." *New York Times Magazine,* Nov. 27, 1927. Rpt. in *Folk-Songs of America,* 71–77.

———. *Folk-Songs of America.* New York: National Service Bureau, 1938.

———. "The Folk-Songs of America: A Hunt on Hidden Trails." *New York Times Magazine,* Jan. 2, 1927. Rpt. in *Folk-Songs of America,* 1–5.

———. "Negro Chants." *New York Times Magazine,* May 8. 1927. Rpt. in *Folk-Songs of America,* 34–39.

———. "Old Songs That Men Have Sung." *Adventure,* July 30, 1923: 191–92.

Green, Archie. "Dobie's Cowboy Friends." *JEMF Quarterly,* no. 41 (Spring 1976): 21–29.

———. *Only a Miner: Studies in Recorded Coal-Mining Songs.* Urbana: University of Illinois Press, 1972.

———. *Torching the Fink Books and Other Essays on Vernacular Culture.* Chapel Hill: University of North Carolina Press, 2001.

———. *Wobblies, Pile Butts, and Other Heroes: Laborlore Explorations.* Urbana: University of Illinois Press, 1993.

Green, Archie, ed. *Songs about Work: Essays in Occupational Culture for Richard A. Reuss.* Special Publication of the Folklore Institute, no. 3. Bloomington: Folklore Institute, Indiana University, 1993.

Green, Douglas B. *Singing in the Saddle: The History of the Singing Cowboy.* Nashville, Tenn.: Country Music Foundation Press and Vanderbilt University Press, 2002.

Green, Stephen. "The Berea Tune Lists: An Archival Resource for the Study of Social Music in Eastern Kentucky and East Tennessee in 1915." *Tennessee Folklore Society Bulletin* 57, no. 2 (1995): 1–18.

Green, William E. *The Dancing Was Lively: Fort Concho, Texas, a Social History, 1867–1882.* San Angelo, Tex.: Fort Concho Sketches Publishing, 1974.

Greene, Bruce. "The Romance of the Kentucky Fiddler." *Fiddler Magazine* 4, no. 2 (Summer 1997): 5–10.

Groom, Bob. "The Library of Congress Blues and Gospel Recordings, Part 2, The Nashville Washboard Band." *Blues World* no. 39 (Summer 1971): 7–9.

———. Notes to *Jack O' Diamonds: 1934 Field Recordings from Texas.* Flyright Matchbox Library of Congress Series, SDM 265 (1976).

Gura, Philip F. *C. F. Martin and His Guitars, 1796–1873.* Chapel Hill: University of North Carolina Press, 2003.

Haley, J. Evetts. *The XIT Ranch of Texas and the Early Days of the Llano Estacado.* 1929. Rpt., Norman: University of Oklahoma Press, 1953.

Hall, Joan Houston. ed. *Dictionary of American Regional English.* Vol. 4. Cambridge, Mass.: Belknap Press/Harvard University Press, 2002.

Halpert, Herbert. "Folk Music Recordings Made in Mississippi by Herbert Halpert, May 1939, AFS 2735-3153." Typed field notes. AFC.

Hand, Wayland D. "The Cowboy's Lament." *Western Folklore* 17, no. 3 (July 1958): 200–205.

Handy, W. C., ed. *Blues: An Anthology.* 1926. Rpt., New York: Da Capo, 1990.

———. *Father of the Blues: An Autobiography.* 1941. Rpt., New York: Da Capo, 1969.

Harris, Emmylou. Notes to *Emmylou Harris: Artist's Choice.* Hear Music OPCD-7656 LMM-209 (2004).

Harris, Trudier. "August Wilson's Folk Traditions." In *August Wilson: A Casebook,* edited by Marilyn Elkins, 49–67. New York: Garland Publishing, 1994.

Hawes, Bess Lomax. "SEM Lecture—2/18/94 revision for *Ethnomusicology.*" 21-page typescript. Later published as "Reminiscences and Exhortations: Growing Up in American Folk Music," *Ethnomusicology* 39, no. 2 (Spring/Summer 1995): 179–92.

Hay, Samuel. "Joe Turner's Come and Gone." In *The Cambridge Companion to August Wilson,* edited by Christopher Bigsby, 89–100. Cambridge: Cambridge University Press, 2007.

Heilbut, Tony. *The Gospel Sound, Good News and Bad Times.* 1971. Rpt., New York: Anchor Doubleday, 1975.

Hentoff, Nat. "American Folk Songs, Direct from the Field." *Wall Street Journal,* Nov. 20, 1997.

———. *American Music Is.* New York: Da Capo Press, 2004.

Herzog, George. "The Study of Folksong in America." *Southern Folklore Quarterly* 2, no. 2 (June 1938): 59–64.

Hill, Dick. "The Grand Ole Opry, 1944–45: A Radio Log Kept by Dick Hill, of Tecumseh, Neb." *Journal of Country Music* 5, nos. 3–4 (1975): 91–122.

Holloway, John, and Joan Black. *Later English Broadside Ballads.* London: Routledge and Kegan Paul, 1957.

Howe, Elias. *Howe's School for the Violin.* Boston: Oliver Ditson, 1851.

Hoy, James. "F. H. Maynard, Author of 'The Cowboy's Lament.'" *Mid-American Folklore* 21, no. 2 (Fall 1993): 61–68.

Huddleston, Ed. *Big Wheels and Little Wagons.* Nashville, Tenn.: Nashville Banner, 1959.

Hughes, Langston, and Milton Meltzer. *Black Magic: A Pictorial History of Black Entertainers in America.* New York: Bonanza Books, 1967.

Hull, Cordell. *Addresses and Statements by the Honorable Cordell Hull in Connection with His Trip to South America to Attend the Inter-American Conference for the Maintenance of Peace Held at Buenos Aires, Argentina, December 1–23, 1936.* Washington, D.C.: Department of State, publication 1019, conference series no. 31.

Hundley, D. R. *Social Relations in Our Southern States.* New York: Henry B. Price, 1860.

Hunter, Lillie Mae. *The Book of Years: A History of Dallam and Hartley Counties.* Hereford, Tex.: Pioneer Book Publishers, 1969.

Hurston, Zora Neale. "High John de Conquer." In *The American Mercury Reader,* edited by Lawrence E. Spivak and Charles Angoff, 106–12. Philadelphia, Pa.: Blakiston, 1944.

Hutchinson, George. *The Harlem Renaissance in Black and White.* Cambridge, Mass.: Belknap Press/Harvard University Press, 1995.

Ives, Edward D. *Joe Scott, the Woodsman-Songmaker.* Urbana: University of Illinois Press, 1978.

———. "A Man and His Song." In *Folksongs and Their Makers,* edited by Ray B.

Browne, 71–148. Bowling Green, Ohio: Bowling Green University Popular Press, 1970.

———. "'The Teamster in Jack MacDonald's Crew': A Song in Context and Its Singing." In *Folklife Annual 1985,* edited by Alan Jabbour and James Hardin, 74–85. Washington, D.C.: American Folklife Center, Library of Congress, 1985.

Jabbour, Alan. "Copland's Kentucky Muse." *Civilization,* June/July 1999, 110.

———. Notes to *American Fiddle Tunes,* AFS L62 (1971). Reissued as Rounder CD 1518 (2000).

Jackson, Bruce, ed. *The Negro and His Folklore in Nineteenth-Century Periodicals.* Publications of the American Folklore Society. Bibliographical and Special Series. Vol. 18. Austin: University of Texas Press, 1967.

———. *Wake Up Dead Man: Afro-American Worksongs from Texas Prisons.* Cambridge, Mass.: Harvard University Press, 1972.

Jackson, Travis A. Review of *Black Appalachia.* In *2000 Yearbook for Traditional Music* 32 (2000): 230–31.

Jamieson, Robert S. "Gribble, Lusk and York: Recording a Black Tennessee Stringband." *Tennessee Folklore Society Bulletin* 53, no. 2 (Summer 1987): 43–57.

Johnson, Charles S. "A Chapel Talk to the Students of Fisk University." Charles S. Johnson Papers, box 158, folder 23, Fisk.

———. *Growing Up in the Black Belt: Negro Youth in the Rural South.* Washington, D.C.: American Council on Education, 1941.

———. "Jazz Poetry and Blues." *Carolina Magazine,* May 1928, 16–20.

———. "Some Notes on a Personal Philosophy of Life." Charles S. Johnson Papers, box 174, folder 5, Fisk.

———. "Some Suggestions for a New Pragmatic Philosophy." Charles S. Johnson Papers, box 174, file 15, Fisk.

———. "A Spiritual Autobiography." Charles S. Johnson Papers, box 144, folder 1, Fisk.

Johnson, James Weldon, and J. Rosamond Johnson. *The Book of American Negro Spirituals.* 1925. Rpt., New York: Da Capo, 1977.

Joint Committee on Folk Arts, WPA. "Folksong Questionnaire." Washington, D.C., Mar. 1939. AFC.

Jones, Bessie, and Bess Lomax Hawes. *Step It Down: Games, Plays, Songs and Stories from the Afro-American Heritage.* New York: Harper and Row, 1972.

Jones, Lewis W. Memorandum to Charles S. Johnson, "The Folk Culture Study in Coahoma County, Mississippi," Aug. 20, 1942. 12-page typescript. LC/Fisk.

———. "The Mississippi Delta." Typescript with handwritten title above printed notation "Social Science Institute, Fisk University, Nashville." ALC.

Jones, Loyal. *Faith and Meaning in the Southern Uplands.* Urbana: University of Illinois Press, 1999.

Kahn, Ed. "The Ballad of Coal Creek." *Sing Out!* 10, no. 1 (Apr.–May 1960): 18.

Kinnard, J., Jr. ("Our Salt-Fish Dinner Correspondent"). "Who Are Our National Poets?" *Knickerbocker Magazine* 26, no. 4 (Oct. 1845): 331–41.

Kittredge, George Lyman. "Ballads and Rhymes from Kentucky." *Journal of American Folklore* 20, no. 79 (Oct.–Dec. 1907): 251–77.

———. "Ballads and Songs." *Journal of American Folklore* 30, no. 117 (Jul.–Sept. 1917): 283–369.

Knapp, Herbert, and Mary Knapp. *One Potato, Two Potato: The Secret Education of Children*. New York: W. W. Norton, 1976.

Kochman, Marilyn. "Tex Logan: Fiddling Around with Mathematics." *Pickin'* 6, no. 9 (Oct. 1979): 44–46, 56.

Korson, George. *Coal Dust on the Fiddle: Songs and Stories of the Bituminous Industry.* 1943. Rpt., Hatboro, Pa.: Folklore Associates, 1965.

Larsen, Mary. "Bruce Greene: Carrying on Kentucky's Old-Time Traditions." *Fiddler Magazine* 4, no. 2 (Summer 1997): 11–17.

Laws, G. Malcolm, Jr. *American Balladry from British Broadsides*. Bibliographical and Special Series, 8. Philadelphia, Pa.: American Folklore Society, 1957.

———. *Native American Balladry: A Descriptive Study and Bibliographical Syllabus.* Bibliographic Series, 1. Philadelphia, Pa.: American Folklore Society, 1950.

Lemann, Nicholas. *The Promised Land: The Great Black Migration and How It Changed America*. New York: Alfred A. Knopf, 1991.

Levine, Lawrence W. *Black Culture and Black Consciousness*. New York: Oxford University Press, 1977.

Levy, Lester S. Levy Collection of Sheet Music, Johns Hopkins University. Baltimore, Maryland. http://levysheetmusic.mse.jhu.edu/.

Limmer, E. A., Jr., ed. *Story of Bell County, Texas*. 2 vols. Austin: Eakin Press, 1988.

Lingenfelter, Richard E., Richard A. Dwyer, and David Cohen, eds. *Songs of the American West*. Berkeley: University of California Press, 1968.

Linn, Karen. *That Half-Barbaric Twang: The Banjo in American Popular Culture*. Urbana: University of Illinois Press, 1991.

Lodewick, Kenneth. "'The Unfortunate Rake' and His Descendants." *Western Folklore* 14, no. 2 (Apr. 1955): 98–109.

Logsdon, Guy. Notes to *Cisco Houston, the Folkways Years 1944–1961*. Smithsonian Folkways SF CD 40059 (1994).

Lomax, Alan. "Field Notes." 1941 and 1942 wire-bound notebooks. ALC.

———. "Field Trips Eastern Kentucky—228 Records." In *Archive of American Folk Song: A History 1928–1939,* 54–57. Compiled from the Annual Reports of the Librarian of Congress, Library of Congress Project, Work Projects Administration, 1940 [for 1938]. AFC.

———. "The Functional Aspects of Folklore." In "Conference on the Character and State of Studies in Folklore." *Journal of American Folklore* 59, no. 234 (Oct.–Dec. 1946): 495–527.

———. "I Got the Blues." *Common Ground* 8 (Summer 1948): 30–52.

———. *The Land Where the Blues Began*. New York: Pantheon, 1993.

———. *Mister Jelly Roll: The Fortunes of Jelly Roll Morton, New Orleans Creole and "Inventor of Jazz."* New York: Grove Press, 1950.

———. Notes to *Afro-American Blues and Game Songs,* Rounder CD 1513 (1999).

———. Notes to *Blues in the Mississippi Night,* Rounder 1860 (2003).

———. "Ohio and Indiana Field Notes, Spring 1938, AFS 1689-1767." AFC.

———. *The Rainbow Sign: A Southern Documentary*. New York: Duell, Sloan and Pearce, 1959.

Lomax, John A. *Adventures of a Ballad Hunter*. New York: Macmillan, 1947.

———. *Cowboy Songs and Other Frontier Ballads*. New York: Sturgis and Walton, 1910. Rev. ed., New York: Macmillan, 1938.

———. "Field Experiences with Recording Machines." *Southern Folklore Quarterly* 1, no. 2 (June 1937): 57–60.

———. "Hunting Negro Songs in the Prisons." *Dallas Morning News*, Oct. 15, 1933.

———. "Self-Pity in Negro Folk-Song." *Nation* 105 (Aug. 9, 1917): 141–45.

———. "Some Types of American Folk Song." *Journal of American Folklore* 28, no. 107 (Jan.–Mar. 1915): 1–17.

———. "Southern Recording Trip by John A. Lomax 1940, 3942-4087." Typed field notes. AFC.

———. "The Story of 'Good-by, Old Paint.'" *Street and Smith's Wild West Weekly* 82 (Feb. 1, 1934): 132–34.

Lomax, John A., and Alan Lomax. *American Ballads and Folk Songs*. New York: Macmillan, 1934.

———. *Folk Song: U.S.A.* New York: Duell, Sloan and Pearce, 1947.

———. *Negro Folk Songs as Sung by Lead Belly*. New York: Macmillan, 1935.

———. *Our Singing Country: A Second Volume of American Ballads and Folk Songs*. Music ed. Ruth Crawford Seeger. New York: Macmillan, 1941.

Lomax, John A., and Ruby T. Lomax. "The John and Ruby Lomax 1939 Southern Recording Trip, AFS 2589-2728 and AFS 3551-3557, March 31–June 14, 1939." Typed field notes. AFC.

Lornell, Kip. *"Happy in the Service of the Lord": African-American Sacred Vocal Harmony Quartets in Memphis*. 2nd ed. Knoxville: University of Tennessee Press, 1995.

Lornell, Kip, and Blanton Owen. Notes to *E. C. Ball and Orna, Through the Years, 1937–1975*. Copper Creek CCCD-0141 (1997).

Love, Louise. "The Dedication of Texas Trail Monuments in Wyoming." *Annals of Wyoming* 21, no. 1 (Jan. 1949): 93–99.

Lunsford, Bascom Lamar, and Lamar Stringfield. *30 and 1 Folksongs (from the Southern Mountains)*. New York: Carl Fischer, 1929.

Malone, Bill C. *Don't Get above Your Raisin': Country Music and the Southern Working Class*. Urbana: University of Illinois Press, 2002.

"Manner of Living of the Inhabitants of Virginia." *American Museum* 1, no. 3 (Mar. 1787): 214–16.

McCallum, Brenda. "Songs of Work and Songs of Worship." *Tributaries, Journal of the Alabama Folklife Association*, premiere issue (Summer 1994): 45–71.

McCormick, Mack. "Mance Lipscomb—Texas Sharecropper and Songster." In *American Folk Music Occasional, No. 1*, edited by Chris Strachwitz, 61–73. Berkeley, Calif.: American Folk Music Occasional, 1964.

McDearman, Karen M. "Black Belt." In *Encyclopedia of Southern Culture*, edited by Charles Reagan Wilson and William Ferris, 567. Chapel Hill: University of North Carolina Press, 1989.

McGregory, Jerrilyn. "Livingston, Alabama, Blues: The Significance of Vera Ward Hall." *Tributaries, Journal of the Alabama Folklife Association*, no. 5 (2002): 72–80.

McKnight, Mark. "Charivaris, Cowbellions, and Sheet Iron Bands: Nineteenth-Century Rough Music in New Orleans." *American Music* 23, no. 4 (Winter 2005): 407–25.

McLean, Ann. Notes to *Freedom at the Library of Congress: The Golden Gate Quartet and Josh White*. Bridge 9114 (2002).

McNutt, James. "Beyond Regionalism: Texas Folklorists and the Emergence of a Post-Regional Consciousness." Ph.D. diss., University of Texas, 1982.

McWhorter, William L. *Inmate Society: Legs, Half-Pants and Gunmen: A Study of Inmate Guards.* Saratoga, Calif.: Century Twenty One Publishing, 1981.

Meade, Guthrie T., Jr., with Dick Spottswood and Douglas S. Meade. *Country Music Sources: A Biblio-Discography of Commercially Recorded Traditional Music.* Chapel Hill: Southern Folklife Collection, University of North Carolina at Chapel Hill Libraries, in association with the John Edwards Memorial Forum, 2002.

Meade, Guthrie T., Jr., and Richard Nevins. Notes to *Wink the Other Eye: Old Time Fiddle Band Music from Kentucky.* Morning Star Records 45003 (1980).

Merrick, George B. "Joseph Reynolds and the Diamond Jo Line Steamers, 1862–1911." *Mississippi Valley Historical Society Proceedings* 8 (1914–15): 217–61.

Meyer, Delores Jan. "Excursion Steamboating on the Mississippi." Ph.D. diss., Saint Louis University, 1967.

Meyer, Donald C. "Toscanini and the Good Neighbor Policy: The NBC Symphony Orchestra's 1940 South American Tour." *American Music* 18, no. 3 (Fall 2000): 233–56.

Mitchell, Elder W. H., comp. *Select Pentecostal Songs of the Kingdom. Special for Revivals Book 13.* Little Rock, Ark.: Church of God in Christ, [1933].

Morris, Jess. "History of Ridin' Ol' Paint and Leadin' Ol' Ball, an Old Cowboy Song, the History Dating Back to: 1871." Typescript, Jan. 10, 1950. Jess Morris file, AFC.

Morris, Vera. "Descendants of Lucy Lee Hughes and Edwards James Morris." Manuscript in her possession, 1983.

Morton, David C., with Charles K. Wolfe. *DeFord Bailey: A Black Star in Early County Music.* Knoxville: University of Tennessee Press, 1991.

Muldoon, Paul. "Blackwatertown." In *The Rose and the Briar: Death, Love and Liberty in the American Ballad,* edited by Sean Wilentz and Greil Marcus, 347–48. New York: W. W. Norton, 2005.

Mullen, Patrick B. *The Man Who Adores the Negro: Race and American Folklore.* Urbana: University of Illinois Press, 2008.

My Old Dad's Woolly Headed Screamer. [New York: Turner and Fisher], 1844. Robert W. Gordon Collection of Nineteenth-Century Songsters, folder 3, AFC.

Nelson, John H., comp. *October, 1922 Rock Island Magazine: A Reprint.* Newton, Iowa: CPM, n.d.

Nemerov, Bruce. "John Wesley Work III: Field Recordings of Southern Black Folk Music, 1935–1942." *Tennessee Folklore Society Bulletin* 53, no. 3 (1987): 82–103.

Nevins, Richard. Notes to *Kentucky Mountain Music.* Yazoo 2200 (2003).

Noonan, Jeffrey J. "The Guitar in America as Reflected in Topical Periodicals, 1882–1933." Ph.D. diss., Washington University, 2004.

Notes (unsigned) to *Ramblin' Jack Elliott Sings Woody Guthrie and Jimmie Rodgers and Cowboy Songs.* Monitor MCD 71380 (1994), expanded reissue of the 1960 LP.

Nulton, Lucy. "Jump Rope Rhymes as Folk Literature." *Journal of American Folklore* 61, no. 239 (1948): 53–67.

Nye, Hermes. Notes to *Texas Folk Songs.* Folkways FA 2128 (1955).

Odum, Howard W. "Folk-Song and Folk-Poetry as Found in the Secular Songs of the Southern Negroes." *Journal of American Folklore* 24, no. 93 (1911): 255–94; no. 94 (1911): 351–96.

Odum, Howard W., and Guy B. Johnson. *The Negro and His Songs.* Chapel Hill: University of North Carolina Press, 1925.

———. *Negro Workaday Songs.* Chapel Hill: University of North Carolina Press, 1926.

Olcott-Bickford, Vahdah. "The Guitarist—'Do You Play the Spanish Fandango?'" *Cadenza* 26, no. 9 (Sept. 1919): 24–25.

Oliver, Paul. *Barrelhouse Blues.* New York: Basic Civitas Books, 2009.

———. *Broadcasting the Blues: Black Blues in the Segregation Era.* New York: Routledge, 2006.

———. *Conversation with the Blues.* 1965. 2nd ed. Cambridge: Cambridge University Press, 1997.

———. Notes to *Bobbie Leecan and Robert Cooksey 1926–27.* Matchbox Bluesmaster Series, MSE 1010 (1986).

———. "Rock Island Line." *Music Mirror* 4, no. 1 (Jan. 1957): 6–8.

———. *Songsters and Saints: Vocal Traditions on Race Records.* Cambridge: Cambridge University Press, 1984.

———. "Tub, Jug, Washboard Bands: Music on Improvised Instruments." Rpt. in Paul Oliver, *Blues Off the Record: Thirty Years of Blues Commentary,* 31–38. New York: Da Capo, 1984.

Oliver, Paul, ed. *Encyclopedia of Vernacular Architecture of the World.* Cambridge: Cambridge University Press, 1997.

Olsson, Bengt. *Memphis Blues and Jug Bands.* London: Studio Vista, 1970.

Ong, Walter J. *Orality and Literacy: The Technologizing of the Word.* London: Routledge, 1982.

Opie, Iona, and Peter Opie. *The Lore and Language of Schoolchildren.* Oxford: Oxford University Press, 1959.

Oshinsky, David M. *"Worse than Slavery": Parchman Farm and the Ordeal of Jim Crow Justice.* New York: Free Press, 1996.

Oster, Harry. Notes to *Prison Worksongs.* Arhoolie CD 448 (1997).

Palmer, Robert. *Deep Blues.* New York: Viking Press, 1981.

Partee, C. L. "Practical Hints on Modern Guitar Playing: Tuning the Guitar." *Cadenza* 4, no. 1 (Sept.–Oct. 1897): 3.

Peel, Alfreda M. "On the Trail of Virginia Folk Lore." Unpublished manuscript. Acquisition number 9829, box 8, AKD.

———. *Witch in the Mill.* Richmond, Va.: Deitz Press, 1947.

Perrow, E. C. "Songs and Rhymes from the South." *Journal of American Folklore* 25, no. 96 (Apr.–June 1912): 137–55; 26, no. 100 (Jan.–Mar. 1913): 123–73; 28, no. 108 (Apr.–June 1915): 129–90.

Petersen, William J. "The Diamond Jo Line." *Palimpsest* 51, no. 4 (Apr. 1970): 169–216.

Phay, John E. *The Report of a Study of the Education for Negroes in Sunflower County, Mississippi.* [Oxford, Miss.]: Bureau of Educational Research, School of Education, University of Mississippi, Mar. 1950.

Pollack, Howard. *Aaron Copland: The Life and Work of an Uncommon Man.* New York: Henry Holt, 1999.

Porterfield, Nolan. *Last Cavalier: The Life and Times of John A. Lomax.* Urbana: University of Illinois Press, 1996.

Raichelson, Richard. "Black Religious Folksong: A Study in Generic and Social Change." Ph.D. diss., University of Pennsylvania, 1975.

Rammel, Hal. *Nowhere in America: The Big Rock Candy Mountain and Other Comic Utopias.* Urbana: University of Illinois Press, 1990.

Ramsey, Buck. "A Revival Meeting and Its Missionaries: The Cowboy Poetry Gathering." In *The Changing Faces of Tradition: A Report on the Folk and Traditional Arts in the United States,* written, edited, and compiled by Elizabeth Peterson. Research Division Report 38, 42–49. Washington, D.C.: National Endowment for the Arts, 1996.

Randolph, Vance. *Ozark Folksongs.* 4 vols. Rev. ed. Columbia: University of Missouri Press, 1980.

Renbourn, John. "The American Steel-String Guitar: Tracing the Early Years." B.A. thesis, Dartington College of Arts, 1986.

Richardson, Ethel Parks. *American Mountain Songs.* Edited and arranged by Sigmund Spaeth. N.p.: Greenberg, 1927.

Riddle, Almeda. *A Singer and Her Songs: Almeda Riddle's Book of Ballads.* Edited by Roger D. Abrahams. Baton Rouge: Louisiana University Press, 1970.

Riggs, Linn. *The Cherokee Night and Other Plays.* Norman: University of Oklahoma Press, 2003.

———. *Green Grow the Lilacs: A Play.* 1930. Rpt., New York: Samuel French, 1958.

Riley, James Whitcomb. *The Complete Works of James Whitcomb Riley.* Vol. 7. New York: Harper and Brothers, 1916.

Robbins, Faye Wellborn. "A World-Within-a-World: Black Nashville, 1880–1915." Ph.D. diss., University of Arkansas, 1980.

Rockwell, John. "Art Rock." In *The Rolling Stone Illustrated History of Rock and Roll,* edited by Jim Miller, 347–52. New York: Random House, 1976.

Romalis, Shelly. *Pistol Packin' Mama: Aunt Molly Jackson and the Politics of Folksong.* Urbana: University of Illinois Press, 1999.

Rooney, James. *Bossmen: Bill Monroe and Muddy Waters.* New York: Da Capo, 1971.

Rosenbaum, Art. *Old-Time Mountain Banjo.* New York: Oak Publications, 1968.

Rosenberg, Bruce A. *Can These Bones Live?: The Art of the American Folk Preacher.* 1970. 2nd ed. Urbana: University of Illinois Press, 1988.

Rosenberg, Neil V. *Bluegrass: A History.* Urbana: University of Illinois Press, 1985.

———. "'An Icy Mountain Brook': Revival, Aesthetics, and the 'Coal Creek March.'" In A. Green, *Songs about Work,* 163–83.

Rosenberg, Neil V., and Charles K. Wolfe. *The Music of Bill Monroe.* Urbana: University of Illinois Press, 2007.

Russell, Tony. *Blacks, Whites and Blues.* New York: Stein and Day, 1970.

———. "Clarksdale Piccolo Blues." *Jazz and Blues* 1, no. 7 (Nov. 1971): 30.

———. *Country Music Records: A Discography, 1921–1942.* New York: Oxford University Press, 2004.

———. Notes to *Georgia Stringbands,* vol. 1. Document Records DOCD-8021 (1998).

Sandburg, Carl. *Good Morning, America.* New York: Harcourt, Brace, 1928.

———. *New American Songbag.* New York: Broadcast Music, 1950.

———. *The People, Yes.* New York: Harcourt Brace and World, 1936.

Sanders, J. Olcutt. "Honor the Fiddler!" In *Texian Stomping Grounds,* 78–90. Texas Folklore Society Publications, no. 17. Austin, 1941.

Scarborough, Dorothy. *On the Trail of Negro Folk-Songs.* Cambridge, Mass.: Harvard University Press, 1925.

Schlappi, Elizabeth. *Roy Acuff: The Smoky Mountain Boy.* 1978. Rpt., Gretna, La.: Pelican, 1997.

Seeger, Charles. "The Importance to Cultural Understanding of Folk and Popular Music." In *Conference on Inter-American Relations in the Field of Music,* 1–10.

———. "Inter-American Relations in the Field of Music: Some Basic Considerations." *Music Educators Journal* 27, no. 5 (Mar.–Apr. 1941): 17–18, 64–65.

———. "Music in America." *Magazine of Art* 31, no. 7 (July 1938): 411–12, 435–36.

Seeger, Pete. *The Goofing-Off Suite.* New York: Hargail Music Press, [1962?].

Seeger, Ruth Crawford. *The Music of American Folk Song and Selected Other Writings on American Folk Music.* Edited by Larry Polansky with Judith Tick. Rochester, N.Y.: University of Rochester Press, 2001.

Seroff, Doug. *Gospel Arts Day, Nashville: A Special Commemoration, Jubilee Hall, Fisk University, June 19, 1988.* Nashville, Tenn.: Nashville Gospel Ministries, 1988.

Sharp, Cecil J. *Cecil Sharp's Collection of English Folk Songs.* 2 vols. Edited by Maud Karpeles. London: Oxford University Press, 1974.

———. *English Folk Songs from the Southern Appalachians.* 2 vols. Edited by Maud Karpeles. London: Oxford University Press, 1932.

Sharpe, John M. "Experiences of a Texas Pioneer." In *The Trail Drivers of Texas,* vol. 2, edited by J. Marvin Hunter, 721–29. 1925. Rpt., New York: Argosy Antiquarian, 1963.

Shettler, C. D. "A Guitarist of European Training." *Cadenza* 5, no. 1. (Sept.–Oct. 1898): 14.

Siegmeister, Elie. "Letter from Alabama." In *The Music Lover's Handbook,* edited by Elie Siegmeister, 23–25. New York: William Morrow, 1943.

Smith, Louis Roycraft, Jr. "A History of Sumter County, Alabama, through 1886." Ph.D. diss., University of Alabama, 1988.

Smith, Margaret, et al. "The Abraham Smith Family of Washington County, Virginia." Undated typescript. Smith family file, Museum of the Middle Appalachians, Saltville, Va.

Smith, Richard D. *Can't You Hear Me Callin': The Life of Bill Monroe, Father of Bluegrass.* Boston: Little, Brown, 2000.

Spaeth, Sigmund. "Dixie, Harlem, and Tin Pan Alley: Who Writes Negro Music—And How?" *Scribners* 99 (1936): 23–26.

———. *A History of Popular Music in America.* New York: Random House, 1948.

———. *Weep Some More, My Lady.* Garden City, N.J.: Doubleday, Page, 1927.

Spottswood, Dick. Notes to *How Low Can You Go: Anthology of the String Bass (1925–1941).* Dust-to-Digital DTD 04 (2006).

———. Notes to "Old Grey Goose." *The Early Days of Bluegrass,* vol. 1, Rounder 1013 (1974).

Spratt, Robert D. *A History of the Town of Livingston, Alabama.* Edited by Nathaniel Reed. Livingston: Livingston Press, University of West Alabama, 1997.

Steinmetz, John. "Goodbye, Old Paint: A Cowboy Song for Bassoon and Piano." Sheet music. Tellevast, Fla.: TrevCo Music, 2000.

Stewart, Samuel Swain. *The Complete American School.* Philadelphia, Pa.: N.p., 1887.

Strachwitz, Chris. Notes to *Blind James Campbell and His Nashville Street Band.* Arhoolie F1015 (1963), reissued as Arhoolie CD 438 (1995).

Sullivan, Dulcie. *The LS Brand: The Story of a Texas Panhandle Ranch.* Austin: University of Texas Press, 1968.

Sutton-Smith, Brian. *Games of New Zealand Children.* Berkeley: University of California Press, 1959.

Talbot, Nancy. "Tex Logan: Fiddler in Two Worlds." *Muleskinner News,* Dec. 1977, 6–11.

Talley, Thomas W. *Negro Folk Rhymes.* 1922. New, expanded edition with music, edited by Charles K. Wolfe. Knoxville: University of Tennessee Press, 1991.

Tallmadge, William H. "Dr. Watts and Mahalia Jackson: The Development, Decline and Survival of a Folk Style in America." *Ethnomusicology* 5, no. 2 (May 1961): 95–99.

Tartt, Ruby Pickens. *Dim Roads and Dark Nights: The Collected Folklore of Ruby Pickens Tartt.* Edited by Alan Brown. Livingston, Ala.: Livingston University Press, 1993.

Taylor, William Banks. *Down on Parchman Farm: The Great Prison on the Mississippi Delta.* Columbus: Ohio State University Press, 1999.

Thede, Marion Unger. "Traditional Fiddling." *Ethnomusicology* 6, no. 1 (Jan. 1962): 19–24.

Thieme, Art. Notes to *Chicago Town and Points West.* Folk-Legacy FSI-135 (2006).

Thomas, Gates. "South Texas Negro Work-Songs: Collected and Uncollected." In *Rainbow in the Morning,* edited by J. Frank Dobie, 154–80. Publications of the Texas Folk-Lore Society, no. 5, 1926.

Thompson, Suzy Rothfield. "Time Traveling." *Strings Magazine* 19, no. 2 (Aug./Sept. 2004): 44–49.

Tick, Judith. "Ruth Crawford, Charles Seeger, and 'The Music of American Folk Songs.'" In *Understanding Charles Seeger, Pioneer in American Musicology,* edited by Bell Yung and Helen Rees, 109–29. Urbana: University of Illinois Press, 1999.

———. *Ruth Crawford Seeger: A Composer's Search for American Music.* New York: Oxford University Press, 1997.

Tinsley, Jim Bob. *He Was Singin' This Song.* Orlando: University of Central Florida, University Presses of Florida, 1981.

Titon, Jeff Todd. *Old-Time Kentucky Fiddle Tunes.* Lexington: University Press of Kentucky, 2001.

Titon, Jeff Todd, ed. *From Blues to Pop: The Autobiography of Leonard "Baby Doo" Caston.* JEMF Special Series, no. 4. Los Angeles: John Edwards Memorial Foundation, 1974.

Tribe, Ivan. "Jimmie Skinner: Country Singer, Bluegrass Composer, Record Retailer." *Bluegrass Unlimited* (Mar. 1977): 34–37.

Valin, Kathy. "Landing on Their Feet: West-End Based Jump Rope Team Continues a Folk Tradition While Learning to Win." *Cincinnati City Beat* 1, no. 25 (May 4–10, 1995): 8–11.

Wade, Stephen. "Ain't No Grave Can Hold My Body Down." *All Things Considered,* National Public Radio, Nov. 26, 1996.

———. "The Beautiful Music All Around Us: Washboards, Street Music, and John W. Work III." *All Things Considered,* National Public Radio, Oct. 22, 1997.

———. *Catching the Music.* WETA-TV public television documentary (1987), available at http://folkstreams.net.

———. "Fleming Brown Interview, May 24, 1983." *Banjo Newsletter* 11, no. 5 (Mar. 1984): 5–10.

———. "New Photos, Old Daguerreotypes: Remembrances of the 1990 Tennessee Banjo Institute." *Southern Quarterly* 31, no. 1 (Fall 1992): 77–84.

———. Notes to *A Treasury of Library of Congress Field Recordings.* Rounder CD 1500 (1997).

———. Notes to *Black Appalachia.* Rounder 1823 (1999).

———. Notes to Hobart Smith, *In Sacred Trust: The 1963 Fleming Brown Tapes.* Smithsonian Folkways SFW CD 40141 (2005).

———. "Tom Paley Interview, Part One." *Banjo Newsletter* 25, no. 5 (Mar. 1998): 14–21.

Wade, Stephen, and Archie Green. "Leadbelly's 'Old Man' and the Worksong Tradition." *All Things Considered,* National Public Radio, Aug. 23, 2006.

Wald, Elijah. *Escaping the Delta: Robert Johnson and the Invention of the Blues.* New York: HarperCollins, Amistad, 2004.

Wardlow, Gayle Dean. "Henry 'Son' Sims." *78 Quarterly* 9 (1995): 11–18.

Ware, Carolina F. *The Cultural Approach to History.* New York: Gordon Press, 1974.

Warren-Findley, Jannelle. "Passports to Change: The Resettlement Administration's Folk Song Sheet Program, 1936–1937." In *Prospects: An Annual of American Cultural Studies* 10, edited by Jack Salzman, 197–241. Cambridge: Cambridge University Press, 1985.

Way, Frederick, Jr., with Joseph W. Rutter. *Way's Packet Directory 1848–1983.* Athens: Ohio University Press, 1983.

———. *Way's Steam Towboat Directory.* Athens: Ohio University Press, 1990.

Weeks, Linton. *Clarksdale and Coahoma County: A History.* Clarksdale, Miss.: Carnegie Public Library, 1982.

Whisnant, David E. *All That Is Native and Fine: The Politics of Culture in an American Region.* Chapel Hill: University of North Carolina Press, 1983.

White, Newman I. *American Negro Folk-Songs,* 1928. Rpt., Hatboro, Pa.: Folklore Associates, 1965.

———. "The White Man in the Woodpile: Some Influences on Negro Secular Folk-Songs." *American Speech* 4, no. 3 (Feb. 1929): 207–15.

Wiggins, Gene. "Not Very Aristocratic." *Old Time Music* 26 (Autumn 1977): 5–9.

Wilgus, D. K. "The *Aisling* and the Cowboy: Some Unnoticed Influences of Irish Vision Poetry on Anglo-American Balladry." *Western Folklore* 44, no. 4 (Oct. 1985): 255–300.

———. *Anglo-American Folksong Scholarship since 1898.* New Brunswick, N.J.: Rutgers University Press, 1959.

———. "Country-Western Music and the Urban Hillbilly." In *The Urban Experience and Folk Tradition,* edited by Américo Paredes and Ellen J. Stekert, 137–64. Austin: University of Texas Press, 1971.

———. "The Hanged Fiddler Legend in Anglo-American Tradition." In *Folklore on Two Continents,* edited by Nikolai Burlakoff and Carl Lindahl, 120–38. Bloomington, Ind.: Trickster Press, 1981.

———. "The Text Is the Thing." *Journal of American Folklore* 86, no. 341 (Jul.–Sept. 1973): 241–52.

Wilgus, D. K., and Eleanor R. Long. "The Blues Ballad and the Genesis of Style in Traditional Narrative Song." In *Narrative Folksong: New Directions (Essays in Appreciation of W. Edson Richmond)*, edited by Carol L. Edwards and Kathleen E. B. Manley, 437–82. Boulder, Colo.: Westview Press, 1985.

Will, G. F. "Songs of the Western Cowboys." *Journal of American Folklore* 22, no. 84 (Apr.–June 1909): 256–61.

Williams, Michael Ann. *Staging Tradition: John Lair and Sarah Gertrude Knott*. Urbana: University of Illinois Press, 2006.

Wilson, August. *Joe Turner's Come and Gone: A Play in Two Acts*. New York: New American Library, 1988.

Wilson, Joe. Notes to the Sunshine Skiffle Band, *Beat It, Blow It, Strum It, Hum It!* Flying Fish FF 70589 (1992).

Wilson, Olly. "The Heterogeneous Sound Ideal in African-American Music." In *New Perspectives on Music: Essays in Honor of Eileen Southern*, edited by Josephine Wright with Samuel A. Floyd Jr., 327–38. Warren, Mich.: Harmony Park Press, 1992.

Wolfe, Charles K. *The Devil's Box: Masters of Southern Fiddling*. Nashville, Tenn.: Country Music Foundation Press and Vanderbilt University Press, 1997.

———. *A Good-Natured Riot: The Birth of the Grand Ole Opry*. Nashville, Tenn.: Country Music Foundation Press and Vanderbilt University Press, 1999.

———. *Kentucky Country: Folk and Country Music of Kentucky*. Lexington: University Press of Kentucky, 1982.

———. "New Light on 'The Coal Creek March.'" *JEMF Quarterly* 12, no. 41 (Spring 1976): 1–8.

———. Notes to *Bill Monroe: Bluegrass 1970–1979*. Bear Family Records BCD 15606 DI (1994).

———. "The Oldest Recorded Fiddling Styles." In Wolfe, *The Devil's Box: Masters of Southern Fiddling*, 3–11. Nashville, Tenn.: Country Music Foundation Press and Vanderbilt University Press, 1997.

———. "Rural Black String Band Music." *Black Music Research Journal* 10, no. 1 (Spring 1990): 32–35.

———. "String." *Bluegrass Unlimited*, June 1982, 45–51.

Wolfe, Jacques. "Short'nin' Bread." Sheet music. New York: Harold Flammer, 1928.

Wood, Stephen E. "The Development of Arkansas Railroads." Pts. 1 and 2. *Arkansas Historical Quarterly* 7, no. 2 (Summer 1948): 103–40; and no. 3 (Autumn 1948): 155–93.

Work, Frederick J. "A Search for a Song." *Tennessee Folklore Society Bulletin* 54, no. 1 (1989): 14–19.

Work, John Wesley. *Folk Song of the American Negro*. Nashville, Tenn.: Fisk University Press, 1915.

———. "Negro Folk Song." *Opportunity* 1, no. 10 (Oct. 1923): 292–94.

Work, John W., III. *American Negro Songs and Spirituals*. New York: Crown, 1940.

———. "The Folk Songs of the American Negro." Master's thesis, Teachers College, Columbia University, 1930.

———. ["In the Bottoms"]. Untitled typescript, informal title conveyed by Beth Howse, Fisk University. Fisk and ALC.

———. "Negro Folk Music." Robinson Music Lecture Series, Mar. 4, 1938. Work Papers, box 3, folder 13, Fisk.

———. "Typescript of Address Given at Negro Folk Music Program at 4:15 P.M., Friday, May 2, 1941 as Part of Fisk's 75th Anniversary." Fisk.

Work, John W., III, Lewis Wade Jones, and Samuel C. Adams Jr. *Lost Delta Found: Rediscovering the Fisk University Library of Congress Coahoma County Study, 1941–1942.* Edited by Robert Gordon and Bruce Nemerov. Nashville, Tenn.: Vanderbilt University Press, 2005.

Worrall, Henry. *The Eclectic Guitar Instructor.* Boston: Oliver Ditson, 1884.

———. Henry Worrall Collection. Library Collection, no. 23, KSHS.

Wynn, Bill. "Old Cox." *Junior Historian* 6, no. 6 (May 1946): 1–4. Published by the Texas State Historical Association, Austin.

In October 1997, a compact disc that I produced and annotated called *A Treasury of Library of Congress Field Recordings* (Rounder CD 1500) went into national release. A full list of its tracks and downloads are available under its title at http://www.rounder.com. For this book I have focused on thirteen of those thirty recordings that appear on the enclosed compact disc:

1. "Bonaparte's Retreat" (1:52). Played on the fiddle by W. H. Stepp, Salyersville, Ky., Oct. 26, 1937.
2. "Rock Island Line" (1:49). Sung by Kelly Pace and group, Gould, Ark., Oct. 2, 1934.
3. "Pullin' the Skiff" (1:06). Sung by Ora Dell Graham, Drew, Miss., Oct. 24, 1940.
4. "Shortenin' Bread" (0:54). Sung by Ora Dell Graham, Drew, Miss., Oct. 24, 1940.
5. "Sea Lion Woman" (1:11). Sung by Christine and Katherine Shipp, Byhalia, Miss., May 13, 1939.
6. "Soldier's Joy" (2:10). Played on washboard, banjo-mandolin, guitar, and tin-can bull fiddle by the Nashville Washboard Band, Nashville, Tenn., July 15, 1942.
7. "Another Man Done Gone" (1:26). Sung by Vera Hall, Livingston, Ala., Oct. 31, 1940.
8. "Ain't No Grave Can Hold My Body Down" (4:10). Sung by Bozie Sturdivant, Clarksdale, Miss., July 25, 1942.
9. "Coal Creek March" (1:30). Played on the five-string banjo by Pete Steele, Hamilton, Ohio, Mar. 29, 1938.
10. "One Morning in May" (3:18). Sung by Texas Gladden, Salem, Va., Sept. 8 or 9, 1941.
11. "Glory in the Meetinghouse" (1:45). Played on the fiddle by Luther Strong, Hazard, Ky., Oct. 18, 1937.
12. "Diamond Joe" (2:14). Sung by Charlie Butler, Parchman, Miss., Mar. 8, 1937.
13. "Goodbye, Old Paint" (4:31). Sung with fiddle by Jess Morris, Dallas, Tex., May 3, 1942.

Bartlett Tribune, 417–18n35

Barton, Uncle Johnny, 290

Basie, William "Count," 124

Battle, Joe, 59

"The Battle of the Nile," 37

"The Battle of Waterloo," 37

Bayard, Samuel, 37–38

Bean Blossom (Ind.) country music park and festival, 290, 293–94

Beatles, 64, 138

The Beautiful Music All Around Us (CD included with book): art and human experience merged in, xii–xiii; case study approach of, 20–21; contents listed, 447; meaning of phrase, 2, 4; origins in *Treasury*, 11–16; tradition and individual creativity in, 21–23

Begley, Big Hiram (or "Black"), 277, 279, 408n39

Begley, Justus, 274–75

Belafonte, Harry, 154

Belcher, Red, 225, 400n84

Belden, Henry M., 352

Berea College (Ky.): Appalachian Center Sound Archive at, 280; fiddle contests of, 277, 279, 280; fiddle tune collecting and, 276

Bertram, Cuje, 142

biblical references: *selah* term in, 116; *specific books*: Isaiah, 183; Matthew, 111, 356, 378n31; Mark, 183; John, 183, 186; 1 Corinthians, 181, 185–86, 391n14; Galatians, 200; Colossians, 200; Revelation, 186. *See also* gospel music; hymns and hymn singing

"Bicycle Built for Two," 214

Biddle Shops Colored Quartette, 52, 53

Big Road Blues (Evans), 100

"The Big Rock Candy Mountain," 83

"Billie in the Lowground," 234

Billy the Kid (Copland), 42, 349

Bingham, James Swan, 331–32

Birmingham (Ala.): gospel quartets in, 60–61

Black Belt: conditions for African Americans in, 155–58, 159–62, 169–71; murders and lynchings in, 163, 164, 170. *See also* occupations; racism and racial segregation; *specific locations and states*

blackface minstrelsy: Acuff and, 136, 139; banjo linked to, 146–47; dialect of, 93; musical caricatures of, 92; "Shortenin' Bread" linked to, 96, 97–98. *See also* minstrelsy; steamboats and river boats

"Blackwatertown" (poem, Muldoon), 402n4

Blanton, Arthur, 194, 198, 199. *See also* Friendship Spirituals

Blaustein, Richard, 150

"The Blind Girl," 260

Blind Lemon (itinerant guitarist), 250

"Blood-Strained Banders," 17

Blue Grass Boys, 291–92

bluegrass music: attitudes toward, 290; "Diamond Joe" as, 317–18; "Glory" and "Jerusalem Ridge" as, 290–93; parts distributed in, 289

blues: emergence of, 5–6; foundation of, 309; history of "Baby Please Don't Go" and, 174, 177; "I'm Alabama Bound" as, 175; museum of, 202; oral history of, 163–64; precursors to gospel type, 192–93. *See also* Oliver, Paul

blues ballad: coining of, 392n33; "Duncan and Brady" as, 314–15; "Railroad Bill" as, 255

Bobbie Leecan's Need-More Band, 94

Boggs, Dock, 224, 225

Boleu, C. B., 303, 305

Bonaparte, Napoleon, 36–39, 340–41

"Bonaparte's Retreat": history of, 36–38; recordings of, 38–39, 368n53

"Bonaparte's Retreat" (Stepp): Copland's incorporation of, 25–26, 40, 42, 44, 45–46; Crawford's transcription of, 44; legacy of, 45–46; others' remembrances of, 32; particularities of, 39; placement in Stepp's performance, 30; *recordings*: Bill Stepp, 11, 36, 38; others mentioned, 37, 38, 368n53

"Bonaparte's Retreat from Moscow," 36

"Boney's in St. Helena," 38

Bonnie and Clyde (film), 284, 286

"Bonyparte," 369n66. *See also* "Bonaparte's Retreat" (Stepp)

Booker, Jim (father), 143

Booker, Jim (son), 142–43, 292

Boone, Eva Grace, 84–86, *85*

booster movement: company instructions for, 51–52; music's role in, 49–50, 52–55, 61. *See also* advertising

border crossings: changing meanings of songs and, 21; cultural exchanges and, 12–13, 115; music as means of, 125–26; shared music across racial-cultural boundaries, 142–45; transcription's role in, 42–46

Botkin, Benjamin: on culture, 359; on Folk Music series, 11; on hunger and poverty, 96; Living Lore project (FWP) of, xi, xiii, 10; on tradition and individual creativity, 22; *work*: *Negro Religious Songs and Services* (album), 190, 390–91n6

Bottoms: use of term, 190

Boudreaux, Ella Hoffpauir, 17–20, *18*, 364n57

Boukeyon, Alissyna, 111

Cannon, Dede, 325, 411n
Cannon, Gus, 139
Cannon, Hal, 357
Cannon, Wendell, 324–25, 415n104
Carl Fischer Inc., 348
Carlisle, Cliff, 273
Carmer, Carl, 166, 387n53
carnival: etymology of, 99
Carolina Chocolate Drops, 154
Carpenter, Nora, 35–36
Carr, B., 397n20
Carroll, Thomas James, 132, 147–48, 151,
    383n36. *See also* Nashville Washboard
    Band
Carson, Jack, 369n
Carter Family, 249, 255, 403n20
Casey, Smith, 16–17
Casey and Mae in the Street (Motley), 361n4
Cash, Johnny, 64, 65, 154, 392n20
Caston, Leonard "Baby Doo," 177
"Catherine's Bar Room," 263
Cattlemen's Beef Board, 365–66n1
Caudill Family, 391n20
Chaffee, Edmund W., 340
Challenger disaster, 187
Champion Coated Paper Company
    (Hamilton, Ohio): Luther Strong working
    at, 270; owner of, 208; Steeles working at,
    209–10, 234–35
"Character and State of Studies in Folklore"
    (conference), 10
Charles, Ray, 193
Charles, Roosevelt, 308
"Charles Guiteau," 220
"Charming Billy," 189
"Chattanooga Choo-Choo," 192
Checker, Chubby, 113
Cherry, Hugh, 151–52
Chicago: Bud Billiken parade in, 361n4;
    childhood adventures in, xii; Johnson's
    studies in, 6; "Living Lore" in, xi; Maxwell
    Street market in, 361n4, 361n8. *See also*
    Jones, Casey, "the Chicken Man"
Chicago, Rock Island, and Pacific Railroad.
    See Rock Island Line
Chicago Cubs fans, 238
Chicago Defender, x
Child, Francis James: ballad collection
    and canon of, 252, 253, 254, 260–61, 287;
    sources of, 256
children's songs and game songs:
    atmosphere of, 13; changes due to
    playground equipment, 87; Drew students
    recorded, 76, 80–82; forbidden actions
    in, 84–86; function of, 86, 116; jump-rope
    rhymes, 87; Kelly Pace's singing of, 69;
    learning of, 83–84; misrule and upended

roles in, 88–89; multiplication table song
    as, 17; personal interpretations of, 86–87,
    90–91, 114; ring plays as, 117–19, 125–26,
    379n55; Vera Hall's recollections of, 161;
    specific: "All Hid," 80, 161–62, 373n13;
    "Coonjine," 167; "Jack, Can I Ride," 90;
    "Little Bitty Man," 174; "Little Girl," 81;
    "Will You Marry Me, My Pretty Little
    Miss," 69. *See also* dance and movement;
    Graham, Ora Dell "Honey"; "Pullin' the
    Skiff"; rhymes and rhyming; "Sea Lion
    Woman"; "Shortenin' Bread"
Choctaw, Oklahoma, and Gulf Railroad,
    415n89
Choctaw Indians, 111
Cincinnati (Ohio): jump-rope rhymes in,
    87; Ohio Valley Folk Festival in, 210–11,
    225, 396n9
Cisle, Lew, 231, 401n106
Civil War: anti-Lincoln songs of, 106;
    Morris family and, 331–32. *See also* Black
    Belt; slavery
Clark, Cortelia, 382n32
Clarksdale (Miss.): appeal for information
    in, 187–88; Bozie Sturdivant's move to,
    189; children's song in, 90–91; Delta Blues
    Museum of, 202; gospel quartet of, 180;
    jukeboxes banned on Sundays, 301; labor
    changes in, 179; Silent Grove Baptist
    Church of, 180–81, 183, 187, 190, 192, 202
"Claude Allen," 220
Claunch, W. E., 13–14
Clay, Beaufort, 134, 135
Clay County (Ky.): "The Last of Callahan"
    linked to, 275–76
Cline, Joe, 291
Clodhoppers, 376n82
close-harmony sacred singing (genre):
    "Rock Island Line" in context of, 60–62
Coahoma County (Miss.): D.A. and county
    sheriff of, 299–301, 302; labor changes in,
    179. *See also* Clarksdale; Fisk University/
    Library of Congress project
Coal Creek (Tenn.). *See* "Coal Creek
    March"; Lake City (Tenn.)
Coal Creek Company, 219
"Coal Creek March": adapted into
    other genres and scenes, 228, 231–33;
    circumstances of LC recording, 3;
    events commemorated by, 217–20; first
    recording of, 225; legacy of, 234–35;
    meanings of, 220–22; origins and
    development, 222–29; other tunes and,
    214–16; *recordings:* Forrest Lewis, 221;
    Frank Lewis and Bailey Briscoe, 224–26,
    227–28; Jesse Spencer, 211, 225; Pete
    Seeger, 229, 231, 232; Pete Steele, 210–11,

214, 217, 221–22; Roscoe Holcomb, 221, 399n65; Sam Gaston, 223–24, 226; Tom Paley, 231. *See also* Steele, Pete (Simon Peter)

Feist, Leslie, 126

Felton, Andrew Jackson, 332

Felton, Jack, 417–18n35

Ferrel, Frank, 38

Ferriss, Abbott: assistance of, 377n; as Halpert's assistant, 105–10, 374n33; photographs by, 120; "Seline" (ring play) recorded by, 117–19, 379n55

Festival of Contemporary American Music, 159, *160*

Feyne, Buddy, 131

fiddle music: alternative intonations in, 284, 286; catgut vs. steel strings, 344; contests of, 277, 279, 280, 288, 292, 337–38, 339, 368n53; cross-tuning or cross-keying of, 282; extending and reworking tunes, 292–93; harmonica vs., 174, 388n85; how to listen to, 7; lonesome sound of, 280–81, 287, 288, 293; oldest fiddler recorded, 338–39; piano accompaniment to, 344; preacher-father's attitude toward, 332; push, pull, and long-bow techniques, 288–90; "Soldier's Joy" ubiquitous in, 142. *See also* Morris, Jess; Stepp, Bill "Fiddler Bill" (W. H.); Strong, Luther

"Fiddle Tune," 410n94

Fiddlin' Powers and Family, 408n34

field hollers. *See* hollers and shouts

Fields, Charlotte Texas Smith, 402n, 403n18

film: blacks as servants in, 97–98; Camelot of the Kennedys and, 268; on Casey the Chicken Man, 361n8; cowboy, 348; "Foggy Mountain Breakdown" in, 284, 286; "Lead Me to the Rock" in, 380n68; local connection to, 45; "Pullin' the Skiff" in, 88; "Rock Island Line" in, 65, 380n68; "Sea Lion Woman" in, *121*, 121–23; "Shortenin' Bread" in, 89; "There Ain't No Grave Gonna Hold My Body Down" in, 391n20. *See also The General's Daughter*; mass media; radio programs; television

Fisk Jubilee Singers, 7, 62, 129, 392n20

Fisk University: anniversary festivities of, 1–2, 4–5, 6–7, 135; Johnson's arrival and lecture at, 5–6

Fisk University/Library of Congress project: accomplishments of, 140; Charles Johnson's role in, 8–9, 362n9; imitation and adaptation of music heard in, 191–93, 202–5; origins of, 5, 8–9; questionnaire and questions of, 10, 192, 240–41, 242–43; recording blanks used, 364n52; sheriff's advice for, 300–301. *See also* Jones, Lewis W.; Lomax, Alan; Work, John, III

Five Blind Boys of Mississippi, 195

Five Soul Stirrers of Denver, Colorado, 195–96, 197, 394n71

Flatt, Lester, 286

Flemmons, Marvin, 99–100

Flying Fish Records, 364n39

Flynt, Althea, 45

Flynt, Larry, 45

"Foggy Mountain Breakdown," 284, 286

Folk Archive. *See* Archive of Folk Culture (earlier, Archive of American Folk Song, then Archive of Folk Song)

Folklife Annual (periodical), 13

folklore: balancing tradition and individual creativity in, 21–23; colors in nature, 125, 380n77; concept of, 1–2; healing in, 108; woman disguised as man in, 40–41. *See also* foodways

folklore and folksong studies: case study approach in, 20; local settings and meanings missing from, 10; songs vs. biographies in, 15, 256; variant interpretations in, 323–24; women singers stereotyped in, 261

folk music: African American contributions celebrated, 177–78; changing preferences for, 146–48; classical aesthetics compared with, 7; commemorative function of, 36–39; common verse in, 313; as communal activity, 58–59; composers' interests in, 41–43; contextual meanings of, 21; Crawford's transcriptions of, 42–44; cross-cultural potential of, 12–13, 115; folk-lyric stream in, 352–53; geographical differences in, 173–74; "heterogeneous sound ideal" of, 144–45; hillbilly music distinguished from, 211–12; ideal form of songs and, 255–56; individual expression in, 86–87, 90–91, 114, 256, 264–65, 287–90; linguistic coincidences in, 116–17; "packing" songs away as child, 249; paradoxical nature of, 264; "piecing together" as process of, 314–15; respect for musicians, 130–31; revival of (1960s), 231, 232; sentimentality in, 252–54; songs as fluid rather than fixed, 256; spoken interludes in, 63; stereotypes of African American, 150, 167; tradition and individual creativity in, 21–23; transmission of, 17. *See also* community; creativity; everyday life

Folk Music of the United States (LC series): ambient or background sounds included, x, xii–xiii, 4, 240, 278–79; art and human experience merged in, xii–xiii; circumstances and equipment of, 3–4; description of, 4, 13–14; editorial choices in, 10; evaluative formula (grading system) for selections, 364n42; funding for, 12–13; goals of, 12, 364n42; official and informal paired in, 22–23; praise for, 11; spoken word exchanges included, 14; tracks selected for, 14–15. *See also* Archive of Folk Culture; Fisk University/Library of Congress project; Library of Congress; *and specific recordings*

Folk Songs from the Southern Appalachian Mountains (album), 231

foodways: canning, 237–38; folklore of, 91–92, 99; shortening bread recipe, 92

Forman, Miloš, 45

Forrester, Howdy, 139, 292

"The Forsaken Girl," 352

Fort Worth Star-Telegram, 327, 335, 340, 341

Foster, Gwen, 273

Foster, Stephen, 83

Four Eagle Gospel Singers, 61

"The Four Marys." *See* "Mary Hamilton"

419 West Main (album), 291

Four Star Quartet, 182, 188

Fox, Curly, 124

Fox, Oscar J., 42, 347–50

"Fox Chase," 142

Francis, Arthur, 284, 286, 410n71

Frank, Michael, 385n

Fraterville (Tenn.): mine explosion in, 217–18, 220; programs commemorating, 398–99n54

Frazier, Ned, 7, 130–31, 146, 363n24

Freberg, Stan, 64

Frederick, Lulah Lee Morris, 329, *334*

"Freedom," 178

Freeny's Barn Dance Band, 415n104

French and Indian War, 141

"French Four," 142. *See also* "Soldier's Joy"

Friars Point (Miss.): musical diversity of, 183–84; students recorded in, 86, 90, 91, 374n34

Friendly Five Harmony Singers, 134–35, 184, 192, 202

Friendship Spirituals (Blanton, J. Dawson, R. Dawson, and Sturdivant): creativity and confidence of, 200–201, 203–4; founding of, 198; musical and performance instructions for, 197–200; photograph of, 194, *199*; *recording*: "Ain't No Grave Gonna Hold My Body Down," 200–201, 202. *See also* Dawson, Ralph; Sturdivant, Bozie

Friends of Music (album), 396n12

"Froggy Went a-Courtin'," 136

"Frog Song," 233

Fulmer, David, 402n4

Fuson, Harvey, 31

Futrell, Junius, 55

FWP (Federal Writers' Project), xi, xiii, 127–28, 166. *See also* Halpert, Herbert

Gabbard, Leona Steele, 210, 229, 234–35, 396n, 400n84

Gabbard, Myron, 396n

Galliher, John, 250, 255, 403n35

Galmore, Savannah, 180, 181, 391n10

games: "Diamond Joe" linked to, 314; hiding (and song), 80, 161–62, 373n13; monkey (copying movements), 248; ring plays as, 117–19, 125–26, 379n55. *See also* children's songs and game songs

Gammon, Vic, 37

Garcia, Jerry, 408n21, 414n70

Garrett, Phil, 49

Gaston, Sam, 223–24, 225, 226, 232, 399n76

The General's Daughter (film): folk music credits of, *121*; other songs in, 380n68; responses to soundtrack, 380n70; "Rock Island Line" in, 65; "Sea Lion Woman" in, *121*, 121–23; trance-beat remixes in, 122, 380n72

Gennett (label), 145, 225

"Gentle on My Mind," 290

Georgia: "Diamond Joe" in, 313–14, 315–16

Georgia Crackers, 315, 316–18, 320

"Georgia Dusk" (Toomer), 6

Gerrard, Alice, 404n41, 408n21

Gevedon, Monroe, 367n36, 408n21

Gibson, Don, 292

Gibson, John (or George?), 134–35

"Gilderoy," 44

"Girls in the Blue Velvet Band," 220

Gist, Morse, 390n

Gladden, Hobart, 239

Gladden, James Clayton "Jim" (Texas's son): on Alfreda Peel, 261; assistance of, 402n; on background noise, 240; death of, 402n1; foodstuffs prepared by, 237–38; memories of, 239–45, 248, 265; on "One Morning in May," 257; photographs of, 241–42, *242*, *243*

Gladden, James Thomas (Texas's husband): elopement and wedding of, 241, 244–47, *247*, 254, 403n20; photographs of, 241–42, *242*, *243*

Gladden, Marvel, 265

Gladden, Mary (James's sister), 241, *243*

Gladden, Mary (Texas's daughter), 241, *243*

Gladden, Texas Anna Smith, 237–65; Alfreda Peel's relationship with, 251–52, 260–63; author's appreciation for, 401–2n; characteristics of, 240, 246–48; circumstances of LC recording, 3, 240, 241; diversity of performance venues, 159, *160*, 239, 253, 256, 262; elopement and wedding of, 241, 244–47, *247*, 254, 403n20; Fleming Brown's connection with, xiii; on ideal form and possession of songs, 255–56, 264; life experiences and everyday singing of, 2, 237–38, 242–44, 265; music in childhood, 248–50, 256–57; name of, 239; occupations of, 247, 250; photographs of, 241–42, *242*, *243*, *251*; poetry of, 245, 404n38; repertory of, 251–58, 260, 405n78; *recordings/performances*: "Come All You Fair and Tender Ladies," 262; "The Devil and the Farmer's Wife" (with Hobart), 250; "The Devil's Nine Questions," 252; "Hangerman Tree," 261; "The House Carpenter," 252; "John Henry," 262; list of LC recordings, 402n8; "Mary Hamilton," 251–52; "Old Kimball," 250, *252*; "One Morning in May," 3, 240, 252, 258–59; "Poor Ellen Smith" (with Hobart), 250, 260; "Rose Connelly" (with Hobart), 250; *Texas Gladden* (CD), 402n9; *Texas Gladden Sings Blue Ridge Ballads* (CD), 403n34; "The Three Babes," 262. *See also* "One Morning in May"

Gladden, William Langstaff "Papa Gladden," 251

Gladden, Wilma Jean: assistance of, 402n; memories of, 239–40, 244–45; name of, 239, 402n7; on parents' elopement and marriage, 245

Gladden family photographs, 241–42, *242*, *243*

"Glory in the Meetinghouse": adapted into other genres and scenes, 290–93; first recording of, 274; function of, 269; lyrics, 281; origins and development, 279–80, 282; purpose and sense of past of, 280–82; significance of LC recordings, 286–90; transcription of Luther Strong's, 284, *285*; *recordings*: Art Stamper, 279–80, 281, 282, 287–88, 292; John Hartford, 290–91; Luther Strong, 269, 279–80, 282, 284, 286, 289–90, 294; Marion Sumner, 280, 292; others' versions, 282–83; Theophilus G. Hoskins, 274, 408n26. *See also* Strong, Luther

Godfrey, Hettie, 167

"Going Away to Make It Lonesome Here," 152

Goins, Melvin, 280–81, 407n

Goins Brothers, 280, 281, 292

Golden Gate Jubilee Quartet (aka Golden Gate Singers), 62, 69, 178, 192, 195, 199

"The Golden State," 53–54

Goldsmith, Oliver, 258

"Goodbye, Old Paint": adapted into other genres and scenes, 349–50; advertisement (postcard) of, *345*; Jess Morris's creative claim to, 354–56; Jess Morris's learning of, 335, 337–38; legacy of, 357–59; lyrics,

348, 351–52; origins and development, 344–49; rehearsals of, 416n; tuning of, 343; waltzing to, 339, 343, 346, 347, 416n; *recordings*: Dick Devall, 356; Jess Morris, 3, 328, 343–46, 350–51, 353; John Steinmetz, 357–58. *See also* Morris, Jess

"Goodbye My Lover Goodbye," 50

"Goodnight Irene," 314

"Good Shepherd," 17

The Goofing-Off Suite (Seeger's songbook), 232

Gordon, Robert Winslow: on "Diamond Joe," 314–15, 316, 318; on "Shortenin' Bread," 96, 376n82

Gorman, James E., 52

gospel music: "Ain't No Grave" as, 180; blues and, 192–93; jug band's performances of, 138; modern solos of, 201; open-door offerings of, 196; oral tradition and making of, 180; secular intent combined with, 60–62; solo-spirituals structure in, 190–92, *191*; transport metaphor in, 56, 57, 61–62; value of black spirituals, 7. *See also* hymns and hymn singing; Shipp sisters; Sturdivant, Bozie; *and specific titles*

gospel quartets: attitudes toward, 182; community-based jubilee style of, 184; company sponsored, 60–61; in Denison (Texas), 194, 195–96, *199*, 200, 203–4. *See also* quartets; *and specific groups*

"Gospel Train," 199

"The Gospel Train is Coming," 62

Graham, Babe, 101–2

Graham, Della, 102

Graham, Martha, 40

Graham, Mary, 102

Graham, Ora Dell "Honey," 75–103; author's search for, 99–100; characteristics of, 100–101, 102; death of, 75–76, 102–3; life experiences of, 2, 80–81; photograph of, *75*, *76*; *recordings*: LC recordings noted, 76, 372n2; "Little Girl," 81; "Pullin' the Skiff," 81–84, 88–89; "Shortenin' Bread," 89–90, 98–99, 377n91. *See also* "Pullin' the Skiff"; "Shortenin' Bread"

Graham, Samuel, 102

Grammy Awards: best folk recording (1966), 382n32

Grand Ole Opry: Bobby Hebb's audition for, 139; Earl Scruggs on, 232; first and second African American performers at, 139, 142; musically skillful hayseed type at, 135–36, 140; radio program of, 124, 131, 289; radio station of, 139

Grant, John, 80, 82

Gray, A. A., 38, 368n53

Henderson, Sylvia, 22
Henderson, Walt, 21–22
Henry, Jim, 308
Henrytown (Va.): Smith-Gladden family in, 241–42, 242
Henry VIII (king of England), 258
Hentoff, Nat, 151
Herrington, J. W., 398n52
Herzog, George, 9–10
Hickerson, Joe, 389n
Hicks, Bobby, 410n94
Higgins, Branch, 35
High John the Conqueror, xii
Hill, Don, 134
hillbilly music: of African Americans, 142; contemporary takes on, 273–74; folk music distinguished from, 211–12; "Too Late" as, 253
Hitler, Adolf, 340–41
Ho, Eugenia, 385n
Hobart, Garret A., 239
Hodges, Ernie, 224, 225–26
"Hoedown" (in Copland's *Rodeo*), 25–26, 40, 42, 44, 45–46
Hoffpauir, Cora Lee, 18, 19
Hoffpauir, Ella (later, Boudreaux), 17–20, 18, 364n57
Hoffpauir, Julien, 18–19
"Hog-Eyed Man," 284, 408n26
"hokum" music, 136–37
Holcomb, Roscoe, 221, 399n65
Holland, Justin, 214
hollers and shouts: for cows and husbands, 106; demonstration of, 167; "Diamond Joe" in context of, 309, 312–13; hog and other farmyard, 410n74; of Kelly Pace, 66–67, 72; of Parchman convicts, 308–9, 413n41; street cries as sung poetry, xi; *specific*: "Black Woman," 158. *See also* spoken-word elements
Homestead steel strike, 226
"Home Sweet Home," 220, 227
"Hometown Skiffle," 133
"Hoochie Coochie Man," xii
Hooker, John Lee, 93
Hoosier Hotshots, 135
Hootenanny (television program), 234
Hopkins, Doc: author's lessons with, 228–29, 396n; birthdate of, 400n94; "Coal Creek March" and, 227–29; on influences, 401n97; songbook of, 229; *recording*: "Trouble at the Coal Creek Mines," 227–28, 232
Hopkins, Lightnin', 93
"Hop Light Ladies," 94
Hopper, Edward, 267
Horton, Johnny, 64

Hoskins, Owen, 30, 34–35
Hoskins, Theophilus G., 274, 287, 408n26
Hot Springs (Ark.): railroad workers' quartets broadcasting from, 52
Hot Springs Railroad, 415n89
House, Eddie "Son," 309, 413n41
"The House Carpenter," 252
"House of the Rising Sun" (or "New Orleans"), 257, 258, 273
"House Rent Scuffle," 133
Houston, Cisco, 319, 320, 414n69
Houston and Texas Central Railroad, 319
Howard, James, 31
Howard, Nannie, 28, 29, 32, 45, 365n
Howard, Peggy, 34, 35, 365n
Howe, Elias, 141
Howlin' Wolf, xi
Howse, Beth M., 381n
Hughes, Earlene, 80
Hughes, Langston, 6
"Hungarian Rhapsody," 139
Hunter, Nancy, 100–101, 372n
Hurricane Ridgerunners, 280
Hutchison, Frank, 215
Hyden (Ky.): Callahan-Deaton feud in, 276; LC recordings in, 273, 274
hymns and hymn singing: "Ain't No Grave" and, 182; congregations as feeling together in, 166; convicts' vocal style linked to, 309; "Old Hundred songs" of, 201; part-singing in, 109; setting the pitch for, 108; Smith family's singing of, 248–49. *See also* biblical references; gospel music

"If He'd Be a Buckaroo," 369n66
"If I Had a Hammer," 320
"If Teardrops Were Pennies," 234
"I'll Be Glad When You're Dead, You Rascal You," 131, 137, 382n30, 394n71
Illinois: bluegrass and Bray Brothers of, 290–93; Steele's move to, 207–9. *See also* Chicago
Illinois River: *Julia Belle Swain* steamboat of, 320
"I'll Never Turn Back," 195
"I'll Twine 'mid the Ringlets" (aka "Wildwood Flower"), 249–50
Il Trovatore (opera), 213
"I'm Alabama Bound," 175, 389n90
"I'm Bound for the Promised Land," 248–49
"I'm Chopping Cotton," 174–75
"I'm Gonna Feast at the Welcome Table," 366n18
"I'm Gonna Walk Your Log," 177
immigration: African diaspora and, 148–49; personal perspective on, 19–20; sharing and appropriating of, 126. *See also*

shops in, 48, 49; Rock Island Line route through, 56, 57–58

"Little Sleeping Negroes," 95–96

Livingston (Ala.): black voters and regulations in, 165, 170; conditions for African Americans in, 155–58, 159–62, 169–71; Pilgrim's Church in, 166; recordings in, 154, 166–68, 171–72, 174–75. *See also* Hall, Vera; Tartt, Ruby Pickens

Lizard Music (play), 361n4

localities: changing conditions of, 1–2; Dewey's concept of, 23

Locke, Alain, 178

Logan, Benjamin "Tex," 316–18, *317*, 324, 411n

"Logan County Blues," 215

"Logan Waters," 140

Logsdon, Guy, 319–20

Lomax, Alan: African American contributions celebration and, 178; Alfreda Peel and, 261; color film footage by, 408n22; Columbia University folk music concert and, 159, *160*; Crawford's work with, 43; evaluative formula (grading system) of, 364n42; Fisk/LC project and, 8–9, 10, 183–84, 241; Kentucky recordings by, summarized, 286–88; permission requests and, 13; Pete Steele and, 234; radio program of, 42, 78; sheriff's advice for, 300–301; Shipp sisters and, 115; Strong home visit of, 272–73; Town Hall concert series of, 163; Vera Hall and, 154, 162–64

—*recordings*: circumstances of, 3; Anne Williams, 379n48; Bev Baker, 278–79; Bill Stepp, 30–32, 34, 36, 273; C. H. Savage, 186; E. C. Ball, 21–22; Ella Hoffpauir Boudreaux, 18; Friars Point students, 86, 90, 91, 374n34; Georgia Turner, 273; Jelly Roll Morton, 15; Luther Strong, 278–79, 286; Nashville Washboard Band, 131–32, 137, 140, 142–44, 147–49, *149*; Oscar Parks, 276; Pete Steele, 211–12, 217, 221–22, 396n12; Ruby Smith, 90; Texas Gladden, 240, 241, 252, 253–55, 256–57; Vera Hall, 153–54, 159, 164, 166, 168–71

—*topical comments*: "Bonaparte's Retreat," 38; "Diamond Joe," 311, 312–13, 318–19; folk vs. hillbilly music, 211–12; Luther Strong and nearby musicians, 275; old-time and commercial music, 274, 286, 290; songs about Napoleon, 36–37; travels for collecting, 274; typicality criterion, 164; "walking the log," 176

—*works*: *American Ballads and Folk Songs* (with John), 31, 42; *Mister Jelly Roll*, 163; *Rainbow Sign*, 163–64. *See also Our*

Singing Country (Alan and John A. Lomax)

Lomax, Bess (later, Hawes), 42, 118–19, 125, 365n, 369n66

Lomax, Elizabeth. *See* Sturz, Elizabeth Lyttleton (earlier, Lomax)

Lomax, John A.: Doc Reed's relationship with, 166–67; Jess Morris and, 327, 346, 347, 350–51, 354; Kelly's last meeting with, 70–72; Ledbetter's travels with, 48, 55–56, 58–59, 62; sheet music editions of, 42; sound effects attempted by, 84; Vera Hall and, 153, 154–55

—*recordings*: Charlie Butler and other Parchman convicts, 308–13; circumstances of, 3; Drew students, 80–81; Elijah Cox, 338; Ella Hoffpauir Boudreaux, 18; Irene Williams, 78, 83, 372n5; J. D. Dillingham, 319; Jess Morris, 350–51; Kelly Pace and other Arkansas convicts, 47–48, 56–57, 58–59, 66–67; McDonald, 118; Ora Dell Graham, 76, 89–90; Rich Brown, 175; Vera Hall, 153–54

—*topical comments*: "Diamond Joe," 414n78; "Goodbye, Old Paint," 347–49; Richard Amerson, 168

—*works*: *American Ballads and Folk Songs* (with Alan), 31, 42; *Ballad Hunter*, 48, 71, 155. *See also Our Singing Country* (Alan and John A. Lomax)

Lomax, Johnny, Jr., 55–56

Lomax, Ruby Terrill (John's wife): on "Diamond Joe," 311; Vera Hall and, 154–55; *recordings*: Irene Williams, 78, 372n5; Kelly Pace, 69; Ora Dell Graham, 89–90; Vera Hall, 153–54, 166–68

Long, Theodocia Bonnet, 106

Lornell, Kip, 60–61, 370n, 371n41

"Lost John," 142, 308

Loughead, Tom, 230–31

Louis, Joe, 195

Louisiana: Angola Prison in, 55, 307, 308; Ella Hoffpauir Boudreaux's childhood in, 17–19

"Love Somebody," 142. *See also* "Soldier's Joy"

"Love's Worse than Sickness," 254

Loyd, O. H., 337

Luallen, Cal, 220

lullabies: memories of, 265; "One Morning in May" as, 240, 243–44; "Shortenin' Bread" as, 96, 98

Lunceford, Jimmie, 129

Lunsford, Bascom Lamar, xiii, 38, 93, 375n64

Lusk, John, 144–45

Lyman, Jeffrey, 358

Macon, Uncle Dave, 215, 286, 397–98n37
MacPherson, James, 275–76
Madison, James, 329
Magoffin County (Ky.): Larry Flynt from, 45; Stepp family in, 28, 29, 29–30, 365n, 366n9
"The Maiden's Lament," 406n98
"The Maid Freed from the Gallows" (aka "Hangerman Tree"), 261
Mainer, Wade, 215, 286
"Makes a Long Time Man Feel Sad," 308
Malone, Bill, 404n41
"The Man of Calvary" (sermon), 190
"Marching Jaybird," 215
Marshall, Edgar, 392n22
Martin, Benny, 289
"Mary Hamilton," 251–52
Mary McDonald, 174
"Mary of the Wild Moor," 251
Mason, Jake, 49
mass media: blacks as servants in, 97–98; bluegrass and Bray Brothers in, 290–93; compartmentalization and, 282–83; concerns about, 274, 286, 287, 290; imitation and adaptation of music heard in, 191–93, 202–5; Kentucky fiddling in, 287–88; learning new songs via, 191–93; mountain families' access to, 273–74. See also film; radio programs; television
"Masubiana," 338
"Matchbox Blues," 124
Mathieson Alkali Works (Saltville), 247, 248, 250
Maxi, Mrs. John, 263
May, Basil, 35, 367n33
Mayall, John, 154
Maynard, F. H., 263
McAuliffe, Christa, 187
McAuliffe, Leon, 234
McCallum, Brenda, 60–61, 371n41
McCartney, Paul, 64
McCord, May Kennedy, 376n82
McCottrell, Fannie, 183–84
McCulloh, Judy, 16
McDonald, Joe, 118
McFarland, Arnold, 33, 34, 35, 365n
McFarland, Lydie, 33, 34
McFarland, Roscoe (R. C. Macfarlane), 32, 33, 34, 35
McGee, Kirk, 215
McGhee, Brownie, 159, 160
McGhee, John, 202, 392n22
McKinley, William, 239
McKinney, Tom, 91
"McLeod's Reel," 44
McMahon, A. J. "Smoky," 52–53, 73

McMichen, Clayton, 368n53
McTell, Blind Willie, 238, 265, 402n4
McWhorter, William, 305
Meade, Guthrie, 383n37, 409n42, 409n46
Medlock, James, 196
Memphis (Tenn.): Rock Island Line route through, 56, 57–58
Memphis Jug Band, 152
Memphis Slim (John Len [or Peter] Chatman), 163–64, 319, 412n23
Mercer, Johnnie, 98
Merrill, Boothe, 347–48, 349
"Midnight Special," 308, 309, 322–23
Miers, A. J., 410n94
military: fiddling for, 339; tune's commemoration of battle, 215–16, 398n42; tunes incorporated into, 37. See also "Bonaparte's Retreat"; "Sebastopol"; "Soldier's Joy"
Mills Brothers, 124
Milton, Kathleen, 86–87, 91
Milton, Leon "Sonny": assistance of, 372n; on Babe Graham's death, 101–2; on Ora Dell Graham, 75–78, 102; on school funds, 80
"The Minery Boys," 220
Minghella, Anthony, 88
minstrelsy: blackface impersonators and caricatures in, 92–93; Casey Jones's evoking of, xiii–xiv; popular culture's incorporation of, 97–98; "Shortenin' Bread" linked to, 96. See also blackface minstrelsy; steamboats and river boats
Misiewicz, Roger, 385n
Mississippi: Bozie Sturdivant born in Swan Lake, 188, 393n43; "Diamond Joe" versions in, 313–15; fiddler and farmer of Watson's Crossroads, 112–13; jump-rope rhymes in, 87; LC recordings in, 78, 84–86, 85, 90, 91, 373n6, 374n34; musical diversity of Friars Point, 183–84; racism and violence in, 76–77; ring play recordings in Edwards, 117–19, 379n55; Shipp family of Miller, 106–7; WPA guide on, 322; WWII-era labor shortage in, 300–301. See also Byhalia; Clarksdale; Coahoma County; Drew; Fisk University/ Library of Congress project
Mississippi Department of Corrections, 305, 325, 411n. See also Parchman Farm
Mississippi Sheiks, 124
Missouri, Kansas & Texas Railroad, 195
Mister Jelly Roll (A. Lomax), 163
Mobile, Annie, 158
"Model Church," 34
Molsky, Bruce, 280

38; later street musicians on, 134, 382n18; life experiences of, 2; street performances of, 131, 151–52; Work III and, 129–32, 140; *recordings*: "Arkansas Traveler," 143–44; "Going Away to Make It Lonesome Here," 152; "I'll Be Glad When You're Dead, You Rascal You," 137; "Soldier's Joy," 132, 140, 142, 143, 147–49, *149*; "You're Bound to Look Like a Monkey When You Grow Old," 137. *See also* skiffle music and ensembles; "Soldier's Joy"

National Barn Dance (WLS program), 124, 227

National Cattlemen's Beef Association, 365–66n1

National Cowboy Poetry Gathering, 357

National Folk Festival (Washington, D.C.), 253

Native Americans, 12, *12*, 26–27, 111, 253

"A Natural Man," 138

Neely, Jerry, 335

Negro Folk Rhymes (Talley), 95–96

Negro Religious Songs and Services (album), 190, 390–91n6

Netherland, John D., 362n

Netter, Jim, 364n39

New Deal: "common man" idea and, 41; Federal Writers' Project of, xi, xiii, 127–28, 166; music programs in, 41–42; Works Progress Administration in, 3, 270, 322

New Iberia (La.): Ella Hoffpauir Boudreaux's childhood in, 17–19

"New Orleans" (or "House of the Rising Sun"), 257, 258, 273

New York (state): Pinkster parades in, 99

New York City: hootenannies in Greenwich Village, 231; "Living Lore" in, xi; modernist circle in, 41; Town Hall concert series in, 163; Vera Hall's visit to, 159, *160*

New York Times Magazine, 314

Nicholls, Ed, 414n78

Nichols, Mrs. W. S., 158

Nicholson, George C., 39, 368n53, 408n36

Niles, John Jacob, 409n51

nonsense tradition, 83, 110. *See also* children's songs and game songs; rhymes and rhyming

Norman Luboff Choir, 238

North Carolina: John Canoe festivities in, 99; "Spanish Fandango" in, 215

Nottaway Indians, 26–27

"Nottingham Fair" (broadside), 83

"Now Your Man Done Gone," 171, 172, 175

O'Brien, Tim and Molly, 391n20

O'Bryant, Jimmy, 149

occupations: alkali (baking soda) plant, 247, 248, 250; barbershop owner, 181, 202; categories of (Lomax), 55; coal mining, 207, 217–22, 396n1; cooks and domestic servants, 154–55, 158, 159, 164, 167; cowboy work (as wolfer), 341–42, 343; drayman and church janitor, 107–8; electricians, 111, 123, 230; freight handling, 330–31; house- and yard "boy," 189; limitations in Black Belt, 155–58; makeshift types (hominy selling and chair caning), 133; minister, 194; moonshine whiskey making, 270–71; rounders, 93; shining shoes, 196, 204; steel work, 226. *See also* farming; railroad workers

Odetta (folk revivalist), 154

Odum, Howard, 313–14, 318

Ohio: Morris family and early history of, 329–30. *See also* Cincinnati; Hamilton

Ohio State Fair, 229

Ohio Valley Folk Festival (Cincinnati), 210–11, 225, 396n9

"Oh Susannah" (Foster), 83, 136

Okeh (label), 94

Oklahoma: "Goodbye, Old Paint" in, 347–48; Riverside Indian School in Anadarko, 12

Oklahoma! (musical), 349–50

Olcott-Bickford, Vahdah, 215, 216–17, 226

"The Old Chisholm Trail," 42

"Old Death March" (aka "Dead March"), 225, 400n84

"Old Hen Cackle," 142

"Old Hundred," 201

"Old Joe," 131, 338

"Old Joe Clark," 13, 142, 231, 267

"Old Kimball," 250, 252

"Old Man," 338, 418n52

"The Old Man and Old Woman Quarrelin'," 38

"Old Paint." *See* "A Ridin' Old Paint"; "Goodbye, Old Paint"; "I Ride an Old Paint"; *Ridin' Old Paint*; "Ridin' Ol' Paint an' Leadin' Ol' Ball"

"The Old Ship of Zion," 35, 61–62

Oliver, Paul: African American blues scholarship of, 297–98, 309; on "Baby Please Don't Go," 174; on "Diamond Joe," 324; on "Rock Island Line," 64; on "Shortenin' Bread" by Bobbie Leecan's Need-More Band, 94; on vernacular, 297, 298, 323

Olson, William Bruce, 383n38, 383n40, 405n69

"One Morning in May": adapted into other genres and scenes, 238; artistic malleability of, 264–65; circumstances

of LC recording, 3, 240; earliest
documentation of, 257; lyrics, 258, 259–
60; meanings of, 238–39, 257, 265; origins
and development, 256, 257–61; *recordings*:
others mentioned, 238; Texas Gladden, 3,
240, 252, 258–59. *See also* Gladden, Texas
Anna Smith

On the Trail of Negro Folk-Songs
(Scarborough), 96–97

"On Top of Old Smoky," 352

Opie, Iona, 83

Opie, Peter, 83

Oprah Winfrey Show, 123

Ordower, Fred, xii

Original Five Blind Boys of Mississippi,
393n38

Osborne (baritone), 196

Ossman, Vess L., 224

Oster, Harry, 308

Our Singing Country (Alan and John A.
Lomax): commercially sourced songs
in, 369n72; introductory stories in, 37,
163; music transcriptions in, 42–44;
contents: "Bonaparte's Retreat," 38;
"Bonyparte," 369n66; "Diamond Joe," 319;
"House of the Rising Sun," 273; "If He'd
Be a Buckaroo," 369n66; "The Last of
Callahan," 408n36; "Sis Joe," 369n66; "The
Vance Song," 35

"Over the Waves," 225, 338

Pace, Eliza, 273, 274, 408n22

Pace, Henry, 68–69

Pace, Kelly (Robert Kelly Pace), 47–73;
childhood and singing of, 58, 66,
68–69; death of, 70; grave marker of, 65;
imprisonment of, 2, 47, 58–59, 66–67,
69–70; legacy of, 70–73; photograph of,
71; *recordings*: field hollers and spoken-
word pieces, 66–67, 72; "Rock Island
Line," 47–48, 58–59, 60, 64, 65, 68, 70;
"Samson," 69, 71. *See also* "Rock Island
Line"

Pace, Lawrence, 67–69, *68*, 70, 369n

Pace, Ruby, 67–68, 369n

Paley, Tom, 231

Pancho (monte dealer), 338, 339

Panic of 1837, 156

Pap's Jug Band, 135–38, 139, 140, 150

"Paradise," 234

Paramount (label), 133

Parchman Farm (penitentiary): cages at,
304; daily routine for inmates, 302–5,
306; desegregation of bands at, 324–25;
documents of, 412n22; location and size
of, 301–2, 412n21; Lomax's visits to, 78,
306–13; mug shots from, *299*, 411n; Ora

Dell's brother in, 102; pardon system of,
322–23; reflections on, 305–6; whistle
of visitors' train to, 322–23; women at,
85–86, 302–3, 325; *recordings*: "Have You
Ever Been to Nashville," 308, 323; "I'm
Alabama Bound," 175; integrated band
(1980s), 325; "Rosie," 308; "Stewball,"
308; women convicts singing "Pullin' the
Skiff," 85–86; work sounds and songs,
306–9, 324–25. *See also* Butler, Charlie;
"Diamond Joe"

Parham, Tiny, 149

Park, Robert E., 6

Parks, Oscar, 276

"Parson Burr," 403n20

Parsons, Gerald E., Jr.: on "Ain't No Grave,"
390–91n6; favorite folk song of, 389n;
on folk musicians' artistry, 22; role in
Treasury, 11–12, 13, 14

Partee, C. L., 398n44

Patterson, Brenda, 390n

Patterson, Frank, 7, 130–31, 146, 338, 363n24

Patton, Charley, 100, 146

"Payday in the Army," 142. *See also* "Soldier's
Joy"

Payne, Sonny, 393n38

Pearsley, Dakota Jack, 224, 227, 228

Peel, Alfreda: childhood inspiration for,
260; Powell's correspondence with, 404–
5n61; songs collected by, 257, 259–61, 262–
63, 405n72; Texas Gladden's relationship
with, 251–52, 260–63

Peer, Ralph, 94

"Peg and Awl," 252

Pell, Paul, 230

Pennsylvania: Homestead strike of, 226

The People vs. Larry Flynt (film), 45

Perkins, Percell, 393n38

Perrow, Eber C.: on "Diamond Joe," 314,
315, 318–19; on Seline verse, 118; on
"Shortenin' Bread," 94–95, 98

Phelan, Catherine E., 354

"Pick a Bale of Cotton," 71

Pickens, Ruby. *See* Tartt, Ruby Pickens

Pickens, William King, 165

Pilgrim Travelers, 200

Pine Mountain Settlement School, 31

Pinkster parades (N.Y.), 99

"Please Don't Drive Me Away," 180

Pollack, Howard, 40, 369n76

"Polly Put the Kettle On," 50

"Po' Mona," 118

Poole, Charlie, 282

"Poor Ellen Smith," 250, 260

Porter, Cletus, 35

Porter, Harvey, 35, 367n33

Porterfield, Nolan, 350

Musician, recording artist, and writer *Stephen Wade* is best known for his long-running stage performances of *Banjo Dancing* and *On the Way Home*. He also produced and annotated the Rounder CD collection that gave rise to this book, *A Treasury of Library of Congress Field Recordings*. Since 1996 his occasional commentaries on folksongs and traditional tunes have appeared on National Public Radio's *All Things Considered*. He lives in Hyattsville, Maryland.

Music in American Life

The University of Illinois Press
is a founding member of the
Association of American University Presses.

Designed by Kelly Gray
Composed in 10.5/15 Adobe Minion Pro
with Centaur MT display
by Barbara Evans
at the University of Illinois Press
Manufactured by Thomson-Shore, Inc.

University of Illinois Press
1325 South Oak Street
Champaign, IL 61820-6903
www.press.uillinois.edu